ORPHANS' COURT REGISTER DOCKET

Mifflin County Pennsylvania

Volume 1
1789–1899

Compiled by
Lorraine Indermill Quillon

HERITAGE BOOKS
2025

HERITAGE BOOKS

AN IMPRINT OF HERITAGE BOOKS, INC.

Books, CDs, and more—Worldwide

For our listing of thousands of titles see our website
at
www.HeritageBooks.com

Published 2025 by
HERITAGE BOOKS, INC.
Publishing Division
5810 Ruatan Street
Berwyn Heights, MD 20740

Sources:
https://www.familysearch.org/ark:/61903/3:1:3QSQ-G9SM-7975-3?i=0&wc=9P
MK-L2Q%3A268494601%2C268510401&cc=1999196 (Film #1026537)

International Standard Book Number
Paperbound: 978-0-7884-5075-4

ORPHANS' COURT
REGISTER'S DOCKET
Mifflin County, Pennsylvania

Volume 1

(1789 - 1899)

Heritage Books by the author

Abstracts of Early Probate Records, Belmont County, Ohio (1802–1827)

Deed Abstracts, Belmont County, Ohio: Volumes A, B, and C (1800–1811)

Deed Abstracts Belmont County, Ohio: Volume D, E, and F (1811–1817)

Deed Abstracts, Belmont County, Ohio: Volume G (1817–1820)

Deed Abstracts Belmont County, Ohio Volumes H and J (1820–1824)

Orphans' Court Register Docket, Mifflin County, Pennsylvania,
Volume 1, 1789–1899

Will Abstracts, Belmont County, Ohio: Volumes A, B, and C (1810–1827)

Will Abstracts, Belmont County, Ohio: Volumes D, E, and F (1827–1839)

Will Abstracts, Belmont County, Ohio: Volumes G and H (1839–1856)

Will Abstracts, Belmont County, Ohio: Volumes I and K (1856–1872)

Will Abstracts, Washington County, Pennsylvania: Volumes 1 and 2

DEDICATION

To Ova John Quillon, Jr., (Johnie)
who endured almost four and a half decades
of living with a companion who was obsessed
with the relentless pursuit of dead people,
and who (in retrospect) didn't complain
very often at all.

❧

INTRODUCTION

This is the second book of Pennsylvania record abstracts I have prepared. The first was wills from early Washington County. This time we are relocating to the place where my elusive third-great-grandfather seems to have made the first surviving records found so far. Even if there are no smoking guns, may there be some new clues hiding in these Orphans' Court records.

It is hoped that family history researchers may find these abstracts helpful in placing their family members on the ground in this county during this time period. Sometimes, that is the only offering the records give—these people were present and serving in various capacities at this time.

Although this is not a source which defines relationships between the parties listed, there may be clues that will yield that information if the individuals are researched further. Readers may want to pay attention if the same group of people seem to be working together on similar projects through this time span.

Names of all participants are given as well as the compiler could interpret the handwriting. Any entry which was particularly difficult to decipher and whose interpretation was doubtful was also enclosed in square brackets, as were generally any notes or additional material inserted by the compiler.

Please keep in mind that the spelling habits of the individuals themselves, the clerks who may have recorded their names, and the fallible skills of the compiler will make for some interesting variations. Frame numbers are indicated to allow for easy access to the actual image from which the information was taken. Please review these images to see if you see something different than the way it was transcribed. Sometimes, very small nuances in the handwriting can lead to a totally different interpretation.

Because this information was presented in a table format, that is how it was copied. Researchers are advised to prepare a card showing the headings of each of the columns (given at the first of Page 1) in order to remember what each of the letters in the manuscript represents. (For example, "b" does not mean birth!) However, the significance of these columns will change at various points in the manuscript.

It is often said that no book of this nature is ever perfect, and no such claim is made for this one. Nevertheless, may the errors not be numerous, and may all that *is* correct help each of us further our knowledge of our ancestors, their families, and their associations.

Lorraine Indermill Quillon

TABLE OF CONTENTS

IMPORTANT NOTE: The way the information is presented changes in the course of the collection. Please see notes on pages 194, 204, and 207, in addition to the original order given on page 1.]

ORPHANS' COURT REGISTER'S DOCKET

Mifflin County, Pennsylvania

Volume 1 (1789-1899)

Information will be presented in the order given on the page under these headings: (**a**)-Names of Decedents [to be implied though not labeled as such in this version], **b**-Time of Granting Letters &c, **c**-Names of Administrators & Executors, **d**-Amount of Bond, **e**-Names of Sureties, **f**-Time of Filing Inventory, **g**-Date of Settlement, **h**-Amount of Debt, **i**-Amount of Credit, **j**-To whom due. If nothing is entered following any of those letters, there was nothing written in those columns. [**NOTE**: *This presentation will change through the 110 years; look for notices in text. Pages 193, 204, and 207.*]

Page 1, frame 6

James WHITE, b-19 Dec 1789, **c**-James BARR, **d**-£400, **e**-James BURNS x, John MEANS, **f**- **g**- **h**- **i**- **j**-

James HUSTON, b-22 Dec 1789, **c**-John HUSTON and Abigail HUSTON, **d**-£350, **e**-John BROWN, Sr., John McCARTY, **f**-22 Dec 1789 **g**- **h**- **i**- **j**-

Judah OGDEN, b-4 Feb 1790, **c**-Hugh SHARON, **d**-£150, **e**-Robert BUCHANAN, Arthur BUCHANAN, **f**- **g**- **h**- **i**- **j**-

James RIPPETH, b-9 Feb 1790, **c**-William RIPPETH, **d**-£200 **e**-Thomas WIGINS, William HOLT, **f**-1 May 1790 **g**-13 Apr 1793 **h**-£46..15..1, **i**-£46..10..3, **j**-£0..4..10, heirs

George CRANE, b-29 Mar 1790, **c**-Mary CRANE, **d**-£700, **e**-Abraham WELLS, John [SHUPER], **f**-29 Mar 1790, **g**- **h**- **i**- **j**-

James CALHOON, b-14 Aug 1790, **c**-James CALHOON, **d**-£400, **e**-William BROWN, William STUART, **f**- **g**- **h**- **i**- **j**-

Thomas WILEY, b-15 Sep 1790, **c**-Samuel WILEY, **d**-£400, **e**-John HENDERSON, Joseph SHARP, **f**- **g**- **h**- **i**- **j**-

Margaret LYTLE, b-27 Nov 1790, **c**-Robert LYTLE, **d**-£200, **e**-William ELLIOTT, John LYTLE, **f**- **g**- **h**- **i**- **j**-

Elizabeth ALLISON, b-24 Dec 1790, **c**-Robert ALLISON, **d**-£100, **e**-William BROWN, Thomas BROWN, **f**-18 Mar 1791, **g**-1 Aug 1791, **h**-£12..1..7, **i**-£12..1..7, **j**-£12..1..7

Lewis LEWIS[sic], **b**-10 Mar 1791, **c**-Jane LEWIS, Joshua WILLIAM, **d**-£1000, **e**-Daniel JONES, Robert BUCHANAN, **f**-16 Jun 1791, **g**-9 Dec 1800, **h**-£1213..16.., **i**-£1212..6..9, **j**-£198..10..8, admrs

Frederick BAUM, **b**-17 Mar 1791, **c**-Rosana BAUM, John BAUM, Frederick WIMAN, **d**-£1000, **e**-Jacob BAUM, Henry BARNTHISEL, **f**-22 Jun 1791, **g**-17 Jul 1805, **h**- **i**- **j**-

Page 2, Frame 7

John McCONNELL, **b**-15 Jun 1791, **c**-David BEALE, **d**-£1000, **e**-George WILSON, John SCHNELL, **f**-Nov 1797, **g**-31 Jan 1800, 21 Apr 1808, **h**-£423..9..7; $122.37, **i**-£423..9..7, $129.63, **j**-£15..8..7; $7.26, admrs

Robert HOWE, **b**-15 Jun 1791, **c**-Hannah HOWE, John SCHNELL, **d**-£600, **e**-Daniel JONES, Joseph McCOY, **f**-30 Jul 1791 [or 1798?], **g**- **h**- **i**- **j**-

David MITCHELL, **b**-17 Jun 1791, **c**-John MITCHELL, Thomas MITCHELL, **d**-£1000, **e**-George MITCHELL, Neal McMANIGIE, **f**- **g**- **h**- **i**- **j**-

Samuel COWAN, **b**-1 Oct 1791, **c**-David WALKER, James MACKLIN, **d**-£1500, **e**-James BANKS, John MOORE, **f**-13 Dec 1791, **g**-26 Aug 1794, **h**-£311..0..9, **i**-£345..4..9, **j**-£57..5..9, admrs

Henry MILROY, **b**-4 Nov 1791, **c**-Agness MILROY, William WILSON, **d**-£1000, **e**-Agnes MILROY, William WILSON, **f**- **g**- **h**- **i**- **j**-

Robert DOUGLASS, **b**-8 Feb 1792, **c**-Robert DOUGLAS, William DOUGLAS, **d**-£1100, **e**-John STONE, James BELL, **f**- **g**- **h**- **i**- **j**-

Insly ANDERSON, **b**-Aug 1792, **c**-Thomas ANDERSON, **d**-£500, **e**-William HOLT, Henry BARNTHISEL, **f**- **g**- **h**- **i**- **j**-

John DUNLAP, **b**-18 Apr 1792, **c**-William THOMPSON, **d**-£500, **e**-John CULBERSON, David WALKER, **f**-29 May 1792, **g**-12 Aug 1796, **h**-£114..4..0, **i**-£41..2..9, **j**-£17..13..9, estate

William PURDY, **b**-28 Aug 1792, **c**-James PURDY, **d**-£1000, **e**-Wm. McCAY, Ebenezer LARIMER, **f**- **g**- **h**- **i**- **j**-

Hugh PURDY, **b**-27 Aug 1792, **c**-James PURDY, **d**-£200, **e**-Ebenezer LARIMER, Wm. McCAY, **f**- **g**- **h**- **i**- **j**-

Page 3, Frame 8

James SMITH, **b**-27 Aug 1792, **c**-William SMITH, **d**-£1000 **e**-Ebenezer LARIMER, William CONEN, **f**-25 Jul 1792, **g**-14 Feb 1797, **h**-£48..0..0, **i**-£17..4..10, **j**-£30..15..2, heirs

Patrick DOYLE, b-29 Sep 1792, c-John PATTERSON, d-£300, e-John CULBERTSON, William ARMSTRONG, f-27 Dec 1792, g-30 Mar 1817, h-£34..16..5, i-£34..17..11, j-£..1..6, admrs

Alexander ROBISON, b-29 Mar 1793, c-James ROBISON, Elizabeth ROBISON, d-£200, e-John McKEE, William ROBISON, f- g- h- i- j-

Arthur McCLEARY, b-1 Apr 1793, c-John McCREARY[sic], Nathan ALLEN, d-£200 e-John BROWN, James BURNS, f- g- h- i- j-

James ALEXANDER, b-19 Nov 1793, c-Robert ALEXANDER, d-£2000, e-William WILSON, William BROWN, f-1 Nov 1791, g-9 Apr 1812, h-$331.10, i-$323.04, j-$8.06, heirs

John MILTON, b-15 Apr 1793, c-Robert BOYLE, d-£50, e-James McCORD, Charles DOUGHERTY, f- g- h- i- j-

Ulrie STEELY, b-11 May 1793, c-Gabriel STEELY, Lazarus STEELY, d-£1000, e-John KEEVER, John MEANS, f- g- h- i- j-

John COLLONS, b-14 Jun 1793, c-Thomas COLLONS, d-£50, e-Arthur BUCHANAN, Jacob YOST, f- g-29 Jun 1794, h-£42..15..2, i-£43..4..8, j-£9..6, admrs

James BROWN, b-13 Nov 1793. c-Benjamin BROWN, William MARSDEN, d-£400, e-George McCLELLAND, William HARPER, f- g- h- i- j-

Samuel MONTGOMERY, b-13 Nov 1793, c-John MONTGOMERY, d-£1000, e-John CULBERTSON, Joseph EDMISTON, f- g- h- i- j-

Page 4, Frame 9

John BEARD, b-3 Dec 1793, c-William STERRETT, d-£100, e-Thomas BEALE, f- g- h- i- j-

Alexander McNITT, b-11 Apr 1794, c-Ann McNITT, Robert McNITT, d-£2000, e-William McNITT, Moses WILLIAMSON, f- g- h- i- j-

Patrick MURPHY, b-12 Apr 1794, c-Hannah MURPHY, Alexander MURPHY, d-£1000 e-Patrick WELDEN, Daniel DEVINNEY, f- g- h- i- j-

James NEVILL, b-24 May 1794, c-Henry NEVILL, Samuel LIPINCOTT, d-£300, e-William CAMPBELL, Thomas COPLAND, f- g- h- i- j-

Henry MOORE, b-27 Jun 1794, c-George PATTERSON, Esq., Robert [McLEER], d-£200, e-George McCLELLAND, Jno. CULBERTSON, f-10 Dec 1794, g-10 Nov 1796, h-£68..9..10, i-£58..18..11.5, j-£8..1..1, heirs

Denis CHRISTY, b-12 Sep 1794, c-Robert CHRISTY, d-£400, e-Hugh HARDY, Charles STEUART, f- g- h- i- j-

John BARRET, b-18 Oct 1794, **c**-Edmund RICHARDSON, **d**-£50, **e**-John CULBERTSON, John BUCHANAN, **f- g- h- i- j-**

Joshua FURGUSON, b-20 Oct 1794, **c**-Samuel McKINSTRY, **d**-£500, **e**-David WALKER, John RANKIN, **f**-19 Jan 1795, **g**-15 Apr 1796, **h**-£162..16..1, **i- j-**

Mathew FURGUSON, b-12 Nov 1794, **c**-Samuel McKINSTRY, **d**-£400, **e**-David WALKER, Abraham LUKENS, **f- g**-15 Apr 1806, **h**-£253..8..6.5, **i- j**-£194..14..4.5, heirs

James PATTERSON, b-9 Dec 1794, **c**-Andrew THOMPSON, **d**-£400, **e**-William McALLISTER, James BANKS, **f**-17 Feb 1795, **g**-11 Dec 1798, **h**-£74..19..10, **i**-£24..19..7, **j**-£50.0..3, heirs

Page 5, Frame 10

Thomas COOKSON, b-13 Jan 1795, **c**-Martha COOKSON, **d**-£300, **e**-David WALKER, Samuel DAVIS, **f- g- h- i- j-**

Jacob WAGGONER, b-17 Feb 1795, **c**-William WEBSTER, **d**-£400, **e**-John FREDERICK, Anthoney [TERNIES], **f- g- h- i- j-**

Joseph SHERK, b-17 Apr 1795, **c**-Jacob SHERK, Frederick LEATHER, **d**-£1000, **e**-Jacob LEATHER, Thomas ERSKINE, **f- g- h- i- j-**

Michael YODER, b-23 Apr 1795, **c**-Jacob YODER, Abraham YODER, **d**-£2000, **e**-Christian ZOOK, John [HASSTLER], **f**-24 Jun 1799, **g**-24 Jun 1799, **h**-£383..13..10, **i**-£66..0..3, **j**-£317..13..7, heirs

Thomas TOLLY [the two capital "T"s are the same, but one has to wonder if it is possibly JOLLY? There is a subsequent entry for a Thomas JOLLY], **b**-25 Apr 1795, **c**-Andrew DUFF, **d**-£1500, **e**-Wm. ELLIOTT, Wm. McCANDLISH, **f- g- h- i- j-**

John BROWN, b-16 May 1795, **c**-John BROWN, Jr., **d**-£600, **e**-William HARPER, Jacob YOST, **f- g- h- i- j-**

James FAIRMAN, b-10 Jul 1795, **c**-James FAIRMAN, **d**-£300, **e**-Andrew GAMBLE, Thomas ERSKIN, **f- g- h- i- j-**

Joseph POULTNEY, b-1 Aug 1795, **c**-Mary POULTNEY, **d**-£1000, **e**-Nath. SIMPSON, John BUCHANAN, **f**-30 Dec 1795, **g- h- i- j-**

Robert RYAN, b-1 Aug 1795, **c**-Thomas RYAN, **d**-£400, **e**-John MEANS, Mathew KELLY, **f- g- h- i- j-**

James BONER, b-1 Nov 1795, **c**-Martha BONER, Thomas [GORMLY], **d- e**-David WALKER, Robert WRAY, **f**-3 Feb 1796, **g**-10 Dec 1799, **h**-£877..10..1.5, **i**-£159..19..1, **j**-£877..10..1.5 [no designation]

Page 6, Frame 11
Hugh GRAY, b-16 Dec 1795, **c**-Mary GRAY, John GRAY, **d**-£1000, **e**-
William GRAHAM, John KERR, **f**-15 Dec 1795, **g**-11 Sep 1798/9 Sep
1809, **h**-£174..17..10/454..4..8, **i**-/152..10..8, **j**-/£301..14..0, heirs
John PAULEY, b-2 Feb 1796, **c**-Thomas PAULEY, Isaac SELLERS, **d**-
£4000, **e**-Samuel SHARON, Hugh McELROY, **f**-2 May 1796, **g**-May
1800, **h**-£622..10..1.75, **i**-£95..19..1, **j**-£526.11.., heirs
Benjamin GREEN, b-28 Mar 1796, **c**-George GREEN,　**d**-£1000, **e**-
Thomas GREEN, Samuel SHARON, **f**- **g**- **h**- **i**- **j**-
George MOY, b-26 Apr 1796, **c**-George MOY, Leonard CRONINGER,
d-£4000, **e**-Benjn. KEPNER, Christian BRANDT, **f**-3 Apr 1799, **g**-10
Dec　1799/17　Oct　1806,　**h**-£1765..16..1.5/859..9..0,　**i**-
£1239..17..6.5/449..18..10, **j**-£409..10..2, heirs
Archibald GILLESPY, b-5 May 1796, **c**-Elijah CRISWELL, James
AITKENS, **d**-£1000, **e**-Moses WILLIAMSON, Doct. Ezra DOTY, **f**-5
Aug　1796,　**g**-10　Sep　1799,　**h**-£183..18..1.75,　**i**-£160..18..10,　**j**-
£22..19..0.75, heirs
Daniel FRY, b-13 May 1796, **c**-Samuel FREY[sic], **d**-£100, **e**-Edward
WILLIAMS, James WELLS, **f**-9 Aug 1796, **g**- **h**- **i**- **j**-
Andrew MOORE, b-9 Jun 1796, **c**-Isabella MOORE, John MOORE, **d**-
£1000, **e**-William ELLIOTT, Robert PATTERSON, **f**- **g**- **h**- **i**- **j**-
Thomas JOLLY, b-10 Nov 1796 **c**-James AITKEN, **d**-£1500, **e**-David
NELSON, John RIDDLE, **f**- **g**- **h**- **i**- **j**-
James MOORE, b-11 February 1796, **c**-George HAYS, **d**-£600, **e**-John
PATTERSON, Andrew NELSON, **f**- **g**- **h**- **i**- **j**-
Jonas BAUM, b-12 Nov 1796, **c**-Margaret BAUM, **d**-£2000, **e**-Melchor
IMDORF, Robert SCOTT, **f**-7 Feb 1791/14 Dec 1802, **g**-13 May
1800/14　Dec　1802,　**h**-£893..9..11/£367..19..5.5,　**i**-
£535..0..5.5/£15..15..9, **j**-£352..3..8.5, J. BAUM'S heirs

Page 7, Frame 12/13 [p. 7 duplicated]
Samuel HENDERSON, b-29 Nov 1796, **c**-Thomas HENDERSON, **d**-
£500, **e**-George WILSON, William ELLIOTT, **f**- **g**- **h**- **i**- **j**-
Thomas HARDY, b-28 Nov 1795, **c**-David HARDY, Alexander HARDY,
d-£3000, **e**-Hugh HARDY, James ROBINSON, **f**- **g**- **h**- **i**- **j**-
Sarah THATCHER, b-30 Dec 1796, **c**-John STONE, Prudence
THATCHER, **d**-£200, **e**-John JOHNSTON, John McWILLIAMS, **f**- 29
Dec 1796, **g**-15 May 1799, **h**-£437..1..4, **i**-£273..2..7, **j**-£163..18..8.5,
heirs

Benjn. ARMSTRONG, **b**-39 Dec 1796, **c**-John ARMSTRONG, **d**-£2000, **e**-William ARMSTRONG, Robert MARTIN, **f**- **g**- **h**- **i**- **j**-

Robert BARNHILL, **b**-21 Feb 1797, **c**-Rebecca BARNHILL, William BARNHILL, **d**-£500, **e**-William MITCHELL, Robert PATTERSON, **f**- **g**- **h**- **i**- **j**-

Herman WARTMAN, **b**-15 Jun 1797, **c**-Peter OYSTER, Jacob GOOSEHORN, **d**-£1000, **e**-Michael FUNCANAN, Adam EBERT, **f**-13 Jun 1797/10 Jan 1804, **g**-14 Feb 1804/22 Apr 1813/30 Oct 1819, **h**-£559..4..9.5/$592.74, **i**-£433..16..9.5, **j**-$108.85, admr

Robert MURDOCK, **b**-30 Jun 1797, **c**-James MURDOCK, **d**-£600 **e**-Alexander WEIR, Charles STEWART, **f**- **g**- **h**- **i**- **j**-

Robert McNITT, **b**-1 Jul 1797, **c**-Jane McNITT, John ALEXANDER, **d**-£1000, **e**-Mathew TAYLOR, John JOHNSTON, **f**-10 Oct 1797//17 Dec 1827, **g**-5 Jul 1810/29 Aug 1810//17 Dec 1827, **h**-£46..5..0/$445.88//$433.63, **i**-£25..2..6/$12.25//$159.75, **j**-£21..2..6, heirs/$433.63, heirs//$273.88, estate of decedent

John HASTINGS, **b**-21 Aug 1797, **c**-Sarah HASTINGS, **d**-£600, **e**-John PATTON, James POTTER, **f**-15 May 1798, **g**-6 Jun 1808, **h**-£916..0..0, **i**-£694..3..8, **j**-£221..16..4, heirs

Englehart BROWN, **b**-30 Aug 1797, **c**-Joseph YODER, John HARTZLER, **d**-£1000, **e**-John [ZOOK], Michael FUNCANAN, **f**- **g**- **h**- **i**- **j**-

Page 8, Frame 14

Samuel DAVIS, **b**-22 Aug 1797, **c**-John DAVIS, **d**-£500, **e**-Elisha CRISWELL, John CULBERTSON, **f**- **g**- **h**- **i**- **j**-

Robert McKONAGHAN, **b**-29 Sep 1797, **c**-David WILEY, **d**-£1000, **e**-James POTTER, James ALEXANDER, **f**-23 Oct 1797, **g**-12 Jul 1805, **h**- **i**-£202..10..5.5, **j**-£2..14..6.5, admrs

James MILES, **b**-3 Oct 1797, **c**-Samuel MILES, **d**-£1000, **e**-William BROWN, George DUFFIELD, **f**- **g**- **h**- **i**- **j**-

Alexander DIVEN, **b**-27 Oct 1797, **c**-James DIVEN, **d**-£600, **e**-John CULBERTSON, Joseph EDMISTON, **f**-6 Nov 1797 **g**-1 Nov 1799, **h**-£344..11..4, **i**-£94..14..0, **j**-£249.17..4, estate

John BOGGS, **b**-11 Jan 1798, **c**-Andrew BOGGS, **d**-£1000, **e**-William SWANEY, William HARRIS, **f**-24 Jan 1798,, **g**-31 Jan 1800, **h**-£226..14..0, **i**-£307..17..0, **j**-£81..03..0, accountant

Samuel FRAMPTON, **b**-18 Jan 1798, **c**-Joseph COWGILL, **d**-£500, **e**-Mathew KELLY, John KELLY, **f**-9 May 1798, **g**-9 Sep 1800, **h**-£163..6..10.75, **i**-£142..3..11.5, **j**-£21..2..10.75, heirs

John PURDY, b-28 Feb 1798, c-Nancy PURDY, David E. [GRIER], d-£1000, e-Thomas TURBETT, William ELLIOTT, f-30 Mar 1798, g-14 May 1810, h-$4,401.66 i-$4401.66, j-

George ARMSTRONG, b-16 Mar 1798, c-John KESTLER, John McCORD, d-£3000, e-Robert PATTERSON, Michael FUNCANEN, f-6 Jan 1805, g-18 Aug 1806, h-£809.. i-£586..18..7.5, j-£222..1..4.5, G. ARMSTRONG's estate

Jacob BOWEN, b-11 May 1798, c-James MAYES, d-£100, e-Moses WILLIAMSON, Robert PATTERSON, f- g- h- i- j-

Samuel JORDAN, b-15 May 1798, c-James GREEN, d-£200, Michael JACK, Isaac McKINNEY, e-18 Jun 1798, f- g- h- i- j-

Page 9, Frame 15/16 [p. 9 duplicated]

James REED, b-8 Sep 1798, c-James REED, d-£200, e-David WALKER, Edward WILLIAMS, f- g-11 Sep 1804, h-£113..15..1, i- j-£79..19..0, heirs

Jacob SNOW, b-29 Nov 1798, c-David HACKEDORN, d-£400, e-Adam SEAWARD, Jacob BEAVER, f- g-22 Apr 1819, h-$261.53, i-$281.84, j-$20.32, extrs

John EMMETT, b-7 Aug 1799, c-James STEEL, d-£120, e-Wm. A. PATTERSON, James CHRISWELL, f- g- h- i- j-

William GUILES, b-2 Sep 1799, c-James BIRD, Jacob KINSER, d-£2000, e-James POTTER, Elias HORNING, f-1 Oct 1799, g-10 May 1803, h-£354..11..9, i-£102..1..3, j-£352..10..6, heirs

Jerman JACOBS, b-3 Sep 1799, c-Catherine JACOB[sic], d-£2000, e-John CULBERTSON, James STEEL, f- g- h- i- j-

William CHRISTY, b-11 Sep 1799, c-John WILLIAMS, John WHARTON, d-£2000, e-William ELLIOTT, David BEALE, f- g- h- i- j-

Andrew GAMBLE, b-30 Sep 1799, c-Agness GAMBLE, d-£400, e-John [PIPER], Michael FORSCANON, f-11 Oct 1799, g-5 Mar 1808, h-£105..0..1.5, i-£99..0..5.5, j-£5..19..8, heirs

John McKINSTRY, b-2 Oct 1799, c-William MAGILL, James McKINSTRY, d-£500, e-Roswell DOTY, William CURRAN, f-2 Nov 1799, g-13 Jan 1806, h-£321..5..0.5, i-£325..6..5.5, j-£4..1..5, admrs

Christian PETERS, b-13 Dec 1799, c-Agness PETERS, William EARLY, d-£300, e-Lewis STUDDS, [Conrad] YOUNG, f-2 Jan 1800 g- h- i- j-

James DAVIDSON, b-28 Dec 1799, c-William THOMPSON, d-£300, e-Neal McMANIGIE, William HARPER, f- g- h- i- j-

Page 10, Frame 17

Samuel BRYSON, b-3 Jan 1800, **c**-Ann BRYSON, William HARRIS, **d**-£600, **e**-Conad[sic] LINTNER, James BANKS, **f**- **g**- **h**- **i**- **j**-

Samuel BRATTON, b-15 Jan 1800, **c**-William BRATTON, William BRATTON Esq., **d**-£1000, **e**-Wm. ROBISON, Jno. VANCE, **f**- **g**- **h**- **i**- **j**-

Maurice McNAMARA, b-31 Jan 1800, **c**-John WILSON, Wm. STEWART, **d**-£400, **e**-Robert PATTERSON, Saml. MILLEGAN, **f**-3 Mar 1800, **g**-7 Jan 1802, **h**-$(£)18..13..4, **i**-£18..13..4, **j**-

Ludwick COOK [looks like COOTE], b-3 Feb 1800, **c**-John MILLHOUSE, **d**-£600, **e**-Michael FUNCANON, John GILLESPY, **f**-16 Apr 1800, **g**-9 May 1808, **h**-£51..13..1.5, **i**-£41..10..2.5, **j**-£10..2..11, estate

William ELLIOTT, b-17 Jun 1800, **c**-Mary ELLIOTT, **d**-£3000, **e**-Robert BUCHANAN, James BURNS, **f**- **g**- **h**- **i**- **j**-

Adam REYNOLDS, b-31 Oct 1800, **c**-Charity REYNOLDS, Robert McKIM, **d**-£500, **e**-Andrew GREGG, Peter SMITH, **f**-28 Nov 1800, **g**-16 Jul 1811, **h**-$635.53, **i**-$233.13, **j**-$402.39, heirs

Thomas TULL, b-6 Nov 1800m **c**-Neal McCOY, **d**-£400, **e**-David BEALE, William WORK, **f**-19 Nov 1806, **g**-23 Apr 1807, **h**-$78.02, **i**-$78.02, **j**-

James CHAMBERS, b-6 Nov 1800, **c**-William BARKLY, **d**-£400, **e**-Joseph McCOY, John WILLIAMS, **f**- **g**- **h**- **i**- **j**-

Alexander STEWART, b-14 Nov 1800, **c**-Alexander STEWART, William BRATTON, **d**-£400, **e**-James BRATTON, James JOHNSTON, **f**- **g**- **h**- **i**- **j**-

Jacob HART, b-15 Nov 1800, **c**-Jacob SMITH, Samuel MIERS, **d**-£500, **e**-Michael [LAUVER], Nicholas MIERS, **f**-15 Nov 1800, **g**-17 Jul 1805/8 Jan 1819, **h**-£428..19..0/$814.00, **i**-£250..17..8.5/$814.00, **j**-

Page 11, Frame 18

Margaret WEAVER, b-19 Feb 1800, **c**-Abraham WEAVER, **d**-£400, **e**-Michael FONCANON, Robert HOPE, **f**- **g**- **h**- **i**- **j**-

Daniel JONES, b-27 Jan 1801, **c**-Susana JONES, **d**-£1000, **e**-Robert BUCHANAN, James CUPPLES, **f**- **g**- **h**- **i**- **j**-

Simon SKOUTEN, b-17 Apr 1801, **c**-Abraham WILT, **d**-£200, **e**-Samuel EDMISTON, William STERRETT, **f**- **g**- **h**- **i**- **j**-

William SCOTT, b-29 Apr 1801, **c**-Susanah SCOTT, Col. William BRATTON, **d**-£800, **e**-Mathew SCOTT, James JOHNSTON, **f**-9 Jun 1801, **g**-3 May 1810, **h**-£319..13..7, **i**-£72..8..9, **j**-£247..4..10, heirs

Elizabeth **HOLT**, **b**-16 May 1801, **c**-John HOLT, **d**-£200, **e**-Wm. MONKS, Wm. LAMB, **f**-17 Jun 1801, **g**-20 Nov 1823, **h**-$60.94 **i**-$49.78, **j**-$11.16, estate

Daniel **OAKESON**, **b**-18 Jun 1801, **c**-Nicholas OAKESON, **d**-£1000, **e**-Joseph AIRA, Geo. CARSNER, **f**-9 Jul 1801, **g**-19 Dec 1806, **h**-£215..6..5, **i**-£207..13..0, **j**-£8..3..5, heirs

John **ALEXANDER**, **b**-30 Jun 1801, **c**-James ALEXANDER, John WHARRY, **d**-£400, **e**-Saml. MILLIGAN, John McMANIGEL, **f**-22 Jul 1801, **g**-9 Sep 1806/10 Sep 1806, **h**-£384.2..7/£384..10..7, **i**-£259..19..4/£249..19..3.25, **j**-£124..3..3/£249..19..3.75, estate

John **DAVIS**, **b**-28 Jul 1801, **c**-Catherine DAVIS, John DAVIS, **d**-£1000, **e**-Elijah CRISWELL, Wm. CUMMINS, **f**-11 Aug 1801, **g**-10 Nov 1809, **h**-£310..15..11, **i**-£308..12..7, **j**-£2..3..4, estate

James **FLEMING**, **b**-11 Dec 1801, **c**-James MAYES, **d**-£2000 **e**-Andrew MAYES, Robert FORSYTHE, **f**-29 May 1819, **g**-18 Mar 1807[sic], **h**-$244.92.5, **i**-$140.04.5, **j**-$104.88, estate

[Tirrel/Tinel] **TULLY**, **b**-2 Jan 1802, **c**-Margaret TULLY, **d**-£100, **e**-Felix LEE, George SNYDER, **f**- **g**- **h**- **i**- **j**-

Page 12, Frame 19/20 (p. 12 duplicated)
Elizabeth **BOND**, **b**-20 Feb 1802, **c**-Abraham WEAVER, **d**-£800 **e**-Henry HOOVER, John ORT, **f**-10 May 1803, **g**-10 May 1803, **h**-£238..2..1.5, **i**-£30..4..10.5, **j**-£238..2..1.5, estate

John **McELVAIN**, **b**-26 Feb 1802, **c**-Mary Ann McELVAIN, John CULBERTSON, **d**-$5000, **e**-James STEEL, Wm. ARMSTRONG, **f**- **g**- **h**- **i**- **j**-

William **WATTSON**, **b**-2 Mar 1802, **c**-William W. LAIRD, **d**-$1000, **e**-John [LUPBE], **f**- **g**- **h**- **i**- **j**-

James **JOHNSTON**, **b**-25 Mar 1802, **c**-Mary JOHNSTON, John VANCE, **d**-£1250, **e**-Wm. BRATTON, John CULBERTSON, **f**-25 Mar 1892, **g**-10 Apr 1810, **h**-$1829.90, **i**-$1333.20, **j**-$495.70, heirs

John **JOHNSTON**, **b**-3 Apr 1802, **c**-Thomas JOHNSTON, **d**-$1200, **e**-Peacock MAJOR, Robert PATTERSON, **f**- **g**- **h**- **i**- **j**-

John **DUNLAP**, **b**-26 Apr 1802, **c**-Thomas BROWN, **d**-$600, **e**-William BROWN, Malc[o]lm [ANDREE], **f**- **g**- **h**- **i**- **j**-

John **JONES**, **b**-2 Sep 1802, **c**-David McCRORY, **d**-$900, **e**-Christian COPELAND, Robert HOPE, **f**-9 Oct 1802, **g**-17 Sep 1804, **h**- **i**- **j**-£96..5..7, heirs

John POSTLETHWAIT, b-3 Nov 1802, **c**-Susanah POSTLETHWAIT, William POSTLETHWAIT, **d**-$800 **e**-Jonathan HAMILTON, Mathew SCOTT, **f**-23 Dec 1802, **g- h- i- j-**

Duncan McLAUGHLIN, b-5 Nov 1802, **c**-Margaret McLAUGHLIN, Elizabeth McLAUGHLIN, **d**-$1500, **e**-David SUNDERLAND, Jeremiah CUNNINGHAM, **f**-26 Sep 1810, **g**-24 Mar 1807, **h**-£48..2..5.5, **i**-£53..7..3, **j**-£5..4..9.25, admrs

George HILL, b-16 Nov 1802, **c**-Elizabeth HILL, Michael FONCANON, **d**-$300, **e**-Abraham WEAVER, Henry HOOVER, **f- g- h- i- j-**

Page 13, Frame 21

William POWER, b-17 Dec 1802, **c**-Catherine POWER, **d**-$1800, **e**-Peacock MAJOR, James McGEE, **f- g- h- i- j-**

Robert HOPE, b-1 Mar 1803 **c**-Jennet HOPE, Richard HOPE, **d**-$1500, **e**-James FLEMING, Joseph COWGIL, **f**-16 Mar 1803, **g**-25 Jun 1803, **h**-£736..8..2, **i**-£621..12..10.5, **j**-£114..15..3.5, heirs

Enoch WILLIAM[S], b-31 May 1803, **c**-Edward WILLIAMS, **d**-$8000, **e**-Joseph EDMISTON, Joseph COWGILL, **f- g- h- i- j-**

Joseph ALEXANDER, b-22 Jun 1803, **c**-Daniel ALEXANDER, William ALEXANDER, **d**-£500, **e**-Thomas ALEXANDER, James STEEL, **f**-**g**-9 Apr 1805, **h**-£181..3..9.5, **i**-£234..5..9.5, **j**-£53..1..4.75, admrs

Alexander SHERLOCK, b-26 Jul 1803, **c**-Catherine SHERLOCK, **d**-$700, **e**-William MARTIN, William GALLAHER, **f- g- h- i- j-**

Christian ZOOK, b-11 Aug 1803, **c**-Christian YODER, Christian HOOLY, **d**-$3000, **e**-Christian ZOOK, James CRISWELL, **f**-17 Aug 1803, **g**-10 Sep 1805, **h**-£537..0..10, **i**-£363..7..11, **j**-£173..12..10, heirs

James MILLIKEN, b-6 Aug 1803, **c**-Robert MILLIGAN[sic], **d**-$800, **e**-William FLEMING, David WILSON, **f- g- h- i- j-**

William THOMPSON, b-14 Sep 1803, **c**-Jane THOMPSON, **d**-£200, **e**-Neal McMANIGIE, Archibald NORRIS, **f**-4 Nov 1803, **g**-8 Dec 1806, **h**-£58..8..11.5, **i**-£39..4..4.5, **j**-£19..4..0, heirs

John JOHNSTON, b-15 Sep 1803, **c**-John JOHNSTON, James KNOX, **d**-$500, **e**-Samuel DAVIDSON [second D has a very short stack), John BEATTY, **f**-2 Nov 1803, **g**-5 Apr 1806, **h**-$391.88, **i**-$365.87.5, **j**-$26.00.5, heirs

John FARRIER, b-2 Nov 1803, **c**-Ann FERRIER[sic], James TENNIS, **d**-$3000, **e**-Joseph BAUGHMAN, James ANDERSON, **f**-2 Dec 1803, **g**-18 Aug 1806/15 Mar 1808, **h**-£1391..10..9.5, **i**-£1464..17..3.5/£53..7.4.5, **j**-£73..6..6, admrs

Page 14, Frame 22

John **McCONNALL**, **b**-2 Nov 1803, **c**-George McCONNELL[sic],
Thomas McCONNELL[sic], **d**-$1800, **e**-Thomas BARRETT, James
McCONNELL[sic], **f**-2 Nov 1803, **g**-7 Nov 1806/17 Mar 1820, **h**-
£195..1..8.5/$297.67, **i**-£114..9..10.5/$433.61.5, **j**-£80..11..10, heirs/
$135.94.5, accountant

John **STEEL**, **b**-22 Nov 1843[1803?], **c**-Jacob STEEL, **d**-$1500, **e**-James
STEEL, John STEEL, **f**-20 Dec 1803, **g**-10 Jun 1807, **h**-£88..5..5.5, **i**-
£22..4..1, **j**-£66..4..4.5, heirs

Andrew JOHNSTON, **b**-23 Nov 1803, **c**-Margaret JOHNSTON,
Alexander JOHNSTON, **d**-$1200, **e**-David JORDAN, Henry
HOOVER, **f**-13 Dec 1803, **g**-5 Apr 1806, **h**-£143..7..0, **i**-£177..17..3,
j-£34..10..3, admrs

Robert LAUGHLIN, **b**-8 Dec 1803, **c**-Mary LAUGHLIN, David
LAUGHLIN, **d**-$2000, **e**-Paul LAUGHLIN, Robert GRAY, **f**-19 Jan
1804, **g**-18 Nov 1806, **h**-£260..6.6.5, **i**-£116..19..9, **j**-£143..6.9.5, heirs

Doct. Thos. LAUGHLIN, **b**-8 Dec 1803, **c**-Nancy LAUGHLIN, Paul
LAUGHLIN, **d**-$2000, **e**-David LAUGHLIN, Robert GRAY, **f**-23 Jan
1804, **g**-19 Dec 19-7, **h**-£613..18..1, **i**-£257..2..6.5, **j**-£356..15..6.5,
heirs

John **STEVENSON**, **b**-12 Dec 1803, **c**-Margaret STEVENSON, John
STEWART, **d**-$1200, **e**-Jacob RICHART, John GILLESPIE **f**-12 Jan
1804, **g**-18 Nov 1806/25 Jan 1811, **h**-/$96.24, **i**-$96.24, **j**-

Samuel DAVIDSON, **b**-12 Dec 1803, **c**-Elizabeth DAVIDSON, John
WATTSON, Esq., **d**-$2000, **e**-James KNOX, Hugh McALLISTER, **f**-6
May 1808, **g**-7 Feb 1814, **h**-$614.45, **i**-$370.13 **j**-$244.32, estate

William HARPER, **b**-17 Dec 1803, **c**-Sarah HARPER, **d**-$1000, **e**-
Peacock MAJOR, Henry HOOVER, **f**- **g**- **h**- **i**- **j**-

James C. RAMSEY, **b**-23 Dec 1803, **c**-Samuel JACKSON, **d**-$1000, **e**-
James BURNS, Edward WILLIAMS, **f**- **g**- **h**- **i**- **j**-

Samuel FEER, **b**-2 Jan 1804, **c**-Thomas FEER, **d**-$1000, **e**-William
BEALE, Robert STARKS, **f**- **g**- **h**- **i**- **j**-

Page 15, Frame 23

Henry FLEMING, **b**-__ Mar 1804, **c**-Jo. HAGERTY, **d**-$400, **e**-James
STEEL, Robert FORSYTHE, **f**- **g**- **h**- **i**- **j**-

Joseph MORGAN, **b**-20 Mar 1804, **c**-Joseph MORGAN, **d**-$1500, **e**-John
WRIGHT, William BEATTY, **f**- **g**-11 Feb 1806, **h**-$414.10, **i**-$208.99,
j-$205.02, heirs

William HARPER, **b**-22 May 1804, **c**-Moses KELLY, Peacock MAJOR, **d**-$1000, **e**-Robert MEANS, Henry HOOVER, **f**- **g**- **h**- **i**- **j**-

Sarah HARPER, **b**-22 May 1804, **c**-Moses KELLY, Peacock MAJOR, **d**-$500, **e**-Robert MEANS, Henry HOOVER, **f**- **g**- **h**- **i**- **j**-

James McGINNES, **b**-29 May 1804, **c**-Mary McGINNES, Joseph MARTIN, **d**-$1000, **e**-John GILLESPIE, James STEEL, **f**-19 Jun 1804, **g**-31 Aug 1808, **h**-$1025.11.5, **i**-$488.85, **j**-$536.26.5, heirs

Noah ABRAHAM, **b**-29 May 1804, **c**-Rebecca ABRAHAM, James SANDERSON, **d**-$8000, **e**-William BEALE, John BROWN, **f**-14 Jan 1805, **g**-4 Mar 1814, **h**-$4046.17, **i**-$3351.05, **j**-$595.12, heirs

Charles KELLY, **b**-2 Jun 1804, **c**-Michael KELLY, **d**-$400, **e**-Nicholas CALDWELL, Jacob WERTZ, **f**-13 Jun 1804, **g**-12 Jan 1807, **h**-£78..7..6, **i**-£33..6..6, **j**-£45..1..0, heirs

James RODMAN, **b**-11 Sep 1804, **c**-Margaret RODMAN, **d**-$1600, **e**-William BEALL, William BEATTY, **f**-9 Apr 1805, **g**-3 Jul 1812, **h**-$1461.36, **i**-$1461.36, **j**-

Robert McDOWELL, **b**-26 Sep 1804, **c**-James BANKS, Frederick SWITZER, **d**-$1800, **e**- Peter LINTNER, **f**- **g**- **h**- **i**- **j**-

John FRYBARGER, **b**-28 Sep 1804, **c**-George BREHMAN, **d**-$1800, **e**-Thos. GALLAHER, L. DOERST, **f**-19 Mar 1805, **g**-9 an 1806, **h**-$1228.02, **i**-$365.89, **j**-$862.13, heirs

Page 16, Frame 34

Alexander STALFORD, **b**-1 Oct 1804, **c**-George BRATTON, John BRATTON, **d**-$2500, **e**-Robert PARKS, James CRISWELL, **f**- **g**- **h**- **i**- **j**-

John DAILY, **b**-5 Oct 1804, **c**-John RODMAN, Alexander McCAHEN, **d**-$1000, **e**-John McCAHEN, Ezra DOTY, **f**-6 Nov 1804, **g**-26 Sep 1812, **h**- **i**-$52.13, **j**-$52.13, admrs

William GROTHOUSE, **b**-10 Oct 1804, **c**-Mary GROTHOUSE, James WOODS, **d**-$4000, **e**-John YOKAM, James MACKLIN, **f**-10 Oct 1804, **g**-29 Dec 1809, **h**-£820..3..3.5, **i**-£218..13..1, **j**-£601..10..2.5, heirs

James STEWART, **b**-13 Oct 1804, **c**-William BRATTON, Esq., **d**-$2400, **e**-John CULBERTSON, Edwd. WILLIAMSON, **f**- **g**-30 Mar 1807, **h**-£248..0..11, **i**-£206..4..11.5, **j**-£41..15..11.5, heirs

William MITCHELL, **b**-4 Oct 1804, **c**-James ALRICKS, Robert WILSON, **d**-$6000, **e**-Robert McMEEN, Thomas STURGEON, **f**-23 Nov 1804, **g**-20 Aug 1808/19 Apr 1819, **h**-£303..16..7.5/225..0..0, **i**-£466..4..1.5/215.3..10, **j**-£9..14..2, heirs

Samuel JACOBS, b-8 Nov 1804, **c**-John PATTERSON, Merch., **d**-$300, **e**-Thos. GILSON, John ARNOLD, **f**- **g**- **h**- **i**- **j**-

John OWENS, b-8 Nov 1804, **c**-Andrew OWENS, David McKEE, **d**-$1500, **e**-Robert FORSYTHE, Edward WILLIAMS, **f**-8 May 1805, **g**-21 Mar 1806, **h**-£400..16..8.75, **i**-£295..5..8.5, **j**-£105..11..0.25, heirs

Christly MYERS, b-21 Nov 1804, **c**-John WRIGHT, George IRVINE, **d**-$4000, **e**-Lewis HORNING, James CURRAN, **f**-6 Aug 1805, **g**-18 Mar 1807, **h**-$941.54.5, **i**-$446.19, **j**-$405/35/5, heirs

David STARRS, b-22 Nov 1804, **c**-Lettice STARRS, **d**-$7000, **e**-Peacock MAJOR, John McCURDY, **f**-26 Nov 1804, **g**-5 Aug 1806, **h**-£138..1..9, **i**-£102..12..5, **j**-£35..9..4, heirs

Jacob SNYDER, b-27 Nov 1804, **c**-George SNYDER, **d**-$1500, **e**-John IRVIN, Michael FONCANON, **f**-28 Nov 1804, **g**-6 Aug 1806, **h**-$195.31, **i**-$196.04, **j**-$.73, admr

Page 17, Frame 26

James STACKPOLE, b-1 Dec 1804, **c**-Dorcas STACKPOLE, **d**-$2400, **e**-George WAKEFIELD, Jacob KURTZ, **f**-27 Dec 1804, **g**-16 Oct 1819, **h**-$1133.31, **i**-$1133.31, **j**-

James RIDDLE, b-5 Dec 1804, **c**-John RIDDLE, **d**-$1600, **e**-James CURRAN, Jas. BANKS, Col., **f**-19 Dec 1804/20 Mar 1828, **g**-15 Apr 1806/19 Nov 1821, **h**-£197..13..7/$66.00, **i**-£288..6..6.5/$1391.15.5, **j**-£90..12..11.5, admr/$1325.53.5, accountant

John ZOOK, b-6 Dec 1804, **c**-Christly YOTTER, Christian COFFMAN, **d**-$15,500, **e**-John ZOOK, Christian ZOOK, **f**-22 Dec 1804, **g**-4 Feb 1806/6 Sep 1811, **h**-£285..7..10.75/$6148.52, **i**-£91..3..9.75/$6536.63, **j**-/$388.11, admr

Samuel REICHART, b-10 Dec 1804, **c**-John ZOOK, John EVANS, **d**-$500, **e**-Christly ZOOK, Jacob YOTTER, **f**- **g**-8 Nov 1806, **h**-£108..10..4, **i**-£40..16..9.5, **j**-£67..13..6.5, heirs

Thomas SMILEY, b-21 Dec 1804, **c**-John SMILEY, **d**-$3200, **e**-John MAHON, Joseph DOUGLASS, **f**-25 Dec 1804, **g**-$1062.11, **h**-8 Mar 1808, **i**-$1137.66, **j**-$75.55, admr

Benjamin KEPNER, b-22 Dec 1804, **c**-John KEPNER, Benjn. KEPNER, **d**-£2000, **e**-Hugh ALEXANDER, Andrew PATTERSON, **f**-20 Dec 1826, **g**-11 Jun 1827, **h**-$480.93, **i**-$315.11.5, **j**-$165.81.5, estate

Andrew RAMSEY, b-14 Jan 1805, **c**-Agness RAMSEY, Andrew RAMSEY, **d**-$500, **e**-David DAVIDSON, James SANDERSON, **f**- **g**- **h**- **i**- **j**-

Ann THOMPSON, b-9 Jan 1805, **c**-Wm. ARBUCKLE, **d**-£200, **e**-John
ARBUCKLE, George GUILLIFORD, **f**-29 Jan 1805, **g**-18 Oct 1811,
h-£106..6..5, **i**-£72..15..4, **j**-£33..11..1, heirs
Isabella NEELY, b-29 Jan 1805, **c**-David NEELY, **d**-£250, **e**-Col. John
McDOWELL, Robert MITCHELL, **f**- **g**- **h**- **i**- **j**-
Jacob CROW, b-15 Feb 1805, **c**-Philip LESOH, **d**-$1600, **e**-Christian
CROW, Henry GRIM, **f**- **g**- **h**- **i**- **j**-

Page 18, Frame 27
John KINGLE, b-16 Mar 1805, **c**-Abraham SNYDER, **d**-$500, **e**-Adam
SIGLER, Wm. STEMPFF, **f**- **g**- **h**- **i**- **j**-
George JACOBS, b-10 May 1805, **c**-John CARLISLE, **d**-$400, **e**-William
BRATTON, George GALBREATH, **f**- **g**- **h**- **i**- **j**-
George IRWIN, b-14 Jun 1805, **c**-Mary IRWIN, David ALLEN, James
SANDERSON, **d**-$8000, **e**-Roswell DOTY, Edward WILLIAMS, **f**-9
Feb 1808, **g**-9 Feb 1808, **h**-$3026.29, **i**-$2144.62, **j**-$881.67, heirs
George PORTER, b-29 Jul 1805, **c**-Mary PORTER, Robert PORTER, **d**-
$10,000, **e**-George McCLELLAND, Wm. A. PATTERSON, **f**-5 Dec
1805/27 Jun 1808, **g**-21 Jan 1807/18 Jun 1808/26 Nov 1808, **h**-
£2248..1..1/1/2154..9..5, **i**-£1160..5..1.5//2154..9..5, **j**-
Robert STALFORD, b-25 Sep 1805, **c**-George BRATTON, **d**-$3500, **e**-
Robert PARKS, John CRISWELL, **f**- **g**- **h**- **i**- **j**-
Saml. Southard DOTY, b-13 Aug 1805, **c**-Ezra DOTY, Roswell DOTY,
d-$2000, **e**-George McCLELLAND, John BROWN, **f**- **g**- **h**- **i**- **j**-
John MYERS, b-5 Oct 1805, **c**-Samuel MYERS, John ROTHROCK, **d**-
£800, **e**-John ORTH, Lazarus STEELY, **f**-13 Feb 1811, **g**-6 Jun
1811/Apr 1823, **h**-$3383.24/$2254.98 **i**-$4420.58/1962.93, **j**-
$1037.34/$292.02, heirs
James BOGGS, b-9 Oct 1805, **c**-Francis BOGGS, Joseph BOGGS, **d**-
$600, **e**-William WILSON, John BEATTY, **f**-24 Oct 1805, **g**-18 Nov
1817, **h**-$529.52, **i**-$1160.73.5, **j**-$708.57, admrs
James HOLMS, b-24 Oct 1805, **c**-John OLIVER, George WAKEFIELD,
d-$1800, **e**-James CRISWELL, James ALEXANDER, **f**-13 May 1806,
g-19 Feb 1808, **h**-£465..4..7, **i**-£261..5..3.5, **j**-£201..19..3.5, heirs
Joseph MULHERREN, b-29 Oct 1805, **c**-Sarah MULHERREN, Isaiah
YOKAM, **d**-$1800, **e**-John YOKAM, James KNOX, **f**-21 Nov 1805,
g-19 Apr 1808/18 Dec 1812, **h**-£68..14..9.5/$194.80, **i**-
£99..18..8.5/$194.80 **j**-

Page 19, Frame 28

Edward WILLIAMS, b-30 Oct 1805, c-Mary WILLIAMS, James CHRISWELL, Andrew KEISER, d-$3000, e-Michl. FONCANON, Elias W. HALE, f-11 May 1815, g-11 May 1815, h-$1778.60, i-$1700.55, j-$78.05, heirs

John ALLEN, b-1 Oct 1805, c-Margaret ALLEN, William ALLEN, d-$2500, e-George HANAWALT, James CHRISWELL, f-8 Jan 1812, g- h- i- j-

Edward McCARTY, b-2 Nov 1805, c-Bathsheba McCARTY, George McCLELLAND, d-$4000, e-Andrew KEIZER, Robert PORTER, f- g-18 Mar 1807, h-$1670.98, i-$1152.01, j-$518.97, estate

John McINTIRE, b-4 Nov 1805, c-Samuel McINTIRE, Alexander McINTIRE, d-$2500, e-Thomas BARRETT, Wm. ARBUCKLE, f-4 Nov 1805, g-14 Mar 1810/9 May 1812, h-$1090.22.5/689.29, i-$434.93/431.31, j-$259.98, heirs

John GARDNER, b-11 Nov 1805, c-Isabella GARDNER, Alexander CAMERON, d-$1800, e-Robert FORSYTHE, John GILLASPIE, f- g- h- i- j-

William PHILIPS, b-14 Nov 1805, c-Ann PHILIPS, d-$1500, e-Aaron COTTER, Thos. GALLAHER, f-26 Dec 1805, g-13 Nov 1806, h-£87..13..9.5, i-£85..14..5, j-£1..19..4.5, heirs

Thomas BEARD, b-15 Nov 1805, c-Jonathan HAMILTON, d-$2000, e-Archibald FERGUSON, Thos. POSTLETHWAIT, f- g- h- i- j-

Jesse GRIFFITH, b-7 Dec 1805, c-John SHIVELY, Isaiah YOKAM, d-$3000, e-Doct. Roswell DOTY, William QUAIL, f-11 Feb 1806, g-3 May 1811, h-$1299.23, i-$462.26, j-$836.96, heirs

John HORRELL, b-17 Dec 1805, c-Sarah HORRELL, John PATTERSON, d-$5000, e-Stewart LAIRD, John McCAUGHAN, f-15 Jan 1806/7 Dec 1805[sic], g-22 May 1807/13 Mar 1816, h-$1606.24, i-$1845.47, j-

John STEWART, b-9 Jan 1806, c-Margaret STEWART, Thos. H. STEWART, William HARRIS, d-$4000, e-John WATTSON, George McCLELLAND, f-2 Aug 1806/23 Jun 1807, g-23 Nov 1810, h-$3097.99, i-$2897.32, j-$200.67, heirs

Page 20, Frame 29

John McCAHEN, b-23 Jan 1806, c-Alexander McCAHEN, d-$3000, e-James ROBISON, Thomas ANDERSON, f- g-19 Mar 1810, h-$316.68, i-$671.55, j-$354.87, admr

William HENDERSON, b-25 Jan 1806, **c**-John HENDERSON, Thomas HENDERSON, **d**-$3000, **e**-James McLAUGHLIN, Griffith THOMAS, **f**-24 Feb 1806, **g**-1- Kim 1924. **h**-$1019.08, **i**-$424.40, **j**-$594.68, estate

Christian STEELY, b-11 Feb 1806, **c**-Henry STEELY, **d**-$2000, **e**-John LANTZ, John EVANS, **f**- **g**- **h**- **i**- **j**-

Daniel ZOOK, b-11 Feb 1806, **c**-John ZOOK, Carpt., **d**-$2000, **e**-Christly ZOOK, John EVANS, **f**-9 Apr 1806/15 Oct 1807, **g**-1 Apr 1809/18 Mar 1811/17 Mar 1817, **h**-£199..1..3/ $1474.66/$1309.11, **i**-£48..2..6/$487.33/$96.50, **j**-$1212,61, heirs

William CAMPBELL, b-11 Mar 1806, **c**-James CAMPBELL, Robert CAMPBELL, **d**-$6000, **e**-John WRIGHT, Martin BYERS, **f**- **g**- **h**- **i**- **j**-

James TAYLOR, b-22 Mar 1806, **c**-Doct. Ezra DOTY, Mathew TAYLOR, **d**-$3000, **e**-Thomas GHORMLY, Andrew BANKS, **f**-5 May 1806, **g**-14 Dec 1814, **h**-$677.48, **i**-$1096.44, **j**-$418.06, admrs

Henry HOUSTETTER, b-27 Mar 1806, **c**-David COFFMAN, **d**-$2000, **e**-John ZOOK, Christly ZOOK, **f**-11 Apr 1806, **g**-3 May 1808, **h**-$916.71, **i**-$998.70, **j**-$81.99, admrs

Nicholas ARNOLD, b-28 Mar 1806, **c**-Jacob REIGHART, Edward HOWARD, **d**-$3000, **e**-John STEWART, Edwd. HOWARD, **f**-28 Apr 1806, **g**-17 Apr 1816, **h**-$913.74, **i**-$1001.92, **j**-$88.18, admrs

Mary CAGHILL, b-10 Apr 1806, **c**-William CORBETT, Sr., **d**-$2000, **e**-Caleb PARSHALL, Abm. HUFFORD, **f**- **g**- **h**- **i**- **j**-

Christian ZOOK, Jr., b-22 Apr 1806, **c**-John EVANS, **d**-$8000, **e**-Christian ZOOK, Christly YODER, **f**- **g**-25 Apr 1807, **h**-$548.89 **i**-$343.88, **j**-$205.01, heirs

Page 21, Frame 30
John REYNOLDS, b-25 Apr 1806, **c**-Jacob SELLERS, **d**-$1500, **e**-Jacob SMITH, Samuel MYERS, **f**-19 Aug 1806, **g**-19 May 1807, **h**-£114..1..0, **i**-£111..10..3.5, **j**-£2..10..8, heirs

Christian LANTZ, b-8 May 1806, **c**-Jacob KING, Jacob YODER, **d**-$4000, **e**-Jacob LANTZ, Christian DETWEILER, **f**-8 May 1806, **g**-26 Nov 1808/25 Feb 1809, **h**-£253..12..2, **i**-£353..12..2, **j**-

William BEATTY, b-30 May 1806, **c**-Isabella BEATTY, **d**-$1800, **e**-Benjamin LAW, James SANDERSON, **f**- **g**- **h**- **i**- **j**-

Nicholas DEHL, b-11 Jun 1806, **c**-Andrew KEISER, **d**-$2500, **e**-Wm. A. PATTERSON, George McCLELLAND, **f**-7 Jul 1806, **g**-25 Apr 1811, **h**-$1577.77, **i**-$1638.89, **j**-$61.12, admr

James IRWIN, b-16 Jun 1806, **c**-James IRWIN, John ROSS, **d**-$8000, **e**-Col. Wm. BEALE, Robert MISKELLY, **f**- **g**- **h**- **i**- **j**-

William BEALE, **b**-20 Aug 1806, **c**-William BEALE, Abner BEALE, **d**-$3000, **e**-David BEALE, John CUMMINGS, **f**-19 Nov 1806, **g**-4 Sep 1813, **h**-$1434.93.5, **i**-$1414.93, **j**-$20.07, estate

Henry BITNER, **b**-11 Oct 1806, **c**-Leonard GRONINGER, Jacob WRIGHT, **d**-$4800, **e**-Zachh. DOERST, Jacob FRYBARGER, **f**-17 Nov 1806, **g**-12 Mar 1808, **h**-$1854.35.5, **ih**-$79.04, **j**-$1775.31.5, heirs

John HARRIS, **b**-18 Oct 1806, **c**-Thomas HARRIS, **d**-$3500, **e**-Robert MISKELLY, Baltzer CROW, **f**- **g**- **h**- **i**- **j**-

David HEISER, **b**-18 Oct 1806, **c**-Jacob AUKER, **d**-$500, **e**-Michael PAGE, Abraham PAGE,, **f**-18 Oct 1806, **g**- 17 Apr 1810, **h**-$288.06, **i**-$267.97, **j**-$20.08.5, heirs

Neal McMANIGIL, **b**-20 Oct 1806, **c**-William McMANIGIL, Robert McMANIGIL, **d**-$4500, **e**-John COOPER, Samuel McNITT, **f**- **g**- **h**- **i**- **j**-

Page 22, Frame 31

John MITCHELL, **b**-28 Oct 1806, **c**-Robert MITCHELL, **d**-$2500, **e**-Robert MITCHELL, James REED, **f**- **g**- **h**- **i**- **j**-

Thomas GREEN, **b**-30 Oct 1806, **c**-Isaac GREEN, **d**-$2000, **e**-Samuel SHARON, Andrew NELSON, **f**- **g**-15 Feb 1808/21 Apr 1813, **h**-$290.84/$134.03, **i**-$235.96/$121.97, **j**-$12.06, heirs

Jacob GUYER, **b**-3 Nov 1806, **c**-Margaret GUYER, Henry GUYER, **d**-$3000, **e**-Jacob HOFFMAN, Henry DUNMIRE, **f**-3 Nov 1806, **g**-27 Jun 1816, **h**-$719.50, **i**-719.50, **j**-

John GLENN, **b**-18 Nov 1806, **c**-Jane GLENN, Paul LAUGHLIN, **d**-$4000, **e**-William DOUGLAS, Joseph DOUGLAS, **f**- **g**- **h**- **i**- **j**-

Letitia SAMPLE, **b**-22 Nov 1806, **c**-James SAMPLE, **d**-$3000, **e**-Joseph SAMPLE, James STEEL, **f**- **g**- **h**- **i**- **j**-

Samuel JACKSON, **b**-21 Jan 1807, **c**-Margaret JACKSON, **d**-$1500, **e**-David DAVIDSON, David WALKER, Esq., **f**-17 Feb 1807, **g**-6 May 1808, **h**-£38..8..9, **i**-£36..9..4.5, **j**-£1..19..4.5, heirs

Aquilla BURCHFIELD, **b**-27 Jan 1807, **c**-Church COX, **d**-$3000, **e**-William BLACK, David WALKER, **f**-11 Nov 1808/23 Jan 1807[sic], **g**-13 May 1808/23 Jun 1809, **h**-£200..14..7/£129..7..0, **i**-£71..7..7/£10..13..8.5, **j**-£108..13..3.5, estate

Jeremiah DAILY, **b**-27 Jan 1807, **c**-Mary DAILY, **d**-$2000, **e**-Robert BUCHANAN, James TURNER, **f**-9 Feb 1807, **g**-5 Mar 1810, **h**-£135..16..7, **i**-£107..8..2.5 **j**-£28..8..4.5, estate

George SHAVER, **b**-21 Feb 1807, **c**-Abner BEALE, **d**-$3400, **e**-Samuel KEEVER, John KEEVER, Esq., **f**- **g**- **h**- **i**- **j**-

Samuel **REEDER**, **b**-24 Feb 1807, **c**-Sarah REEDER, Azzur WRIGHT, **d**-$2000, **e**-Edward HOWARD, Samuel BURGE, **f**-21 Mar 1807, **g**-2 May 1809, **h**-$1576.52, **i**-£267..12..6, **j**-£343..11..4, heirs

Page 23, Frame 32
Hugh MAGILL, **b**-6 Mar 1807, **c**-Robert MAGILL, **d**-$2800, **e**-Wm. MAGILL, Doct. Roswell DOTY, **f**- **g**- **h**- **i**- **j**-
Richard CONLEY, **b**-18 Mar 1807, **c**-Elijah CRISWELL, **d**-$1500, **e**-John BRISBIN, Joseph KYLE, **f**- **g**- **h**- **i**- **j**-
William WORLEY, **b**-30 Mar 1807, **c**-Jacob REIGHAT, Esq., **d**-$1500, **e**-Jacob YOST, John WATTSON, Esq., **f**-23 Apr 1807, **g**-3 Sep 1813, **h**-$774.21.5, **i**-382.42.5, **j**-$391.79, heirs
John McCLELLAND, **b**-31 Mar 1807, **c**-Catherine LYON, John WATTSON, **d**-£1000, **e**-William CUNNINGHAM, John STEWART, **f**- **g**- **h**- **i**- **j**-
West KINSLOE, **b**-20 Apr 1807, **c**-James KINSLOE, **d**-$2000, **e**-James MACKEY, Martin BYERS, **f**- **g**- **h**- **i**- **j**-
Michael CHRISWELL, **b**-20 Apr 1807, **c**-Isabella CHRISWELL, **d**-$2000, **e**-Col. Wm. BRATTON, Alexander STEWART, **f**- **g**- **h**- **i**- **j**-
William HARRIS, **b**-24 Apr 1807, **c**-James HARRIS, Esq., **d**-$2800, **e**-James CHRISWELL, Wm. CORBETT, **f**- **g**- **h**- **i**- **j**-
Thomas RAMSEY, **b**-12 May 1807, **c**-John SMITH, **d**-$1000, **e**-George McCLELLAND, William SCOTT, **f**- **g**- **h**- **i**- **j**-
Rev. Alexr. McILWAIN, **b**-22 May 1807, **c**-Moses CARRAN, **d**-$2800, **e**-E. W. HALE, John BROWN, **f**- **g**- **h**- **i**- **j**-
Patrick McCALEB, **b**-26 May 1807, **c**-Alexander WORK, **d**-$1000, **e**-Daniel McCALEB, Roswell DOTY, **f**- **g**- **h**- **i**- **j**-

Page 24, Frame 33
Joseph SWARTZELL, **b**-9 Jun 1807, **c**-George SWARTZELL, **d**-$2000, **e**-Henry SWARTZELL, John STEEL, **f**- **g**- **h**- **i**- **j**-
Daniel HOSEA, **b**-16 Jun 1807, **c**-Col. John McDOWELL, **d**-$1000, **e**-John COOPER, Wm. A. PATTERSON, **f**- **g**- **h**- **i**- **j**-
Christian ZOOK, **b**-23 Jun1807, **c**-David KAUFMAN, **d**-$8000, **e**-Isaac CARVER, Michael HOSTETLER, **f**- **g**-19 Jun 1809, **h**-$1985.86, **i**-£347..9..7.5, **j**-£397..4..3.5, heirs
Stephen TUCKMAN, **b**-25 Jun 1807, **c**-George TUCKMAN, Stephen TUCKMAN, **d**-$6000, **e**-Hugh HARDY, Patrick McCAHEN, **f**- **g**-10 Nov 1826, **h**-$3018.66.5, **i**-$33.48.5, **j**-$2985.18, estate

George CASNER, **b**-26 Dec 1807, **c**-William BEALE, Nicholas OAKESON, **d**-$1400, **e**-John KINZER, Valentine WEISHAUPT, **f**- **g**-5 Oct 1821, **h**-$4700.52, **i**-$4456.36, **j**-$244.16, estate

John HOSTETLER, **b**-27 Jun 1807, **c**-Barbara HOSTETLER, John KAUFMAN, **d**-$4000, **e**-Christley HOOLY, Jacob ZOOK, **f**- **g**-20 Jun 1809/3 May 1813, **h**-$1169.70/$5642.82, **i**-$2322.05 **j**-$3319.77, heirs

Thomas GALLACHER, **b**-4 Jul 1807, **c**-Lydia GALLAHER[sic], James KNOX, **d**-$4800, **e**-William BROWN, Francis ELLIS, **f**- **g**-3 May 1813, **h**-$916.62, **i**-$769.55, **j**-$147.09, heirs

Henry BITNER, **b**-19 Aug 1807, **c**-Michael McMONAHON, **d**-$8500, **e**-John PATTERSON, John HARDY, **f**-18 Jun 1808, **g**-24 Jul 1809/8 Mar 1810, **h**-£1333..13..5/$790.13, **i**-£1038..17..5/$159.41, **j**-$630.72, heirs

Samuel HOLLIDAY, **b**-19 Nov 1807, **c**-Sarah HOLLIDAY, Adam HOLLIDAY, John HOLLIDAY, **d**-$6000, **e**-George CALBREATH[sic], Col. Wm. BRATTON, Esq., **f**- **g**- **h**- **i**- **j**-

James LOCKERT, **b**-19 Nov 1807, **c**-Col. Wm. BRATTON, **d**-$1000, **e**-Adam HOLLIDAY, Geo. CALBREATH, **f**- **g**- **h**- **i**- **j**-

Page 25, Frame 34

William McNAIR, **b**-24 Nov 1807, **c**-Andrew KEISER, Esq., **d**-$6000, **e**-James CHRISWELL, John STEEL, **f**-1 Dec 1807, **g**-16 Nov 1811, **h**-$2098.76, **i**-$2098.76, **j**-

William MARTIN, **b**-11 Dec 1807, **c**-Nathan MARTIN, James SANDERSON, **d**-$1000, **e**-Thos. WILSON, Geo. MULHOLLEN, **f**- **g**- **h**- **i**- **j**-

John PAULUM, **b**-1 Jan 1808, **c**-William BEALE, Jacob MOHLER, **d**-$1000, **e**-Wm. WALLSMITH, Abraham HAMAKER, **f**-20 Jan 1808, **g**-25 Aug 1815, **h**-$2382.23, **i**-$2264.13, **j**-$118.10, heirs

William MONTGOMERY, **b**-18 Jan 1808, **c**-David HUNTER, **d**-$6000, **e**-Robert STERRETT, David STERRETT, **f**- **g**- **h**- **i**- **j**-

James JOHNSTON, **b**-30 Jan 1808, **c**-William JOHNSTON, **d**-$2000, **e**-Michael CUNNINGHAM, James A. KINKEAD, **f**- **g**-22 Jan 1811, **h**-$73.93, **i**-$73.93, **j**-

John HAMILTON, **b**-24 Feb 1808, **c**-Wm. CUNNINGHAM, John PARSONS, **d**-$8000, **e**-George BRAHMAN, Hugh HARDY, **f**-18 Apr 1808, **g**-12 Mar 1811, **h**-$716.76, **i**-$448.18, **j**-$268.58, heirs

Christopher WIMER, **b**-15 Apr 1808, **c**-Esther WIMER, **d**-$1000, **e**-Mathew TAYLOR, Doct. Roswell DOTY, **f**- **g**- **h**- **i**- **j**-

William **COOKSON**, **b**-27 Apr 1808, **c**-Mary COOKSON, Joseph
  COOKSON, **d**-$2000, **e**-David WALKER, Isaac YOST, **f**-27 Apr 1808
  g-22 Nov 1809/21 Nov 1810, **h**-$599.83/310.03, **i**-£113..17..8/$109.31,
  j-$200.72, estate

Enoch **WILLIAMS**, **b**-14 May 1808, **c**-David WILLIAMS, **d**-$8000, **e**-
  Robt. MEANS, Philip ROTHROCK, **f**- **g**- **h**- **i**- **j**-

William **STEWART**, **b**-17 Aug 1808, **c**-Alice STEWART, William
  GRAHAM, **d**-$5000, **e**-John PATTERSON, Thomas HENDERSON,
  f- **g**-22 Apr 1817, **h**-$1013.57, **i**- **j**-

Page 26, Frame 35

Christian **COPELAND**, **b**-17 Aug 1808, **c**-Nicholas ICKES, Thomas
  HENDERSON, **d**-$5000, **e**-John SMITH, Valentine WEISHAUPT, **f**-
  17 Mar 1819, **g**-17 Mar 1819/21 Nov 1826, **h**-$901.44, **i**-
  $901.44/$40.62.5, **j**-$40.62.5, accountant

Lazarus **STEELY**, **b**-18 Aug 1808, **c**-Jonathan ROTHROCK, **d**-$8000, **e**-
  Wm. MITCHELL, Geo. McCLELLAND, **f**- **g**- **h**- **i**- **j**-

Stephen **TENNIS**, **b**-29 Aug 1808, **c**-Jacob REIGART, **d**-$4000, **e**-James
  ALRICKS, John JAMESON, **f**-27 Dec 1808, **g**-14 Mar 1810, **h**-
  $386.63, **i**-$374.25.5, **j**-$12.37.5, heirs

Samuel **McCRORY**, **b**-30 Aug 1808, **c**-Mary McCRORY, John
  McCRORY, **d**-$2000, **e**-David BARNHILL, Robert GLASS, **f**- **g**- **h**-
  i- **j**-

Alexander **ROBISON, Jr.**, **b**-21 Sep 1808, **c**-Jane ROBISON, **d**-$3000,
  e-Hugh HARDY, John HARDY, **f**-14 Nov 1808, **g**-14 May 1816, **h**-
  $242.67, **i**-$243.29, **j**-$.62, admr

William **SCOTT**, **b**-7 Nov 1808, **c**-Jasper COWGILL, Esq., **d**-$2000, **e**-
  James CHRISWELL, Wm. CORBETT, **f**-3 Dec 1808, **g**-16 Mar 1810,
  h-$324.25, **i**-$199/04. **j**-$135.30, heirs

Elizabeth **GROVE**, **b**-13 Feb 1809, **c**-Windle GROVE, **d**-$1000, **e**-
  Nicholas OAKESON, Jacob COON, **f**- **g**- **h**- **i**- **j**-

Melchoir **SEGNER**, **b**-9 Mar 1809, **c**-Andrew SEGNER, **d**-$1000, **e**-Peter
  SPRINGER, Michael FUNK, **f**- **g**- **h**- **i**- **j**-

Jacob **YOST**, **b**-11 Mar 1809, **c**-James ALEXANDER **d**-$1600, **e**-Robert
  BUCHANAN, Joseph COWGILL, **f**-20 Mar 1809, **g**-30 Mar 1813, **h**-
  $386.05, **i**-$386.05 **j**-

Rebecca **ROBISON**, **b**-18 Mar 1809, **c**-Thomas ROBISON, **d**-$2000, **e**-
  James ROBISON, John HARDY, **f**- **g**- **h**- **i**- **j**-

Page 27, Frame 36

Michael MULLEN, **b**-23 Sep 1809, **c**-Mary MULLEN, **d**-$1000, **e**-Andrew CALDWELL, Jacob KURTS, **f**- **g**- **h**- **i**- **j**-

Joseph IRWIN, **b**-29 Aug 1809, **c**-James IRWIN, **d**-$800, **e**-James CRISWELL, Peter LANGTON, **f**-7 Oct 1809, **g**-24 Oct 1809, **h**-$131.74, **i**-$131.74, **j**-

Jane EDMISTON, **b**-5 April 1809, **c**-George McCLELLAND, Esq., **d**-$3000, **e**-Wm. A. PATTERSON, Andw. KEISER, Esq., **f**-13 Mar 1811, **g**-13 Mar 1811, **h**-$2464.32, **i**-$2154.64, **j**-$309.68, estate

Mary JOHNSTON, **b**-19 Apr 1809, **c**-Philip GRAFT, **d**-$3000, **e**-Philip SHUPE, David JORDAN, **f**- **g**- **h**- **i**- **j**-

Jacob BEAVER, **b**-15 May 1809, **c**-Samuel BARNHILL, **d**-$2000, **e**-Samuel WALLICK, Samuel DUNCAN, **f**-15 May 1809, **g**-13 Mar 1809, **h**-$112.26, **i**-$127.50, **j**-$15.24, admr

Henry HOOVER, **b**-24 Jul 1809, **c**-Elizabeth HOOVER, **d**-$2000, **e**-Peacock MAJOR, Philip RUPERT, **f**- **g**- **h**- **i**- **j**-

Mathias LICHTENTHALER, **b**-5 Aug 1809, **c**-Jacob REIGHART, **d**-$5000, **e**-Daniel [SHEITLE], Isaac YOST, **f**- **g**- **h**- **i**- **j**-

Michael MULLEN, **b**-26 Aug 1809, **c**-Mary MULLIN[sic], George BRATTON, **d**-$1000, **e**-William BRATTON, William W. LAIRD, **f**- **g**- **h**- **i**- **j**-

William MONTOOTH, **b**-11 Dec 1809, **c**-William McCORMICK, Mary MONTOOTH, **d**-£100, **e**-Alexr. WALKER, David CLAYTON, **f**- **g**- **h**- **i**- **j**-

Thomas SWEARINGEN, **b**-27 Oct 1809, **c**-Evan VAN SWEARINGEN, **d**-$4000, **e**-William BEALE (written BEALE William], William BELL, **f**- **g**- **h**- **i**- **j**-

Robert WORK, **b**-22 Nov 1809, **c**-Joseph BOGGS, **d**-$2000. **e**-Joseph B. ARD, Hugh WREKFORD, **f**- **g**- **h**- **i**- **j**-

Samuel ANDERSON, **b**-19 Jan 1809, **c**-James CRAWFORD, **d**-$5000, **e**-William W. LAIRD, Elias W. HALE, **f**- **g**- **h**- **i**- **j**-

Page 28, Frame 37

James IRWIN, **b**-1 Feb 1810, **c**-William BRATTON, Jeremiah CARNEY, **d**-$5000, **e**-John CARLISLE, Alexr. McKINSTRY, **f**- **g**-24 Nov 1820, **h**-$441.08.5, **i**-$374.38 **j**-$66.70.5, estate

Mary MURRAY, **b**-3 Feb 1810, **c**-Theodore MEMINGER, **d**-$1000, **e**-John [NONIS, NORRIS?], Jos. B. ARD, **f**- **g**- **h**- **i**- **j**-

Alexander McNITT, **b**-26 Feb 1810, **c**-Samuel McNITT, **d**-$1800, **e**-Francis BOGGS, Crawford KYLE, Robert TAYLOR **f**-26 Feb 1810, **g**-26 Feb 1810, **h**-$1083.07, **i**-$240.60, **j**-$842.47, heirs

William CUNNINGHAM, **b**-10 Apr 1810, **c**-Robert FORSYTHE, **d**-$1000, **e**-Peacock MAJOR, Anthoney [FESES], **f**- **g**-28 Sep 1813, **h**-$632.85, **i**-$563.74 **j**-$69.09, estate

Henry KREIDER, **b**-13 Apr 1810, **c**-Elizabeth KREIDER, Tobias KREIDER, **d**-$500, **e**-Henry HARTMAN, John CLYMER, **f**-16 Apr 1810, **g**-24 Jan 1811, **h**-$272.71, **i**-$161.07, **j**-$111.64, heirs

David BEALE, **b**-18 Apr 1810, **c**-David BEALE, **d**-$600, **e**-Abner BEALE, Samuel WALLICK, **f**- **g**-21 Aug 1811, **h**-£55..1..4, **i**-£55..1..4 **j**-

David LAUGHLIN, **b**-17 Jan 1810, **c**-John PATTERSON, Esq., Joseph STEWART, **d**-$2000, **e**-James KNOX, Esq., James McCONNELL, **f**-17 Jan 1810, **g**-13 Mar 1816, **h**-$936.54, **i**-$637.52, **j**-$299.15, heirs

Melchoir IMTORF, **b**-18 May 1810, **c**-John ROTHROCK, **d**-$2000, **e**-John [NORRIS?], James CHRISWELL, **f**- **g**- **h**- **i**- **j**-

William SCOTT, **b**-25 May 1810, **c**-Jane SCOTT, Samuel EDMISTON, John BROWN, **d**-$5000, **e**-E. W. HALE, Wm. A. PATTERSON, **f**-3 Dec 1808[sic], **g**- **h**- **i**- **j**-

James ATKINS, **b**-1 Jun 1810, **c**-William BELL, **d**-$2500, **e**-David ALLEN, William WILSON, **f**-22 Aug 1810, **g**- **h**- **i**- **j**-

John CLIMER, **b**-12 Jun 1810, **c**-Tobias KREIDER, Sr., **d**-$600 **e**-Tobias KREIDER, Jr., Roswell DOTY, **f**-7 Jul 1810, **g**-15 Apr 1811, **h**-$733.88.5, **i**-$459.70, **j**-$274.18.5, estate

William HUNTER, **b**-21 Aug 1810, **c**-Margaret HUNTER, James KIRK, **d**-$1200, **e**-Thomas BARRETT, William KERR, **f**-22 Aug 1810, **g**-29 Sep 1810, **h**-$635.23, **i**-$138.77, **j**-$496.46, heirs

Page 29, Frame 38

Sarah McLAUGHLIN, **b**-22 Aug 1810, **c**-Elizabeth McLAUGHLIN, **d**-$200, **e**-Wm. FLEMING, John HANAWALT, **f**- **g**- **h**- **i**- **j**-

Charles McGEE, **b**-28 Sep 1810, **c**-Frederick KELLER, **d**-$200, **e**-Walter CHARLES, Michael PAGE, **f**- **g**- **h**- **i**- **j**-

Joseph CEEVER, **b**-30 Oct 1810, **c**-John CEEVER, Esq., **d**-$1500, **e**-William FRAMPTON, Andrew KEISER, **f**-19 Nov 1810, **g**-5 Oct 1813, **h**-$1427.40, **i**-$508.71, **j**-$918.69, estate

James BRATTON, **b**-8 Jan 1811, **c**-William BRATTON, Wallace BRATTON, **d**-$800, **e**-Nicholas CALDWELL, Benjn. [WALKEE? WALKER?] **f**- **g**- **h**- **i**- **j**-

Edward NICHOLSON, b-24 Jan 1811, c-David BEALE d-$200, e-Wm. BEALE, M. M, MONAHON, f- g- h- i- j-

George JOHNSTON, b-6 Mar 1811, c-Peacock MAJOR, Roswell DOTY, d-$200, e-Andrew MAYS, Henry BARTHOLEMEW, f- g- h- i- j-

Arthur BUCHANAN, b-15 Mar 1811, c-Robert BUCHANAN, d-$500, e-John NONIS [NORRIS?], Andrew GREGG, f-4 Feb 1792, g-18 Dec 1806, h- i- j-

Edey LUKENS, b-23 Mar 1811, c-John LUKENS, d-$600, e-James ALRICKS, John McDOWELL, f- g-26 May 1812, h-$388.05, i-$35.82, j-$352.23, heirs

John PURDY, b-18 Apr 1811, c-Levi REYNOLDS, James BANKS, d-$1000, e-Stephen REYNOLDS, M. M. MONAHON, f- g-19 Jan 1814, h-$7395.89 i-$7398.37, j- $2.48, admrs

Alexander SHERLOCK, b-17 May 1811, c-William MARTIN, d-$300, e-Roswell DOTY, Samuel ANDERSON f- g- h- i- j-

John CULBERTSON, b-3 Jul 1811, c-Mary CULBERTSON, William PORTER, Charles DANIEL, d-$10,000, e-George BRATTON, John VANCE, James STEEL, f- g- h- i- j-

Bastian HASLER, b-16 Aug 1811, c-Ann HASLER, Wm. WALLSMITH, d-$1500, e-Robert MISCELLY, Leonard GLONINGER, f-30 Apr 1813, g-30 Apr 1813, h-$1897.40, i-$406.13.5, j-$1491.26.5, heirs

Page 30, Frame 39

Mathias SWARTZ, b-26 Aug 1811, c-John SNYDER, d-$300, e-Benjn. LANDES, Peter SWARTZ, f-26 Aug 1811, g-19 Jan 1813, h-$105.04, i-$41.97, j-$63.07, heirs

William McLAUGHLIN, b-11 Sep 1811, c-George VANCE, d-$400, e-John MEVEY, George MITCHELL, f- g-23 Oct 1818, h-$68.01, i-74.18, j-6.17, accountant

Jeremiah LINDSEY, b-18 Sep 1818, c-Mary LINDSEY, d-$400, e-James MACKEY, Anthoney YOUNG, f- g- h- i- j-

Zachariah RICE, b-21 Nov 1811, c-John RICE, d-$5000, e-Thomas TURBETT, Stewart LAIRD, f-23 Dec 1811, g-12 Oct 1812, h-£744..17.3, i-£37..2..11, j-£707..14..4 [no designation]

Samuel EDMISTON, b-23 Nov 1811, c-John EDMISTON, d-$10,000, e-Elias W. HALE, Jos. B. ARD, f-30 Jul 1804, g-20 Aug 1813, h-$956.66, i-$1854.67, j-$898.1, admr

John HARDY, b-5 Dec 1811. c-James KNOX, Esq., d-$1000, e-Samuel CHRISTY, Andrew KEISER, f-17 Mar 1801, g-18 Jan 1813/19 Nov 1813, h-$1491.87.5/$116.22, i-$1536.54/$456.03, j-$339.41, admr

William BUCHANAN, b-31 Jan 1812, **c**-David STEWART, **d**-$300, **e**-
David JORDAN, Robert FORSYTHE, **f**-20 Feb 1812, **g**-18 Mar 1819,
h-$683.91.5, **i**-$788.46, **j**-$104.56.5, admr

Lydia SCOTT, b-25 Feb 1812, **c**-William BRISBIN, **d**-$600, **e**-James
BRISBEN, James MILLIKEN, **f**- **g**- **h**- **i**- **j**-

John CARLISLE, b-5 Mar 1812, **c**-George BRATTON, John CARLISLE,
d-$5000, **e**-Wm. BRATTON, Esq., Francis ELLIS, **f**-4 Apr 1812, **g**-3
Sep 1814, **h**-$828.37.5, **i**-$896.73, **j**-$303.28.5, admrs

Peter MOOREHOUSE, b-6 Apr 1812, **c**-Arthur McNIGHT, **d**-$400, **e**-
James NORTH, Andrew KEISER, **f**-14 Oct 1840, **g**-14 Oct 1820, **h**-
$322.35.5, **i**-$323.80, **j**-$1.44.5, estate

Robert PATTERSON, b-20 Apr 1812, **c**-Moses PATTERSON, **d**-$600,
e-John SNYDER, Jacob HOFFMAN, **f**- **g**- **h**- **i**- **j**-

James MAGILL, b-20 Apr 1812, **c**-Charles MAGILL, **d**-$300, **e**-Roswell
DOTY, Elias W. HALE, **f**- **g**- **h**- **i**- **j**-

Page 31, Frame 40

Daniel MILLER, b-18 May 1812, **c**-John BRUBAKER, Jr., **d**-$300, **e**-
David SHELLEBARGER, Conrad ORT, **f**-18 May 1812, **g**-16 May
1814, **h**-$156.82, **i**-$178.46, **j**-$21.64, admrs

John JOHNSTON, b-23 May 1812, **c**-Ezekiel BROWN, **d**-$100, **e**-John
WRIGHT, Azzur WRIGHT, **f**- **g**- **h**- **i**- **j**-

William [LARS? SARS?], b-28 May 1812, **c**-William PORTER, **d**-$300,
e-John SIMPSON, Robert FORSYTHE, **f**- **g**- **h**- **i**- **j**-

Eleanor JOHNSTON, b-29 Jun 1812, **c**-Adam JOHNSTON, **d**-$2000, **e**-
David JORDAN, David STEWART, **f**- **g**- **h**- **i**- **j**-

Joseph HOSTETLER, b-8 Aug 1812, **c**-David CAUFMAN, Sr., Michael
HOSTETLER, David CAUFMAN, Jr., **d**-$2000, **e**-Wm. HENRY,
Christly ZOOK, **f**-24 Aug 1812, 15 Dec 1812, **g**-14 Dec 1814/17 Jan
1815/4 Jul 1821, **h**-$4093.07/182.51/3419.54, **i**-
$674.53/118.50/3404.17, **j**-$3419.54/64.01, heirs/$15.37, estate

Sarah THOMPSON, b-17 Aug 1812, **c**-Mitchell THOMPSON, **d**-$2000,
e-Peter THOMPSON, Jacob REIGHART, **f**- **g**- **h**- **i**- **j**-

John PEXLER, b-24 Aug 1812, **c**-Jacob PEXLER, **d**-$500, **e**-Frederick
NIPPLE, James MILLIKEN, **f**- **g**- **h**- **i**- **j**-

Thomas GRAHAM, b-14 Oct 1812, **c**-James CUPPLES, **d**-$300, **e**-Robert
FORSYTHE, Anthoney YOUNG, **f**- **g**- **h**- **i**- **j**-

Elizabeth McDOWELL, b-2 Nov 1812, **c**-James McDOWELL, **d**-$600,
e-Abraham [HUFFERD], **f**- **g**-16 Apr 1814, **h**-$309.20, **i**-$112.79, **j**-
$186.23, heirs

Joseph [WAHOB] , b-28 Nov 1812, c-Robert RANKEN, d-$2000, e-John MEVEY, George CALBRAITH, f- g- h- i- j-

Robert MOORE, b-17 Jan 1813, c-Francis MOORE, d-$500, e-James MOORE, Christopher [HORRELL], f- g- h- i- j-

Aaron COLTER, b-19 Jan 1813, c-Benjamin LAW, Moses COLTER, d-$1000, e-M. M. MONAHAN, Geo. BREHMAN, f- g- h- i- j-

Page 32, Frame 41

John FIGHT, b-12 Feb 1813, c-James MACKEY, Esq., d-$300, e-Anthoney YOUNG, Christian HONALL, f- g-24 Jul 1820, h-$106.09, i-$136.09, j-$30.98, accountant

Barbara BITNER, b-18 Feb 1813, c-Jacob REIGART, Esq., d-$800, e-Danl. CHRISTY, James JOHNSTON, f-22 Mar 1813, g-14 Dec 1814, h-$380.09, i-$222.32, j-$157.77, estate

Isaac HUNTSLINGER, b-27 Feb 1813, c-Abm. HUNTSLINGER, d-$2000, e-Tobias KREIDER, David LAPP, f-17 Mar 1813, g-29 Jun 1814, h-$976.18, i-$439.77, j-$536.41, estate

William SPEEDY, b-13 Mar 1813, c-Alexander SANDERSON, d-$500, e-M. McMONAHON, John GUSTINE, f- g- h- i- j-

James SANDERSON, b-13 Mar 1813, c-Alexander SANDERSON, d-$2000, e-M. McMONAHON, John GUSTINE, f- g- h- i- j-

James MULLEN, b-13 Mar 1813, c-Roswell DOTY, d-$500 e-Peacock MAJOR, Christn. HONALL, f- g- h- i- j-

James ROBISON, b-2 Apr 1813, c-Jane ROBISON, d-$1000, e-Hugh HARDY, James HENDERSON, f-18 Sep 1816, g-18 Sep 1816, h-$415.93, i-$574.05, j-$148.12, admx

Sarah STEWART, b-13 Apr 1813, c-Alexander STEWART, d-$500, e-John JACOBS, Elias W. HALE, f- g- h- i- j-

William HAMILTON, b-16 Apr 1813, c-William HAMILTON, d-Robert FORSYTHE, Peacock MAJOR, e- f- g- h- i- j-

James WALKER, b-19 Apr 1813, c-David WALKER, d-$2000, e-Stephen REYNOLDS, Saml. [VERRURNER], f- g- h- i- j-

William BROWN, b-19 Apr 1813, c-Elizabeth BROWN, John PATTERSON, d-$3000, e-Wm. PATTON, Stephen REYNOLDS, f- g- h- i- j-

William PEACOCK, b-20 Apr 1813, c-James KNOX, Esq., d-$500, e-Jacob REIGHART, John SNYDER, f-18 Aug 1817, g-18 Aug 1817, h-$111.06, i-$79.87.5, j-$31.18.5, heirs

Page 33, Frame 42

Samuel REED, **b**-20 Apr 1820, **c**-Samuel REED, **d**-$500, **e**-David REED, Andrew STROUP, **f**- **g**- **h**- **i**- **j**-

James CUNNINGHAM, **b**-21 Apr 1813, **c**-Martha CUNNINGHAM, Alexander McCAHEN, **d**-$1000, **e**-Hugh HARDY, Wm. BEALE, **f**- **g**- **h**- **i**- **j**-

Michael McCOLLUM, **b**-17 May 1813, **c**-Daniel McDONALD, **d**-$800, **e**-Jos. B. ARD, Christ. HONNEL, **f**-31 May 1813, **g**-27 Aug 1825 **h**-$402.84, **i**-$542.73, **j**-$139.89, accountant

William CHESTNUT, **b**-13 May 1813, **c**-Samuel CHESTNUT, **d**-$1000, **e**-Francis BOGGS, James CUPPLES, **f**-14 Apr 1814, **g**-14 Apr 1814, **h**-$321.82, **i**-$203.99, **j**-$117.83, estate

Alexander TAYLOR, **b**-4 Jun 1813, **c**-Ezra DOTY, **d**-$1000, **e**-E. W. HALE, C. HORRELL, **f**- **g**-28 Feb 1822, **h**-$37.17, **i**-$293.26.5 **j**-$256.09.5, accountant

Benjn. FRY, **b**-16 Jun 1813, **c**-Jonathan FRY, Gabriel FRY, **d**-$200, **e**-Joseph SELLERS, David WALKER, **f**-18 Sep 1813, **g**-2 Mar 1815, **h**-$306.71, **i**-$172.65, **j**-$134.06, accountant

Samuel FRY, **b**-16 Jun 1813, **c**-Jonathan FRY, Gabriel FRY, **d**-$500, **e**-Joseph SELLERS, David WALKER, **f**- **g**- **h**- **i**- **j**-

Jacob WIANT, **b**-30 Jul 1813, **c**-John STUMPFF, Esq., Michael MOURER, **d**-$1000, **e**-Jacob KEARNS, George FRY, **f**-30 Jul 1813, **g**-16 Nov 1812/13 Jun 1825, **h**-$600.97/$1182.65, **i**-$352.86/$852.99.5, **j**-$248.11, heirs/$329.52.5, estate

Benjamin HALL, **b**-12 Aug 1813, **c**-William HALL, **d**-$1000, **e**-Robert McKEE, David McKEE, **f**- **g**- **h**- **i**- **j**-

Henry LUKEN, **b**-16 Aug 1813, **c**-John STEWART, **d**-$2000, **e**-Andrew THOMPSON, James NIXON, **f**- **g**-25 Nov 1819, **h**-$1731.94.5, **i**-$1824.72, **j**-$92.87, admr

Thomas BEALE, **b**-16 Aug 1813, **c**-John PERSONS, **d**-$300, **e**-James HENDERSON, C. HORRELL, **f**-14 Sep 1813, **g**- **h**- **i**- **j**-

John CALDWELL, **b**-17 Aug 1813, **c**-James GARDNER, **d**-$300, **e**-Thomas BARRETT, Daniel CHRISTY, **f**- **g**- **h**- **i**- **j**-

Page 34, Frame 43

Charles MORROW, **b**-1 Sep 1813, **c**-Alse MORROW **d**-$2000, **e**-John PATTERSON, William MAGILL, **f**-1 Sep 1813, **g**-17 Aug 1814, **h**-$1095.81, **i**-$111.94, **j**-$983.87, heirs

John THOMAS, b-6 Sep 1813, **c**-Margaret THOMAS, John THOMAS, **d**-$1000, **e**-John [LAUVER]. Jacob [FEES], **f**-1 Oct 1813, **g**-13 Jan 1815, **h**-$1214.91, **i**-$390.65, **j**-$824.25, heirs

John SMITH, b-10 Sep 1813, **c**-John SHNELL, **d**-$100, **e**-Samuel WALLICK, Andrew MURPHY, **f**- **g**- **h**- **i**- **j**-

John STEEL, b-24 Sep 1813, **c**-Robert STEEL, Mary STEEL, Robert ROBISON, William SHADE, **d**-$10,000, **e**-James ROBISON, Roswell DOTY, Peacock MAJOR, **f**- **g**-11 Apr 1815, **h**-$510.92, **i**-$209.18, **j**-$301.73, heirs

Abraham YOTTER, b-28 Sep 1813, **c**-Christian CAUFMAN, Christian ZOOK, **d**-$3000, **e**-Jacob YOTTER, Eli SMITH, **f**-9 Oct 1813, **g**-25 Nov 1816, **h**-$864.60, **i**-$843.43, **j**-$21.17, heirs

James HOLLIDAY, b-26 Oct 1813, **c**-Adam HOLLIDAY, **d**-$2000, **e**-E. W. HALE, Francis ELLIS, **f**- **g**- **h**- **i**- **j**-

Thomas McCONNALL, b-19 Nov 1813, **c**-Henry McCONNALL, **d**-$300, **e**-Jacob HOFFMAN, John SNYDER, **f**- **g**- **h**- **i**- **j**-

Noah ABRAHAM, b-20 Nov 1813, **c**-M. M. MONAHON, **d**-$1000, **e**-William BEALE, Alexr. SANDERSON, **f**- **g**-17 Jan 1831, **h**-$924.28, **i**-$1001.28, **j**-$76.99, accountant (real balance due acct. $1.88.5)

Alexander METLEN, b-23 Nov 1813, **c**-Samuel METLEN, **d**-$1000, **e**-John WRIGHT, Chrisr. HORRELL **f**- **g**- **h**- **i**- **j**-

Frederick SWITZER, b-6 Dec 1813, **c**-David SWITZER, **d**-$2000, **e**-John YEIGH, John SHIVELY, **f**- **g**- **h**- **i**- **j**-

William [McFETERAGE], b-1 Jan 1814, **c**-Christena McFETTERAGE, Jos. B. ARD, **d**-$100, **e**-David JORDAN, James [SLAYSMAN], **f**- **g**- **h**- **i**- **j**-

William JOHNSTON, b-18 Jan 1814, **c**-Michael JOHNSTON, **d**-$1000, **e**-Daniel CHRISTY, Wm. McALLISTER, **f**- **g**-4 Nov 1825, **h**-$410.81.5, **i**-$343.34, **j**-67.47.5, estate

Page 35, Frame 44

John CULBERTSON, b-22 Jan 1814, **c**-William ARMSTRONG, **d**-$10,000, **e**-George CALBREATH, James CHRISWELL, **f**-16 Aug 1811, **g**-20 Jan 1816, 9 May 1825, **h**-$15–/$2160.94, **i**-$135.58/$1676.03, **j**-$120.58, admr/$484.91, estate

Saml. MONTGOMERY, b-27 Jan 1814, **c**-John P. HELFENSTINE, **d**-$1000, **e**-Christian LEONARD, Robert ROBISON, **f**- **g**-25 Aug 1815, **h**-$850.00, **i**-$346.39, **j**-$503.61, heirs

Michael STOFFER, b-10 Mar 1814, **c**-Christian [LANTES], **d**-$1000, **e**-Christian CROW, Charles MAGILL, **f**- **g**- **h**- **i**- **j**-

Barbara AULLY, b-19 Mar 1814, **c**-Andrew HOSEA, **d**-$1000, **e**-William BRISBEN, David MILLIKEN, **f- g- h- i- j-**
John KREBBS, b-25 Mar 1814, **c**-John SNYDER, **d**-$1000, **e**-John NEIMAN, Elias W. HALE, **f**-18 Apr 1814, **g**-17 Apr 1815, **h**-$441.80, **i**-$36.18, **j**-$385.62, estate
John KEEVER, b-7 Apr 1814, **c**-John KEEVER, William KEEVER, **d**-$8000, **e**-Saml. MACLAY, Andrew KEISER, **f- g- h- i- j-**
John VANCE, b-13 May 1814, **c**-James CRISWELL, Archibald MOORE, **d**-$1000, **e**-John HORNING, Thomas MITCHELL, **f**-11 Jun 1814, **g**-12 Feb 1815/5 Mar 1818/4 Dec 1818/4 Nov 1837, **h**-$3091.90/ /$3777.04/ $3946.69, **i**-$2219.21/ /$170.20/$3756.16.5, **j**-$2219.21 due ___/ /$3606.84.5, heirs/$81.79, heirs
Susannah STEELY, b-5 Jul 1814, **c**-Robert ROBISON, **d**-$500, **e**-James ROBISON, Samuel EISENBISE, **f- g- h- i- j-**
Hannah BEAVER, b-15 Aug 1814, **c**-John OWENS, John SHNELL, **d**-$1000, **e**-James GRAY, George DAUGHMAN, **f**-12 Sep 1814, **g**-16 Mar 1820, **h**-$346.03, **i**-$370.08, **j**-$24.05, accountant
John FUNK, b-15 Sep 1814, **c**-15 Sep 1814, **d**-Elizabeth FUNK, James MILLIKEN, **e**-Samuel EISENBISE, James ROBISON, **f- g- h- i- j-**
Samuel COCHRAN, b-17 Sep 1814, **c**-Alexander COCHRAN, **d**-$500, **e**-William BROWN, James MILLIKEN, **f- g- h- i- j-**

Page 36, Frame 45
Alexander McCAHEN, b-22 Sep 1814, **c**-John McCAHEN, **d**-$1000, **e**-John STERRETT, E. W. HALE, **f- g- h- i- j-**
Franey ZOOK, b-13 Oct 1814, **c**-David ZOOK, **d**-$2000, **e**-Christian ZOOK, Christian COFFMAN, **f**-8 Nov 1814, **g**-29 Mar 1816, **h**-$2964.75, **i**-$2152.37, **j**-$812.28, heirs
James BURNS, b-2 Nov 1814, **c**-Hugh BURNS, M. M. MONAHON, **d**-$5000, **e**-James MILLIKEN, Wm. A. PATTERSON, **f- g**-15 Oct 1825, **h- i- j-**
Mathew REIGHLY, b-14 Nov 1814, **c**-Susanah REIGHLY, John SMITH, **d**-$3000, **e**-Wm. McDOWELL, David MILLIKEN, **f**-21 May 1816, **g**-21 May 1816, **h**-$1988.14, **i**-$1177.31, **j**-$810.83, heirs
Barbara AULTZ, b-24 Nov 1814, **c**-John CLAYTON, **d**-$800, **e**-Jacob SHET, James MILLIKEN, **f**-9 Apr 1814, **g**-3 Dec 1816, **h**-$424.38, **i**-$263.03, **j**-$161.35, heirs
Barbara HOSTETLER, b-7 Jan 1815, **c**-Michael HOSTETLER, **d**-$1000, **e**-Andrew KEISER, Samuel MORTON, **f**-16 Jan 1815, **g**-18 Apr 1818, **h**-$257.63, **i**-$257.63, **j-**

John McFADDEN, **b**-15 Feb 1815, **c**-Hugh McFADDEN, **d**-$500, **e**-Samuel MARTIN, Francis McCOY, **f**- **g**- **h**- **i**- **j**-

George BRIDGE, **b**-14 Mar 1815, **c**-Elizabeth BRIDGE, Henry CLOSE, **d**-$800, **e**-Jacob BRIDGE, Thomas ORR, **f**-7 Apr 1815, **g**-9 Aug 1823, **h**-$1032.64.5, **i**-1049.26, **j**-$16.61.5, accountant

James WILKEN, **b**-10 Apr 1815, **c**-William PORTER, **d**-$5000, **e**-Robert FORSYTHE, Peacock MAJOR, **f**- **g**-23 Jun 1815, **h**-$248.63, **i**-$248.63, **j**-

Jacob REED, **b**-3 May 1815, **c**-John STUMPF, **d**-$200, **e**-Wright HANY, John KNAPP, **f**- **g**- **h**- **i**- **j**-

James WILKEN, **b**-23 Kim 1815, **c**-George HANAWALT, **d**-$5000, **e**-Robt. ROBISON, Anthoney ELTON, **f**- **g**-18 Mar 1824/8 Dec 1828, **h**-$2722.62.5/$1257,23, **i**-$3688.80.5, **j**-$1257.23, accountant

Elnathan GREGORY, **b**-14 Jul 1815, **c**-Michael HOLMAN, **d**-$500, **e**-Wm. P. ELLIOTT, Thos. GALLAHER, **f**-15 Aug 1816, **g**-15 Aug 1816, **h**-$39.00 **i**-$30.81, **j**-$8.69, heirs

Page 37, Frame 46

Alexander McDONALD, **b**-17 Jul 1815, **c**-Amelia BRATTON, **d**-$500, **e**-James CRISWELL, John STINSON, **f**- **g**- **h**- **i**- **j**-

John REYNOLDS, **b**-22 Jul 1815, **c**-Robert U. ELLIOTT, **d**-$500, **e**-Samuel EISENBISE, Wm. FRAZER, **f**- **g**- **h**- **i**- **j**-

Joseph McCLELLAND, **b**-16 Aug 1815, **c**-William SANDERSON, **d**-$500, **e**-James KINSLOE, Jesse JENNINGS, **f**- **g**- **h**- **i**- **j**-

Negro Sam, **b**-17 Aug 1815, **c**-Henry KENNEDY, **d**-$300, **e**-Peacock MAJOR, James ROBISON, **f**- **g**- **h**- **i**- **j**-

Oliver CLARK, **b**-21 Aug 1815, **c**-Polly CLARK, **d**-$1000, **e**-David GLENN, David THATCHER, **f**- **g**- **h**- **i**- **j**-

Solomon STEEL, **b**-2 Sep 1815, **c**-Peter LONG, **d**-$1000, **e**-Jacob STOOLL, Jacob STEELE, Jr., **f**-10 Jul 1818, **g**-10 Jul 1818/4 Oct 1820/15 Apr 1828, **h**-$640.51/$172.51/$831.57, **i**-$467.99/$68.22/$96.16. **j**-$172.52, heirs/Bal $735.41, estate

Wm. TONER, **b**-5 Sep 1815, **c**-Jeremiah CUNNINGHAM, **d**-$1000, **e**-Peacock MAJOR, James ROBISON, **f**- **g**- **h**- **i**- **j**-

Thomas MARTIN, **b**-20 Sep 1815, **c**-Elizabeth MARTIN, Wm. A. PATTERSON, **d**-$2000, **e**-Wm. ARMSTRONG, James CHRISWELL, **f**-25 Mar 1820, **g**-16 Mar 1820, **h**-$2651.68.5, **i**-$472.94.5, **j**-$2178.74, estate

James MAYES, **b**-21 Sep 1815, **c**-Rebecca MAYES, Mathew TAYLOR, **d**-$5000, **e**-James SHERARD, Wm. P. MACLAY, **f**- **g**- **h**- **i**- **j**-

John GILLESPIE, b-13 Oct 1815, c-Joseph MARTIN, d-$2000, e-David
STEWART, Anthoney YOUNG, f- g-8 May 1829, h-$3107.35, i-
$2628.53.5, j-$478.81.5, estate

James BELL, b-21 Oct 1815, c-George BELL, d-$500,00[sic], e-John
McCLENAHEN, Chas. McCLENAHAN, f-21 Nov 1815, g-Sep
[nothing else], h- i- j-

Abraham CAUFMAN, b-26 Oct 1815, c-David CAUFMAN, d-$500, e-A.
A. ANDERSON, Robt. ROBISON, f- g- h- i- j-

Page 38, Frame 47

John HIGHLAND, b-21 Nov 1815, c-William GRAHAM, d-$100, e-Wm.
WHARTON, Israel HOOPS, f-30 Dec 1815, g-18 Apr 1822, h-
$213.53, i-$202.75.5, j-$10.79.5, estate

Ann McKEE, b-1 Nov 1815, c-Robert MEANS, Robert STINSON, d-
$1000, e-James ROBISON, Samuel MARTIN, f- g-25 Jul 1828/13 Oct
1830, h-$136.29/$1669.79, i-$43.52/$931.66, j-$92.77,
estate/$738.13.5, estate

John CARLISLE, b-6 Jan 1815, c-Samuel CARLISLE, d-$1000, e-E. W.
HALE, Jerema. CUNNINGHAM, f- g- h- i- j-

Peter BROWN, b-24 Nov 1815, c-Patrick BROWN, d-$1000, e-Jas.
JUNKIN, George BRATTON, f- g- h- i- j-

Jos. DYSART, b-24 Nov 1815, c-Jas. DYSART, Wm. DYSART, d-$5000,
e-Thos. MITCHELL, Jas. KINSLOE, f- g- h- i- j-

Henry [DRING], b-25 Nov 1815, c-James MACKEY, David
CRAWFORD, d-$2000, e-Jos. DOUGLAS, Wm. BEALE, f- g- h- i- j-

Andrew NELSON, b-28 Nov 1815, c-Ephraim BANTES, James
KINSLOE, d-$1000, Andrew KEYSER, David MILLIKEN, e- f- g- h-
i- j-

Joseph STEWART, b-22 Dec 1815, c-George STEWART, Joseph
STEWART, Wm. ARBUCKLE, d-$3000, e-Hugh HART, Robert
KIDD, f-17 Jan 1816, g-13 Mar 1818, h-$1894.62.5, i-$1240.79, j-
$653.83.5, heirs

Jacob BRIDGE, b-2 Jan 1816, c-Rebecca BRIDGE, Michael KNULL, d-
$2000, e-Felix LEE, Robt. LONGWELL, f-15 Jan 1816, g-10 Dec
1817/23 Nov 1818/20 Apr 1819/17 Mar 1823, h-$901.23/
/$791.72/$166.64, i-$775.77/ /$750.33/$180.90.5, j-$125.46,
heirs/$41.39, heirs/$14.62.5 estate

Edward COLE, b-15 Jan 1816, c-Nancy COLE, d-$500, e-James STEEL,
Samuel STEWART, f- g- h- i- j-

Church COX, b-29 Jan 1816, c-Jacob REIGHART, d-$1000, e-Wm. THOMPSON, James KINSLOE, f-5 Apr 1816, g- h- i- j-

James DAILY, b-31 Jan 1816, c-Anthoney YOUNG, d-$300, e-David STEWART, David R. REYNOLDS, f- g-16 Apr 1819, h-$43.39, i-$43.39, j-no balance

Page 39, Frame 48

Valentine BRIDGE, b-5 Feb 1816, c-John BRIDGE, d-$1000, e-Henry WORKINGER, Wm. POTTER, f-13 Feb 1816, g-20 Apr 1818, h-$464.04, i-$428.08, j-$35.96, estate

Mark KERR, b-15 Feb 1816, c-William GILSON, d-$1000, e-James MARKEY, Robt. M. ELLIOTT, f- g- h- i- j-

John ROBISON, b-20 Feb 1816, c-Thos. ROBISON, Francis McCOY, d-$1000, e-James ROBISON, Henry KULP, f- g- h- i- j-

Moses PEACHEY, b-21 Feb 1816, c-Jacob HARTZLER, David HARTZLER d-$2000, e-Wm. P. MACLAY, John FLEMING, f- g-17 Feb 1825, h-$3602.30, i-$45.55, j-$3556.75, estate

Moses OSBORNE, b-24 Feb 1816, c-Catherine OSBOURN[sic] d-$100, e-Levi REYNOLDS, David R. REYNOLDS, f- g- h- i- j-

Joseph STEWART, b-7 Mar 1816, c-Thomas STEWART, d-$500, e-Wm. BROWN, Esq., David MILLIKEN, f- g- h- i- j-

William FAULS, b-9 Mar 1816, c-William BRISBIN, d-$500, e-Foster MILLIKEN, James ROBISON, f-, g- h- i- j-

Nancy CAUFMAN, b-18 Apr 1816, c-David CAUFMAN, d-$1000, e-Jacob SELLERS, Frederick KITLER f- g- h- i- j-

John RITTER, b-25 Apr 1816, c-Henry RITTER, Andrew ULSH, d-$2000, e-George KNEPP, Daniel MOSHER, f-14 May 1816, g-20 Apr 1818, h-$1147.02, i-$885.51, j-$261.50, heirs

Samuel KEPNER, b-9 May 1816, c-Benjn. KEPNER, Henry GROCE, d-$5000, e-Jacob KEPNER, Wm. BELL, f-20 Nov 1821, g-20 Nov 1821, h-$1585.52, i-$47.29, j-$1537.23, estate

Ann REED, b-25 Jun 1816, c-Charles REED, d-$1000, e-Wm. KENNEDY, James KINSLOE, f- g- h- i- j-

James FERRER, b-19 Aug 1816, c-Jane FERRER, James POLLOCK, d-$1000, e-Wm. OWENS, Robert MAGILL, f- g-22 May 1821, h-$1261.93, i-$1494.18, j-$232.25, accountants

Page 40, Frame 49

Wm. McELHANEY, b-23 Aug 1816, c-John McELHANEY, d-$1000, e-John CUMMIN, Jas. MACKEY, f- g- h- i- j-

George McELHANEY, b-23 Aug 1816, c-John McELHANEY, d-$1000, e-Jas. MACKEY, Jno. CUMMIN, f- g- h- i- j-

Adam BECKET, b-30 Aug 1816, c-John BECKET, William CUMMIN, d-$2000, e-Jos. EDMISTON, James MILLIKEN, f-26 Sep 1816, g-13 Aug 1818, h-$1705.88, i-$1705.88, j-

Wm. MOORE, b-9 Oct 1816, c-Moses MOORE, d-$500, e-Henry BARKLEY, Thomas HOPPER, f- g- h- i- j-

Wm. CHRISWELL, b-14 Oct 1816, c-Margaret CHRISWELL, d-$500, e-Henry SILLS, John JONES, f- g- h- i- j-

Mary JOHNSTON, b-18 Oct 1816, c-Michael JOHNSTON, d-$1000, e-Robert JOHNSTON, James KINSLOE, f- g-22 Aug 1828, h-$1137.77, i-$2195.89, j-$1058.12, accountant

Volentine BRIDGE, b-21 Oct 1816, c-Michael [KNOLL], d-$2000, e-John McDOWELL, James McNITT, f- g- h- i- j-

Jesse JENNINGS, b-8 Nov 1816, c-Arthur McNAUGHT, d-$1000, e-John YOCUM, Wm. JENNINGS, f-23 Feb 1827, g-27 Feb 1827 h-$1316.52.5, i-$1798.22, j-$481.69.5, accountant

Amos HARPER, b-15 Nov 1816, c-Isaac WILEY, d-$500, e-Jos. BROTHERS, Geo. WILEY, f- g- h- i- j-

John WILEY, b-18 Nov 1816, c-Isaac WILEY, d-$500 e-Geo. WILEY, Henry KULP, f- g- h- i- j-

Catherine NORTH, b-18 Nov 1818, c-Charles COOKSON, d-$1000, e-Lewis EVANS, M. M. MONAHON, f- g- h- i- j-

John STERRETT, b-2 Dec 1816, c-Rebecca STERRETT, Robert STERRETT, Elias W. HALE, James CHRISWELL, d-$10,000, e-Samuel MACLAY, James MILLIKEN, f- g- h- i- j-

Page 41, Frame 50

Bernard FULTZ, b-29 Dec 1816, c-Michael LAUVER, d-$1000, e-Henry ACKER, Jacob LAUVER, f-29 Dec 1816, g-16 Jul 1819, h-$347.45, i-$319.60, j-$27.85, estate

Catherine WIANT, b-30 Dec 1816, c-George WIANT, d-$1000, e-Jesse ANDERSON, Henry REMICH, f- g-19 Nov 1824, h-$167.18, i-$111.16, j-$56.02, estate

Christian [ROOKY], b-24 Jan 1817, c-Saml. W. STEWART, d-$500, e-Francis McCOY, Robt. STEVENSON, f- g- h- i- j-

Hugh McCALLY, b-12 Feb 1817, c-John McCALLY, d-$1000, e-Henry HOOVER, David REYNOLDS, f-16 Feb 1816, g-15 Dec 1819, h-$250.78, i-$187.82.5, j-$62.95.5, heirs

David CAUFMAN, b-14 Feb 1817, c-John TURNER, d-$500, e-Michael HOLMAN, Jas. MILLIKEN, f- g- h- i- j-

Wm. LEWIS, b-24 Mar 1817, c-David REYNOLDS, d-$4000, e-James ROBISON, M. M. MONAHON, Robt. ROBISON, David JORDAN, Peacock MAJOR, f- g-7 Feb 1821, h-$2927.19, i-$3094.69, j-$167.50, accountant

Jacob SMITH, b-27 Mar 1817, c-S. MYERS, J. SMITH, d-$10,000, e-E. HORNING, Wm. McALLISTER, f-22 Apr 1817, g-20 Mar 1821/20 Apr 1825, h-$3283.75/$1761.70.5, i-$2046.60/$1604.47, j-$157.23.5, estate

James MAGILL, b-7 Apr 1817, c-Michael M. MONAHON, d-$1000, e-David REYNOLDS, Robert ROBISON, f- g- h- i- j-

Charles MAGILL, b-7 Apr 1817, c-M. M. MONAHON, d-$1000, e-David REYNOLDS, Robert ROBISON, f- g-18 Nov 1824, h-$134.54, i-$143.18, j-$8.64, accountant

Jane McCONING, b-7 Apr 1817, c-M. M. MONAHON, d-$1000, e-David REYNOLDS, Robert ROBISON, f-19 Aug 1823 g- h- i- j-

George SAILOR, b-21 Apr 1817, c-Philip SAILOR, d-$1000, e-Samuel SAILOR, Silas SAILOR, f- g- h- i- j-

John WILSON, b-22 Apr 1817, c-Wm. MORRISON, d-$1000, e-Wm. CUMMIN, John MAXWELL, f- g-23 Jul 1822, h-$320.64, i-$251.29.5, j-$69.34.5, estate

Page 42, Frame 51

John HAUN, b-22 Apr 1817, c-Catherine HAUN, Jacob HAUN, John HAUN, d-$5000, e-William McMANIGIL, f- g- h- i- j-

Margaret ALLEN, b-25 Apr 1817, c-Joel HANY, d-$1000, e-J. B. ARD, R. FORSYTH, f-24 May 1817, g-18 Mar 1819, h-$377.68, i-$388.68, j-

William REED, b-19 Jun 1817, c-James REED, Jane REED, d-$2000, e-Saml. MARTIN, Saml. MACLAY, f- g- h- i- j-

John WITMER, b-11 Jul 1817, c-Jacob WITMER, George WILT, d-$3000, e-H. GROCE, A. WITMER, f- 6 Aug 1817, g- 12 Aug 1818/22 Apr 1821/13 Dec 1821, h-$2471.46/$435.46.75/$6632.57.5, i-$1597.85.75/$571.29/$6340.99.75, j-$873.60.25, heirs; bal. $117.83

Daniel CRAWFORD, b-15 Jul 1817, c-James KNOX, Esq., d-$1000, e-Wm. A. PATTERSON, Francis McCOY, f-19 Aug 1817, g-19 Nov 1829, h-$998.98, i-$998.98, j-no balance

Robert **GEMMILL b-**23 Jul 1817, **c-**Christian GEMMILL, Francis McCOY- **d-**$2000, **e-**Joseph MARTIN, Robert ROBISON, **f- g-**12 Jan 1827, **h-**$3171.12, **i-**$2151.45 **j-**$1009.67, estate

Christian HARTZLER, b-16 Aug 1817, **c-**Jacob HARTZLER, **d-**$2000, **e-**Christian YODER, Jacob ZOOK, **f-**19 Aug 1817, 1 Sep 1817, **g-**28 May 1818, **h-**$1246.20, **i-**$213.90, **j-**$1032.30, heirs

Nathan ALLEN, b-11 Sep 1817, **c-**William KIRK, **d-**$12,000, **e-**D. REYNOLDS, J. NORTON, **f-**27 Dec 1806, April ___, **g-**22 Jan 1807, 19 Apr 1808, **h-**£289..16..5.5, $377.87, **i-**£191..16..4.5, $20.70, **j-**$357.17, heirs

Robert WHARTON, b-24 Sep 1817, **c-**John PATTERSON, **d-**$2000, **e-**Benjamin LAW, Wm. McALLISTER, **f- g- h- i- j-**

Martin STAGER, b-10 Nov 1817, **c-**James KNOX, Esq., **d-**$1000, **e-**Benj. PATTON, D. W. AITKEN, **f-**22 Apr 1818, **g-**27 Oct 1819, **h-**$588.67, **i-**$442.34, **j-**$146.33, heirs

Anthoney DECK, b-17 Nov 1817, **c-**F. MILLIKEN, S. CUNNINGHAM, **d-**$1000, **e-**Crawford KYL, J. MILLIKEN, **f-**5 Dec 1817, **g-**16 Jan 1821, **h-**$329.94, **i-**286.47, **j-**$43.47, estate

Isaiah WILLIS, b-6 Dec 1817, **c-**Sarah WILLIS, James CHRISWELL, **d-**$4000, **e-**E. W. HALE, Robt. MILLIKEN, **f- g-**14 Mar 1820/2 Apr 1822, **h-**$7707.71/$4175.93, **i-**$3986.54/$703.65, **j-**$3492.28, estate

Page 43, Frame 52

Wm. HALL, b-20 Dec 1817, **c-**Samuel P. LILLEY, **d-**$1000, **e-**William SHAW, David McKEE, **f- g- h- i- j-**

Daniel McCONAHY, b-14 Jan 1818, **c-**M. McCONAHY, **d-**$2000, **e-**James McKINSTRY, John BARD, **f-**7 Feb 1818, **g-**Aug 1819/28 May 1823, **h-**$613.40/$524.47.5 **i-**$210.51.5/$490.20,5, **j-**$393.88.5, heirs/ $34.26.25, estate

Sarah JACOBS, b-21 Jan 1818, **c-**Jesse JACOBS, **d-**$2000, **e-**James SHERARD, John WRIGHT, **f- g- h- i- j-**

Nicholas COLDWELL, b-23 Feb 1818, **c-**William TODD, Wm. A. PATTERSON, **d-**$1000, **e-**N. CALDWELL, A. McILVAIN, **f- g- h- i- j-**

Barbara MILLER, b-24 Feb 1818, **c-**Jacob CLICK, **d-**$2000, **e-**Christian HONALL, James McDOWELL, **f-**10 Mar 1818, **g-**18 Mar 1819, **h-**$1391.62, **i-**$100.31, **j-**$1291.31, heirs

John SMITH, b-26 Feb 1818, **c-**Andrew SMITH, **d-**$4000, **e-**John PATTERSON, Henry HACKET, **f- g- h- i- j-**

William HORRALL, **b**-10 Mar 1818, **c**-James HORRALL, **d**-$500, **e**-T. HORRALL, Wm. BELL, **f**- **g**- **h**- **i**- **j**-

George SUNDAY, **b**-15 Nov 1823, **c**-John RITTER, Geo. BILLMAN, **d**-$800, **e**-John BILMAN, Jacob RITTER, **f**- **g**- **h**- **i**- **j**-

William KNOX, **b**-23 Mar 1818, **c**-George PETERS, **d**-$1000, **e**-Peacock MAJOR, William ROBISON, **f**- **g**- **h**- **i**- **j**-

Sarah BURNS, **b**-21 Apr 1818, **c**-[Y.] {probably Z.} DURST, **d**-$1000, **e**-M. M. MONAHON, J. CUPPLES, **f**- **g**- **h**- **i**- **j**-

Samuel LINDSEY, **b**-21 Apr 1818, **c**-Mary LINDSAY, **d**-$1000, **e**-A. ELTON, F. MITCHELL, **f**- **g**- **h**- **i**- **j**-

Jacob REIGHART, **b**-5 Aug 1818, **c**-John REIGHART, **d**-$5000, **e**-David REIGHART, Fleming STEWART, **f**-17 Aug 1818, **g**-11 Nov 1821, **h**-$3019.82, **i**-$2730.46, **j**-$289.36, estate

Page 44, Frame 53

William STRAWBRIDGE, **b**-8 Aug 1818, **c**-William STRAWBRIDGE, **d**-$1000, **e**-Francis BOGGS, F. GOODFELLOW, **f**- **g**-23 Aug 1820, **h**-$220.29, **i**-$220.29, **j**-

Daniel PRICE, **b**-10 Aug 1818, **c**-John PRICE, James PRICE, **d**-$1000, **e**-Isaac PRICE, Francis BOGGS, **f**-11 Sep 1818, **g**- **h**- **i**- **j**-

John CUNNINGHAM, **b**-11 Aug 1818, **c**-James CARMICHAEL, Elizabeth CARMICHAEL, **d**-$600, **e**-Wm. DYSERT, John OLIVER, Robert CEVER, **f**- **g**- **h**- **i**- **j**-

Nicholas ARNOLD, **b**-21 Jan 1817, **c**-Jacob REIGHART, **d**-$3000, **e**-David CAUFMAN, Hugh McALLISTER, **f**- **g**- **h**- **i**- **j**-

Michael MARKLY, **b**-15 Dec 1820, **c**-John REED, Esq., **d**-$500, **e**-George REED, Andrew McILVAIN, **f**- **g**- **h**- **i**- **j**-

Mary LOVE, **b**-18 Aug 1818, **c**-Thomas HIGHLANDS, **d**-$500, **e**-Wm. BEALE, John McAVEY, **f**- **g**- **h**- **i**- **j**-

William ENSLOW, **b**-3 Sep 1818, **c**-Enoch BARTON, John McDONALD, **d**-$1000, **e**-Thomas [SHAVER/SHARER], Charles TOWER, **f**-2 Oct 1812/19 Feb 1828, **g**-18 Jul 1819/19 Feb 1828, **h**-$26.20/$1099.45, **i**-$24.62/$605.73, **j**-$1.58, heirs/$493.72, estate

William STUMP, **b**-16 Nov 1818, **c**-William STUMP, John McCALLY, **d**-$2000, **e**-John STUMP, Michael [MOURER], **f**- **g**-15 Apr 1825, **h**-$1530.70, **i**-$1970.27, **j**-$439.50, accountant

Isabella NICHOLASON, **b**-18 Nov 1818, **c**-George KERR, **d**-$500, **e**-John CUMMIN, Jos. B. ARD, **f**- **g**- **h**- **i**- **j**-

Mathias **LICHTENTHALER**, **b**-20 Nov 1818, **c**-Albert LICHTENTHALER, **d**-$1000, **e**-John HOLMAN, James ROSS, **f**- **g**- **h**- **i**- **j**-

Anthoney DUNLEVY, **b**-20 Nov 1818, **c**-Jeremiah CUNNINGHAM, **d**-$500, **e**-Charles DANIEL, John HOLLIDAY, **f**- **g**- **h**- **i**- **j**-

Jesse FRY, **b**-26 Nov 1818, **c**-Abraham FRY, Jesse FRY, **d**-$500, **e**-Benj. KEPNER, David STRAUSE, **f**- **g**-13 Mar 1822, **h**-$1491.50, **i**-$238.44, **j**-$1208.06, estate

Page 45, Frame 54

Jacob NOSS, **b**-27 Nov 1818, **c**-Philip SHOOP, **d**-$1000, **e**-George NOSS, David REYNOLDS, **f**-27 Nov 1818, **g**-30 Oct 1819, **h**-$103.48, **i**-$145.18, **j**-$41.70, admr.

Patrick PRY, **b**-4 Feb 1819, **c**-Patrick McKENON, Mary PRY, **d**-$1000, **e**-John CROUSE, James WOODWARD, **f**-17 Feb 1819, **g**- **h**- **i**- **j**-

George SAILOR, **b**-5 Feb 1819, **c**-John SAILOR, **d**-$500, **e**-Richard WILSON, Philip KILMORE, **f**- **g**- **h**- **i**- **j**-

John GRAY, **b**-8 Feb 1819, **c**-Mary GRAY, John KINZER, **d**-$3000, **e**-George HOOBAUGH, James HUGHS, **f**-16 Apr 1822, **g**-21 Jul 1823, **h**-$2226.84.5, **i**-$2311.44, **j**-$84.55.5, accountant

William KEYS, **b**-19 Feb 1819, **c**-Edward KEYS, **d**-$500, **e**-John KEYS, John LOVE, **f**-8 Mar 1819, **g**-21 May 1821, **h**-$539.32.5, **i**-$634.81, **j**-$95.49, accountant

Frederick FLICK, **b**-10 Mar 1819, **c**-George FLICK, **d**-$500, **e**-William BEALE, Thomas BEALE, **f**- **g**- **h**- **i**- **j**-

Lazarus STEELY. **b**-10 Mar 1819, **c**-James ROBISON, **d**-$20,000, **e**-Robert ROBISON, David REYNOLDS, **f**- **g**-15 Mar 1824, **h**- **i**-$128.51, **j**-$128.51, accountant

Nicholas ARNOLD, **b**-18 Mar 1819, **c**-John WARNTZ, **d**-$1000, **e**-Thos. GALLAHER, Wm. LINTON, **f**- **g**-22 Jan 1828, **h**-$1800.26 **i**-$201.85, **j**-$1598.41, heirs

William MITCHELL, **b**-19 Apr 1819, **c**-David MITCHELL, Robert COOPER, James CHRISWELL, **d**-$10,000, **e**-John McDOWELL, Thomas MITCHELL, Saml. MITCHELL, **f**-11 Dec 1823, **g**-13 Mar 1827, **h**-$1978.41, **i**-$1934.65, **j**-$43.78, estate

David LAUGHLIN, **b**-20 Apr 1819, **c**-Mathew LAUGHLIN, **d**-$500, **e**-Paul LAUGHLIN, Manasses RAMSEY, **f**- **g**- **h**- **i**- **j**-

John POLLOCK, **b**-22 Apr 1819, **c**-James POLLOCK, **d**-$1000, **e**-Wm. OWENS, John CUMMIN, **f**- **g**- **h**- **i**- **j**-

John PATTON, Jr., **b**-22 Apr 1819, **c**-William A. PATTON, Saml. S. PATTON, **d**-$500, **e**-Thos. HORRALL, James DICKSON, **f**-20 May 1819, 13 Jul 1819, **g**- **h**- **i**- **j**-

Page 46, Frame 55
Joseph FLEMING, **b**-30 Apr 1819, **c**-David FLEMING, William FLEMING, **d**-$5000, **e**-James FLEMING, John FLEMING, **f**-7 May 1819,   **g**-15 Mar 1822/30 Nov 1825/29 Aug 1831, **h**-$2940.64/$4454.92/$6559.39, **i**-$1404.28.5/$3530.40, **j**-$1536.36 due ___/$924.52, estate
Edward KENNEDY, **b**-19 May 1819, **c**-John HENRY, James KENNEDY, **d**-$400, **e**-Robert TAYLOR, **f**- **g**- **h**- **i**- **j**-
David GRIFFITH, **b**-4 Jun 1819, **c**-David GRIFFITH, **d**-$1000, **e**-Charles COOKSON, James ROSS, **f**- **g**- **h**- **i**- **j**-
Church COX, **b**-4 Jun 1819, **c**-Charles COOKSON, **d**-$1000, **e**-David GRIFFITH, Jr., John ROSS, **f**- **g**-23 Apr 1823, **h**-$341.30.5, **i**-$348.15.75, **j**-$6.85.75, accountant
Robert LONGWELL, **b**-14 Jun 1819, **c**-Michael KNOLL, James LONGWELL, **d**-$1000, **e**-Foster MILLIKEN, John CRISSMAN, **f**- **g**- **h**- **i**- **j**-
John HAYS, Sr., **b**-23 Jul 1819, **c**-Robert BLACK, **d**-$1000, **e**-Abraham COPLIN, Randolph WOODEN, **f**- **g**- **h**- **i**- **j**-
Richard WILSON, **b**-3 Aug 1819, **c**-Robert WOODS, David STRAUSE, **d**-$1000, **e**-Benjn. KEPNER, James WILSON, **f**- **g**-16 Dec 1825, **h**-$1185.21.5, **i**-$1346.44.5, **j**-$161.23, accountant
James McCRACKEN, **b**-17 Aug 1819, **c**-David WALKER, Esq., **d**-$1500, **e**-David HOFFMAN, John RIDDLE, **f**-30 Aug 1819, **g**-19 Nov 1823, **h**-$160.12.5, **i**-$127.02.5, **j**-$33.10, estate
John HAYS, **b**-17 Aug 1819, **c**-William HAYS, Samuel HAYS, **d**-$1000, **e**-Robert MILLIKEN, Andrew JUNKIN, **f**-16 Aug 1819, **g**-24 Jan 1828, **h**-$996.06, **i**-$785.14, **j**-$210.92, estate
Samuel MULLEN, **b**-28 Aug 1819, **c**-George WARD, **d**-$1000, **e**-James ROBISON, Mark KULP, **f**- **g**- **h**- **i**- **j**-
Lewis STUDDS, **b**-3 Sep 1819, **c**-Dorothy STUDDS, Christian HOOVER, **d**-$500, **e**-William SHAW, John SMITH, **f**- **g**- **h**- **i**- **j**-
Margaret McKINLY, **b**-16 Sep 1819, **c**-John McKINLY, **d**-$2000, **e**-E. W. HALE, Thomas MELOY, **f**- **g**- **h**- **i**- **j**-

Page 47, Frame 56

Caleb PARSHALL, b-13 Oct 1819, **c**-Caleb PARSHALL, **d**-$2000 **e**-Jos. B. ARD, James GLASGOW, **f**-28 Aug 1820, **g**-2 Aug 1825, **h**-$380.63.5, **i**-$392.00, **j**-$11.36.5, accountant

John WOODS, b-15 Oct 1819, **c**-Robert WOODS, **d**-$1000, **e**-Jas. McGLAUGHLIN, Edward [CRINEN] **f**-15 Nov 1819, **g**- **h**- **i**- **j**-

David S. CUMMINGS, b-26 Oct 1819, **c**-Robert CUMMINS[sic], **d**-$1000, **e**-Robert U. JACOBS, David REYNOLDS, **f**- **g**- **h**- **i**- **j**-

Magdalen LANTZ, b-3 Nov 1819, **c**-John LANTZ, **d**-$2000, **e**-James KENNY, Jos. MARTIN, **f**- **g**- **h**- **i**- **j**-

John INGLES, b-11 Dec 1819, **c**-Jesse INGLES, **d**-$1000, **e**-Chas. HARDY, Wm. JENNINGS, **f**-19 Jan 1820, **g**- **h**- **i**- **j**-

Henry SHULER, b-12 Jan 1820, **c**-William SHULER, James PIERCE, **d**-$200, **e**-David REYNOLDS, James ROBISON, **f**-17 Jan 1820, **g**- **h**- **i**- **j**-

Julia Ann WILAND, b-14 Jan 1820, **c**-John LANDES. **d**-$2000, **e**-Benjn. LANDIS, M. RUMBAUGH, **f**-15 Jan 1820, **g**-26 Feb 1824, **h**-$853.51, **i**-$568.68.5 **j**-$284.82.5, estate

John McKINSTRY, b-20 Jan 1820, **c**-Richard MONTGOMERY, **d**-$5000, **e**-Thos. HONALL, John HARMAN, **f**- **g**- **h**- **i**- **j**-

Rev. Jas. JOHNSTON, b-19 Jan 1820, **c**-John JOHNSTON, **d**-$2000, **e**-Saml. MACLAY, James CRISWELL, **f**- **g**- **h**- **i**- **j**-

James JOHNSTON, b-20 Jan 1820, **c**-Daniel JOHNSTON, Wm. McCRUM, **d**-$1000, **e**-William BEALE, Pat. McKENON, **f**-20 Feb 1820, **g**-23 Apr 1823, **h**-$905.77.5, **i**-$353.84, **j**-$551.93.5, estate

Sarah HOLMS, b-20 Jan 1820, **c**-John OLIVER, **d**-$3000, **e**-William LYON, John HOLMS, **f**- **g**- **h**- **i**- **j**-

Rodolph BOLINGER, b-5 Feb 1820, **c**-Daniel BOLLINGER, Jacob MOHLER, **d**-$1000, **e**-Samuel MYER, D. SHALLEBARGER, **f**-19 Apr 1820, **g**- **h**- **i**- **j**-

Page 48, Frame 57

John SCOTT, b-26 Feb 1820, **c**-Samuel EDMISTON, **d**-$2000, **e**-R. U. JACOBS, E. W. HALE, **f**- **g**- **h**- **i**- **j**-

[Johmael] OWENS, b-28 Feb 1820, **c**-[Monis] OWENS, **d**-$500, **e**-David STEWART, Isaac WILEY, **f**-15 Mar 1820, **g**- **h**- **i**- **j**-

Daniel CRAWFORD, b-1 Mar 1820, **c**-M. M. MONAHON, **d**-$2000, **e**-David REYNOLDS, Wm. BRISBIN, **f**- **g**-18 Aug 1829, **h**-$498.51, **i**-$806.28.5, **j**-$307.77.5, accountant

Catherine LANTZ, **b**-8 Mar 1820, **c**-Christian SMOKER, Abraham STUTZMAN, **d**-$1000, **e**-Robert ROBISON, Christian KING, **f**-6 Aprr 1820, **g**-24 Jun 1836, **h**-$5182.65, **i**-$5986.31.5, **j**-$803.66.5, accountant

Roswell DOTY, **b**-4 Apr 1820, **c**-Ellen DOTY, Robert U. JACOBS, A. A. ANDERSON, Esq., **d**-$3,000, **e**-James CHRISWELL, Wm. ARMSTRONG, **f**- **g**- **h**- **i**- **j**-

William MARTIN, **b**-12 Apr 1820, **c**-Robert M. MARTIN, **d**-$500, **e**-William PATTON, William BEALE, **f**-19 May 1820, **g**- **h**- **i**- **j**-

William STEWART. **b**-22 Apr 1820, **c**-William REED, **d**-$500, **e**-Samuel REED, David REED, **f**- **g**- **h**- **i**- **j**-

Elias BIDLEMAN, **b**-20 Apr 1820, **c**-George BECK, **d**-$500, **e**-John BROWN, Henry SPANGLER, **f**-3 Aug 1820, **g**- **h**- **i**- **j**-

William McKINLY, **b**-9 Jun 1820, **c**-John McKINLY, **d**-$500, **e**-John McAVOY, E. W. HALE, Esq., **f**- **g**- **h**- **i**- **j**-

William McCOY, **b**-21 Jun 1820, **c**-Mary McCOY, William S. WILLIAMS, **d**-$6000, **e**-James CHRISWELL, James DICKSON, **f**- **g**- **h**- **i**- **j**-

Mary RUBLE, **b**-12 Jul 1820, **c**-Michael RUBLE, **d**-$1000, **e**-Robt. ROBISON, William KENNEDY, **f**- **g**-17 Jul 1820, **h**-$150.20, **i**-$94.51, **j**-$55.69, estate

Mary WILSON, **b**-13 Jul 1820, **c**-David REYNOLDS, Stewart TURBETT, **d**-$1000, **e**-Wm. BRISBEN, Christ[r] HORRELL, **f**- **g**- **h**- **i**- **j**-

Page 49, Frame 58

Robert McNITT, **b**-14 Aug 1820, **c**-John BROWN, William McNITT, **d**- —, **e**-James MILLIKEN, **f**- **g**- **h**- **i**- **j**-

David W. AITKENS, **b**-21 Aug 1820, **c**-Jonathan W. AITKEN[sic], **d**-$1000, **e**-Wm. AITKEN, Thos. BEALE, **f**-19 Nov 1821, **g**-15 Mar 1822, **h**-$304.75, **i**-$304.82.5, **j**-$.07.5, accountant

Jane SMITH, **b**-24 Aug 1820, **c**-Andrew SMITH, **d**-$500, **e**-Saml. STERRETT, Thos. BEALE, **f**- **g**- **h**- **i**- **j**-

Elizabeth STEEL, **b**-8 Sep 1820, **c**-Alexander STEEL, **d**-$1000, **e**-David JORDAN, Geo. GREEN, **f**- **g**- **h**- **i**- **j**-

John ALEXANDER, **b**-9 Oct 1820, **c**-Josiah ALEXANDER, Saml. W. TAYLOR, **d**-$3000, **e**-Robt. TAYLOR, Robt. ROBISON, **f**-8 Nov 1820, **g**-19 Jul 1825, **h**-$3964.23, **i**-$1198.86, **j**-$2765.37, estate

Isaac TURNER, b-23 Oct 1820, c-Jesse REYNOLDS, d-$500, e-David REYNOLDS, Levi REYNOLDS, f-21 Nov 1820, g-20 Jan 1826, h-$446.29.5, i-$400.77, j-$45.52.5, estate

James LOVE, b-10 Nov 1820, c-John LOVE, d-$2000, e-Jesse REYNOLDS, Thos. ROBISON, f-9 Dec 1820, g-31 Jul 1826, h-$2368.13.5, i-$1735.45.5, j-$632.68, estate

Ignatius ROMER, b-9 Dec 1820 c-Joseph DYSER [DYSERT?], d-$2000, e-Andrew KISER, Jos. MARTIN, f-11 Dec 1820, g-21 Feb 1824, h-$1002.00, i-$152.31, j-$49.69, estate

Michael MARKEY, b-15 Dec 1820, c-John REED, Esq., d-$500, e-George MEANS, Andrew McILVAIN, f- g- h- i- j-

Page 50, Frame 59 [NOTE: Dates revert back to 1789 at this point]
William MONTOOTH, b-11 Dec 1789, c-Mary MONTOOTH, Wm. McCORMICK, d- e- f- g- h- i- j-

Charles OHARA, b-12 Dec 1789, c-William BROWN, d- e- f- g-6 Dec 1806, h-£105..13..9, i-£106..5..7, j-£0..11..4, extr

Alexander BROWN, b-12 Dec 1789, c-William BROWN, Jane BROWN, d- e- f-17 Oct 1789, g-9 Sep 1800, h-£467..7..10, i-£836..16..8, j-£369..5..10

James POTTER, b-15 Dec 1789, c-James POTTER, Andrew GREGG, James POE, d- e- f- g- h- i- j-

John BOWER, b-19 Dec 1789, c-John COY, d- e- f- g- h- i- j-

George SIGLER, b-9 Mar 1790, c-George SIGLER, d- e- f- g- h- i- j-

John COLLINS, b-6 Apr 1790, c-Catherine COLLINS, Brice COLLINS, d- e- f-3 Apr 1830, g-22 Jan 1808, h-£376..2..3.75, i-£48..2..7.5, j-£327..19..8.25, estate

David MITCHELL, b-14 Jun 1790. c-John MITCHELL, Francis MITCHELL, d- e- f- g- h- i- j-

Charles HUNTER, b-18 Oct 1791, c- d- e- f- g- h- i- j-

Duncan CAMERON, b-14 Jan 1792, c-John BAIRD, William McDOWELL, d- e- f-15 Aug 1792, g-9 Apr 1802 h-£138..11..7, i-£142..3..4, j-£3..11..9, extrs

Arthur BUCHANAN, b-14 Feb 1792, c-Isabella BUCHANAN, William STROUD, William LYON, d- e- f-4 Feb 1792, g-18 Dec 1806, h-£39..13..1, i-£66..8..9.5, j-£26..15..8.5, extrs

Zephaniah STARKS, b-2 Jul 1792, c-Nancy STARKS, Joseph COWGILL, d- e- f-30 Aug 1792, g-12 Sep 1797, h-£249..6..1, i-£245..8..9, j-£3..17..3, heirs

Page 51, Frame 60

Mary DICK, b-12 Nov 1792 **c**-Joseph CASTLE, **d- e- f- g- h- i- j-**

John GLASGOW, b-20 Nov 1792, **c**-Margaret GLASGOW, James GLASGOW, John WATTSON, **d- e- f- g- h- i- j-**

Hugh MARTIN, b-11 Feb 1793, **c**-Elijah CRISWELL, John FLEMING, **d- e- f**-22 Sep 1795, **g**-23 Sep 1795, **h**-£121..2..1, **i**-£121..2..1, **j-**

Benjamin WELLS, b-28 Feb 1793, **c**-Jane WELLS, **d- e- f**-9 May 1796, **g**-9 May 1796, **h**-£360..8..1, **i**-£360..8..1, **j-**

Hercules CAMPBELL, b-20 Mar 1793, **c**-George BELL, Jane CAMPBELL, **d- e- f- g- h- i- j-**

Robert BROTHERTON, b-25 Mar 1793, **c**-John CAMPBELL, **d- e- f**-7 May 1795, **g**-14 Sep 1795, **h**-£63..12..5, **i**-£63..12..5, **j-**

John WAKEFIELD, b-3 Mar 1794, **c**-Martha WAKEFIELD, William WAKEFIELD, **d- e- f**-20 Oct 1806, **g**-17 Jan 1807, **h**-£31..17..6, **i**-£34..19..4.5, **j**-£3..1..10.5, extrs

Robert CRAWFORD, b-29 Jul 1793, **c**-Elizabeth CRAWFORD, **d- e- f- g- h- i- j-**

James WILLIAMS, b-24 Aug 1793, **c**-Rebecca WILLIAMS, **d- e- f- g- h- i- j-**

John YOUNG, b-3 Oct 1793, **c**-Mary YOUNG, **d- e- f- g- h- i- j-**

Henry COLLINS, b-7 Nov 1793, **c**-Rachel COLLINS, Aaron COLLINS, Henry COLLINS, **d- e- f- g- h- i- j-**

Henry HANIWALT, b-25 Mar 1794, **c**-George HANIWALT, John HANIWALT, **d- e- f**-25 Jun 1794, **g**-11 May 1807, **h**-£52..11..9, **i**-£161..2..7.5, **j**-£108..10..10.5, extrs

Page 52, Frame 61

John HARRIS, b-22 Apr 1794, **c**-Jane HARRIS, James HARRIS, William HARRIS, **d- e- f**-29 Jul 1794, **g**-24 Nov 1808/3 Oct 1832, **h**-£1432..5..11.5/$1758.22, **i**-£1434..12..10, **j**-£2..6..10.5, extrs/$880.45, accountant

Samuel DITTERLINE, b-27 Apr 1794, **c**-William DITTERLINE, **d- e- f- g- h- i- j-**

John MILLIGAN, b-6 Aug 1794, **c**-John FLEMING, James WILSON, **d- e- f- g- h- i- j-**

John JOHNSTON, b-17 Nov 1794, **c**-James JOHNSTON, Isabella JOHNSTON, **d- e- f- g- h- i- j-**

Rebecca ARMSTRONG, b-10 Dec 1794, **c**-James ARMSTRONG **d- e- f- g- h- i- j-**

William SANKEY, b-30 Dec 1794, c-Elizabeth SANKEY, Ezekiel SANKEY, d- e- f- g- h- i- j-

Jonathan PARSHALL, b-23 Jan 1795, c-Caleb PARSHAL[sic], d- e- f-15 Apr 1795, g- h- i- j-

John TURBETT, b-16 Apr 1795, c-Samuel TURBETT, d- e- f-23 May 1795, g-10 Dec 1799, h-£430..16..11.5, i-£291..1..2, j-£131..15..9.5, heirs

James CHAMBERS, b-2 May 1795, c-William CHAMBERS, Thomas BEALE, d- e- f- g- h- i- j-

Hugh WATT, b-13 May 1795, c-Jane WATT, Hugh WATT, d- e- f- g- h- i- j-

James McCOWN, b-10 Aug 1795, c-Jane McCOWN, Robert BUCHANAN, d- e- f- g- h- i- j-

Thomas THOMPSON, b-25 Aug 1795, c-John BARBER, John [McKIMM], d- e- f- g- h- i- j-

Page 53, Frame 62

William SMITH, b-25 Sep 1795, c-Joseph STRODE, William WAKEFIELD, d- e- f- g- h- i- j-

James GRAY, b-15 Dec 1795, c-Rachel GRAY, John GRAY, d- e- f-11 Oct 1798, g- h- i- j-

James HENDERSON, b-16 Dec 1795, c-Sarah HENDERSON, Robert HUNTER, d- e- f- g- h- i- j-

William STEWART, b-16 Jan 1796, c-William BELL, Esq., d- e- f- g- h- i- j-

William KENNISON, b-15 Feb 1796, c-Henry KENNISON, Mary KENNISON, d- e- f- g- h- i- j-

Edward McCONNELL, b-16 Mar 1796, c-Henry McCONNELL, d- e- f- g- h- i- j-

William MARSDEN, b-13 Apr 1796, c-William MARSDEN, Jacob MARSDEN, d- e- f-21 May 1798, g-11 Mar 1816, h-$972.67, i-$972.67, j-

William JENNINGS, b-14 Jun 1796, c-Elizabeth JENNINGS, John YOCAM, d- e- f-10 Sep 1796, g-9 Dec 1800, h-£121..15..4, i-£149..19..3, j-£28..3..11.5, admrs

Andrew DUFF, b-31 Aug 1796, c-July DUFF, Thomas JOHNSTON, James AITKEN, d- e- f- g- h- i- j-

Griffith THOMAS, b-8 Oct 1796, c-Mariah THOMAS, Griffith THOMAS, d- e- f- g- h- i- j-

Marshall STANLEY, **b**-29 Nov 1796, **c**-Nathaniel STANLEY, John BRATTON, **d- e- f- g- h- i- j-**

James SCOTT, **b**-30 Nov 1796, **c**-John SCOTT, John BROWN, Crawford KYLE, James McCLURE, **d- e- f- g- h- i- j-**

Page 54, Frame 63

Thomas WILSON, **b**-6 Dec 1796, **c**-George WILSON, Josiah WILSON, Thomas WILSON, **d- e- f- g- h- i- j-**

Joseph FOSTER, **b**-10 Dec 1796, **c**-Moses MOORE, **d- e- f- g- h- i- j-**

Frederick LEATHER, **b**-14 Dec 1794, **c**-Jane LEATHERS[sic], James WILLIAMSON, **d- e- f- g- h- i- j-**

John MIERS, **b**-19 Mar 1797, **c**-John MYERS[sic], **d- e- f- g- h- i- j-**

William CHRISTY, **b**-18 Feb 1797, **c**-Catherine CHRISTY, **d- e- f- g- h- i- j-**

Robert BARNHILL, **b**-21 Feb 1797, **c**-Rebecca BARNHILL, William BARNHILL, **d- e- f- g- h- i- j-**

Jesse MOORE, **b**-16 Jun 1797, **c**-William HUKEY, **d- e- f**-12 Jun 1797, **g**-21 Sep 1799, **h**-£180..0..2.5, **i- j**-£24..10..4.5, heirs

George BRATTON, **b**-24 May 1797, **c**-George BRATTON, Wm. BRATTON, **d- e- f- g- h- i- j-**

John TENNIS, **b**-31 Jul 1797, **c**-Stephen TENNIS, **d- e- f- g- h- i- j-**

Christian SHROIRER, **b**-9 Aug 1797, **c**-Mary SHROIRER, Abraham WEAVER, Jacob SHROIRER, **d- e- f**-10 Aug 1797, **g- h- i- j-**

Joseph ALLENDER, **b**-14 Aug 1797, **c**-Thomas McCOMMON, Alexander ALLENDER, William RANKIN, **d- e- f**-7 Sep 1797, **g**-15 Jun 1808, **h**-$3257.68, **i**-$2045.66, **j**-$1212.02, heirs

James McCRUM, **b**-26 Aug 1797, **c**-William McCRUM, John WRIGHT, **d- e- f**-23 Sep 1797, **g**-25 Feb 1807/15 Jan 1800, **h**-$1277.51/£778..12..4, **i**-$1456.46/£305..10..2.5, **j**-$178.95, extrs, £473..2..1.5, heirs

Page 55, Frame 64

Joseph BROWN, **b**-29 Sep 1797, **c**-Hugh McCLELLAND, **d- e- f- g- h- i- j-**

Robert MOORE, **b**-2 Oct 1797, **c**-Andrew BANKS, William W. MOORE, **d- e- f**-19 Oct 1797, **g**-11 Apr 1818, **h**-£151..0..10, **i**-£186..12..0.5, **j**-£35..11.2.5, extr

Stephen BETTY [probably BEATTY], b-21 Nov 1797, c-John BETTY, William BETTY, d- e- f-12 Dec 1798, g-8 Aug 1805, h-£654..10..2, i-£375..4..2, j-£289..6..0, estate

Abraham WELLS, b-30 Nov 1797, c-James WELLS, d- e- f- g- h- i- j-

George ARMSTRONG, b-8 Feb 1798, c-John McCORD, John KISTLER, d- e- f- g- h- i- j-

James KINNEAR, b-8 Aug 1798, c-Ann KINNEAR, d- e- f- g- h- i- j-

Jacob KISTLER, b-13 Oct 1798 c- d- e- f- g- h- i- j-

Alexander KENNY, b-15 Aug 1798, c-James WELLS, d- e- f-15 Aug 1798, g-17 Jul 1805, h-£179..19..4.5, i-£165..6..6.5, j-£14..12..10, heirs

William RIDDLE, b-17 Jan 1799, c-David WALKER, Esq. d- e- f-1 Mar 1799, g-11 May 1802, h-£234..12..2 i- j-£72..18..8, extr

David SAMPLE, b-8 Mar 1799, c-Francis SAMPLE, David SAMPLE, d- e- f- g- h- i- j-

John WOODS, b-8 Mar 1799, c-John WOODS, d- e- f- g- h- i- j-

Judiath ACHINGER, b-3 Apr 1799, c-Alexander McKETRICK, Catherine McKETRICK, d- e- f-20 May 1799, g-24 Apr 1804, h-£430..18..4, i- j-£304..13..8, heirs

Page 56, Frame 65

James ROSS, b-23 May 1799, c-James ROSS, Wm. McCINSTRY, d- e- f- g- h- i- j-

Thomas SANKEY, b-5 Jun 1799, c-Jeremiah SANKEY, Thomas SANKEY, d- e- f- g- h- i- j-

James SNODGRASS, b-13 Aug 1799, c-Jane SNODGRASS, William GRAHAM, Thomas ANDERSON d- e- f-13 Aug 1799, g-13 Sep 1803, h-£411..8..0.5, i- j-

Thomas BRATTON, b-28 Dec 1799, c- d- e- f- g- h- i- j-

Samuel BRATTON. b-31 Dec 1799, c-William BRATTON, William BRATTON, Esq., d- e- f-15 Jan 1800, g-2 May 1824, h-$5005.91, i-$5885.75, j-$877.87, accountants

Morris [McKAMARA], b-31 Jan 1800, c-John WILSON, William STEWART, d- e- f-17 Dec 1801, g-13 Dec 1808, h-$453.34, i-$296.76, j-$156.57, heirs

James LYON, b-13 Aug 1800, c-William LYON, John OLIVER, d- e- f- g- h- i- j-

Valentine CARBERRY, b-27 Aug 1800, c-Ann CARBERRY, d- e- f-28 Aug 1800, g-13 Nov 1806, h-£10..0..0, i-£11..19..4.5, j-£1..19..4.5, extrs

Christian BROWN, b-10 Nov 1800, c-Hugh McCLELLAND, d- e- f- g- h- i- j-

James HUSTON, b-30 Dec 1800, c-Isabella HUSTON, David McKIM, d- e- f- g- h- i- j-

Daniel JONES, b-27 Jan 1801, c-Susannah JONES, d- e- f- g- h- i- j-

John HARDY, b-6 Feb 1801, c-John HARDY, d- e- f- g- h- i- j-

Page 57, Frame 66

Mathew KELLY, b-1 Apr 1801, c-John KELLY, George KELLY, d- e- f- g- h- i- j-

Thomas ANDERSON, b-14 Apr 1801, c-Eleanor ANDERSON, Joseph STEWART, James McCONNELL, d- e- f-14 Apr 1801, g-19 Dec 1806, h-£248..19..5.5, i-£101..4..11, j-£147..14..6.5, heirs

John SHAVER, b-3 Jun 1801, c-Thomas SHAVER, James BOGGS, d- e- f-19 Nov 1806, g-19 Nov 1806, h-£549..18..3.5, i-£417..15..8 j- £132..2..7, heirs

Henry DIXON, b-19 Sep 1801, c-Ann DIXON, William LYON, William STRODE, d- e- f-19 Oct 1801, g-18 Dec 1806, h-£513..5..4.5 i- £254..12..5, j-£258..12..11.5, estate

Samuel AITKEN, b-6 Oct 1801, c-John PATTERSON, d- e- f-5 Mar 1803, g-17 Feb 1803, h-£68..17..1.5, i-£65..10..1.5, j-£3..7..0, due —

William SILVERTHORN, b-5 Nov 1801, c-Ann SILVERTHORN, John WILLIAMS, d- e- f- g- h- i- j-

Martin KERNER, b-19 Nov 1801, c-George KERNER, Margaret KERNER, d- e- f- g- h- i- j-

John HANGE, b-19 Dec 1801, c-John RICE, Jacob HENCH, d- e- f-8 Jan 1802, g-20 Jan 1807, h-£1087..19..10, i-£730..19..3, j-£351..00..7, heirs

John DAVIS, b-15 Jan 1802, c-John DAVIS, d- e- f- g-1 Apr 1812, h- $581.70, i-$572.90, j-$9.80, estate

William THOMPSON, b-23 Mar 1802, c-George GUILLIFORD, William ARBUCKLE, d- e- f-12 Apr 1802, g-11 Dec 1806/22 Jan 1812, h- £423..18..6/$152.81.5, i-£389..9..4/$304.92.5, j-$152.11, extrs

Joseph DAVIS, b-24 Mar 1802, c-Hannah DAVIS, John WATTSON, Esq., d- e- f- g- h- i- j-

Edward JOHNSTON, b-14 Apr 1802, c- d- e- f- g- h- i- j-

Page 58, Frame 67

Patrick MURPHY, b-14 Apr 1802, c-Alexander MURPHY, d- e- f-7 Jun 1802, g-18 Nov 1806, h- i- j-

Andrew McKEE, **b**-25 May 1802, **c**-Ann McKEE, Robert MEANS, **d**- **e**- **f**-19 Jun 1802, **g**-13 Mar 1807, **h**-$873.58, **i**-$429.61, **j**-$443.97, heirs

John McKEE, **b**-28 May 1802, **c**-David McKEE, **d**- **e**- **f**-26 Jun 1802, **g**-26 Feb 1807, **h**-£640..8..7, **i**-£108..5..11, **j**-£532..2..8, heirs

Thomas KERR, **b**-25 Jun 1802, **c**-John KERR, William DEVOR, **d**- **e**- **f**-26 Oct 1804, **g**-12 Feb 1813, **h**-$2771.98, **i**-$452.94, **j**-$2319.04, heirs

James KYLE, **b**-29 Oct 1802, **c**-Joseph KYLE, Thomas BROWN, **d**- **e**- **f**- **g**- **h**- **i**- **j**-

John STONE, **b**-2 Nov 1802, **c**-John McCONNELL, Thomas BARRITT, **d**- **e**- **f**-2 Nov 1802, **g**-17 Nov 1806, **h**-£241..18..11, **i**-£209..15..2.5, **j**-£32..3..8.5, extrs

Enoch WILLIAMS, **b**-28 Dec 1802, **c**Thomas MENIONGER,- **d**- **e**- **f**- **g**- **h**- **i**- **j**-

Robert MARTIN, **b**-12 Apr 1803, **c**-William ARMSTRONG, Jr., John OLIVER, **d**- **e**- **f**-27 May 1803, **g**-6 Jul 1810, **h**-$3142.45, **i**-$1226.83, **j**-$1915.62, heirs

Christian LINTNER, **b**-12 Apr 1803, **c**-Peter LINTNER, Conrad LINTNER, **d**- **e**- **f**- **g**- **h**- **i**- **j**-

William TEMPLETON, **b**-13 Apr 1803, **c**-Peter EYSTER, Thomas MORROW, **d**- **e**- **f**-11 Jan 1804, **g**-14 Feb 1804, **h**-£56..13..1, **i**-£84..10..7, **j**-£27..19..6, extrs

John McFADDIN, **b**-17 Jun 1803, **c**-Samuel McFADDIN, **d**- **e**- **f**- **g**- **h**- **i**- **j**-

Page 59, Frame 68

James MICHELTREE, **b**-17 Jun 1803, **c**-James McLINN, David WALKER, Esq. **d**- **e**- **f**-17 Jun 1803, **g**-17 Feb 1807, **h**-$3430.20, **i**-$856.69, **j**-$2573.71, heirs

James MILLIKEN, **b**-6 Aug 1803, **c**-Robert MILLIKEN, **d**- **e**- **f**- **g**- **h**- **i**- **j**-

George SHAVER, **b**-11 Aug 1803, **c**-William BEALE, Jr. **d**- **e**- **f**- **g**- **h**- **i**- **j**-

Abraham MILLER, **b**-13 Sep 1803, **c**-Catherine MILLER, Joseph ROTHROCK, Jacob KINSEL, **d**- **e**- **f**-3 Oct 1803, **g**-31 Oct 1806/6 Sep 1823, **h**-£344..18..2/$7402.98, **i**-£316..7..8/$7449.98, **j**-£28..10..6, heirs/$47.00, accountant

Jacob ADAMS, **b**-27 Sep 1803, **c**-Robert WILSON, William MITCHELL, **d**- **e**- **f**-24 Oct 1804, **g**- **h**- **i**- **j**-

Joseph YODER, **b**-8 Oct 1803, **c**-Christian YOTTER, David HARTZLER, **d**- **e**- **f**-28 Oct 1803, **g**- **h**- **i**- **j**-

James IRWIN, b-2 Nov 1803, c-George IRWIN, d- e- f-21Nov 1803, g-14 May 1805, h-£466..19..2.5, i-£201..15..6.5, j-£265..3..8, heirs

James REED, b-19 Nov 1803, c-Alexander REED, John REED, d- e- f-23 Dec 1803, g-18 Mar 1811, h- i- j-

Michael ECKHART, b-1 Feb 1804, c-John ARNOLD, Nicholas ARNOLD, d- e- f-14 Mar 1804, g-26 Jul 1805, h-£274..16..4, i-£42..6..2.5, j-£232..10..1.5, estate

Joseph COOKSON, b-9 Apr 1804, c-David WALKER, Esq. d- e- f-6 Apr 1806, g-17 Feb 1807, h-$955.87.5, i-$544.55, j-$411.32.5, estate

James SMILEY, b-9 Apr 1804, c-Patrick SMILEY, d- e- f- g- h- i- j-

John WHARRY, b-11 Apr 1804, c-Agness WHARRY, John McDOWELL, d- e- f- g- h- i- j-

Page 60, Frame 69

William ARMSTRONG, b-25 May 1804, c-William ARMSTRONG, d- e- f-20 Jun 1804 g- h- i- j-

ßhufanna?] ALEXANDER, b-2 Jun 1804, c-George BRATTON, d- e- f-19 Jan 1807, g-15 Mar 1809, h-$1314.46 i-$1114.22, j-$200.25, heirs

Samuel EDMISTON, b-12 Jul 1804, c-Jane EDMISTON, George McCLELLAND, d- e- f- g- h- i- j-

Andrew FRYBARGER, b-5 Sep 1804, c-John KEPNER, d- e- f-22 Dec 1804, g-7 Jun 1806/15 Mar 1823/20 Mar 1829, h-$1182.61/$4406.42.5 /$2909.80, i-$92.16.5/$4147.76/$3841.28, j-$258.66.5, heirs/$931.48, accountant

Anthoney DEARDUFF, b-17 Sep 1804, c-Benjamin DEARDORF[sic], Mathias LICHENTHALER, d- e- f- g- h- i- j-

Thomas KERR, b-19 Sep 1804, c-John KERR, d- e- f- g-17 Jan 1820/4 Mar 1823, h-$4707.67.5/$8186.43, i-$1007.76/$1561.26, j-$6625.17, estate

Francis ALEXANDER, b-16 Oct 1804, c-James ALEXANDER, d- e- f-17 Jan 1805, g- h- i- j-

Alexander STALFORD, b-19 Oct 1804, c-George BRATTON, d- e- f-19 Jan 1807, g-15 Mar 1809, h-$1314.46, i-$1114.22, j-$200.23, heirs

John QUAIL, b-20 Oct 1804, c-William QUAIL, d- e- f-5 Nov 1804, g- h- i- j-

Mathew SCOTT, b-26 Oct 1804, c-Archibald FERGUSON, Christian FERGUSON, Joseph DYSERT, Jonathan HAMILTON, d- e- f- g- h- i- j-

Samuel MILLIKEN, b-31 Oct 1804, **c**-James MILLIKEN, John WILSON, John BROWN, **d- e- f- g**-20 Nov 1820, **h**-$6996.80, **i**-$6996.80, **j**-

John McFEE, b-22 Nov 1804, **c**-Jane McFEE, **d- e- f- g- h- i- j**-

Page 61, Frame 70

Mary BROWN, b-15 Apr 1805, **c**-James KINSLOE, **d- e- f- g- h- i- j**-

William McKEE, b-9 May 1805, **c**-Robert McKEE, **d- e- f- g- h- i- j**-

William LOGAN, b-13 Jun 1805, **c**-Margaret LOGAN, **d- e- f- g- h- i- j**-

John McCLELLAND, b-19 Jun 1805, **c**-Catherine McCLELLAND, **d- e- f**-11 Sep 1890, **g**-15 Jan1816, **h**-$342.67, **i**-$372.85, **j**-$30.81, admr

Nathan ALLEN, b-19 Jun 1805, **c**-Margaret ALLEN, William ALEXANDER, **d- e- f- g- h- i- j**-

Mary ADAMS, b-5 Jul 1805, **c- d- e- f- g- h- i- j**-

William MORRISON, b-15 Jul 1805, **c**-William MORRISON, James MORRISON, **d- e- f- g- h- i- j**-

Christian CLAY, b-7 Aug 1805, **c**-Mathias CLAY, Zachh DURST, **d- e- f**-7 Aug 1805, **g**-11 Jul 1807/28 Feb 1810/15 Mar 1814, **h**-£1002..19..5/$802.88/$645.40.5, **i**-£901..17..8.5/$474.14.5/$49.65, **j**-$595.75.5, estate

William MOSS, b-12 Aug 1805, **c**-Lewis EVANS, **d- e- f**-18 Aug 1807, **g**-27 Sep 1816, **h**-$484.20, **i**-$265.95, **j**-$72.75, heirs

Mathew CRUNK, b-8 Oct 1805, **c**-Mary BARNHILL, **d- e- f- g- h- i- j**-

James McLIN, b-23 Oct 1805, **c**-Thomas McLIN, **d- e- f- g- h- i- j**-

Jacob MILLER, b-29 Oct 1805, **c**-John MILLER, John ZOOK (carpt) **d- e- f- g**-21 Aug 1811/31 May 1831, **h**-$765.33/$665.40/ **i**-$117.09/$678.73, **j**-$765.33, heirs/$13.33, accountant

Page 62, Frame 71

John HOLLY, b-15 Nov 1805, **c**-John HARTZLER, Jacob YODER, **d- e- f- g- h- i- j**-

Rebecca ABRAHAM, b-11 Jan 1806, **c**-Jacob WRIGHT, James KNOX, **d- e- f**-15 Apr 1806/10 Feb 1807, **g**-18 Dec 1811/24 Apr 1813/21 Aug 1815, **h**-$583.60.5/$27.50/$401.66, **i**-$181.94/$27.50/$133.77, **j**-$567.89, heirs

Samuel McCRORY, b-23 Feb 1806, **c**-Solomon McCRORY, John McCRORY, **d- e- f**-31 Aug 1809, **g**-3 Feb 1813, **h**-$224.09, **i**-$127.42. **j**-$96.67, heirs

James WOOD, b-17 Apr 1806, c-17 Apr 1806, d-David WALKER, Esq., Thomas WOOD, e- f- g-19 Jan 1821, h-$2661.99, i-$3017.15, j-$1440.96, accountant

Abraham LUKEN, b-14 May 1806, c-Mary LUKEN, Gabriel LUKEN, d- e- f-27 May 1806, g-13 Jul 1807/22 Mar 1811/[same], h-£402..11..5.5/ $1635.35/$677.68, i-£47..7..1.5/$217.74/$70.19, j-£355..4..4/ $1447.60/$607.49, heirs

Jonas KELSO, b-23 May 1806, c-Enos KELSEY, Esther KELSEY, d- e- f- g- h- i- j-

William BEATTY, b-30 May 1806, c-Isabella BEATTY, d- e- f- g- h- i- j-

William WEBSTER, b-5 Jun 1806, c-Jacob REIGHART, Arthur McNIGHT, d- e- f-19 Aug 1806, g-14 Dec 1811, h-$406.06, i-294.97, j-$109.09, heirs

Joseph COULTER, b-1 Oct 1806, c-William WAKEFIELD, David CRISWELL, d- e- f-15 May 1821, g-15 May 1821, h-$2885.82 i-$1325.83.5, j-$1559.98, estate

James GLASS, b-31 Oct 1806, c-Robert GLASS, d- e- f- g- h- i- j-

John MEAN, b-14 Nov 1806, c-William HENRY, d- e- f- g-9 Dec 1818, h-$728.39, i-$1255.14.5, j-$526.75, admr

Mary McINTIRE, b-7 Nov 1806, c-James McINTIRE, d- e- f- g- h- i- j-

Page 63, Frame 72

John SWIGER, b-17 Nov 1806, c-George HANAWALT, John SWIGERT, d- e- f- g- h- i- j-

Henry BITNER, b-17 Nov 1806, c-M. M. MONAHON, d- e- f- g-4 Dec 1826, h-$675.72, i-$817.13, j-$141.41, accountant

Samuel DAVIS, b-18 Nov 1806, c-Lewis EVANS, d- e- f-18 Aug 1807, g- h- i- j-

John BORRIS, b-10 Dec 1806, c-Peter BORRIS, John SHIBLY, d- e- f-6 Mar 1807, g-11 Mar 1809, h-£1289..8..0, i-£1290..12..2.5, j-£1..4.2.5. extr

Robina DUNLOP, b-16 Feb 1811, c-Geo. DUNLOP, d- e- f-23 May 1811, g-2 Jan 1813, h-$109.74, i-$9.09, j-$100.65, estate

Jane HARRIS, b-14 Feb 1807, c-James HARRIS, d- e- f-23 Apr 1807, g-6 May 1817, h-$8185.62, i-$8185.62, j-

John McDOWELL, b-27 Feb 1807, c- d- e- f- g- h- i- j-

John [COMFORT/COMFERT], b-7 Mar 1807, c-Andrew KEISER, Esq. d- e- f-18 Mar 1807, g-2 Jul 1812, h-$662.64, i-$748.39, j-$85.75, extr

Samuel OSBORNE, b-13 Mar 1807, **c**-George WOOD, Jr., **d- e- f- g- h-i- j-**

Mary WILSON, b-16 Mar 1807, **c**-Thomas WILSON, Thomas TURBETT **d- e- f- g- h- i- j-**

William QUALE [possibly QUAIL], **b**-24 Apr 1807, **c**-M. M. MONAHON, **d- e- f**-19 Aug 1808, **g- h- i- j-**

Thomas RAMSEY, b-9 May 1807, **c**-John SMITH, **d- e- f- g- h- i- j-**

Page 64, Frame 73

George WOOD, b-18 Jun 1807, **c**-George WOOD, William WOOD, Thomas WOOD, **d- e- f- g- h- i- j-**

Wm. CUNNINGHAM, b-30 Sep 1807, **c**-Margaret CUNNINGHAM, Michael CUNNINGHAM, **d- e- f- g- h- i- j-**

Alexander COCHRAN, b-3 Oct 1807, **c**-Joseph COCHRAN, James COCHRAN, **d- e- f**-16 Oct 1807, **g**-6 Nov 1810, **h**-$1151.72, **i**-$1151.72, **j**-no balance

John COOPER, b-24 Oct 1807, **c**-John McDOWELL, David FLEMING, Robert COOPER, **d- e- f**-5 Jul 1811, **g**-[4 or 11] Sep 1811, **h**-$1857.77, **i**-$387.82, **j**-$1469.95, heirs

Robert PATTERSON, b-12 Dec 1807, **c**-John PATTERSON, **d- e- f- g-h- i- j-**

William MONTGOMERY, b-18 Jan 1808, **c**-David HUNTER, **d- e- f- g-h- i- j-**

Edward BATES, b-2 Apr 1808, **c**-John BATES, **d- e- f**-20 Apr 1808, **g**-27 Feb 1809, **h**-$1107.17, **i**-$93.88, **j**-$1013.29, estate

Alexander KERR, b-20 Apr 1808, **c**-James McCONNELL, Robert KERR, **d- e- f**-21 Apr 1808, **g**-9 Oct 1815, **h**-$1935.40, **i**-$229.48, **j**-$1705.92, heirs

Hannah WILLIAMS, b-17 May 1808, **c**-David NUGENT, **d- e- f**-20 Nov 1811, **g**-20 Nov 1811, **h**-$283.92, **i**-$79.89, **j**-$204.03, heirs

Theophilus McDONALD, b-6 Jun 1808, **c**-Theophilus McDONALD, Thomas McDONALD, **d- e- f- g- h- i- j-**

Stephen WHITE, b-9 Jun 1808, **c**-Thomas WHITE, **d- e- f- g- h- i- j-**

Daniel VINES, b-10 Jun 1808, **c**-Peter THOMPSON, **d- e- f- g**-5 Jan 1826, **h**-$207.41.25, **i**-$131.04, **j**-$76.37.25, accountant

Page 65, Frame 74

Mark KERR, b-22 Jun 1808, **c**-Thomas GILSON, **d- e- f**-15 Aug 1808, **g**-11 May 1810, **h**-$1489.49, **i**-$554.69, **j**-$925.79, heirs

Philip STROUSE, **b-**20 Sep 1808, **c-**Benjamin KEPNER, John STROUSE, **d- e- f- g- h- i- j-**
Peter FISCHER, b-15 Oct 1808, **c-**Eve FISCHER, Peter SCHWARTS, **d- e- f-**17 Oct 1808, **g-**16 Nov 1813, **h-**$191.94, **i-**$234.62, **j-**$42.68, extrs
Robert PATTERSON, b-16 Nov 1808, **c- d- e- f- g- h- i- j-**
John KYLE, b-16 Jan 1809, **c-**Crawford KYLE, Joseph KYLE, **d- e- f- g- h- i- j-**
Christopher IRWIN, b-18 Mar 1809, **c-**William IRWIN, **d- e- f- g- h- i- j-**
James GRAY, b-28 Mar 1809, **c-**Thomas GRAY, **d- e- f-**6 Jun 1809, **g-**25 Oct 1809, **h-**$113.17, **i-**$113.17, **j-**
Joseph COULTER, b-28 Dec 1809 [7?], **c- d- e- f- g- h- i- j-**
Margaret CUNNINGHAM, b-9 Oct 1809, **c-**Michael CUNNINGHAM, M. M. MONAHON, **d- e- f- g- h- i- j-**
Henry NIPPLE, b-31 Oct 1809, **c-**Charles HITE, **d- e- f- g- h- i- j-**
David SUNDERLAND, b-7 Nov 1809, **c-**David SUNDERLAND, Jeremiah CUNNINGHAM, **d- e- f-**7 Dec 1809, **g-**29 Sep 1810, **h-**$629.69, **i-**$34.63, **j-**$595.05, heirs
John McDOWELL, b-7 Dec 1809, **c-**William McDOWELL, James McDOWELL, **d- e- f- g- h- i- j-**

Page 66, Frame 75
Samuel WALKER, b-17 Dec 1809, **c-**David WALKER, Esq., **d- e- f- g- h- i- j-**
David LOGHLIN, b-17 Jan 1810, **c-**Thomas HARRIS, William DILLEN, **d- e- f- g- h- i- j-**
Mary MURRAY, b-22 Sep 1809, **c-**Theodore MEMINGER, **d- e- f- g- h- i- j-**
Jane REED, b-30 Feb[???] 1810, **c-**Alexander REED, **d- e- f- g- h- i- j-**
Dorothy TURBETT, b-30 Mar 1810, **c-**Samuel FOULTON, **d- e- f-**8 May 1810, **g-**3 Jan 1811, **h-**$5262.56, **i-**$2983.39, **j-**$2279.17, heirs
Robert GLASS, b-29 Mar 1810, **c-**Agness GLASS, John STERRETT, John BEATTY, **d- e- f-**3 Oct 1810, **g-**18 Oct 1816, **h-**$5535.78, **i-**$558.77, **j-**$4977.01, heirs
James TURBETT, b-31 May 1810, **c-**Thomas TURBETT, **d- e- f- g- h- i- j-**
Joseph CORBETT, b-15 Jun 1810, **c-**William CORBETT, **d- e- f- g- h- i- j-**

William LEWIS, b-6 Aug 1810, **c**-Ellen LEWIS, John BRATTON, Wm. W. LAIRD, Esq., **d- e- f**-17 Sep 1810, **g**-28 Jan 1814, **h**-$24.00, **i**-167.65, **j**-$143.65, admr

Christian HANAWALT, b-24 Aug 1810, **c**-George HANAWALT, John HANAWALT, William BRATTON, **d- e- f- g- h- i- j-**

Peter CLOSE, b-13 Sep 1810, **c**-Catherine CLOSE, Mathew RILEY, **d- e- f**-14 Sep 1811, **g**-18 Oct 1811, **h**-$539.25, **i**-$90.80.5, **j**-$448.44.5, estate

Hugh McALLISTER, b-2 Oct 1810, **c**-Hugh McALLISTER, James KNOX, Esq., **d- e- f**-23 Jan 1811, **g**-20 Aug 1816, **h**-$5265.51, **i**-$4046.58, **j**-$1218.93, heirs

Page 67, Frame 76

Michael GARBER, b-11 Dec 1810, **c**-Magdalen GARBER, **d- e- f- g- h- i- j-**

William SINKEY, b-28 Feb 1811, **c**-Jeremiah SINKEY, John CLAYTON, **d- e- f**-28 Feb 1828, **g**-14 Mar 1829, **h**-$3667.13.5, **i**-$600.62.5, **j**-$3066.51, estate

Elijah CRISWELL, b-12 Mar 1811, **c**-Elijah CRISWELL, James MILLIKEN, John CRISWELL, **d- e- f**-27 Jun 1812, **g**-2 Mar 1819/13 Feb 1839, **h**-$1114.42/$2557.83, **i**-$1215.70/$2557.83, **j**-$101.28, estate

James TURNER, b-29 Apr 1811, **c**-Mary TURNER, William TURNER, William A. PATTERSON, **d- e- f**-3 May 1811, **g**-27 May 1814, **h**-$620.10, **i**-$428.40, **j**-$191.70, extrs

John CRISWELL, b-21 May 1811, **c**-James CRISWELL, **d- e- f**-14 Jun 1811, **g**-20 Apr 1822, **h**-$1566.99.5, **i**-$1189.40.5, **j**-$377.59, estate

George MOORE, b-27 May 1811, **c**-Elizabeth MOORE, Howard MOORE, **d- e- f- g- h- i- j-**

Mathias SWARTS, b-26 Aug 1811, **c**-John SNYDER, Jr., **d- e- f- g- h- i- j-**

Andrew DOUGLAS, b-20 Aug 1811, **c**-Hugh McALLISTER, Daniel CHRISTY, **d- e- f**-4 Aug 1812, **g**-22 Apr 1818, **h**-$1689.69, **i**-$1657.91, **j**-$21.78, estate

Abraham KEPNER, b-22 Aug 1811, **c**-Samuel KEPNER, Arthur McNIGHT, **d- e- f**-5 Oct 1811, **g**-20 Apr 1813, **h**-$34.94, **i**-$63.77, **j**-$28.83, extrs

Thomas JOHNSTON, b-2 Oct 1811, **c**-Mary JOHNSTON, Andrew NELSON, **d- e- f**-12 Oct 1815, **g**-12 Oct 1815, **h**-$211.71.5, **i**-$248.93, **j**-$37.21.5, extrs

George McCLELLAND, b-4 Nov 1811, **c**-Robert McCLELLAND, John DOWELL, **d- e- f- g**-17 Mar 1814, **h- i- j**-$1158.53, estate

Alexander ROBISON, b-18 Nov 1811, **c**-James ROBISON, Thomas ROBISON, **d- e- f- g- h- i- j-**

Page 68, Frame 77

Mathew KENNY, b-17 Dec 1811, **c**-James KENNY, Margaret KENNY, **d- e- f**-16 Dec 1812, **g**-16 Dec 1812, **h**-$1525.56, **i**-$1334.38, **j**-$201.18, heirs

Mary WILLIAMS, b-26 Feb 1812, **c**-Andrew KEISER, Wm. S. WILLIAMS, **d- e- f- g- h- i- j-**

Peter DEHEVEN, b-19 Jan 1812, **c**-John HANAWALT, Jesse INGLES, **d- e- f- g- h- i- j-**

William SHADDEN, b-22 Jan 1812, **c**-Samuel SHARRON, Esq., **d- e- f- g- h- i- j-**

David CARGILL, b-8 Apr 1812, **c**-James CORGILL[sic], **d- e- f- g- h- i- j-**

David COULTER, b-21 Apr 1812, **c**-Irwin COULTER, **d- e- f- g- h- i- j-**

William SAWERS, b-28 May 1812, **c**-William PORTER, **d- e- f**-7 Jan 1815, **g**-7 Jan 1815, **h**-$296.57, **i**-$312.25, **j**-$15.68, admrs

James STERRETT, b-4 Jul 1812, **c**-Robert STERRETT, John STERRETT, **d- e- f**-3 Aug 1813, **g**-26 Jun 1824, **h**-$5046.11, **i**-$5046.11, **j-**

Jane KERR, b-11 Aug 1812, **c**-William DEVER, **d- e- f- g- h- i- j-**

Sarah THOMPSON, b-17 Aug 1812, **c**-Mitchell THOMPSON, **d- e- f- g- h- i- j-**

William McNITT, b-17 Aug 1812, **c**-Robert McNITT, **d- e- f- g- h- i- j-**

William FLEMING, b-13 Nov 1812, **c**-Joseph FLEMING, **d- e- f**-15 Dec 1812, **g**-7 Mar 1814/5 May 1815, **h**-$6647.03/$7895.93 **i**-$1172.48/$73.75, **j**-$7895.93, heirs

Page 69, Frame 78

Alexander McKINSTRY, b-19 Jan 1813, **c**-James McKINSTRY, **d- e- f- g- h- i- j-**

Caleb [WORLEY], b-6 Feb 1813, **c**-Lewis EVANS, **d- e- f**-19 Aug 1819, **g**-17 Jul 1819, **h**-$561.07, **i**-$643.28, **j**-$82.21, extrs

James RAMSEY, b-6 Feb 1813, c-Manasses RAMSEY, Arthur
  McNIGHT, d- e- f-14 Mar 1822, g-14 Mar 1822, h-$6345.16, i-
  $6114.28, j-$230.88, estate
William THOMPSON, b-6 Feb 1813, c-James THOMPSON, d- e- f- g-
  h- i- j-
Hugh McELROY, b-22 Mar 1813, c-Alexander McELROY, d- e- f-20
  Apr 1819, g-21 Apr 1819/14 Jul 1825 h-$2236.82.5, i-$1024.53, j-
  $1212.29.5, heirs/$2080.32, estate
John KELLY, b-7 Apr 1813, c-Rebecca KELLY, William C. KELLY,
  Moses KELLY, d- e- f- g- h- i- j-
Henry BRIDGE, b-10 Apr 1813, c-John ORT, Henry ORT, d- e- f-28 Apr
  1813, g-24 Dec 1815, h-$662.97, i-$355.57, j-$307.40, heirs
John PATTERSON, b-20 Apr 1813, c-Hugh HOIT [probably HART],
  Charles TOWERS, d- e- f-20 Apr 1813/19 Apr 1814, g-20 Apr 1814/24
  Nov 1825, h-$565.05/$239.29.5, i-$449.27/$597.85.5, j-$115.78,
  heirs/$358.56, accountant
Jacob AUKER, b-20 Apr 1813, c-John SNYDER, d- e- f-8 May 1813, g-
  22 Jun 1818, h-$696.21, i-$536.96, j-$235.20, heirs
Samuel SHARRON, b-20 Apr 1813, c-John JAMISON, Samuel
  SHARRON, d- e- f- g- h- i- j-
William GRAHAM, b-20 Apr 1813, c-John GRAHAM, William
  GRAHAM, d- e- f- g- h- i- j-
Thomas STURGEON, b-21 May 1813, c-James KNOX, Esq., Moses
  STURGEON, d- e- f-16 Aug 1813, g-21 Jan 1819, h-$8001.64, i-
  $6063.55, j-$1938.09, heirs

Page 70, Frame 79
Samuel FRY, b-16 Jun 1813, c-Jonathan FRY, Gabriel FRY, d- e- f- g- h-
  i- j-
Samuel LEONARD, b-23 Jun 1813, c-Elijah LEONARD, d- e- f- g- h- i-
  j-
John STROUSE, b-30 Aug 1813, c-David STROUSE, d- e- f- g- h- i- j-
John RIDDLE, b-18 Aug 1813, c-Sarah RIDDLE, d- e- f- g- h- i- j-
Henry LUKEN, b-16 Aug 1813, c-John STEWART d- e- f- g- h- i- j-
Robert [VERNOR], b-16 Aug 1813, c-John STEWART, d- e- f- g- h- i-
  j-
John STEEL, b-12 Aug 1813, c-Robert STEEL, Mary STEEL, Robert
  ROBISON, William SHAW, d- e- f- g- h- i- j-

John THOMAS, b-6 Sep 1813, c-Margaret THOMAS, John THOMAS, d- e- f- g- h- i- j-

Henry SHARLOCK, b-16 Nov 1813, c-Abraham SHARLOCK, d- e- f- g- h- i- j-

Henry TAYLOR, b-4 Dec 1819, c-Rhoda TAYLOR, Mathew TAYLOR, Samuel W. TAYLOR, d- e- f- g- h- i- j-

Thomas WILSON, b-14 Jan 1814, c- d- e- f- g- h- i- j-

William LAW, b-17 Jan 1814, c-Ann LAW, Joseph Stewart McCOY, d- e- f-17 Jan 1814, g-15 Dec 1815, h-$471.71.5, i-$205.97, j-$265.74.5, heirs

Page 71, Frame 80

John McFADDEN, b-30 Jan 1814, c-Joseph MATHERS, John McFADDEN, d- e- f- g- h- i- j-

John JOHNSTON, b-24 May 1814, c-James JOHNSTON, d- e- f- g- h- i- j-

Lanclott JOHNSTON, b-24 May 1814, c-James JOHNSTON, d- e- f- g- h- i- j-

William BLACK, b-15 Jun 1814, c-Joseph WEAVER, d- e- f-15 Jun 1814, g-30 Apr 1820, h-$247.94.5, i-$172.44.5, j-$75.50.5, estate

Adam WILT, b-5 Sep 1814, c-John RUMBAUGH, Henry DIM, d- e- f- g- h- i- j-

Philip KILMORE, b-5 Sep 1814, c-Tobias KREIDER, Philip KILMORE, d- e- f-25 Oct 1814, g-19 Aug 1816, h-$3624.62, i-$1287.09, j-$2337.53, heirs

James BURNS, Sr., b-1814, c-Elizabeth BURNS, Samuel BURNS, John STERRETT, d- e- f- g- -h- i- j-

John ERSKINE, b-7 Oct 1814, c-Thompson SMITH, John ERSKINE, d- e- f-21 Nov 1814, g-23 Apr 1816/7 May 1818, h-$1802.04.5/$3376.58.5, i-$1262.08/$3214.00, j-$162.58, heirs

Catherine COLLINS, b-17 Apr 1815, c-Daniel COLLINS, d- e- f- g- h- i- j-

Valentine BRIDGE, b-1815, c-Jacob BRIDGE, Peter CLOSE, d- e- f- g- h- i- j-

Silas MARTIN, b-13 May 1815, c-Sarah MARTIN, John KENNER, d- e- f-20 Jul 1824, g-20 Jul 1824, h-$487.47, i-$513.95, j-$26.46, accountant

Robert ELLIOTT, b-10 Jun 1715m c-Elizabeth ELLIOTT, George HANAWALT, d- e- f- g- h- i- j-

Page 72, Frame 81

Mary McCLELLAND, b-3 Jul 1815, **c-**Robert McCLELLAND, William BELL, **d- e- f- g-**17 Mar 1826, **h-**$1292.70.5, **i-**$1498.59.25, **j-**$105.88.25, accountant

Thomas MEMINGER, b-6 Sep 1815, **c-**Joseph B. ARD, **d- e- f- g- h- i- j-**

Alexander REED, b-21 Nov 1815, **c-**Abner REED, Samuel W. TAYLOR, **d- e- f-**1 Dec 1824, **g-**1 Dec 1824, **h-**$1916.68.5, **i-**$3261.24.5, **j-**$1344.56, accountant

Mathias KOPLIN, b-15 Jan 1816, **c-**Catherine KOPLIN, Abraham KOPLIN, **d- e- f-**26 Jan 1818, **g-**3 Apr 1824/1 Jul 1833, **h-**$2961.50/ $1547.86, **i-**$2725.15.25/$177.25, **j-**$236.34.75, estate/$1370.61, estate

James THOMPSON, b-5 Jan 1816, **c-**Samuel McCOLLOUGH, William NESBETT, **d- e- f- g-**19 Nov 1819, **h-**$471.80, **i-**$572.26, **j-**$100.46, accountant

George BELL, b-15 Apr 1816, **c-**William BELL, George BELL, **d- e- f- g- h- i- j-**

Melchoir PLANK, b-17 Apr 1816, **c-**Jacob PLANK, John WILSON, **d- e- f- g- h- i- j-**

John RITTER, b-23 Apr 1816, **c-**Henry RITTER, Andrew [UTZ, ULZ {probably ULSH}] **d- e- f- g- h- i- j-**

Elijah CHRISWELL, b-27 Jun 1816, **c-**John STERRETT, David FLEMING, Robert COOPER, **d- e- f- g-**6 May 1824, **h-**$3659.47, **i-**$4125.75, **j-**$466.28, accountant

Thomas KEARNS, b-10 Jul 1816, **c-**Abraham KEARNS, John KEARNS, **d- e- f- g- h- i- j-**

Valentine BRIDGE, b-19 Aug 1816, **c-**Jacob BRIDGE, Peter CLOSE, **d- e- f- g- h- i- j-**

Moses THOMPSON, b-21 Aug 1816, **c-**John THOMPSON, William THOMPSON, James POTTER, **d- e- f- g- h- i- j-**

Page 73, Frame 82

James McCLURE, b-21 Aug 1816, **c-**James McCLURE, Robert ALEXANDER, Samuel McNITT, **d- e- f-**24 Oct 1817, **g-**19 Jan 1825, **h-**$1609.73, **i-**$378.15, **j-**$1231.58, estate

Jane REED, b-24 Nov 1816, **c-**John REED, Abner REED, **d- e- f- g- h- i- j-**

Mary WALLACE, b-30 Nov 1816, **c-**Henry KENNEDY, **d- e- f- g- h- i- j-**

John McFARLAND, b-30 Dec 1816, c-Juda McFARLAND, d- e- f- g- h- i- j-

Andrew ISEMENGER, b-5 May 1817, c-John ISEMENGER, George HUBAUGH, d- e- f-24 Oct 1821, g-24 Oct 1821, h-$308.73, i-$153.67, j-$155.06, estate

William FLEMING, b-3 Apr 1817, c-Sarah FLEMING, d- e- f- g-26 Oct 1836, h-$2053.77, i-$1306.83.75, j-$746.88.25, estate

William BUCHANAN, b-17 Feb 1817, c-Abraham BUCHANAN, Evans BUCHANAN, d- e- f- g- h- i- j-

John ALEXANDER, b-13 Mar 1817, c-Margaret ALEXANDER, d- e- f- g- h- i- j-

James STEEL, b-Ann STEEL, Hugh McCLELLAND, Wm. P. MACLAY, c- d- e- f- g-21 Apr 1821, h-$213.32.25, i-$215.14.25, j-$1.82, accountant

William CUMMINS, b-25 Jun 1817, c-Robert CUMMINS, Charles CUMMINS, William CUMMINS, d- e- f- g- h- i- j-

Henry DIEHL, b-21 Aug 1817, c-Michael MOURER, Adam RAGER, Sr., d- e- f-12 Jul 1830, g-12 Jul 1830, h-$501.50.5, i-$591.46.5, j-$89.96, accountant

Margaret ALLEN, b-20 Aug 1817, c- d- e- f- g- h- i- j-

Page 74, Frame 83

Lazarus WAGNER, b-12 Sep 1817, c-Peter BEAVER, d- e- f- g- h- i- j-

Mathias RUBLE, b-12 Sep 1817, c-Michael RUBLE, William BROWN, Jr., d- e- f-17 Jul 1820, g-24 Aug 1820/28 Feb 1837, h-$225.86/1089.37, i-$225.95.5/$1089.37, j-no balance

John ELLIOTT, b-17 Nov 1817, c-James KNOX, Esq., d- e- f-22 Apr 1818, g-21 Jan 1819/31 Jul 1824, h-$18.50/$182.57, i-$34.75/$158.48.5 j-$16.25, heirs/$24.08.5, estate

James THOMPSON, b-5 Jan 1818, c-William MORRISON, David SAMPLE, d- e- f-21 Jan 1818, g-21 Jan 1819/31 Jul 1824, h-$18.50/$182.57, i-$34.75/$158.48.5, j-$16.25, heirs/$24.08.5, estate

John BEATTY, b-12 Feb 1818, c-James KNOX, Esq., d- e- f- g- h- i- j-

Philip EVERHARD, b-14 Jul 1818, c-Elizabeth EVERHARD, John DREES, d- e- f- g- h- i- j-

Jacob KINZER, b-16 Nov 1818, c-John KINZER, Jacob KINZER, d- e- f- g- h- i- j-

John BOGGS, b-7 Dec 1818, c-James McCONNELL, d- e- f- g- h- i- j-

David NEELY, b-17 Aug 1818, c-James MILLIKEN, d- e- f- g-5 Jun 1830, h-$572.34, i-$581.52.25 j-$9.18.25, accountant

George SHITZ, b-18 Sep 1818, c-Peter SHITZ, d- e- f-8 Mar 1824, g-18 Mar 1824, h-$1175.45.25, i-$822.47, j-$352.98.75, estate

Margaret STURGEON, b-9 Oct 1818, c-James KNOX, Esq., d- e- f-21 Jan 1819, g-21 Jan 1819, h-$2460.73, i-$907.59, j-$1553.14, heirs

Frederick HARPSTER, b-16 Nov 1818, c-Susanah HARPSTER, Isaac GILL, d- e- f- g- h- i- j-

Page 75, Frame 84

Benjamin CRISWELL, b-2 Jan 1819, c-Robert CRISWELL, Robert MILLIKEN, d- e- f- g-20 Oct 1825, h-$1068.98.5, i-$944.63.5, j-$124.35, estate

James MACKLIN, b-16 Feb 1819, c-George MACKLIN, Joseph HOWARD, d- e- f- g-7 Mar 1820, h-$680.77.5, i-$272.61, j-$408.16.5, estate

Esther DUNN, b-22 Feb 1819, c-David WALKER, d- e- f-22 Feb 1819, g-9 Aug 1933. h-$147.71, i-$168.82, j-$21.11, accountant

William IRWIN, b-27 Feb 1819, c-Thomas STINSON, William IRWIN, d- e- f-29 Mar 1819 [looks like a 1 written over a 2 in the year], g-16 Sep 1825/14 Sep 1827, h-$3668.00/$1350.36, i-$2659.94/$346.89.5, j-$1003.46.5, estate

Robert STOGDELL, b-10 Mar 1819, c-George HYCUS, d- e- f- g- h- I- j-

William KERR, b-19 Jan1819, c-James WALLICK, Sarah KERR, d- e- f-17 Jan 1827, g-17 Jan1827, h-$1818.20.5, i-$1286.55.5 j-$531.65. estate

Lefferd HOUGHAWOUT, b-20 Jan 1819, c-Lefferd HOUGHAWOUT, Peter HOUGHAWOUT, Robert WILSON, d- e- f- g-19 Oct 1831, h-$586.79, i-$643.98, j-$57.19, accountant

Agness THOMPSON, b-21 Apr 1819, c-Thomas McCONNELL, d- e- f-17 Apr 1821, g- h- i- j-

George STOGDELL, b-10 Mar 1819, c-George HIKES, d- e- f-10 Mar 1819, g-23 Jul 1822, h-$275.73.5, i-$245.55, j-$30.18.5, estate

William BELL, b-10 May 1819, c-David BELL, William BELL, d- e- f-19 Oct 1821, g-5 Jul 1833, h-$12,400.00, i-$1156.77, j-$843.23, estate

Jane McKEE, b-18 May 1819, c-David McKEE, Robert ROBISON, d- e- f-7 Aug 1819, g-18 Sep 1834, h-$1811.46.25, i-$374.37, j-$1437.09.25, estate

Robert **LONGWELL**, **b**-12 Jun 1819, **c**-Michael KNOLL, James LONGWELL, **d- e- f- g- h- i- j-**

Page 76, Frame 85
Ann **WOLFINGTON**, **b**-3 Jul 1819, **c**-A. A. ANDERSON, Esq., Jane WOLFINGTON, **d- e- f- g- h- i- j-**
Robert **BUCHANAN**, **b**-27 Jul 1819, **c**-Robert BUCHANAN, Wm. A. PATTERSON, **d- e- f- g**-15 Apr 1826/7 Jun 1831, **h**-$100.00/ $1225.88.5, **i**-$233.31/$1301.34.5, **j**-$926.54, estate
Jane **ELLIOTT**, **b**-2 Aug 1819, **c**-James KNOX, Esq., **d- e- f- g- h- i- j-**
William **McALLISTER**, **b**-2 Aug 1819, **c**-John McALLISTER, William McALLISTER, **d- e- f**-2 Jul 1838, **g**-2 Jun 1838, **h**-$8406.15.5, **i**-$4481.32, **j**-$3924.83.5, estate
Barbara **SPRINGER**, **b**-16 Aug 1819, **c**-John BRUBAKER, **d- e- f**-4 Oct 1819, **g**-1 Mar 1823, **h**-$424.87.5 **i**-$434.80.5, **j**-$9.93, accountant
William **McCLURE**, **b**-17 Aug 1819, **c**-Alexander McCLURE, Samuel WALLICK, **d- e- f- g- h- i- j-**
Rebecca **BROWN**, **b**-15 Sep 1819, **c**-Doct. David CRAWFORD, **d- e- f- g- h- i- j-**
Peter **RAPP**, **b**-15 Oct 1819, **c**-Abraham HARNER, **d- e- f- g**-21 Mar 1825/14 Oct 1835, **h**-$882.79/$598.71, **i**-$828.26.5/$538.15, **j**-$60.56, estate
Archibald **MOORE**, **b**-7 Jan 1820, **c**-David CRISWELL, David LUSK **d- e- f**-29 Apr 1820/21 Aug 1821, **g**-22 Aug 1826. **h**-$1739.12.5, **i**-$1040.37, **j**-$698.75, estate
James **KNOX, Esq.**, **b**-6 Jan 1820, **c**-Calvin BLYTHE, Doct. John HARRIS, **d- e- f**-21 Aug 1820, **g- h- i- j-**
Mary **RIDDLE**, **b**-8 Apr 1820, **c**-David WALKER, Esq. **d- e- f**-17 Apr 1820, **g**-21 Dec 1832, **h**-$42.67, **i**-$108.52, **j**-$65.85, accountant
Thomas **TURBETT**, **b**-28 Jun 1820, **c**-Stewart TURBETT, William TURBETT, **d- e- f- g- h- i- j-**

Page 77, Frame 86
Robert **McNITT**, **b**-14 Aug 1820, **c**-William McNITT, **d- e- f- g- h- i- j-**
George **VANCE**, **b**-23 Aug 1820, **c**-James CRISWELL, Andrew BRATTON, **d- e- f- g- h- i- j-**
Anna **WRIGHT**, **b**-20 Nov 1820, **c**-Anna WRIGHT, **d- e- f- g- h- i- j-**
Fanny **HOWDER**, **b**-2 Nov 1820, **c**-Mathew RODGERS, **d- e- f- g- h- i- j-**

William BEALE, b-20 Jan 1821, **c**-Thomas BEALE, Benjamin KEPNER, Jacob MOHLER, **d**- **e**- **f**-21 May 1827, **g**-21 May 1827, **h**-$4316.75, **i**-$4068.27, **j**-$252.10, accountants

Page 78, Frame 87 [Page 78 repeated on Frame 88]
Michael HOLLIDAY, b-19 Jan 1821, **c**-Adam HOLLIDAY **d**- **e**- **f**- **g**- **h**- **i**- **j**-
Sarah HOLLIDAY, b-19 Jan 1821, **c**-John HOLLIDAY, Samuel HOLLIDAY, **d**- **e**- **f**- **g**-4 Jul 1828, **h**-$30.37.5, **i**-$503.75, **j**-$473.37,5, accountant
Robert ALLISON, b-13 Jan 1821/13 Feb 1821, **c**-Richard ALLISON, **d**- **e**- **f**-27 Oct 1821, **g**-22 Apr 1822, **h**-$510.89, **i**-$334.15, **j**-$176.74, heirs
Robert LEWIS, b-6 Jan 1821, **c**-Mary LEWIS, Charles COOKSON, **d**-$500, **e**-James KINSLOE, Joseph MATHEWS, **f**-22 Apr 1823, **g**-23 Apr 1823, **h**-$81.25, **i**-$70.80, **j**-$10.40, estate
Philip POWELL, b-1 Feb 1821, **c**-John HANAWALT, John NORTON, **d**-$2000, **e**-Francis BOGGS, David REYNOLDS, **f**-26 Feb 1821, **g**-17 Sep 1825/31 Jan 1831, **h**-$817.57/$2344,23, **i**-$652.69/$412.31.5, **j**-$1932.12.5, estate
John KAUFMAN, b-8 Feb 1821, **c**-M. M. MONAHON, Daniel KAUFMAN, **d**-$300, **e**-James CRISWELL, David REYNOLDS, **f**- **g**-16 Mar 1827, **h**-$60.37, **i**-$45.13.5, **j**-$15.23.5, estate
Christian LAPP, b-16 Feb 1821, **c**-Christian KAUFMAN, **d**-$10,000, **e**-Daniel SMOKER, C. DETWEILER, **f**- **g**- **h**- **i**- **j**-
Christian ZOOK, b-17 Feb 1821, **c**-Jacob ZOOK, Abraham ZOOK, **d**- **e**- **f**-7 Mar 1821, **g**-6 May 1822, **h**-$345.02.5, **i**- **j**-$345.02.5, estate
Hugh GARDNER, b-3 Mar 1821, **c**-Thomas J. McCONNELL, Enoch BARTON, **d**-$1000, **e**-David BEALE, Jr., Alexander BOGGS, **f**- **g**-22 Nov 1826, **h**-$702.48.5, **i**-$468.66.5, **j**-$236.15, estate
Martin STEGER, b-22 Mar 1821, **c**-Hugh HARDY, Jr., **d**-$1000, **e**-George DAUGHMAN, David JORDAN, **f**- **g**-4 Aug 1832, **h**-$1146.31.5, **i**-$145.71, **j**-$1000.60.5, estate
James SMITH, b-28 Mar 1821, **c**-David REYNOLDS, E. B. PATTERSON, **d**-$500, **e**-Philip SMITH, **f**-15 Jan 1827, **g**- **h**- **i**- **j**-
William CURREN, b-19 Apr 1821, **c**-Samuel McKINSTRY, **d**-$1500, **e**-Christopher IRVIN, Lewis EVANS, **f**-18 May 1821, **g**-12 Sep 1823, **h**-$2739.34, **i**-$340.09, **j**-$2399.27, estate

Page 79, Frame 89

Thomas McCORD, b-21 May 1821, c-James McCORD, Jr., d-$1400, e-Joseph MARTIN, David MILLIKEN, f-20 Jun 1821, g- h- i- j-

William KINSLOE, b-21 May 1821, c-Cornelius HESKINS, d-$500, e-Henry G. HESSER, Daniel RADALAP, f- g- h- i- j-

John STEELY, b-2 Jun 1821, c-David REYNOLDS, d-$1500, e-John ROTHROCK, William BRISBIN, f- g- h- i- j-

Michael FUNK, b-27 Jun 1821, c-John FUNK, Michael FUNK, Michael SHELLY, d-$3000, e-John [MOOTZER? MOOLZER?], f-26 Jul 1821, g-20 Dec 1822, h-$2205.06, i-$378.885.75, j-$1826.20.25, estate

Joseph KEISER, b-4 Aug 1821, c-William PENNEPACKER, d-$1000, e-Joseph CUSTER, Elias CORNING, f-25 Aug 1821, g-18 Nov 1823, h-$771.32.5, i-$702.10, j-$69.22.5, estate

David WILSON, b-7 Aug 1821, c-John WILSON, George WILSON, d-$1000, e-James MILLIKEN, David FLEMING, f-28 Aug 1821, g-16 Jun 1824, h-$377.74, i-$187.65.5, j-$190.08.5, estate

Adam THOMPSON, b-9 Aug 1821, c-Adam THOMPSON, d-$1000, e-Stewart LAIRD, John PATTERSON, Joseph DOUGLASS, f-21 Aug 1821/1 Dec 1823, g-15 Mar 1824, h-$1143.20.25, i-$347.62.5, j-$795.57.75, estate

John DILLEN, b-9 Aug 1821, c-John DILLEN, d-$200, e-Joseph DILLEN, Adam THOMPSON, f-30 May 1822, g- h- i- j-

George SIGLER, b-22 Aug 1821, c-Jacob SIGLER, George SIGLER, d-$2000, e-Stephen HINDS, Samuel SIGLER, f-4 Sep 1821, g- h- i- j-

Thomas BEALE, b-14 Sep 1821, c-Elizabeth BEALE, Joshua BEALE, William GILSON, d-$8000, e-Thomas TODD, David GILSON, f-5 Oct 1821, g-2 Jun 1825, h-$2434.52.25, i-$1731.02, j-$702.90.25, estate

William BELL, b-24 Sep 1821, c-John HAMAN, Thomas STINSON, Sarah BELL, d-$4000, e-Joseph ARD, William ARMSTRONG, f- g-13 Dec 1825/4 Oct 1831/15 Jun 1837, h-$9999.43/$9256.87/$2827.99, i-$10,462.61.5/$8892.84.5/$3292.42.5, j-$463.18.5/$364.02.5/$464.43.5, accountants

Samuel HOUDER, b-24 Sep 1821, c-John JAMEISON, d- e- f-20 Apr 1820, g-19 Apr 1824, h-$466.33.5, i-$209.68, j-$256.65.5, estate

Page 80, Frame 90

Jacob WEAVER, b-6 Apr 1821, c-James BRISBIN, Esq., d- e- f-24 Nov 1821, g-16 Apr 1829, h-$179.65.5, i-$168.09, j-$11.56.5, estate

Thomas PATTON, **b**-23 May 1821, **c**-Isaac HENDERSHOT, **d**- **e**- **f**-10 Mar 1823, **g**-11 Mar 1823, **h**-$73.57.5, **i**-$80.87.5, **j**-$7.30, accountant

James MACKEY, Esq., **b**-23 May 1821, **c**-Mary MACKEY, **d**- **e**- **f**-22 Apr 1823, **g**- **h**- **i**- **j**-

William O'BOURN, **b**-18 Jun 1821, **c**-Richard HOPE, **d**- **e**- **f**-3 Oct 1836, **g**-1 Oct 1836, **h**-$839.65, **i**-$422.54, **j**-$417.11, estate

David STEEL, **b**-29 Jun 1821, **c**-Alexander STEEL, David W. HULINGS, **d**- **e**- **f**-24 Jul 1821, **g**-14 Mar 1829, **h**-$291.67, **i**-$314.07, **j**-$22.40, accountant

Adam TRESSLER, **b**-22 Aug 1821, **c**-Mary Julian TRESSLER, **d**- **e**- **f**-22 Jul 1826/21 Aug 1821, **g**-22 Jul 1826, **h**-$722.90.5, **i**-$731.30, **j**-$8.39.5, accountant

George MITCHELL, Sr., **b**-14 Sep 1821, **c**-William McMANIGIL, James McDONALD, **d**- **e**- **f**-20 Apr 1822, **g**-20 May 1829, **h**-$1156.81, **i**-$1143.69, **j**-$13.12, estate

Abraham KAUFMAN, **b**-26 Sep 1821, **c**-Daniel KREIDER, Abraham KAUFMAN, **d**- **e**- **f**- **g**- **h**- **i**- **j**-

John WAGGONER, **b**-28 Sep 1821, **c**-Henry BURKHOLDER, Philip ROTHROCK, **d**-$2000, **e**-David MILLIKEN, Robert ROBISON, **f**-30 Oct 1821, **g**-11 Dec 1830, **h**-$3233.36.5, **i**-$2773.08.25, **j**-$460.28.25, estate

Bernard McDONALD, **b**-2 Oct 1821, **c**-Ann McDONALD, **d**- **e**- **f**-30 Nov 1821, **g**- **h**- **i**- **j**-

George PETERS, **b**-11 Oct 1821, **c**-Thomas FEAR, **d**-$700, **e**-Francis BOGGS, James MITCHELL, **f**-6 Apr 1822, **g**- **h**- **i**- **j**-

Thomas COLLINS, **b**-23 Oct 1821, **c**-Andrew BRATTON, **d**-$400, **e**-Robert ROBISON, A. A. ANDERSON, **f**- 23 Jan 1824, **g**-20 Aug 1824, **h**-$243.90, **i**-$250.90 **j**-$7.00, accountant

Page 81, Frame 91

Dennis McCOOL, **b**-2 Oct 1821, **c**-John McGARVERN, **d**-$1000, **e**-James DICKSON, William MITCHELL, **f**- **g**-21 May 1823, **h**-$148.14, **i**-$53.64, **j**-$94.50, estate

Charles HARDY, **b**-2 Nov 1821, **c**-Margaret HARDY, John SNYDER, **d**- **e**- **f**-31 Dec 1821, **g**-4 Mar 1834, **h**-$295.02, **i**-$320.44.5, **j**-$25.42.5, accountant

Arthur BELL, **b**-2 Nov 1821, **c**-Stewart LAIRD, **d**-$500, **e**-Ephraim BANKS, Geo. McCULLOCH, **f**-5 Dec 1821, **g**-16 Apr 1827/13 Mar

1838, **h**-$445.20/$651.98, **i**-$428.82.5/$645.14, **j**-$17.54.5, estate/$6.84, estate

Henry YODER. **b**-9 Nov 1821, **c**-Daniel YODER, John HARTZLER, **d**-$2000, **e**-Nicholas MILLER, Abraham STUTZMAN, **f**-19 Nov 1821, **g**-4 Jul 1831, **h**-$1617.89.5 **i**-$1595.21, **j**-$22.68.5, estate

David YODER, **b**-14 Nov 1821, **c**-David HARTZLER, John HARTZLER, Jonathan YODER, **d**- **e**- **f**-8 Dec 1821, **g**-16 Oct 1826,18 Jul 1828, **h**-$536.88/$1060.32, **i**-$619.60.5/$854.65.25, **j**-$205.66.25, estate

Jane CRISWELL, **b**-15 Jan 1822, **c**-Joseph STEWART, James DAVIS, **d**- **e**- **f**-25 May 1822, **g**-23 Jun 1832, **h**-$2292.20.5, **i**-$678.15.5, **j**-$1614.05, estate

Morris MURPHY, **b**-16 Nov 1821, **c**-Jeremiah TOLAND, Michael O'BRIEN, **d**-$400, **e**-James DICKSON, David REYNOLDS, **f**- **g**- **h**- **i**- **j**-

George KERR, **b**-19 Nov 1821, **c**-Thomas KERR, Hugh HART, **d**-$3000, **e**-Jos. B. ARD, Geo. McCULLOCH, **f**-18 Apr 1822, **g**-16 Mar 1825, **h**-$1607.96, **i**-$771.39, **j**-$836.57, estate

Margaret STEWART, **b**-21 Nov 1821, **c**-Eleanor STEWART, **d**-$500, **e**-William WHARTON, Stewart LAIRD, **f**- **g**- **h**- **i**- **j**-

Mary ARMSTRONG, **b**-27 Nov 1821, **c**-William ARMSTRONG, **d**-$1500, **e**-James MILLIKEN, Francis McCOY, **f**-28 Jan 1822, **g**- **h**- **i**- **j**-

Jacob [STAGER], **b**-28 Nov 1821, **c**-John McCAHEN, **d**-$1000, **e**-Patrick McCAHEN, Wm. SILHEIMER, **f**-27 Dec 1824, **g**-9 Mar 1824/16 Jan1827, **h**-$344.00, **i**-$351.00, **j**-$7.00, accountant

Terance GLANCY, **b**-29 Nov 1821, **c**-Joseph B. ARD, James DICKSON, **d**-$300, **e**-James MILLIKEN, John IRVINE, **f**- **g**- **h**- **i**- **j**-

Page 82, Frame 92

John HOOKER, **b**-29 Nov 1821, **c**-Joseph B. ARD, James DICKSON, **d**-$200, **e**-James MILLIKEN, John IRVINE, **f**- **g**- **h**- **i**- **j**-

John McCLINTIC, **b**-5 Dec 1821, **c**-James McCLINTIC, James NIXON, **d**-$500, **e**-George BECK, Andrew KEISER, **f**-4 Jan 1822, **g**-14 Apr 1832, **h**-$1173.36, **i**-$800.03 **j**-$373.33, estate

Daniel MOSER, **b**-6 Dec 1821, **c**-John ROTHROCK, William SHAW, **d**-$2000, **e**-John SHUG, James ROBISON, **f**-21 Jan 1824, **g**- **h**- **i**- **j**-

George MARKLEY, **b**-31 Dec 1821, **c**-George MARKLEY, George MATHEWS, **d**-$1500, **e**-Henry [MAAS?], William ROBB, **f**-8 Apr 1822, **g**-29 Nov 1824, **h**-$978.50, **i**-$685.13, **j**-$715.13, estate

George McGREGOR, **b**-9 Jan 1822, **c**-Robert McKEE, **d**-$500, **e**-E. W. HALE, James DICKSON, **f**-19 Feb 1823, **g**-21 Jul 1823, **h**-$48.91.5 **i**-$110.77.5, **j**-$61.86, accountant

James SHIELDS, **b**-21 Jan 1822, **c**-John PIERCE, **d**-$800, **e**-James MILLIKEN, James DICKSON, **f**-30 Jan 1822, **g**- **h**- **i**- **j**-

Thomas HENRY, **b**-23 Jan 1822, **c**-John HENRY, **d**-$500, **e**-George ELLIOTT, Wm. HENRY, **f**- **g**- **h**- **i**- **j**-

Michael CROW, **b**-24 Jan 1822, **c**-James LYON, **d**-$500, **e**-James PATTERSON, Wm. C. KELLY, **f**- **g**- **h**- **i**- **j**-

Michael COFFMAN, **b**-2 Feb 1822, **c**-Joseph RENNELS, **d**-$1800, **e**-Isaac COFFMAN, Joseph MATHERS, **f**-4 Mar 1822, **g**-21 Feb 1824, **h**-$690.56.5, **i**-$248.48.5, **j**-$442.12, estate

Hugh McCLELLAND, Esq., **b**-9 Feb 1822, **c**-Margaret McCLELLAND, Robert McCLELLAND, **d**-$10,000, **e**-Robert FORSYTHE, Adam HOLLIDAY, **f**-8 Mar 1822, **g**-16 Mar 1832, **h**-$6629.14, **i**-$6449.60, **j**-$179.54, estate

Alexander STEWART, **b**-12 Feb 1822, **c**-Thomas MITCHELL, William SWANZEY, **d**-$1000, **e**-David COULTER, James ROBISON, **f**-30 Jun 1826, **g**-30 Jun 1826, **h**-$237.93, **i**-$243.11, **j**-$5.18, accountant

Henry HALLER, **b**-2 Mar 1822, **c**-Samuel HALLER, **d**-$2000, **e**-Francis McCOY, James GLASS, **f**-16 Mar 1822, **g**- **h**- **i**- **j**-

Page 83, Frame 93

Joseph STRODE, **b**-9 Mar 1822, **c**-Amor STRODE, William STRODE, Isaac STRODE, **d**- **e**- **f**-2 Nov 1822, **g**- **h**- **i**- **j**-

Jacob STOUFER, **b**-9 Mar 1822, **c**-John STOUFER, **d**-$1000, **e**-John FUNK, John YOKEM, **f**-2 Apr 1822, **g**-6 Sep 1824, **h**-$94.09.5, **i**-$43.56.5, **j**- $50.53, estate

Thomas BRADY, **b**-9 Mar 1822, **c**-Philip BRADY, **d**-$2000, **e**-James DICKSON, Peacock MAJOR, **f**- **g**-18 Nov 1823, **h**-$770.00, **i**-$758.26, **j**-$11.74, estate

Jane PATTERSON, **b**-15 Mar 1822, **c**-Samuel BRYSON, Joseph CUMMINS, **d**- **e**- **f**- **g**- **h**- **i**- **j**-

John FLEMING, **b**-26 Mar 1822, **c**-James FLEMING, John FLEMING, **d**- **e**- **f**- **g**- **h**- **i**- **j**-

Jacob KING, **b**-17 Apr 1822, **c**-John KING, Samuel KING, **d**- **e**- **f**-10 Jun 1822, **g**- **h**- **i**- **j**-

Valentine WISEHOUPT, b-18 Apr 1822, **c-**Valentine WISEHOUPT, Andrew SMITH, **d-**$4000, **e-**Henry HACKET, John ARNOLD, **f-**23 May 1822, **g-**21 May 1828, **h- i- j-**

John SMITH, b-31 May 1822, **c-**James PATTERSON, **d- e- f- g- h- i- j-**

George HARPSTER, b-6 Jun 1822, **c-**Thomas MAGEE, Stephen HINDS, **d-**$1000, **e-**Robert McCLELLAND, Jacob SIGLER, **f-**1 Jul 1822, **g- h- i- j-**

William HENRY, b-8 Jun 1822, **c-**William HENRY, John HENRY, Francis HENRY, **d- e- f- g-**31 Aug 1833, **h-**$6900.64, **i-**$9249.56, **j-**$2348.92, accountants

George MELOY, Esq., b-8 Jun 1822, **c-**Jacob MELOY, Adam THOMPSON, **d-**$1000, **e-**Thomas ELLIOTT, John KINSER, **f- g- h- i- j-**

Jane PORTER, b-18 Jun 1822, **c-**David PORTER, **d-**$600, **e-**James MILLIKEN, John IRVINE, **f- g- h- i- j-**

Page 84, Frame 94

William McCOY, b-1 Jul 1822, **c-**James McDOWELL, **d-**$6000 **e-**James CRISWELL, Samuel EDMISTON, **f- g- h- i- j-**

Joseph FETTERMAN, b-9 Jul 1822, **c-**Mary FETTERMAN, **d-**$2000, **e-**Robert C. GALLAHER, Wm. NESBETT, **f-**25 Mar 1824, **g-**3 Dec 1824, **h-**$122.50, **i-**$418.12, **j-**$295.62, accountant

James BURNS, Esq., b-17 Dec 1825, **c-**Samuel BURNS, **d- e- f- g-**30 Oct 1833, **h-**$1199.73, **i-**$1057.65, **j-**$142.08, estate

Robert CAMPBELL, Sr., b-29 Jul 1822, **c-**Robert CAMPBELL, Joseph CAMPBELL, **d- e- f- g-**7 Mar 1834, **h-**$399.66, **i-**$511.66 **j-**$112.00, accountant

Robert CROSSETT, b-1 Aug 1822, **c-**Jane CROSSETT, Wm. LYON, William JONES, **d-**$2500, **e-**James ROBISON, David JORDAN, **f-**9 Aug 1822, **g-**30 Dec 1826/30 Jun 1827, **h-**$1126.23.5/$401.62.5, **i-**$733.67/$288.01.75, **j-**$392.56.5/$137.05.25, accountant

James NORTON, b-6 Aug 1822, **c-**John NORTON, **d-**$11,000, **e-**Peacock MAJOR, James ROBISON, **f-**8 Aug 1822, **g-**15 Jul 1826/22 Feb 1823/12 Feb 1833, **h-**$5069.60.75/$4295.08.75/$282.40, **i-**$5333.94/$72.08/$562.30, **j-**$278.90, accountant

Rebecca KELLY, b-9 Aug 1822, **c-**James PATTERSON, **d-**$1000, **e-**John PATTERSON, Esq., Moses KELLY, **f-**6 Sep 1822, **g- h- i- j-**

James KELLY, b-9 Aug 1822, **c-**James PATTERSON, **d-**$1000, **e-**John PATTERSON, Esq., Moses KELLY, **f-**6 Sep 1822, **g- h- i- j-**

Margaret GLASSFORD, **b**-20 Aug 1822, **c**-Henry GLASSFORD, **d**-$600, **e**-George BRATTON, Robert STEWART **f**- **g**- **h**- **i**- **j**-

John WILLIAMS, **b**-22 Aug 1822, **c**-James PATTERSON, John GRAHAM, **d**-$1000, **e**-John PATTERSON, Benjn. LAW, **f**-21 Sep 1822, **g**-28 Jun 1830/23 Feb 1832, **h**-$478.24/$2339.68.5, **i**-$4515.50.75/$441.35, **j**-$898.37.5, estate

Isaiah WILLIS, **b**-22 Aug 1822, **c**-William SWANZEY, **d**-$4000, **e**-Anthoney ELTON, Andrew JUNKIN, **f**- **g**-21 Apr 1824/28 Jun 1825, **h**-$2976.75/$2748.03, **i**-$2966.94/$1860.16, **j**-$887.87, estate

Francis JOHNSON, **b**-23 Aug 1822, **c**-John STEWART, **d**- **e**- **f**-11 Ja 1828, **g**- **h**- **i**- **j**-

Page 85, Frame 95

James CUMMINS, **b**-1 Apr 1823, **c**-John CUMMIN [sic], **d**- **e**- **f**- **g**- **h**- **i**- **j**-

Jeremiah CUNNINGHAM, **b**-2 Sep 1822, **c**-Jeremiah CUNNINGHAM, **d**-$4,000, **e**-Nathl. CUNNINGHAM, Wm. A. PATTERSON, **f**-1 Oct 1822, **g**-5 Mar 1825, **h**-$2169.31.5, **i**-$1753.79 **j**-$415.52.5, estate

David McCORMICK, **b**-21 Sep 1822, **c**-Jane McCORMICK, Ephraim BANKS, **d**-$10,000, **e**-James MILLIKEN, Jos. B. ARD, **f**-8 Sep 1823, **g**-18 Sep 1827, **h**-$9466.75.75, **i**-$4502.52.5, **j**-$4964.23.25, estate

John LYTLE, Esq., **b**-2 Oct 1822, **c**-James LYTLE, Calvin BLYTHE, Esq., **d**- **e**- **f**-19 Apr 1932/30 Jun 1836, **g**-4 Mar 1840, **h**-$1501.60.5 **i**-$200.13.5, **j**-$1300.47, estate

Jacob MAST, **b**-3 Oct 1822, **c**-John MAST, Abraham COFFMAN, **d**-$2500, **e**-Daniel KREIDER, C. COFFMAN, **f**-3 Dec 1822, **g**-30 Dec 1826/12 Oct 1829, **h**-$1112.60/$382.86, **i**-$933.05.5/$515.60, **j**-$179.56, estate/$932.74, accountant

Sarah STERRETT, **b**-6 Oct 1822, **c**-Robert STERRETT, **d**- **e**- **f**-12 Dec 1822, **g**- **h**- **i**- **j**-

Jesse KEISER, **b**-7 Oct 1822, **c**-William R. POWER, **d**-$200, **e**-Jos. MARTIN, John IRVINE, **f**-1 Nov 1822, **g**- **h**- **i**- **j**-

James MATEER, **b**-11 Oct 1822, **c**-James MATEER, **d**-$1000, **e**-John HOUGHAWOUT, S. W. TAYLOR, **f**-2 Nov 1822, **g**-13 Mar 1826/24 Jun 1834, **h**-$455.19, **i**-$528.51.75/$619.90.5, **j**-$619.90.5, accountant

John OPLINGER, **b**-12 Sep 1822, **c**-William GEORGE, **d**- **e**- **f**-18 Sep 1822, **g**- **h**- **i**- **j**-

Joseph CUSTER, b-18 Oct 1822, c-Elizabeth CUSTER, Amor STRODE, Samuel EISENBISE, d-$5000, e-James ROBISON, James MILLIKEN, f-20 Nov 1822, g-17 Mar 1831, h-$1408.27, i- j-

Jacob DOUDLE, b-1 Oct 1822, c-George DOUDLE, d-$2000, e-F. A. MELTZHEIMER, Jos. [MARTIN], f-11 Nov 1822, g-19 Nov 1825, h-$1387.32, i-$1098.35, j-$288.97, estate

Page 86, Frame 96

Joseph MATHERS, b-20 Oct 1822, c-James MATHERS, d-$1500, e-Robert TURNER, Samuel EDMISTON, f-20 Nov 1822, g- h- i- j-

William TYSON, b-31 Oct 1822, c-Mathew TYSON, Joseph KINGERICH, d-$2500, e-Christn. ALSDORF, Wm. RENNELS, f-2 Nov 1822, g-19 Jan 1824/6 Oct 1831, h-$1103.17.5/$683.77.5, i-$503.41.5/$683.77.5, j-$529.76.25, estate

John FERGUSON, b-2 Nov 1822, c-David WALKER, Esq., d-$11,500, e-Andrew WALKER, George CRANE, f- g- h- i- j-

John CAMPBELL, b-2 Nov 1822, c-Margaret CAMPBELL, William HARRIS, d-$1300, e-Francis BOGGS, James MILLIKEN, f-30 Nov 1822, g- h- i- j-

John JACOBS, b-11 Nov 1822, c-Alexander JACOBS, Elias W. HALE, d-$1000, e-John IRVINE, Saml. EDMISTON, f-30 Dec 1822, g- h- i- j-

John SHOOKE, Sr., b-5 Nov 1822, c-Henry BURKHOLDER, Henry SNYDER, d-$8000, e-Samuel MARTIN, James MILLIKEN, f-8 Jan 1823, g-4 Oct 1832, h-$5240.78.5, i-$1562.04, j-$3678.74.5, estate

Samuel CUSTER, b-11 Nov 1822, c-Daniel CHRISTY, d-$2000, e-C. [SEIBER], f-19 Nov 1822, g-7 Jun 1826, h-$6902.17.5, i-$6210.64, j-$691.53.5, estate

Henry THOMPSON, b-12 Nov 1822, c-Daniel CHRISTY, d-$2000, e-Benjn. WALLACE, Charles HOFF, f-7 Dec 1822, g-16 Jul 1829, h-$300.92, i-$434.55, j-$153.63, accountant

Christian BRANDT, b-13 Nov 1822, c-Martin BRANDT, Leonard GRONINGER, d-$3000, e-Jacob KEPNER, Leonard GROCE, f-13 Nov 1822, g-10 Mar 1829, h-$2473.12, i-$1994.95, j-$478.17, estate

James McCULLEY, b-15 Nov 1822, c-Thomas McCULLEY, Foster MILLIKEN, d-$2000, e-Robert CRESWELL, Joseph MILLIKEN, f-14 Dec 1832[sic], g-9 Mar 1829, h-$1328.68.5, i-$1201.26.5, j-$127.42, estate

Andrew DOUGLASS, b-18 Nov 1822, c-David CRAWFORD, d-$2000, e-Jos. DOUGLASS, David REYNOLDS, f-22 Jul 1829, g-22 Jul 1829 h-$258.26, i-$119.32.5, j-$138.93.5, estate

Peter CASNER, b-18 Nov 1822, c-James CASNER, d-$3000, e-E. R. KELLOGG, John [McCOLLISTER], f-20 Nov 1823, g- h- i- j-

Page 87, Frame 97

Thomas ALEXANDER, b-18 Nov 1822, c-Saml. W. TAYLOR, Francis McCOY, d-$4000, e-James MILLIKEN, Joseph MARTIN, f-30 Nov 1822, g-7 Mar 1827, h-$2696.33.5, i-$342.11.75, j-$2354.21.75, estate

Mary GREATHOUSE, b-19 Nov 1822, c-Arthur McNIGHT, d- e- f-25 Dec 1822/22 Jan 1841, g-22 Feb 1833, h-$738.61, i-$406.51, j-$332.10, estate

Christian EISENBISE, b-29 Nov 1822, c-Samuel EISENBISE, d-$4000, e-Anthoney YOUNG, Ephraim BANKS, f-30 Nov 1822, g- h- i- j-

William BRISBIN, b-28 Nov 1822, c-James BRISBIN, Foster MILLIKEN, d-$1000, e-David HAWN, David REYNOLDS, f-12 Dec 1822, g-16 Apr 1824, h-$387.79, i-$323.77.75, j-$264.01.25, estate

Jacob REEL, b-3 Dec 1822, c-John REEL, Christian YODER, d-$2000, e-Peter HERSHBARGER, John CLICK, f-17 Dec 1822, g-21 Jul 1828, h-$817.46, i-$838.02.5, j-$20.56.5, accountant

John IRVINE, b-10 Dec 1822, c-Henry IRVINE, Joseph HOWARD, d-$8000, e-E. B. PATTERSON, E. W. HALE, f-16 Dec 1822, g-24 Jul 1824, h-$2406.37.5, i-$2719.28.5, j-$312.91, accountant

Henry HOOVEN, b-12 Dec 1822, c-Lewis EVANS, d-$400, e-Calvin BLYTHE, Robert C. GALLAHER, f- g-11 Nov 1823, h-$719.70, i-$695.12, j-$245.8, estate

Godfried WOMER, b-16 Dec 1822, c-Henry WOOMER [sic], d-$250, e-David HARSHBARGER, Wm. PATTON, f-16 Dec 1822, g- h- i- j-

David JORDAN, b-16 Dec 1822, c-William McCOY, Ephraim BANKS, d- e- f-23 Feb 1825, g-23 Feb 1825, h-$173.91, i-$266.77.5, j-$92.26.5, accountant

John BUSHEY, b-18 Dec 1822, c-Samuel MYERS, d-$2000, e-Andrew KEISER, Ephraim BANKS, f-4 Mar 1829, g-19 Apr 1830/4 Mar 1829, h-$100.60/$1598.59, i-$124.65/$1740.00, j-$24.05, accountant/ $141.41, accountants

James MATHEWS, b-31 Dec 1822, c-William MATHEWS, d-$500, e-John McAVOY, Henry SPANGLER, f-23 Jan 1823, g-19 Apr 1825, h-$738.30, i-$508.84.5, j-$229.45.5, estate

George **HOOBAUGH**, **b**-23 Jan 1822, **c**-John HOOBAUGH, Peter KOCHENDERFER, **d**-$4000, **e**-David BEALE, Evan VAN SWEARENGEN, **f**-23 Apr 1823, **g**-27 Jun 1825, **h**-$3743.74.5, **i**-$1529.4.5, **j**-$2214.35, estate

Page 88, Frame 98
John BEATTY, **b**-4 Feb 1823, **c**-Robert FORGY, James CRISWELL, **d**- **e**- **f**-17 Oct 1829, **g**-17 Oct 1829, **h**-$3113.29, **i**-$812.50, **j**-$2300.79, estate

Jacob SELLERS, **b**-7 Feb 1823, **c**-Joseph SELLERS, Jacob SELLERS, **d**- **e**- **f**-20 Nov 1826, **g**-21 Apr 1829, **h**-$1082.02.5, **i**-$1107.93, **j**-$25.60.5, accountant

Mary MONAHON, **b**-12 Feb 1823, **c**-Michael M. MONAHON, **d**-$3000, **e**-James DICKSON, Robt. ROBISON, **f**- **g**- **h**- **i**- **j**-

Robert KENNY, **b**-12 Feb 1823, **c**-James KENNY, **d**-$500, **e**-James MILLIKEN, Joseph MILLIKEN, **f**-22 Aug 1829/13 Mar 1823, **g**-22 Aug 1829, **h**-$732.45, **i**-$518.91.5, **j**-$213.53.5, estate

Ann MOORE, **b**-12 Feb 1823, **c**-John MOORE, **d**-$2000, **e**-Wm. McCOY, Ephraim BANKS, **f**-26 Aug 1823, **g**- **h**- **i**- **j**-

Azzur WRIGHT, **b**-13 Feb 1823, **c**-David WRIGHT, Levi YOUNG, Jr., **d**- **e**- **f**- **g**- **h**- **i**- **j**-

James McBRIDE, **b**-14 Feb 1823, **c**-Henry KULP, **d**-$800, **e**-Joseph BROTHERS, Henry ORT, **f**- **g**- **h**- **i**- **j**-

Hannah FOREST, **b**-17 Feb 1823, **c**-James FOREST, **d**-$600, **e**-David COULTER, George JOHNSTON, **f**- **g**- **h**- **i**- **j**-

Thomas BURCHFIELD, **b**-19 Feb 1823, **c**-Aquilla BURCHFIELD, **d**-$1000, **e**-Jas. BURCHFIELD, Jos. EDMISTON, **f**-28 Mar 1823, **g**- **h**- **i**- **j**-

John CRISWELL, **b**-5 Mar 1823, **c**-William CUMMIN, William BARR, **d**-$1500, **e**-John HENRY, Francis HENRY, **f**-20 Nov 1826, **g**-17 Nov 1826/25 Feb 1837, **h**-$581.79/$335.33, **i**-$403.76.5/$378.48, **j**-$207.65.5, estate/$43.15, accountant

David YODER, **b**-10 Mar 1823, **c**-John YODER, Peter YODER, **d**-$1000, **e**-Jacob KING, James MILLIKEN, **f**-3 Apr 1823, **g**-14 Aug 1824, **h**-$654.61.5, **i**-$155.91.25, **j**-$498.60.25, estate

John ZOOK, **b**-11 Mar 1823, **c**-Christian ZOOK, **d**- **e**- **f**-17 Mar 1823, **g**-16 May 1827, **h**-$4234.22, **i**-$155.46, **j**-$4078.76, estate

Page 89, Frame 99

John CEVER, b-15 Mar 1823, **c-**Henry LONG, John ROTHROCK, **d-**$2500, **e-**James MILLIKEN, Francis BOGGS, **f-**10 Nov 1824, **g-**17 Mar 1832, **h-**$1053.19.5, **i-**$952.79, **j-**$100.40, estate

Jacob KINSER, b-21 Mar 1823, **c-**David KINSER, **d-**$800, **e-**Joel KINSER, Thos. MACLIN, **f- g- h- i- j-**

Abraham KEARNS, b-22 Mar 1823, **c-**Thomas MAGEE, Stephen HINDS, **d-**$1000, **e-**Peacock MAJOR, Robt. McCLELLAND, **f- g- h- i- j-**

Andrew N. GALLAHER, b-9 Apr 1823, **c-**Robert C. GALLAHER, **d-**$2000, **e-**Thomas KNOX, John KAUFMAN, **f-**8 May 1823, **g-**20 Dec 1827, **h-**$1519.36, **i-**$1214.05, **j-**$269.13.5, estate

Catherine SWILER, b-10 Apr 1823, **c-**William SWILER, Adam SWILER, **d- e- f-**10 Apr 1823, **g- h- i- j-**

Catherine DAVIS, b-18 Apr 1823, **c-**James DAVIS, Sr., William BARR, **d- e- f-**20 Aug 1823, **g- h- i- j-**

Rosanah MITCHELL, b-21 Apr 1823, **c-**William RAMSEY, David MITCHELL, **d- e- f- g- h- i- j-**

Mary MINSHALL, b-21 Apr 1823, **c-**John STEWART, **d-**$800, **e-**John RIDDLE, James RIDDLE, **f- g- h- i- j-**

Lydia GALLAHER, b-24 Apr 1823, **c-**Robert C. GALLAHER, **d- e- f-**5 Jun 1823, **g- h- i- j-**

Alexander McKINSTRY, b-26 Apr 1823, **c-**Elizabeth McKINSTRY, **d-**$1000, **e-**Saml. SUNDERLAND, Alexr. McKINSTRY, **f-**26 May 1823, **g- h- i- j-**

Michael McMULLEN, b-29 Apr 1823, **c-**James MILLIKEN, **d-**$300, **e-**Jas. or Jos. MILLIKEN, David McCLURE, **f- g-**15 Apr 1828, **h-**$212.19.5, **i-**$149.28.5, **j-**$62.91, estate

Alexander A. ANDERSON, b-30 Apr 1823, **c-**Thomas BURNSIDE, Wm. P. MACLAY, **d- e- f-**24 Apr 1824, **g-**30 Jun 1836, **h-**$12,078.11.5, **i-**$9947.78.25, **j-**$2130.33.25, accountant

Page 90, Frame 100

Susannah SHELLENBARGER, b-19 May 1823, **c-**Michael LABES, Sr., **d- e- f-**9 Jun 1823, **g-**19 Jul 1825, **h-**$2686.97, **i-**$58.06, **j-**$2628.90.5, estate

George CALBRAITH, b-31 Oct 1822, **c-**Hannah CALBRAITH, John HAMAN, **d- e- f- g-**23 Nov 1843, **h-**$9904.33, **i-**$9775,36, **j-**$128.97, estate

Isabella CROZIER, **b**-22 Nov 1823, **c**-John CROZIER, Jr. **d**- **e**- **f**- **g**-22 Apr 1831, **h**-$181.21, **i**-$228.30, **j**-$47.09, accountant
Samuel McENTIRE, **b**-21 Jul 1823, **c**-Robert McKEE, David McKEE, Sr., David [GLENN], **d**-$2500, **e**-John KINZER, H. BUTLER, **f**-18 Aug 1823, **g**- **h**- **i**- **j**-
Mary ROOP, **b**-2 Aug 1823, **c**-George ROOP, **d**-$700, **e**-John KAUFMAN, Isaac KAUFMAN, **f**-5 Sep 1823, **g**-2 Mar 1824, **h**-$200.78.5, **i**-$61.80, **j**-$138.98.5, estate
Thomas GLISSON, **b**-7 Aug 1823, **c**-Richard LATCHFORD, **d**-$1000, **e**-Francis JORDAN, David MILLER, **f**-10 Sep 1823, **g**-3 Jan 1828, **h**-$165.22, **i**-$170.74, **j**-$5.51, accountant
William MARLEY, **b**-20 Aug 1823, **c**-Joseph CUMMINS, **d**-$600, **e**-Thos. McDONALD, Calvin BLYTHE, **f**-20 Sep 1823/21 Apr 1826, **g**-21 Apr 1826, **h**-$466.98.5, **i**-$438.93.5, **j**-$24.27, estate
Benjamin REYNOLDS, **b**-27 Aug 1823, **c**-Stephen REYNOLDS, **d**-$1200, **e**-Evan EVANS, D. R. REYNOLDS, **f**-27 Sep 1823/23 Aug 1826, **g**-23 Aug 1826, **h**-$853.04, **i**-$225.88, **j**-$627.16, estate
John MICK, **b**-29 Aug 1823, **c**-Michael LEPLEY, John WALES, **d**-$600, **e**-Henry WAGNER, Jacob GILL, **f**-5 Jan 1824, **g**-23 Aug 1826, **h**-$853.04, **i**-$225.88, **j**-$627.16, estate
James McLAUGHLIN, **b**-30 Aug 1823, **c**-Archibald RANKIN, **d**-$500, **e**-Patrick BYRNE, E. W. HALE, Esq., **f**-6 Oct 1823, **g**- **h**- **i**- **j**-
John FIELDS, **b**-10 Sep 1823, **c**-Henry BARRICK, **d**-$1500, **e**-John HANAWALT, John NIECE, **f**-4 Oct 1823, **g**-7 Jan 1826, **h**-$853.68.5, **i**-$711.14.5, **j**-$142.54, estate
James McKEEHAN, **b**-10 Sep 1823, **c**-John NIECE, **d**-$1000, **e**-Henry BARRICK, John HANAWALT, **f**-4 Oct 1823, **g**-27 Feb 1827, **h**-$341.71.5, **i**-$416.79, **j**-$75.07.5, accountant

Page 91, Frame 101
Samuel BROWN, **b**-12 Sep 1823, **c**-Agnes BROWN, **d**- **e**- **f**-9 Oct 1823, **g**- **h**- **i**- **j**-
William BRICE, **b**-19 Sep 1823, **c**-Thomas McVITTY, Thomas MORROW, **d**-$2000, **e**-Peter COOK, Elias W. HALE, **f**-19 Sep 1823, **g**-25 Aug 1826, **h**-$538.21, **i**-$639.38, **j**-$101.17, accountant
Richard BELL, **b**-7 Oct 1823, **c**-Andrew BANKS, **d**- **e**- **f**-20 Jan 1824, **g**-6 Sep 1825, **h**-$4934.71, **i**-$217.54, **j**-$4717.17, estate

Samuel WEAVER, b-7 Oct 1823, **c-**David WEAVER, John WEAVER, **d-**$1000, **e-**Thomas STINSON, David REYNOLDS, **f-**28 Oct 1823, **g-**9 May 1825, **h-**$330.24.5, **i-**$141.26, **j-**$188.98.5, estate

Alice STEWART, b-17 Oct 1823, **c-**Henry HACKET, **d- e- f-**28 Nov 1823, **g-**23 Nov 1833, **h-**$1165.48.5, **i-**$300.40, **j-**$865.08.5, estate

Jacob SCHREDER, b-21 Oct 1823, **c-**Joseph RITTENHOUSE, John McFADDEN, **d- e- f-**18 Nov 1823, **g-**12 Jan 1828, **h-**$266.76, **i-**$365.95, **j-**$55.19, accountant

James CASSNER, b-21 Oct 1823, **c-**John McALLISTER, **d-**$300, **e-**John JAMISON, Wm. McALLISTER, **f- g- h- i- j-**

Joseph ZOOK, b-27 Oct 1823, **c-**Christly ZOOK, Samuel KING, **d-**$800, **e-**Joseph MARTIN, Samuel MARTIN, **f-**4 Dec 1823, **g-**21 Mar 1825, **h-**$899.21.5, **i-**$187.18.5, **j-**$712.05, estate

William STALL, b-28 Oct 1823, **c-**John BOLE, **d-**$600, **e-**John BAKER, Wm. P. ELLIOTT, **f-**28 Oct 1823, **g-**23 Nov 1826, **h-**$538.31, **i-**$538.35.5, **j-**$.04.5 balance

Rachel McKINSTRY, b-30 Oct 1823, **c-**Alexander McKINSTRY, **d-**$2000, **e-**Thos. MITCHELL, George MARKLEY, **f- g- h- i- j-**

John HOSTETLER, b-14 Nov 1823, **c-**John KURTZ, David HARTZLER, **d-**$2000, **e-**Stephen KURTZ, James MILLIKEN, **f-**13 Dec 1823, **g-**16 Oct 1826, **h-**$729.38.5, **i-**$440.33.5, **j-**$289.05, estate

George SUNDAY, b-17 Nov 1823, **c-**John RITTER, George BILLMAN, **d-**$800, **e-**John BILLMAN, Jacob RITTER, **f-**4 Dec 1823, **g-**19 Apr 1826, **h-**$361.26, **i-**$253.41, **j-**$107.85, estate

Page 92, Frame 102 [duplicated on Frame 103]
Mathew TAYLOR, b-20 Nov 1823, **c-**John TAYLOR, Henry TAYLOR, **d- e- f-**5 Mar 1835/9 Jan 1836, **g-**20 Oct 1828, **h-**$1799.23, **i-**$2434.32, **j-**$635.09, accountant

Peter CASNER, b-20 Nov 1823, **c-**John McALLISTER, **d-**$2000, **e-**John JAMISON, Danl. CHRISTY, Esq., **f- g- h- i- j-**

Joseph YODER, b-20 Nov 1823, **c-**Christian YODER, John HARTZLER, **d-**$4000, **e-**Abraham STUTZMAN, John YODER, **f-**18 Dec 1823, **g-**12 Mar 1827/20 Jul 1829/14 Mar 1831, **h-**$1425.96.25/$747.54.25/ $3127.72, **i-**$766.96/$748.02.25/$1627.46.5, **j-**$1500.26.5, estate

George MOORE, b-20 Nov 1823, **c-**Jane MOORE, **d-**$10,000, **e-**Francis MOORE, John HOLMAN, **f- g- h- i- j-**

Mary CRISWELL, b-6 Dec 1823, **c-**James DAVIS, William CUMMINS, **d- e- f- g- h- i- j-**

John SMITH, **b**-27 Dec 1823, **c**-Samuel PENCE, **d**-$1500, **e**-Wm. SHERLOCK, Thomas HANLIN, **f**-31 May 1822, **g**-22 Sep 1824, **h**-$336.24, **i**-$411.48, **j**-$75.34, accountant

James WINNING, **b**-7 Jan 1824, **c**-David ~~WALKER~~, Robert THOMPSON, **d**-~~$200~~, **e**-James McDOWELL, Esq., Joseph MILLIKEN, **f**-20 Jan 1824, **g**- **h**- **i**- **j**-

Elizabeth KINZER, **b**-13 Jan 1824, **c**-John KINZER, **d**-$500, **e**-Wm. McCAY, David REYNOLDS, **f**-2 Jun 1824, **g**-18 Jan 1832, **h**-$367.96.25, **i**-$98.39, **j**-$269.57.25, estate

William SIMMS, **b**-19 Jan 1824, **c**-Samuel KERLAND, **d**-$1000, **e**-John BEALE, Benjn. KEPNER, **f**-18 Feb 1824, **g**-28 Feb 1828, **h**-$74.52.5, **i**-$77.87.5, **j**-$3.35, accountant

Elisha CHRISWELL, **b**-28 Jan 1824, **c**-Samuel W. TAYLOR, James DAVIS, **d**-$4000, **e**-Saml. EISENBISE, James MILLIKEN, **f**-18 Aug 1829, **g**-16 Mar 1831, **h**-$398.51, **i**-$574.54, **j**-$210.85, accountant

John McNITT, **b**-3 Feb 1824, **c**-Alexander B. McNITT **d**- **e**- **f**- **g**- **h**- **i**- **j**-

Henry ORT, **b**-4 Feb 1824, **c**-John ORT, Jr., Jacob ORT, **d**-$4000, **e**-John ORT, James MILLIKEN, **f**-22 Jun 1825, **g**-23 Dec 1828, **h**-$3334.06, **i**-$2776.21.25, **j**-$557.84.75, estate

Page 93, Frame 104

Isaac HAMLIN, **b**-13 Feb 1824, **c**-Stephen REYNOLDS, **d**-$300, **e**-William McCAY, James DEVINNEY, **f**-13 Mar 1824, **g**-23 Aug 1826, **h**-$145.63, **i**-$122.13, **j**-$23.49, estate

Robert FORSYTHE, **b**-17 Feb 1824, **c**-William LYON, Mathew FORSYTHE, **d**-$10,000, **e**-Jos. B. ARD, Wm. P. MACLAY, **f**- **g**- **h**- **i**- **j**-

Leonard COCHEL, **b**-21 Feb 1824, **c**-William HAZLETT, **d**- **e**- **f**-19 Apr 1924. **g**-3 Jun 1826, **h**-$794.84, **i**-$686.86.5, **j**-$107.97.5, estate

Benjamin WILLIAMS, **b**-9 Mar 1824, **c**-J. or I. Stewart WILLIAMS, **d**-$500, **e**-John KINZER, Wm. BARKLEY, **f**- **g**- **h**- **i**- **j**-

Robert MITCHELL, **b**-25 Feb 1824, **c**-William M. INGREM, Robert INGREM **d**- **e**- **f**- **g**- **h**- **i**- **j**-

Jacob HARTZLER, **b**-10 Mar 1824, **c**-David HARTZLER, Joseph HARTZLER, **d**-$5000, **e**-Henry [STONER], **f**-27 Mar 1824, **g**-18 Oct 1828, **h**-$3621.12, **i**-$3557.29, **j**-$63.83, estate

Valentine WISEHAUBT, **b**-11 Mar 1824, **c**-Valentine WISEHAUBT **d**- **e**- **f**-23 May 1822[sic], **g**-21 May 1828, **h**-$2937.49.5, **i**-$1177.32.5, **j**-$1760.17.25, estate

Barbara HARNER, b-11 Mar 1824, c-Michael HARNER, d- e- f- g- h- i-
j-

David WHARRY, b-13 Mar 1824, c-Wm. M. INGRAM, d-$500, e-
Hamilton LONGWELL, James MILLIKEN, f- g- h- i- j-

Leonard MELCHOIR, b-17 Mar 1824, c-John STINE, Cyrus STINE, d-
$800, e-Rachel MELCHOIR, Elias W. HALE, Robert STEWART, f-29
Mar 1824, g-30 Oct 1833, h-$993.39.5, i-$1016.61.75, j-$23.22.25,
accountants

Mark KULP, b-29 Mar 1824, c-Elias KULP, d-$500, e-Henry
EISENBISE, Robert LEAPBLE, f- g- h- i- j-

George MACKLIN, b-3 Apr 1824, c-Luken ATKINS, Wm.
ARMSTRONG, d- e- f-15 Jun 1824/1 Jul 1831, g-10 Mar 1828/30 Dec
1829/19 Jun 1834, 1 Jul 1831, h-$1286.45/$275.49/$2677.14,
$110.47.5, i-$1031.13/$69.80.5/$1677.14, $35.38, j-$75.09.5, estate

Page 94, Frame 105

Alexander GIVENS, b-20 Apr 1824, c-Samuel McCOLLOCK, d- e- f-20
Apr 1824, g-19 Apr 1826, h-$364.68, i-$374.87, j-$10.19, accountant

Samuel WHARTON, b-20 Apr 1824, c-Samuel WHARTON, d-$400, e-
William WHARTON, John WILLIAMS, Jr., f-13 May 1824, g- h- i-
j-

Elizabeth WISCHAUBT [possibly WISEHAUPT], b-21 Apr 1824, c-
David WISCHAUBT, d-$1400, e-John PATTERSON, Wm.
GRAHAM, f- g- h- i- j-

James GELANEY, b-22 Apr 1824, c-Jesse ADAMS, d-$1000, e-Jos.
CAMPBELL, Wm. McCULLOCH, f-21 May 1824, g-23 Feb 1827, h-
$232.63, i-$119.65.5, j-$112.97.5, estate

Thomas BEALE, b-27 Apr 1824, c-Thomas TODD, d-$5000, e-Samuel
STERRETT, Patrick McKENNON, f- g-4 Jul 1833, h- i- j-

John RAUSH, b-17 May 1824, c-Ulrick RUMBACH, d-$500, e-Peter
THOMPSON, James GILFILLEN, f-17 May 1824, g-12 May 1825, h-
$232.87, i-$129.20, j-$101.70.5, estate

Mena COMFORT, b-22 May 1824, c-William CHARTERS, John
COMFORT, d-$500, e-Jos. MILLIKEN, James CHRISWELL, f-22 Jun
1824, g-22 Oct 1825, h-$450.23.5, i-$150.60.75, j-$299.62.75, estate

Daniel THATCHER, b-22 May 1824, c-Sarah THATCHER, George
McCULLOCH, d-$600, e-Alexander COULTER, James DICKSON,
f-18 Aug 1824, g-22 Nov 1834, h-$2233.88, i-$2334.74, j-$100.86,
accountant

James MATHEWS, b-1 Jun 1824, c-Daniel McDONALD, d- e- f- g- h- i- j-

Samuel VINES, b-5 Jun 1824, c-Charles COX, d-$1000, e-John HAMMOND, Andrew BRATTON, f-27 Jul 1824, g-17 Mar 1826, h-$388.57.5, i-$325.24.75, j-$63.32.75, estate

Thomas PLOWMAN, b-16 Jun 1824, c-Sarah PLOWMAN, Hezekiah PLOWMAN, d-$800, e-Robert BURNS, Benjamin MAJOR, f-17 Jul 1824, g- h- i- j-

Theodore MEMINGER, b-9 Jul 1824, c-John NORRIS, d- e- f-19 Aug 1824, g-9 Jan 1843, h- i- j-$12,950.74, estate

Page 95, Frame 106

Dorothy STUDDS, b-19 Jul 1824, c-Christian HUBER, d-$3000, e-James MILLIKEN, David REYNOLDS, f-17 Aug 1824, g- h- i- j-

Enoch ANDERSON, b-2 Aug 1824, c-E. L. ANDERSON, d- e- f- g- h- i- j-

Andrew McELWAYNE, b-24 Aug 1824, c-Robert CHRISWELL, d-$600, e-James MILLIKEN, Alexander COULTER, f-23 Sep 1824, g- h- i- j-

James BURCHFIELD, b-27 Aug 1824, c-Robert BURCHFIELD, d-$200, e-William MOSS, f- g- h- i- j-

Mary WILSON, b-2 Sep 1824, c-Josiah WILSON, d-$2000, e-David REYNOLDS, Mary ELLIS, f- g- h- i- j-

Isaiah VANZANT, b-7 Sep 1824, c-George VANZANT, Casper DULL, d-$1000, e-Wm. MITCHELL, John NIECE, f-25 Sep 1824, g- h- i- j-

John REED, b-9 Sep 1824, c-Abner REED, d- e- f- g- h- i- j-

Mary ALLISON, b-14 Sep 1824, c-William ALLISON, d- e- f- g- h- i- j-

Elisabeth FLEMING, b-14 Sep 1824, c-John FLEMING, d- e- f- g-4 Jul 1827, h-$767.11, i-$1117.08, j-$349.97, accountant

Henry KENNEDY, b-16 Sep 1824, c-James ROBISON, John ROTHROCK, d-$2500, e-Robert ROBISON, James McDONAHY, f-8 Nov 1824, g-22 Mar 1831/7 Mar 1834, h-$1407.61.5/$273.11, i-$1231.17/$154.32.5, j-$176.44, estate/$119.82.5, estate

Thomas BAIRD, b-18 Sep 1824, c-George MITCHELL, James McDONALD, d-$1200, e-Alexr. McKINSTRY, Irvin COULTER, f-18 Oct 1824, g-3 Nov 1827, h-$1214.27, i-$653.99.5, j-$560.27.5, estate

William HYMPHRYS, b-9 Oct 1824, c-John GALLOWAY, Thomas FRITZ, d-$5000, e-James CHRISWELL, David HARTZLER, f- g- h- i- j-

Page 96, Frame 107

John REED, b-11 Oct 1824, c-Christopher HORRELL, d-$600, e-David STEWART, Samuel EDMISTON, f-10 Nov 1824, g- h- i- j-

Jacob CODER, b-13 Oct 1824, c-Joshua BEALE, d-$100, e-John BEALE, Francis BOGGS, f-18 Jan 1825, g- h- i- j-

James ADAMS, b-30 Oct 1824, c-Jesse ADAMS, James THOMPSON, d- e- f-26 Nov 1824, g-11 Dec 1830, h- i- j-

Nathaniel CUNNINGHAM, b-30 Oct 1824, c-Jeremiah CUNNINGHAM, [I. J.] CUNNINGHAM, d-$2000, e-John DYSERT, John NIECE, f-6 Jan 1825, g-7 Aug 1827, h-$1367.65.5, i-$561.67.5, j-$805.98, estate

Daniel REIGLE, b-22 Oct 1824, c-Benjamin REIGLE, d-$200, e-John THOMPSON, Samuel EISENBISE, f-19 Jan 1825, g-24 Jun 1825, h-$215.04.35, i-$215.04.25, j-

Henry MAST, b-30 Oct 1924, c-Joseph RANNELS, d-$3000, e-Samuel RANNELLS[sic], David RICKABAUGH, f-20 Nov 1824, g-11 Mar 1826, h-$1197.51.5, i-$411.21, j-$786.30.5, estate

Jacob KAUFFMAN, b-2 Nov 1824, c-Joseph RENNELS, Isaac KAUFFMAN, d-4000 e-John KAUFMAN, Daniel KAUFMAN, f-26 Nov 1824, g-11 Mar 1826, h-$734.71, i-$168.05.5, j-$566.55.5, estate

Caleb GRIFFITH, b-16 Nov 1824, c-Lewis EVANS, d-$500, e-Nathan GRIFFETH, Charles COOKSON, f-16 Jan 1826, g-18 Nov 1828, h-$1224.85.5, i-$1077.44, j-$147.41.5, estate

Hannah STUTZMAN, b-16 Nov 1824, c-Michael STUTZMAN, d-$1500, e-John STUTZMAN, Henry STUTZMAN, f- g- h- i- j-

George BOUSEY, b-16 Nov 1824, c-Cornelius BARKLEY, d-$500, e-John WILSON, James GARDNER, f-17 Dec 1824, g- h- i- j-

John PARSONS, b-16 Nov 1824, c-Sarah PARSONS, d- e- f- g- h- i- j-

Mary GREEN, b-18 Nov 1824, c-James CHRISWELL, d- e- f- g- h- i- j-

Page 97, Frame 108

Maj. John IRWIN, b-7 Dec 1824, c-Joseph HOWARD, E. B. PATTERSON, A. S. WILSON, d-$8000, e-Sarah HALL, Wm. M. HALL, f- g-20 Mar 1828, h-$2725.20.25, i-$2870.32.25, j-$145.12, accountant

Robert MITCHELL, b-15 Dec 1824, c-Samuel McDOWELL, Joseph MILLIKEN, d-$1000, e-Samuel MITCHELL, John ORT, f- g- h- i- j-

Jacob BIXLER, b-27 Dec 1824, c-Barbara BIXLER, Jacob BIXLER, d-$ e- f- g- h- i- j-

Barbara SELLERS, b- 4 Jan 1825, c-William SELLERS, d-$1200, e-John GEISINGER, James KINSLOE, f-24 Jan 1825, g-24 Oct 1825, h-$657.01.75, i-$162.27.75 j-$494.74, estate

William [FALLZ], b-13 Jan 1825, c-Jonathan W. ELLIOTT, d-$200, e-William SANDOE, Jacob MILLER, f- g-30 Mar 1826, h-$46.– i-$46.–, j-

Samuel EISENBISE, b-15 Jan 1825, c-Henry EISENBISE, Henry KULP, d-$4000, e-Alexander EISENBISE, William MARKS, f- g- h- i- j-

Margaret STEWART, b-18 Jan 1825, c-Francis STEWART, d-$600, e-William GILSON, Andrew SMITH, f-22 Jan 1822, g- h- i- j-

Mary ROBISON, b-18 Jan 1825, c-William STRODE, John OLIVER, d-$ e- f- g- h- i- j-

John REED (of Chester), b-19 Jan 1825, c-Robert REED, d-$1000, e-James MILLIKEN, Francis BOGGS, f- g- h- i- j-

William WAKEFIELD, b-26 Jan 1825, c-William WAKEFIELD, d- e- f-7 Mar 1825, g- h- i- j-

John MUSER, b-29 Jan 1825, c-Samuel KURTZ, d- e- f-14 Jul 1828 g-14 Jul 1828, h-$9200.04, i-$191.79.5, j-$.24.5, estate

James CUMMIN, b-19 Jan 1825, c-John CUMMIN, d- e- f- g- h- i- j-

Page 98, Frame 109

Robert ARMSTRONG, b-15 Feb 1825, c-Catherine ARMSTRONG, d-$1000, e-Jesse REYNOLDS, John ROBISON, f-1 Dec 1825, g-5 Feb 1833, h-$1129.14.5, i-$161.60, j-$967.54.5, heirs

Daniel BROUGHT, b-16 Feb 1825, c-John BROUGHT, d-$200, e-John BROUGHT, Wm. ROBB, f-14 Dec 1827, g-14 Dec 1827, h-$2550.91.5, i-$3131.96, j-$546.24.5, accountant

Simon CODER, b-19 Feb 1825, c-Samuel STERRETT, Catherine CODER, d- e- f-19 Feb 1825, g-20 Jan 1829, h-$173.18.5, i-$232.94, j-$59.76, accountant

Francis SAMPLE, b-19 Feb 1825, c-Agnes SAMPLE, John SAMPLE, d- e- f- g- h- i- j-

Henry AUGHY, b-23 Feb 1825, c-Benjamin LAW, Abraham GUSS, d- e- f-9 Nov 1825, g-30 Sep 1829/15 Dec 1837, h-$4496.98.5/$1613.41, i-$4469.28.5/$1613,41, j-no bal.

Samuel ANDERSON, b-25 Feb 1825, c-Joseph ANDERSON, Robert ROBISON, d-$25, e-James ROBISON, John ROBISON, f-3 Feb 1826, g-17 Aug 1829, h-$1277.82, i-$477.70.5, j-$800.11.5, heirs

Benjamin M. DULL, b-3 Mar 1825, c-Casper DULL, d-$300, e-D. W. JEFFERS, James KELLOGG, f-2 Mar 1826, g- h- i- j-

Thomas HENDERSON, b-7 Mar 1825, c-Stewart TURBETT, Thomas KNOX, d-$1000, e-Wm. C. KELLY, Levi REYNOLDS, f-7 Mar 1825, g-21 Jun 1826, h-$255.68, i-$221.31, j-$64.16, estate

Alexander WILKEN, b-18 Mar 1825, c-William PORTER, James PORTER, d-$500, e-Robert WILKEN, David JENKIN, f-18 Apr 1825, g- h- i- j-

Isaac YOST, b-14 Mar 1825, c-John HAMILTON, John STEWERT [sic], d- e- f-12 Apr 1825, g-19 Jun 1829, h-$2684.66, i-$2562.55, j-$122.11, estate

Mary YOST, b-22 Mar 1825, c-Rinehard [WITZEL], d-$800, e-James McCORD, Joseph HENDERSON, f-9 Apr 1825, g- h- i- j-

Thomas BROWN, b-25 Mar 1825, c-John BROWN, James WILLS, d-$, e- f- g-1 Sep 1829, h- i-$536.48, j-$536.48 [no designation given]

Page 99, Frame 110

John KESHOUER, b-9 Apr 1825, c-Peter HERSHBARGER, d-$500, e-Thomas MITCHELL, William McVEY, f-5 Dec 1829, g-5 Dec 1829, h-$90.27, i-$124.42, j-$34.15, accountant

Joseph MOSS, b-12 Apr 1825, c-John STEWART, d-$500, e-David REYNOLDS, John CUMMIN, f-17 May 1825, g- h- i- j-

Peter GAUFF, b-18 Apr 1825, c-Philip ROTHROCK, d-$200, e-Henry BURKHOLDER, John BURKHOLDER, f- g- h- i- j-

Philip MINEHART, b-20 Apr 1825, c-John WERTS, d-$3000, e-Joseph MARTIN, James MILLIKEN, f-30 Oct 1824[sic], g-20 Aug 1829, h-$401.07.5, i-$405.99.5, j-$4.92, accountant

Charles COOKSON, b-20 Apr 1825, c-Lewis EVANS, d- e- f-19 Feb 1825, g-16 Apr 1832, h-$2722.65, i-$9591.38, j-$6768.73, accountant

Elizabeth KINGERICH, b-21 Apr 1825, c-John KINGERICH, Evan EVANS, d-$2000, e-Jesse JACOBS, Joseph CUMMINS, f-24 May 1825, g-28 Jul 1827, h-$836.54.5, i-$844.57.5, j-$8.03, accountant

George McCLELLAND, b-25 Apr 1825, c-Joseph B. ARD, Abraham S. WILSON, d-$2000, e-Robt. McCLELLAND, James MILLIKEN, f-25 May 1825, g- h- i- j-

Margaret CEEVER, b-16 Jun 1825, c-Robert CEEVER, d-$ e- f- g- h- i- j-

William BRATTON, b-20 Apr 1825, c-Andrew BRATTON, James LANGTON, d- e- f- g- h- i- j-

William JUNKEN, b-16 May 1825, **c**-David LUSK **d**- **e**- **f**-18 Apr 1826, **g**-20 Jul 1829, **h**-$3640.92, **i**-$6019.75.5, **j**-$2378.83.5, accountant

Stephen REYNOLDS, b-18 May 1825, **c**-Mary REYNOLDS, Leonard LINGLE, **d**-$300, **e**-Foster MILLIKEN, Henry HALL, **f**-3 Jun 1825/27 Feb 1826, **g**-22 Apr 1829, **h**-$609.33.5, **i**-$318.64.5, **j**-$290.69, estate

George SHREFFLER, b-24 May 1825, **c**-Margaret SHREFFLER, **d**-$400, **e**-Christopher HORRELL, David REYNOLDS, **f**-6 Jun 1825, **g**-16 Mar 1829, **h**-$190.38, **i**-$171.46, **j**-$18.92, estate

Page 100, Frame 111

Benjamin KEPNER, b-19 Jul 1825, **c**-John KEPNER, John FRYBARGER, **d**-$800, **e**-Benjn. KEPNER, Thomas TODD, **f**- **g**- **h**- **i**- **j**-

Jane HUMPHRY[S], b-15 Aug 1825, **c**-Thomas FRITZ, **d**- **e**- **f**- **g**- **h**- **i**- **j**-

James WOODWARD, b-19 Aug 1825, **c**-Adam THOMPSON, Thomas TODD, **d**-$1000, **e**-Thos. HARRIS, John PATTERSON, **f**-30 Aug 1825, **g**-4 Apr 1849/9 Nov 1836, **h**-$346.50/$357.76, **i**-$544.03/ $453.53, **j**-$33.90, accountant

Robert RICHIE, b-20 Aug 1825, **c**-Martha [McCLEAR], **d**- **e**- **f**- **g**- **h**- **i**- **j**-

Anthoney ELTON, b-23 Aug 1825, **c**-Revel ELTON, **d**-$800, **e**-David LUSK, Richard MONTGOMERY, **f**-8 Nov 1825, **g**- **h**- **i**- **j**-

Barnabas RAMSEY, b-1 Sep 1825, **c**-Samuel McCULLOCH, Paul LAUGHLIN, **d**-$, **e**- **f**-1 Sep 1825, **g**-24 Jan 1828/7 May 1836, **h**-$576.20.5/$150.08, **i**-$587.08.5/$185.15.25, **j**-$35.07.25, accountant

John WRIGHT, b-10 Sep 1825, **c**-James NIXON, John WRIGHT, Samuel HORNING, **d**- **e**- **f**-21 May 1827, **g**-21 Feb 1827, **h**-$1542.96 **i**- **j**-$991.35, estate

Alexander STEWART, b-10 Sep 1825, **c**-William ARMSTRONG, William FORGY, **d**- **e**- **f**-17 Mar 1828, **g**-17 Mar 1828, **h**-$375.10, **i**-$425.12.5, **j**-$50.02.5, accountant

David STROUSE, b-14 Sep 1825, **c**-Henry HARTMAN, John WALLACE, **d**- **e**- **f**-24 Oct 1825, **g**-21 May 1832, **h**-$1919.93, **i**-$2220.26, **j**-$300.33, accountant

Eleanor GLASGOW, b-14 Sep 1825, **c**-John GLASGOW, **d**-$1100, **e**-John WALLACE, George JACOBS, **f**- **g**- **h**- **i**- **j**-

Rachel JOHNSTON, b-23 Sep 1825, **c**-John OLIVER, Jr., **d**-$1200, **e**-Ephraim BANKS, Wm. WAKEFIELD, **f**-21 Oct 1825, **g**- **h**- **i**- **j**-

Christian YODER, b-26 Sep 1825, c-John YODER, Samuel KING, d-$12,000, e-Joseph MILLIKEN, Joseph MARTIN, f- g-1 Oct 1839, h-$13,177.08, i-$2861.48, j-$10,305.60, estate

Page 101, Frame 112

Nancy FERGUSON, b-28 Sep 1825, c-Andrew BRATTON, d-$1000, e-James LANGTON, Andrew JUNKIN, f-24 Feb 1829, g-7 Aug 1829, h-$657.08, i-$242.75.5, j-$414.32.5, estate

John MOORE, b-3 Oct 1825, c-Thomas W. MOORE, d-$1000, e-Christopher MARK [or MACK], Francis McCOY, f-19 Aug 1826, g-10 Nov 1830, h-$762.70, i-$1507.37.5, j-$744.67.5, accountant

Daniel SWARTZENTRUVER, b-8 Oct 1825, c-Henry SWARTZENTRUVER, d-$1000, e-John CROUSE, Thomas ROBISON, f-2 Nov 1825, g-14 Feb 1828, h-$458.04, i-$657.76.5, j-$199.72.5, accountant

Edward HAGENEY, b-12 Oct 1825, c-Sarah HAGENY[sic], d-$100, e-James LANGSTON, David ROSS, f- g- h- i- j-

George DIXON, b-15 Oct 1825, c-Amor STRODE, William WAKEFIELD, d-$3000, e-Ephraim BANKS, Francis McCOY, f-17 Nov 1825, g-21 Oct 1827/26 Jun 1847, h-$769.77/$325.73, i-$514.72/$424.73, j-$255.05, estate/$108.97, accountant

Gabriel FRY, b-20 Oct 1825, c-Abraham KURTZ, d-$500, e-Jonathan FRY, John STUTZMAN, f-19 Nov 1825, g-11 Oct 1828, h-$637.23, i-$564.14, j-$73.10, estate

William MARSDEN, b-31 Oct 1825, c-John MARSDEN, Jacob MARSDEN, d-$ e- f-29 Aug 1826, g- h- i- j-

James JOHNSTON, b-6 Oct 1825, c-William LYON, James CRISWELL, d- e- f-3 Dec 1825, g-12 Feb 1830, h-$1848.28, i-$1019.67, j-$828.61, estate

John HENRY, b-28 Oct 1825, c-Richard DOYLE, Alexander BOGGS, d- e- f-8 Nov 1825, g-20 Jan 1829, h-$298.00, i-$314.81, j-$16.81, accountant

Isabella MOORE, b-9 Nov 1825, c-David LUSK, d-$800, e-Revel ELTON, John RIEHL, f- g- h- i- j-

Isaiah WILLIS, b-9 Nov 1825, c-Francis McCOY, d-$8000, e-Jos. MARTIN, James McCORD, f- g-24 Oct 1831, h-$6668.45.75, i-$337.58, j-$6330.87.25, estate

Christian STUTZMAN, b-9 Nov 1825, c-Abraham STUTZMAN, Daniel STUTZMAN, d-$12,000, e-Michael STUTZMAN, John HARTZLER, f-6 Dec 1825, **g**-19 Mar 1831/28 June 1836, **h**-$7032.48/$1418.12, **i**-$5960.03/!$1528.79.5, **j**-$110.67.5, accountant

<u>Page 102, Frame 113</u>
James JOHNSTON, **b**-10 Nov 1825, **c**-William LYON, James CRISWELL, **d**-$6000, **e**-Casper DULL, Samuel EDMISTON, **f**- **g**- **h**- **i**- **j**-

James JUNKEN, **b**-10 Nov 1825, **c**-Andrew BRATTON, **d**-$2000, **e**-Nancy JUNKEN, James LANGTON, **f**- **g**- **h**- **i**- **j**-

John BRATTON, **b**-10 Nov 1825, **c**-Andrew BRATTON, **d**-$500, **e**-James LANGTON, Andrew JUNKEN, **f**-3 Nov 1827 **g**-3 Nov 1827 **h**-$80.43, **i**-$49.53, **j**-$30.90, estate

Sarah PERSON, **b**-25 Nov 1825, **c**-Samuel STERRETT, **d**-$300, **e**-Thomas TODD, Carrol REYNOLDS, **f**-16 Dec 1825, **g**-18 Mar 1829, **h**-$142.75, **i**-$208.39, **j**-$65.64, accountant

Elizabeth BELL, **b**-6 Dec 1825, **c**-David BELL, **d**-$3000, **e**-Thomas MITCHELL, Charles WORRALL, **f**-7 Feb 1826, **g**- **h**- **i**- **j**-

William GALLAGHER, **b**-22 Dec 1825, **c**-Henry BARKLEY, **d**-$500, **e**-John ROTHROCK, David REYNOLDS, **f**- **g**- **h**- **i**- **j**-

Abraham KAUFMAN, **b**-3 Jan 1826, **c**-William KAUFMAN, John SASMAN, **d**-$3000, **e**-Christian SEIBER, Jonas KAUFMAN, **f**-3 Feb 1826, **g**-17 Mar 1832, **h**-$199.49.5, **i**-$1868.27, **j**-$131.22.5, estate

Israel HOOPS, **b**-5 Jan 1826, **c**-Robert MARTIN, John PATTERSON, **d**- **e**- **f**-19 Jan 1826, **g**-18 Nov 1828, **h**-$4291.34.5, **i**-$4288.37, **j**-$2.97.5, estate

John SHIVELY, **b**-16 Jan 1826, **c**-John POTTER, **d**-$300, **e**-John THOMPSON, Isaac SHIVELY, **f**-17 Feb 1826, **g**-27 Nov 1830, **h**-$738.36, **i**-$673.01.75, **j**-$65.34.25, estate

Abraham KEARNS, **b**-18 Jan 1826, **c**-James McCLINTIC, **d**-$1500, **e**-James NIXON, Adam GREER, **f**-12 Jun 1823[sic], **g**-16 Apr 1832, **h**-$187.78.5, **i**-$242.90.75, **j**-$55.12.25, accountant

Jeremiah CUNNINGHAM, **b**-19 Jan 1826, **c**-William IRWIN, **d**-$4000, **e**-James CRISWELL, Jonathan CUNNINGHAM, **f**- **g**- **h**- **i**- **j**-

William BROWN, Esq., **b**-23 Jan 1826, **c**-John BROWN, William BROWN, **d**-$, **e**- **f**-9 Feb 1826, **g**- **h**- **i**- **j**-

<u>Page 103, Frame 114</u>
Abraham WILSON, **b**-24 Jan 1826, **c**-Hugh WILSON, **d**-$1500, **e**-Nathl. WILSON, John McNAIR, **f**-23 Feb 1826, **g**- **h**- **i**- **j**-

Mary DEARDORF, **b**-11 Feb 1826, **c**-Benjamin YODER, **d**- **e**- **f**-18 Apr 1826, **g**- **h**- **i**- **j**-

John MILLER, **b**-17 Feb 1826, **c**-David HARTZLER, **d**-$300, **e**-John REEL, John JACOBS, **f**-13 Mar 1826, **g**- **h**- **i**- **j**-

Richard JONES, **b**-20 Feb 1826, **c**-Thomas JONES, **d**-$200 **e**-Lydia JONES, John BUMBAUGH, **f**-15 May 1826, **g**-16 Jan 1827, **h**-$24.02, **i**-$37.85, **j**-$13.83, accountant

Michael GARBER, **b**-7 Mar 1826, **c**-Stephen KURTZ, **d**-$300, **e**-David HARTZLER, James KELLOGG, **f**- **g**- **h**- **i**- **j**-

Jacob COMFORT, **b**-8 Mar 1826, **c**-Henry COMFORT, Samuel COMFORT, **d**-$3500, **e**-Andrew MAYES, John McFADDEN, **f**-1 Apr 1826, **g**-2 Apr 1832, **h**-$671.07.5, **i**-$2735.94, **j**-$2064.86.5 accountant

Robert HAYES, **b**-3 Apr 1826, **c**-Joseph MATHEWS, **d**-$400, **e**-Henry BUTLER, Enoch BEALE, **f**-3 May 1826, **g**- **h**- **i**- **j**-

Henry SPANGLER, **b**-4 Apr 1826, **c**-Martha SPANGLER, John WALLACE, **d**-$1200, **e**-Lewis EVANS, Christopher MACK, **f**-8 Apr 1826, **g**-15 Jul 1828, **h**-$652.60, **i**-$565.09.25, **j**-$87.60.75, estate

Robert CRAIG, **b**-10 Apr 1826, **c**-William McCAY, William MITCHELL, **d**-$ **e**- **f**-16 Mar 1831, **g**-16 Mar 1831, **h**-$398.69, **i**-$406.90.75, **j**-$8.21.75, accountants

Mary REYNOLDS, **b**-21 Apr 1826, **c**-John REYNOLDS, **d**-$500, **e**-James ALEXANDER, Sr., Wm. K. TOWNSEND, **f**-28 Apr 1826 **g**- **h**- **i**- **j**-

Robert BUCHANAN, **b**-11 May 1826, **c**-David STEWART, Edmund B. PATTERSON, **g**-22 Dec 1829, **h**-$732.14, **i**-$625.35.75, **j**-$106.78.25, estate

William HUMPHRY, **b**-17 May 1826, **c**-James CRISWELL, **d**-$3000, **e**-Thomas FRITZ, Jane GALLOWAY, **f**-21 Oct 1824, **g**-17 Mar 1826, **h**-$2300.97, **i**-$1530.32, **j**-$770.65, estate

Page 104, Frame 115

Michael RAUCH, **b**-25 May 1826, **c**-John RAUCH, **d**-$1000, **e**-Henry GROCE, Jr., Ephraim BANKS, **f**-25 May 1826, **g**-16 Apr 1830, **h**-$1082.07.75, **i**-$1073.29, **j**-$8.78.75, estate

William LEWIS, **b**-29 May 1826, **c**-Levi REYNOLDS, Jr. **d**-$5000, **e**- **f**- **g**- **h**- **i**- **j**-

Caleb WHITE, **b**-12 Jun 1826, **c**-Jacob KEISER, **d**-$200, **e**-James KELLOGG, Jr., Levi REYNOLD, Jr., **f**-4 Jul 1826 **g**- **h**- **i**- **j**-

John KANN, **b**-19 Jun 1826, **c**-George KANN, **d**-$1000, **e**-Alexander COULTER, Robert McCLELLAND, **f**-19 Jun 1926, **g**- **h**- **i**- **j**-

Nicholas CALDWELL, b-21 Jun 1826, **c**-Robert CHRISWELL, **d**-$1000, **e**-Foster MILLIKEN, David REYNOLDS, **f**- **g**-16 Jul 1828, **h**-$150.00, **i**-$58.93.5, **j**-$91.06.5, estate

Elias HORNING, b-18 Jul 1826, **c**-John HORNING, Samuel MYERS, **d**-$4000, **e**-Saml. HORNING, Jacob HORNING, **f**- **g**- **h**- **i**- **j**-

Isabella JORDAN, b-5 Aug 1826, **c**-Wm. McCAY, Henry KULP, **e**- **f**-14 May 1835, **g**-14 May 1835, **h**-$1123.43.25, **i**-$762.08.25, **j**-$361.35, estate

Jane TURBETT, b-3 Aug 1826, **c**-Stewart TURBETT, **d**- **e**- **f**- **g**- **h**- **i**- **j**-

Catherine ARNOLD, b-7 Aug 1826, **c**-Jacob ARNOLD, **d**-$150, **e**-John ARNOLD, John McCONNELL, **f**- **g**- **h**- **i**- **j**-

John BROWN, b-22 Aug 1826, **c**-Rhoda BROWN, Samuel MACLAY, **d**-$1500, **e**-Samuel McNITT, Foster MILLIKEN, **f**-19 Feb 1827 **g**-31 Jul 1827, **h**-$973.49.75, **i**-$476.91.25, **j**-$496.58.5 to estate

Rhoda TAYLOR, b-22 Aug 1826, **c**-Rhoda TAYLOR, Samuel MACLAY, **d**-$ **e**- **f**- **g**- **h**- **i**- **j**-

John HASSLER, b-26 Aug 1826, **c**-Russel BROOKE, **d**-$500, **e**-Henry [STONER], James McCORD, **f**- **g**- **h**- **i**- **j**-

Page 105, Frame 116

William ROSS, b-26 Aug 1826, **c**-John HANAWALT, Thos. POSTLETHWAIT, **d**- **e**- **f**-21 Nov 1826 **g**-23 Jan 1829, **h**-$453.39.5, **i**-$454.83, **j**-$1.43.5, accountant

William MORRISON, b-26 Aug 1826, **c**-Henry BARRICK, John MORRISON, **d**- **e**- **f**-10 Nov 1826, **g**-22 Aug 1828/16 Jun 1837/2 Jul 1847, **h**-$2200.52/$5703.61, **i**-$2393.01/2386.90.5, **j**-$336.70.5, estate

William HENRY, b-2 Sep 1826, **c**-Robert MILLIKEN, John HENRY, **d**- **e**- **f**-8 Nov 1826, **g**-7 Mar 1834/21 Feb 1840, **h**-$2835.80.5/$2253.22.5, **i**-$2253.22.5, **j**-$1151.83, estate

James WARD, b-4 Sep 1811[sic], **c**-Foster MILLIKEN, **d**- **e**- **f**-4 Dec 1826, **g**- **h**- **i**- **j**-

Henry SNYDER, b-4 Nov 1811, **c**-Abraham ROTHROCK, Joseph KINSER, **d**- **e**- **f**-13 Apr 1827, **g**-$743.07/$6879.74/$356.43 **h**-$859.60/$8992.46/$123.99, **i**-$743.67/$6879.74/$356.43, **j**-$115.93/$2112.72/$232.44, estate

James THOMPSON, b-11 Sep 1826, **c**-James CRISWELL, **d**-$300, **e**-James MILLIKEN, Wm. MITCHELL, **f**- **g**- **h**- **i**- **j**-

William SELHEIMER, b-23 Sep 1826, **c**-Absolum SELHEIMER, **d**-$800, **e**-David REYNOLDS, Isaac FISHER, **f**-7 Oct 1826, **g**-22 Aug

1823/4 Jun 1833, **h**-$318.65/$79.85.75, **i**-$293.02.5/$88.99.75, **j**-$9.14, accountant

Christian EISENBISE, **b**-28 Sep 1826, **c**-David R. REYNOLDS, **d**-$3000, **e**-James MILLIKEN, E. B. PATTERSON, **f**- **g**- **h**- **i**- **j**-

Jonathan HAMILTON, **b**-12 Oct 1826, **c**-Alexander HAMILTON, John LOWTHER, **d**-$300, **e**-D. W. HULINGS, David REYNOLDS, **f**-9 Nov 1826, **g**-20 Oct 1827/25 Sep 1835, **h**-$396.77/$526.29, **i**-$248.23/ $536.74, **j**-$10.45.25, accountant

George HANAWALT, **b**-16 Oct 1826, **c**-Henry HANAWALT, John OLIVER, Jr., **d**-$4000, **e**-Joseph KINSEL, Joseph MILLIKEN, **f**- **g**-4 Mar 1836/4 Mar 1837, **h**-$3499.14/$116.01, **i**-$5317.71/$3599.61, **j**- $1818.57, accountant/$3483.60, accountant

James W. LYON, **b**-31 Oct 1826, **c**-William LYON, **d**-$1500, **e**-R. U. JACOBS, W. A. PATTERSON, Esq. **f**- **g**- **h**- **i**- **j**-

John MEVEY. Jr., **b**-4 Nov 1826, **c**-James CRISWELL, John WALTERS, **d**-$1000, **e**-Wm. WAKEFIELD, John HORNING, **f**-1 Dec 1826, **g**-11 Jan 1834/30 Jun 1843, **h**-$1413.63/$2268.11, **i**-$263.67/$1781.80, **j**- $486.31, estate

Page106, Frame 117

Elizabeth KAUFMAN, **b**-4 Nov 1826, **c**-Elijah DAVIS, **d**-$100, **e**-D. W. HULINGS, James CRISWELL, **f**-16 Jul 1831, **g**-16 Jul 1831, **h**- $144.69, **i**-$101.11, **j**-$43.58, estate

Joseph ORT, **b**-9 Nov 1826, **c**-David ORNER, **d**-$500, **e**-Zach DUERST, John HOFFMAN, **f**-23 Nov 1826, **g**-16 Apr 1827, **h**-$308.32, **i**- $289.07, **j**-$19.25, estate

Hezlett WRIGHT, **b**-10 Nov 1826, **c**-Samuel HORNING, **d**-$500, **e**- George WRIGHT, Christopher MACK, **f**-17 Oct 1827, **g**-17 Oct 1827, **h**-$236.80, **i**-$175.74, **j**-$61.06, estate

John YODER, **b**-17 Nov 1826, **c**-Shem ZOOK, **d**-$2500, **e**-Christian YODER, David MILLIKEN, **f**-9 Dec 1826, **g**-19 Oct 1829/3 May 1830, **h**-$1513.89/$257.04, **i**-$1266.96/$38.76, **j**-$218.27.25, estate

William STRODE, **b**-20 Nov 1826, **c**-Amor STRODE, William WAKEFIELD [order reversed in original], **d**-$1200, **e**-Jos. B. ARD, Joseph MILLIKEN, **f**-12 Dec 1826, **g**-29 Sep 1846/6 Dec 1846, **h**$2792.22.5/$260.66.5, **i**-$2483.04/$121.81, **j**-$309.18.5, estate/ $158.85.5, estate

John FRYBERGER, **b**-20 Nov 1826, **c**-Samuel MYERS, **d**-$1200, **e**-Wm. PENNEBAKER, Michael BESHOAR, **f**- **g**- **h**- **i**- **j**-

John UTLEY, b-21 Nov 1826, **c**-Thos. J. POSTLETHWAIT, **d**-$200, **e**-James DICKSON, Samuel EDMISTON, **f**-15 Dec 1826, **g**-28 Feb 1831, **h**-$254.56.25, **i**-$253.21.25, **j**-$.65.5,estate

Elias HORNING, b-21 Nov 1826, **c**-John HORNING, Joseph HORNING, **d- e- f**-20 Dec 1826/17 Dec 1827, **g**-17 Dec 1827/17 Dec 1827, **h**-$1214.09/$1312.51, **i**-$98.36.5/$1738.97, **j**-$1115.72.5, estate/$426.46.5, accountant

Patrick McCAHEN, b-21 Nov 1826, **c**-Patrick McCANNON, **d- e- f**-11 Dec 1826, **g- h- i- j-**

Joseph HOWARD, b-1 Dec 1826, **c**-Ephraim BANKS, Esq., **d- e- f- g**-30 Nov 1835, **h**-$1919.14.5, **i**-$1733.42.5, **j**-$185.72, accountant

John SPEICHER, b-8 Dec 1826, **c**-Christian SEIBER, Abraham KURTZ, **d- e- f**-15 Jan 1827, **g**-11 Oct 1828, **h**-$727.72.5, **i**-$377.23.5, **j**-$250.49, estate

Anthoney YOUNG, b-16 Dec 1826, **c**-Elizabeth YOUNG, **d- e- f- g- h- i- j-**

Page 107, Frame 118

Adam HOLLIDAY, b-18 Dec 1826, **c**-Samuel HOLLIDAY, **d- e- f- g- h- i- j-**

Robert MONTGOMERY, b-3 Jan 1827, **c**-Moses KELLY, Samuel HALLER, **d**-$1500, **e**-Philip ROTHROCK, D. W. HULINGS, **f**-1 Feb 1827, **g**-7 Mar 1831, **h**-$991.92.75, **i**-$981.91.75, **j**-$10.01, estate

William DOUGLASS, b-4 Jan 1827, **c**-Robert DOUGLASS, **d**-$200, **e**-James DOUGLASS, John MILLIKEN, **f- g- h- i- j-**

Joseph HAZLETT, b-20 Jan 1827, **c**-John HAZLETT, **d- e- f- g- h- i- j-**

Mary ROOK, b-6 Feb 1827, **c**-Amos ROOK, **d**-$100, **e**-Christopher MACK, Jos. HORNING, **f- g- h- i- j-**

Robert McCLELLAND, b-14 Feb 1827, **c**-Martha McCLELLAND, William M. HALL, **d**-$3000, **e**-Jas. KELLOGG, Jr., E. B. PATTERSON, **f**-23 Feb 1827, **g**-14 Feb 1828/10 Mar 1852, **h**-$1253.07.5/$4114.21, **i**-$1266.07/$061.03.25, **j**-$53.12.25, estate

Thomas DAVIS, b-21 Feb 1827, **c**-Francis BOGGS, George BELL, Jr., **d**-$500, **e**-Samuel MITCHELL, John HOYT, **f**-16 Dec 1828, **g**-18 Dec 1828/23 Jun 1834, **h**-$384.18/$195.31, **i**-$237.70/$157.25, **j**-$38.08, estate

Nancy GIBSON, b-6 Mar 1827, **c**-Jacob HOOVER, Christian HOOVER, Jr., **d**-$400, **e**-Christian HOOVER, James MILLIKEN, **f**-6 Apr 1827, **g**-14 Mar 1829, **h**-$269.36.5, **i**-$136.23.5, **j**-$133.13, estate

Thomas BOYD, b-16 Mar 1827, **c**-Arthur McKNIGHT, **d**-$200, **e**-Jonathan FRY, Stephen REYNOLDS, **f**-21 May 1827, **g**-17 Oct 1828, **h**-$58.27.5, **i**-$59.31, **j**-$1.05.5, accountant

Randolph WOODEN, b-17 Apr 1827, **c**-John M. BARTON, **d**-$600, **e**-John HAMOND[sic], Nathl. WILSON, **f**-5 May 1827, **g**-5 Oct 1833, **h**-$916.66.5, **i**-$837.72, **j**-$78.94.5, estate

Michael REIGLE, b-23 Mar 1827, **c**- **d**- **e**- **f**- **g**- **h**- **i**- **j**-

Abraham BRUBAKER, b-17 Mar 1827, **c**-David WEAVER, **d**- **e**- **f**-4 Apr 1827. **g**-3- Kim 1929. **h**-$975/38/5. **i**-$121.65,,**j**-$743.72.5, estate

Page 108, Frame 119
James INNIS, b-22 Nov 1826, **c**-Samuel McCULLOCH, Charles TOWER, **d**- **e**- **f**-22 Nov 1826, **g**-23 Jan 1828, **h**-$694.47, **i**-$392.29, **j**-$202.18, estate

Henry ALEXANDER, b-19 Apr 1827, **c**-Josiah ALEXANDER, **d**-$200, **e**-Saml. W. TAYLOR, Francis BOGGS, **f**- **g**- **h**- **i**- **j**-

Andrew MAYES, b-15 May 1827, **c**-William P. [MACLERY], William SHAW, **d**-$ **e**- **f**-29 Jun 1827 **g**- **h**- **i**- **j**-

Robert McMEEN, b-26 Apr 1827, **c**- **d**- **e**- **f**- **g**- **h**- **i**- **j**-

Manasses RAMSEY, b-19 Jun 1827, **c**-Nancy RAMSEY, **d**-$800, **e**-Paul LAUGHLIN, Mathew LAUGHLIN, **f**-4 Jul 1827, **g**- **h**- **i**- **j**-

Michael GARBER, b-20 Jun 1827, **c**-Shem SHARP, **d**-$2000, **e**-Jos. HOSTETLER, Stephen KURTZ, **f**- **g**- **h**- **i**- **j**-

Elizabeth MITCHELL, b-10 Aug 1827, **c**-James MITCHELL, **d**- **e**- **f**- **g**- **h**- **i**- **j**-

Lydia COOKSON, b-20 Aug 1827, **c**- **d**- **e**- **f**- **g**- **h**- **i**- **j**-

Jacob BRIDGE, b-22 Aug 1827, **c**-James ALEXANDER, **d**-$500, **e**-D. W. HULINGS, Henry SWARTZELL, **f**- **g**- **h**- **i**- **j**-

James WILKIN, b-23 Aug 1827, **c**-Samuel COUCH, **d**-$500, **e**-Edward COUCH, Richard MONTGOMERY, **f**- **g**- **h**- **i**- **j**-

Catherine MARKLEY, b-4 Sep 1827, **c**-James McCLINTIC, **d**-$1200, **e**-Joseph MARTIN, John THOMPSON, **f**- **g**- **h**- **i**- **j**-

William LYON, b-7 Sep 1827, **c**-Joseph B. ARD, George A. LYON, **d**- **e**- **f**-17 Nov 1827, **g**-26 Jul 1832, **h**-$1789.10.5, **i**-$1155.89.5, **j**-$633.21, estate

Page 109, Frame 120 [duplicated on Frame 121]
George MOORE, b-11 Sep 1827, **c**-Francis MOORE, **d**- **e**- **f**- **g**- **h**- **i**- **j**-

Robert HIEGHET [reversed in original], **b**-25 Sep 1827, **c**-Francis McCOY, Esq., **d- e- f- g**-18 Nov 1827, **h- i- j-**

John MAXWELL, **b**-30 Sep 1827, **c**-William HORRELL, **d**-$500, **e**-Jos. MARTIN, Saml. EDMISTON, **f**-11 Oct 1827, **g**-13 Sep 1828/19 Jan 1830, **h**-$312.87.5/173.34, **i**-$147.53/173.32, **j**-$.02, [no assignment]

Jacob STOLL [or STOTT], **b**-15 Sep 1827, **C**-William TOWNSEND, **d**-$500, **e**-Magdalena STOLL, D. W. HULINGS, **f**-12 Oct 1827, **g- h- i- j-**

Stephen GEORGE, **b**-19 Sep 1827, **c**-William McALLISTER, **d**-$400, **e**-Joseph MILLIKEN, Wm. McCAY, Esq., **f**-21 Nov 1827, **g**-29 Jun 1829, **h**-$1269.80, **i**-$999.93, **j**-$279.87, estate

George HOOPS, **b**-22 Sep 1827, **c**-Samuel GRAHAM, **d**-$1500, **e**-Jos. B. ARD, Geo. McCULLOCH, **f**-5 Oct 1827, **g**-10 Mar 1829, **h**-$131.70.5, **i**-$107.26.5,**j**-$24.44, estate

James W. LYON, **b**-13 Oct 1827, **c**-George A. LYON, **d**-$1500, **e**-James CRISWELL, Casper DULL, **f**-21 Nov 1826/25 Dec 1827, **g**-20 Dec 1828/19 Feb 1829, **h**-$699.69/$434.00.75, **i**-$272.09.25/$167.19, **j**-$266.81.25, estate

William BELL, **b**-18 Oct 1827, **c**-John H. BELL, Johnston BELL, **d**-$1500, **e**-Margaret BELL, George SIGLER, **f**-27 Nov 1827, **g**-17 Mar 1830, **h**-$851.88, **i**-$372.42, **j**-$479.46. estate

Samuel ALEXANDER, **b**-19 Oct 1827, **c**-Ann ALEXANDER, Henry B. TAYLOR, **d**-$1500, **e**-S. W. TAYLOR, James MILLIKEN, **f- g- h- i- j-**

John SHULTZ, **b**-26 Oct 1827, **c**-Henry MATTOCKS, **d**-$300, **e**-William STEWART, Thos. JOHNSTON, **f**-21 Nov 1827, **g- h- i- j-**

Martha BEATTY, **b**-26 Oct 1827, **c**-David COULTER, **d- e- f- g- h- i- j-**

David SEMPLE, **b**-30 Oct 1827, **c**-Rachel SEMPLE, **d**-$1000, **e**-Hugh ALEXANDER, James MILLIKEN, **f- g- h- i- j-**

Page 110, Frame 122

George BRATTON, **b**-31 Oct 1827, **c**-John DOUGHERTY, **d**-$1500, **e**-J. H. STACKPOLE, James BRATTON, **f**-22 Nov 1827, **g**-13 Dec 1830, **h**-$1247.10, **i**-$1360.69, **j**-$113.59, accountant

Christian SEIBER, Jr., **b**-3 Nov 1827, **c**-Christian SEIBER, Sr., **d**-$2000, **e**-Christian [KING], D. W. HULINGS, **f**-1 Dec 1827, **g**-18 Mar 1829, **h**-$838.68.5, **i**-$379.85, **j**-$458.83.5, estate

George SWARTZ, **b**-8 Nov 1827, **c**-Sophia SWARTZ, **d- e- f- g- h- i- j-**

Andrew CALDWELL, **b**-14 Nov 1827, **c**-John OLIVER, Jr., Amor STRODE, **d**-$3000, **e**-Wm. MITCHELL, Wm. McCAY, **f**-18 Dec 1827, **g**- **h**- **i**- **j**-

Henry RICKEBAUGH, **b**-21 Nov 1827, **c**-John JAMEISON, Esq., **d**- **e**- **f**- **g**- **h**- **i**- **j**-

Philip AULTZ, **b**-15 Dec 1827, **c**-John HARTZLER, **d**-$400, **e**-Joseph KENNEGY, Jacob BECK, **f**-12 Jan 1828, **g**- **h**- **i**- **j**-

Jacob WISE, **b**-11 Jan 1828, **c**-Emanuel WISE, **d**-$500, **e**-S. RODEBAUGH, F. W. KINSLOE, **f**-11 Feb 1828, **g**- **h**- **i**- **j**-

James ALLISON, **b**-14 Jan 1828, **c**-Robert THOMPSON, Robert MILLIKEN, **d**-$1000, **e**-Joseph KYLE, Joseph MILLIKEN, **f**-12 Feb 1828, **g**-17 Jun 1829, **h**-$764.86, **i**-$57.39, **j**-$707.47, heirs

Edward O'FRIEL, **b**-14 Jan 1828, **c**-Arthur O'FRIEL, Charles DUFFY,**d**-$1500, **e**-James MILLIKEN, Joseph MILLIKEN, **f**- **g**- **h**- **i**- **j**-

Daniel [GASTWINT], **b**-14 Jan 1828, **c**-Magdalena [GASTWINT], John SELMAN, **d**-$, **e**-11 Feb 1828, **f**-9 Sep 1831/26 Dec 1836, **g**- **h**- **i**-$8.37, **j**-$8.37, accountant

Christian YODER, **b**-22 Jan 1828, **c**-David ZOOK, John PEACHY, **d**-$3000, **e**-Jacob BYLER, Jacob ZOOK, **f**-19 Oct 1829, **g**-13 Oct 1829, **h**-$3043.36.5, **i**-$1613.73.5, **j**-$1429.63, estate

James KIRK, **b**-23 Jan 1828, **c**-William KIRK, **d**-$3000, **e**-Samuel McCULLOCH, James WALLACE, **f**-22 Feb 1828, **g**-24 Mar 1837, **h**-$4225.64.75, **i**-$564.61.5, **j**-$3661.03.25, estate

Page 111, Frame 123
James MACKLIN, **b**-24 Jan 1828, **c**-John ATKINSON, **d**-$1500, **e**-David LUSK, Cyrus STINE, **f**- **g**- **h**- **i**- **j**-

Thomas SMITH, **b**-26 Jan 1828, **c**-James B. SMITH, Peter SMITH, **d**-$2000, **e**-James KELLOGG, C. MARK, **f**- **g**- **h**- **i**- **j**-

Joseph JACOBS, **b**-28 Jan 1828, **c**-Robert U. JACOBS, William M. HALL, **d**-$5000, **e**-James MILLIKEN, Joseph MILLIKEN, **f**-5 Feb 1828, **g**-4 Jan 1829/6 Apr 1833, **h**-$589.61.25/$1736.79, **i**-$632.08/$1508.11.25, **j**-$42.47, accountant/$228.67.5, estate

Sarah WILLIS, **b**-13 Feb 1828, **c**-Hiram WILLIS, James McCORD, **d**-$500, **e**-Francis McCOY, F. W. KINSLOE, **f**-11 Mar 1828, **g**- **h**- **i**- **j**-

David BEALE, Esq., **b**-14 Feb 1828, **c**-David BEALE, Joshua BEALE, Jesse BEALE, **d**- **e**- **f**-10 Mar 1828, **g**-20 Feb 1839, **h**-$2280.66/$2648.12/$5306.43/$2079.73, **i**-$596.47/$348.47/$2612.48/$824.52, **j**-$1683.19/$2299.65/$2694.95/1255.21, estate

William PICKENS, **b**-16 Feb 1828, **c**-John HANTZLER, **d**-$400, **e**-Wm. P. ELLIOTT, Joshua WAY, **f**-4 Apr 1828, **g**- **h**- **i**- **j**-

James NORTH, **b**-16 Feb 1828, **c**-Lewis E. NORTH, **d**-$1500, **e**-Francis JORDAN, Henry EISENBISE, **f**-7 Mar 1828, **g**-13 Jan 1829, **h**-$191.24, **i**-$114.86.5, **j**-$76.57.5, estate

James BELL, **b**-23 Jan 1828, **c**-John BELL, Samuel BELL, **d**- **e**- **f**- **g**-23 Dec 1830, **h**-$23.40, **i**-$81.70.75, **j**-$58.20, accountant

Thomas RIDER, **b**-26 Feb 1828, **c**-William GILSON, **d**-$1500, **e**-George GILLIFORD, John WILLIAMS, Jr., **f**- **g**-22 Jan 1827, **h**-$473.94.5, **i**-$106.47.5, **j**-$307.47, estate

Thomas ORR, **b**-1 Mar 1828, **c**-William BEATTY, John McDOWELL, **d**-$800, **e**-James MILLIKEN, James KELLOGG, **f**-29 Mar 1828, **g**-18 Mar 1830/19 Oct 1831, **h**-$611.03.5/$544.61.5, **i**-$258.74.5/103.12/ **j**-$441.49.5, estate

Samuel MYERS, **b**-7 Mar 1828, **c**-John MYERS, Samuel MYERS, Jacob [ELIF], **d**-$5000, **e**-Wm. PENNEBAKER, James MILLIKEN, **f**-31 Mar 1828, **g**-6 Nov 1830/7 Dec 1833/ /15 Jan 1838/23 Jan 1828, **h**-$7268.61/$29.56/$4135.06/$2473.48.5/$3779.45, **i**-$5743.52/$33.00/ $1317.62/$2573.86/$1378.34, **j**-$2401.11, estate

Doct. Ezra DOTY, **b**-12 Mar 1828, **c**-Daniel CHRISTY, **d**-$10,000, **e**-Amos GUSTINE, Christian SEIBER, **f**-22 Apr 1828, **g**- **h**- **i**- **j**-

Page 112, Frame 124

John A. CRANE, **b**-15 Mar 1828, **c**-Joseph [CASTLE], **d**-$100, **e**-David REYNOLDS, James KINSLOE, **f**- **g**- **h**- **i**- **j**-

Ferdinand A. MELSHEIMER], **b**-15 Mar 1828, **c**-Mary MELSHEIMER, William M. HALL, **d**-$5000, **e**-Joseph MARTIN, James MILLIKEN, **f**-20 Mar 1828, **g**-6 Mar 1829/14 Mar 1832, **h**-$2859.05/$2949.50.5, **i**-$670.20.25/$243.19.5, **j**-$2706.58.75, estate

Alexander COULTER, **b**-19 Mar 1828, **c**-George McCULLOCH, Francis McCLURE, **d**-$2000, **e**-Joseph MARTIN, Francis McCOY, **f**-30 Apr 1828, **g**-18 Mar 1829,3 Dec 1835, **h**-$541.17/$179.28, **i**-$440.73/$730.11, **j**-$550.82, accountants

Daniel SHREFFLER, **b**-19 Mar 1828, **c**-Andrew McDONALD, **d**-$1200, **e**-David SHEITZ, Robert JONES, **f**-17 Apr 1828, **g**-11 Mar 1831, **h**-$600.81, **i**-$407.00, **j**-$193.84, estate

John RIDDLE, **b**-5 Apr 1828, **c**-Samuel RIDDLE, **d**- **e**- **f**- **g**- **h**- **i**- **j**-

Abraham GARBER, **b**-7 Apr 1828, **c**-Jacob GARBER, Benjamin GARBER, **d**- **e**- **f**-28 Nov 1828, **g**-9 Sep 1829, **h**-$1938.90, **i**-$917.67, **j**-$1021.23, estate

David HOOLY, **b**-7 Apr 1828, **c**-David ZOOK, John KING, **d**-$5000, **e**-Samuel KING, Shem ZOOK, **f**-22 Apr 1828, **g**-10 Aug 1829, **h**-$1222.52, **i**-$611.72.5, **j**-$610.79.5, estate

John SHOOK, **b**-15 Apr 1828, **c**-Philip POWELL, John ROTHROCK, **d**-$1500, **e**-Robert ROBISON, John [FILSON], **f**-17 May 1828, **g**-8 Feb 1831/2 May 1835, **h**-$1146.51.25/$1159.37.25, **i**-$581.61/$1041.12, **j**-$118.25.25, estate

Thomas HENDERSON, **b**-22 Apr 1828, **c**-David GILSON, **d**-$200, **e**-William GILSON, John CROZIER, **f**- **g**- **h**- **i**- **j**-

John BRANISHOLS, **b**-22 Apr 1828, **c**-Frederick BRENISHOLS[sic], **d**-$500, **e**-Andrew COLER, Lewis EVANS, **f**- **g**- **h**- **i**- **j**-

Robert STEVENSON, **b**-23 Apr 1828, **c**-Thomas R. McKEE, John McKEE, **d**-$1500, **e**-James POE, James MILLIKEN, **f**-20 May 1828, **g**-19 Mar 1832, **h**-$743.17.75, **i**-$521.61.5, **j**- $221.56.25, estate

Joseph JONES, **b**-26 Apr 1828, **c**-James GALBRAITH, **d**-$500, **e**-David GLENN, David BARTON, **f**-18 Oct 1828, **g**-5 Jun 1829, **h**-$218.68, **i**-$156.15.25, **j**-$62.52.75, estate

Page 113, Frame 125

William OWENS, **b**-6 May 1828, **c**-Daniel OWENS, **d**-$600, **e**-James POLLOCK, William OWENS, **f**-5 Jun 1828/17 Jan 1844, **g**-30 Apr 1845, **h**- **i**-$217.29, **j**-$217.29, account

John FRYBARGER, **b**-13 May 1828, **c**-John FRYBARGER, **d**-$1200, **e**-Henry G. HESSER, David PICKEBAUGH, **f**-4 Mar 1829, **g**-4 Mar 1829/13 Jan 1828, **h**-$633.36.5/$141.10, **i**-$677.87/$287.14, **j**-$44.50.5/$135.54, accountant

John BUSHY, **b**-15 May 1828, **c**-William PENNEBAKER, **d**-$1000, **e**-John MYERS, Henry G. HESSER, **f**- **g**- **h**- **i**- **j**-

Samuel BELFORD, **b**-26 May 1828, **c**-John WRIGHT, **d**-$200, **e**-James DICKSON, Jane BELFORD, **f**-23 Jun 1828, **g**-4 Mar 1829, **h**-$120.19.5, **i**-$117.48.5, **j**-$2.71.5, estate

William C. KELLY, **b**-4 Jun 1828, **c**-Robert PATTERSON, **d**-$1000, **e**-George McCULLOCH, Christ. MARK, **f**-30 Aug 1828, **g**-2 Oct 1827, **h**- **i**- **j**-$2809.45.5, accountant

Robert McALLISTER, b-4 Jun 1828, c-Robert PATTERSON, d- e- f-16 Apr 1829, g-13 Feb 1832, h-$631.28.5, i-$1130.98, j-$499.69.5, accountant

Jacob YODER, Jr., b-17 Jun 1828, c-John YODER, David KAUFMAN, d-$2000, e-Jacob YODER, James MILLIKEN, f-1 Jul 1828, g-9 Nov 1830, h-$1987.27, i-$450.39, j-$1536.90, estate

George DUNCAN, b-20 Jun 1828, c-Joseph ANDERSON, d-$200, e-James McCORD, Francis McCOY, f-19 Jul 1828, g- h- i- j-

Samuel BRYSON, b-4 Jul 1828, c-James BRYSON, d-$1000, e-Saml. McDOWELL, E. B. PATTERSON, f- g- h- i- j-

Thomas McDONALD, b-14 Jul 1828, c- d- e- f- g- h- i- j-

Hugh REED, b-24 Jul 1828, c-Robert REED, d-$600, e-Geo. McCULLOCH, Saml. EDMISTON, f- g- h- i- j-

Henry RICKEBACH, b-2 Aug 1828, c-David RICKEBACH, d-$200, e-Samuel REYNOLDS, F. W. KINSLOE, f-21 Nov 1827, g- h- i- j-

Page 114, Frame 126

John JAMISON, b-8 Aug 1828, c-David McCLURE, William SHARRON, d-$2000, e-David SHELLEBARGER, Henry [LAURER or LAUVER?], f-18 Aug 1828, g- h- i- j-

James REED, b-13 Aug 1828, c-William REED, Thomas REED, d-$, e- f- g- h- i- j-

John HOYT, b-16 Aug 1828, c-John HOYT, d- e- f- g- h- i- j-

Andrew THOMPSON, b-18 Aug 1828, c-John THOMPSON, d-$500, e-Benjn. WALLACE, David OWENS, f-18 Sep 1828, g- h- i- j-

Alexander WORK, b-18 Aug 1828, c-Robert WORK, d-$200, e-David GLENN, Enoch BARTON, f-19 Sep 1828, g- h- i- j-

Sarah MAGILL, b-19 Aug 1828, c-William TURNER, d- e- f- g- h- i- j-

Robert ELTON, b-20 Aug 1828, c-Revel ELTON, d- e- f- g- h- i- j-

Philip MARKS, b-29 Aug 1828, c-Christopher MARK[sic], d-$400, e-James KELLOGG, Nancy MARK, f-2 Sep 1828, g-28 Dec 1829, h-$591.15, i-$219.62.5, j-$371.53, estate

Joseph SIGLE[sic] [suspect SIGLER, clerk error?], b-29 Aug 1828, c-William ROBISON, John M. FULLER, d-$500, e-James MILLIKEN, Joseph MILLIKEN, f-29 Aug 1828/27 Oct 1828, g- h- i- j-

Daniel KESSLER, b-3 Nov 1828, c-William PENNEBAKER, d- e- f-20 Aug 1832, g-20 Aug 1832, h-$895.88, i-$834.45, j-$61.43, estate

David COULTER, b-20 Aug 1828, c-Irwin COULTER, d- e- f- g- h- i- j-

Henry **HILTERBRAND, b**-13 Sep 1828, **c**-Mary HILTERBRAND, Jacob
MARKS, **d**-$1000, **e**-Robert JONES, F. W. KINSLOE, **f**-6 Oct 1828,
g-23 Nov 1830, **h**-$603.10.25, **i**-$372.42.25, **j**-$230.68, estate

<u>Page 115, Frame 127</u>
William ALLISON, b-18 Sep 1828, **c**-Elizabeth ALLISON, James
BRISBEN, William McMANIGIL, **d**-$4000, **e**-Foster MILLIKEN,
James THOMPSON, **f**-18 Jan 1840, **g**-1 Jul 1840/7 Dec 1840, **h**-
$424.08/$2377.12.25, **i**-$191.14/$2567.47, **j**-$190.35, administrators
Thomas WHERRY, b-19 Sep 1828, **c**-Thomas KERR, **d**-$600, **e**-Neal
McCOY, David REYNOLDS, **f**-13 Oct 1828, **g- h- i- j-**
John McCOY, b-19 Sep 1828, **c**-Neal McCOY, **d**-$1000, **e**-Thomas
KERR, Geo. McCULLOCH, **f**-17 Oct 1828, **g**-20 Apr 1831, **h**-
$1123.34.75, **i**-$472.72.5, **j**-$650.62.25, estate
William F. McMILLEN, b-19 Sep 1828, **c**-Thomas KERR, **d**-$1000, **e**-
Neal McCOY, Wm. McMILLEN, **f**-13 Oct 1828, **g**-6 Aug 1840, **h**-
$198.32, **i**-$58.50, **j**-$139.82, estate
Peter CAVENAUGH, b-23 Sep 1828, **c**-Francis MURPHY, **d**-$200, **e**-Jos.
B. ARD, F. W. KINSLOE, **f- g- h- i- j-**
Bartholemew DAVIS, b-25 Sep 1828, **c**-Richard MILES, **d**-$300, **e**-James
MILLIKEN, John MONTGOMERY, **f- g- h- i- j-**
Alexander WALLACE, b-1 Oct 1828, **c**-Benjamin WALLACE, **d**-$500,
e-M. H. WEAVER, D. W. HULINGS, **f**-31 Oct 1828, **g- h- i- j-**
James McHARY, b-4 Oct 1828, **c**-James McMURY [Compiler's note:
These two names seem to be quite similar. Neither one appears to be
a dominant name in the area. Possible clerk error?] **d**-$500, **e**-F. W.
KINSLOE, Wm. CARTER, **f**-9 Oct 1828, **g**-9 Oct 1828, **h**-$134.50, **i**-
$18.94, **j**-$115.56, estate
John OBERHOLSER, b-4 Oct 1828, **c**-Joseph RENNOLDS, **d**-$400, **e**-
David CLEGG, Philip KAUFMAN, **f**-21 Nov 1828, **g**-17 Nov 1829, **h**-
$459.59, **i**-$459.59, **j-**
Josiah McMEEN, b-11 Oct 1828, **c**-Samuel McMEEN, **d**-$2000, **e**-Wm.
McALLISTER, Ephraim BANKS, **f**-23 Apr 1830/3 Nov 1828, **g**-23
Apr 1830, **h**-$1595.10, **i**-$1376.06.5, **j**-$219.02.5, estate
Mary McCOY, b-21 Oct 1828, **c**-William McLAUGHLIN, **d**-$, **e- f**-30
Jun 1837/15 Dec 1828, **g- h- i- j-**
Elizabeth FLEMING, b-29 Oct 1828, **c**-Joseph GETTYS, **d**-$500, **e**-
James GIBBONEY, John SMITH, **f**-19 Nov 1828, **g**-17 May 1837, **h**-
$307.04.5, **i**-$305.32, **j**-$1.72.5, estate

Page 116, Frame 128

James P. BARTON, b-16 Nov 1828, c-David GLENN, d-$300, e-Enoch BARTON, John BURDGE, f-16 Nov 1829, g-19 Feb 1835/3 Dec 1839, h-$261.80/$103.00, i-$330.15/$141.99, j-$39.99, accountant

Joseph ANDERSON, b-8 Nov 1828, c-James McCORD, Geo. A. LYON, d-$2000, e-Jos. MARTIN, Francis McCOY, f-26 Nov 1828, g-3 Oct 1835, h-$1624.97, i-$1687.15, j-$62.18, accountants

Major John IRWIN, b-8 Nov 1828, c-Samuel PURVIANCE, d-$8000, e-Sarah IRWIN, E. B. PATTERSON, f- g- h- i- j-

Thomas LEONARD, b-10 Nov 1828, c-Alexander BAILEY, d-$500, e-A. S. WILSON, Wm. COGGSHALL, f-10 Dec 1828, g-15 Oct 1829, h-$89.08, i-$47.31, j-$41.77, estate

Catherine E. CLOSE, b-19 Nov 1828, c-Peter CLOSE, Adam CLOSE, d- e- f-30 Dec 1828, g- h- i- j-

Jacob STOLL, b-1 Dec 1828, c-Michael H. WEAVER, d-$500, e-Foster MILLIKEN, M. H. WEAVER, f- g-7 Nov 1834, h-$344.96, i-$218.56, j-$126.40, estate

Robert SCOTT, b-6 Dec 1828, c-Robert FARRELL, d-$300, e-John H. POOL, G. YODER, f-6 Dec 1828, g- h- i- j-

John KYLE, b-9 Dec 1828, c-Andrew KYLE, Moses KYLE, d-$1000, e-Samuel HIME, Francis JORDAN, f-21 Jan 1829, g-3 Feb 1824/12 Sep 1837, h-$2217.64/$3122.84, i-$2985.61.5/$1019.45, j-$2103.39, estate

Alexander McKINSTRY, b-9 Dec 1828, c-Sarah McKINSTRY, James McDONALD, d- e- f-30 Dec 1828, g- h- i- j-

Charlotte WOLBERT, b-31 Dec 1828, c-Elijah DAVIS, Solomon SEACHRIST, d-$100, e-Solomon SEAGRIST[sic], John NIECE, f-16 Jul 1831, g-16 Jul 1831, h-$74.44, i-$61.41.5, j-$13.03.5, accountant

Joshua DAVIS, b-7 Jan 1829, c-James DAVIS, Samuel SHARON, d-$1500, e-John McALLISTER, Abraham [VERNORNEER], f-21 Jan 1829, g- h- i- j-

Benjn. KEPNER (Mercht.), b-12 Jan 1829, c-John RICE, d-$15,000, e-Benjn. KEPNER, Geo. RICE, f-9 Feb 1829, g-26 Jun 1840, h-$15,172.54, i-$2046.02, j-$13,126.52, estate

Page 117, Frame 129

Margaret CUNEN, b-16 Jan 1829, c-John McMINN, d- e- f-22 Apr 1829, g-5 Oct 1829, h-$1823.45.5, i-$473.10, j-$1350.35.5, estate

John HOUDER, b-20 Jan 1829, c-David ZOOK, Joseph HAFFLEY, d- e- f-2 Jan 1838, g-25 Sep 1841, h-$5940.35, i-$232.97, j-$5707.38, estate

Peter CAPP, b-21 Jan 1829, c-George CAPP, Henry GROCE, d-$1500, e-Joseph LEIDER, John ELDER, f-21 Jan 1829, g-15 Mar 1831, h-$1824.66.75, i-$1892.04, j-$67.32.25, accountant

Zephaniah STARKS, b-24 Jan 1829, c-Robert STARKS, d-$500, E-R. U. JACOBS, Saml. COMFORT, f- g- h- i- j-

James MAYES, b-18 Feb 1829, c-James MILLIKEN, d-$1000, e-A. S. WILSON, James CRISWELL, f- 26 Feb 1829, g-20 Mar 1830, h-$600.40, i-$392.32, j-$208.08, estate

Charles B. MELDRUM, b-21 Feb 1829, c-James KINSLOE, d-$500, e-F. W. KINSLOE, James KELLOGG, f-21 Mar 1829, g- h- i- j-

Mary PATTERSON, b-25 Feb 1829, c-Samuel [KINSELY], d-$100, e-Wm. PATTERSON, F. W. KINSLOE, f-4 Mar 1829, g- h- i- j-

John HANAWALT, b-3 Mar 1829, c-George HANAWALT, Thos. J. POSTLETHWAIT, d- e- f-31 Mar 1829, g-28 Sep 1832, h-$2120.78.75, i-$2084.92, j-$35.86.75, estate

Gawin FROW, b-6 Mar 1829, c-James FREW[sic], d-$800, e-Foster MILLIKEN, Christn. MARK, f-28 Mar 1829, g-5 Mar 1830, h-$386.60, i-$307.76, j-$78.84, estate

Jane RIDDLE, b-11 Mar 1829, c-Thomas RIDDLE, d-$, e- f-19 Aug 1829, g- h- i- j-

Charles BURKHOLDER, b-17 Mar 1829, c-Mariah BURKHOLDER, John BURKHOLDER, d-$1000, e-Henry BURKHOLDER, Jos. MILLIKEN, f-4 Apr 1829, g-28 Jun 1833, h-$1307.96.5, i-$286.88.5, j-$1021.08, estate

Thomas MITCHELL, b-23 Mar 1829, c-George MITCHELL, James McDONALD, Andrew BRATTON, d- e- f-22 Apr 1829, g-3 Dec 1836/28 Feb 1838, h-$6739.73/$1003.70, i-$7611.07.75/$1175.40, j-$871.34.75/$171.70, accountants

Page 118, Frame 130

John SAILOR, b-14 Apr 1829, c-Elizabeth SAILOR, d- e- f-18 Nov 1829/25 May 1829, g- h- i- j-

William McCRUM, b-14 Apr 1829, c-Joseph McCRUM, John McCRUM, d- e- f-11 May 1829, g-19 Jan 1830, h-$1417.51, i-$629.62.5, j-$809.88.5, estate

Margaret MILLER, b-22 Apr 1829, c-David HARSHBARGER, d-$2000, e-Henry WILSON, John MONTGOMERY, f-19 May 1829, g-6 Nov 1830, h-$155.16, i-$43.20, j-$111.96, estate

Adam C. SMITH, **b**-22 Apr 1829, **c**-James McDONALD, James WHARTON, **d**-$1000, **e**-Irwin COULTER, Charles BRATTON, **f**-19 May 1829, **g**-29 Aug 1832, **h**-$986.24.25, **i**-$384.73, **j**-$591.51.25, estate

John WITMER, **b**-2 May 1829, **c**-Joseph LEIDER, **d**-$750, **e**-Christian SEACHRIST, John [EPPRICH, EPPRICT?], **f**- **g**- **h**- **i**- **j**-

Mary WITMER, **b**-2 May 1829, **c**-Joseph LEIDER, **d**-$1500, **e**-Christian SEACHRIST, John EPPRICT, **f**-2 May 1829, **g**-22 Apr 1831, **h**-$130.69, **i**-$207.04.25, **j**-$76.35.25, accountant

John MILLER, **b**-5 May 1829, **c**-David MILLER, **d**-$12,000, **e**-Nicholas MILLER, Michael YUTZEY, **f**-15 May 1829, **g**-5 May 1830, **h**-$3112.79, **i**-$2680.50, **j**-$432.29, estate

Robert JONES, **b**-6 May 1829, **c**-Edmund JONES, **d**-$500, **e**-Simon JONES, David MILLIKEN, **f**-5 Jun 1829, **g**- **h**- **i**- **j**-

Jacob MYERS, **b**-18 May 1829, **c**-Michael MYERS, **d**-$400, **e**-Alexander BOGGS, John DILLEN, **f**-16 Jun 1829, **g**-2 Oct 1833, **h**-$225.07, **i**-$217.73.75, **j**-$7.33.5, estate

John AKELY, **b**-25 May 1829, **c**-Benjamin AKELY, **d**-$200, **e**-Amos GUSTINE, Jesse JACOBS, **f**-19 Jun 1829, **g**- **h**- **i**- **j**-

James ALLISON, **b**-27 May 1829, **c**-Joseph KYLE, **d**- **e**- **f**-22 Apr 1828, **g**-6 Dec 1839, **h**-$1873.98, **i**-$1691.00, **j**-$1882.98, heirs

John ALLISON, **b**-27 May 1829, **c**-George LEITER, **d**-$4000, **e**-Michael SHELEY, Jacob GRABILL, **f**-27 May 1829, **g**-1 Jun 1830/17 Dec 1830, **h**-$1108.22.5/$998.73, **i**-$883.27.5/$967.70, **j**-$31.03, estate

John ARNOLD, **b**- **c**-Nicholas ARNOLD, John ARNOLD, **d**- **e**- **f**-18 Jun 1829, **g**-19 Apr 1830, **h**-$876.19, **i**-$566.83.5, **j**-$309.25, estate

Page 119, Frame 131
E. B. PATTERSON, **b**-30 May 1829, **c**-Mary M. PATTERSON, **d**- **e**- **f**-6 Jul 1829, **g**- **h**- **i**- **j**-

John DOUGHERTY, **b**-14 Jul 1829, **c**-John DOUGHERTY, **d**-$1000, **e**-Peter DOUGHERTY, Thos. OSBOURN, **f**-14 Aug 1830, **g**- **h**- **i**- **j**-

William KENNARD, **b**-20 Jul 1829, **c**-George KENNARD, **d**-$300, **e**-Henry SWARTZELL, Christian HOFFMAN, **f**- **g**- **h**- **i**- **j**-

Francis FLANEGAN [FLANOGAN?], **b**-30 Jul 1829, **c**-David LUSK, **d**-$500, **e**-Jacob SPEAR, James DICKSON, **f**- **g**- **h**- **i**- **j**-

Augustus HARR, **b**-23 Jul 1829, **c**-Albert LICHTENTHALER, **d**-$400, **e**-Samuel [HEIM], **f**-19 Aug 1829, **g**-5 Dec 1832, **h**-$543.80.75, **i**-$481.11, **j**-$62.69.75, estate

James BRYSON, **b**-25 Jul 1829, **c**-Samuel McDOWELL, **d**-$200, **e**-David MILLIKEN, James CHRISTY, **f**-22 Aug 1829, **g**- **h**- **i**- **j**-

John HOLMAN, **b**-29 Jul 1829, **c**-John WALLACE, **d**-$300, **e**-William KIRK, Geo. McCULLOCH, **f**- **g**- **h**- **i**- **j**-

Peter [McGIME?], **b**-4 Aug 1829, **c**-Peter McGIME, **d**-$100, **e**-John McLAUGHLIN, Patrick HUGHS, **f**- **g**- **h**- **i**- **j**-

Robert GLASS, **b**-5 Aug 1829, **c**-John STERRETT, **d**-$4000, **e**-Wm. RAMSEY, Geo. W. CRISSMAN, **f**- **g**-7 Oct 1845, **h**-$1597.94, **i**-$792.88.5, **j**-$805.05, accountant

Samuel CAMPBELL, **b**-14 Aug 1829, **c**-Michael H. WEAVER, **d**-$1000, **e**-Foster MILLIKEN, Andrew BARR, **f**-2 Sep 1829, **g**- **h**- **i**- **j**-

John GRABIL, **b**-17 Aug 1829, **c**-Solomon HAAS, **d**-$300, **e**-Valentine HAAS, Wm. PENNEBAKER, **f**-19 Sep 1829, **g**-5 Oct 1833, **h**-$179.67, **i**-$95.44.5, **j**-$84.22.5, estate

Michael SHERK, **b**-28 Aug 1829, **c**-Joseph RENNELS, John HOFFMAN, **d**-$6000, **e**-Joseph SHERK, Michael SHERK, **f**-19 Oct 1829, **g**-20 Apr 1830, **h**-$6264.27, **i**-$6264.27, **j**-

Page 120, Frame 132

Margaret BEARD, **b**-18 Aug 1829, **c**-George MITCHELL, **d**-$300, **e**-James McDONALD, Elijah DAVIS, **f**- **g**- **h**- **i**- **j**-

Bartholomew MURPHY, **b**-31 Aug 1829, **c**-Patrick BELLEW, **d**-$300, **e**-Francis MURPHY, Christn. GLINNEN, **f**- **g**- **h**- **i**- **j**-

Robert STURGEON, **b**-2 Sep 1829, **c**-John JOHNSTON, **d**-$600, **e**-Levi REYNOLDS, Foster MILLIKEN, **f**-21 Jan 1830, **g**-9 May 1831, **h**-$337.82, **i**-$352.77, **j**-$14.95, accountant

John WHITE, **b**-10 Sep 1829, **c**-Mary WHITE, **d**-$200, **c**-C. GLENNEN, Thos. HATFIELD, **f**- **g**- **h**- **i**- **j**-

Barbara BEALE, **b**-12 Sep 1829, **c**-William MILLIKEN, **d**-$2000, **e**-James HUGH, Stewart LAW, **f**-12 Oct 1829, **g**- **h**- **i**- **j**-

James KENNAN, **b**-16 Sep 1829, **c**-Henry STONER, **d**-$1000, **e**-Ephraim BANKS, Jos. B. ARD, **f**- **g**-18 Sep 1830, **h**-$124.75, **i**-$71.68.5, **j**-$53.06.5, paid

Joseph McCRUM, **b**-5 Oct 1829, **c**-Samuel McDOWELL, John McCRUM, Jr., **d**-$1000, **e**-Foster MILLIKEN, Michael H. WEAVER, **f**-2 Nov 1829, **g**-25 Sep 1830, **h**-$651.24.5, **i**-$619.49, **j**-$31.73.5, estate

James HORRELL, b-9 Oct 1829, c-Hugh HARDY, Jr., d-$200, e-S. W. STEWART, David STEWART, f-16 Nov 1829, g-10 Aug 1833, h-$95.83, i-$70.81.25, j-$25.01.75, estate

Elias HORNING, Jr., b-14 Oct 1829, c-Isabella HORNING, William HORNING, d-$1500, e-Jacob HORNING, John HORNING, f-10 Nov 1829, g-11 Oct 1830/2 Apr 1831, h-$926.62.5/$370.13.5, i-$597.98.5/$370.13.5, j-No Balance

Robert LEVI, b-15 Oct 1829, c-William LEVI, d-$500, e-John LEVI, Wm. BROTHERS, f- g-14 Oct 1830, h-$304.38.5, i-$127.89.25, j-$176.49.25, estate

Martha BEATTY, b-17 Oct 1829, c-William FORGY, d-$500, e-Robert FORGY, James CRISWELL, f-16 May 1828, g-2 Jul 1831, h-$278.12.5, i-$275,63,5 j-$8.61, accountant

John SAYLOR, b-21 Oct 1829, c-David WALKER, d-$1000, e-William HENDERSON, Hugh BURNS, f-18 Nov 1829, g- h- i- j-

Page 121, Frame 133
Michael [McGURRON], b-6 Nov 1829, c-Andrew MURPHY, John BURGE, d- e- f- g- h- i- j-

George KUHNS, b-6 Nov 1829, c-James McLAUGHLIN, d-$1500, e-Jacob KEPNER, Michael BOYER, f-16 Nov 1829, g-14 Dec 1831, h-$1452.52.5, i-$1133.44.25, j-$319.08.25, estate

Ephraim McDOWELL, b-7 Nov 1829, c-William PATTON, d-$1000, e-Wm. BROTHERS, John STONEROAD, f-5 Dec 1829, g- h- i- j-

George WAKEFIELD, b-11 Nov 1829, c-John WAKEFIELD, Augustine WAKEFIELD, George WAKEFIELD, d- e- f- g- h- i- j-

Irwin COULTER, b-17 Nov 1829, c-James McDONALD, d- e- f-16 Aug 1830, g-8 Sep 1834, h-$1284.10, i-$860.20.25, j-R413.89.25, estate

James WATTSON, b-17 Nov 1829, c-Geo. A. LYON, d-$500, e-Jos. MARTIN, John McFADDEN, f-23 Dec 1829, g- h- i- j-

Margaret BRATTON, b-18 Nov 1829, c-John OLIVER, Jr., d- e- f-1 Nov 1830, g-27 Nov 1837, h-$456.69, i-$197.75, j-$258.94, estate

John McKEE, Jr., b-27 Nov 1829, c-Robert McKEE, David L. McKEE, d-$300, e-John McKEE, Sr., Foster MILLIKEN, f-25 Dec 1829, g-22 Mar 1831/29 Oct 1833/2 Aug 1836, h-$156.47.25//$3622.84.333, i-$349.52.5//$847.89, j-$2774.95.333, estate

James BUCHANAN, b-7 Dec 1829, c-David STEWART, d-$300, e-James DICKSON, Christopher MARK, f- g- h- i- j-

Thomas BUCHANAN, b-7 Dec 1829, c-David STEWART, d-$300, e-James DICKSON, Christopher MARK, f- g- h- i- j-

Nancy SAMPLE, b-8 Dec 1829, c-Michael H. WEAVER, d-$300, e-David MILLIKEN, James MURRAY, f-5 Jan 1830, g-10 Jan 1831, h-$259.72.5, i-$207.19.5, j-$52.53, estate

Jacob WALTERS, b-10 Dec 1829, c-Martha WALTERS, d-$1000, e-Margaret WALTERS, Samuel W. STEWART, f- g- h- i- j-

Page 122, Frame 134

John HOOBAUGH, b-16 Dec 1829, c-Solomon BOWER, Thomas MARTIN, d- e- f-10 Jun 1830, g-22 Feb 1833, h-$6243.28, i-$2232.29.5, j-$4010.98.5, estate

James HUNTER, b-21 Dec 1829, c-Jacob HUNTER, Martha HUNTER, William BROWN, d-$400, e-James MILLIKEN, Saml. ALEXANDER, f-15 Jan 1830, g- h- i- j-

David COULTER, Sr., b-28 Dec 1829, c-James McDONALD, Nathl. WILSON, d-$500, e-James MITCHELL, Elial McVEY, f- g-1 Jul 1843/1 Jul 1843/17 Feb 1844, h-$1562.87/$2129.45/$1567.53, i-$1469.39/$1740.55/$1515.16, j-$93.47/$378.90/$42.37, [no recipient]

Thomas McCULLEY, b-30 Dec 1829, c-Samuel MACLAY, James McCULLEY, d-$2000, e-John STERRET, Adam GREER, f- g- h- i- j-

Peacock MAJOR, b-30 Dec 1829, c-Martha MAJOR, David R. REYNOLDS, d- e- f- g- h- i- j-

Henry BARNTHISLE, b-1 Jan 1830, c-Tobias KREIDER, Elias BECK, d- e- f-17 Jan 1843, g-20 Dec 1830, h-$43.18.25, i-$246.21, j-$203.02.5, accountants

Robert McMEEN, b-4 Jan 1830, c-Philip KILMORE, d-$200, e-Stewart TURBETT, f-4 Jan 1830, g-25 Feb 1831, h-$151.17, i-$149.66.5, j-$1.51, estate

[Farmen] S. COOK, b-6 Jan 1830, c-Jonathan COOK, Jonathan LESLIE, d-$5000, e-Christopher MARK, Joseph MILLIKEN, f-26 Apr 1830, g- h- i- j-

Jacob BEAVER, b-11 Jan 1830, c-John JOHNSTON, d-$300, e-Christian BEAVER, Wm. J. BROWN, f- g- h- i- j-

Charles TOWERS, b-18 Jan 1830, c-Jeremiah TOWERS, James ANDERSON, d-$3000, e-James PATTERSON, John BELL, f-30 Jan 1830, g-16 Dec 1830, h-$2854.98, i-$923.93, j-$1931.05, estate

Jacob [KITCHNER], b-30 Jan 1830, c-John HARTZLER, d-$400, e-John THOMPSON, John SMOKER, f-20 Feb 1830, g-13 Mar 1832, h-$226.14.5, i-$261.60.5, j-$35.46, accountant

Edward KELLY, b-3 Feb 1830, c-John MURRAY, Alexander BRADLEY, d- e- f- g- h- i- j-

Page 123, Frame 135

Frederick AILMAN, b-6 Feb 1830, c-David AILMAN, d-$1000, e-Samuel KIME, David KREIDER, f-6 Feb 1830, g-8 Oct 1832, h-$528.07, i-$486.37, j-$41.73, heirs

Dorothy KINSLOE, b-6 Feb 1830, c-David WALKER, d- e- f-8 Mar 1830, g-29 Jan 1835, h-$212.81, i-$229.95, j-$17.14, accountant

Jacob RICE, b-10 Feb 1830, c-Samuel RICE, Alexander McGONIGLE, d- e- f-8 Mar 1830, g- h- i- j-

John BARRY, b-17 Feb 1830, c-William ARBUCKLE, John BELL, d- e- f-31 Mar 1830, g-18 Nov 1830, h-$446.25.75, i-$134.30, j-$311.95.75, estate

James CURRAN, b-19 Feb 1830, c-James CURREN[sic], Richard CURREN[sic], d-$500, e-David CRAWFORD, Saml. RIDDLE, f-18 Mar 1830, g-5 Nov 1834, h-$110.20, i-$185.58.5, j-$75.83.5, accountants

John CULLIN, b-4 Mar 1830, c-Cyrus STINE, d-$500, e-Lukin ATKINSON, S. W. STEWART, f- g- h- i- j-

Christian ASH, b-6 Mar 1830, c-John ASH, d-$, e- f-30 Jan 1830, g-16 Dec 1830, h-$2854.98, i-$923.93, j-$1931.05, estate

John WALKER, b-13 Mar 1830, c-Michael WALKER, d-$200, e-Mathias GISH, Saml. STERRETT, f-3 Apr 1830, g-10 Jan 1833, h-$72.32, i-$70.09, j-$2.22, estate

Christian KAUFMAN, b-15 Mar 1830, c-David KAUFMAN, Samuel KAUFMAN, d-$5000, e-Christian YETER, David HARTZLER, f-7 May 1830, g-3 Mar 1831, h-$227.37, i-$264.71.5, j-$37.31.5, accountant

John L. McCORD, b-19 Mar 1830, c-Samuel W. STEWART, d-$1500, e-David STEWART, James DICKSON, f- g- h- i- j-

James KENNY, b-1 Apr 1830, c-Martha KENNY, d- e- f-15 Apr 1830, g- h- i- j-

Page 124, Frame 136

Jacob YODER, **b**-2 Apr 1830, **c**-Christian YODER, Joseph YODER, **d**-$1000, **e**-Abraham STUTZMAN, William SHEARER, **f**- **g**- **h**- **i**- **j**-

George BLACK, **b**-9 Apr 1830, **c**-William OAKISON, **d**-$500, **e**- Samuel ALLEN, Thomas KERR, **f**-9 Apr 1830, **g**- **h**- **i**- **j**-

Robert GLENN, **b**-17 Apr 1830, **c**-Lewis LEWIS, **d**-$500, **e**-John [NINIS?], Samuel PATTON, **f**-5 May 1830, **g**- **h**- **i**- **j**-

John WARWICK, **b**-21 Apr 1830, **c**-Daniel CHRISTY, **d**- **e**- **f**-5 Aug 1835, **g**- **h**- **i**- **j**-

William McCOY, **b**-22 May 1830, **c**-James KINSLOE, **d**-$2000, **e**-Jos. B. ARD, James DICKSON, **f**- **g**-28 Feb 1833, **h**- **i**-$59.98, **j**-$59.98, accountant

Michael AUMAN, **b**-29 May 1830, **c**-Abraham HARNER, **d**-$, **e**- **f**- **g**- **h**- **i**- **j**-

Arthur McNIGHT, **b**-10 Jun 1830, **c**-John HAMILTON, **d**- **e**- **f**-29 Jun 1830, **g**-3 Dec 1833, **h**-$789.42, **i**-$1100.63, **j**-$311.21, accountant

Charles McLAUGHLIN, **b**-12 Jun 1830, **c**-John McLAUGHLIN, Eleanore McLAUGHLIN, **d**- **e**- **f**- **g**- **h**- **i**- **j**-

Henry WALLACE, **b**-17 Jun 1830, **c**-Sally WALLACE, **d**-$1200, **e**-Benjn. CARVER, Jacob CARVER, **f**-16 Aug 1830, **g**- **h**- **i**- **j**-

William SWENEY, **b**-19 Jun 1830, **c**-Jona. J. CUNNINGHAM, Francis McGRATH, **d**-$, **e**- **f**- **g**- **h**- **i**- **j**-

Felix LEE, **b**-3 Jul 1830, **c**-John LEE, Henry LEE, William McMANIGIL, **d**- **e**- **f**-6 Oct 1830, **g**-1 Mar 1836/27 Jun 1843 **h**-$2110.28/$3189.44, **i**-$1467.55/$368.23, **j**-$2821.21, estate

Daniel DAVIS, **b**-13 Jul 1830, **c**-Jane DAVIS, **d**-$100, **e**-James MILLIKEN, Henry BURKHOLDER, **f**-21 Aug 1830, **g**- **h**- **i**- **j**-

Page 125, Frame 137

Conrad TREWITZ, **b**-31 Jul 1830, **c**-Philip LEININGER, **d**-$200, **e**-Bastian KERSTETER, Valentine KELLY, **f**-31 Jul 1830, **g**-9 Aug 1831, **h**-$47.90 **i**-$59.28, **j**-$11.58, accountant

Robert BURNS, **b**-20 Aug 1830, **c**-Michael M. MONAHON, **d**-$200 **e**-Hugh BURNS, Thomas KERR, **f**- **g**- **h**- **i**- **j**-

Sophia LEONARD, **b**-17 Aug 1830, **c**-Lewis EVANS, **d**- **e**- **f**- **g**-8 Jan 1833, **h**-$282.00, **i**-$112.87.5, **j**-$169.12.5, estate

Jane THOMPSON, **b**-23 Aug 1830, **c**-Standish BARRY, John FRANCISCUS, **d**- **e**- **f**- **g**- **h**- **i**- **j**-

John SHELLEBARGER, **b**-6 Sep 1830, **c**-Christian SHELLEBARGER, Michael SHELLEBARGER, **d**- **e**- **f**-2 Oct 1830, **g**-17 Feb 1834, **h**- **i**- **j**-$5389.04, estate

Bernard McDONALD, **b**-13 Sep 1830, **c**-Dennis McDONALD, **d**-$400, **e**-Francis MURPHY, Michael STAFFORD, **f**- **g**- **h**- **i**- **j**-

Michael REDMOND, **b**-13 EP 1830, **c**-John MURPHY, **d**- **e**- **f**- **g**- **h**- **i**- **j**-

Samuel THOMPSON, **b**-21 Sep 1830, **c**-Thomas KERR, **d**-$200, **e**-Thomas TODD, Isaac FISHER, **f**-26 Oct 1830, **g**- **h**- **i**- **j**-

John ORT, **b**-9 Oct 1830, **c**-Joseph RANNELS, **d**-$600, **e**-Conrad ORT, John ORT, Jr., **f**-15 Nov 1830, **g**-17 Oct 1831, **h**-$507.87, **i**- **j**-$159.35.5, estate (by Decree of Court)

Patrick LEATTOR, **b**-11 Oct 1830, **c**-James LEATTOR, Henry LEATTOR, **d**-$, **e**- **f**- **g**- **h**- **i**- **j**-

Catherine LEVY, **b**-20 Oct 1830, **c**-John LEIPLE, **d**-$200, **e**-William LEVY, James MILLIKEN, **f**-4 Nov 1830, **g**- **h**- **i**- **j**-

Fleming STEWART, **b**-26 Oct 1830, **c**-Albert LICHTENTHALER, **d**-$400, **e**-Tobias KREIDER, Jr., Jos. MILLIKEN, **f**-29 Nov 1830, **g**-29 Jun 1833, **h**-$868.54.5, **i**-$356.68.25, **j**-$481.86.25, estate

<u>Page 126, Frame 138</u>

John JOHNSTON, **b**-15 Nov 1830, **c**-William B. JOHNSTON, **d**-$4000, **e**-Samuel MACLAY, James PARKER, **f**-15 Dec 1830, **g**-5 Jul 1833, **h**-$7416.17.5, **i**-$5388.83, **j**-$2027.62.5, estate

Robert DOUGLASS, **b**-18 Nov 1830, **c**-William ARBUCKLE, Jonas THATCHER, **d**-$, **e**- **f**-17 Dec 1830, **g**-24 Apr 1832, **h**-$662.10.5, **i**-$362.13.5, **j**-$299.97.25, estate

John McKEE, **b**-18 Nov 1830, **c**- **d**- **e**- **f**- **g**- **h**- **i**- **j**-

Samuel BRYSON, **b**-20 Nov 1830, **c**-Samuel McDOWELL, **d**-$200, **e**-Foster MILLIKEN, Hugh KNOX, **f**-2 Aug 1828[sic], **g**- **h**- **i**- **j**-

Mary LAPP, **b**-13 Dec 1830, **c**-Samuel KAUFMAN, **d**-$5000, **e**-David SMOKER, Foster MILLIKEN, **f**-13 Jan 1831, **g**-3 Mar 1831, **h**-$2855.26, **i**-$83.19.5, **j**-$2772.06.5, estate

Jesse JENNINGS, **b**-13 Dec 1830, **c**-Daniel CHRISTY, **d**-$500, **e**-John KNOX, William ARD, **f**- **g**- **h**- **i**- **j**-

Sylvanus MOSS, **b**-17 Dec 1830, **c**-Thomas TODD, **d**-$1000, **e**-Jesse BEALE, John SELHEIMER, George DILL, **f**-6 Apr 1842, **g**-6 Apr 1842, **h**- **i**-$35.56.25, **j**-$35.56.25, accountant

Samuel REEDER, b-21 Dec 1830, **c**-James MATHERS, **d**-$100, **e**-Daniel CHRISTY, John HAMILTON, **f**-17 Jan 1831, **g**-16 Jul 1831, **h**-$212.87.5, **i**-$212.87.5, **j**-

Margaret MELOY, b-22 Dec 1830, **c**- **d**- **e**- **f**- **g**- **h**- **i**- **j**-

Michell THOMPSON, b-19 Jan 1831, **c**-William THOMPSON, **d**-$3000, **e**-Daniel CHRISTY, A. LICHTENTHALER, **f**-18 Feb 1831, **g**-4 Dec 1832, **h**-$2543.64, **i**-$291.67, **j**-$2151.97, estate

William STEEL, b-29 Jan 1831, **c**-Alexander STEEL, **d**-$1000, **e**-Wm. J. McCOY, John McFADDEN, **f**-5 Jan 1833, **g**-5 Jan 1833, **h**-$153.69, **i**-$203.51, **j**-$49.82, accountant

Frederick VEIGH, b-21 Feb 1831, **c**-John McMINN, **d**-$1000, **e**-John VEIGH, John O'NIEL, **f**-21 Mar 1831, **g**-16 Mar 1832, **h**-$466.82.5, **i**-$208.82.5, **j**-$257.86.5, estate

Page 127, Frame 139

Hugh McDONALD, b-11 Mar 1831, **c**-Hugh McDONALD, **d**-$300, **e**-Andrew McDONALD , James McCRUM, **f**-7 Apr 1831, **g**-9 Mar 1832, **h**-$76.96.5, **i**-$76.78.5, **j**-$.08 [no assignment]

John McCLENAHAN, b-12 Mar 1831, **c**-John McCLENAHAN, Stephen HINDS, **d**-$1000, **e**-John STONEROAD, James MILLIKEN, **f**-18 Apr 1831, **g**- **h**- **i**- **j**-

Sarah SAMPLE, b-19 Mar 1831, **c**-Andrew SAMPLE, **d**-$1000, **e**-E. W. HALE, James MILLIKEN, **f**-12 Apr 1831, **g**-17 Jun 1833, **h**-$547.93.5, **i**-$179.06.75, **j**-$368.86.75, estate

Philip STROUP, b-19 Mar 1831, **c**-John STROUP, **d**-$1000, **e**-Ludwick YEATTER, George WILEY, **f**-18 Apr 1834, **g**-23 Aug 1833, **h**-$558.69, **i**-$537.91, **j**-$20.78, estate

Joseph HORNING, b-2 Apr 1831, **c**-Jacob HORNING, **d**-$1000, **e**-William HORNING, James STEPHENSON, **f**-2 May 1831, **g**-7 Feb 1832, **h**-$516.79, **i**-$621.72, **j**-$104.93, accountant

James McCULLEY, b-4 Apr 1831, **c**-James McCULLY[sic], **d**-$800 **e**-Mathew TAYLOR, David MILLIKEN, **f**- **g**- **h**- **i**- **j**-

Foster MILLIKEN, b-8 Apr 1831, **c**-James DICKSON, **d**-$15,000, **e**-James MILLIKEN, Joseph MILLIKEN, **f**-28 Apr 1831, **g**-6 Apr 1832/ 2 Jul 1838, **h**-$4031.62.5/$6606.45, **i**-$3370.63/$6817.89, **j**-$211.44, accountant

Stephen REYNOLDS, b-16 Apr 1831, **c**-Samuel MACLAY, **d**-$1000, **e**-Wm. M. HALL, A. S. WILSON, **f**-6 May 1831, **g**- **h**- **i**- **j**-

John STEWART, Esq., **b**-20 Apr 1831, **c**-David WALKER, Esq., David STEWART, William STEWART, **d**- **e**- **f**- **g**-5 Sep 1832, **h**-$2376.98.25, **i**-$662.05.5, **j**-$1714.93, estate

David STERRETT, **b**-27 Apr 1831, **c**-James STERRETT, **d**- **e**- **f**-15 Mar 1832, **g**-5 Jul 1832, **h**- **i**-$133.59, **j**-$133.59, accountant

Zachariah DOERST, **b**-27 Apr 1831, **c**-Henry HARTMAN, John HOFFMAN, **d**- **e**- **f**-25 May 1831, **g**-29 May 1833, **h**-$3761.35.5, **i**-$276.78.5, **j**-$3448.57.25, estate

Samuel MARSHALL, **b**-29 Apr 1831, **c**-David MARSHALL, Martin LANAIS, **d**-$400, **e**-Wm. CULBERTSON, Tobias KREIDER, **f**-30 Apr 1831, **g**- **h**- **i**- **j**-

Page 128, Frame 140

Jacob COFFMAN, **b**-30 Apr 1831, **c**-William BROTHERS, **d**-$800, **e**-Jos. BROTHERS, E. W. KULP, **f**-27 May 1831, **g**- **h**- **i**- **j**-

John IRVIN, **b**-30 Apr 1831, **c**-William M. HALL, **d**-$1000, **e**-A. S. WILSON, John LYON, **f**-25 Apr 1838, **g**-26 Apr 1838, **h**-$342.04, **i**-$31.50, **j**-$310.54, estate

David KAUFFMAN, Jr., **b**-9 May 1831, **c**-John ADAMS, **d**-$2000, **e**-George KAUFMAN, Abraham KNISELY, **f**-9 Jun 1831, **g**-7 Dec 1832, **h**-$1287.05, **i**-$1279.02.5, **j**-$8.52, estate

Joseph LIGHTER, **b**-7 Jun 1831, **c**-Owen OWENS, Samuel MEALY, **d**-$2000, **e**-Christian SEACHRIST, George LIGHTER, **f**-7 Jun 1831, **g**-26 Sep 1834, **h**-$1943.27, **i**-$2551.31, **j**-$438.04, accountant

Washington BURNS, **b**-23 Jun 1831, **c**-William SHAW, Liberty BURNS, **d**-$1000, **e**-James BURNS, James TURNER, **f**-24 Jun 1831, **g**- **h**- **i**- **j**-

Christopher MARK, **b**-10 Jun 1831, **c**-E. L. BENEDICT, William CULBERTSON, **d**-$, **e**- **f**-4 Sep 1831, **g**-11 Feb 1837/24 Aug 1847, **h**-$1001.14.5/$10,287.21, **i**-$988.49.25/$10,287.21, **j**-$12.65.25, estate

Esther HORNING, **b**-20 Jun 1831, **c**-William HORNING, **d**- **e**- **f**-26 Feb 1832, **g**-7 Feb 1832/24 Aug 1847, **h**-$230.75, **i**-$108.33, **j**-$122.42, estate

Richard KENNEDY, **b**-2 Jul 1831, **c**-Mary KENNEDY, **d**-$1000, **e**-Jesse REYNOLDS, Philo HAMBLIN, **f**-1 Aug 1831, **g**- **h**- **i**- **j**-

Susannah POTTER, **b**-12 Jul 1831, **c**-Eli POTTER, **d**-$1000, **e**- E. W. HALE, Thos. KERR, **f**- **g**- **h**- **i**- **j**-

Robert STURGEON, **b**-12 Jul 1831, **c**-William B. JOHNSTON, **d**-$300, **e**-Samuel MACLAY, Robert U. JACOBS, **f**-9 May 1831, **g**-11 Jul

1832/7 Oct 1833, **h**-$387.00/$116.74.5, **i**-$295.27.25/$116.09, **j**-$.65.25, [no designation]

John BRUBAKER, b-22 Jul 1831, **c**-John BRUBAKER, Jr., **d- e- f**-23 Jul 1821[sic], **g**-29 Feb 1832, **h**-$205.33, **i**-$117.88, **j**-$87.45, estate

Mathias FOOS, b-27 Jul 1831, **c**-John JACOBS, **d**-$500, **e**-Tobias KREIDER, Saml. McFADDEN, **f**-15 Aug 1831, **g**-30 Sep 1833, **h**-$234.65.75, **i**-$261.00.5, **j**-$26.35, accountant

Page 129, Frame 141

Francis SAMPLE, Sr., b-18 Aug 1831, **c**-Josiah ALEXANDER, **d**-$1000, **e**-Jos. MILLIKEN, S. W. TAYLOR, **f- g- h- i- j-**

James JOHNSTON, b-19 Aug 1831, **c**-William BROWN, **d**-$10,000, **e**-Wm. B. JOHNSTON, Samuel MACLAY, **f- g- h- i- j-**

Thomas McCULLEY, b-22 Aug 1831, **c**-James McCULLY, **d**-$2000, **e**-G. W. PATTON, D. S. LAW, **f**-5 Feb 1830/12 Sep 1831, **g**-25 Dec 1830/12 Jul 1831, **h**-$1078.76/$314.12, **i**-$793.21.5/$137.45, **j**-$176.67, estate

Hugh McFADDEN, b-25 Aug 1831, **c**-James MILLIKEN, **d**-$2000, **e**-Jos. MILLIKEN, A. S. WILSON, **f**-10 Nov 1831, **g- h- i- j-**

Isaac WILEY, b-29 Sep 1831, **c**-Elizabeth WILEY, James DICKSON, **d**-$300, **e**-George McCULLOCH, A. S. WILSON, **f**-10 Oct 1831, **g**-1 Apr 1833/28 Feb 1837, **h**-$2280.25/$2730.67, **i**-$1413.91/$1223.65, **j**-$1507.02, estate

Frederick CANNER, b-12 Oct 1831, **c**-James HALL, **d**-$1000, **e**-Samuel PATTON, John NORRIS, **f**-12 Nov 1831, **g**-5 Oct 1832/29 Feb 1836, **h**-$230.68.5/$293.57, **i**-$132.96/$112.12.5, **j**-$281.44.5, estate

William ROBB, b-8 Nov 1831, **c**-John ROBB, **d- e- f**-15 Nov 1832, **g- h- i- j-**

Jacob GINGER, b-11 Nov 1831, **c**-David GINGER, Thomas HAMILTON, **d**-$1000, **e**-Wm. BROTHERS, John GINGER, **f**-14 Nov 1831 **g- h- i- j-**

John MOTHERSBAUGH, Jr., b-2 Dec 1831, **c**-Robert COOPER, **d**-$2000, **e**-Jno. MOTHERSBAUGH, Francis BOGGS, **f**-30 Dec 1831, **g**-6 Mar 1834, **h**-$554.23, **i**-$254.38.5, **j**-$299.84.5, estate

Daniel DUNMIRE, b-20 Dec 1831, **c**-Jacob CARVER, S. W. TAYLOR, **d**-$1500, **e**-Henry STONER, Joseph MILLIKEN, **f**-7 Mar 1835, **g**-7 Mar 1835, **h**-$820.64, **i**-$360.65, **j**-$450.99, estate

Elizabeth STUMPFF, b-31 Dec 1831, **c**-John McCAULEY, **d- e- f- g- h- i- j-**

Joseph MARTIN, b-21 Dec 1831, c-Francis McCOY, d- e- f-19 Feb 1841, g- h- i- j-

Page 130, Frame 142 [duplicated on Frame 143]
David LUSK, b-7 Jan 1832, c-James McDONALD, Augustine WAKEFIELD, d-$2000, e-A. S. WILSON, Jos. A. BELL, f-6 Feb 1832, g-4 Jan 1833, h-$450.22, i-$64.74, j-$385.48, estate

Jacob STEEL, b-14 Jan 1832, c-Henry BECK, William MAYES, d-$2000, e-Richard PEARSON, Joseph MILLIKEN, f-8 Feb 1832, g-1 Mar 1833, h-$856.47, i-$940.36, j-$83.89, accountant

William JONES, b-16 Jan 1832, c-Thomas JONES, d-$1000, e-James McCORD, William BROTHERS, f-31 Jan 1832, g-27 Feb 1837, h-$108.60, i-$130.42.25, j-$21.82.25, accountant

Jacob HARTZLER, b-17 Jan 1832, c-Daniel YODER, David HARTZLER, d- e- f-9 Feb 1832, g- h- i- j-

Mathew TAYLOR, b-18 Jan 1832, c-Henry B. TAYLOR, Samuel W. TAYLOR, d-$3000, e-A. B. McNITT, Wm. CUMMINS, f- g-29 Jun 1835, h-$1427.37.5, i-$1737.69, j-$310.31.5, accountants

Rebecca MOORE, b-18 Jan 1832, c-William A. MOORE, d-$2000, e-Richard MILES, John WALTERS, f- g- h- i- j-

William JUNKEN, b-18 Jan 1832, c-Richard MILES, d-$8000, e-Wm. A. MOORE, Nathl. WILSON, f- g-15 Jun 1838/15 May 1839/18 Apr 1843/5 Aug 1847, h-$2496.33/$6958.36/$8287.13/$40.74, i-$792.19.75/$1135.32/$399.56/$500.74, j-$7887.57, estate

William STEPHEN, b-19 Jan 1832, c-Moses KELLY, d-$500, e-John McCAULEY, Jacob HOOVER, f-18 Feb 1832, g- h- i- j-

William CLARK, b-19 Jan 1832, c-Elijah DAVIS, d-$500, e-Nathl. WILSON, James CORBETT, f- g- h- i- j-

Noah ABRAHAM, b-20 Jan 1832, c-James MATHERS, d-$1000, e-Thomas KERR, A. S. WILSON, f-7 Feb 1832, g-18 Jan 1833, h- i-$8.06, j-

Leonard SHULER, b-14 Feb 1832, c-Sarah SHULER, d- e- f-20 Feb 1832, g- h- i- j-

Samuel TIBBETTS, b-14 Feb 1832, c-Richard PEARSON, d-$500, e-Tobias KREIDER, Isaac FISHER, f-20 Feb 1832, g-3 Sep 1832, h-$172.14.5, i-$171.75, j-$.39, [no designation]

Page 131, Frame 144

Elias W. HALE, Esq., **b**-15 Feb 1832, **c**-Abraham S. WILSON, James T. HALE, **d**-$15,000, **e**-James MILLIKEN, Benjn. PATTON, **f**- **g**- **h**- **i**- **j**-

Tobias KREIDER, Esq., **b**-15 Mar 1832, **c**-Daniel KREIDER, William CULBERTSON, **d**-$1000, **e**-Christian HOFFMAN, Alexander BAILY, **f**-20 Mar 1832, **g**-28 Feb 1833, **h**-$204.35, **i**-$187.00.25, **j**-$1724.25, estate

Peter LANGTON, **b**-17 Apr 1832, **c**-James LANGTON, **d**-$1000, **e**-Andrew BRATTON, Tobias KREIDER, **f**-12 May 1832, **g**-6 Apr 1833, **h**-$373.09.5, **i**-$71.76.25, **j**-$301.33.25, estate

Samuel McDOWELL, Esq., **b**-17 Apr 1832, **c**-John McDOWELL, **d**-$2000, **e**-John McDOWELL, Wm. JOHNSTON, **f**-25 Apr 1832 **g**- **h**- **i**- **j**-

Jacob KINZELL, **b**-18 Apr 1832, **c**-Joseph KINZELL, **d**-$3000, **e**-Elijah DAVIS, Henry HANAWALT, **f**-18 May 1832, **g**-30 Sep 1835, **h**-$1166.00, **i**-$54.56, **j**-$1111.44, estate

Robert McALLISTER, **b**-19 Apr 1832, **c**-Hugh McALLISTER, **d**-$3000, **e**-John NORTH, Geo. McCULLOCH, **f**- **g**-4 Mar 1835, **h**-$1394.57, **i**-$1195.37.5, **j**-$199.19.5, estate

James STERRETT, **b**-20 Apr 1832, **c**-Robert STERRETT, Alexander PATTERSON, **d**-$10,000, **e**-Geo. McCULLOCH, John GRAHAM, **f**-10 May 1832, **g**- **h**- **i**- **j**-

Robert ROBISON, **b**-25 April 1832, **c**-Ephraim BANKS, Esq., **d**- **e**- **f**-12 May 1832, **g**-27 Nov 1835/15 Nov 1838/4 Mar 1843, **h**-$2431.78.5/ $4470.04/$6811.67, **i**-$1947.25/$2746.45/$990.19.5, **j**-$7982.93, estate

John FERGUSON, **b**-12 May 1832, **c**-John KNOX, **d**-$1000, **e**-John [MOOTZER], John FUNK, **f**- **g**- **h**- **i**- **j**-

John STEWART, Esq., **b**-16 May 1832, **c**-Daniel CHRISTY, **d**-$5000, **e**-Jos. MILLIKEN, Francis McCOY, **f**-6 May 1831, **g**-5 Aug 1835, **h**-$876.08, **i**-$898.02, **j**-$21.94, accountant

Jane POWER, **b**-23 May 1832, **c**-John DAVIDSON, **d**- **e**- **f**- **g**- **h**- **i**- **j**-

Robert CRAIG, **b**-1 Jun 1832, **c**-Alfred KEISER, ~~Andrew KEISER~~, **d**-$1000, **e**-Andrew KEISER, Henry STONER, **f**- **g**- **h**- **i**- **j**-

Page 132, Frame 145

Robert M. ALEXANDER, **b**-11 Jun 1832, **c**-James ALEXANDER, Cyrus ALEXANDER, Alexander GIBBONEY, **d**-$8000, **e**-Joseph

MILLIKEN, James ALEXANDER [appears to be MK after the name], f-9 Jan 1833, g- h- i- j-

John G. RIAN, b-16 Jun 1832, **c-**Sarah RIAN, **d-**$200, **e-**Samuel NICKEL, David CUMMINS, **f- g- h- i- j-**

John [WITNCER/WITNSER?], Jr., b-20 Jun 1832, c-John HOFFMAN, d-$5000, e-Henry HARNER, Henry GUYER, f- g-25 Nov 1833, h-$1170.00.25, i-$642.92, j-$527.08.5, estate

Ferdinand A. MELSHEIMER, b-12 Jul 1832, **c-**Mary MELSHEIMER, Benjn. PATTEN, Jr., **d-**$2000, **e-**James KINSLOE, Daniel KREIDER, **f- g- h- i- j-**

Philip SMITH, b-19 Jul 1832, **c-**Thomas ROBISON, **d-**$1000, **e-**Thos. M. ELLIOTT, D. R. REYNOLDS, **f-**3 Aug 1832, **g-**2 Mar 1835, **h-**$113.89.25, **i-**$158.05, **j-**$44.15.25, accountant

[Onro?] McNABB, b-16 Aug 1832, **c-**Crawford KYLE, **d-**$200, **e-**Henry TAYLOR, John McCAULEY, **f-**11 Sep 1832, **g- h- i- j-**

Elizabeth MATEER, b-6 Oct 1832, **c-**Zachariah ALBRIGHT, **d-**$100, **e-**John MATEER, Jacob HARTZLER, **f-**3 Nov 1832, **g- h- i- j-**

John WILSON, b-19 Sep 1832, **c-**Robert MILLIKEN, Wm. Brown MACLAY, **d-**$, **e- f-**19 Oct 1832, **g-**4 Aug 1853, **h-**$2972.43.5, **i-**$2886.20, **j-**$86.23.5, accountants

Samuel JORDAN, b-2 Nov 1832, **c-**William CUSTER, **d- e- f-**25 Dec 1832, **g-**5 Mar 1839, **h-**$643.79, **i-**$740.43, **j-**$96.64, accountant

John FLEMING, b-5 Nov 1832, **c-**Mary FLEMING, Robert MILLIKEN, **d-**$8000, **e-**James BRISBIN, Henry TAYLOR, **f-**12 Dec 1832, **g-**6 Mar 1834/21 Feb 1840, **h-**$2997.79/$9882.77, **i-**$1805.18.25/$9426.15, **j-**$370.57, estate

Robert STARKS, b-22 Nov 1832, **c-**Theodore STARKS, Ephraim BANKS, **d-**$, **e- f-**22 Dec 1832, **g-**27 Nov 1835, **h-**$94.09, **i-**$577.52, **j-**$370.57, estate

Anthoney YOUNG, b-1 Dec 1832, **c-**Joseph BROWER, **d-**$2000, **e-**Joseph MILLIKEN, Wm. REED, **f- g- h- i- j-**

Page 133, Frame 146

John COMFORT, b-3 Jan 1833, **c-**John McFADDEN, **d-**$500 **e-**Samuel CHESNUT, Wm. CHARTERS, **f-**26 Jan 1833, **g- h- i- j-**

George B. KREEMER, b-4 Jan 1833, **c-**[I. P. F.] KREEMER, **d-**$500, **e-**D. W. HULING, Benjn. MASON, **f- g- h- i- j-**

James MARKLIN, b-10 Jan 1833, c-Ephraim BANKS, d-$2000, e-Lukens ATKINSON, Saml. WITHEROW, f- g-29 Feb 1836, h-$911.89, i-$591.64, j-$320.25, estate

Esther DUNN, b-7 Feb 1833, c-James DUNN, d-$1000, e-Peter EBY, John YODER, f- g-3 Jun 1839, h-$907.47, i-$394.54, j-$512.93, estate

MaryTURNER, b-16 Feb 1833, c-Robert B. TURNER, d-$500, e-James BURNS, Samuel CHESNUT, f- g- h- i- j-

Robert MORGAN, b-26 Feb 1833, c-Samuel MYERS, William WAKEFIELD, d-$5000, e-James ROBISON, Francis McCOY, f-22 Mar 1833, g-27 Feb 1837, h-$773.51, i-$546.10, j-$227.40, estate

Daniel PEFFER, b-1 Mar 1833, c-Philip PEFFER, d-$200, e-William BROTHERS, Wm. PEFFER, f-19 Mar 1833, g- h- i- j-

Catherine HOOVER, b-27 Feb 1833, c-Hannah KEYSER, d-$, e- f- g- h- i- j-

Elizabeth YOUNG, b-4 Mar 1833, c-William BROTHERS, d-$5000, e-Jos. B. ARD, Wm. LEVI, f- g- h- i- j-

George PEFFER, b-9 Mar 1833, c-Philip PEFFER, d-$500, e-William PEFFER, William BROTHERS, f-19 Mar 1833, g-1 Mar 1834, h-$28.00, i-$32.65.25, j-$4.65.25, accountant

Jacob MILLER, b-22 Mar 1833, c-David KAUFMAN, Joseph HEFFLY, d-$500, e-James MILLIKEN, Joseph ZOOK, f-13 Apr 1833, g-27 Feb 1835/1 Mar 1845, h-$294.72/$1594.38.5, i-$43.97.5/$1490.01, j-$104.37.5, estate

John O'CONNER, b-6 May 1833, c-Thomas OSBOURN, d-$1000, e-Wm. P. COWLING, Christian SWARTZ, f-25 May 1833, g-6 May 1834, h-$322.12.5, i-$173.10.75, j-$149.01.75, estate

Robert McCLELLAND, b-18 Nov 1833, c- d- e- f- g- h- i- j-

Page 134, Frame 147

Frederick BAUM, b-17 May 1833, c-David MILLIKEN, d-$500, e-James McCULLEY, Geo. W. PATTON, f- g- h- i- j-

David YODER, b-25 May 1833, c-David ZOOK, d-$6000, e-Jacob ZOOK, Robert LOWERY, f-12 Sep 1833, g-2 Mar 1835/1 Jun 1835, h-$1270.15.5/$1307.58, i-$1041.48/$17.00, j-$1290.58, estate

Elzabeth GARBER, b-12 Aug 1833, c-Samuel W. TAYLOR, Moses GARBER, d-$2000, e-Jos. MILLIKEN, Jos. A. TAYLOR, f-20 Sep 1833, g- h- i- j-

Charles HICKENBOTHOM, **b**-6 Aug 1833, **c**-Jona. J. CUNNINGHAM, **d**-$1000, **e**-George DULL, John McLAUGHLIN, **f**-11 Oct 1833, **g**-7 Aug 1837, **h**-$201.92.5, **i**-$112.73, **j**-$89.18.5, estate

Joseph ANDERSON, **b**-7 Aug 1833, **c**-James CRAWFORD, **d**-$500, **e**-John ROBISON, Isaac FISHER, **f**-24 Aug 1833, **g**-30 Nov 1840, **h**-$360.76, **i**-$177.50.75, **j**-$183.26, heirs

Alexander SANDERSON, **b**-8 Aug 1833, **c**-James MATHERS, **d**-$200 [possible strike out of this figure?], **e**-Saml. W. STUART, Isaac FISHER, **f**-6 Sep 1833, **g**- **h**- **i**- **j**-

Abraham KOPLIN, **b**-16 Aug 1833, **c**-J. J. CUNNINGHAM, **d**-$2000, **e**-Ralph BOGLE, William ROSS, **f**-11 Oct 1833, **g**- **h**- **i**- **j**-

John SWISHER, **b**-20 Aug 1833, **c**-Jacob SWISHER, **d**-$500, **e**-[J. I.] McCOY, Jacob EVERICH, **f**-5 Sep 1833, **g**-11 Aug 1834, **h**-$31.36, **i**-$39.38.5, **j**-$8.02.5, accountant

Solomon YODER, **b**-21 Aug 1833, **c**-John YODER, Gideon YODER, **d**-[$3000], **e**-John BYLER, Joseph MILLIKEN, **f**-7 Sep 1833, **g**-28 Feb 1835, **h**-$2023.63.5, **i**-$1004.05, **j**-$1019.59, estate

Dorothy KINSLOE, **b**-6 Sep 1833, **c**-Thomas KINSLOE, **d**-$500, **e**-Geo. W. PATTON, James MATHERS, **f**- **g**- **h**- **i**- **j**-

Joseph ROHREBACHER, **b**-13 Sep 1833, **c**-Elizabeth ROHREBACHER, **d**-$1000, **e**-D. W. HULINGS, Isaac FISHER, **f**-4 Feb 1837, **g**- **h**- **i**- **j**-

Benjamin CLICK, **b**-17 Sep 1833, **c**-Shem ZOOK, **d**-$1000, **e**-James MILLIKEN, Wm. P. MACLAY, **f**-16 Oct 1833, **g**-4 Nov 1834, **h**-$523.98.5, **i**-$439.65, **j**-$84.33.5, estate

Page 135, Frame 148

Ralph BOGLE, **b**-11 Oct 1833, **c**-Ralph BOGLE, **d**-$3000, **e**-J. J. CUNNINGHAM, William ROSS, **f**-9 Nov 1833, **g**-2 Jan 1849, **h**- **i**- **j**-

Robert McCLELLAND, **b**-2 Nov 1833, **c**-James McDOWELL, **d**-$4000, **e**-Francis McCLURE, Thomas McCLURE, **f**-27 Jun 1835, **g**-27 Jun 1835, **h**-$981.95, **i**-$45.60.75, **j**-$936.24.25, estate

William McDOWELL, **b**-18 Nov 1833, **c**-William McDOWELL, **d**-$6000, **e**-Joseph MILLIKEN, John STERRETT, **f**- **g**-2 Jul 1838, **h**-$3369,49, **i**-$739.55, **j**-$2630.85, estate

Robert TAYLOR, **b**-21 Sep 1833, **c**-George WILSON, **d**- **e**- **f**-2 Feb 1842, **g**- **h**- **i**- **j**-

James ALEXANDER, b-26 Oct 1833, c-Thomas REED, William ALEXANDER, d- e- f-12 Dec 1833, g-6 Mar 1841, h-$2143.90.75, i-$1970.77, j-$173.60, heirs

Margaret WILLS, b-14 Dec 1833, c- d- e- f- g- h- i- j-

Benjamin WILLIAMS, b-9 Jan 1834, c-John PATTERSON, Jr., d-$500, e-Andrew PARKER, A. S. WILSON, f-8 Feb 1834, g- h- i- j-

Elizabeth SHIMP, b-24 Jan 1834, c-Frederick SHIMP, d-$500, e-John McFADDEN, Alexander STEEL, f- g- h- i- j-

David LUKENS, b-30 Jan 1834, c-Joseph LANGTON, d-$3000, e-James CRISWELL, Joseph MILLIKEN, f-12 Apr 1834, g-3 Apr 1845, h-$2531.92, i-$1126.98, j-$1404.94, estate

William STUMPFF, b-10 Feb 1834, c-William SHAW, d-$1000, e-John STUMPFF, Jacob STUMPFF, f-2 Dec 1834, g- h- i- j-

John SUMMERS, b-11 Mar 1834, c-Abraham ZOOK, d-$2000, e-Joseph YODER, David HARTZLER, f-5 Apr 1834, g-4 Jul 1835, h-$538.80, i-$295.31.25, j-$253.48.75, estate

Joseph McFADDEN, b-25 Mar 1834, c-John McFADDEN, d-$1000, e-Andrew MAYES, Robert MATHEWS, f-24 Apr 1834, g-28 Nov 1837, h-$544.46, i-$919.70.5, j-$375.24.5, accountant

Page 136, Frame 149

Eleanor ENGLISH, b-5 Apr 1834, c-David McCONAHY, d-$500, e-James McCONAHY, Isaac FISHER, f-9 Aug 1820[sic], g- h- i- j-

George MARKLIN, b-8 Apr 1834, c-Lukins[sic] ATKISSON[sic], d-$4000, e-James CRISWELL, A. S. WILSON, f- g- h- i- j-

Joshua MORRISON, b-19 Apr 1834, c-John MORRISON, Elijah MORRISON, d-$, e- f-3 May 1834, g-2 Sep 1835/20 May 1847, h-$1838.50/$3209.51, i-$191.92/$3237.38.5, j-$1646.58, estate/$27.87.5, accountant

Richard JOHNSTON, b-3 May 1834, c-William BROWN, d-$5000, E-A. S. WILSON, Wm. B. JOHNSTON, f-9 May 1834, g- h- i- j-

William CORBETT, b-17 May 1834, c-James CORBETT, d- e- f-14 Jun 1834, g-3 Feb 1836, h-$535.03.75, i-$495.71.25, j-$39.32.5, estate

William BROWN, b-4 Jun 1834, c-Rachel BROWN, Wm. W. POTTER, d- e- f-20 Jun 1834, g-17 Jun 1846, 23 Oct 1844, h-$6684.02, i-$7887.50, j-$1203.48, accountants

John POTTER, b-1 Aug 1834, c-George STRUNK, d-$1500, e-George POTTER, Joseph MILLIKEN, f-27 Aug 1834, g-28 Mar 1840/8 Jul

1844, h-$1071.64.5/$193.62, i-$358.13.5/$61.50, j-$713.51, estate/$132.12, estate

Lilley McFARLAND, b-7 Aug 1834, c-James McFARLAND, d-$6000, e-James MILLIKEN, Wm. THOMPSON, f- g-5 Sep 1835, h-$4800.00, i-$174.10.25, j-$4625.90.75, estate

George TRIMNELL, b-3 Sep 1834, c-Nathaniel WILSON, d-$1000, e- f-5 Feb 1841, g-2 Jul 1841[sic], h-$1252.10.75, i-$1638.00.75, j-$385.90, accountant

Robert ALEXANDER, b-10 Sep 1834, c-James ALEXANDER, Cyrus ALEXANDER, Silas ALEXANDER, d-$, e- f-10 Oct 1834, g- h- i- j-

William PENDLETON, b-4 Oct 1834, c-Geo. W. PATTON, d-$500, e-A. S. WILSON, J. C. AGNEW, f-3 Nov 1834/25 Apr 1835, g- h- i- j-

David STEWART, b-29 Oct 1834, c-George McCULLOCH, Joseph MILLIKEN, d- e- f- g-17 Jul 1844/26 Mar 1849, h-$13,441.29/$1081.24, i-$11646.67.5/$115.90, j-$1794.61.5, estate/[no amount given, just "Bal due Estate of Decedent"]

Page 137, Frame 150

Rev. James JOHNSTON, b-6 Nov 1834, c-Dr. Samuel MACLAY, d-$3000, e-Wm. P. MACLAY, James BROWN, f- g- h- i- j-

William LINGLE, b-20 Nov 1834, c-Leonard LINGLE, d-$500, e-Abraham KENNAGY, Jos. HAWN f- g- h- i- j-

Mary SEILIGH, b-2 Dec 1834, c-William SHAW, d- e- f-7 May 1835, g-20 Jun 1838, h-$617.32.5, i-$321.92.25, j-$295.40.25, estate

William SWANZEY, b-13 Nov 1834, c-James CRISWELL, Geo. H. GALBRAITH, d- e- f-23 Dec 1834, g- h- i- j-

William ARMSTRONG, b-13 Nov 1834, c-James CRISWELL, Amor STRODE, d- e- f-23 Dec 1834, g- h- i- j-

Margaret HORNING, b-12 Dec 1834, c-John HORNING [although the "R" appears to have been meticulously crossed out–?], d-$1000, e-James ROBISON, S. W. STEWART, f-19 Dec 1834, g- h- i- j-

Samuel EDMISTON, Esq., b-24 Dec 1834, c-William MITCHELL, d-$6000, e-Joseph MILLIKEN, James GIBBONEY, f- g- h- i- j-

Tobias KREIDER, b-29 Dec 1834, c-Samuel W. STEWART, d-$1000, e-James T. HALE, Geo. McCULLOCH, f- g- h- i- j-

Alexander STEWART, b-5 Jan 1835, c-Thomas WATTSON, d-$2000, e-John McDOWELL, Jr., Joseph ROTHROCK, f- g- h- i- j-

William BEALE, b-7 Jan 1835, c-John BEALE, d-$3000, e-Saml. STERRETT, David REYNOLDS, f- g-4 Apr 1842/30 Sep 1844/1 Apr

1856,   h-$2684.27/$114.69/$3254.68,   i-$5224.97.5/$2031.02.5/ $3265.19, j-$1916.56.25, accountant/$10.51, estate

John WORTS, **b**-20 Jan 1835, **c**-Dr. Jos. B. ARD, Martin WORTS, **d**- **e**- **f**- **g**- **h**- **i**- **j**-

James McCLINTIC, **b**-9 Feb 1835, **c**-Giles CARPENTER, Charles RITZ, **d**-$3000, **e**-James MILLIKEN, James KINSLOE, **f**-9 Mar 1835, **g**-29 Feb 1836/2 Jul 1839, **h**-$1223.57.25/$2177.88, **i**-$365.69.25/$2299.92, **j**-$122.04, accountant

Page 138, Frame 151

Christian DITWEILER, **b**-10 Feb 1835, **c**-David ZOOK, Christian DITWEILER, **d**-$4,000, **e**-Abraham PEACHY, Shem YODER, **f**-28 Feb 1833, **g**-24 Jun 1836/7 Jun 1842, **h**-$1739.80/$1739.18, **i**-$463.19.5/$37.41, **j**-$1701.77, estate

John MOFFAT, **b**-10 Feb 1935. **c**-Robert MOFFAT, **d**-$200, **e**-S. W. TAYLOR, David ZOOK, **f**-28 Nov 1835, **g**-28 Nov 1835, **h**-$95.67, **i**-$81.82.5, **j**-$13.79.5, estate

Gotleib SATTLER, **b**-9 Mar 1835, **c**-Joseph SNYDER, **d**-$300, **e**-Jacob SNYDER, [T. KECKA], **f**-21 Apr 1835, **g**-23 Apr 1835, **h**-$303.83.5, **i**-$303.83.5, **j**-

Thomas VASHON, **b**-17 Mar 1835, **c**-Nancy VASHON, **d**-$2000, **e**-James T. HALL, D. R. REYNOLDS, **f**-7 Apr 1835, **g**-27 Feb 1836, **h**-$208.11.75, **i**-$226.03.75, **j**-$17.92, accountant

Jane DAVIS, **b**-8 Apr 1835, **c**-Moses KELLY, **d**-$500, **e**-Valentine STONEROAD, Saml. MITCHELL, **f**- **g**- **h**- **i**- **j**-

Isaac PRICE, **b**-10 Apr 1835, **c**-Isaac PRICE, **d**-$1000, **e**-Abraham ROTHROCK, Francis McCLURE, **f**-19 May 1835, **g**-27 Feb 1836, **h**-$326.80.5, **i**-$283.44.75, **j**-$43.35.25, estate

Richard PINDELL [nothing afterward, the appearance of a Richard PINDELL in the following record makes me a little suspicious of a clerk's error?]

Samuel EDMISTON, **b**-16 Apr 1835, **c**-Richard PINDELL, **d**-$500, **e**-A. S. WILSON, Wm. MITCHELL, **f**- **g**- **h**- **i**- **j**-

James McCORD, **b**-11 Jun 1835, **c**-Thomas McCORD, **d**-$, **e**- **f**- **g**- **h**- **i**- **j**-

William A. STERRETT, **b**-8 Jul 1835, **c**-John STERRETT, **d**-$1200, **e**-Robert STERRETT, James T. HALL, **f**-5 Aug 1835, **g**-15 Feb 1837, **h**-$1580.66.5, **i**-$864.39.75, **j**-$716.26.25, estate

James JOHNSTON, **b**-5 Aug 1835, **c**-Augustine WAKEFIELD, **d**-$500, **e**-James CRISWELL, John V. CRISWELL, **f**- **g**- **h**- **i**- **j**-

Jacob BUMBAUGH, **b**-17 Aug 1835, **c**-George BUMBAUGH, **d**-$1000, **e**-Joseph MILLIKEN, S. H. BERRYHILL, **f**-25 Aug 1835, **g**-9 Aug 1836, **h**-$174.85, **i**-$51.51.25, **j**-$123.34.75, estate

Page 139, Frame 152

Ann JOHNSTON, **b**-28 Sep 1835, **c**-Dr. J. B. ARD, Ephraim BANKS, Esq., **d**- **e**- **f**-23 May 1833[sic], **g**-21 Feb 1840, **h**-$271.37, **i**-$183.37, **j**-$88.00, estate

William MITCHELL, **b**-25 Aug 1835, **c**-John MITCHELL, **d**-$, **e**- **f**-21 Dec 1835, **g**-15 Oct 1840/29 Jun 1842, **h**-$9152.86.5/$1889.50.25, **i**-$7797.15.5/$1363.40, **j**-$1355.71, estate/$526.10.5, estate

Nancy REED, **b**-27 Nov 1835, **c**-Robert COOPER, **d**-$2000, **e**-Moses KELLY, Saml. MITCHELL, **f**-21 Jan 1836, **g**- **h**- **i**- **j**-

Mathew TAYLOR, **b**-8 Dec 1835, **c**-William SHAW, **d**-$1000, **e**-Robert SHAW, A. B. LONG, **f**- **g**-29 Jun 1840, **h**-$3109.18, **i**- **j**-$66.51, estate

Robert McCLELLAND, **b**-22 Dec 1835, **c**-Reuben C. HALE, **d**-$5000, **e**-Joseph MILLIKEN, Francis McCLURE, **f**-13 Jan 1836, **g**-2 Oct 1840, **h**-$2334.71, **i**-$2593.58, **j**-$258.87, accountant

Samuel EDMISTON, Esq., **b**-6 Jan 1836, **c**-James DICKSON, **d**-$6000, **e**-D. W. HULINGS, Joseph MILLIKEN, **f**- **g**-2 Jul 1842, **h**-$2336.57, **i**-$2317.69, **j**-$18.90, estate

Hugh BEATTY, **b**-27 Jan 1836, **c**-James BRISBIN, Samuel KYLE, **d**-$2000, **e**-Jos. KYLE, Jos. MILLIKEN, **f**-2 Aug 1836, **g**-27 Feb 1841, **h**-$4798.38, **i**-$3164.08, **j**-$1634.50, estate

Isaac W. DONAHOO, **b**-23 Feb 1836, **c**-David RITTENHOUSE, Samuel RITTENHOUSE, **d**-$1500, **e**-D. R. REYNOLDS, Michael BRANON, **f**-12 Mar 1836, **g**-22 Feb 1837, **h**-$548.39.5, **i**-$493.84.5, **j**-$155.05, estate

Samuel MACLAY, Esq., **b**-1 Mar 1836, **c**-Samuel MACLAY, Wm. B. JOHNSTON, **d**-$3000, **e**-Jas. E. JOHNSTON, Jos. MILLIKEN, **f**-30 Mar 1836, **g**-27 Feb 1844/3 Jul 1846, **h**-$5647.86, **i**-$6229.49/$688.92, **j**-$688.92, accountant

Christian YODER (Butcher), **b**-7 Mar 1836, **c**-Shem YODER, Nicholas YODER, **d**-$4000, **e**-Shem ZOOK, Joseph MILLIKEN, **f**-4 Apr 1836, **g**-6 Mar 1838, **h**-$18,663.48, **i**-$18,678.48, **j**-$15.00, accountants

Christian HOFFMAN, **b**-7 Mar 1836, **c**-Elizabeth HOFFMAN, William HOFFMAN, **d**-$, **e**- **f**- **g**- **h**- **i**- **j**-

Catherine BAHN, **b**-10 Mar 1836, **c**-Henry BAHN, **d**-$12,000, **e**-Samuel COMFERT, Nathl. COMFERT, **f**-8 Apr 1836, **g**-24 Jun 1837, **h**-$6670.62.5, **i**-$6670.62.5, **j**-

Page 140, Frame 153
James CRISWELL, **b**-16 Mar 1836, **c**-Samuel PATTON, **d**-$1000, **e**-John NORRIS, A. S. WILSON, **f**-8 Apr 1836, **g**-18 Jun 1842, **h**-$487.23, **i**-$506.80, **j**-$18.97, accountant
Mariah BEAVER, **b**-12 Mar 1836, **c**-Joseph FLEMING, **d**- **e**- **f**- **g**- **h**- **i**-**j**-
Francis Boggs McNITT, **b**-24 Mar 1836, **c**-Robert M. THOMPSON, **d**-$1000, **e**-James MILLIKEN, Thompson McMANIGEL, **f**-23 Apr 1836/2 Apr 1838, **g**-29 Jun 1839, **h**-$716.45, **i**-$692.04, **j**-$24.41, estate
John HARTZLER, Sr., **b**-28 Mar 1836, **c**-David COFFMAN, **d**-$500, **e**-David HARTZLER, R. U. JACOBS, **f**-15 Apr 1836, **g**-24 Feb 1838/21 Feb 1844, **h**-$2363.38.5/$1971.01.5, **i**-$1446.55.25/$1082.30, **j**-$856.83.25, estate/$888.71.5, estate
David GRAHAM, **b**-30 Mar 1836, **c**-Robert MILLIKEN, **d**-$3000, **e**-John KAUFMAN, James WILSON, **f**-28 Apr 1836, **g**-2 Jul 1839/3 Mar 1843/2 Oct 1843, **h**-$2311.30/$2909.43/$3672.25.75, **i**-$476.46/$162.00, **j**-$3886.85, estate
John McFADDEN, **b**-2 May 1836, **c**-Robert MATHEWS, William MAYES, **d**-$2000, **e**-Joseph MILLIKEN, James GIBBONEY, **f**-5 May 1836, **g**-29 Feb 1840/3 Jul 1843, **h**-$2367.97/$991.03.5, **i**-$3153.52/$1158.52, **j**-$167.44, accountant
John SIGLER, **b**-4 May 1836, **c**-Samuel SIGLER, **d**- **e**- **f**- **g**- **h**- **i**- **j**-
Jacob YODER, **b**-12 May 1836, **c**-Isaac PLANK, Nicholas YODER, **d**-$, **e**- **f**-1 Jul 1828/30 Apr 1856, **g**-9 Nov 1830/$6 Apr 1857, **h**-$1987.29/$492.39.5, **i**-$450.39/$2955.23.75, **j**-$1536.90, state/$2462.84, estate
Joseph GETTYS, **b**-3 Jun 1836, **c**-John GETTYS, David ZOOK, **d**-$500, **e**-James GIBBONEY, Geo. MATHIAS, **f**-24 Jun 1836, **g**-17 May 1837, **h**-$437.70.5, **i**-$193.47.5, **j**-$244.23.5, estate
William MEVEY, **b**-2 Jul 1836, **c**-John ROBB, **d**-$1000, **e**-Geo. MITCHELL, S. W. STEWART, **f**-3 Aug 1836, **g**-17 Apr 1841,6 Nov 1844, **h**-$1846.38/$6433.28, **i**-$778.13/$883.66, **j**-$5549.62, estate
Nancy L. HORRELL, **b**-27 Jul 1836, **c**-James GIBBONEY, **d**-$500, **e**-Wm. B. JOHNSTON, R. C. HALE, **f**-22 Aug 1836, **g**- **h**- **i**- **j**-
Elias W. HALE, Esq., **b**-5 Aug 1836, **c**-Reuben C. HALE, **d**-$15,000, **e**-James GIBBONEY, D. W. HULINGS, **f**- **g**- **h**- **i**- **j**-

Page 141, Frame 154

John WHITESIDE, **b**-22 Aug 1836, **c**-Ruth E. WHITESIDE, **d**-$1000, **e**-Wm. WHITESIDE, Hugh McILVAINE, **f**-8 Sep 1836, **g**- **h**- **i**- **j**-

Richard B. ROPER, **b**-`10 Sep 1836, **c**-Joseph ROPER, **d**-$500, **e**-Isaac ARMSTRONG, James BICE, **f**-29 Sep 1836, **g**-6 Jul 1837, **h**-$83.00.25, **i**-$30.79.5, **j**-$52.20.75, estate

John RIDEN, Jr., **b**-19 Sep 1836, **c**-George MYERS, **d**-$500, **e**-Francis McCLURE, Jacob ALBRIGHT, **f**-3 Oct 1836, **g**-23 Jun 1838, **h**-$617.09, **i**-$392.52.25, **j**-$214.56.25, estate

John McLENAHAN, **b**-25 Oct 1836, **c**-John McCAULEY, Samuel BARR, **d**-$700, **e**-Francis McCLURE, J. MUTHERSBAUGH, **f**-21 Nov 1836/30 Dec 1837/11 Apr 1840, **g**-30 Dec 1837/5 Mar 1838, **h**-$374.68.75/$529.63, **i**-$157.10.25/$160.96, **j**-$217.58.5/$367.68.5, estate

David SAMPLE, **b**-11 Nov 1836, **c**-Josiah ALEXANDER, **d**-$1000, **e**-John ALEXANDER, Robert HUGHS, **f**- **g**- **h**- **i**- **j**-

Alexander A. ANDERSON, **b**-25 Nov 1836, **c**-Ephraim BANKS, **d**-$2000, **e**-Henry STONER, James ROBISON, **f**- **g**- **h**- **i**- **j**-

Richard PRYER, **b**-7 Dec 1836, **c**-Jonas SEWELL, **d**-$600, **e**-James BURNS, S. W. STEWART, **f**-31 Dec 1837, **g**-2 May 1837, **h**-$453.35, **i**-$169.88.75, **j**-$283.47.25, estate

Alexander GIBBONEY, **b**-15 Dec 1836, **c**-Alexander GIBBONEY, James GIBBONEY, **d**- **e**- **f**-12 Jan 1837, **g**- **h**- **i**- **j**-

John ZOOK, **b**-17 Dec 1836, **c**-David ZOOK, **d**- **e**- **f**-5 Apr 1837, **g**-28 Feb 1838, **h**-$634.01.75, **i**-$167.52, **j**-$466.69.75, estate

James WILSON, **b**-10 Jan 1837, **c**-Thomas J. WILSON, **d**- **e**- **f**-17 Feb 1837, **g**-2 Jul 1841, **h**-$3952.96, **i**-$3807.92.5, **j**-$145.03.5, estate

Joseph BROTHERS, **b**-25 Jan 1837, **c**-William BROTHERS, Samuel COMFERT, **d**- **e**- **f**-16 Feb 1837, **g**- **h**- **i**- **j**-

Frederick SETZLER, **b**-21 Feb 1837, **c**-John SETZLER, Daniel YODER, **d**-$300, **e**-Christian KAUFMAN, Samuel BRATTON, **f**-14 Mar 1837, **g**-10 Feb 18839, **h**-$290.86.25, **i**-$229.12.5, **j**-$61.73.75, estate

Page 142, Frame 155

Charles McLENAHAN, **b**-22 Feb 1837, **c**-John McLENAHAN, **d**-$500, **e**-John HOOVER, Alexander ORR, **f**-20 Mar 1837, **g**- **h**- **i**- **j**-

George ESPY, **b**-22 Feb 1837, **c**-John McLAUGHLIN, **d**-$200, **e**-Wm. S. WOODEN, Wm. J. McCOY, **f**- **g**- **h**- **i**- **j**-

William P. STITT, **b**-1 Mar 1837, **c**-John W. STITT, **d**-$1000, **e**-Archibald STITT, Cyrus STINE, **f**-3 Apr 1837, **g**- **h**- **i**- **j**-

George G. HALE [could be HALL], **b**-3 Mar 1837, **c**-John M. HALE, **d**-$1000, **e**-R. C. HALE, Geo. McCULLOCH, **f**- **g**- **h**- **i**- **j**-

Abraham LUKENS, **b**-7 Mar 1837, **c**-Geo. W. COULTER, William LAUGHLIN, **d**-$1000, **e**-James GIBBONEY, John THOMPSON, **f**-3 Apr 1837, **g**-26 Jun 1843, **h**- **i**- **j**-

William ROBISON, **b**-29 Mar 1837, **c**-James ROBISON, **d**-$1000, **e**-John ROBISON, D. R. REYNOLDS, **f**- **g**- **h**- **i**- **j**-

Jacob KENEGY, **b**-5 Apr 1837, **c**-David ZOOK, **d**- **e**- **f**-17 May 1837, **g**-20 Jun 1843/30 Jun 1847, **h**-$4550.63/$1215.92, **i**-$529.08/$81.81.5, **j**-$4021.55, estate/$1134.09.5, estate

Phoebe DILWORTH, **b**-11 Apr 1837, **c**-Charles DILWORTH, **d**-$4000, **e**-Charles WORRALL, Brinton DILWORTH, **f**-29 Apr 1837, **g**-28 Feb 1838, **h**-$2100.00, **i**-$97.68, **j**-$2002.32, estate

Jackson WATTSON, **b**-6 May 1837, **c**-Lewis T. WATTSON, Nathan B. WATTSON, **d**-$12,000, **e**-Joseph MILLIKEN, James BURNS, **f**-10 Jun 1837, **g**-2 Jul 1839, **h**-$1098.06, **i**-$871.77, **j**-$226.29, accountant

John GRAHAM, **b**-20 May 1837, **c**-John McDOWELL, **d**-$1000, **e**-Thomas REED, James MILLIKEN, **f**-17 Jun 1837, **g**-25 Feb 194-. **h**-$647.15.5, **i**-$147.43, **j**-$500.72.5, estate

Ann VANCE, **b**-14 Jun 1827, **c**-James CRISWELL **d**- **e**- **f**- **g**- **h**- **i**- **j**-

Mary McCOY, **b**-18 Jun 1837, **c**-Lewis HOOVER, **d**-$2000, **e**-Christian HOOVER, Wm. P. ELLIOTT, **f**- **g**- **h**- **i**- **j**-

Page 143, Frame 156

Samuel PATTON, **b**-22 Jul 1837, **c**-Mary B. PATTON, **d**-$1000, **e**-Wm. B. NORRIS, Adam GREER, **f**-10 Aug 1837, **g**- **h**- **i**- **j**-

Robert MEANS, **b**-17 Aug 1837, **c**-Andrew MEANS, Robert A. MEANS, **d**- **e**- **f**-23 Sep 1837, **g**- **h**- **i**- **j**-

James CRISWELL, **b**-17 Aug 1837, **c**-James DICKSON, **d**-$4000, **e**-Jno. NORRIS, R. U. JACOBS, **f**- **g**-18 Jun 1842, **h**-$48.13.5, **i**-$48.89, **j**-

Joseph McFADDEN, **b**-23 Aug 1837, **c**-Charles RITZ, **d**-$800, **e**-Andrew MAYES, A. B. LONG, **f**- **g**- **h**- **i**- **j**-

Adam CRISSMAN, **b**-21 Sep 1837, **C**-A. B. McNITT, John McDOWELL, **d**-$, **e**- **f**- **g**- **h**- **i**- **j**-

John B. IRWIN, **b**-27 Sep 1837, **c**-John OLIVER, Jr., **d**-$500 **e**-James CRISWELL, Joseph MILLIKEN, **f**-27 Nov 1837, **g**-13 Mar 1839, **h**-$65.87.5, **i**-$57.93.75, **j**-$7.93.75, estate

John H. JONES, **b**-7 Jan 1837, **c**-Jos. LOUGHERY, Jane W. JONES, **d**-$2000, **e**-Geo. McCULLOCH, S. W. STEWART, **f**-2 Feb 1838, **g**-5 May 1843, **h**-$32.70, **i**-$27.60, **j**-$5.10, estate

Thomas OSBOURN, **b**-13 Dec 1837, **c**-Mary OSBOURN, **d**-$500, **e**- **f**- **g**-24 Jul 1843, **h**-$414.50, **i**-$73.50, **j**-$32.00, accountant

John HAFFLEY, **b**-16 Dec 1837, **c**-Joseph HAFFLEY, David ZOOK, **d**-$900, **e**-John KAUFMAN, Francis McCOY, **f**-2 Jan 1838, **g**-2 Jan 1838/1 Mar 1845, **h**-$13,831.91, **i**-$8.81.25/$7470.61, **j**-$6361.30, estate

Josiah AULTZ, **b**-6 Dec 1837, **c**-Joseph HAFFLEY, **d**-$100, **e**-David KAUFMAN, John ZOOK, **f**- **g**- **h**- **i**- **j**-

Arthur BELL, **b**-17 Dec 1837, **c**-John H. BELL, **d**-$1000, **e**-Isaac TOWNSEND, John WILLS, **f**-15 Jan 1838, **g**-15 Sep 1838, **h**-$189.85, **i**-$154.65.5, **j**-$35.19.5, estate

William ALLISON, **b**-4 Jan 1838, **c**-Shem ZOOK, **d**-$5000, **e**-James MILLIKEN, John McDOWELL, **f**-18 Jan 1838, **g**-1 Jul 1840, **h**-$224.08, **i**-$191.14, **j**-$232.96, estate

Page 144, Frame 157

Robert GLASS, **b**-15 Mar 1838, **c**-William MONTGOMERY, **d**-$800, **e**-Robt. MATHEWS, Robt. McNEAL, **f**-28 Mar 1838, **g**-28 Mar 1840/7 Oct 1845, **h**-$617.47.5, **i**-$502.21.5, **j**-$115.26, [no designation but probably estate]

Peter CLOSE, **b**-2 Apr 1838, **c**-John McDOWELL, Henry L. CLOSE, **d**-$, **e**- **f**-8 Jun 1838, **g**-25 Feb 1840, **h**-$1082.79, **i**-$676.88.75, **j**-$465.75.25, estate

Joseph COCHRAN, **b**-3 Apr 1838, **c**-Thomas M. COCHRAN, **d**-$1600, **e**-Samuel CHESNUT, Joseph MILLIKEN, **f**-3 Apr 1838, **g**- **h**- **i**- **j**-

Stephen HINDS, **b**-18 Apr 1838, **c**-Thaddeus BANKS, **d**-$1000, **e**-Andrew KEISER, Thos. ROBISON, **f**-14 May 1838, **g**-18 Nov 1840/20 Jun 1845, **h**-$1497.24.5, **i**-$1566.05.5, **j**-$69.81, accountant

John IRWIN, **b**-25 Apr 1838, **c**-William M. HALL, **d**-$700, **e**-Joseph MILLIKEN, James McDOWELL, **f**- **g**- **h**- **i**- **j**-

Michael RUBLE, Sr., **b**-10 May 1838, **c**-John SNYDER, Henry HANAWALT, **d**- **e**- **f**-26 May 1838, **g**-20 Feb 1833[sic–1843?] **h**-$1729.28, **i**-$1768.96.5, **j**-$39.68, accountant

Thomas OSBOURN, **b**-22 May 1838, **c**-William BROTHERS, **d**-$600, **e**- **f**- **g**- **h**- **i**- **j**-

Henry SIGLER, b-30 May 1838, c-Geo. H. SIGLER, John SIGLER, Thomas B. CODER, d-$, e- f-25 Jun 1838, g-1 Jun 1839, h-$835.57, i-$461.74, j-$374.83, estate

John H. BELL, b-22 Jun 1838, c-William S. BELL, Thompson G. BELL, d-$2000, e-Geo. SIGLER, James MILLIKEN, f-17 Jul 1838, g-28 Jun 1839, h-$1648.70, i-$474.42, j-$1174.28, estate

Joseph RIDEN, b-28 Jun 1838, c-Henry LONG, d-$200, e-John H. LONG, Wm. BROTHERS, f-4 Aug 1838, g-28 Nov 1839, h-$35.57.5, i-$35.57.5, j-

Thomas OSBOURN, b-3 Jul 1838, c-Alexander OSBOURN, d-$500, e-Wm. BROTHERS, Robt. BURNS, f- g- h- i- j-

Martha KENNY, b-7 Jul 1838, c-James HEMPHILL, d-$800, e-Jos. MILLIKEN, Chas. RITZ, f-24 Mar 1845, g-24 Mar 1845, h-$1008.45.75, i-$593.22, j-$415.23.75, estate

Page 145, Frame 158

George PENNEPACKER, b-5 Aug 1838, c-Elias PENNEPACKER, d-$1000, e-Hugh McKEE, Henry LEATTOR, f-10 Aug 1838, g-2 Oct 1840, h-$292.03.25, i-$482.07.25, j-$90.06, accountant

John ORT, b-18 Aug 1838, c-William KEPPERLING, d-$800, e-William BROTHERS, John HOYT, f-5 Nov 1838, g-2 Oct 1839, h-$80.90 i-$121.31, j-$40.41, accountant

Joseph FLEMING, b-12 Sep 1838, c-Martin FLEMING, John WILSON, d-$2000, e-James MILLIKEN, John FLEMING, f- g-2 Oct 1839, h-$2009.43, i-$1445.73, j-$563.70, estate

Henry STEELY, b-2 Oct 1838, c-Mary STEELY, Hugh MORAN, d-$, e-f- g- h- i- j-

Thomas WILLIAMS, b-5 Oct 1838, c-Catherine WILLIAMS, d-$150, e-J. G. SMITH, J. CRAWFORD, f-18 Oct 1838, g-6 Aug1839, h-$140.81, i-$236.77, j-$95.96, accountant

William MAYES, b-10 Oct 1838, c-Thomas McCLURE, d-$1000, e-Francis McCLURE, David R. REYNOLDS, f-2 Nov 1838, g-24 Jun 1843/19 Feb 1847, h-$2693.99/$2471.92.5, i-$1560.00/$95.57, j-$2376.35.25, [no designation, but probably estate]

Parker DURBURROW, b-15 Oct 1838, c-David McCLURE, d-$500, e-Joseph MILLIKEN, John CRAWFORD, f-23 Oct 1838, g-2 Mar 1841, h-$493.56, i-$601.16, j-$149.03, accountant

Dr. J. P. MORRISON, b-26 Oct 1838, c-E. BANKS, Esq., d-$500, e-Henry STONER, Wm. McCAY, f-9 Nov 1838, g- h- i- j-

John POWERS, **b**-30 Oct 1838, **c**-M. M. MONAHON, **d**-$50, **e**-J. S. McEUEN, James TURNER, **f**-28 Nov 1838, **g**- **h**- **i**- **j**-

James FLEMING, **b**-30 Oct 1838, **c**-John WATT, **d**- **e**- **f**-4 Jul 1839, **g**-28 Jun 1843, **h**-$5695.56, **i**-$5735.56, **j**-$40.00, accountant

John EVERHART, **b**-28 Nov 1838, **c**-Robert McDONELL, **d**-$400, **e**-James HEMPHILL, Geo. PATTON, Jr., **f**-8 Jan 1839, **g**-13 Jun 1840, **h**-$312.97.75, **i**-$302.75.5, **j**-$10.22.25, accountant

Jane SCOTT, **b**-8 Dec 1838, **c**-William SCOTT, **d**-$600, **e**-Geo. W. PATTON, R. SCOTT, **f**- **g**- **h**- **i**- **j**-

Page 146, Frame 159 [duplicated on frame 160]
Henry MILLER, **b**-31 Dec 1838, **c**-Michael MILLER, **d**-$1000, **e**-James PARKER, Ludwig YEATTER, **f**- **g**-27 Mar 1843, **h**-$792.42, **i**-$80.33, **j**-$712.09, estate

Foster MILLIKEN, **b**-18 Jan 1839, **c**-Reuben C. HALE, **d**-$5000, **e**-James MILLIKEN, Joseph MILLIKEN, **f**- **g**- **h**- **i**- **j**-

Jacob JOHNSTON (Negro), **b**-28 Jan 1839, **c**-Catherine JOHNSTON, **d**- **e**- **f**- **g**- **h**- **i**- **j**-

David McKEE, **b**-11 Feb 1839, **c**-John OLIVER, Jr., Hugh McKEE, **d**- **e**- **f**- **g**- **h**- **i**- **j**-

Henry MILLER, **b**-14 Feb 1839, **c**-John GRAHAM, **d**-$200, **e**-Francis McCAIN, John CUPPLES, **f**-6 Apr 1839, **g**-26 Feb 1841, **h**-$216.20, **i**-$215.66, **j**-$.54, estate

Ann McKEE, **b**-19 Feb 1839, **c**-William H. SMITH, **d**-$300, **e**-Thos. R. McKEE, John McKEE, **f**- **g**- **h**- **i**- **j**-

Christian SCOTT, **b**-11 Mar 1839, **c**-David W. HULINGS, **d**-$200, **e**-Jacob WINDER, D. R. REYNOLDS, **f**- **g**- **h**- **i**- **j**-

Richard PRYER, **b**-14 Mar 1839, **c**-E. L. BENEDICT, **d**-$300, **e**-Jos. MILLIKEN, Robt. MATHEWS, **f**- **g**- **h**- **i**- **j**-

John WERTZ, Jr., **b**-18 Mar 1839, **c**-David McCLURE, **d**-$400, **e**-James MILLIKEN, Saml. COMFERT, **f**- **g**- **h**- **i**- **j**-

Jacob SNIDER, **b**-25 Mar 1839, **c**-James THOMPSON, **d**- **e**- **f**- **g**- **h**- **i**- **j**-

John KING, **b**-1 Apr 1839, **c**-Yost KING, **d**- **e**- **f**-3 Jul 1841, **g**- **h**- **i**- **j**-

William DYSART, **b**-2 Apr 1839, **c**-John DYSART, Samuel WHARTON, **d**-$2000, **e**-J. J. CUNNINGHAM, Elisha BRATTON, **f**-23 Apr 1839, **g**-11 Sep 1840, **h**-$2060.23.25, **i**-$1731.57, **j**-$328.66, estate

Page 147, Frame 161

Isaac KAUFMAN, **b**-27 Apr 1839, **c**-Peter HERSHBARGER, **d**- **e**- **f**-20 May 1839, **g**-8 Nov 1851, **h**-$2002.38, **i**-$1926.05, **j**-$76.33, executor

John GRAHAM, **b**-3 May 1839, **c**-Peter HARSHBARGER, **d**- **e**- **f**-20 May 1839, **g**-22 Jun 1842, **h**-$1461.59, **i**-$1457.74.25, **j**-$3.84.75, estate

Hannah MEANS, **b**-6 May 1839, **c**-Robert McKEE, Andrew MEANS, **d**- **e**- **f**- **g**- **h**- **i**- **j**-

Joseph LEEHEY, **b**-2 Jul 1839, **c**-Charles RITZ, **d**-$300, **e**-James BURNS, Wm. J. STEEL, **f**- **g**- **h**- **i**- **j**-

John COX, **b**-6 Jul 1839, **c**-Edward COX, **d**-$2000, **e**-Wm. THOMPSON, Adam GREER, **f**-5 Aug 1839, **g**- **h**- **i**- **j**-

David WINSKEY, **b**-4 Sep 1839, **c**-Henry WICKS, **d**-$150, **e**-Robert McMANIGIL, James TURNER, **f**- **g**- **h**- **i**- **j**-

James BOGLE, **b**-7 Dec 1839, **c**-Michael CRISWELL, **d**-$2400, **e**-James MILLIKEN, R. E. HALL, **f**-11 Jan 1840, **g**- **h**- **i**- **j**-

Christian LAPP, **b**-20 Dec 1839, **c**-Nancy YODER, **d**-$12,000, **e**-John KAUFMAN, William REED, **f**-20 Jan 1840, **g**-6 Apr 1842, **h**-$7276.67.5, **i**-$88.54.25, **j**-$7188.13.25, estate

Henry WILSON, **b**-4 Jan 1840, **c**-Mary WILSON, **d**-$400, **e**-Geo. MILLER, James McCORD, **f**- **g**-24 Feb 1843, **h**-$132.42, **i**-$301.60, **j**-$256.08, accountant

William C. WAKER[sic], **b**-18 Jan 1840, **c**-Robert MATHEWS, **d**-$100, **e**-John KEITH, Nathl. McELCAR, **f**- **g**- **h**- **i**- **j**-

James LEATTOR, **b**-24 Feb 1840, **c**-Thomas FRITZ, Charles BRATTON, **d**-$, **e**- **f**-12 Jun 1840, **g**- **h**- **i**- **j**-

George BECK, **b**-20 Feb 1840, **c**-John ORT, Jr., **d**-$2000, **e**- Geo. DAVIS, Henry KULP, **f**-14 May 1840, **g**- **h**- **i**- **j**-

Page 148, Frame 162

David YERGER, **b**-2 Mar 1840, **c**-Samuel WHARTON, **d**- **e**- **f**-6 Apr 1840, **g**-22 Feb 1841, **h**-$285.59.5, **i**-$197.84.5, **j**-$88.75, estate

John McLENAHEN, **b**-14 Mar 1840, **c**-Samuel BARR, **d**-$1000, **e**-James MILLIKEN, Jacob MURTHERSBAUGH, **f**- **g**-7 Mar 1846, **h**-$648.76, **i**-$191.57.5, **j**-$457.38.5, estate

Henry SEACHRIST, **b**-6 Apr 1840, **c**-Owen OWENS, **d**-$500, **e**-Lewis OWENS, Geo. MITCHELL, Sr., **f**-6 May 1840, **g**-29 Oct 1841, **h**-$97.21, **i**-$393.84.5, **j**-$296.63.5, accountant

James McDOWELL, b-7 Apr 1840, c-Henry LONG, A. [L., probably S.] WILSON, d-$, e- f-28 Mar 1840, g-25 Feb 1842, h-$445.58.75, i-$95.75, j-$349.83.75, estate

James McDOWELL, Esq., b-17 Mar 1840, c-Reuben C. HALE, d- e- f-17 Apr 1840, g-7 Aug 1840, h-$5233.70, i-$4854.30.5, j-$379.39.5, estate

Ellen TOWNSEND, b-1 May 1840, c-Joseph BURKHOLDER, d- e- f-6 Jun 1841, g-12 Jun 1845, h-$399.32, i-$309.36.5, j-$117.34.5, estate

George BUOY, b-11 May 1840, c-Mary BUOY, Martin GAMBLE, d-$300, e-John STERRETT, Geo. MILLER, f-2 Jun 1840, g-1 Jul 1842, h-$96.50, i-$92.98, j-$3.52, estate

Thomas JONES, b-20 May 1840, c-John McCORD, d-$300, e-James McCORD, Geo. WILEY, f-2 Jun 1840, g- h- i- j-

William MAYES, b-27 Jun 1840, c-Samuel BARR, Esq., d-$600, e-Geo. SIGLER, Peter LEHR, f-25 Jul 1843, g-28 Feb 1843, h-$371.70, i-$237.79, j-$133.93, estate

John BEATTY, b-2 Jul 1840, c-Dr. Saml. MACLAY, William BEATTY, James BEATTY, d-$, e- f-11 Jul 1840, g- h- i- j-

Jacob SNIDER, b-17 Jul 1840, c-Lewis BERGSTRESSER, d-$500, e-James MILLIKEN, Jesse WINKET, f- g-28 Jun 1842/" " ", h-$357.96.25/$189.94, i-$290.49.5/$157.72.5, j-$99.68, estate

Joseph TRIMBLE, b-31 Jul 1840, c-Dr. A. ROTHROCK, Harriet B. CORBETT, d-$14,000, e-Jane H. TRIMBLE, Ann H. TRIMBLE, Esther B. TRIMBLE, f-17 Aug 1840, g-2 Jul 1841, h-$8777.58, i-$232.54, j-$8545.04, estate

Page 149, Frame 163

Claudius DONNELLY, b-5 Aug 1840, c-James CORBETT, d-$500, e-P. STROUSE, J. M. BARTON, f-6 Jan 1845, g-31 Mar 1845, h-$321.36, i-$328.19, j-$6.83, accountant

Andrew LANGTON, b-3 Aug 1840, c-Michael CRISWELL, d- e- f- g- h- i- j-

James McCORMICK, b-6 Aug 1840, c-Robert McCORMICK, d- e- f-2 Nov 1840, g- h- i- j-

William STALL, b-7 Sep 1840, c-Mathias RUMBAUGH, d-$1400, e-Martin [KISEY], Amos [STOLL], f- g- h- i- j-

George SWARTZELL, b-19 Sep 1840, c-George SWARTZELL, Jacob KRISE, d- e- f- g-29 Jun 1849, h-$1590.95, i-$336.65, j-$1254.30, estate

James GLASGOW, b-15 Oct 1840, **c**-Francis McCLURE, **d- e- f**-16 Feb 1841, **g- h- i- j-**

Allen ARNOLD, b-23 Oct 1840, **c**-John CUPPLES, **d**-$200, **e**-Hugh McKEE, James SHEHEN, **f**-21 Nov 1840, **g**-23 Oct 1841/16 Feb 1846, **h**-$209.45.25/$213.57, **i**-$209.45.25/$219.42.5, **j**-$5.85.5, administrator

Jonathan ALEXANDER, b-14 Dec 1840, **c**-William SMITH, William McDOWELL, **d**-$1000, **e**-R. C. HALL, James BEATTY, **f**-7 Jan 1841, **g**-19 Feb 1842, **h**-$958.83, **i**-$944.18, **j**-$14.65, heirs

David CRISWELL, b-14 Dec 1840, **c**-Cyrus CRISWELL, David JENKINS, **d**-$1600, **e**-A. S. WILSON, John ROSS, **f**-6 Jan 1841, **g**-4 Mar 1842/16 Oct 1844, **h**-$2568.68/$1541.54, **i**-$681.76/$1627.62, **j**-$86.08, accountant

Robert McNITT, b-21 Dec 1840, **c**-William McNITT, James McNITT, John McNITT, **d**-$ **e- f- g- h- i- j-**

Isaac JONES, b-6 Jan 1841, **c**-William T. BELL **d**-$4000, **e**-Robert PATTERSON, John KAUFMAN, **f**-4 Feb 1841, **g**-16 Dec 1844/13 Feb 1846, **h**-$2105.62/$1364.47, **i**-$1464.57/$493.55.75, **j**-$870.91.25, estate

Mary GREATHOUSE, b-8 Jan 1841, **c**-Andrew PARKER, Esq., **d**-$3000, **e**-James PARKER, Wm. PARKER, **f- g- h- i- j-**

Page 150, Frame 164

Joseph MARTIN, b-13 Jan 1841, **c**-J. J. CUNNINGHAM, **d**-$600, **e**-Geo. W. PATTON, S. P. LILLEY, **f- g- h- i- j-**

William HORRELL, b-22 Jan 1841, **c**-Robert McDOWELL, **d**-$400, **e**-Frederick SWARTZ, Jno. J. McCOY, **f**-11 Feb 1841, **g**-7 Apr 1843, **h**-$381.61.5, **i**-353.38.5 **j**-$28.23, estate

Richard JOHNSTON, b-27 Jan 1841, **c**-John SHAW, **d**-$100, **e**-C. HOOVER, Sr., Jacob SMITH, **f- g- h- i- j-**

Johl. F. ROOT, b-28 Jan 1841, **c**-John R. WEEKS, **d**-$3200, **e**-Johnston THOMAS, John A. STERRETT, **f**-15 Feb 1841, **g**-8 Jul 1844, **h**-$1172.00.25, **i**-$668.39.25, **j**-$503.61, estate

Jane REED, b-29 Jan 1841, **c**-Alexander GIBBONEY, George WILSON, **d**-$, **e- f**-30 Mar 1841, **g- h- i- j-**

William BEATTY, b-30 Jan 1841, **c**-William McDOWELL, **d**-$600, **e**-R. C. HALL, James TURNER, **f**-8 Feb 1841, **g**-25 Feb 1843, **h**-$201.63.25, **i**-$139.18.75, **j**-62.44.5, estate

John McDOWELL, b-6 Feb 1841, **c**-John FLEMING, **d**-$, **e- f**-2 Mar 1841, **g**-28 Feb 1842, **h**-$1665.23, **i**-$220.35.25, **j**-$1263.93.75, estate

Jacob ZOOK, b-11 Feb 1841, c-David ZOOK, d- e- f-8 Feb 1844, g-8 Feb 1844, h-$4313.55, i-$3663.48, j-$650.07 [or $656.67], estate

John OLIVER, Jr., b-16 Feb 1841, c-Geo. W. OLIVER, d-$3000, e-Casper DULL, Geo. A. LYON, f-9 Mar 1841, g-3 Jul 1843, h-$1742.15.5, i-$1983.93.25, j-$241.77.75, accountant

Allen CAVENAUGH, b-5 Feb 1841, c-Sarah CAVENAUGH, d-$400, e-A. BLYMYER, Isaac AULTZ, f-20 Feb 1841, g-4 Feb 1842, h-$116.81.5, i-$113.06.5, j-$4.75, estate

William STRUNK, b-2 Mar 1841, c-Rebecca STRUNK, d-$600, e-Benjn. STRUNK, Wm. McDOWELL, f-27 Mar 1841, g- h- i- j-

John NORRIS, b-10 Mar 1841, c-Wm. B. NORRIS, John NORRIS, Jas. C. NORRIS, d-$, e- f-13 Apr 1841, g- h- i- j-

Page 151, Frame 165

Margaret GRAHAM, b-18 Mar 1841, c-Philip STROUSE, d-$400, e-Michael SEACHRIST, Mathias MOODY, f-27 Mar 1841, g-1 Jul 1842, h-$392.87, i-$392.87, j-

John FERTIG, b-7 Apr 1841, c-Ephraim BANKS, d-$400, e-R. C. HALE, Saml. P. LILLEY, f-1 Jan 1842, g- h- i- j-

Samuel CEEVER, b-11 May 1841, c-John SNYDER, Henry AURAND, d-$, e- f-19 May 1841, g-1 Mar 1842, h-$52.46.5, i-$80.35, j-$27.88.5, accountant

James GIBBONEY, b-19 May 1841, c-David CANDOR, d-$2000, e-Jas. McCONNELL, Robt. PATTERSON, f-10 Jun 1841 g-3 Mar 1846, h-$400.90.25, i-$407.49.25, j-$3.41.5, estate

Theodore MEMINGER, b-22 Jun 1841, c-Wm. B. NORRIS, John NORRIS, d-$1200, e-Wm. McCAY, Adam GREER, f- g- h- i- j-

James McDONALD, b-1 Jul 1841, c-James McDONALD, d- e- f-16 Jul 1841, g-6 Dec 1844, h-$2845.55, i-$77.11, j-$2768.44, estate

James BROWN, b-6 Jul 1841, c-Thomas BROWN, James BROWN, Wm. B. JOHNSTON, d-$8000, e-John STERRETT, Cyrus ALEXANDER, f-2 Aug 1841, g-3 Jun 1846, h-$2573.50, i-$, j-

James C. CLARK, b-5 Jul 1841, c-Andrew WATTS, d-$500, e-Shem ZOOK, Robt. PATTERSON, f-2 Aug 1841, g- h- i- j-

John RIDEN, b-10 Jul 1841, c-Jacob MILLER, d-$500, e-D. REYNOLDS, James MILLIKEN, f-10 Aug 1841, g- h- i- j-

Rudolph POLGER, b-17 Sep 1841, c-Samuel HOPPER, d-$100, e-Wm. H. IRWIN, J. [BOARLY], f-11 Oct 1841, g- h- i- j-

William MATHEWS, b-30 Aug 1841, c-Ephraim BANKS, d- e- f- g-4
   Dec 1853, h-$198.09, i-$2645.47.5, j-$2447.38.5, estate
Rebecca STERRETT, b-11 Sep 1841, c-Nathl. W. STERRETT, d- e- f-29
   Jan 1842, g- h- i- j-
Mary ELLIS, b-6 Apr 1841, c-Geo. McCULLOCH, d- e- f-16 Apr 1841,
   g- h- i- j-

Page 152, Frame 166
Elizabeth SHOOK, b-20 Sep 1841, c-John FILSON, d-$200, e-R. U.
   JACOBS, Jos. MILLIKEN, f- 4 Dec 1843, g-4 Dec 1843, h-$147.56.5,
   i-$32.98.25, j-$114.58.25, estate
Frederick KINERLY, b-9 Oct 1841, c-William ROSS, d-$2000, e-James
   BURNS, John ROSS, f-2 Nov 1841, g- h- i- j-
Margaret COOPER, b-27 Sep 1841, c-Robert McNEAL, d-$, e- f- g- h-
   i- j-
James E. APPLEBAUGH, b-12 Oct 1841, c-John R. APPLEBAUGH, d-
   $3000, e-James BURNS, James McCONNELL, f-8 Nov 1841, g-9 Dec
   1844, h-$333.99.5, i-$167.23.5, j-$166.76, estate
Edward McNUTT, b-2 Nov 1841, c-Wm. CUMMINGS, d-$1600, e-
   Francis McCLURE, S. W. TAYLOR, f- g- h- i- j-
Samuel SWITZER, b-2 Novo 1841, c-Elijah MORRISON, d-$600, e-John
   POSTLETHWAIT, John GAYTON, f-24 Nov 1841, g-10 Nov 1842,
   h-$321.59, i-$347.38, j-$25.79, accountant
Christian BUMGARNER, b-27 Nov 1841, c-John BEATTY, d-$500, e-
   James BEATTY, Jos. MILLIKEN, f-13 Dec 1841, g- h- i- j-
Isabella McCARTY, b-6 Dec 1841, c-R. C. HALE, Henry EISENBISE,
   d-$, e- f- g- h- i- j-
William McCAY, Esq., b-16 Dec 1841, c-Henry KULP, Abraham
   McCAY, d-$, e- f-11 Jan 1842/3 Mar 1842, g-12 Oct 1844, h-
   $5536.71, i-$5316.33, j-$220.38, estate
James McINTIRE, b-3 Jan 1842, c-Francis THOMPSON, d-$300, e-
   Francis McCOY, James WAREAM, f-3 Feb 1842, g-10 Oct 1843, h-
   $146.33.75, i-$126.42.25, j-$19.92.5, estate
John POWELL, b-3 Jan 1842, c-Joel ZOOK, d-$, e- f-27 Jan 1842, g-27
   Feb 1843, h-$675.38, i-$570.72.5, j-$104.65.5, estate
Jacob RUBLE, b-4 Jan 1842, c-William McDOWELL, Geo. RUBLE, d-$,
   e- f-1 Feb 1842, g- h- i- j-

Page 153, Frame 167

Edmund LOCKERD, b-19 Jan 1842, **c**-William LEVY, **d**-$100, **e**- **f**- **g**-4 Jan 1843/16 Mar 1844, **h**-$20.00/$76.32, **i**-$27.00/$49.58.5, **j**-$7.00, [accountant]/$26.73.5, estate

Doct. L. G. SNOWDEN, b-2 Feb 1842, **c**-John FORSTER, **d**-$1200, **e**-Wm. ERWIN, D. R. REYNOLDS, **f**- **g**- **h**- **i**- **j**-

Edward DOUGHERTY, b-3 Feb 1842, **c**-William BAKER, **d**- **e**- **f**- **g**- **h**- **i**- **j**-

John LAMARD, b-9 Feb 1842, **c**-Geo. H. ALLEN, **d**-$600, **e**-Michael CRISWELL, Wm. R. LILLEY, **f**-9 Nov 1842, **g**- **h**- **i**- **j**-

John FOSTER, b-22 Feb 1842, **c**-Henry LEATTOR, Wm. HARDY, **d**-$7000, **e**-John McCORD, R. C. HALE, **f**-8 Mar 1842, **g**-30 Sep 1845, **h**-$4097.26.25, **i**-$803.38, **j**-$3283.88.25, estate

Jacob BROWER, b-22 Feb 1842, **c**-A.. B. NORRIS, **d**-$400, **e**-Benjn. BROWER, Jos. BROWER, **f**- **g**-6 Nov 1843/10 Mar 1845, **h**-$89.87/$42.52, **i**-$47.35/$42.00, **j**-$42.52, estate

Michael YODER, b-5 Mar 1842, **c**-Peter YODER, Gideon YODER, **d**-$, **e**- **f**-19 Mar 1842/16 Jan 1843, **g**-13 May 1844/22 Aug 1846, **h**-$641.35/$9473.73, **i**-$609.11.75/$1233.47, **j**-$32.23.5, estate/$8240.26, estate

Doct. L. G. SNOWDEN, b-7 Mar 1842, **c**-Margaret SNOWDEN, **d**-$1200, **e**-Casper DULL, Jas. LANGTON, **f**-5 Apr 1842, **g**- **h**- **i**- **j**-

Crawford KYLE, b-11 Mar 1842, **c**-Joseph KYLE, Ephraim BANKS, **d**- **e**- **f**-26 Mar 1842, **g**- **h**- **i**- **j**-

Jacob MILLER, b-1 Apr 1842, **c**-David HARTLER, Joshua KING, **d**- **e**- **f**- **g**- **h**- **i**- **j**-

Jane COCHRAN, b-7 Apr 1842, **c**-James BEATTY, **d**-$1000, **e**-Robt. STERRETT, Josiah KERR, **f**-13 Apr 1842, **g**-6 May 1843, **h**-$479.29, **i**-$38.11.75, **j**-$441.17.25, estate

George MARKS, b-5 Apr 1842, **c**-Christian MARKS, William B. JOHNSTON, Jacob MARKS, **d**-$800, **e**-Wm. A. McMANIGIL, Thomas BROWN, **f**-4 May 1842, **g**- **h**- **i**- **j**-

Page 154, Frame 168

Solomon PECHT, b-16 Apr 1842, **c**-William A. PECHT, **d**-$300, **e**-Robt. McMANIGIL, Adam GREER, **f**-14 May 1842, **g**-4 Aug 1853, **h**-$357.28, **i**-$579.80, **j**-$168.52, estate

James ROBISON, b-16 Apr 1842, **c**-David CANDOR, David McCLURE, **d**-$, **e- f**-1 Sep 1842, **g**-3 Mar 1846, **h**-$4096.50, **i**-$3756.46.5, **j**-$340.04.5, estate

Elizabeth STARKS, b-7 Apr 1842, **c**-Charles RITZ, **d- e- f**-28 May 1842, **g**-11 Mar 1845, **h**-$911.64, **i**-$281.65, **j**-$629.99, estate

John BATES, b-14 Apr 1842, **c**-Davis BATES, **d- e- f**-15 Apr 1843, **g- h- i- j**-

Henry BURKHOLDER, b-18 Apr 1842, **c**-John BURKHOLDER, Ephraim BANKS, **d- e- f**-17 Jun 1842, **g**-4 Aug 1845/10 Jan 1856/ " " ", **h**-$3437.23/$379.76/$3207.62, **i**-$667.51.5/$4174.34/$17,483,28.5, **j**-$1769.71.5, estate/$794.58, estate/$14,275.66.5, estate

Phoebe GILSON, b-30 Apr 1842, **c**-Ephraim BANKS, **d**-$2000, **e**-Wm. GILSON, Jos. MILLIKEN, **f**-25 May 1842, **g- h- i- j**-

Philip STROUP, b-7 May 1842, **c**-George DAVIS, **d**-$1200, **e**-James McCORD, Geo. WILEY, **f**-11 Jun 1842, **g**-4 Mar 1844, **h**-$743.19.75, **i**-$664.47.75, **j**-$78.72, estate

James EAGER, b-17 May 1842, **c**-David W. McCORMICK, **d**-$600, **e**-Ephraim BANKS, James BURNS, **f**-1 Jun 1842, **g**-16 Jul 1844, **h**-$753.30.75, **i**-$397.84.5, **j**-$355.46.25, estate

James McDONALD, Jr., b-25 Jun 1842, **c**-Cyrus CRISWELL, **d**-$800, **e**-James COOPER, Saml. BROWN, **f**-1 Aug 1842, **g**-5 Nov 1844/2 Dec 1845, **h**-$3229.75/$142.81, **i**-$3143.68/$153.46.5, **j**-$86.70, [no designation, possibly estate?], $10.65.5, accountant

James McDONALD, Sr., b-25 Jun 1842 [although the "2" has a heavy "1" marked through it–?], **c**-Cyrus CRISWELL, **d**-$800, **e**-James COOPER, Saml. BROWN, **f- g- h- i- j**-

Peter RUBLE, b-21 Jul 1842, **c**-Gabriel DUNMIRE, Jacob GARVER, **d**-$1200, **e**-Saml. P. LILLEY, Francis McCLURE, **f**-26 Aug 1842, **g- h- i- j**-

John BYLER, b-8 Aug 1842, **c**-John KESMEGY, Christian BYLER, **d**-$, **e- f**-8 Aug 1842, **g**-5 Jan 1849, **h**-$1823.75, **i**-$1805.45, **j**-$18.30, accountants

Page 155, Frame 169

James ANDERSON, b-24 Sep 1842, **c**-John L. ICKES, **d**-$200, **e**-David McCLURE, James McCONNELL, **f- g- h- i- j**-

William P. MACLAY, b-1 Oct 1842, **c**-Samuel MACLAY, Wm. B. MACLAY, David MACLAY, Holms MACLAY, **d- e- f**-28 Oct 1842, **g- h- i- j**-

Henry McCONKEY, b-16 Oct 1842, c-William McCONKEY, d-$1700, e-Robert PATTERSON, Jos. HOSTETLER, f-9 Nov 1842, g-29 Nov 1843, h-$1219.05, i-$30.79, j-$1188.26, estate

Samuel MATTER, b-18 Oct 1842, c-William B. MACLAY, d-$2600, e-Christian MYERS, John McDOWELL, f-8 Nov 1842, g-11 Mar 1845, h-$765.58.75, i-$811.14, j-$45.55.25, accountant

Robert E. SMITH, b-18 Oct 1842, c-E. J. SMITH, Adam GREER, d-$2000, e-J. E. JOHNSTON, F. McCOY, Jr., f-8 Dec 1842, g- h- i- j-

Moses YODER, b-3 Nov 1842, c-John KENNEGY, Joel ZOOK, d-$2000, e-James MILLIKEN, S. W. TAYLOR, f-28 Nov 1842, g-2 Nov 1843/ 30 Jun 1847, h-$1088.63.75/$5533.99, i-$575.56/$6130.70, j-$513.07.75, estate/$596.70, accountants

Mathias MOODY, b-17 Dec 1842, c-John MORRISON, d-$300, e-Philip STROUSE, f-5 Jan 1843, g-2 Jul 1847, h-$712.48.5, i-$311.80, j-$400.68.5, estate

James RIPPY, b-9 Dec 1842, c-David MACLAY, d-$300, e-William WILSON, Adam GREER, f-17 Jan 1843, g- h- i- j-

William MATHEWS, b-17 Dec 1842, c-Joseph MATHEWS, Eleanor MATHEWS, d-$1000, e-Robt. MATHEWS, Saml. COMFORT, f-30 Apr 1841/3 Jun 1843, g- h- i- j-

Christian GROW, b-16 Dec 1842, c-Ephraim BANKS, Esq., d- e- f-21 Mar 1843, g- h- i- j-

Philip WEILER, b-22 Dec 1842, c-George WEILER, David WEILER, d-$6000, e-J. R. McDOWELL, David YODER, f-20 Jan 1843, g-3 Jul 1847, h-$7020.98.5, i-$1336.28.75, j-$5684.69.75, estate

Sarah MORRISON, b-28 Jan 1843, c-George ASKINS, d-$800, e-Thos. ASKINS, Jno. J. McCOY, f-24 Feb 1843, g- h- i- j-

Richard HOPE, b-13 Oct 1842[sic], c-Mathew B. HOPE, Abraham CRISWELL, Jos. W. HERSHBERGER, d- e- f-19 Oct 1842, g- h- i- j-

Page 156, Frame 170

Margaret BELL, b-16 Feb 1843, c-Samuel BARR, Esq., d-$400, e-Johnston BELL, Wm. S. BELL, f-3 Mar 1843, g-6 Jan 1853, h-$161.06, i-$547.24, j-$386.18 [no designation]

Hannah GALBRAITH/CALBRAITH, b-24 Feb 1843, c-Augustin WAKEFIELD, d-$8000, e-G. H. CALBRAITH, f-21 Mar 1843, g- h- i- j-

James GLASGOW, b-20 Mar 1843, c-John PURCELL, d-$1000, e-Mathew GLASGOW, J. C. SECHLER, f-1 May 1843, g-21 Feb

1845/18 Jun 1849, **h**-$714.51/$133.39, **i**-$807.99/$134.39, **j**-$93.43, accountant/$4.00, accountant

John DYSERT, Sr., **b**-28 Feb 1943. **c**-James DYSERT, **d**- **e**- **f**-21 Mar 1843, **g**-7 Feb 1844, **h**-$2979.77.5, **i**-$116.81, **j**-$2862.96.5, estate

William HAZLETT, **b**-23 Mar 1843, **c**-Wilson HAZLETT, **d**- **e**- **f**-12 May 1843, **g**- **h**- **i**- **j**-

Rachel LONGWELL, **b**-25 Mar 1843, **c**-Alexander LONGWELL, **d**-$200, **e**-Thomas REED, Jos. BROWER, **f**- **g**- **h**- **i**- **j**-

David LANTZ, **b**-12 Apr 1843, **c**-Jacob MILLER, **d**-$150, **e**-Samuel LANTZ, **f**-4 May 1843, **g**-1 Apr 1844, **h**-$44.32, **i**-$47.06, **j**-$2.64, accountant

John WERTZ, **b**-25 Apr 1843, **c**-David McCLURE, Francis McCORD, **d**-$500, **e**-James McCORD, Samuel MILLIKEN, **f**- **g**- **h**- **i**- **j**-

William P. FLOYD, **b**-26 Apr 1843, **c**-Mathias NIECE, **d**-$500, **e**-John R. McDOWELL, Wm. J. McCOY, **f**-26 May 1843, **g**- **h**- **i**- **j**-

Samuel GILMORE, **b**-26 Apr 1843, **c**-William W. GILMORE, Robt. M. GILMORE, **d**-$, **e**- **f**- **g**- **h**- **i**- **j**-

Yost HARTZLER, **b**-22 Apr 1843, **c**-Jacob HARTZLER, Enoch ZOOK, John HARTZLER, **d**- **e**- **f**-6 May 1843, **g**-1 Jun 1844, **h**-$3016.38, **i**-$1024.80, **j**-$1991.58, estate

Robert STERRETT, **b**-8 May 1843, **c**-Robert STERRETT, **d**- **e**- **f**-5 Jun 1843, **g**- **h**- **i**- **j**-

Samuel MARTIN, **b**-18 Oct 1842, **c**-James M. MARTIN, Francis MARTIN, **d**- **e**- **f**- **g**-9 Dec 1845, **h**-$853.83, **i**-$2551.09.25, **j**-$1697.26.25, accountants

Page 157, Frame 171

Alexander B. McNITT, **b**-26 May 1843, **c**-Brown McNITT, John McNITT, **d**- **e**- **f**-22 Jun 1843, **g**- **h**- **i**- **j**-

James T. ALEXANDER, **b**-10 Jun 1843, **c**-John HENRY, **d**-$600, **e**-Francis McCLURE, Wm. CUMMINS, **f**-10 Feb 1843, **g**- **h**- **i**- **j**-

Isaac STRODE, **b**-22 Jun 1843, **c**-Joseph STRODE, Saml. WOODS, **d**-$3000, **e**-Jas. PARKER, James S. WOODS, **f**- **g**-26 Nov 1844, **h**-$2193.03, **i**-$575.60, **j**-$1617.43, estate

Isabella DAVIS, **b**-1 Jul 1843, **c**-Ephraim BANKS, **d**- **e**- **f**-4 Aug 1843, **g**-6 Oct 1845, **h**-$601,38, **i**-$112.31, **j**-$489.08, estate

John MILLER, **b**-25 Jul 1843, **c**-William REED, **d**-$600, **e**-James McINTIRE, Jacob [KIPP], **f**- **g**- **h**- **i**- **j**-

Abraham McCAY, b-1 Aug 1843, **c**-Samuel S. WOODS, **d**-$6000, **e**-John STERRETT, J. S. WOODS, **f**-6 Sep 1843, **g**-18 Oct 1844/1 Jul 1847, **h**-$1908.79.5/$1135.16, **I**-$,/$469.20, **j**-$431.48.5, estate/$665.96, estate

James CUPPLES, b-7 Aug 1843, **c**-George DAVIS, **d**-$12,000, **e**-John STERRETT, Jos. B. ARD, **f**-10 Nov 1843, **g**- **h**- **i**- **j**-

William McCAY, Esq., b-9 Aug 1843, **c**-David McCAY, **d**-$14,000, **e**-Jos. B. ARD, Jos. MILLIKEN, **f**-15 Mar 1844, **g**-24 Jun 1845, **h**-$3580.31.5, **i**-$2546.00.75, **j**-$1934,31, estate

Henry LONG, b-21 Aug 1843, **c**-Thomas REED, James M. MARTIN, **d**- **e**- **f**- **g**- **h**- **i**- **j**-

James HAMILTON, b-29 Aug 1843, **c**-David HAMILTON, **d**- **e**- **f**-19 Sep 1843, **g**- **h**- **i**- **j**-

Richard GIBBS, b-28 Sep 1843, **c**-David McCLURE, **d**-$150, **e**-James McCONNELL, **f**- **g**-10 Dec 1844, **h**-$308.27, **i**-$123.62.5, **j**-$184.64.5, estate

John EALY, b-30 Oct 1843, **c**-John KOSER, Margaret ELY[sic], **d**- **e**- **f**-21 Nov 1843, **g**- **h**- **i**- **j**-

Page 158, Frame 172

John LAUVER, b-7 Nov 1843, **c**-Elizabeth LAUVER, **d**-$600, **e**-Jacob LAUVER, L. T. WATTSON, **f**-4 Dec 1843, **g**-4 Mar 1845, **h**-$989.16, **i**-$827.37.25, **j**-$171.78.75, estate

John TAYLOR, b-10 Nov 1843, **c**-Elizabeth TAYLOR, Mathew TAYLOR, Joseph MILLIKEN, **d**-$, **e**- **f**- **g**- **h**- **i**- **j**-

Margaret CRISSMAN, b-21 Nov 1843, **c**-Geo. W. CRISSMAN, **d**-$1000, **e**-Joseph MILLIKEN, Robt. M. THOMPSON, **f**-27 Jan 1843, **g**- **h**- **i**- **j**-

Abraham KEARNS, b-4 Dec 1843, **c**-Jacob BALSBACH, **d**-$500, **e**-Abraham ROTHROCK, Wm. KEPPERLING, **f**-4 Dec 1843, **g**-5 Apr 1849, **h**-$48.37, **i**-$165.97, **j**-$117.60, estate

Daniel GONZALES, b-15 Dec 1843, **c**-Cyrus STINE, **d**-$1000, **e**-Jos. M. COGLEY, Saml. WITHEROW, **f**-5 Jan 1844, **g**-10 Apr 1847, **h**- **i**- **j**-

William ORNER, b-19 Dec 1843, **c**-James K. KELLY, **d**-$1000, **e**-James POTTER, Adam GREER, **f**- **g**- **h**- **i**- **j**-

Thomas THOMPSON, b-28 Dec 1843, **c**-Francis THOMPSON, Margaret THOMPSON, **d**-$2000, **e**-Francis McCOY, Jos. MILLIKEN, **f**-1 Feb 1844, **g**-8 Oct 1845, **h**-$1554.89.5, **i**-$1139.29.5, **j**-$415.60, estate

John UTLEY, **b**-3 Jan 1844, **c**-John PURCELL, **d**-$1000, **e**-Jacob NORTON, Robt. A. McDOWELL, **f**-20 Jan 1844, **g**- **h**- **i**- **j**-

Jacob HARTZELL, **b**-10 Jan 1844, **c**-Elizabeth HARTZELL, **d**-$200, **e**-J. A. CUNNINGHAM, A. BLYMYER, **f**-27 Jan 1844, **g**- **h**- **i**- **j**-

John NORTON, **b**-10 Jan 1844, **c**-Felix NORTON, **d**- **e**- **f**-9 Feb 1844, **g**-6 Aug 1845, **h**-$910.90.5, **i**-$29.10.5, **j**-$881.80, estate

Geo. W. HAMILTON, **b**-20 Feb 1844, **c**-Mary HAMILTON, **d**- **e**- **f**-19 Mar 1844, **g**- **h**- **i**- **j**-

Mary SHIRK, **b**-20 Feb 1844, **c**-Jas. A. CUNNINGHAM, **d**-$500, **e**-James BURNS, James TURNER, **f**-1 Mar 1844, **g**-20 Oct 1845, **h**-$72.70, **i**-$140.93, **j**-$68.23, accountant

Page 159, Frame 173

Catherine STRODE, **b**-24 Feb 1844, **c**-Saml. S. WOODS, Esq., Jos. STRODE, Sr., **d**- **e**- **f**-29 Mar 1844, **g**-2 Mar 1847, **h**-$1341.12.5, **i**-$63.66, **j**-$1277.46.5, estate

George VANZANDT, **b**-26 Feb 1844, **c**-John VANZANT[sic], Jr., John PURCELL, **d**- **e**- **f**-27 Mar 1844, **g**-21 Feb 1845, **h**-$597.22, **i**-$597.24, **j**-$.02 [undesignated]

John WALLS, **b**-6 Mar 1844, **c**-John ALLEN, Isaac WALLS, Jr. **d**-$800, **e**-John ROSS, Andrew MAYES, **f**-25 Mar 1844, **g**-5 Apr 1855, **h**-$1140.93, **i**-$1026.88, **j**-$114.05, accountant

Bethsheba EVANS, **b**-1 May 1844, **c**-John B. COTTLE, **d**- **e**- **f**- **g**- **h**- **i**- **j**-

James NIXON, **b**-23 Feb 1744, **c**-Mary NIXON, **d**- **e**- **f**- **g**- **h**- **i**- **j**-

James BROGAN, **b**-13 May 1844, **c**-James BURNS, **d**-$600, **e**-James TURNER, John R. McDOWELL, **f**- **g**- **h**- **i**- **j**-

Nancy BEATTY, **b**-23 May 1844, **C**-A. B. NORRIS, **d**-$2500 [a decimal makes it look more like $25.00), **e**-John NORRIS, **f**- **g**- **h**- **i**- **j**-

Elizabeth MOURER, **b**-21 May 1844, **c**-Jacob LITER, **d**-$400, **e**-Benjn. CLAY, Jno. STONEROAD, **f**-18 Jun 1844, **g**-11 Sep 1845, **h**-$340.93, **i**-$69.06, **j**-$271.87, estate

David HARTZLER, **b**-31 May 1844, **c**-David HARTZLER, **d**- **e**- **f**-13 Jun 1844, **g**- **h**- **i**- **j**-

Nancy SUMERVILLE, **b**-1 Jun 1844, **c**-Joshua MORRISON, **d**- **e**- **f**- **g**-16 Oct 1845, **h**-$50.93, **i**-$48.83, **j**-$2.10, estate

Samuel McNITT, **b**-8 Jun 1844, **c**-Will. B. NORRIS, **d**-$1000, **e**-Wm. McKINNEY, Jacob MARKS, **f**-6 Jul 1844, **g**- **h**- **i**- **j**-

Mathew TAYLOR, b-14 Jun 1844, c-David McCLURE, d-$1000, e-James MILLIKEN, James TURNER, f- g-8 Jan 1850, h-$7667.29, i-$1134.24, j-$6533.05, estate

Page 160, Frame 174
Conrad ORT, b-14 Jun 1844, c-David CANDOR, Esq., d-$500, e-C. BAYER, Lydia ORT, f-8 Jul 1844, g-2 Mar 1848, h-$211,45 i-$516.01, j-$304.55 [no designation]
Margaret FOSTER, b-19 Jun 1844, c-Henry LEATTOR, d-$6000, e-Wm. HARDY, Jno. R. McDOWELL, f- g- h- i- j-
William GROW, b-27 Jun 1844, c-Nancy GROW, Robert BURNS, d-$600, e-James TURNER, James BURNS, f- g- h- i- j-
Margaret MATHEWS, b-17 Jul 1844, c-Isaac HEINS, d- e- f-9 Aug 1844, g-8 Nov 1851, h-$426.39, i-$357.75, j-$68.64, executor
James McDOWELL, b-16 Jul 1844, c-John PURCELL d-$2000, e-Jacob NORTON, Jno. R. McDOWELL, f-8 Aug 1844, g-19 Jun 1849, h-$605.88, i-$605.88, j-
Henry STITZER, b-7 Aug 1844, c-Thomas SWANGER, d-$2000, e-John SWANGER, William SWANGER, f- g- h- i- j-
Isaac WILEY, b-8 Aug 1844, c-David McCLURE, d-$600, e-James MILLIKEN, James TURNER, f- g- h- i- j-
Philip SMITH, b-9 Aug 1844, c-Joseph ALEXANDER, d-$100, e-Daniel ZIGLER, Samuel HOPPER, f- g- h- i- j-
John MITCHELL, b-19 Aug 1844, c-Jacob ROLAND, d- $80, e- Jos. HUDSON, A. B. NORRIS, f- g- h- i- j-
Alexander [CRUMMY], b-29 Aug 1844, c-John McDOWELL, d-$700, e-James MILLIKEN, Adam GREER, f-13 Sep 1844, g- h- i- j-
William BROWN, b-13 Sep 1844, c-William B. JOHNSTON, d-$1000, e-Saml. McNITT, John R. McDOWELL, f-12 Oct 1844, g- h- i- j-
Robert THRELKET, b-19 Sep 1844, c-Caleb PARKER, d-$200, e-N. A. ELDER, James MATHERS, f-24 Dec 1844, g- h- i- j-

Page 161, Frame 175
Isaac TOWNSEND, b-13 Sep 1844, c-Arthur B. LONG, d-$1600, e-James MILLIKEN, Wm. E. FOWLER, f-28 Oct 1844, g-28 Feb 1846, h-$1430.90, i-$1082.85.75, j-$348.04.25, estate
Richard BRIMMER, b-30 Sep 1844, c-Ralph BOGLE, Ellis GRIFFITH, d-$3000, e-Wm. WAKEFIELD, James TURNER, f- g-2 Apr 1847, h-$673.25.5, i-$420.63, j-$252.62.5, estate

Henry **BEAR**, **b**-19 Oct 1844, **c**-Geo. A. LYON, John BEAR, **d**-$800, **e**-James MILLIKEN, Jos. MILLIKEN, **f**-16 Nov 1844, **g**-18 Oct 1845, **h**-$551.84.25, **i**-$260.67, **j**-$291.17.75, estate

Nancy **SKIPTON**, **b**-1 Nov 1844, **c**-George SKIPTON, **d**-$300, **e**-James MILLIKEN, **f**- **g**- **h**- **i**- **j**-

John **SHOOK**, **b**-8 Nov 1844, **c**-Henry SHOOK, **d**-$100, **e**-Isaac REIFSNYDER, John STEWART, **f**- **g**- **h**- **i**- **j**-

Mary **MAGINNES**, **b**-15 Nov 1844, **c**-Francis McCOY, **d**- **e**- **f**- **g**- **h**- **i**- **j**-

Henry **DUNMIRE**, **b**-21 Sep 1844, **c**-Gabriel DUNMIRE, Jacob GARVER, **d**- **e**- **f**-16 Oct 1844, **g**- **h**- **i**- **j**-

James **PRESTON**, **b**-7 Dec 1844, **c**-John PRESTON, **d**- **e**- **f**-2 Jan 1845, **g**- **h**- **i**- **j**-

Michael **HOSTETLER**, **b**-16 Dec 1844, **c**-Jos. HOSTETLER, Jacob PEACHY, **d**- **e**- **f**-3 Jan 1845, **g**-27 Feb 1846, **h**-$9056.34.75, **i**-$2027.24, **j**-$7029.10.75, estate

George S. **BOGLE**, **b**-19 Aug 1844, **c**-James CRISWELL, **d**- **e**- **f**-18 Sep 1844, **g**- **h**- **i**- **j**-

Joseph **FISHER**, **b**-24 Dec 1844, **c**-Jacob FULTZ, **d**-$1000, **e**-Peter ALBRIGHT, Jos. GOODHART, **f**-23 Jan 1845, **g**- **h**- **i**- **j**-

Jos. **McELHANEY**, **b**-27 Dec 1844, **c**-Shem ZOOK, **d**-$1000, **e**-D. C. MILLER, David ZOOK, **f**-16 Jan 1845/18 Feb 1845, **g**-27 Jun 1846, **h**-$302.34, **i**-$79.27.5, **j**-$229.06.5, estate

James **DRAKE**, **b**-30 Dec 1844, **c**-John PURCELL, **d**-$, **e**- **f**-16 Jan 1845, **g**- **h**- **i**- **j**-

Page 162, Frame 176

Thos. J. **HYNEMAN**, **b**-8 Feb 1845, **c**-William BUTLER, **d**-$200, **e**-James MORRISON, M. MORRISON, **f**-26 Feb 1845, **g**-6 Jul 1846, **h**-$79.77, **i**-$78.56, **j**-$1.11, estate

Adam **HARTZLER**, **b**-10 Feb 1845, **c**-John PEACHY, **d**-$1000, **e**-David ZOOK, Jos. MILLIKEN, **f**-10 Mar 1845, **g**-10 Feb 1845/30 Apr 1847, **h**-$1716.97.25/$6084.55, **i**-$1692.53/$2140.55, **j**-$24.44.75, estate/$3944.00, estate

James **WIGHTMAN**, **b**-19 Mar 1845, **c**-David HOUGH, Esq., **d**-$200, **e**-Andrew MAYES, John R. WEEKS, **f**- **g**- **h**- **i**- **j**-

John **CAMPBELL**, **b**-1 Apr 1845, **c**-Robert CAMPBELL, John O. CAMPBELL, Geo. W. OLIVER, **d**- **e**- **f**-24 Apr 1845, **g**- **h**- **i**- **j**-

Joseph TOWNSEND, **b**-8 Apr 1845, **c**-Peter TOWNSEND, **d**-$200, **e**-Geo. SIGLER, James CRAWFORD, **f**- 29 Apr 1845, **g**-25 Jun 1846, **h**-$42.69.25, **i**-$47.75, **j**-$5.05.75, accountant

Geo. WORRALL, **b**-12 Apr 1845, **c**-David HOUGH, **d**-$400, **e**-Joshua MORRISON, Jas. A. CUNNINGHAM, **f**-$16 Apr 1845, **g**-4 Jan 1847, **h**-$306.41.5, **i**-$361.78.5, **j**-$55.37, accountant

Mathew FORSYTHE, **b**-18 Apr 1845, **c**-Saml. S. WOODS, **d**-$100, **e**-Jas. S. WOODS, Jos. M. COGLEY, **f**-18 Jun 1845, **g**-1 Jul 1847, **h**-$247.69, **i**-$247.69.5 **j**-

John HINDS, **b**-21 Apr 1845, **c**-Stephen HINDS, Robert SIMS, **d**-$400, **e**-L. T. WATTSON, Jos. M. COGLEY, **f**- 21 May 1845, **g**- **h**- **i**- **j**-

Thomas McCORD, **b**-23 Apr 1845, **c**-Enoch BEALE, **d**-$200, **e**-James McCORD, Joshua MORRISON, **f**-9 Jun 1845, **g**-20 Apr 1846, **h**-$1182.89.5, **i**-$1185.55.25, **j**-$2.99.75, accountant

Robert McKEE, **b**-26 Apr 1845, **c**-Andrew W. McKEE, Robt. A. McKEE, **d**-$, **e**- **f**-21 May 1845, **g**-14 Nov 1853, **h**-$162.19.75, **i**-$550.82, **j**-$388.62.25, estate

John MARTIN, **b**-5 May 1845, **c**-John CUPPLES, **d**-$200, **e**-James TURNER, John McCAULEY, **f**-17 May 1845, **g**-8 May 1846, **h**-$235.71, **i**-$87.10, **j**-$148.61, estate

Nicholas LOTZ, **b**-13 May 1845, **c**-John ALBRIGHT, Josiah KERR, **d**-$600, **e**-J. A. CUNNINGHAM, Chas. COLFELT, **f**-7 Jun 1845, **g**-2 Mar 1847, **h**-$150.93, **i**-$147.03, **j**-$3.90, estate

Page 163, Frame 177

David YODER, **b**-15 May 1845, **c**-Thomas B. CODER, **d**-$400, **e**-Robert BURNS, James TURNER, **f**-2 Jun 1845, **g**-21 Feb 1846, **h**-$2914.5, **i**-$35.84.5, **j**-$6.70, accountant

Jacob COMFORT, **b**-17 May 1845, **c**-Samuel COMFORT, **d**-$800, **e**-Nathl. COMFORT, Henry COMFORT, **f**-16 Jun 1845, **g**- **h**- **i**- **j**-

Alexander CAMERON, **b**-7 Jun 1845, **c**-Thomas WATTSON, **d**-$400, **e**-John STERRETT, Robt. M. THOMPSON, **f**- **g**-30 Dec 1848, **h**-$4707.34, **i**-$4394.43, **j**-$312.91, accountant

Martha WORRALL, **b**-28 Jun 1845, **c**-David HOUGH, **d**-$1000, **e**-Joshua MORRISON, J. A. CUNNINGHAM, **f**-28 Jul 1845, **g**- **h**- **i**- **j**-

Charles MOWERY, **b**-30 Jun 1845, **c**-Jacob SCHOFFNER, **d**-$300, **e**-Frederick SWARTZ, Jno. R. McDOWELL, **f**-5 Aug 1845, **g**-19 Jun 1846, **h**-$628.81, **i**-$486.19, **j**-$142.62, estate

Jacob KISHLER, b-25 Jul 1845, c-John CRAWFORD, d-$100, e-Wm. SCOTT, Wm. SHIMP, f- g- h- i- j-

Thomas GIBBONEY, b-2 Aug 1845, c-Henry GIBBONEY, d-$300, e-Geo. CONSER, Thos. MILLER, f- g-3 Jul 1847, h-$245.00, i-$, j-

William McMANIGIL, b-4 Aug 1845, c-William McMANIGIL, Robt. M. THOMPSON, d-$, e- f- g- h- i- j-

Amor STRODE, b-25 Aug 1845, c-Joseph STRODE, Geo. WAKEFIELD, d-$1500 e-Jos. MILLIKEN, Jas. POTTER, Jr., f-20 Sep 1845, g-26 Jun 1847, h-$1433.59, i-$1336.57, j-$97.02, estate

Sophia SWARTS, b-6 Sep 1845, c-Roswell D. SWARTS, d-$600, e-Noble NORTON, David HOUGH, f-26 Sep 1845, g- h- i- j-

Mathew MAYES, b-10 Sep 1845, c-David McCLURE, d-$3000, e-Joshua MORRISON, James TURNER, f-10 Oct 1845, g- h- i- j-

John ENTREKEN, b-17 Sep 1845, c-John H. SWEENEY, d-$1600, e-Milton EARLY, Robert SIMS, f-15 Oct 1845, g- h- i- j-

Page 164, Frame 178
Susannah STEELY, b-15 Oct 1845, c-Benjamin F. ROBISON, d-$200, e-Hiram HANTS, C. RINEHOLD, f-14 Nov 1845, g- h- i- j-

Catherine MILLER, b-3 Nov 1845, c-Charles BRATTON, d-$1000, e-Richeson BRATTON, Henry LEATTOR, f- g- h- i- j-

Joseph McKINSTRY, b-2 Dec 1845, c-James CORBETT, d-$, e- f-5 Jan 1846, g-23 Jun 1847, h-$850.43.5, i-$795.29, j-$55.14.5, estate

Henry BUTLER, b-13 Dec 1845, c-John PURCELL, d-$800, e-W. BUTLER, D. C. FREEBURN, f-6 Jan 1846, g- h- i- j-

Henry CASTOR, b-3 Jan 1846 c-George CULLEN, d-$400, e-Augustus STINE, Robert GEORGE, f-24 Jan 1846, g-28 Nov 1846, h-$250.48, i-$202.31.5, j-$48.16.5, estate

Adam C. SHAW, b-5 Jan 1846, c-Robert G. SHAW, d- e- f-31 Jan 1846, g-7 Apr 1852, h-$296.19, i-$430.14, j-$133.95, estate

Isaac CORNELIUS, b-26 Dec 1845, c-Randolph CORNELIUS, d- e- f- g- h- i- j-

Henry CASTER, b-3 Jan 1846, c-Geo. CULLEN, d- e- f- g- h- i- j-

Samuel MATTER, b-6 Jan 1846, c-John MATTER, William RAMSEY (admin De Bonis Non), G. W. ELDER (admin De Bonis Non), d-$800, e-Jas. BEATTY, E. E. LOCKE, f- g-14 Nov 1853, h-$1157.21.75, i-$1831.57, j-$674.35.25, estate (given Wm. RAMSEY, ADB)

Samuel KENNEDY, b-10 Jan 1846, c-William KENNEDY, d-$1000, e-F. W. RAWLE, f-10 Feb 1846, g- h- i- j-

Rosanah STERRETT, b-31 Jan 1846, c-Robert STERRETT, d- e- f- g- h- i- j-

James WILLS, b-6 Feb 1846, c-Saml. B. WILLS, Joseph J. WILLS, d- e- f-12 Mar 1846, g- h- i- j-

Page 165, Frame 179

William McDOWELL, b-23 Feb 1846, c-John McDOWELL, Jr., d-$6000, e-John McDOWELL, f-19 Mar 1846, g-8 Nov 1855, h-$6235.46.5, i-$7354.75.25, j-$1119.28.75, accountant

John LEVY, Sr., b-2 Mar 1846, c-Geo. DAVIS, Esq., d- e- f- g- h- i- j-

Samuel D. BUCHANAN, b-3 Mar 1846, c-John P. ASHCOM, d-$3500, e-Jas. B. COOK, Jas. HEMPHILL, f-26 Mar 1846, g-7 Oct 1846, h-$212.10.75, i-$183.47, j-$28.63.25, estate

Peter SWAGGART, b-3 Mar 1846, c-William ROSS, Samuel MYERS, d-$1400, e-D. R. REYNOLDS, Robt. McFARLAND, f- g- h- i- j-

Elizabeth McLENAHAN, b-25 Mar 1846, c-James DORMAN, d-$100, e-Wm. INGRAM, A. MUTHERSBAUGH, f- g- h- i- j-

John WILLS, b-24 Mar 1846, c-Jos. H. WILLS, David ROTHROCK, d-$, e- f-14 Apr 1846, g- h- i- j-

Anthony DEAN, b-9 Apr 1846, c-James CALDWELL, d-$200, e-Wm. ROSS, A. F. McNAIR, f-8 May 1846, g-9 Apr 1847, h-$111.03, i-$47.13.5, j-$63.89.75, estate

Richard WORRALL, b-14 Apr 1846, c-Geo. W. THOMAS, d-$4000, e-M. MONTGOMERY, W. BUTLER, f-27 Apr 1846, g-27 Sep 1847, h-$2425.23.5, i-$2585.59, j-$160.36.25, estate

Amos SMOKER, b-21 Apr 1846, c-Jacob SHOFFNER, d-$1000, e-David ESHELMAN, f-20 May 1846, g-25 Jun 1847, h-$916,88, i-$708.45, j-$208.43, estate

Edward SCHACHT, b-18 May 1846, c-Yost KING, d- e- f- g- h- i- j-

Lewis STONEROAD, b-21 May 1846, c-John STONEROAD, Ephraim BANKS, d- e- f-27 Jun 1846, g-6 Apr 1857, h-$2400.45.5, i-$3362,37, j-$961.91.5, estate

Jane COULTER, b-21 May 1846, c-Nathaniel WILSON, d- e- f-29 Jul 1846, g- h- i- j-

Page 166, Frame 180

James GIBBONEY, b-3 Jun 1846, c-David R. REYNOLDS, d-$400, e-D. CUMMINGS, Jno. STONEROAD, f- g- h- i- j-

James WHARTON, b-20 Jul 1846, **c**-Henry WHARTON, **d**-$1400, **e**-
Geo. B. WHARTON, **f- g- h- i- j-**
Cynthia McKINSTRY, b-25 Jul 1846, **c**-Margaret McKINSTRY, John
WICKS, **d**-$500, **e**-James TURNER, John R. WEEKS, **f- g- h- i- j-**
John B. IRWIN, b-11 Aug 1846, **c**-R. R. FRANKS, **d**-$200, **e**-Geo.
CARNEY, R. H. McCLINTIC, **f- g- h- i- j-**
Adam SIGLER, b-5 Aug 1846, **c**-Johnston SIGLER, **d**-$2000, **e**-Thos.
VANVALZAH, Jos. MILLIKEN, **f**-3 Sep 1846, **g- h- i- j-**
Robert SANKEY, b-12 Sep 1846, **c**-James GILLAM, **d**-$500, **e**-John
SNYDER, Jr., L. T. WATTSON, **f**-24 Sep 1846, **g- h- i- j-**
Charles RAMSEY, b-19 Sep 1846, **c**-James BROWN, Jr., **d- e- f**-22 Oct
1846, **g**-6 Apr 1854, **h**-$604.23, **i**-$595.49, **j**-$8.74, accountant
George AULTZ, b-11 Nov 1846, **c**-John PEACHY, **d- e- f**-11 Dec 1846,
g-3 Aug 1847, **h**-$72.98, **i**-$72.98, **j**-
Samuel SUNDERLAND, b-23 Sep 1846, **c**-Cyrus STINE, **d**-$1000, **e**-
Augustus STINE, Saml. SUNDERLAND, **f**-21 Oct 1846, **g- h- i- j-**
John HENDERSON, b-29 Oct 1846, **c**-Mary HENDERSON, **d**-$800, **e**-
Jos. B. ARD, John SNYDER, **f**-23 Dec 1846, **g- h- i- j-**
Robert McKEAG, b-12 Nov 1846, **c**-John KAUFMAN, **d**-$3000, **e**-Jos.
MILLIKEN, Jas. McKEAG, **f**-18 Nov 1846, **g- h- i- j-**
Catherine HAWN, a-3 Dec 1846, **c**-Joseph HAWN, **d**-$1600, **e**-Jos.
MILLIKEN, F. T. HOFFMAN, **f- g- h- i- j-**

Page 167, Frame 181
John FIELDS, b-10 Dec 1846, **c**-Samuel DRAKE, **d**-$650, **e**-J. F.
COTTRELL, George LANE, **f**-5 Jan 1847, **g- h- i- j-**
James RIDEN, b-17 Dec 1846, **c**-James RIDEN, **d**-$400, **e**-Saml. RIDEN,
J. JACOB[sic], **f**-25 Dec 1846, **g- h- i- j-**
John BEAR, b-19 Dec 1846, **c**-Charles BRATTON, **d**-$600, **e**-R. BOGLE,
Henry FORER, **f- g**-5 Jan 1849, **h**-$208.86.75, **i**-$613.83.75, **j**-$404.97,
estate
Jacob RIGGLE, b-19 Dec 1846, **c**-John RIGGLE, George SIGLER, **d**-$,
e- f-7 Jan 1847, **g- h- i- j-**
Eleanor VANCE, b-2 Jan 1847, **c**-Geo. V. MITCHELL, Robt. HORNING,
d-$1000, **e**-James TURNER, W. BUTLER, **f**-1 Feb 1847, **g- h- i- j-**
Mariah SHERDEN, b-11 Jan 1847, **c**-John LEVY, **d**-$100, **e**-Wm. LEVY,
Saml. GRANDEN, **f**-26 Sep 1848, **g**-5 Jan 1849, **h**-$94.23, **i**-$186.55,
j-$92.32, estate – NOTE: See a/c—The above balance paid in full by

Sarah Jane LEVY, exrx. of Jno. LEVY to Jos. ALEXANDER, Esq., atty. for James SHERIDEN – Dec 13 1864, Amt. $189.59.

Samuel KING, b-11 Jan 1847, **c**-Levi KING, **d- e- f**-1 Feb 1847, **g**-9 [Nov] 1854, **h**-$13,165.29, **i**-$18,643.30, **j**-$5478.01, estate

Jason COAN, b-14 Jan 1847, **c**-George DAVIS, **d**-$300 **e**-Joshua MORRISON, L. RITTENHOUSE, **f**-10 Feb 1847, **g- h- i- j-**

David KREIDER, b-20 Jan 1847, **c**-James PARKER, **d- e- f**-15 Feb 1847, **g- h- i- j-**

Barbara YODER, b-15 Jan 1847, **c**-Shem HARTZLER, **d**-$2000, **e**-Abraham ZOOK, Fredr. SWARTZ, **f**-12 Feb 1847, **g- h- i- j-**

John MATHEWS, b-21 Jan 1847, **c**-Geo. B. MATHEWS, **d**-$1000, **e**-Wm. GEORGE, Jacob KNEPP, **f- g**-8 Nov 1851, **h**-$119.34, **i**-$187.26, **j**-$67.92, estate

George WAKEFIELD, b-11 Feb 1847, **c**-Eli WAKEFIELD, **d**-$3000, **e**-A. WAKEFIELD, Chas. BRATTON, **f**-3 Mar 1847, **g**-10 Jan 1850, **h**-$815.88, **i**-$792.16, **j**-$23.72, accountant

Page 168, Frame 182

Elizabeth McDOWELL, b-13 Feb 1847, **c**-James BEATTY, **d**-$500, **e**-Thos. BROWN, James M. BROWN, **f**-11 Mar 1847. **g**-(See Deed Book GG, p. 662, for Release) **h- i- j-**

Hugh JOHNSTON, b-13 Feb 1847, **c**-J. D. MORRISON, Jas. G. McCOY, **d- e- f**-13 Mar 1847, **g**-1 Mar 1857, **h**-$5445.21, **i**-$6459.61.75, **j**-$1014.40.75, estate

James LEECH, b-19 Feb 1847, **c**-Wm. LEECH, J. [G.] LEECH, **d**-$600, **e**-J. A. ROSS, Wm. F. MOYER, **f**-19 Feb 1847, **g- h- i- j-**

Robert M. THOMPSON, b-19 Feb 1847, **c**-Samuel THOMPSON, **d**-$8000, **e**-John McDOWELL, Jos. MILLIKEN, **f**-17 Mar 1847, **g- h- i- j-**

William SMITH, b-24 Feb 1847, **c**-Andrew McFARLAND, Thos. BROWN, **d**-$4000, **e**-Jos. MILLIKEN, James BEATTY, Jr. **f**-22 Mar 1847, **g- h- i- j-**

Atlee PRICE, b-12 Mar 1847, **c**-Wm. J. McCOY, **d**-$3000, **e**-John A. STEEL, James TURNER, **f**-12 Apr 1847, **g- h- i- j-**

James EWING, b-23 Mar 1847, **c**-Samuel DRAKE, **d- e- f**-21 Apr 1847, **g- h- i- j-**

David MILLER, b-26 Mar 1847, **c**-Jesse MILLER, Henry EBY, **d**-$2000, **e**-D. HARSHBARGER, Mathias BOAS, **f**-24 Apr 1847, **g**-4 Nov 1852, **h**-$1213.39.75, **i**-$1375.81, **j**-$162.41.25, estate

Robert McCORMICK, b-20 Apr 1847, c-Huston McCORMICK, d-$800, e-James McCORMICK, A. ROTHROCK, f-17 May 1847, g- h- i- j-
Robert ALEXANDER, b-15 May 1847, c-Sarah ALEXANDER, d-$1000, e-Alexander McKEE, f- g- h- i- j-
Eliza MORRISON, b-20 May 1847, c-Elijah MORRISON, d-$1800, e-Jos. MILLIKEN, David McCLURE, f-22 Jun 1847, g- h- i- j-
Philip ROTHROCK, b-10 Jun 1847, c-William CREIGHTON, d-$800, e-Philip ROTHROCK, J. JACOB[sic], f-22 Jun 1847, g- h- i- j-
Rebecca ARMSTRONG, b-12 Jun 1847, c-Benjamin CHANDLER, d- e- f-24 Jun 1847, g-3 Apr 1849, h-$3766.02, i-$1010.88, j-$2755.14, estate

Page 169, Frame 183 [repeated on Frame 184]
William WARD, b-22 Jul 1847, c-Jacob GARVER, William WILSON, d-$500, e-Jacob KREPS, Robert FORGY, f-4 Sep 1847, g-24 Jul 1849, h-$2125.80, i-$, j-$1307.35, estate
Stephen KISTLER, b-11 Aug 1847, c-William MITCHELL, d-$200, e-S. S. CUMMINGS, D. W. HULINGS, f- g- h- i- j-
Samuel BRILHART, b-12 Aug 1847, c-Jacob BRILLHART[sic], d-$250, e-Henry [ZERBE], George COUSER, f-20 Sep 1847, g- h- i- j-
Patrick BYRNE, b-26 Aug 1847, c-David McCLURE, d-$300, e-Jas. A. CUNNINGHAM, f-4 Sep 1847, g-1 Oct 1847, h-$18.50, i-$120.40, j-$101.90, estate
Michael YUTSEY, b-27 Jul 1847, c-Elijah YUTZEY, Michael YUTSEY, d- e- f- g-13 Sep 1847, h-4 Nov 1855, i- j-
Joshia[sic] ALEXANDER, b-2 Oct 1847, c-Samuel MACLAY, William McMANIGIL, d-$4000, e-Joseph MILLIKEN, Robert McMANIGIL, f-22 Oct 1847, g- h- i- j-
James McGEIGER, b-4 Oct 1847, c-James McGEIGER, d-$100, e-Jno. R. McDOWELL, D. R. REYNOLDS, f- g- h- i- j-
David MORRISON, b-15 Oct 1847, c-Joel MORRISON, d-$1000, e-Abram MORRISON, D. R. REYNOLDS, f- g- h- i- j-
Jacob PRICE, b-16 Oct 1847, c-David McCLURE, d-$1500, e-Joseph MILLIKEN, Jas. A. CUNNINGHAM, f-19 Oct 1847, g- h- i- j-
David SUNDERLAND, b-1 Nov 1847, c-Wm. A. MOOR, d-$1000, e-Robert FORGY, Jona. J. CUNNINGHAM, f-24 Dec 1847, g-5 Apr 1849/10 Jan 1856, h-$180.98/$536.82, i-$531.75/$536.82, j-$350.77, estate

Samuel AITKINS, b-4 Nov 1847, c-Hugh CONLEY, d-$600, e-Johnston SIGLER, f-4 Dec 1847, g- h- i- j-

Page 170, Frame 185
Philip PEFFER, b-23 Nov 1847, c-John McCORD, d-$300, e-Owen [OWNS, OWENS?], Joseph TICE, f-13 Dec 1847, g-8 Dec 1849, h-$428.80, i-$365.44, j-$63.36, estate
Joseph HUDSON, b-14 Dec 1847, c-Samuel HOPPER, d-$100, e-John HAMILTON, D. R. REYNOLDS, f- g- h- i- j-
Wilson STONE, b-24 Jan 1848, c-Lewis T. WATTSON, d-$1000, e-Frederick SWARTZ, A. P. JACOBS, f-31 Jan 1848, g-5 Apr 1849, h-$277.61, i-$615.87, j-$338.26, estate
Robert McCLELLAND, b-5 Jan 1848, c-Augustine WAKEFIELD, exor, d-(Will), e- f-1 Feb 1848, g-4 Aug 1853, h-$2658.10, i-$963.74, j-$1694.36, accountant
Henry CONLEY, b-19 Feb 1848, c-Hugh CONLEY, Josiah KERR, d-$4000, e-James BURNS, Robt. STERRETT, f-18 Mar 1848, amt. $2303.38, g- h- i- j-
Joseph BARTHOLEMEW, b-2 Mar 1848, c-John BARTHOLEMEW, d-$1200, e-George BLYMYER, Samuel P. NASH, f-6 Mar 1848, amt. $917.62.5, g-6 Dec 1849, h-$1821.33.5, i-$1376.82.5, j-$444.53.75, estate
George WAGNER, b-26 Feb 1848, c-Samuel BARR, Esq., d-$300, e-John RAGAR, Jacob H. COOK, f-20 Mar 1848, amt. $174.80.5, g-7 Aug 1851, h-$166.97.5, i-$170.70.5, j-$3.10, estate
Robert CORGILL, b-11 Mar 1848, c-William CORGILL, d- $200, e-David WEITZ, Joseph H. RITTENHOUSE, f- g- h- i- j-
James ALEXANDER, Sr., [Union], b-3 Apr 1848, c-Jas. & N. B. ALEXANDER, exors, d- e- f-2 May 1848, g- h- i- j-

Page 171, Frame 186
Maj. David CUMMINGS, b-24 Mar 1848, c-Hannah M. TOWNSEND, d-$1000, e-Doct. Joseph B. ARD, James K. KELLY, f- g-24 Mar 1848, h- i- j-
Jacob HARTZEL, b-20 Mar 1848, c-Joseph ALEXANDER, Esq., de bonis &c, d-$200, e-Daniel ZEIGLER, f- g-8 Jan 1852/20 Mar 1848, h-$130.44, i-$457.35, j-$326.91, estate
Isabella Jane CUMMINGS, b- c-S. S. CUMMINGS, admr., d-$200, e-A. S. CUMMMINGS, f- g- h- i- j-

James **MITCHELL**, **b**-31 Mar 1848, **c**-Doct. Geo. V. MITCHELL, **d**-$300, **e**-Ralph BOGLE, Michl. BUOY, **f**-22 Apr 1848, **g**-20 Jun 1849, **h**-$4195.82.5, **i**-$229.84, **j**-$34.02, accountant

John **SMITH**, **b**-3 Apr 1848, **c**-Andw. McFARLAND, Saml. KYLE, James B. SMITH, exors., **d**-no bail on bond, **e**-Ralph BOGLE, Michl. BUOY, **f**-27 Apr 1848, **g**-10 Aug 1854/3 Mar 1848, **h**-$2961.07, **i**-$5977.91, **j**-$3016.84, estate

James **TODD**, **b**-6 Apr 1848, **c**-Thomas WILSON (Columbia), **d**-$800, **e**-Joseph BROUGHT, Saml. GRUNDEN, **f**-8 Apr 1848, **g**-5 Aug 1853, **h**-$103.22, **i**-$67.03, **j**-$36.19, accountant

David **YOUNG**, **b**-8 Apr 1848, **c**-John PEACHY, **d**-$800, **e**-Christian PEACHY, Joseph HAFFLEY, **f**-9 May 1848 (invy & vendue paper), **g**-6 Jan 1853, **h**-$407.22.25, **i**-$457.48.75, **j**-$50.26.5, estate

Benjamin **WALTERS, Sr.**, **b**-20 Apr 1848, **c**-Jno. & S. H. WALTERS **d**-$300, **e**-Michl. AULTZ, Geo. CONELL, **f**-20 May 1848, **g**- **h**- **i**- **j**-

Joseph **ROTHROCK**, **b**-1 Apr 1848, **c**-Isaac PRICE, Danl. BASHORE, exors., **d**-Exors No Bond, **e**- **f**-22 Apr 1848, **g**- **h**- **i**- **j**-

John **SMITH**, **b**-3 Apr 1848, **c**-Andw. McFARLAND, Saml. KYLE, Jas. B. SMITH, **d**-Exors No Bond, **e**- **f**-37 Apr 1848, **g**- **h**- **i**- **j**-

Jacob **MARSDEN**, **b**-17 Apr 1848, **c**-John MARSDEN, John GROSS, Exors, **d**-No Bond, **e**-No Sureties, **f**-13 May 1848, **g**- **h**- **i**- **j**-

James **INGRAM**, **b**-9 May 1848, **c**-William INGRAM, **d**-$500, **e**-James DORMAN, John HOOVER, **f**- **g**-6 Jan 1853, **h**-$575.69, **i**-$384.04, **j**-$191.65, accountant

Page 172, Frame 187

Samuel **BOLLINGER**, **b**-10 Jun 1848, **c**-Michael BOLLINGER, **d**-$200, **e**-John SWINT, Daniel YODER, **f**-10 Jul 1848, **g**- **h**- **i**- **j**-

Charles S. **CARPENTER**, **b**-10 Jun 1848 **c**-Laura W. CARPENTER, **d**-$400, **e**-Thomas VANVALZAH, **f**- **g**- **h**- **i**- **j**-

David **HARTZLER**, **b**-23 Jun 1848, **c**-Daniel YODER, **d**-$2000, **e**-John HARTZLER, Christian KAUFMAN, **f**-8 Jul 1848/26 Jul 1848, **g**- **h**- **i**- **j**-

Samuel **SWIGART**, **b**-29 Jul 1848, **c**-Christian SWIGART, Henry SWIGART, **d**-$200, **e**-Samuel MYERS, **f**-26 Aug 1848, **g**- **h**- **i**- **j**-

Elizabeth **CARMICHAELS[sic]**, **b**-3 Jul 1848, **c**-exors James D. CARMICHAL, Abigail DYSART, **d**- **e**- **f**- **g**- **h**- **i**- **j**-

Henry **HANAWALT (Wayne Twp)**, **b**-31 Jul 1848, **c**-Extrs. Elisha FIELDS & Catharine HANAWALT, **d**- **e**- **f**-31 Aug 1848, **g**- **h**- **i**- **j**-

Jacob ICKES, b-23 Aug 1848, c-exor. Peter BAKER of Perry County, d-
e- f-1 Sep 1848/12 Oct 1848, g-23 Aug 1849, h-$1574.43.25, i-
$1624.68.5, j-$50.25.25, accountant

Sarah B. MILLIKEN, wife of Robert, b-3 Jun 1848, will, proven, c- d-
e- f- g- h- i- j-

George McCLANAHAN, b-30 Aug 1848, c-E. E. LOCKE, d-$200, e-Jas.
[H. or K.? probably H.] KELLY, f-4 Sep 1848, g- h- i- j-

Hugh SPROLE, b-28 Sep 1848, c-John SPROLE, d-$200, e-Archabald
McCAHAN, Thomas COCHRAN, f-4 Oct 1848, g- h- i- j-

Andrew KEISER, Esq., b-5 Sep 1848, c-Ephraim BANKS, Henry
STONER, exors. d- e- f-5 Oct 1848, g- h- i- j-

John WHARTON, b-11 Oct 1848, c-Saml. WHARTON, Wm.
WHARTON, d- e- f-30 Nov 1848 amended account, g-14 Nov
1853/10 Aug 1854, h-$2665.83.25/$2831.39, i-$3322.73/$3322.73, j-
$656.90.75, estate/$491.34 [acct. due?]

George SHADE, b-25 Oct 1848, c-Andrew WISE & John SHADE, d-
$1500, e-Frederick SCHWARTZ, Jacob WISE, f-25 Dec 1848, g- h-
i- j-

James BRISBIN, Esq., b-28 Nov 1848, c-Hugh CONLEY, James S.
BRISBIN, d-$3000, e-Robert MILLIKEN, Andrew McFARLANE, f-
27 Dec 1848, g- h- i- j-

Page 173, Frame 188

Joseph MATHEWS, b-8 Dec 1848, c-Robert MATHEWS, d-$500, e-J. C.
SIGLER, John DAVIS, f- g- h- i- j-

Stephen KURTZ, b-9 Dec 1848, c-John KURTZ, exor., d-No Bond, e- f-
13 Jan 1849, g-8 Nov 1851, h-$356.36, i-$6391.00, j-$6034.64, estate

Jane COULTER, b-25 Dec 1848, c-Robert FORGY, d-$1000, e-John
STINE, James TURNER, f-26 Jan 1849, g- h- i- j-

Catharine DUNMIRE, b-22 Dec 1848, c-John ALLEN, exor, d-No Bond,
e- f-16 Feb 1849, g- h- i- j-

Philip WAGONER, b-28 Sep 1848, c-Samuel BARR, Esq., d-No Bond,
e- f-9 Jan 1849, g-7 Aug 1851, h-$139.97.75, i-$149.84, j-$9.86.75,
estate

John KAYS, Sr., b-6 Jan 1849, c-John KAYS, Jr., d-No Bond, e- f-27 Jan
1849, g- h- i- j-

William MORRISON, b-23 Jan 1849, c-William MORRISON, Albert
GIBBONY, d-$1400, e-James TURNER, Montgomery MORRISON,
f-6 Feb 1849, g- h- i- j-

James H. SUMMERS, **b**-26 Dec 1848, **c**-Geo. W. THOMAS, **d**-$1000, **e**-
Moses MONTGOMERY, Chas. STRATFORD, **f**-24 Jan 1849, **g**- **h**- **i**-
j-

John HAMMEL, **b**-3 Feb 1849, **c**-John PETER, Sr., **d**-no bond, **e**- **f**-2 Mar
1849, **g**-4 Nov 1852, **h**-$554.88.5, **i**-$667.96.75, **j**-$113.08.25, estate

Page 174, Frame 189 [repeated on Frame 190]
Joseph STEVENSON, **b**-17 Feb 1849, **c**-Margaret STEVENSON, **d**-
$2000, **e**-John LEVY, David M. DAVIDSON, **f**-16 Mar 1849, **g**- **h**- **i**-
j-

John HARTZLER, **b**-27 Feb 1849, **c**-Samuel YODER, Daniel YODER,
d-No Bond, **e**- **f**-24 Jul 1849, **g**-10 Jan 1856, **h**-$693.53, **i**-$2067.49, **j**-
$1373.96, estate

Henry EISENBISE, **b**-30 Jan 1849, **c**-Jesse R. CRAWFORD, **d**-$100, **e**-
Saml. S. WOODS, **f**- **g**- **h**- **i**- **j**-

Ezekiel JACKSON, **b**-3 Mar 1849, **c**-Harriet JACKSON, **d**-$2000, **e**-
James WAREAM, Daniel ZEIGLER, **f**-16 Mar 1849, **g**- **h**- **i**- **j**-

Nancy HARTZLER, **b**-12 Mar 1849, **c**-Jacob DETWEILER, **d**-$2000, **e**-
David ZOOK, Yost KING, **f**-2 Apr 1849, **g**- **h**- **i**- **j**-

David MARSHALL, **b**-15 Mar 1849, **c**-Doct. James CULBERTSON, **d**-no
bond **e**- **f**-24 Mar 1849, **g**-8 Nov 1851/8 Nov 1855, **h**-$749.87/$5.00,
i-$773.79/$34.60, **j**-$23.92, estate/$29.60, estate

Descartes S. ALEXANDER, **b**-17 Mar 1849, **c**-Hugh CONLEY, **d**-$2000,
e-Davis BATES, Perry W. McDOWELL, **f**-7 Sep 1849, **g**- **h**- **i**- **j**-

William DECKER, **b**-19 Mar 1849, **c**-William DECKER, **d**-$400, **e**-
Thomas JOHNSTON, Alfred DECKER, **f**-16 Apr 1849, **g**-9 Nov 1854,
h-$2588.74.5, **i**-$1956.67, **j**-$632.07.5, accountant

William BAREFOOT, **b**-21 Mar 1849, **c**-Peter BAREFOOT, John
BAREFOOT, James BAREFOOT, Exors., **d**- **e**- **f**-20 Apr 1849, **g**-2 Oct
1852, **h**-$9879.60.5, **i**-$9729.51, **j**-$150.09.5, accountant; ball in hands
of accts. as per Auditor's report: $12.82

John McCLENAHEN, **b**-22 Mar 1849, **c**-James DORMAN, **d**-$200, **e**-
George T. BELL, **f**-20 Apr 1849, **g**- **h**- **i**- **j**-

Jesse B. MORRIS, **b**-30 Mar 1849, **c**-Michael YOUTZY, **d**-$150, **e**-Robt.
H. MONTGOMERY, David WERTZ, **f**-27 Apr 1849, **g**- **h**- **i**- **j**-

Page 175, Frame 191

Eliza MORRISON, **b**-20 May 1847, **c**-Elijah MORRISON, **d**-$1800, **e**-
Jno. MORRISON, Joseph MILLIKEN, David McCLURE, **f**- **g**-5 Apr
1849, **h**-$1126.27, **i**-$1126.27, **j**-

John C. REYNOLDS, **b**-7 Apr 1849, **c**-Ellen M. REYNOLDS, **d**-no bond,
e- **f**-1 May 1849, **g**- **h**- **i**- **j**-

Eleanor M. REYNOLDS, **b**-30 Apr 1849, **c**-Levi REYNOLDS, Jr., David
CANDOR, **d**-no bond, **e**- **f**-1 May 1849, **g**-4 Nov 1852/14 Nov 1853,
h-$159.57/$3149.00, **i**-$159.57/$2846.59, **j**- --- -- /$302.41, exor. Levi
REYNOLDS

James D. MORRISON, **b**-24 May 1849, **c**-Samuel MORRISON, **d**-$2000,
e-Jona. J. CUNNINGHAM, Stephen HINDS, **f**-16 Jun 1849, **g**- **h**- **i**- **j**-

James ROBISON, **b**-29 May 1849, **c**-David CANDOR, **d**-$7000, **e**-Thos.
R. McKEE, James J. ROBINSON, **f**-18 Jun 1849, **g**- **h**- **i**- **j**-

Charles McLENAHEN, **b**-31 May 1849, **c**-Jesse R. CRAWFORD, **d**-
$400, **e**-Jesse WINGATE, David R. REYNOLDS, **f**-18 Jun 1849, **g**- **h**-
i- **j**-

Mathew GLASGOW, **b**-31 May 1849, **c**-Robert LAUGHLIN, **d**-$4000,
e-Geo. W. COULTER, Saml. LAUGHLIN, **f**-13 Jun 1849, **g**- **h**- **i**- **j**-

William LAUGHLIN, **b**-31 May 1849, **c**-George W. COULTER, **d**-$600,
e-Robert LAUGHLIN, Saml. LAUGHLIN, **f**-13 Jun 1849, **g**- **h**- **i**- **j**-

Enoch BEALE, **b**-23 Jun 1849, **c**-Dorothy Ann BEALE, **d**-no bond, **e**- **f**-18
Jul 1849, **g**- **h**- **i**- **j**-

Nancy CUNNINGHAM, **b**-5 Jun 1849, **c**-Hugh CONLEY, **d**-No Bond, **e**-
f- **g**- **h**- **i**- **j**-

George FIELDS, **b**-7 Aug 1849, **c**-William FIELDS, **d**-$400, **e**-David
JENKINS, John ROSS, **f**-7 Sep 1849, **g**- **h**- **i**- **j**-

Emanuel BECHT, **b**-8 Aug 1849, **c**-John K. METZ, **d**-$1600, **e**- James
McDONALD, William SMITH, **f**-8 Aug ----, **g**- **h**- **i**- **j**-

Daniel ROW, **b**-22 Aug 1849, **c**-Robert ROW, Charles STRATFORD,
exors, **d**-no bond, **e**- **f**-26 Sep 1849, **g**- **h**- **i**- **j**-

Page 176, Frame 192

William MARKS, **b**- 12 Sep 1849, **c**-Alfred MARKS, John W. SHAW, **d**-
$5000, **e**-Frederick SCHWARTZ, Robt. McMANIGIL, **f**-1 Oct 1849,
g-7 Aug 1851, **h**-$5276.65.5, **i**-$5300.24, **j**-$23.58.5, estate

Thomas STERRETT, **b**-20 Sep 1849, **C**-S. P. & W. J. STERRETT, **d**-
$14,000, **e**-Saml. S. WOODS, Robert M, KINSLOE, **f**-23 Oct 1849, **g**-
h- **i**- **j**-

David RITTENHOUSE, b-27 Sep 1849, **c**-Saml. & T. RITTENHOUSE, **d**-$1000, **e**-Nath. FEAR, Robt. H. McCLINTIC, **f**-11 Oct 1849, **g**-4 Aug 1853, **h**-$2608.03, **i**-$3166.98, **j**-$558.95, estate

Louis P. FRANCISCUS, b-1 Oct 1849, **c**-Francis G. FRANCISCUS, **d**-$1000, **e**-L. T. WATTSON, James PARKER, **f**- **g**- **h**- **i**- **j**-

George SUTTLE, b-1 Oct 1849, **c**-John SUTTLE, **d**- **e**- **f**-26 Oct 1849, **g**- **h**- **i**- **j**-

Enoch AURAND, b-4 Oct 1849, **c**-Elias AURAND, **d**-$1200, **e**-Samuel AURAND, Henry FELGER, **f**-9 Oct 1849, **g**- **h**- **i**- **j**-

John SIGLER, b-13 Oct 1849, **c**-John PURCELL, **d**-$2000, **e**-Benjamin NORTON, **f**-30 Oct 1849, **g**-7 Aug 1851/14 Nov 1853, **h**-$587.37.5/ $1573.34, **i**-$1628.04.5/$1573.34, **j**-$1040.67, estate/ 0 0 0

George W. OLIVER, b-17 Oct 1849, **c**-Joseph HAFFLEY, Jos. CAMPBELL, **d**-$4000, **e**-John KAUFFMAN, Robert CAMPBELL, **f**-5 Nov 1849, **g**-4 Aug 1853, **h**-$7509.66, **i**-$10,117.93.5, **j**-$2608.27.5, estate

Ann PEFFER, b-1 Dec 1849, **c**-Enoch MOYER, **d**-$400, **e**-Jacob MAURER, Jonas KEELER, **f**-24 Dec 1849, **g**-6 Jan 1853, **h**-$249.04.25, **i**-$388.11, **j**-$139.06.75, estate

Isaac HOOPES, b-20 Dec 1849, **c**-Henry ORR, **d**-$800, **e**-Alfred MARKS, **f**-15 Jan 1850, **g**- **h**- **i**- **j**-

Agness STERRETT, b-29 Oct 1849 **c**-Charles COLFELT, **d**-no bond, **e**- **f**- **g**-10 Aug 1854, **h**-$6917.00, **i**-$6917.00, **j**-00.00

Richard MONTGOMERY, b-19 Jan 1850, **c**-James McKINSTRY, **d**-$150, **e**-Elias PENEPACKER[sic], Ralph BOGLE, **f**-16 Mar 1850, **g**- **h**- **i**- **j**-

Henry TODD, b-31 Jan 1850, **c**-Joseph ROBINSON, John SWIGART, **d**-no bond, **e**- **f**-2 Sep 1850, **g**- **h**- **i**- **j**-

Page 177, Frame 193

Robert FORGY, Sr., b-12 Feb 1850, **c**-Robert FORGY, James FORGY, **d**-no bond, **e**- **f**-11 Mar 1850, **g**- **h**- **i**- **j**-

Godfrey BAILEY, b-26 Feb 1850, **c**-Samuel BARR, **d**-$1600, **e**-John [LAUVER] [NOTE: The "S"s and "L"s often look a lot alike, but there are LAUVERs in the area at this time, no SAUVERs], Isaac HOUGH, **f**-19 Mar 1850, **g**-7 Aug 1851/5 Feb 1854, **h**-$623.13/$282.05, **i**-$935.35.75/$423.92, **j**-$309.22.75, estate/$141.87, heirs

George LUKENS, b-12 Mar 1850, **c**-John LUKENS, **d**-$75, **e**-Jacob KNEPP, **f**-12 Apr 1850, **g**- **h**- **i**- **j**-

John R. APPLEBAUGH, **b**-14 Mar 1850, **c**-Edmund S. FAXON, John J. APPLEBAUGH, **d**-$1000, **e**-John A. WEEKS, James BURNS, **f**-13 Apr 1850, **g**- **h**- **i**- **j**-

David S. SHAW, **b**-15 Mar 1850, **c**-Robert STEWART, **d**-$200, **e**-J. M. LEECH, John WALT, **f**-1 Apr 1850, **g**- **h**- **i**- **j**-

Margaret TAYLOR, **b**-3 Apr 1850, **c**-Robert TAYLOR, George WILSON, **d**- **e**- **f**-25 Jun 1850, **g**- **h**- **i**- **j**-

David BAIR, **b**-16 Apr 1850, **c**-James HOOD, N. B. BRATTON, **d**-$800, **e**-John [ROSS] [NOTE: The presence of Napoleon Bonaparte BRATTON in the extended family of John ROSS would bode well for his identification], John WALTERS,**f**- 10 May 1850, **g**-9 Aug 1855, **h**-$1927.00.75, **i**-$3126.40, **j**-$1927.00.75, heirs

James GAMBLE, **b**-25 Apr 1850, **c**-Thomas J. POSTLETHWAIT, **d**-$1500, **e**-John PURCELL, Samuel DRAKE, **f**-18 May 1850, **g**-8 Jan 1852, **h**-$720.53.5, **i**-$335.78, **j**-$384.75.5, estate

B. F. COULTER, **b**-27 Apr 1850, **c**-G. W. COULTER, **d**-$300, **e**-Jacob GARVER, John POWELL, **f**-25 May 1850, **g**-4 Nov 1852, **h**-$1944.06.75, **i**-$1900.60, **j**-$43.46.75, [no designation]

Sarah SHILLING, **b**-9 Apr 1850, **c**-George SHILLING, **d**-$120, **e**-John [WONIER], Peter HULL, **f**-8 May 1850/1 Jun 1850, **g**-6 Apr 1854, **h**-$10,243.25, **i**-$10,584.07, **j**-$340.82, estate

Daniel SEACHRIST, **b**-11 May 1850, **c**-James KERR, **d**-$1000, **e**-J. R. McDOWELL, Adam HOSEA, **f**- These Letters revoked & Letters issued to John PERCELL, see page 178, **g**- **h**- **i**- **j**-

Samuel SUNDERLAND, **b**-11 Jun 1850, **c**-Mary SUNDERLAND, **d**-$1000, **e**-Wm. STINE, W. S. POSTLETHWAIT, **f**-1 Jul 1850, **g**-8 Nov 1851, **h**-$39.67, **i**-$250.20, **j**-$210.53, estate

Jacob GRUBER, **b**-28 May 1850, **c**-Rachel GRUBER [NOTE: Testator's name looks like GRUBEE, but Rachel's seems to be GRUBER], **d**- **e**- **f**-3 Jun 1850, **g**-8 Nov 1851, **h**-$7365.73, **i**-$11,784.48, **j**-$4418.75, estate

Page 178, Frame 194

James CALDWELL, **b**-19 Jun 1850, **c**-Samuel DRAKE, **d**-$1000, **e**-J. R. McDOWELL, John PURCELL, **f**- **g**- **h**- **i**- **j**-

Daniel SEACHRIST, **b**-19 Jun 1850, **c**-John PURCELL, **d**-$2000, **e**-Samuel DRAKE, David JENKINS, **f**-13 Jul 1850, **g**-7 Nov 1851, **h**-$67.00, **i**-$1074.22, **j**-$1007.22, estate

William P. ALEXANDER, b-24 Jun 1850, **c**-W. A. McMANIGIL, W. B. MACLAY, **d**-no bond, **e- f**-17 Jul 1850, **g**-9 Aug 1853, **h**-$1648.96.5, **i**-$1315.64, **j**- $333.32.5, accountants

Jacob WAGGONER, b-29 Jun 1850, **c**-George ROSS, **d**-$400, **e**-Christian ZOOK, Fred SCHWARTZ, **f- g**-2 Dec 1852, **h**-$254.33.75, **i**-$239.00, **j**-$15.33.75, accountant

Rebecca McVEY, b-29 Jun 1850, **c**-William M. COULTER, **d**-$200, **e**-R. D. JACOB, James COOPER, **f**-31 Jul 1850, **g**-4 Nov 1852, **h**-$105.07, **i**-$85.45, **j**-$19.62, accountant

James COCHRAN, b-29 Jul 1850, **c**-James COCHRAN, **d**-$1200, **e**-L. T. WATTSON, James BURNS, **f**-21 Aug 1850, **g**-8 Nov 1851, **h**-$431.19.75, **i**-$1047.78, **j**-$616,58.25, estate

Robert FIELDS, b-5 Aug 1850, **c**-John PURCELL, Elijah MORRISON, **d**-no bond, **e- , f**-1 Oct 1850, **g**-5 Aug 1852/5 Apr 1855, **h**-$2318.72/ $2172.21, **i**-$2410.90.5/$2596.48.5, **j**-$92.18.5, estate/$424.27.5, heirs

Bernard STOHL, b-5 Aug 1850, **c**-Saml. BARR,, **d**-$800, **e**-Joseph YEATTER, Simon KREPS, **f**-28 Aug 1850, **g**-7 Apr 1852, **h**-$364.62.5, **i**-$614.51.75, **j**-$256.48.25, estate

William MILLER, b-14 Sep 1850, **c**-A. J. MILLER, **d**-no bond, **e- f**-16 Oct 1850, **g- h- i- j-**

Dorothy A. BEALE, b-20 Sep 1850, **c**-Margaret ASTON, **d**-no bond, **e- f**-20 Sep 1850, **g- h- i- j-**

Michael HOSTETLER, b-24 Sep 1850, **c**-Jacob PEACHY, Isaac YODER, **d**-$1600, **e**-Alfred MARKS, Jerman JACOB[sic], **f**-22 Oct 1850, **g**-8 Jan 1852, **h**-$122.38.5, **i**-$1971.86.5, **j**-$549.48, estate

John MARTIN, b-2 Oct 1850, **c**-James DAVIS, Sr., **d**-$800, **e**-George DAVIS, Jno. KAUFFMAN, **f**-23 Oct 1850, **g**-25 Aug 1852, **h**-$222.52, **i**-$454.02.5, **j**-$231.50.5, heirs

Nathaniel FEAR, b-11 Oct 1850, **c**-Saml. BARR, **d**-$500, **e**-Henry ORT, Robert A. MEANS, **f**-8 Nov 1850, **g- h- i- j-**

Page 179, Frame 195

Mary SHULTZ, b-18 Oct 1850, **c**-William MORRISON, **d**-no bond, **e- f**-23 Oct 1851, **g**-10 Aug 1854, **h**-$113.31.5, **i**-$63.08.75, **j**-$50.22.75, accountant

William T. JAMES, b-21 Oct 1850, **c**-James SUMMERVILLE, **d**-$100, **e**-John LEHR, James WAREAM, **f**-22 Oct 1850, **g**-7 Aug 1851, **h**-$72.91.5, **i**-$29.70, **j**-$43.21.5, adms

John F. DAVIS, **b**-12 Oct 1850, **c**-James DAVIS, **d**-no bond, **e**- **f**-6 Nov 1850, **g**- **h**-$1406.51, **i**-$1637.64, **j**-$231.13, estate
Michael CRISWELL, **b**-25 Oct 1850, **c**-John ROSS, **d**-$1000, **e**-Saml. S. WOODS, Lewis HOOVER, **f**- **g**- **h**- **i**- **j**-
Elijah DAVIS, **b**-6 Nov 1850, **c**-William MACKLIN, **d**-Will &c, **e**- **f**- **g**-3 Dec 1850, **h**-9 Aug 1855, **i**-$3056.47, **j**-$1955.48, heirs
Christopher WOLFLEY, **b**-10 Jan 1851, **c**-Henry KOHLER, **d**-$120, **e**-Saml. BELFORDT, Philip BARGER, **f**-1 Feb 1851, **g**-8 Jan 1857, **h**-$862.45.25, **i**-$690.26, **j**-$172.19.25, accountant
James A. SAMPLE, **b**-10 Jan 1851, **c**-Robert M. KINSLOE, **d**-$300, **e**-Samuel BARR, James M. BROWN, **f**-10 Feb 1851, **g**-14 Nov 1853, **h**-$601.55, **i**-$601.41, **j**-$00.14, [no designation]
Christian ZOOK, **b**-20 Jan 1851, **c**-Joseph HAFFLEY, Isaac YODER, **d**-$4000, **e**-L. T. WATTSON, Alfred MARKS, **f**-10 Feb 1851, **g**-9 Nov 1854, **h**-$4662.78, **i**-$20,615.62, **j**-$15,952.84, estate
Moses WATTS, **b**-25 Jan 1851, **c**-W. J. McCOY, **d**-$2000, **e**-T. F. McCOY, W. J. JACOBS, **f**- **g**- **h**- **i**- **j**-
Michael NORTON, **b**-27 Jan 1851, **c**-Wm. MACKLIN, **d**-$800, **e**-S. HAMAN, T. F. McCOY, **f**-17 Feb 1851, **g**-4 Aug 1853, **h**-$1939.30, **i**-$1838.50, **j**-$100.80, accountant
Jacob CARSON, **b**-28 Jan 1851, **c**-William J. GLASS, William A. CARSON, **d**-$1000, **e**-George BELL, Saml. BARR, **f**-27 Feb 1851, **g**- **h**- **i**- **j**-
William R. ALEXANDER, **b**-29 Jan 1851, **c**-George WILSON, **d**-$2000, **e**-Robert TAYLOR, L. T. WATTSON, **f**-6 Mar 1851, **g**-6 Apr 1854, **h**-$906.97.25, **i**-$1104.36.25, **j**-$197.39, estate
Samuel ZOOK, **b**-12 Feb 1851, **c**-David HOSTETLER, **d**-$1000, **e**-Jno. KAUFFMAN, Solomon ZOOK, **f**-16 Feb 1851, **g**-4 Nov 1852, **h**-$2163.92, **i**-$2093.88, **j**-$70.04, accountant

Page 180, Frame 196
William JENNINGS, **b**-17 Feb 1851, **c**-Henry BOOK, **d**-$4000, **e**-George STRUNK, L. T. WATTSON, **f**-7 Mar 1851, **g**-5 Jan 1854, **h**-$391.27, **i**-$1968.77, **j**-$1577.50, in hands of accountant
Samuel SIGLER, **b**-22 Feb 1851, **c**-John C. SIGLER, **d**-$1200, **e**-George W. SIGLER, **f**-8 Mar 1851, **g**-4 Nov 1852, **h**-$756.05, **i**-$756.05, **j**-00
Thomas G. KEARNS, **b**-4 Mar 1851, **c**-John W. KEARNS, **d**-$2000, **e**-John PRESTON, Jacob MOHLER, **f**-14 Mar 1851, **g**-8 Nov 1851, **h**-$479.31, **i**-$2568.27.5, **j**-$2088.96.5, estate

Fairfax GOODALL, b-24 Mar 1851, **c**-John ROSS, **d**-$1500, **e**-James COOPER, Jno. A. ROSS, **f**-19 Apr 1851, **g- h- i- j-**

Henry WILSON, b- c- d- e- f-25 Oct 1851, **g- h- i- j-**

Frances HUTCHINSON, b-31 Mar 1851, **c**-Samuel DRAKE, **d- e- f**-15 Apr 1851, **g- h- i- j-**

Margaret LUKENS, b-9 Apr 1851, **c**-John LUKENS, **d- e- f**-8 May 1851, **g- h- i- j-**

Christian BYLER, b-15 Apr 1851, **c**-Jacob BYLER, **d**-$1600, **e**-L. T. WATTSON, Jonas BYLER, **f**-8 May 1851, **g**-15 Jan 1853 [5 looks a little like an 8], **h**-$1665.40.25, **i**-$1665.40.25, **j-**

John C. JENNINGS, b-10 May 1851, **c**-George W. STEWART, **d**-$1000, **e**-Robt. MATHEWS, D. ZEIGLER, **f**-16 May 1851, **g**-1 Apr 1856, **h**-$973.21, **i**-$906.33, **j**-$66.88, accountant,

Jane TAYLOR, b-22 May 1851, **c**-George. W. THOMAS, **d**-$6000, **e**-M. MONTGOMERY, W. H. IRWIN, **f- g- h- i- j-**

Christian PLANK, b-9 May 1851, **c**-Isaac PLANK, Joseph HAFFLEY, **d**-no bond, **e- f**-2 Jun 1851, **g**-1 Dec 1852, **h**-$401.39.5, **i**-$4688.69.5, **j**-$4287.30, estate

John EDMISTON, b- c- d- e- f- g- h- i- j-

Page 181, Frame 197

William [COMMER], b-24 May 1851, **c**-William J. McCOY, **d**-$700, **e**-Wm. J. JACOBS, T. F. McCOY, **f**-6 Jun 1851, **g- h- i- j-**

Daniel REEL, b-24 May 1851, **c**-William W. GILMORE, Henry STEELY, **d**-$500, **e**-Jno. R. McDOWELL, **f**-10 Jun 1851, **g**-7 Apr 1852, **h**-$96.08.5, **i**-$226.25.25, **j**-$130.16.75, estate

Catharine CEEVER, b- c- d- e- f- g- h- i- j-

John KEARNS, b-28 May 1851, **c**-Philip S. KEARNS, John W. KEARNS, **d**-no bond, **e- f**-14 Jun 1851/3 Jan 1852, **g**-30 Nov 1852, **h**-$602.27, **i**-$6363.09, **j**-$5760.82/$4017.00 paid Legatees/$1743.82, estate

Thomas ROBINSON, b-30 May 1851, **c**-Christian HOOVER, **d**-$300, **e**-Daniel FICHTHORN, Joseph SMITH, **f**-20 Jun 1851, **g**-5 Jan 1854, **h**-$105.07.5, **i**-$788.64, **j**-$683.56.5, in hands of accountant

James McCLUNEY, b-8 Jul 1851, **c**-John McCORD, **d**-$200, **e**-John WILLIAMS, R. MATHEWS, **f**-5 Aug 1851, **g- h- i- j-**

Geo. M. BOWMAN, b-4 Aug 1851, **c**-G. W. McBRIDE, A. HARSHBARGER, **d**-$800, **e**-John ROSS, **f**-28 Aug 1851, **g- h- i- j-**

Isaac WAGGONER, b-14 Aug 1851, **c**-Henry MOWRY, **d**-$2000, **e**-John HUMMELL, David [T.] KLINE, **f**-18 Aug 1851, **g**-4 Aug 1853, **h**-$729.31, **i**-$893.57.75, **j**-$164.26.75, estate

Christian MOIST, b-14 Aug 1851, **c**-Wm. J. McCOY, Samuel YODER, **d**-$5000, **e**-Jacob KAUFFMAN, T. F. McCOY, **f**-15 Sep 1851, **g- h- i- j-**

Martin DIXON, b- 12 Sep 1851,**c**- Elias W. DIXON, **d**-$800, **e**-Robert DIXON, S. ROBINSON, **f**-4 Oct 1851, **g**-7 Apr 1852, **h**-$235.34, **i**-$1659.32, **j**-$1423.98, estate

Catharine SHIMP, b-3 Oct 1851, **c**-John DAILEY, **d**-$100, **e**-Wm. BUTLER, C. HOOVER, **f**-3 Nov 1851, **g- h- i- j-**

Thompson J. MITCHELL, b-7 Oct 1851, **c**-Robert McMANIGLE[sic], **d**-$1000, **e**-Z. RITTENHOUSE, G. W. STEWART, **f- g- h- i- j-**

George MULHOLLAN, b-15 Oct 1851, **c**-R. C. HALE, **d**-$5000, **e**-Jane HALE, James T. HALE, **f- g- h- i- j-**

Page 182, Frame 198

Philip ROTHROCK, b-21 Oct 1851, **c**-Abraham ROTHROCK, **d- e- f**-3 Nov 1851, **g**-4 Aug 1853/11 Jan 1861, **h**-$1335.89/$3482.52, **i**-$996.87/$7672.71, **j**-$339.02/$4190.19, heirs

Sarah ROBINSON, b-11 Nov 1851, **c**-William R. McCAY, **d- e- f**-12 Nov 1851, **g- h- i- j-**

John P. STROUP, b-22 Nov 1851, **c**-John YEALTER, **d**-$600, **e**-John KANE, Levi SULTZBOUGH, **f**-10 Dec 1851, **g- h- i- j-**

Nicholas MILLER, b-22 Nov 1851, **c**-Joshua KING, **d**-$5000, **e**-Daniel MILLER, Jacob KAUFFMAN, **f**-18 Dec 1851, **g- h- i- j-**

Jacob MARKS, b-29 Nov 1851, **c**-William B. JOHNSTON, **d**-$400, **e**-William MARKS, And. McFARLANE, **f**- 26 Dec 1851, **g**-9 Aug 1855, **h**-$1028.06.5, **i**-$968.35, **j**-$59.71.5, accountant

Joseph COULTER, b-4 Nov 1851, **c**-George W. COULTER, **d- e- f**-3 Dec 1851, **g**-4 Aug 1853, **h**-$184.77.75, **i**-$580.76, **j**-$395.98.25, estate

Peter SNOOK, b-8 Dec 1851, **c**-Abraham SNOOK, **d- e- f**-27 Dec 1851, **g**-4 Jan 1855, **h**-$176.96.5, **i**-$170.54.5, **j**-$6.42, accountant

Michael BEAR, b-13 Dec 1851, **c**-Joseph E. BEAR, William MONTGOMERY, **d**-$600, **e**-Jacob BEAR, Robert MATTHEWS, **f**-13 Jan 1852, **g- h- i- j-**

Mary NIXON, b-16 Dec 1851, **c**-Samuel BARR, Henry BRIDGE, **d- e- f**-13 Jan 1852, **g**-8 Nov 1855, **h**-$547.36, **i**-$1793.84, **j**-$1246.48, heirs

Jacob SMITH, b-3 Jan 1852, c-Samuel DRAKE, d-$600, e-David HAMILTON, David HEISLER, f-31 Jan 1852, g-3 Dec 1852, h-$123.38, i-$482.45, j-$359.07, estate

John CHESTER, b-8 Jan 1852, c-Susan CHESTER, d- e- f-30 Jan 1852, g- h- i- j-

John KLINE, b-5 Jan 1852, c-Christian HOOVER, d-$50, e- f- g-6 Jan 1853, h-$120.00, i-$120.00, j- —

Susan WAGGONER, b-9 Jan [1852], c-Isaac SMITH, d-$600, e- f- g- h- i- j-

Page 183, Frame 199

Rebecca McCLELLAN, b-26 Jan 1852, c-David ZOOK, d- e- f-12 Feb 1852, g-4 Aug 1853/8 Nov 1855, h-$2975.70.5/$3137.12, i-$4865.33.75/$9083.89, j-$1889.63.25, estate/$5946.77, heirs

R. H. ALEXANDER, b-26 Jan 1852, c-Joseph MILLIKEN, d-$1500, e-Robert ALEXANDER, John R. McDOWELL, f-17 Mar 1852, g-8 Nov 1855, h-$788.59, i-$2401.49, j-$1612.90, heirs

Samuel J. GEORGE, b-29 Jan 1852, c-William J. JACOBS, d-$300, e-Samuel FRANK, John SHAW, f- g-6 Jan 1853, h-$45.37.5, i-$182.55, j-$137.17.5, estate

John KENNAGY, b-3 Feb 1852, c-Jacob ZOOK, d-$4000, e-Jacob KING, David HOSTETLER, f-27 Feb 1852, g-9 Nov 1854, h-$5490.08 i-$5210.60, j-$279.48, accountant

Rachel JOHNSTON, b-19 Feb 1852, c-Joseph RHODES, George STRODE, d- e- f-8 Mar 1852, g-9 Nov 1854, h-$3504.73, i-$5046.04, j-$1541.31, estate

John HOFFMAN, b-17 Feb 1952. c-John & Michael HOFFMAN, d- e- f-6 Mar 1852, g-14 Nov 1853, h-$334.34, i-$813.87, j-$479.53, estate

James HOOD, Esq., b-30 Mar 1852, c-John BROWN, d-$2000, e-N. B. BRATTON, H. J. WALTERS, f-30 Apr 1852, g-9 Nov 1854, h-$380.47.5, i-$1329.07.5, j-$949.20, estate

Henry MILLER, b-16 Apr 1852, c-George B. WHARTON, d-$500, e-James McKINSTRY, f-10 Jun 1852, g-4 Jan 1855, h-$1122.61, i-$1846.66, j-$724.05, heirs

William J. GLASS, b-13 May 1852, c-Henry L. CLOSE, d-$3000, e-Davis BATES, f-31 May 1852 g- h- i- j-

Catharine JACOB, b-26 May 1852, c-A. P. JACOB, Esq., James PARKER, d- e- f- g-14 Nov 1853, h-$2240.00, i-$2241.67, j-$1.67, estate

Henry KULP, Esq., **b-**1 Jun 1852, **c-**James IRVIN, **d-**$300, **e-**William BUTLER, Christian HOOVER, **f-**29 Jun 1852, **g-**4 Jan 1855, **h-**$487.86.5, **i-**$1794.26, **j-**$1306.39.5, heirs

Keever WHARTON, M.D., **b-**1 Jun 1852, **c-**Samuel WHARTON, **d-**$2000, **e-**John NORTON, Jr., George B. WHARTON, **f-**1 Jul 1852, **g- h- i- j-**

George STOUT, **b-**2 Jul 1852, **c-**Samuel BARR, **d-**$800, **e-**Zebulon PHILIPS, **f-**31 Jul 1852, **g-**8 Nov 1855, **h-**$353.42, **i-**$728.37, **j-**$374.95 in hands of accountant, less $187.64 to heirs

Page 184, Frame 200

Joseph BEAR, **b-**6 Jul 1852, **c-**Jacob BEAR, **d-**$100, **e-**Robt. H. McCLINTIC, **f-**2 Aug 1852, **g- h- i- j-**

James McDOWELL, **b-**13 Jul 1852, **c-**Joseph MILLIKEN, **d-**$800, **e-**Robert MILLIKEN, John McDOWELL, **f- g- h- i- j-**

Robert McNEAL, **b-**14 Jul 1851[sic], **c-**David BLOOM, **d-**$1500, **e-**Joseph ALEXANDER, Alexander McNEAL, **f-**10 Aug 1852, **g-**14 Nov 1853, **h-**$203.36.5, **i-**$200.55, **j-**$2.81.5, accountant

Isaac CORRELL, **b-**21 Jul 1852, **c-**Rebecca Ann CORRELL, **d-**$1000, **e-**William HARDY, T. F. McCOY, **f-**2 Aug 1852, **g- h- i- j-**

John YODER, **b-**3 Aug 1852, **c-**John PEACHY, adm., **d-**$2000, **e-**John KAUFFMAN, D. M. [CONTERER or CONTERES?], **f-**28 Aug 1852, **g-**5 Jan 1854, **h-**$13537.5, **i-**$1275.85.5, **j-**$1140.48, heirs

William WILLS, **b-**28 Aug 1852, **c-**Samuel WILLS (son of James), **d- e- f-**24 Sep 1852, **g-**29 Oct 1852, **h-**$3878.91, **i-**$8305.03, **j-**$4426.12, estate

David [BURIGHT], **b-**27 Sep 1852, **c-**Joseph C. BURIGHT, C. HOOVER, admrs., **d-**$500, **e-**William BUTLER, Daniel BURIGHT, **f-**27 Oct 1852, **g-**8 Nov 1855, **h-**$767.74, **i-**$1209.17 **j-**$441.43, in hands of accountants

James COOPER, **b-**22 Oct 1852, **c-**William J. McCOY, **d-**$2000, **e-**Thos. F. McCOY, Wm. J. JACOBS, Esq., **f- g- h- i- j-**

[NOTE: This section is a little confusing. It appears that a couple of records have been inserted, and the lines aren't always totally clear as to which belongs to which. Will do my best.]

Mary Ann FLEMING, **b**-4 Nov 1852, **c**-William M. FLEMING, **d**- **e**- **f**-6 Dec 1852, **g**-14 Nov 1853, **h**-$476.00, **i**-$2336.00, **j**-$1860–, estate

Charles NAGENEY, **b**-4 Nov 1852, **c**-Charles NAGENEY, John D. NAGENEY, **d**- **e**- **f**- **g**- **h**- **i**- **j**-

William A. JINKINS, **b**-8 Nov 1852, **c**-John PURCELL, **d**-$1000, **e**-David JINKINS, Jno. R. McDOWELL, **f**-26 Nov 1852, **g**-9 Nov 1854, **h**-$279.33.5, **i**-$1122.90, **j**-$843.66.5, estate

Mary KEARNS, **b**-13 Nov 1852, **c**-John W. KEARNS, **d**-$2000, **e**-John [LITTLE?], Jacob MILLER, **f**-20 Jan 1853, **g**-5 Jan 1854, **h**-$382.43, **i**-$2161.78, **j**-$1779.36, heirs

Abraham EAST, **b**-17 Nov 1852, **c**-Christian HOOVER, Esq., **d**-$100, **e**-R. H. McCLINTICK, H. J. WALTERS, **f**- **g**-5 Jan 1854, **h**-$160.14.75, **i**-$266.37.5, **j**-$106.23, in hands of administrator

Francis THOMPSON, **b**-19 Nov 1852, **c**-Christian HOOVER, Esq., Hannah C. THOMPSON, **d**-$3000, **e**-Wm. BUTLER, Michael BUOY, **f**-28 Dec 1852, **g**-8 Nov 1855, **h**-$2053.27.5 **i**-$1861.48, **j**-$191.79.5, accountants

Mary Ann BEATTY, **b**-19 Nov 1852, **c**-Perry W. McDOWELL, **d**-$400, **e**-Geo. BELL, Jno. R. McDOWELL, **f**-18 Dec 1852, **g**- **h**- **i**- **j**-

Page 185, Frame 201

Henry TIPPEL, **b**-20 Nov 1852, **c**-Jesse WINGATE, **d**-$400, **e**-Wm. A. McMANIGLE, Michael BUOY, **f**-14 Dec 1852, **g**-9 Aug 1855, **h**-$72.89, **i**-$171.08, **j**-$98.19, heirs

John ROBISON, **b**-20 Nov 1852, **c**-William P. ROBISON, James J. ROBISON, David CANDOR, **d**- **e**- **f**-17 Nov 1852, **g**- **h**- **i**- **j**-

Joshua PRICE, **b**-30 Nov 1852, **c**-Elias HUFFNAGLE, **d**-$1200, **e**-Samuel FRANKS, Lewis T. WATTSON, **f**-28 Dec 1852, **g**-6 Apr 1854, **h**-$617.18, **i**-$1136.38, **j**-$519.20, estate

Henry STONER, Esq., **b**-30 Nov 1852, **c**-John C. SIGLER, **d**-$1000, **e**-Francis McCOY, **f**-4 Mar 1853, **g**-4 Aug 1853, **h**-$293.02, **i**-$263.71.5, **j**-$29.30.5, accountant

Isaac HAINES, **b**-3 Dec 1853, **c**-John McCORD, Esq., **d**-$300, **e**-Elias PENEPACKER, **f**-13 Jan 1853, **g**- **h**- **i**- **j**-

James CRISWELL, **b**-11 Dec 1852, **c**-Michael BUOY, **d**-$500, **e**-Saml. FUNK, Jno. A. ROSS, **f**- **g**- **h**- **i**- **j**-

Col. John McDOWELL, **b**-14 Dec 1852, **c**-William J. JACOBS, Esq., **d**-$100, **e**-Saml. S. WOODS, Charles COLFELT, These Letters revoked and Letters granted to Joseph MILLIKEN, **f**- **g**- **h**- **i**- **j**-

George **ALBRIGHT**, b-30 Dec 1852, c-Elizabeth ALBRIGHT, Excr., d-e- f- g- h- i- j-

Col. Jno. **McDOWELL**, b-5 Jan 1853, c-Joseph MILLIKEN, d-$200, e-Jno. McDOWELL, Thomas REED, f- g- h- i- j-

Noble **NORTON**, b-11 Jan 1853, c-Mary NORTON, d-$6000, e-George N. NORTON, Edmund S. NORTON, f- g- h- i- j-

Margaret **MATTHEWS**, b-12 Jan 1853, c-Joseph MILLIKEN, admr, C. T. annexr, d-$1000, e-Robert MILLIKEN, Wm. MITCHELL, f- g- h- i- j-

Christian **KAUFFMAN**, b-31 Jan 1853, c-Jonathan KAUFFMAN, d-$1200, e-Daniel YODER, Reuben KAUFFMAN, f-17 Feb 1853, g-10 Aug 1854, h-$940.52, i-$1171.27, j-$230.75, estate

Hugh **SAMPLE**, b-7 Feb 1853, c-Moses A. SAMPLE, d-$200, e-Jno. W. SHAW, Esq., Thomas MAYES, f-18 Feb 1853, g-10 Jan 1856, h-$387.63.75, i-$1056.48.25, j-$668.84.5 Bal. to which add as fee $19.50, decree of [cenit?], $688.34.5 [no designation]

Page 186, Frame 202 [duplicated on Frame 203]

Catharine **STRODE**, b-9 Feb 1853, c-Joseph STRODE, Jr., exor, d-no bond, e- f- g- h- i- j-

George B. **MATTHEWS**, b-10 Feb 1853, c-George LANE, d-$1500, e-Samuel DRAKE, Jno. A. ROSS, f-7 Mar 1853, g-10 Jan 1856/6 Nov 1856, h-$482.24/$501.93.5, i-$910.52/$428.30 j-$428.30, estate/$73.63.5, admr

Feronica **ZOOK**, b-23 Feb 1853, c-Eli ZOOK, Simon KENAGY, Exors, d-no bond, e- f-26 Feb 1853, g-5 Apr 1855, h-$465.05, i-$2656.27, j-$2191.22, heirs

John **SIGLER**, b-22 Mar 1853, c-George H. SIGLER, Joseph BURKHOLDER, d-$2000, e-Adam SIGLER, Thomas G. BELL, f-20 Apr 1853, g-4 Jan 1855, h-$292.34.25, i-$849.80.5, j-$557.46.25, heirs

John **MATTHEWS**, b-1 Apr 1853, c-William ERWIN, D.B.M., d-$500, e-Cyrus STINE, Richard GALLAHER, f- g- h- i- j-

Hugh **MORAN**, b-5 Apr 1853, c-William W. GILMORE, Esq., d-$8000, e-James HEMPHILL, Thomas [STROUPE], f-27 Apr 1853, g-9 Nov 1854/9 Aug 1855, h-$1002.98.5/$49.50, i-$1288.89/$1095.71.5, j-$285.90.5/$1046.21.5, estate

Henry A. **HEMPHILL** b-5 Apr 1853, c-Joseph HAFFLY, Esq., d-$800, e-Christian C. ZOOK, Joseph CAMPBELL, Jr., f-22 Apr 1853, g-10 Aug 1854, h-$359.38, i-$990.56.5, j-$631.18.5, no designation

James CUPPLES, **b**-5 Apr 1853, **c**-Joseph MILLIKEN, admr De Bonis non, **d**-$1000, **e**-James CUPPLES, James THOMPSON, **f**- **g**- **h**- **i**- **j**-

William B. MACLAY, **b**-5 Apr 1853, **c**-Holmes MACLAY, Jos. H. MACLAY, **d**-$16,000, **e**-Saml. MACLAY, Wm. A. MANIGLE, **f**-18 Apr 1853, **g**- **h**- **i**- **j**-

George DAVIS, **b**-7 Apr 1853, **c**-John W. SHAW, **d**-$1000, **e**-Alfred MARKS, Samuel FRANK, **f**-21 May 1853, **g**-9 Nov 1854, **h**-$398.92, **i**-$429.46, **j**-$30.54, estate

James J. MACLAY, **b**-8 Apr 1853, **c**-Jno. MACLAY, **d**-$500, **e**-William REED, Thomas BUNN, W. B. JOHNSTON, **f**- **g**- **h**- **i**- **j**-

Jacob MILLER, **b**-23 Apr 1853, **c**-Miller A. McILVAINE, **d**-no bond, **e**- **f**-12 May 1853, **g**-5 Apr 1855, **h**-$1052.60, **i**-$1272.93, **j**-$220.33, heirs

Samuel MITCHELL, **b**-27 Apr _____, **c**-Samuel MITCHELL, Joseph MILLIKIN, exors, **d**-no bond, **e**- **f**- **g**- **h**- **i**- **j**-

Page 187, Frame 204

Abraham ZOOK, **b**-24 May 1853, **c**-David ZOOK, Jacob ZOOK, **d**-no bond, **e**- **f**-3 Jun 1853, **g**-8 Nov 1855, **h**-$9175.86, **i**-$923607, **j**-$60.21, heirs

Dr. Lewis HOOVER, **b**-24 May 1853, **c**-Christian HOOVER, Jr., **d**-$2000, **e**-R. U. JACOB[sic], Jacob MUTHERSBAUGH, **f**-27 May 1853, **g**-5 Aug 1857/4 Apr 1861, **h**-$884.97, **i**-$1051.58.25/$88.43, **j**-$166.61.5, heirs

Catharine OATENKIRK, **b**-18 Jun 1853, **c**-Adam HOSEA, Exr. **d**-no bond, **e**- **f**-18 Jul 1853, **g**- **h**- **i**- **j**-

Henry LEATTOR, Esq., **b**-20 Jul 1853, **c**-Jno. C. LEATTOR, Elisha BRATTON, admrs cum testamento annexo, **d**-$9000, **e**-Wm. ERWIN, Esq., Wm. A. MOORE, **f**-filed 20 Aug 1853, **g**- **h**- **i**- **j**-

Ephraim SWANGER, **b**-1 Aug 1853, **c**-Jefferson SWANGER, admr., **d**-$800, **e**-David HOOLEY, Hugh CONLEY, **f**-27 Aug 1853, **g**-4 Jan 1855, **h**-$538.70, **i**-$971.29, **j**-$432.59, estate

Margaret Jane WIESON, **b**-1 Aug 1853, **c**-William M. FLEMING, **d**-no bond, **e**- **f**-2 Jan 1854, **g**- **h**- **i**- **j**-

Moses KELLY, **b**-3 Aug 1853, **c**-Matthew KELLY, admr., **d**-$400, **e**-Wm. MITCHELL, Jas. M. MARTIN, **f**-30 Aug 1853, **g**-8 Nov 1855, **h**-$357.89, **i**-$327.58.75, **j**-$30.30.25, accountant

John LEVY, **b**-24 May 1853, **c**-Joseph ALEXANDER, Esq., admr de bonis non, **d**-$500, **e**-Daniel ZEIGLER, **f**- **g**- **h**- **i**- **j**-

Jacob MAURER, b-15 Sep 1853, c-Christian HOOVER, Esq., d-$100, e-Daniel EISENBISE, Michael BUOY, f- g-9 Nov 1854, h-$114.82.5, i-$565.00, j-$450.17.5, estate

Peter CHRISTIANA, b-27 Sep 1853, c-Christian HOOVER, Esq., d-$200, e-Chas. C. STEINBARGER, Amos [ROOT], f-3 Nov 1853, g- h- i- j-

Christian GRUNAWALT, b-8 Oct 1853, c-Joseph GRUNAWALT, d-$2400, e-Joshua KING, Elijah YOUTZEY, f-28 Oct 1853, g-5 Apr 1855, h-$136.03, i-$1663.94, j-$152791, heirs

James MONAHON, b-21 Oct 1853, c-Christian HOOVER, admr., d-$500, e-Samuel S. WOODS, Samuel COMFERT, f- g- h- i- j-

William McCONKEY, b-8 Nov 1853, c-William W. GILMORE, d-$800, e-James McFARLAND, Thomas HAZLETT, f-Filed 15 Nov 1853, g-10 Jan 1856, h-$1997.27, i-$487.25, j-$289.98, estate

<u>Page 188, Frame 205</u>

Ann ALEXANDER, b-23 Nov 1853, c-Henry P. TAYLOR, exor., d- e- f-29 Nov 1853, g-2 Mar 1865, h-$3462.93, i-$16,490.60, j-$13,027.67, heirs

[do] b-28 Nov 1853, c-Dr. Hugh ALEXANDER ([Ohio]), d-$16,000, e-James ALEXANDER, Joseph ALEXANDER, Esq., f- g- h- i- j-

Jason CONE, b-8 Dec 1853, c-Joshua MORRISON, admn D B N, d-$400, e-William MORRISON, Jno. STONEROAD, f- g- h- i- j-

Mary C. COULTER, b-2 Jan 1854, c-David G. COULTER, Wm. M. COULTER, exors., d-no bond e- f- g- h- i- j-

James MORRISON, b-9 Jan 1854, c-George MILLER, Esq., d-$150, e-William MORRISON, Samuel RITTENHOUSE, f- g- h- i- j-

Martha STEEL, b-25 Jan 1854, c-C. C. HEMPHILL, d-$200, e-John A. ROSS, T. F. McCOY, f-27 Jan 1854, g- h- i- j-

Rachel GRUBER, b-6 Feb 1854, c-John C. SIGLER, Thompson G. BELL, exors., d-no bond, e- f-8 Feb 1854, g- h- i- j-

Sarah STRODE, b-9 Feb 1854, c-Joseph STRODE, Sr., d- e- f- g- h- i- j-

Dorothy Ann BEALE, b-14 Feb 1854, c-Joseph MILLIKEN, admr., Dr Bonis nom C. T. Annexo, d-$700, e-Robert M. MILLIKEN, Jos. ALEXANDER, f- g- h- i- j-

George LANDIS, b-28 Feb 1854, c-Saml. WATTS, Christopher HOOLEY, admrs. cum testamento annexo, d-$5000, e-David HOOLEY, Andrew [WATT], f-20 Mar 1854, g-9 Aug 1855, h-$3490.04.5, i-$3953.83, j-$473.78.5, heirs

McCluny RADCLIFF, b-1 Mar 1854, **c**-Sarah RADCLIFF, exrx., **d- e- f-
g- h- i- j-**

William JACKSON, b-4 Mar 1854, **c**-William JACKSON, **d**-$700, **e**-John
STINE, Jr., Daniel ZEIGLER, **f- g- h- i- j-**

John SHILLING, b-21 Mar 1854, **c**-Frederick SCHWARTZ, **d**-$400, **e**-
John HAMILTON, John W. SHAW, **f**-15 Apr 1854, **g**-10 Apr 1856, **h**-
$784.94, **i**-$831.55.25, **j**-$46.61.25, in hands of accountant

Geo. BUMBAUGH, b-25 Mar 1854, **c**-C. HOOVER, Jacob
BUMBAUGH, exors., **d**-no bond, **e- f- g- h- i- j-**

Page 189, Frame 206

Dr. James CULBERTSON, b-4 Apr 1854, **c**-Mrs. Mary CULBERTSON,
exor., **d**-$4000, **e**-John EVANS, Dr. Elias W. HALE, **f**-13 Jun 1854, **g**-
6 Nov 1856, **h**-$1454.37, **i**-$2741.47, **j**-$138710, heirs

Revd. Joshua MOORE, b-22 Apr 1854, **c**-Robert MILLIKEN, admr., **d**-
$1000, **e**-Wm. P. MILLIKEN, James ALEXANDER, **f**-16 May 1854,
g-8 Nov 1855, **h**-$238.26, **i**-$409.55, **j**-$171.29, heirs

John McCORD, Esq., b-13 Jun 1854, **c**-Thos. McCORD, John ADAIR,
exors., **d- e- f**-11 Jul 1854, **g- h- i- j-**

Dorcas STACKPOLE, b-7 Aug 1854, **c**-James H. ROSS, admr., **d**-$200,
e-John ROSS, Wm. M. COULTER, **f- g**-27 Nov 1855, **h**-$130.31, **i**-
$662.41, **j**-$532.10, heirs

David ROTHROCK, Esq., b-9 Aug 1854, **c**-Jacob HOOVER, **d**-$600, **e**-
David MUTHERSBAUGH, William R. WILLS, **f**-29 Aug 1854, **g**-9
Nov 1861, **h**-$835.29, **i**-$988.33, **j**-$153.04, estate

Nancy Jane GONZALES, b-9 Aug 1854, **c**-William WILSON, **d**-$1500,
e-Cyrus STINE, James FLEMING, **f**-filed 23 Oct 1854, **g- h- i- j-**

Jonathan COLLER, b-21 Aug 1854, **c**-Abram B. ALBERT, **d**-$800, **e**-
Daniel YODER, George SWOYER **f**-4 Oct 1854, **g**-6 Nov 1856, **h**-
$472.87, **i**-$472.33, **j**-$.54, administrator

Susannah HANAWALT, b-21 Aug 1854, **c**-Hugh McKEE, exor., **d**-no
bond, **e- f**-6 Sep 1854, **g**-5 Dec 1855, **h**-$315.54, **i**-$436.81.5, **j**-
$121.27.5, heirs

Martha MILLER, b-2 Sep 1854, **c**-Andrew J. MILLER, admr., **d**-$400,
e-William S. CUSTER, C. HOOVER, Esq., **f**-12 Sep 1854, **g**-31 Aug
1857, **h- i- j-**

Miller A. McILVAINE, b-4 Sep 1854, **c**-Mrs. Eliza McILVAINE, **d**-
$4000, **e**-Peter ALBRIGHT, Joseph ALEXANDER, **f**-9 Oct 1854, **g**-7
Apr 1857, **h**-$1965.88, **i**-$1438.74, **j**-$472.86, in hands of accountant

Henry SMITH, b-22 Sep 1854, **c**-Jacob SMITH, exor., **d**-no bond, **e**- **f**-30 Sep 1854, **g**- **h**- **i**- **j**-

John GIBBS, b-30 Sep 1854, **c**-Joseph GRUVER, **d**-$200, **e**-James BURNS, Wm. R. McCAY, **f**-2 Oct 1854, **g**- **h**- **i**- **j**-

Jacob MILLER, b-16 Oct 1854, **c**-Samuel AURAND, A.D.N.C.T.A., **d**-$1000, **e**-John DAVIS, Henry ALBRIGHT, **f**- **g**-20 Sep 1856, **h**-$37.30, **i**-$255.93, **j**-$218.63, in hands of accountant

Page 190, Frame 207

John HUMMEL, b-21 Oct 1854, **c**-Abraham KLURE, John HUMMEL, **d**-no bond, **e**- **f**-23 Oct 1854, **g**-4 Mar 1856, **h**-$4062.25, **i**-$6498.48, **j**-$2436, heirs

Joseph GOCHENOUR, b-28 Oct 1854, **c**-Christian HOOVER, Esq., **d**-$1000, **e**-Wm. H. ERWIN, John HAMILTON, **f**-filed 15 Nov 1854, **g**-9 Mar 1857, **h**-$570.41, **i**-$591/93. **j**-$11.42, estate

Elizabeth DRAKE, b-1 Nov 1854, **c**-Samuel DRAKE, exor., **d**-no bond, **e**- **f**-6 Nov 1854, **g**-10 Mar 1857, **h**-$1101.69, **i**-$1020.60, **j**-$81.09, estate

William R. McCAY, b-4 Nov 1854, **c**-Michael BUOY, **d**-$3,000, **e**-James BURNS, C. HOOVER, **f**-2 Dec 1854, **g**- **h**- **i**- **j**-

William LATHEROW, b-7 Nov 1854, **c**-Elijah MORRISON, **d**-$1000, **e**-John PURCELL, Wm. R. MORRISON, **f**-4 Dec 1854, **g**-10 Apr 1856, **h**-$660.81, **i**-$650.72, **j**-$10.09, in hands of accountant

Daniel BATES, b-8 Nov 1854, **c**-Davis BATES, exor., **d**-no bond, **e**- **f**- **g**-9 Mar 1858, **h**-$1592.33, **i**-$1455.00, **j**-$137.33, accountant

Mary MILLER, b-11 Nov 1854, **c**-John A. STERRETT, admr., **d**-$2000, **e**-Henry ORT, Jerman JACOB, **f**-29 Nov 1854, **g**-9 Aug 1855, **h**-$117.21, **i**-$1141.75, **j**-$1024.54, estate

Daniel SWITZER, b-28 Nov 1854, **c**-Henry BOOK, **d**-$1500, **e**-Elias PENEPACKER, Geo. MILLER, **f**-26 Dec 1854, **g**- **h**- **i**- **j**-

Thomas R. McKEE, b-12 Dec 1854, **c**-Jno. McKEE, H. J. WALTERS, **d**-$10,000, **e**-Robt. McCLINTIC, Francis McCOY, **f**- **g**-9 Mar 1858, **h**-$$15,961.85, **i**-$11,059.54, **j**-$4902.31 [NOTE: The numbers were severely overwritten; I believe this is accurate; the math works.]

John DYSART, b-22 Dec 1854, **c**-Samuel DRAKE, admr., **d**-$1000, **e**-Jacob GAFF, George LANE, **f**-19 Jan 1855, **g**-8 Dec 1856, **h**-$558.16.75, **i**-$904.58.75, **j**-$346.42, heirs

George GAFF, **b**-22 Dec 1854, **c**-Jacob GAFF, admr., **d**-$800, **e**-Samuel DRAKE, George LANE, **f**-19 Jan 1855, **g**-6 Feb 1856, **h**-$140.28.5, **i**-$691.74, **j**-$551.45.5, accountant

William RIDEN, **b**-26 Dec 1854, **c**-John RIDEN, **d**-$1200, **e**-Aaron RIDEN, James BURNS, **f**-5 Jan 1855, **g**-6 Nov 1856, **h**-$1016.25, **i**-$2245.84, **j**-$1229.59, heirs

Charles HEISLER, **b**-22 Jan 1855, **c**-George W. STEWART, **d**-$2000, **e**-Geo. W. WILEY, Joseph ALEXANDER, Esq., **f**-12 Apr 1855, **g**- **h**- **i**- **j**-

Page 191, Frame 208

James ELLIOTT, **b**-29 Jan 1855, **c**-Christian HOOVER, Esq., **d**-$100, **e**-David WASSON, Geo. W. WILEY, **f**-21 Feb 1855, **g**-9 Mar 1858, **h**-$574.83, **i**-$316.04, **j**-$258.83, heirs

John ERWIN, **b**-8 Feb 1855, **c**-Wm. ERWIN, Geo. W. COULTER, **d**-$300, **e**-Napoleon B. BRATTON, Wm. J. JACOBS, **f**-7 Mar 1855, **g**- **h**- **i**- **j**-

Robert McCORMICK, **b**-24 Feb 1855, **c**-Thomas McCORMICK, **d**-$800, **e**-Moses A. SAMPLE, Amor W. WAKEFIELD, **f**-24 Mar 1855, **g**-29 Aug 1861, **h**- **i**-$350.03, **j**-

Harriet JACKSON, **b**-2 Mar 1855, **c**-Thos. STEWART, **d**-$[5]00, **e**-Adam SIGLER, John STERRETT, **f**- **g**- **h**- **i**- **j**-

Jared IRVIN, **b**-3 Mar 1855, **c**-Adam GREER, **d**-$1500, **e**-Thos. VANVALZAHL, **f**-2 Jun 1855, **g**- **h**- **i**- **j**-

Robert SIMS, **b**-27 Mar 1855, **c**-George W. THOMAS, Esq., **d**-$1000, **e**-Moses MONTGOMERY, George MILLER, **f**-24 Apr 1855, **g**- **h**- **i**- **j**-

Henry SNOOK, **b**-31 Mar 1855, **c**-William SNOOK, admr., **d**-$800, **e**-Samuel BROWER, Zebulon PHILLIPS, **f**-27 Apr 1855, **g**- **h**- **i**- **j**-

Mary Ann HINDS, **b**-9 Apr 1855, **c**-Thomas HAMILTON, admr. cum Testamento annexo, **d**-$1000, **e**-Stephen A. HINDS, Jacob HOOVER, **f**-28 Apr 1855, **g**-10 Aug 1857, **h**-$1001. **i**-$1368.20, **j**-$366.49, estate

George SWOYER, **b**-18 May 1855, **c**-Genl. John ROSS, Daniel YODER, exors., **d**- **e**- **f**-25 May 1855, **g**- **h**- **i**- **j**-

William McFARLAND, **b**-31 May 1855, **c**-Robert MEANS, Andrew McFARLAND, exors., **d**-no bond, **e**- **f**-25 Jun 1855, **g**- **h**- **i**- **j**-

Isaac CORRELL, **b**-8 Jun 1855, **c**-Wm. J. McCOY, admin. D. B. N, ,**d**-$500, **e**-N. B. BRATTON, T. F. McCOY, **f**- **g**- **h**- **i**- **j**-

Ludwick YEATES, **b**-11 Jun 1855, **c**-John WILLIAMS, exor., **d**-no bond, **e**- **f**-1 Oct 1855, **g**- **h**- **i**- **j**-

William MANN, b-15 Jun 1855, **c**-Thos. HUTCHISON, John HOYT, admrs., **d**-$50,000, **e**-Harvey MANN, Francis McCOY, **f**-27 Jun 1855, **g- h- i- j-**

Page 192, Frame 209
Isabella JOHNSTON, b-21 Jun 1855, **c**-Samuel DRAKE, exor., **d**-no bond, **e- f**-28 Jul 1855, **g**-10 Mar 1857, **h**-$178.33, **i**-$215.80.5, **j**-$27.47.5, estate
James WAREAM, b-30 Jun 1855, **c**-Joseph WAREAM, **d**-$1000, **e**-James BURNS, F. G. FRANCISCUS, **f**-30 Jul 1855, **g**-12 Mar 1857, **h**-$2019.73, **i**-$2102.30, **j**-$82.57, in hands of accountant
John COMFERT, b-7 Jul 1855, **c**-Samuel COMFERT, **d**-$1000, **e**-Henry COMFERT, Saml. S. WOODS, **f**-6 Aug 1855, **g- h- i- j-**
Margaret ELLIOTT, b-18 Jul 1855, **c**-Henry J. WALTERS, Esq., **d**-$500, **e**-James BURNS, Jas. A. CUNNINGHAM, **f- g- h- i- j-**
Ezekiel JACKSON, b-21 Jul 1855, **c**-Thomas STUART, **d**-$500, **e**-Adam V. SIGLER, John STERRETT, **f- g**-6 Nov 1856, **h**-$43.27, **i**-$899.25, **j**-$855.98, heirs
John McAULEY, b-21 Jul 1855, **c**-Henry McAULEY, admr Cum Testo Annexo., **d**-$7000, **e**-Henry BOOK, John STONEROAD, **f**-18 Aug 1855, **g**-5 Mar 1858, **h**-$1960.87 [no further designation], **i- j-**
Andrew BRATTON, b-6 Aug 1855, **c**-Genl. John ROSS, **d**-$6000, **e**-N. B. BRATTON, Daniel M. DULL, **f**-4 Sep 1855, **g- h- i- j-**
Nancy POSTLETHWAIT, b-7 Sep 1855 **c**-Joseph POSTLETHWAIT, Samuel DRAKE, exors., **d**-no bond, **e- f- g- h- i- j-**
Christian HOOVER, Sr., b-1 Sep 1855, **c**-Jacob HOOVER, Robt. MATHEWS, exors., **d**-no bond, **e- f**-15 Sep 1855, **g- h- i- j-**
John YODER, b-13 Oct 1855, **c**-Yost KING, one of exors., **d**-no bond, **e- f- g**-28 Feb 1857, **h**-$60.67, **i**-$697.78, **j**-$637.11, in hands of accountant
John GRAHAM, b-27 Oct 1855, **c**-William R. GRAHAM, exor., **d**-no bond, **e- f- g- h- i- j-**
Christiana FERGUSON, b-8 Nov 1855, **c**-William WILSON, admr., **d**-$1000, **e**-William HENRY, William ERWIN, Esq., **f**-18 Dec 1855, **g- h- i- j-**
Abner REED, b-12 Nov 1855, **c**-Andrew REED, Esq., admr., **d**-$5000, **e**-William HENRY, John REED, **f**-8 Dec 1855, **g- h- i- j-**

Page 193, Frame 210

David MARSHALL, b-20 Nov 1855, **c-**Mary MARSHALL, admx., D.B.N., Cum Testamento Annex., **d-**$5000, **e-**Fred. R. SCHWARTZ, Jos. PARKER, **f- g-**4 Apr 1868, **h-**$756.34, **i-**$2205.00, **j-**$1448.66, estate (see Auditor's Report)

Robert MILLIKEN, b-14 Dec 1855, **c-**David F. MILLIKEN, Samuel MILLIKEN, exors., **d-**no bond, **e- f-**24 Jan 1856, **g- h- i- j-**

William WATERS, b-19 Dec 1855, **c-**Mary E. WATERS, **d-**$10,000, **e-**Joseph ALEXANDER, George BLYMYER, **f-**11 Jan 1856, **g- h- i- j-**

Andrew SAMPLE, b-31 Dec 1855, **c-**William CUMMINS, admr., **d-**$9000, **e-**David W. WOODS, Dr. Saml. MACLAY, **f- g- h- i- j-**

Thomas STONEROAD, b-21 Jan 1856, **c-**Margaret STONEROAD, admx, Adam V. SIGLER, admr., **d-**$3500, **e-**Thos. REED, Henry BOOK, **f-**16 Feb 1856, **g-**7 Oct 1857, **h-**$2069.52, **i-**$5011.25, **j-**$2941.73, estate

William SHAW, b-28 Jan 1856, **c-**John W. SHAW, Arthur B. LONG, exors., **d-**no bond, **e- f-**21 Feb 1856, **g- h- i- j-**

Andrew SOMMERS, b-28 Feb 1856, **c-**Thomas STROUP, admr., **d-**$1600, **e-**R. M. KINSLOE, David W. WOODS, **f-**27 Mar 1856, **g-**3 Aug 1857, **h-**$435.28.25, **i-**$1856.25, **j-**$1420.96.75, estate

Samuel KYLE, b-1 Mar 1856, **c-**James KYLE, Moses T. MITCHELL, M.D., exors., **d-**no bond, **e-**" " **f-**29 Mar 1856, **g-**6 Mar 1866, **h-**$3003.45, **i-**$2986.47, **j-**$16.58, accountant

Robert A. GIBBONEY, b-24 Mar 1856, **c-**Joseph HAFFLY, Esq., admr cum t. annexo, **d-**$6000, **e-**Alfred MARKS, Alexr. GIBBONEY, **f-**31 Mar 1856, **g-**20 Feb 1857, **h-**$1260.73, **i-**$2833.43, **j-**$1572.70, in hands of accountant

Robert MELOY, b-24 Mar 1856, **c-**Christian HOOVER, Esq., **d-**$100, **e-**Thomas MAYES, D. W. WOODS, **f- g-**15 Jan 1857, **h-**$215.37.5, **i-**$220.00, **j-**$4.62.5, in hands of accountant

James R. KIMBERLY, b-1 Apr 1856, **c-**Wm. WILSON, Wm. ROSS, **d-**$600, **e-**David JINKINS, Richeson BRATTON, **f-**19 May 1856, **g- h- i- j-**

Magdalena MERST, b-2 Apr 1856, **c-**Daniel YODER, admr., **d-**$2000, **e-**Christian MERST, Lewis HESSER. **f-**24 Apr 1856, **g-**8 Dec 1856, **h-**$271.34, **i-**$1035.09, **j-**$763.75, in hands of accountant

Hannah ALLISON, b-4 Apr 1856, **c-**Joseph ALLISON, exor., **d- e- f-**3 May 1856, **g- h- i- j-**

Page 194, Frame 211

Joseph KEISER, **b**-12 Apr 1856, **c**-William HARSHBARGER, exor., **d**-no bond, **e**-" ", **f**-24 Apr 1856, **g**- **h**- **i**- **j**-

Arthur H. CLARKE, **b**-17 May 1856, **c**-Rowan CLARKE, M.D., **d**-$800, **e**-Michael BUOY, David JINKINS, **f**-Filed 13 Jun 1856, **g**- **h**- **i**- **j**-

John SNYDER, Sr., **b**-3 Jun 1856, **c**-John SNYDER, Jr., **d**-$2000, **e**-George HYMYER, Samuel ORT, **f**-28 Jun 1856, **g**-Filed 31 Oct 1857, **h**-$772.13.5, **i**-$2365.40.75, **j**-$1593.27.25, estate

Nancy DOUGHERTY, **b**-14 Jun 1856, **c**-Wm. BAKER, exor., **d**-no bond, **e**- **f**-23 Jun 1856, **g**- **h**- **i**- **j**- [Revoked, See O.C. D. p. 217]

David HARTZLER, **b**-8 Jul 1856, **c**-Joseph HARTZLER, admr., **d**-$5000, **e**-David HOOLEY, Solomon K. BYLER, **f**-2 Aug 1856, **g**-25 Feb 1858, **h**-$2977.33, **i**-$166.94, **j**-$2810.39, estate

George CARNEY, Esq., **b**-16 Aug 1856, **c**-John C. SIGLER, **d**-$4000 **e**-David BLOOM, John CUBBISON, **f**- **g**- **h**- **i**- **j**-

James DAVIS, **b**-20 Aug 1856, **c**-Chas. K. DAVIS, Geo. M. DAVIS, **d**-$2500, **e**-William CUMMINS, Alexander REED, **f**-19 Sep 1856, **g**- **h**- **i**- **j**-

Thomas BROWN, **b**-21 Aug 1856, **c**-Wm. B. JOHNSTON, Dr. Saml. MACLAY, **d**-$5000, **e**-Jno. R. McDOWELL, Jas. M. BROWN, **f**-20 Sep 1856/24 Sep 1856, **g**-7 Nov 1861, of Wm. B. JOHNSTON, **h**- **i**- **j**-$1880.19, accountant

John SHADE, Sr., **b**-6 Sep 1856, **c**-John SHADE, Jr., Wm. SHADE, **d**-$2500, **e**-Cyrus STINE, [Thos.] JOHNSTON, **f**-2 Oct 1856, **g**- **h**- **i**- **j**-

Nancy McCURDY, **b**-25 Sep 1856, **c**-William McKEE, **d**-$800, **e**-Wm. SHIMP, James IRVIN, **f**-Filed 2 Oct 1856, **g**- **h**- **i**- **j**-

James C. NORRIS, **b**-23 Oct 1856, **c**-A. B. NORRIS, **d**-$200, **e**-James BURNS, **f**- **g**- **h**- **i**- **j**-

John W. HAYES, **b**-31 Oct 1856, **c**-David BLOOM, **d**-$100, **e**-Peter PRINTZ, Geo. W. ELDER, **f**- **g**-26 Sep 1857, **h**-$365.11, **i**-$365.11, **j**-

William RAMSEY, **b**-1 Nov 1856, **c**-Henry L. CLOSE, **d**-$200, **e**-Oliver P. SMITH, **f**-21 Nov 1856, **g**- **h**- **i**- **j**-

Page 195, Frame 212

Samuel McNITT, **b**-29 Oct 1856, **c**-James M. BROWN, John McDOWELL, exors., **d**-no bond, **e**- **f**-28 Nov 1856, **g**- **h**- **i**- **j**-

Robert STEWART, **b**-12 Nov 1856, **c**-Samuel MITCHELL, **d**-$4000, **e**-John M. MITCHELL, Nathanl. FRANK, **f**- **g**- **h**- **i**- **j**-

William CUMMINS, **b**-1 Nov 1856, **c**-John ROSS, **d**-$100, **e**-John STINE, **f**-28 Nov 1856, **g**-1 Mar 1866, **h**-$399.85, **i**-$487.37, **j**-$87.52, estate

Jacob DOUGHERTY, **b**-28 Nov 1856, **c**-Mrs. Mary DOUGHERTY, **d**-$1000, **e**-A. J. ATKINSON, M.D., James S. GALBRAITH, **f**- 27 Dec 1856, **g**- **h**- **i**- **j**-

Thos. J. POSTLETHWAIT, Sr., **b**-8 Dec 1856, **c**-Saml. D. POSTLETHWAIT, John PURCELL, exors., **d**-no bond, **e**- **f**-6 Jan 1857, **g**- **h**- **i**- **j**-

Mary CLARK, **b**-18 Dec 1856, **c**-Kirk HAINES, exor. **d**-no bond, **e**- **f**- **g**- **h**- **i**- **j**-

John T. STERITT[sic], **b**-22 Dec 1856, **c**-Francis R. STERRETT, **d**- " ", **e**- **f**- **g**- **h**- **i**- **j**-

Wilson HAZELETT, **b**-12 Dec 1856, **c**-Margaret HAZELETT **d**-$8000, **e**-Robert M. GILMORE, Yost KING, **f**-10 Jan 1857, **g**- **h**- **i**- **j**-

John GETTYS, **b**-7 Jan 1857, **c**-Thomas J. WILSON, extr., **d**-no bond, **e**- **f**-6 Feb 1857, **g**- **h**- **i**- **j**-

A. P. JACOB, Esq., **b**-9 Jan 1857, **c**-Mrs. Mary E. JACOB, exrx., **d**-no bond, **e**- **f**- **g**- **h**- **i**- **j**-

Christian KAUFFMAN, **b**-28 Jan 1857, **c**-William HARSHBARGER, extr., **d**-no bond, **e**- **f**- **g**- **h**- **i**- **j**-

John C. LEATTOR, **b**-28 Feb 1857, **c**-Margaret LEATTOR, exrx., **d**-no bond, **e**- **f**-27 Mar 1857, **g**- **h**- **i**- **j**-

Joseph MORROW, **b**-26 Mar 1857, **c**-Jas. CRAWFORD, Saml. MORROW, admrs., **d**-$4000, **e**-Christn. HOOVER, Esq., David WASSON, **f**-11 Mar 1857, **g**- **h**- **i**- **j**-

Page 196, Frame 213

Jacob KENAGY, **b**-1 Apr 1857, **c**-Jacob ZOOK, admr., **d**-$3000, **e**-Peter YODER, Thos. MAYES, **f**-7 Apr 1857, **g**- **h**- **i**- **j**-

Francis BOGGS, **b**-6 Apr 1857, **c**-William CREIGHTON, **d**-[several ditto marks, but I don't know if that means the same amount of bond???], **e**- **f**-2 May 1857, **g**- **h**- **i**- **j**-

Jane LONG, **b**-11 Apr 1857, **c**-James H. ALEXANDER, exor., **d**- **e**- **f**-12 May 1857, **g**-9 Jan 1862, **h**-$1204.48, **i**-$1235.05, **j**-$28.57, estate

Henry ALLEN, **b**-14 Apr 1857, **c**-Rebecca ALLEN, exrx., **d**- **e**- **f**- **g**- **h**- **i**- **j**-

Joseph KINSEL, **b**-25 Apr 1857, **c**-Jacob KINSEL, Michael KINSEL, admrs., **d**-$4000, **e**-Michael RUBLE, John RUBLE, **f**-23 May 1857, **g**-

10 Jan 1861, partial; 2 Mar 1865, final **h**-$6547.93/$3236.68, **i**-$4861.90.5/$890.91, **j**-$1686.02.5/$2345.77, accountants

Robert RANKIN, **b**-4 May 1857, **c**-Genl. John ROSS, exor., **d**-no bond, **e**- **f**- **g**- **h**- **i**- **j**-

Robert McMANIGLE, **b**-21 May 1857, **c**-Wm. A. McMANIGLE, Samuel S. WOODS, Esq., **d**-$4000, **e**-Davis BATES, Wm. BUTLER, **f**-19 Jun 1857, **g**- **h**- **i**- **j**-

Andrew W. MOSS, **b**-1 Jun 1857, **c**-Ephraim BANKS, Esq., **d**-$2000, **e**-N. J. RUDISILL, Geo. W. THOMAS, **f**-29 Jun 1857, **g**- **h**- **i**- **j**-

Peter B. D. GRAY, **b**-15 Jun 1857, **c**-Henry J. WATTERS, Esq., **d**-$5000, **e**-James BURNS, Robt. H. McCLINTICK, **f**- **g**- **h**- **i**- **j**-

Christiana SNYDER, **b**-27 Jun 1857, **c**-Henry SNYDER, **d**-$1500, **e**-Reuben MYERS, George MYERS, **f**-16 Jul 1857, **g**- **h**- **i**- **j**-

Peter LICHTEL, **b**-18 Jul 1857, **c**-David G. LANTZ, **d**-$600, **e**-Lewis WOLFLEY, Harrison MANBECK, **f**-6 Aug 1857, **g**- **h**- **i**- **j**-

John L. WHERRY, **b**-26 Aug 1857, **c**-Mary Ann WHERRY, **d**-$300, **e**-William SAGER, Geo. A. WHERRY, **f**-24 Sep 1857, **g**- **h**- **i**- **j**-

Jacob FOLTZ, **b**-22 Aug 1857, **c**-Abraham FOLTZ, exor., **d**-" ", **e**-" ", **f**-29 Sep 1857, **g**- **h**- **i**- **j**-

Page 197, Frame 214

Andrew GLASS, **b**-16 Sep 1857, **c**-Levi GLASS, admr., **d**-$800, **e**-H. J. WALTERS, Jacob HAMAKER, **f**-7 Oct 1857, **g**- **h**- **i**- **j**-

John KIBE, **b**-19 Sep 1857, **c**-Isaiah COPLIN, admr., **d**-$800, **e**-Joseph ALEXANDER, Esq., John W. SHAW, **f**-filed 19 Oct 1857, **g**- **h**- **i**- **j**-

William McCORMICK, **b**-21 Sep 1857, **c**-John HOYT, Jr., admr., **d**-$2000, **e**-Geo. W. ELDER, Wm. BUTLER, **f**-16 Oct 1857, **g**- **h**- **i**- **j**-

Nancy ESSEX, **b**-19 Oct 1857, **c**-John T. PLOWMAN, **d**-$300, **e**-James YEAMAN, Henry STRUNK, **f**-31 or 21 Oct 1857, **g**- **h**- **i**- **j**-

Melissa STINE, **b**-22 Oct 1857, **c**-Geo. W. STEWART, Esq., **d**-$100, **e**-Saml. COMFERT, H. J. WALTERS, **f**- **g**-9 Mar 1858, **h**-$316.27.5, **i**-$316.03, **j**-$.24.5, accountants

John OATENKIRK, **b**-22 Oct 1857, **c**-Isaac OATENKIRK, exor., **d**-no bond, **e**-" ", **f**-16 Nov 1857, **g**- **h**- **i**- **j**-

George ROTHROCK, **b**-30 Oct 1857, **c**-Henry BRIDGE, exor., **d**-no bond, **e**-" ", **f**-27 Nov 1857, **g**- **h**- **i**- **j**-

Joseph CAMPBELL, **b**-14 Nov 1857, **c**-Jos. CAMPBELL A. W. CAMPBELL, R. D. CAMPBELL, exors., **d**-no bond, **e**- **f**- **g**- **h**- **i**- **j**-

James COULTER, b-22 Nov 1857, c-Samuel DRAKE, admr., d-$1000, e-Jas. A. CUNNINGHAM, Robert H. McCLINTIC, f-16 Dec 1857, g-9 Jan 1862, h-$480.96, i-$1049.00, j-$568.06, estate

Thomas KERR, b-28 Nov 1857, c-David WASSON, admr., d-$100, e-Jacob SMITH, Zacharia OMER, f- g- h- i- j-

Christian HOOLEY, b-30 Nov 1857, c-David HOOLEY, exor., d-no bond, e- f-10 Dec 1857, g- h- i- j-

John W. HART, b-16 Dec 1857, c-Joseph HART, admr., d-$1000, e-Elijah MORRISON, James NICHOLS, f-6 Jan 1858, g- h- i- j-

James STACKPOLE, b-28 Dec 1857, c-James B. STACKPOLE, admr., d-$50, e-John CUBBISON, George FRYSINGER, f- g- h- i- j-

Daniel M. YEAGER, b-29 Dec 1857, c-Elias HUFFNAGLE, admr., d-$800, e-John DAVIS, Frank MOYER, f-20 Jan 1858, g- h- i- j-

Jacob GARVER, b-29 Dec 1857, c-Benjamin GARVER, Henry GARVER, Elisha BRATTON, admrs., d-$1600, e-G. H. GALBRAITH, George BLYMYER, f-26 Jan 1858, g-3 Oct 1865, h-$1225.19, i-$1984.22, j-$759.03 in hands of E. BRATTON, due estate

Page 198, Frame 215
George W. BREHMAN, b-5 Jan 1858, c-Mary T. BREHMAN, John ROSS, admrs., d-$1500, e-John WALTERS, Jacob CORRELL, f-14 Jan 1858, g- h- i- j-

John W. PRICE, b-9 Jan 1858, c-Jane M. PRICE, admx., d-$3200, e-John ROSS, James BURNS, f-29 Jan 1858, g- h- i- j-

Magdalina EBERHART, b-14 Jan 1858, c-Fredr. EBERHART, exor., d-no bond, e- f-8 Feb 1858, g- h- i- j-

Benjamin McCOY, b-29 Jan 1858, c-Thompson G. BELL, exor., d-no bond, e- f-3 Feb 1858, g- h- i- j-

Jacob BYLER, b-16 Feb 1858, c-John KANAGY, admr., d-$3000, e-Isaac YODER, John G. KAUFFMAN, f-2 Mar 1858, g- h- i- j-

Jane McCORMICK, b-26 Feb 1858, c-Thomas STUART, admn., d-$1200, e-Theo. FRANKS, J. T. McCORMICK, f-17 May 1858, g- h- i- j-

Bruce McNILE, b-26 Feb 1858, c-J. P. TAYLOR, admr., d-$1200, e-Joseph HAWN, f- g- h- i- j-

James FLEMING, b-2 Mar 1858, c-Thomas J. WILSON, exor., d-no bond, e- f-31 Mar 1858, g- h- i- j-

Jacob HAZLETT, b-4 Mar 1858, c-W. W. GILMORE, Esq., d-$5000, e-R. M. GILMORE, Ephraim HAZLETT, f-8 Apr 1858, g- h- i- j-

John BYLER, b-4 Mar 1858, c-Shem ZOOK, d-$1000, e-James PARKER, Z. MUTTHERSBAUGH, f-18 Mar 1858, g-7 Nov 1861, h- i-$6407.68, j-$6202.34, estate

Molly ROTHROCK, b-6 Apr 1858, c-Abraham ROTHROCK, exor, d-no bond, e- f-Filed 5 May 1858, g- h- i- j-

Joshua WILEY, b-10 Apr 1858, c-Alice WILEY, admrx., d-$150, e-I. T. CORDELL, Jos. ALEXANDER, f- g- h- i- j-

John SMITH (or SCHMIDT), b-12 Apr 1858, c-George SMITH, admr., d-$200, e-James BURNS, Charles RITZ, f- g- h- i- j-

James A. CUNNINGHAM, b-29 Apr 1858, c-Joseph M. STEVENS, John M. CUNNINGHAM, admrs., d-$8000, e-M. BUOY, R. H. McCLINTIC, f-14 May 1858, g- h- i- j-

Page 199, Frame 216

David KOPLIN, b-30 Apr 1858, c-John T. COLDWELL, exor., d-no bond, e- f-20 May 1858, g- h- i- j-

Francis McCOY, b-4 May 1858, c-R. F. ELLIS, C. S. McCOY, Mary McCOY, exors, d-no bond, e- f-4 Jun 1858, g- h- i- j-

Deterick HOBAUGH, b-5 Jun 1858, c-Conrad HOBAUGH, Andrew [McKEE], d-no bond, e- f-27 Oct 1858, g-3 Mar 1866, h-$2367.00, i-$2367.00 j- - - -

John ZOOK, b-14 Jun 1858, c-Shem ZOOK, exor., d-no bond, e- f-8 Jul 1858, g- h- i- j-

John LEATTOR, b-23 Jun 1838, c-[Lauren] S. LEATTOR, admr., d-$300, e- f- g- h- i- j-

Daniel FICHTHORN, b-30 Jun 1858, c-John C. SIGLER, admr., d-$6000, e- f-16 Jul 1858, g- h- i- j-

Glass D. HARPER, b-3 Aug 1858, c-John SWARTZELL, exor., d-no bond, e- f-5 Aug 1858, g- h- i- j-

John STINE, Jr., b-3 Aug 1858, c-Cyrus STINE, Samuel STINE, admrs., d-$20,000, e-John ROSS, James BURNS, f-1 Sep 1858, g-10 Jan 1861/ 9 Jan 1862, h-$9620.79/$6874.25, i-$9331.88/$8379.00 j-$288.91, accountant

James McKINSTRY, b-3 Aug 1858, c-David McKINSTRY, Joseph McKINSTRY, exors., d-no bond, e-17 Aug 1858, f- g- h- i- j-

Sarah HAFFLEY, b-14 Sep 1858, c-Joseph HAFFLEY, exor., d-no bond, e- f-filed 14 Oct 1858, g- h- i- j-

John BOWERSOX, Jr., **b**-20 Sep 1858, **c**-John BOWERSOX, Sr., Elizabeth BOWERSOX, admrs., **d**-$1200, **e**-John GOSS, Saml. BARR, **f**-Filed 6 Mar 1862, **g**- **h**- **i**- **j**-

James T. AITKEN, **b**-13 Oct 1858, **c**-George W. CRISSMAN, Jr., **d**-$1600, **e**-Jac. MUTTHERSBAUGH, John AITKEN, **f**-Filed 19 Nov 1858, **g**- **h**- **i**- **j**-

William MARKS, **b**-11 Nov 1858, **c**-Wm. B. JOHNSTON, Exor., **d**-no bond, **e**- **f**- **g**-7 Nov 1861, **h**-$1629.82, **i**-$1468.93, **j**-

William STEWART, **b**-5 Nov 1858, **c**-Wm. S. WILSON, admr., **d**-$2000, **e**-John McDOWELL, [James] M. BROWN, **f**- **g**- **h**- **i**- **j**-

Page 200, Frame 217

Levi SULTZBAUGH, **b**-6 Nov 1858, **c**-Hetti SULTZBAUGH, Benjamin JACOB, admrs., **d**-$4000, **e**-Frank MOYER, George BLYMYER, **f**-22 Nov 1858, **g**- **h**- **i**- **j**-

David M. BAKER (revoked), **b**-6 Nov 1858, **c**-Benjamin F. BAKER, admr., **d**-$900, **e**-Ephraim BAKER, David A. BAKER, **f**- **g**- **h**- **i**- **j**-

Isaac SMITH, **b**-8 Nov 1858, **c**-Daniel BESHOAR, **d**-$300, **e**-James BURNS, H. J. WALTERS, **f**-27 Nov 1858, **g**- **h**- **i**- **j**-

David M. BAKER, **b**-23 Nov 1858, **c**-George W. ELDER, Esq., admr., **d**-$900, **e**-Wm. BUTLER, Joseph M. COGLEY, **f**- **g**- **h**- **i**- **j**-

Alexander TAYLOR, **b**-6 Dec 1858, **c**-Samuel DRAKE, exor., **d**-no bond, **e**- **f**-24 Dec 1858, [addia?] filed 12 Oct 1860, **g**-29 Aug 1861, **h**-$364.60, **i**-$465.28, **j**-$100.68, estate

Nancy DOUGHERTY, **b**-16 Dec 1858, **c**-T. F. McCOY, Esq., admr. D. B. N. C. T. A., **d**-$300, **e**-Wm. MACKLIN, H. J. WALTERS, **f**-15 Jan 1859, **g**- **h**- **i**- **j**-

Edward BOWLES, **b**-9 Jan 1859, **c**-Christian HOOVER, Esq., **d**-$100, **e**-Daniel ALBRIGHT, John KAYS, **f**- **g**- **h**- **i**- **j**-

Lewis WOLFLEY, **b**-24 Jan 1859, **c**-Catharine WOLFLEY, **d**-$300, **e**-Peter LICHTEL, Harrison MANBECK, **f**-24 Feb 1859, **g**- **h**- **i**- **j**-

John STROUP, **b**-27 Jan 1859, **c**-Albert G. GIBBONEY, William F. STROUP, John STROUP, admrs., **d**-$5000, **e**-Thomas MAYES, Saml. B. WELLS, **f**-Filed 11 Feb 1859, **g**- **h**- **i**- **j**-

Jerman JACOB, **b**-29 Jan 1859, **c**-Elizabeth J. JACOB, admrx., **d**-$1500, **e**-Saml. S. WOODS, A. C. WILSON, **f**-28 Feb 1859, **g**- **h**- **i**- **j**-

Andrew CASTER, **b**-29 Jan 1859, **c**-Isaac STINE, admr. C. T. A., **d**-$200, **e**-Wm. ERWIN, John KIEFOBER, **f**-23 Feb 1859, **g**- **h**- **i**- **j**-

James **DEVINNEY**, b-5 Mar 1859, c-Jacob MUTTHERSBAUGH, d-$3000, e-Daniel BESHOAR, Shem ZOOK, f- g- h- i- j-

Catherine LUSK, b-22 Mar 1859, c-Christian HOOVER, admr., d-$100, e-Wm. A. MOORE, S. M. AULTZ, f- g- h- i- j-

Stephen DIFFENDERFER, b-24 Mar 1859, c-Nicholas HARTZLER, d-$800, e-Yost KING, J. M. LASHELL, f-25 Apr 1859, g- h- i- j-

<u>Page 201, Frame 218</u> [repeated on Frame 219]

David W. HULINGS, b-26 Apr 1859, c-Thomas M. HULINGS, admr., d-$3000, e-Maria H. HULINGS, Elizh. W. HULINGS, Lloyd W. WILLIAMS, f- g- h- i- j-

Thomas WILLS, b-2 May 1859, c-Robert E. WILLS, Samuel WILLS, exors., d-no bond, e- f-17 May 1859, g- h- i- j-

Christian KING, b-6 May 1859, c-Joseph HARTZLER, admr., d-$5000, e-Joel ZOOK, Jr., Solomon ZOOK, f-25 May 1859, g- h- i- j-

Daniel REEL, b-6 May 1859, c-Joel ZOOK, Jr., d-$1000, e-Joseph HARTZLER, Soloman ZOOK, f-25 May 1859, g-4 Apr 1861, h-$284.73, i-$287.41, j-$2.68, estate

Isabella REYNOLDS, b-17 May 1859, c-James M. BROWN, exor., d-no bond, e- f- g- h- i- j-

David BYLER, b-17 May 1859, c-Jacob HARTZLER, admr., d-$3000, e-John HARTZLER, Enoch ZOOK, f-3 Jun 1859, g- h- i- j-

William WALLS, b-23 May 1859, c-David STEFFEY, admr. d-$800, e-Daniel DECKER, John WALLS, f-14 Jun 1859, g- h- i- j-

Jacob [SHANELOPE], b-2 Aug 1859, c-C. HOOVER, admr., d-$100, e-James BURNS, John ROSS, f- g- h- i- j-

Elizabeth E. GRAHAM, b-15 Aug 1859, c-David S. GRAHAM, d-$200, e-George GUTHRIE, Ira THOMPSON, f-9 Sep 1859, g- h- i- j-

John GLICK, Sr., b-24 Aug 1859, c-John PEACHEY, Yost KING, exors., d-no bond, e- f-[24] Sep 1859, g-7 Nov 1861, h-$6154.95, i-$7275.42, j-$1120.47, estate

John AURAND, b-15 Oct 1859, c-Isaac AURAND, exor., d-no bond, e- f-22 Oct 1859, g- h- i- j-

James IRWIN, b-25 Oct 1859, c-Henry J. WALTERS, admr., d-$600, e-G. W. ELDER, T. M. UTLEY, f-14 Nov 1859, g- h- i- j-

John SWIGART, b-25 Oct 1859, c-Levi SWIGART, Elisha BRATTON, admrs., d-$1000, e-S. M. AULTZ, Jos. CLINGER, f-23 Nov 1859, g- h- i- j-

Ann KENNEGY, b-31 Oct 1859, c-John KENNEGY, d-$[500], e-Shem YODER, Seiver YODER, f- g- h- i- j-

Mary Ann STROUP, b-8 Nov 1859, c-Samuel WATT, d-$800, e-John STROUP, Wm. F. STROUP, f-6 Dec 1859, g- h- i- j-

Page 202, Frame 220

Zebulon PHILIPS, b-10 Nov 1859, c-John SWARTZELL, exor., d-no bond, e- f-30 Nov 1859, g-16 Feb 1866, h-$4697.64, i-$4791.39, j-$93.75, estate

Yost KING, b-10 Dec 1859, c-Jacob S. KING, David J. ZOOK, admrs., d-$5000, e-David HERTZLER, Jonas ZOOK, f-3 Jan 1860, g-29 Aug 1861, h- i-$7717.88, j-$2606.84, estate

Michael SHOUGHENCY, b-15 Dec 1859, c-John HOYT, Jr., admr., d-$1400, e-William MANN, H. J. WALTERS, f-17 Jan 1860, g- h- i- j-

Andrew MAYES, b-27 Dec 1859, c-Andrew MAYES, Wm. MAYES, admrs., d-$2000, e-G. W. ELDER, Wm. BUTLER, f- g- h- i- j-

Mary SIGLER, b-27 Dec 1859, c-George SIGLER, admr., d-$500, e-Wm. BUTLER, John C. SIGLER, f-2 Jan 1860, g-4 Apr 1861, h-$28.94, i-$404.70, j-$375.76, heirs and legatees

John HAZLETT, b-2 Jan 1860, c-Nicholas HARTZLER, admr., d-no bond, e- f-20 Jan 1860 g-4 Apr 1861, h-$519.55, i-$1948.62, j-$1429.07, estate

Thomas J. WILSON, b-27 Jan 1860, c-Joseph C. WILSON, John F. WILSON, admrs., d-$6000, e-George WILSON, Thomas MAYES, f-17 Feb 1860, g-7 Nov 1861/21 Mar 1865, h-$3241.41/$1024.18, i-$3285.16/$3385.34, j-$44.68/$1361.16, heirs, less $654.00 paid them, $707.16, heirs

Margret FIELDS, b-6 Feb 1860, c-William FIELDS, J. L. JEFFRIES, exors., d-no bond, e- f- g- h- i- j-

Mary BAREFOOT, b-8 Feb 1860, c-Peter BAREFOOT, admr., d-$800, e-Samuel MACLAY, John BAREFOOT, f-3 Mar 1860, g-7 Nov 1861, h-$357.66, i-$814.43, j-

James FLEMING, b-17 Feb 1860, c-Joseph M. FLEMING, A.D.N.C.T.A., d-$5000, e-John FLEMING, S. McK. FLEMING, f-14 Mar 1860, g- h- i- j-

Lazarus STEELY, Sr., b-24 Feb 1860, c-Catharine A. STEELY, d-$500, e-John LEVY, David WASSON, f-24 Mar 1860, g- h- i- j-

Moses T. **MITCHELL**, b-12 Mar 1860, c-John H. MITCHELL, Maria B. MITCHELL, admrs., d-$4000, e-E. E. LOCKE, Saml. S. WOODS, f-12 Apr 1860, g- h- i- j-

David **MILLIKEN**, b-30 Mar 1860, c-David F. MILLIKEN, d-$100, e-Saml. MILLIKEN, James THOMPSON, f- g- h- i- j-

James **POE**, b-9 Apr 1860, c-John McDOWELL, Jr., William STROUP, exors., d-no bond, e- f-30 Apr 1860, g- h- i- j-

John **BIGELOW**, b-14 Apr 1860, c-Catharine BIGELOW, admx., d-$600, e-James M. BROWN, Cyrus ALEXANDER, f-14 May 1860, g- h- i- j-

Page 203, Frame 221

John **WILLIAMS**, b-12 May 1860, c-Willis C. WILLIAMS, Hartman PHILIPS, admrs., d-$100, e-Philip MARTZ, John W. WILLIAMS, f-26 May 1860, g- h- i- j-

Samuel **MATTER**, b-6 Jun 1860, c-G. W. ELDER, Esq., admr. de bonis non, d-$600, e-Wm. WILLIS, Wm. BUTLER, f- g- h- i- j-

John C. **DANILS [probably DANIELS]**, b-9 Jun 1860, c-William WILSON, exor., d-no bond, e- f- g-4 Apr 1868, h-$1164.25, i-$1534.83.5, j-$374.58.5, estate

David **SWITZER**, b-13 Jun 1860, c-James THOMPSON, Crawford SWITZER, admrs., d-$200, e-Saml. MILLIKEN, W. A. McMANIGAL, f- g- h- i- j-

Jacob **BOBB**, b-13 Jun 1860, c-Isaac WAGNER, exor., d-no bond, e- f-1 Aug 1860, g- h- i- j-

J. Campbell **WILSON**, b-23 Jun 1860, c-Henry J. WALTERS, admr., d-$100, e-W. SHIMP, I. T. CORDELL, f- g- h- i- j-

Henry B. **TAYLOR**, b-25 Jun 1860, c-William CUMMINS, admr., d-$3000, e-J. MUTTHERSBAUGH, Matthew TAYLOR, f-28 Jul 1860, g- h- i- j-

[Forgritta] **NOTTER**, b-26 Jul 1860, c-Peter CLUM, exor., d-no bond, e- f-13 Jul 1861, g-7 Nov 1861, h-$130.45, i-$353.65, j-$223.20, estate

William **ANDERSON**, b-28 Jul 1860, c-Samuel McCOY, John ADAIR, exors., d-no bond, e- f-25 Aug 1860, g- h- i- j-

Benjamin **GARVER**, b-8 Aug 1860, c-Elizabeth GARVER, admx., David MILLIKEN, admr., d-$5000, e-J. MUTTHERSBAUGH, George BLYMYER, f-28 Aug 1860, g-[w-7-1871 & 4-16-62], h- i- j-

Cain **KENNEDY**, b-17 Aug 1860, c-John HAMILTON, admr., d-$100, e-A. T. HAMILTON, M. BUOY, f- g- h- i- j-

James C. DELLETT, **b**-29 Aug 1860, **c**-John TAYLOR, exor., **d**-no bond, **e**- **f**-29 Dec 1860, **g**- **h**- **i**- **j**-

Daniel BROUGHT, **b**-21 Sep 1860, **c**-Sarah BROUGHT, Daniel BROUGHT, admrs., **d**-$3000, **e**-George FETZER, C. C. STANBARGER, **f**-1 or 5 Nov 1860, **g**- **h**- **i**- **j**-

Robert HOPE, **b**-22 Sep 1860, **c**-Samuel G. McCOY, admr., **d**-$1500, **e**-G. B. PENEPACKER, Wm. BUTLER, **f**-22 Oct 1860, **g**- **h**- **i**- **j**-

John R. McDOWELL, **b**-24 Sep 1860, **c**-John McDOWELL, Perry W. McDOWELL, admrs., **d**-$2000, **e**-Davis BATES, R. A. MEANS, **f**-19 Oct 1860, **g**-1 Mar 1865, **h**-$8752.76, **i**-$11,307.41, **j**-$2554.65, estate

Page 204, Frame 222

Esther ZOOK, **b**-1 Oct 1860, **c**-Joel ZOOK, exor., **d**-no bond, **e**- **f**-8 Nov 1860, **g**- **h**- **i**- **j**-

Esther THOMAS. **b**-8 Oct 1860, **c**-John FLEMING, exor., **d**-no bond, **e**- **f**-7 Nov 1860, **g**- **h**- **i**- **j**-

Susan SIGLER, **b**-10 Oct 1860, **c**-Henry P. SIGLER, admr., **d**-$400, **e**-George H. SIGLER, Joseph SIGLER, **f**-23 Oct 1860, **g**- **h**- **i**- **j**-

Abraham BLYMYER, **b**-19 Oct 1860, **c**-John C. SIGLER, admr., **d**-$20,000, **e**-John CUBBISON, Saml. S. WOODS, **f**-6 Nov 1860, **g**- **h**- **i**- **j**-

Dickson S. BURNS, **b**-20 Oct 1860, **c**-Robt. H. McCLINTIC, admr., **d**-$200, **e**-James BURNS, Wm. SHIMP, **f**-6 Nov 1860, **g**- **h**- **i**- **j**-

Elias HUMMEL, **b**-23 Oct 1860, **c**-John W. KEARNS, admr., **d**-$1500, **e**-Moses SAMPLE, Joseph SIGLER, **f**-7 Nov 1860, **g**-9 Jan 1862, **h**-$1113.65, **i**-$1384.94, **j**-$271.34, estate

George MITCHELL, **b**-24 Oct 1860, **c**-Mary Ann MITCHELL, admrx. cum testamento annexor, **d**-$200, **e**-John ROSS, Jos. ALEXANDER, **f**-22 Nov 1860, **g**-30 Sep 1864/1 Apr 1868, **h**-$1078.87/$5839.68, **i**-$1067.02/$7536.40, **j**-$11.85, administrator/$1696.72, bal. paid heirs

Mathew T. REYNOLDS, **b**-12 Nov 1860, **c**-David R. REYNOLDS, exor., **d**-no bond, **e**- **f**- **g**- **h**- **i**- **j**-

Jesse RICE, **b**-16 Novo 1860, **c**-Charles CAUGHLING, Sr., **d**-$600, **e**-Geo. MACKLIN, W. C. VINES, **f**- **g**- **h**- **i**- **j**-

Mary SNYDER. **b**-14 Dec 1860, **c**-Lucien T. SNYDER, admr. cum testamento annexo, **d**-$200, **e**-C. HOOVER, George WILEY, **f**-17 Dec 1860, **g**- **h**- **i**- **j**-

John STINE, Sr., **b**-17 Dec 1860, **c**-Jacob STINE, Augustus STINE, admrs., **d**-$500, **e**-Moses A. SAMPLE, C. C. STANBARGER, **f**- **g**- **h**- **i**- **j**-

Joseph A. TAYLOR, **b**-31 Dec 1860, **c**-Hannah TAYLOR, admx., **d**-$2000, **e**-Henry J. TAYLOR, Moses A. SAMPLE, **f**-28 Jan 1861, **g**- **h**- **i**- **j**-

George LEOPOLD, **b**-23 Jan 1861, **c**-Lewis H. LEOPOLD, admr., **d**-$1500, **e**-Anna LEOPOLD, Hugh McKEE, **f**-19 Feb 1861, **g**- **h**- **i**- **j**-

Page 205, Frame 223

John AITKEN, **b**-14 Feb 1861, **c**-Hugh AITKIN, John M. AITKIN, exors., **d**- **e**- **f**-12 Mar 1861, **g**- **h**- **i**- **j**-

Joseph KYLE, **b**-22 Feb 1861, **c**-Crawford & James KYLE, exors., **d**- **e**- **f**- **g**- **h**- **i**- **j**-

Nancy BROWN, **b**-23 Feb 1861, **c**-H. H. GIBBONEY, admr., **d**-$5000, **e**-James M. BROWN, W. A. McMANIGEL, **f**-8 Mar 1861, **g**- **h**- **i**- **j**-

Samuel GRAHAM, **b**-25 Feb 1861, **c**-John T. GRAHAM, Walter GRAHAM, admrs., **d**-$1000, **e**-Jacob HOOVER, Saml. S. WOODS, **f**-23 Mar 1861, **g**- **h**- **i**- **j**-

David MUTTHERSBOUGH, **b**-25 Feb 1861, **c**-William CREIGHTON, exor., **d**-no bond, **e**- **f**-25 Mar 1861, **g**- **h**- **i**- **j**-

John BROWN, **b**-4 Mar 1861, **c**-Susan BROWN, admx., **d**-$100, **e**-Jacob SMITH, A. MAYES, **f**- **g**- **h**- **i**- **j**-

Siever YODER, **b**-[12] Mar 1861, **c**-Christian B. YODER, admr., **d**-$700, **e**-Joel ZOOK, Jr., Christian C. ZOOK, **f**-27 Mar 1861, **g**- **h**- **i**- **j**-

Mary FORSYTHE, **b**-12 Mar 1861, **c**-[Marg] FORSYTH, Charlotte FORSYTHE, admrxs Cum Testamento annexo, **d**-$5000, **e**-Matthew FORSYTHE, Francis McCLURE, **f**-10 Apr 1861, **g**- **h**- **i**- **j**-

Mary Jane ROBISON, **b**-15 Mar 1861, **c**-Joseph BROUGHT, exor., **d**-no bond, **e**- **f**- **g**- **h**- **i**- **j**-

Thomas C. ALEXANDER, **b**-20 Mar 1861, **c**-Samuel COMFERT, **d**-$100, **e**-M. BUOY, D. W. WOODS, **f**- **g**- **h**- **i**- **j**-

Alfred McCARTNEY, **b**-3 Apr 1861, **c**-Barbara McCARTNEY, admx., **d**-$700, **e**-J. M. MARTIN, Henry ALBRIGHT, **f**-3 May 1861, **g**- **h**- **i**- **j**-

Ann McCLINTICK[sic], **b**-11 Apr 1861, **c**-George W. FISHER, extr., **d**-no bond, **e**- **f**-17 May 1861, **g**- **h**- **i**- **j**-

Maria McNITT, b-19 Apr 1861, c-William McNITT, J. J. LINGLE, d-$600, e-William WILLIS, Joseph ZEIGLER, f-[18] May 1861, g- h- i- j-

Page 206, Frame 224

William SHADE, b-27 Apr 1861, c-John S. REED, admr., d-$250, e-Samuel McCOY, John J. McCORD, f-9 May 1861, g- h- i- j-

Valentine STONEROAD, b-13 May 1861, c-John Thomas STONEROAD, extr., d-no bond, e- f- g- h- i- j-

John HUMMEL, b-25 May 1861, c-Abraham F. KLINE, admr. D.B.N.C.T.A., d-$3000, e-Rebecca KLINE, David F. KLINE, f- g-11 Jan 1861, h-$1452.23, i-$1452.23, j-$80.98, estate

Peter TOWNSEND, b-1 Jun 1861, c-John PRESTON, extr., d-no bond, e- f-27 Jun 1861, g- h- i- j-

Joseph REED, b-13 Jun 1861, c-Alexander REED, Abner THOMPSON, admrs., d-$1200, e-John HENRY, H. J. WALTERS, f-12 Jul 1861, g- h- i- j-

Isaac THOMPSON, b-21 Jun 1861, c-Simeon K. ZOOK, extr., d-no bond, e- f-25 Jul 1861, g- h- i- j-

Mary DEVINNEY, b-19 Jul 1861, c-Jacob MUTTHERSBOUGH, d-$400, e-Wm. JOHNSTON, John DAVIS, f-17 Aug 1861, g- h- i- j-

James YEAMAN, b-27 Jul 1861, c-John STRUNK, d-$600, e-H. J. WALTERS, John T. PLOWMAN, f-29 Aug 1861, g- h- i- j-

Daniel MILLER, b-31 Jul 1861, c-David MILLER, Simon GRO, d-$5000, e-Daniel YODER, John HARSHBARGER, f-19 Aug 1861, g- h- i- j-

Jacob HAWN, b-14 Aug 1861, c-Peter BAREFOOT, Joseph HAWN, d-$1200, e-George GUTHRIE, John McDOWELL, Jr., f-8 Sep1861, g- h- i- j-

Samuel SMITH, b-24 Aug 1861, c-John SMITH, d-$600, e-John GAFF, Thomas JOHNSTON, f-16 Sep 1861, g- h- i- j-

Catharine STOY, b-10 Sep 1861, c-John HAMILTON, Joseph STOY, d-$400, e-C. HOOVER, A. G. HAMILTON, f-10 Oct 1861, g- h- i- j-

Ann C. HAZLETT, b-11 Sep 1861, c-John D. BARR, d-$2000, e-William CUMMINGS, David YODER, f-10 Oct 1861, g- h- i- j-

Page 207, Frame 225

Jacob MUTTHERSBOUGH, b-3 or 5 Oct 1861, c-Daniel D. MUTTHERSBOUGH, William CREIGHTON, d-$1500, e-Henry BOOK, Jeremiah M. YEAGER, f-1 Nov 1861, g- h- i- j-

John WALTERS, b-14 Oct 1861, **c**-Hugh M. WALTERS, **d**-$400, **e**-Saml. M. AULTS, Wm. BUTLER, **f**- **g**- **h**- **i**- **j**-

Nathaniel WISE, b-21 Oct 1861, **c**-Davis McKean CONTNER **d**-$100, **e**-Robert CAMPBELL, William CUSTER, **f**-20 Nov 1861, **g**- **h**- **i**- **j**-

Eli K. WAGNER, b-5 Nov 1861, **c**-Solomon S. WAGNER, **d**-$1000, **e**-Jacob DIEN, John SNOOK, **f**-3 Dec 1861, **g**-4 Apr 1868, **h**-$1671.45, **i**-$1457.92, **j**-$213.93, accountant

David HARSHBARGER, b-27 Nov 1861, **c**-Daniel HARSHBARGER, **d**-$300, **e**-David McKINSTRY, Henry H. KAUFFMAN, **f**-1 Jan 1862, **g**- **h**- **i**- **j**-

John KENNEDY, b-30 Nov 1861, **c**-Theodosia KENNEDY, **d**-no bond, **e**- **f**- **g**- **h**- **i**- **j**-

Mary CLAYTON, b-16 Dec 1861, **c**-William MITCHELL, **d**-$500, **e**-John R. MITCHELL, William ALBRIGHT, **f**-15 Jan 1862, **g**- **h**- **i**- **j**-

James McCLINTICK, b-31 Dec 1861, **c**-Robert BARR, Catharine McCLINTICK, **d**-$4000, **e**-George BLYMYER, Joseph MILLIKEN, **f**-1 or 21 Jan 1862, **g**- **h**- **i**- **j**-

Isaac ARMSTRONG, b-3 Jan 1862, **c**-David WEILER, **d**-$50, **e**-H. J. WALTERS, H. FRYSINGER, **f**-3 Feb 1862, **g**- **h**- **i**- **j**-

John RAGER, b-1 Jan 1862, **c**-Christian HOOVER, **d**-$3500, **e**-Daniel ALBRIGHT, Michael BUOY, **f**-1 Feb 1862, **g**- **h**- **i**- **j**-

Elizabeth HEISLER, b-7 Jan 1862, **c**-John J. HEISLER, extr., **d**-no bond, **e**- **f**-11 Jan 1862, **g**- **h**- **i**- **j**-

Reuben MYERS, b-11 Jan 1862, **c**-Abraham MYERS, extr., **d**-no bond, **e**- **f**-18 Feb 1862, **g**- **h**- **i**- **j**-

Saml. S. ALEXANDER, b-13 Jan 1862, **c**-Mary S. ALEXANDER, No. 2513 Poplar Street, Phila., **d**-$800 **e**-Geo. H. MOORE, Phila., Saml. M. AULTS, **f**-14 Jan 1862, **g**- **h**- **i**- **j**-

Page 208, Frame 226

Samuel ALEXANDER, b-20 Jan 1862, **c**-James H. ALEXANDER, William A. ALEXANDER, exors., **d**-no bond, **e**- **f**-18 Feb 1862, **g**- **h**- **i**- **j**-

Jacob LINTHURST, b-11 Feb 1862, **c**-Mary Ann LINTHURST, extx., **d**-no bond, **e**- **f**-19 Feb 1862, **g**- **h**- **i**- **j**-

John WELSH, b-18 Feb 1862, **c**-Wilson WELSH, **d**-$100, **e**-James WELSH, Michael BUOY, **f**- **g**- **h**- **i**- **j**-

Catharine BYLER, b-10 Mar 1862, **c**-Christian C. ZOOK, **d**-$400, **e**-David HOOLEY, Jr., Robert DUNN, **f**-29 Mar 1862, **g**- **h**- **i**- **j**-

Benewell MILLER, **b**-11 Mar 1862, **c**-Simon GRO, **d**-$400, **e**-John [HARSBARGER?], Jacob KAUFFMAN, **f**- **g**- **h**- **i**- **j**-

Joseph S. KENNEDY, **b**-15 Mar 1862, **c**-Nathaniel KENNEDY, **d**-$500, **e**-Henry J. WALTERS, William SHIMP, **f**- **g**- **h**- **i**- **j**-

Martha J. McNITT, **b**-19 Mar 1862, **c**-James C. McNITT, **d**-$1000, **e**-Dr. Saml. MACLAY, Catharine ALEXANDER, **f**- **g**- **h**- **i**- **j**-

Robert STILLS, **b**-22 Mar 1862, **c**-Geo. W. ELDER, Esq., **d**-$250, **e**-J. W. BUTLER, Saml. W. EISENBISE, **f**-22 Mar 1862, **g**-See Deed Book NN, pp. 696 & 697 [if not there, try 496 & 497] for release **h**- **i**- **j**-

Sarah KENNAGY, **b**-14 Apr 1862, **c**-Solomon D. BYLER, **d**-$1000, **e**-Simeon YODER, Joel ZOOK, Jr., **f**-2 May 1862, **g**- **h**- **i**- **j**-

Mary DEVINNEY, **b**-25 Apr 1862, **c**-Daniel D. MUTTHERSBOUGH, admin de bonus non, **d**-$400, **e**-William BUTLER, David MUTTHERSBOUGH, **f**- **g**- **h**- **i**- **j**-

George GUTHRIE, **b**-3 May 1862, **c**-Peter BAREFOOT, Holmes MACLAY, admrs., **d**-$3500, **e**-John McDOWELL, Sr., Danl. D. MUTTHERSBOUGH, **f**-7 Jun 1862, **g**- **h**- **i**- **j**-

David KENNAGY, **b**-12 May 1862, **c**-Joel ZOOK, extr., **d**-no bond, **e**- **f**-24 May 1862, **g**- **h**- **i**- **j**-

Page 209, Frame 227

William McCULLOUGH, **b**-22 May 1862, **c**-John STROUP, **d**-$800, **e**-John YODER, David WEILER, **f**- **g**-31 Jul 1866, **h**-$184.28, **i**-$109.93, **j**-$74.25, estate

Lydia KING, **b**-27 May 1862, **c**-Jacob S. KING, **d**-$600, **e**-David J. ZOOK, Joseph KING, **f**-19 Jun 1862, **g**- **h**- **i**- **j**-

Jacob HORST, **b**-29 May 1862, **c**-George B. PENEPACKER, **d**-$500, **e**-Adam BRENEMAN, Samuel J. BRISBEN, **f**- **g**- **h**- **i**- **j**-

Sarah WILSON, **b**-30 May 1862, **c**-Thomas M. UTLEY, **d**-$600, **e**-A. S. WILSON, Daniel EISENBISE, **f**- **g**-29 Jul 1865, **h**-$208.80, **i**-$204.00, **j**-$4.80, administrator

Benjamin SCOTT, **b**-3 Jun 1862, **c**-John BARR, extr., **d**-no bond, **e**- **f**-25 Jun 1862, **g**- **h**- **i**- **j**-

Sarah ZOOK, **b**-20 Jun 1862, **c**-Jacob S. KING, extr., **d**-no bond, **e**- **f**-17 Jul 1862, **g**- **h**- **i**- **j**-

Veronica YODER, **b**-3 Jul 1862, **c**-Gideon YODER, **d**-$1000, **e**-Davis BATES, David ZOOK, **f**-14 Jul 1862, **g**- **h**- **i**- **j**-

Rev. James S. WOODS, D.D., **b**-7 Jul 1862, **c**-David W. WOODS, **d**-$1000, **e**-William H. WOODS, Alexander M. WOODS, **f**- **g**- **h**- **i**- **j**-

Henry STRUNK, b-12 Jul 1862, **c**-Mary STRUNK, John STRUNK, **d**-$1000, **e**-H. J. WALTERS, Moses A. SAMPLE, **f**-7 Aug 1862, **g**- **h**- **i**- **j**-

Sarah LINKE, b-22 Jul 1862, **c**-Moses ENGLE, **d**-$100, **e**-C. C. STEINBERGER, H. J. WALTERS, **f**-25 Jul 1862, **g**- **h**- **i**- **j**-

Theodore WAREAM, b-12 Aug 1862, **c**-Joseph S. WAREAM, **d**-$200, **e**-Michael BUOY, William BUTLER, **f**- **g**- **h**- **i**- **j**-

Wm. A. McKEE, b-16 Aug 1862, **c**-Geo. HANAWALT, **d**-$800, **e**-John ROSS, Saml. BELFORD, **f**-16 Sep 1862, **g**- **h**- **i**- **j**-

Page 210, Frame 228

Jas. H. HASINGPLUG, b-26 Aug 1862, **c**-Will. J. McMANIGAL[sic], **d**-$300, **e**-William J. McMANIGLE, Wm. A. McMANIGLE, Joseph HAWN, **f**-30 Sep 1862, **g**- **h**- **i**- **j**-

Saml. W. TAYLOR, b-29 Aug 1862, **c**-John D. BARR, **d**-$8000, **e**-John D. BARR, Saml. W. TAYLOR, Robt. M. TAYLOR, **f**-25 Sep 1862, **g**- **h**- **i**- **j**-

Samuel BARR, b-17 Sep 1862, **c**-T. G. BELL, **d**-$1000, **e**-T. G. BELL, J. W. McCORD, H. J. WALTERS, **f**-30 Sep 1862, **g**- **h**- **i**- **j**-

John WEILER, b-23 Sep 1862, **c**-George WEILER, **d**-$3000, **e**-George WEILER, Francis MORGAN, Wm. M. GILMORE, **f**-7 Oct 1862, **g**- **h**- **i**- **j**-

George WILSON, b-29 Sep 1862, **c**-J. T. WILSON, J. W. WILSON, extrs., **d**-no bond, **e**- **f**-25 Oct 1862, **g**- **h**- **i**- **j**-

Thomas POSTLETHWAIT, b-29 Sep 1862, **c**-Wm. J. POSTLETHWAIT, extr., **d**-no bond, **e**- **f**-10 Nov 1862, **g**- **h**- **i**- **j**-

Henry COBLENTZ, b-28 Oct 1862, **c**-Jacob KURTZ, Peter YODER, extrs., **d**-no bond, **e**- **f**-21 Nov 1862, **g**- **h**- **i**- **j**-

Henry SNYDER, b-8 Nov 1862, **c**-Henry J. WALTERS, **d**-$200, **e**-C. C. STANBARGER, John A. McKEE, **f**-13 Nov 1862, **g**- **h**- **i**- **j**-

I[s]aac GOSS, b-10 Nov 1862, **c**-Jacob [SAWVER], **d**-$800, **e**-John SAWVER, George BLYMYER, **f**-28 Nov 1862, **g**- **h**- **i**- **j**-

Catharine MYERS, b-13 Nov 1862, **c**-Andrew W. McKEE, **d**-$1800, **e**-A. W. McKEE, R. A. McKEE, John KEEVER, **f**-1 Dec 1862, **g**- **h**- **i**- **j**-

Jacob PEACHEY, b-15 Nov 1862, **c**-Christian PEACHEY, Sr., Moses PEACHEY, **d**-$5000, **e**-D. W. WOODS, Francis McCLURE, **f**-11 Dec 1862, **g**- **h**- **i**- **j**-

George TREISTER[sic], b-25 Nov 1862, **c**-Daniel R. FERSTER[sic], **d**-$2000, **e**-H. J. WALTERS, John RUBLE, **f**-16 Dec 1862, **g**- **h**- **i**- **j**-

Page 211, Frame 229

Benjamin RAGER, **b**-5 Dec 1862, **c**-Michael RAGER, **d**-$400, **e**-Benjamin GILL, Michael BOWERSOX, **f**-24 Dec 1862, **g**- **h**- **i**- **j**-

William ERWIN, **b**-5 Dec 1862, **c**-Elisha BRATTON, Franklin CALDWELL, **d**-$1000, **e**-John T. CALDWELL, John CUPPLES, **f**-5 Jan 1863, **g**- **h**- **i**- **j**-

Adam KAUFFMAN, **b**-13 Dec 1862, **c**-Abraham KAUFFMAN, admn., **d**-$300, **e**-Simon GRO, Jonathan K. MILLER, **f**-6 Jan 1863, **g**- **h**- **i**- **j**-

John McKEE, **b**-6 Jan 1863, **c**-John A. McKEE, Robert A. McKEE, **d**-$10,000, **e**-R. A. MEANS, Jno. B. SELHEIMER, John DAVIS, Wm. R. McKEE, H. J. WALTERS, Hugh McKEE, **f**-6 Feb 1863, **g**-1 Apr 1867, **h**-$17,420.22, **i**-$32,507.69, **j**-$15.087.22, estate; see auditor's report for distribution

Henry TAYLOR, **b**-12 Jan 1863, **c**-Mathew TAYLOR, Henry TAYLOR, exrs., **d**-no bond **e**- **f**-20 Feb 1863, **g**- **h**- **i**- **j**-

William BEATTY, **b**-14 Feb 1863, **c**-John M. BEATTY, James R. BEATTY, exrs., **d**-no bond, **e**- **f**-6 Mar 1863, **g**- **h**- **i**- **j**-

John LEVY, **b**-18 Feb 1863 (Will proven 5 Dec 1862), **c**-Sarah J. LEVY, extx., **d**-no bond, **e**- **f**-20 Feb 1863, **g**- **h**- **i**- **j**-

Lukens ATKINSON, **b**-6 Mar 1863, **c**-John ATKINSON, Cyrus STINE, exors, **d**-no bond, **e**- **f**-3 Apr 1863, **g**- **h**- **i**- **j**-

Isaac T. CORDELL, **b**-6 Mar 1863, **c**-Mary M. CORDELL, admr., **d**-$250, **e**-Jane COFFMAN, Jos. McFADDEN, **f**- **g**- **h**- **i**- **j**-

Joseph C. BROUGHT, **b**-20 Mar 1863, **c**-Jane BROUGHT, **d**-$500, **e**-Wm. WILLIS, [O.?] HOOVER, **f**- **g**- **h**- **i**- **j**-

David ROBINOLD, **b**-21 Mar 1863, **c**-Geo. W. FISHER, **d**-$300, **e**-Michael BOWERSOX, Jacob HOOK, **f**-27 Apr 1863, **g**-5 Oct 1865, **h**-$1474.42, **i**-$1626.71, **j**-$152.29, heirs

John KLEPPER, **b**-10 Apr 1863, **c**-Joel ZOOK, **d**-$400, **e**-Abner THOMPSON, Sh. ZOOK, **f**-9 May 1863, **g**- **h**- **i**- **j**-

Page 212, Frame 230

Col. John McDOWELL, **b**-11 Apr 1863, **c**-D. W. WOODS, James KYLE, admrs., **d**-$20,000, **e**-Mary B. McDOWELL, Wm. RUSSELL, **f**-25 Apr 1863, **g**-5 Mar 1866, **h**-$16,184.61.5, **i**-$50,856.53, **j**-$34,671.93.5, estate, paid to widow & heirs

Joseph STRODE, Sr., **b**-21 Apr 1863, **c**-Rebecca J. STRODE, exr., **d**-no bond, **e**- **f**-22 May 1863, **g**- **h**- **i**- **j**-

Joseph H. SMITH, b-27 Apr 1863, c-William T. SMITH, admr., d-$250, e-Wm. F. STROUP, Jacob HAFFLY, f-18 May 1863, g- h- i- j-

Samuel WEST, b-9 May 1863, c-Christian HOOVER, [admr.], d-$400 e-Jacob HOOVER, Wm. T. BURNS, f-10 Jun 1863, g- h- i- j-

Solomon ZOOK, b-30 May 1863, c-Joseph HARTZLER, exor., d-no bond, e- f-17 Jun 1863, g- h- i- j-

Jacob STINE, b-6 Jun 1863, c-Noah RUDY, admr., d-$400, e-John M. McAULEY, Henry STETLER, f-20 Jun 1863, g- h- i- j-

John SWIGART, b-20 Jun 1863, c-M. F. H. KINSEL, d-$1600 e-Wm. BUTLER, Thomas MAYES, f-13 Jul 1863, g-30 Nov 1865, h-$1303.44, i-$1423.29, j-$119.85, estate

Henry KEMMERLING, b-18 Jul 1863, c-George W. FISHER, d-$200, e-Jacob HOOK, John KEMMERLING, f-25 Aug 1863, g-5 Oct 1865, h-$486.57, i-$691.61, j-$205.04, estate

John McNEAR, b-8 Aug 1863, c-James F. McNEAR, d-$400, e-Jos. S. WAREAM, Jas S. GALBRAITH, f-24 Aug 1863, g- h- i- j-

Samuel HORNING, b-24 Aug 1863, c-Maggie E. HORNING, Daniel M. DULL, exrs., d-no bond, e- f-17 Sep 1863, g- h- i- j-

Mary E. WHARTON, b-25 Aug 1863, c-Joseph G. WHARTON, d-$100, e-Saml. DRAKE, Elijah MORRISON, f- g- h- i- j-

Saml. T. DAVIS, b-12 Sep 1863, c-Thompson G. BELL, d-$500, e-J. H. BELL, J. W. McCORD, f-30 Sep 1863, g- h- i- j-

William SHIMP, Esq., b-15 Sep 1863, c-Henry J. WALTERS, Esq., d-$2000, e-John A. McKEE, R. H. McCLINTIC, f-30 Sep 1863, g- h- i- j-

Page 213, Frame 231

Gilbert WATERS, b-17 Sep 1863, c-Christian HOOVER, d-$400, e-James NICHOLS, Geo. BLYMYER, f-28 Jan 1864, g- h- i- j-

William S. WILSON, b-30 Sep 1863, c-J. W. WILSON, d-$2000, e-John WILSON, Sr., John ROSS, f- 21 Oct 1863, g- h- i- j-

William FLEMING, b-10 Oct 1863, c-William M. FLEMING, d-$1200, e-R. M. KINSLOE, Davis BATES, f-21 Nov 1863, g-1 Mar 1865, h-$1063.73, i-$1333.85, j-$270.12, estate

Jacob BEAR, b-20 Oct 1863, c-Christian HOOVER, Esq., d-$100, e-Albert H. BEAR, Wm. BUTLER, f- g- h- i- j-

John JOHNSTON, b-22 Oct 1863, c-John POWELL, d-$3000, e-D. W. WOODS, N. C. WILSON, f-19 Dec 1863, g-11 Jun 1866, h-$1299.30, i-$2357.70, j-$1058.40, estate

Sarah W. WILSON, **b**-27 Oct 1863, **c**-A. W. CAMPBELL, exor., **d**-no bond, **e**- **f**-25 Nov 1863, **g**- **h**- **i**- **j**-

Thomas J. DRAKE, **b**-31 Oct 1863, **c**-Catharine E. DRAKE, James WHARTON, exors., **d**-no bond, **e**- **f**-4 Jan 1864, **g**- **h**- **i**- **j**-

Catharine ZOOK, **b**-4 Nov 1863, **c**-Magdalena SHARP, exrx., **d**-no bond, **e**- **f**- **g**- **h**- **i**- **j**-

Margaret SMITH, **b**-5 Nov 1863, **c**-Thomas M. UTTLEY, **d**-$3000, **e**-R. H. McCLINTIC, N. J. RUDISILL, **f**-28 Nov 1863, **g**- **h**- **i**- **j**-

Mary WILSON, **b**-7 Nov 1863, **c**-George HANAWALT, **d**-$500, **e**-Chas. STRATFORD, John A. SHELLER, **f**-5 Dec 1863, **g**- **h**- **i**- **j**-

William McCAY, Esq., **b**-24 Nov 1863, **c**-D. W. WOODS, Esq., **d**-$3000, **e**-C. C. STANBARGER, R. W. PATTON, **f**-1 Dec 1863, **g**-See Release in Deed Book LL, pp. 544-548, **h**- **i**- **j**-

Samuel WHARTON (Is not entered in proper place. Was overlooked as Letters were issued Some months after the will was proven– by the Register), **b**-9 Oct 1863, **c**-William WHARTON, exor., **d**-no bond, **e**- **f**-3 Nov 1863, **g**- **h**- **i**- **j**-

Page 214, Frame 232

John Y. KING, **b**-27 Nov 1863, **c**-David M. ZOOK, Jacob S. KING, admrs., **d**-$10,000, **e**-[J.] C. BLYMYER, D. W. WOODS, **f**-18 Dec 1864, **g**- **h**- **i**- **j**-

George H. SIGLER, **b**-14 Dec 1863, **c**-Henry P. SIGLER, **d**-$3000, **e**-Henry McCAULEY, Henry ZERBE, **f**-4 Jan 1864, **g**- **h**- **i**- **j**-

Michael AULTZ, **b**-2 Dec 1863, **c**-Elijah AULTZ, admr. cum &c., **d**-$300, **e**-Hugh McKEE, Gabriel DUNMIRE, **f**- **g**- **h**- **i**- **j**-

Joel DEVAULT, **b**-5 Dec 1863, **c**-C. HOOVER, Esq., exor., **d**-no bond, **e**- **f**-9 Jan 1864, **g**- **h**- **i**- **j**-

Samuel WILLS, **b**-7 Dec 1863, **c**-Wm. J. FLEMING, **d**-$1500, **e**-H. S. McNABB, Wilson S. UTTS, **f**-25 Dec 1863, **g**- **h**- **i**- **j**-

James STERRETT, **b**-26 Dec 1863, **c**-Davis BATES, **d**-$4000, **e**-T. G. BELL, Thomas MAYES, **f**-5 Jan 1864, **g**- **h**- **i**- **j**-

Isabella CAMPBELL, **b**-6 Jan 1864, **c**-John A. CAMPBELL, **d**-no bond, **e**- **f**- 25 Jan 1864, **g**- **h**- **i**- **j**-

Margaret F. WILSON, **b**-6 Jan 1864, **c**-John W. WILSON, exor., **d**-no bond, **e**- **f**-19 Jan 1864, **g**-See Release in Deed Book MM, p. 668, dated 18 Nov 1865, **h**- **i**- **j**-

James STERRETT, **b**-14 Jan 1864, **c**-Mrs. Mary STERRETT, **d**-$4000, **e**-Davis BATES, Jas. M. BROWN, **f**-30 Jan 1864, **g**-17 Aug 1867, **h**-$720.54, **i**-$3146.98, **j**-$2420.64, estate in hands of admx.
William WAKEFIELD, **b**-16 Jan 1864, **c**-H. J.WALTERS, Esq., **d**-$1000, **e**-James BURNS, Amor W. WAKEFIELD, **f**-10 Feb 1864, **g**- **h**- **i**- **j**-
William TODD, **b**-23 Jan 1864, **c**-Hugh McKEE, **d**-$1000, **e**-M. BUOY, R. S. McKEE, **f**- **g**-29 Jul 1865, **h**-$210.856, **i**-$390.40, **j**-$179.54, in hands of admr, due creditors
David WERTZ, **b**-23 Jan 1864, **c**-Nancy Jane WERTZ, **d**-$1000, **e**-James WILSON, James BURNS, **f**-17 Feb 1864, **g**- **h**- **i**- **j**-

Page 215, Frame 233
Joseph HENDERSON, M.D., **b**-27 Jan 1864, **c**-Margaret HENDERSON, exrx., **d**-no bond, **e**- **f**-6 Feb 1864, **g**- **h**- **i**- **j**-
Sarah Jane McDOWELL, **b**-29 Jan `1864, **c**-Mrs. Jane McDOWELL, exox., **d**-no bond, **e**- **f**-9 Mar 1864, **g**- **h**- **i**- **j**-
Peter RHODES, Sr., **b**-2 Feb 1864, **c**-Joseph RHODES, Peter RHODES, Jr., admrs., **d**-$1200, **e**-Moses A. SAMPLE, J. T. STONEROAD, **f**-27 Feb 1864, **g**- **h**- **i**- **j**-
George RUBLE, **b**-6 Feb 1864, **c**-Peter BAREFOOT, **d**-$800, **e**-Christian MYERS, Thomas MAYES, **f**-28 Apr 1864, **g**-2 Mar 1865, **h**-$158.45, **i**-$164.11, **j**-$5.66, widow
Catharine REIGLE, **b**-10 Feb 1864, **c**-John REIGLE, exor., **d**-no bond, **e**- **f**-1 Mar 1864, **g**- **h**- **i**- **j**-
James H. McKEE, M.D., **b**-20 Feb 1864, **c**-Alexander McKEE, **d**-$1600, **e**-John McKEE, Wm. F. SHAW, **f**- **g**- **h**- **i**- **j**-
John STONEROAD, Esq., **b**-24 Feb 1864, **c**-John T. STONEROAD, **d**-$500, **e**-Joseph SIGLER, T. G. BALL, **f**-1 Apr 1864, **g**-29 Jul 1865, **h**-$503.14, **i**-$29.30, **j**-$473.94, administrator
Joseph McKIRK, **b**-26 Feb 1864, **c**-Andrew W. McKEE, **d**-$1600, **e**-Wm. R. GRAHAM, Wm. McKIRK, **f**-18 Mar 1864, **g**- **h**- **i**- **j**-
Jacob L. KING, **b**-8 Mar 1864, **c**-Yost HARTZLER, exor., **d**-no bond, **e**- **f**-28 Mar 1864, **g**- **h**- **i**- **j**-
Jonas KAUFFMAN, **b**-18 Mar 1864, **c**-William KAUFFMAN, exr., **d**-no bond, **e**- **f**-19 Mar 1864, **g**- **h**- **i**- **j**-
Annie SHAUP, **b**-21 Mar 1864, **c**-Mrs. Nancy WARTMAN, ex., **d**-no bond, **e**- **f**- **g**- **h**- **i**- **j**-

Christian BURKHOLDER, b-24 Mar 1864, c-Mrs. Matilda BURKHOLDER, d-$800, e-Jacob McAULAY, Simon KREPS, f-4 Apr 1864, g- h- i- j-

Page 216, Frame 234
Andrew WATT, b-9 Apr 1864, c-John D. BARR, d-$3000, e-William GREER, Geo. BLYMYER, f-9 May 1864, g- h- i- j-
John STERRETT, b-15 Apr 1864, c-William REED, d-$50, e-J. W. McLAUGHLIN, John SMITH, f- g- h- i- j-
Christiana WILLS, b-25 Apr 1864, c-William R. WILLS, d-$600, e-Elias HUFFNAGLE, J. T. STONEROAD, f-16 May 1864, g- h- i- j-
John BUCHANAN. b-3 May 1864, c-Mrs. Matilda BUCHANAN, d-$500, e-John STRUNK, George POTTER, f-28 May 1864, g- h- i- j-
Robert WALLACE, b-2 May 1864, c-William WALLACE, John PURCELL, exrs., d-no bond, e- f-6 Jun 1864, g- h- i- j-
Adam BRENEMAN, b-4 Jun 1864, c-Frances BRENEMAN, D. W. WOODS, Esq., exrs., d-no bond, e- f-13 Jun 1864, g-5 Mar 1866, h-$7229.37, i-$7229.37, j-
Franklin CALDWELL, b-13 Jun 1864, c-S. Isabella CALDWELL, d-$2000, e-Wm. S. CALDWELL, Richd. GALLAHER, f-5 Jul 1864, g- h- i- j-
Nancy WEEKES, b-15 Jun 1864, c-John BARGER, exr., d-no bond, e- f-15 Jul 1864, g- h- i- j-
Alexander McKEE, b-18 Jun 1864, c-[Mary] M. SHAW, Elizabeth B. McKEE, exrxs., d-no bond, e- f-24 Jun 1864, g- h- i- j-
Mary SEMPLE, b-9 Jul 1864, c-G. W. FISHER, admr. conn, &c, d-2000, e-Saml. YODER, Ezra D. SAMPLE, f-22 Aug 1864, g-1 Dec 1865, h-$359.78, i-$1623.88, j-$1264.10, heirs
Benjamin INGLE, b-15 Jul 1864, c-John BARGER, d-$1000, e-John CUPPLES, Wm. BUTLER, f-18 Aug 1864, g- h- i- j-
Henry ROTHROCK, b-18 Jul 1864, c-Moses ROTHROCK, exr., d-no bond, e- f-9 Aug 1864, g-29 Jul 1865, h-$433.73, i-$1217.51, j-$783.78, heirs

Page 217, Frame 235
William BELL, Esq., b-5 Aug 1864, c-Mrs. Ann BELL, d-$200, e-Jno. D. TAYLOR, Wm. A. McMANIGLE, f-1 Sep 1864, g- h- i- j-

John M. HORRELL, b-22 Aig 1864, c-Ann HORRELL, d-$1800, e-
Daniel KING, Wm. W. GILMORE, f-9 Sep 1864, g-6 Mar 1866, h-
$812.88, i-$712.25, j-$100.63, accountant

Isabella CAMPBELL, b-22 Aug 1864, c-John O. CAMPBELL, exr., d-no
bond, e- f-14 Sep 1864, g-2 Mar 1865, h-$658.70, i-$979.80, j-$321.10,
estate

William McNABB, Sr., b-23 Aug 1864, c-David WEILER, d-$1600, e-
Joseph HAFFLY, Robert CAMPBELL, f- g- h- i- j-

William COWDEN, b-23 Aug 1864, c-Christ. HOOVER, Esq., d-$100,
e-C. BECK, Henry BOOK, f-24 Aug 1864, g- h- i- j-

James DORMAN. b-1 Sep 1864, c-H. J. WALTERS, Esq., exr., d-no
bond, e- f- g- h- i- j-

Rachel RIDDLE, b-15 Sep 1864, c-Alexander EISENBISE, d-$800, e-
Saml. J. BRISBIN, C. HOOVER, Esq., f-30 Sep 1864, g- h- i- j-

Mrs. Catharine RAMSEY, b-1 Oct 1864, c-Wm. H. RAMSEY, C. P.
RAMSEY, admrs., d-$4000, e-D. A. McMANIGAL, C. A. SAMPLE,
f-29 Oct 1864, g- h- i- j-

Francis HENRY, b-4 Oct 1864, c-William HENRY, Alex. REED, admrs.,
d-$600[sic], e-Jno. HAYES, Jr., Abner THOMPSON, f-31 Oct 1864,
g-27 Nov 1865, h-$10,915.74, i-$20,187.00, j-$9271.26, heirs (see
exhibit on account)

Margaretta McVEY, b-9 Nov 1864, c-George G. COUCH, exor., d-no
bond, e- f- g- h- i- j-

John MILLER, Sr.. b-11 Nov 1864, c-John MILLER, Jesse MILLER,
extrs., d-no bond, e- f- 9 Dec 1864, g-28 Feb 1866, h-$1590.00, i-
$970.66, j-$619.34, estate (see auditor report)

John CUBBISON, b-22 Nov 1864, c-John C. SIBLER, ad., d-$1200, e-D.
M. CONTNER, G. W. SIGLER, f-28 Nov 1864, g-5 Oct 1865, h-
$1095.51, i-$1904.68, j-$809.17, estate

Mary M. SIEGRIST, b-14 Dec 1864, c-Sallie E. SIEGRIST, ad. cum &c.,
d-$100, e-John A. McKEE, Joseph ALEXANDER, f- g- h- i- j-

Page 218, Frame 236

S. S. CUMMINGS, M.D., b-30 Dec 1864, c-Oliver C. CHESNEY, d-
$1000, e-Thomas MAYS, Nathan FRANK, f-1 May 1865, g-4 Nov
1868, h-$1878.79, i-$1188.28, j-$1000.49, in hands of accountant

Peter RHODES, Sr., b-30 Dec 1864, c-Joseph RHODES, admr. cum &c,
d-$500, e-Peter RHODES, Jr., Levi RHODES, f-28 Jan 1865, g-6 Oct
1865, h-$429.92, i-$1354.94, j-$928.02, estate

John MAGILL, **b**-3 Jan 1865, **c**-William MACKLIN, Jas H. ROSS, exors., **d**-no bond, **e**- **f**-1 Feb 1865, **g**-5 Oct 1866, **h**-$1606.88, **i**-$1488.30, **j**-$118.28, estate

John PURCELL, **b**-27 Jan 1865, **c**-Edward R. PURCELL, **d**-$30,000, **e**-David JENKINS, Samuel DRAKE, **f**-27 Feb 1865, **g**- **h**- **i**- **j**-

John FILSON, Jr., **b**-30 Jan 1865, **c**-Joseph FILSON, **d**-$500, **e**-M. A. SAMPLE, John FILSON, Sr., **f**-7 Feb 1865, **g**-2 Oct 1865, **h**-$104.06, **i**-$288.21, **j**-$184.15, in accountant's hands

Christiana SWIGART, **b**-1 Feb 1865, **c**-Jos. R. HANAWALT, exr., **d**-no bond, **e**- **f**-22 Feb 1865, **g**- **h**- **i**- **j**-

Joseph P. POSTLETHWAIT, **b**-14 Feb 1865, **c**-Wm. J. POSTLETHWAIT, **d**-$1000, **e**-T. F. POSTLETHWAIT, Jacob SHADE, **f**-29 Mar 1865, **g**- **h**- **i**- **j**-

Jacob KURTZ, **b**-17 Feb 1865, **c**-Jacob S. KING, Nicholas HARTZLER, exrs., **d**-no bond, **e**- **f**-20 Mar 1865, **g**-2 Dec 1865, **h**-$1365.54, **i**-$1370.80, **j**-$5.26, estate and paid to widow

Adam W. BRIMMER, **b**-20 Feb 1865, **c**-Geo. L. CALDERWOOD, **d**-$800, **e**-D. E. ROBISON, William S. McKEE, **f**-3 Mar 1865, **g**- **h**- **i**- **j**-

Geo. W. CRISSMAN, **b**-21 Feb 1975. **c**-W. J. McCARTHY, Wm. C. CRISSMAN, **d**-$2000, **e**-Wm. McNITT, Ira THOMPSON, **f**-1 Mar 1865, **g**-30 Jul 1866, **h**-$2372.87, **i**-$5167.69, **j**-$2794.82, heirs, paid by admrs.

John MILLER, **b**-25 Feb 1865, **c**-David T. KLINE, Francis H. MILLER, exrs., **d**-no bond, **e**- **f**-3 Apr 1865, **g**-27 Feb 1866, **h**-$2313.72, **i**-$3955.23, **j**-$1641.51, estate, paid to widow and heirs

Elizabeth JOHNSTON, **b**-1 Mar 1865, **c**-Rev. James SMITH, Rev. Saml. M. MOORE, exrs., **d**-no bond, **e**- **f**-2 Mar 1865, **g**- **h**- **i**- **j**-

John B. WILSON, **b**-4 Mar 1865, **c**-Thomas M. UTTLEY, Esq., **d**-$500, **e**-James BURNS, Peter SPANGLER, **f**-6 Mar 1865, **g**-29 Jul 1865, **h**-$127.00, **i**-$121.00, **j**-$6.00, administrator

Page 219, Frame 237

Clement H. SMITH, **b**-11 Mar 1865, **c**-Samuel L. ZELNER, **d**-$1600, **e**-Enoch MOYER, Saml. H. McCOY, **f**-20 Mar 1865, **g**-27 Aug 1866, **h**-$427.86, **i**-$734.92, **j**-$307.06, to creditors by audit

Ormond WHITWORTH, **b**-13 Mar 1865, **c**-Mrs. Mary M. WHITWORTH, **d**-$2000, **e**-Michael AULTZ, Henry S. PRICE, **f**-16 Mar 1865, **g**-29 Oct 1868, **h**-$1205.62, **i**-$2202.77, **j**-$997.15, in accountant's hands

William FURGASON[sic], **b**-1 Apr 1865, **c**-Leonard MELCHER, **d**-$600, **e**-Samuel MILLIKEN, William J. [PRICE], **f**-5 Apr 1865, **g**-24 Oct 1865, **h**-$391.27, **i**-$411.55, **j**-$20.28; $20.28, heirs; admr. has paid heirs $40; overpaid $19.72

Col. Wm. CUMMINS, **b**-8 Apr 1865, **c**-Charles K. DAVIS, Robert CUMMINS, conn teste &c, **d**-$8000, **e**-John D. TAYLOR, Robert M. TAYLOR, **f**-1 May 1865, **g**- **h**- **i**- **j**-

Alfred MARKS, **b**-15 Apr 1865, **c**-John W. SHAW, Esq., **d**-$5000, **e**-Henry ZERBE, William RUSSELL, **f**-10 May 1865, **g**- **h**- **i**- **j**-

William WILLS, **b**-15 Apr 1865, **c**-Joseph J. WILLS, **d**-$8000, **e**-Joseph M. FLEMING, William [HOOVER], **f**-10 May 1865, **g**-30 Nov 1867, **h**-$6827.37.5, **i**-$6827.38, **j**-[can't interpret last notation, not numbers]

John HIMES, **b**-2 May 1865, **c**-John L. HIMES, cum testa &c., **d**-$12,000, **e**-Amos HOOT, Henry M. PRATT, **f**-15 Nov 1865, **g**- **h**- **i**- **j**-

Sarah C. PRICE, **b**-4 May 1865, **c**-George W. ELDER, Esq., **d**-$000, **e**-Andrew MAYES, Christian HOOVER, Esq., **f**-4 May 1865, **g**-See Release &c in Deed Book MM, pp. 544 & 545, **h**- **i**- **j**-

Christian ALLGYER, **b**-6 May 1865, **c**-Benjamin ZOOK, Joseph HARSHBARGER, **d**-$5000, **e**-Joseph HAFFLY, Levi HARTZLER, **f**-23 May 1865, **g**-24 Sep 1866, **h**-$578.90, **i**-$3269.46, **j**-$2620.56, estate

Peter YODER, **b**-12 May 1865, **c**-Christian G. YODER, exr., **d**-no bond, **e**- **f**-18 May 1865, **g**-18 Dec 1868, **h**-$2380.99, **i**-$23,050.84, **j**-$20.669.85, heirs; auditor appointed to make distribution

Nancy J. WERTZ, **b**-20 May 1865, **c**-J. H. WILSON, James WILSON, **d**-$125, **e**-John STRONG, **f**-21 Jun1865, **g**- **h**- **i**- **j**-

John ALEXANDER, **b**-2 Jun 1865, **c**-Jane B. ALEXANDER, exor., **d**-no bond, **e**- **f**-21 Jun 1865, **g**- **h**- **i**- **j**-

John H. GARTHOFF, **b**-5 Jun 1865, **c**-David BENFER, **d**-$3000, **e**-Henry BENFER, Joseph YEATTOR, **f**-15 Jun 1865, **g**-28 Jul 1866, **h**-$3820.20, **i**-$3973.66, **j**-$153.46, estate

Page 220, Frame 238
Elijah McVEY, **b**-17 Jun 1865, **c**-John R. McVEY, exor., **d**-no bond, **e**- **f**-15 Jul 1865, **g**-30 May 1866, **h**-$1216.45, **i**-$1206.45, **j**-$16.00, estate

Mary Ann MILLIKEN, **b**-30 Jun 1865, **c**-Arria FLOYD, exrx., **d**-no bond, **e**- **f**-26 Jul 1865, **g**-30 Jul 1867, **h**-$4315.07, **i**-$1956.78.5, **j**-$2358.28.5, estate, paid to heirs

John L. SETTLEMYER, b-8 Jul 1865, c-N. J. RUDISILL, Esq., d-$200, e-Henry J. WALTERS, Wm., T. BURNS, f-18 Aug 1865, g- h- i- j-

Jacob MICKEY, b-10 Jul 1865, c-Peter BAREFOOT, d-$1200, e-Moses R. THOMPSON, John COX, f- g-24 Jul 1866, h-$950.43, i-$699.85, j-$250.58, estate

Christian HOUSEHOLDER, b-20 Jul 1865, c-Henry S. WILSON, exor, d-no bond, e- f-15 Aug 1865, g- h- i- j-

Joseph COULTER, b-26 Jul 1865, c-Jas. H. ROSS, A. R. HESSER, exrs., d-no bond, e- f-26 Aug 1865, g- h- i- j-

George LANE, b-28 Jul 1865, c-Michael K. LANE, Samuel DRAKE, exors., d-no bond, e- f- g-14 Aug 1865, h- i- j-

Rev. James WILLIAMSON, b-31 Jul 1865, c-C. WILLIAMSON, W. WILLIAMSON, exors., d-no bond, e- f-2 Aug 1865, g- h- i- j-

Christian HOOVER, Esq., b-1 Aug 1865, c-Robert B. HOOVER, d-$2000, e-Wm. WILLIS, John A. McKEE, f-4 Sep 1865, g- h- i- j-

Henry BUCKLEY, b-3 Aug 1865, c-John Allen BUCKLEY, d-$2000, e-Geo. BUCKLEY, E. B. PURCELL, f-15 Aug 1865, g- h- i- j-

John JOHNSTON, b-19 Aug 1865, c-Saml. B. STINE, admr. de bonis &c, d-$1000, e-Thos. JOHNSTON, Thos. McCORMICK, f-11 Jun 1866, g- h- i- j-

George W. FISHER, Esq., b-19 Aug 1865, c-Thompson G. BELL, d-$3000, e-Wm. S. BELL, Saml. H. McCOY, f-2 Sep 1865, g- h- i- j-

Thomas M. HULINGS, b-28 Aug 1865, c-J. F. REYNOLDS, d-$500, e-L. W. WILLIAMS, C. A. REYNOLDS, f- g- h- i- j-

Page 221, Frame 239

David BLOOM, b-11 Sep 1865, c-John HAMILTON, exor., d-no bond, e- f-12 Sep 1865, g- h- i- j-

Mrs. Margaret PHILLIPS, b-12 Sep 1865, c-Thomas PHILLIPS, d-$1200, e-John A. McKEE, Adam HAMAKER, f- g- h- i- j-

Sarah W. McDOWELL, b-19 Sep 1865, c-Ephraim HAZLETT, d-$2000, e-D. McK. CONTNER, Henry STEELY, f-13 Oct 1865, g-19 Sep 1866, h-$2614.30, i-$1115.75, j-$1498.35, estate

Samuel LOWRIE, b-21 Sep 1865, c-Nicholas HARTZLER, exor., d-no bond, e- f-21 Oct 1865, g-5 Oct 1866, h-$274.96, i-$354.49, j-$79.53, estate

Henry KEMERLING, b-27 Sep 1865, c-Mrs. Mary KEMERLING, d-$600, e-Jno. W. SHERIFF, Saml. J. BRISBIN, f-30 Sep 1865, g- h- i- j-

Wilson Irwin LAWVER, b-6 Oct 1865, **c**-D. W. WOODS, Esq., **d**-$600, **e**-Robt. W. PATTON, Saml. COMFORT, **f**-18 Oct 1865, **g**-1 Dec 1865, **h**-$41.53, **i**-$328.53, **j**-$287.00, due and paid to Sarah A. CUPP

Col. Wm. BUTLER, b-17 Oct 1865, **c**-John C. SIGLER, **d**-$4000, **e**-James BURNS, Thomas MAYES, **f**-2 Nov 1865, **g**-4 Apr 1868, **h**-$5933.17, **i**-$9332.68, **j**-$3399.51, creditors; see auditor's report

George G. GIBSON, b-17 Oct 1865, **c**-John C. SIGLER, **d**-$500, **e**-Jacob HOOVER, D. McK. CONTNER, **f**-23 Oct 1865, **g**- **h**- **i**- **j**-

Mrs. Sarah FREEBURN, b-18 Oct 1865, **c**-D. D. MUTTHERSBOUGH, **d**-$100, **e**-Geo. M. FREEBURN, Barger FREEBURN, **f**- **g**- **h**- **i**- **j**-

Elizabeth CLARKE, b-19 Oct 1865, **c**-James A. DYSART, **d**-$1200, **e**-Thos. M. UTTLEY, John DIPPLE, **f**-21 Nov 1865, **g**- **h**- **i**- **j**-

Margaret McCALLOUGH, b-24 Oct 1865, **c**-David WEILER, **d**-$1400, **e**-D. McK. CONTNER, Chas. K. DAVIS, **f**-24 Nov 1865, **g**-27 Sep 1866, **h**-$789,81, **i**-$132.06, **j**-$657.75, estate, paid to heirs

Daniel BEAVER, b-3 Nov 1865, **c**-Peter BAREFOOT, **d**-$500, **e**-Ira THOMPSON, Wm. H. McNITT, **f**-20 Jan 1866, **g**- **h**- **i**- **j**-

Patrick McKINNEY, b-7 Nov 1865, **c**-Thomas ROOP, **d**-$300, **e**-John ROSS, John J. KIMERLY, **f**-22 Nov 1865, **g**- **h**- **i**- **j**-

Page 222, Frame 240

Elizabeth BURKHOLDER, b-21 Nov 1865, **c**-William MITCHELL, **d**-$1000, **e**-Henry BOOK, Thomas REED, **f**- **g**-30 Jul 1866, **h**-$160.43, **i**-$183.55, **j**-$23.12, estate

Jacob BRINER, b-29 Nov 1865, **c**-Wm. W. GILMORE, **d**-$600, **e**-Albert HAZLETT, Geo. W. HAZLETT, **f**-30 Dec 1865, **g**- **h**- **i**- **j**-

Jacob HEINLEY, b-8 Dec 1865, **c**-Samuel MITCHELL, Elizabeth HEINLEY, exors., **d**-no bond, **e**- **f**- **g**- **h**- **i**- **j**-

Mary S. JUNKIN, b-24 Dec 1865, **c**-H. W. JUNKIN, **d**-$100, **e**-John EVANS, Edmund MURPHY, **f**- **g**- **h**- **i**- **j**-

James McFARLAND, b-27 Dec 1865, **c**-James F. MATEER, exr., **d**-no bond, **e**- **f**-8 Jan 1866, **g**-6 Oct 1866, **h**-$3277.48, **i**-$819.91, **j**-$2457.57, estate (see audtr report filed)

George BUBB, b-29 Dec 1865, **c**-Nicholas HARTZLER, admr., **d**-$300, **e**-Edward WHEATON, J. K. HARTZLER, **f**-29 Jan 1866, **g**- **h**- **i**- **j**-

Joseph HART, b-3 Jan 1866, **c**-Elijah MORRISON, exor., **d**-no bond, **e**- **f**-10 Feb 1866, **g**- **h**- **i**- **j**-

Revd. D. D. CLARK, **b**-4 Jan 1866, **c**-William MACKLIN, Robert A. CLARK, exors., **d**-no bond, **e**- **f**-13 Feb 1866, **g**-4 Apr 1868, **h**-$4683.60, **i**-$4683.60, **j**-

Cyrus STINE, **b**-4 Jan 1866, **c**-David STINE, Wm. MACKLIN, **d**-$8000, **e**-Wm. STINE, W. A. MOORE, **f**-5 Feb 1866, **g**- **h**- **i**- **j**-

Roberts[sic] **BURNS**, **b**-12 Jan 1866, **c**-Peter SPANGLER, **d**-$2000, **e**-James BURNS, M. MORRISON, **f**-19 Jan 1866, **g**- **h**- **i**- **j**-

John HAMAN, **b**-9 Feb 1866, **c**-William MACKLIN, John H. HAMAN, exors., **d**-no bond, **e**- **f**-28 Feb 1866, **g**-4 Apr 1979. **h**-$23,130.02, **i**-$23,607.06, **j**-$477.04, estate

John CARNEY, **b**-20 Feb 1866, **c**-John C. SIGLER, **d**-$4000, **e**-D. M. CONTNER, Adam HAMAKER, **f**-5 Feb 1867, **g**- **h**- **i**- **j**-

Daniel BESHOAR, **b**-21 Feb 1866, **c**-William CREIGHTON, **d**-$3000, **e**-Jeremiah YEAGER, Hartman PHILLIPS, **f**- **g**- **h**- **i**- **j**-

Page 223, Frame 241

John NORTON, **b**-21 Feb 1866, **c**-Samuel NORTON, Jacob NORTON, adms., **d**-$10,000, **e**-David WITHROW, John DIPPLE, **f**-24 Mar 1866, **g**- **h**- **i**- **j**-

Henry SWARTZELL, **b**-17 Mar 1866, **c**-John SWARTZELL, George SWARTZELL, admrs., **d**-$30,000, **e**-Davis BATES, Andrew SWARTZELL, James BURNS, **f**-6 Apr 1866, **g**-24 Aug 1868, **h**-$3474.71, **i**-$15,836.74, **j**-$13,362.03, estate

Rachel McINTIRE, **b**-26 Mar 1866, **c**-Joseph STEWART, (Exect), **d**-no bond, **e**- **f**-16 Apr 1866, **g**- **h**- **i**- **j**-

William MORRISON, **b**-3 Apr 1866, **c**-Albert G. GIBBONEY, Exct., **d**-no bond, **e**- **f**-1 May 1866, **g**-4 Dec 1867, **h**-$408.37, **i**-$399.90, **j**-$8.47, executor

Margery FISHER, **b**-30 Apr 1866, **c**-Thompson G. BELL, ex., **d**-no bond, **e**- **f**-4 May 1866, **g**- **h**- **i**- **j**-

Wesley McCOY, **b**-2 Jun 1866, **c**-Saml. H. McCOY, admr., **d**-$1000, **e**-T. G. BELL, Joshua MORRISON, **f**-9 Jun 1866, **g**-16 Jul 1866, **h**-$281.60, **i**-$839.86, **j**-$558.26, estate, paid to widow and heirs

Geo. W. MATTHEWS, **b**-27 Jun 1866, **c**-Samuel DRAKE, admr., **d**-$1000, **e**-Joseph HAFFLY, Robt. CAMPBELL, **f**- **g**- **h**- **i**- **j**-

Jacob ESTERLINE, **b**-30 Jun 1866, **c**-David A. ESTERLINE, admr., **d**-$600, **e**-Nathan ZIMERMAN[sic], Saml. H. McCOY, **f**-30 Jul 1866, **g**- **h**- **i**- **j**-

William MAYES, b-23 Jul 1866, c-Sarah A. MAYES, admrx., d-$20,000, e-Geo. W. ELDER, William WILLIS, f-25 Jul 1866, g-24 Aug 1868, h-$1554.27, i-$12,017.05, j-$10.462.78, estate

Mathew TAYLOR, b-28 Jul 1866, c-Mrs. E. J. TAYLOR, admx., d-$3000, e-R. M. TAYLOR, J. D. TAYLOR, f-25 Aug 1866, g- h- i- j-

George SIGLER, b-2 Aug 1866, c-A. W. SIGLER, G. T. SIGLER, extrs., d-no bond, e- f-31 Aug 1866, g- h- i- j-

Page 224, Frame 242

John SPEICHER, b-15 Aug 1866, c-William SPEICHER, admr., d-$6000, e-Emanuel SPEICHER, Geo. W. HOOVER, f- g- h- i- j-

Enoch MOYER, b-18 Aug 1866, c-Henry BOOK, admr., d-$1200, e-Isaac PRICE, Moses MILLER, f-15 Sep 1866, g- h- i- j-

John H. MOORE, b-30 Aug 1866, c-David WEILER, admr., d-$1200, e-George WEILER, John PEACHEY, f-3 Oct 1866, g- h- i- j-

Margaret T. BRISBIN, b-4 Sep 1866, c-James S. BRISBIN, Wm. J. W. BRISBIN, exrs., d-no bond, e- f-3 Oct 1866, g- h- i- j-

John C. WOLF, b-8 Sep 1866, c-James T. SMITH, Eliza WOLF, d-$2000, e-Moses A. SAMPLE, Chas. K. DAVIS, f-5 Oct 1866, g- h- i- j-

Charles C. PARKER, b-18 Sep 1866, c-John HOYT, Jr., admr., d-$800, e-James H. MANN, f-18 Oct 1866, g- h- i- j-

David A. POSTLETHWAIT, b-19 Sep 1866, c-Saml. D. POSTLETHWAIT, admr., d-$1200, e-James BURNS, John GAFF, f-13 Oct 1866, g-11 Oct 1867, h-$1102.28, i-$1710.68, j-$608.40, admr.

Elias WAGGONER, b-9 Oct 1866, c-William CREIGHTON, exor., d-no bond, e- f-27 Oct 1866, g- h- i- j-

Prudence BLYMYER, b-26 Oct 1866, c-James NICHOLS, exor., d-no bond, e- f-15 Nov 1866, g- h- i- j-

William LOWRIE, b-5 Nov 1866, c-Daniel LOWRIE, extr., d-no bond, e- f-4 Dec 1866, g-4 Apr 1868, h-$676.42, i-$686.20, j-$8.78, estate

Nina M. KEARNS, b-19 Nov 1866, c-Joseph KEARNS, admr., d-$600, e-Thomas KEARNS, D. M. CONTNER, f-12 Dec 1866, g-4 Apr 1868, h-$126.37, i-$227.79, j-$31.42, estate

Geo. B. PENEPACKER, b-23 Nov 1866, c-Saml. H. McCOY, admr., d-$2000, e-T. G. BELL, John S. REED, f-24 Nov 1867, g-4 Apr 1868, h-$2927.64, i-$3385.85, j-$458.21, estate; see audit. report

Bernard GARRETTY, b-30 Nov 1866, c-John ROBERTSON, admr., d-$600, e- f-24 Jan 1867, g- h- i- j-

Page 225, Frame 243

Catharine [YAPEL], b-1 Dec 1866, c-Jas. F. McNEAR, admr., d-$500, e-D. M. CONTNER, Jos. S. WAREAM, f- g- h- i- j-

Albert T. BRATTON, b-1 Dec 1866, c-Richeson BRATTON, admr., d-$800, e-John RUBLE, Jacob KAUFFMAN, f-7 Jan 1867, g-7 Oct 1868, h-$209.37, i-$618.00, j-$408,63, estate

John EDMISTON, b-20 Dec 1866, c-Jos. S. WAREAM, admr., d-$100, e-W. H. WEBER, Abner THOMPSON, f- g- h- i- j-

Geo. H. CALBRAITH, b-24 Dec 1866, c-John ATKINSON, admr., d-$10,000, e-John ROSS, James BURNS, f-8 Jan 1867, g- h- i- j-

Abigail DYSART, b-16 Jan 1867, c-Jas. F. McNEARE, admr., d-$5000, e-John TAYLOR, Richard GALLAHER, f- g- h- i- j-

John L. BYLER, b-6 Feb 1867, c-Benjamin BYLER, exr., d-no bond, e- f-15 Feb 1867, g-4 Apr 1868, h-$1620.08, i-$1687.20, j-$67.28, estate

Jenkins B. SMITH, b-9 Feb 1867, c-Saml. J. BRISBIN, admr., d-$1200, e-G. W. ELDER, W. H. BRATTON, f-11 Feb 1867, g- h- i- j-

Henry STEELY, b-11 Feb 1867, c-Ephraim HAZLETT, admr., d-$12,000, e-J. T. WILSON, Jacob FOCHT, f-11 Mar 1867, g- h- i- j-

James POLLOCK, b-19 Feb 1867, c-Mary POLLOCK, d-$2000, e-Jos. S. STRUNK, B. J. SILLS, f-1 Apr 1867, g-24 Aug 1868, h-$524.85, i-$525.25, j-$.40, admrx.

James & Joseph BARNETT, b-9 Mar 1867, c-Mary MOURY, d-$600, e-Jacob MOURY, Saml. MOURY, f- g- h- i- j-

Catharine KAUFFMAN, b-9 Mar 1867, c-Joseph WINTER, Jr., d-$1600, e-Jacob KAUFFMAN, Jno. K. MILLER, f-23 Mar 1867, g-4 Mar 1868, h-$750.04, i-$1634.33, j-$884.29, heir (paid)

John U. HAMILTON, b-9 Mar 1867, c-John ROBERTSON, d-$600, e-Jos. B. EWING, Jas. F. McNEAR, f-5 Apr 1867, g-4 Apr 1868, h-$120.08, i-$302.20, j-$182.12, estate

Abner THOMPSON, b-12 Mar 1867, c-Nancy M. THOMPSON, admrx., d-$12,000, e-Alexander REED, R. M. KINSLOE, f-8 Apr 1867, g- h- i- j-

Page 226, Frame 244

Isabella FULTZ, b-2 Apr 1867, c-Philip FULTZ, admr., d-$200, e-Geo. WEILER, And. COOK, f-24 Apr 1867, g- h- i- j-

Henry SELICK, Sr., b-17 Apr 1867, c-John SELICK, admr., d-$300, e-R. A. McKEE, J. H. McKEE, f-2 May 1867, g- h- i- j-

Daniel HERRINGTON, b-17 May 1867, c-Joshua MORRISON, admr., d-$1000, e-J. W. SHERIFF, G. W. WILEY, f-3 Jun 1867, g- h- i- j-

Martha SEACHRIST, b-27 May 1867, c-Saml. W. NORTON, exor., d-no bond, e- f- g- h- i- j-

George SETTLE, b-4 Jun 1867, c-Martha H. SETTLE, admx., d-$6000, e-Saml. M. AULTZ, Thos. M. UTTLEY, f-19 Jun 1867, g-4 Dec 1867, h-$2764.08, i-$1418.90 j-$1345.18, accountant

Abraham MUTHERSBOUGH[sic], b-27 Jun 1867, c-Jemima MUTHERSBOUGH, Johnston MUTHERSBOUGH, admrs., d-$5000, E-Wm. CREIGHTON, Henry ZERBE, f-22 Jul 1867, g- h- i- j-

Jacob KAUFFMAN, b-28 Jun 1867, c-Henry HARTZLER, [Jnotn.] KAUFFMAN, admrs., d-$1000, e-John HARSHBERGER, Saml. STAYROOK, f-23 Jul 1867, g-Estate settled; releases of heirs to admr. filed 1 Aug 1868, recorded Deed Book TT, pp. 208 & 687, h- i- j-

J. W. BRODY, b-1 Jul 1867, c-Elijah MORRISON, admr., d-$1500, e-Jos. MILLIKEN, A. J. ATKINSON, f-2 Aug 1867, g-24 Aug 1868, h-$517.89, i-$1586.53, j-$1068.68, estate

Mary POSTLETHWAIT, b-5 Jul 1867, c-John POSTLETHWAIT, exor., d-no bond, e- f-3 Aug 1867, g- h- i- j-

Mary INGRAM, b-10 Jul 1867, c-Robt. INGRAM, exor., d-no bond, e- f- g- h- i- j-

William COWDEN, b-10 Aug 1867, c-Elizabeth COWDEN, extx., d-no bond, e- f- g- h- i- j-

Robert WASSON, b-13 Aug 1867, c-Mary A. WASSON, admx., d-$500, e-Robert WASSON, John HAYES, Jr., f- g- h- i- j-

Samuel ORT, b-10 Sep 1867, c-Melancthon ORT, admr., d-$1200, e-Jacob BLYMYER, Peter ORT, f-13 Sep 1867, g- h- i- j-

William McNITT, b-12 Sep 1867, c-R. J. McNITT, admr., d-$4000, e-Jno. D. NAGANY, J. M. AITKIN, f-12 Oct 1867, g- h- i- j-

Page 227, Frame 245

David MILLER, b-28 Sep 1867, c-Jacob & Wm. MILLER, admrs., d-$4000, e-John HARSHBERGER, Jared KAUFFMAN, f-18 Oct 1867, g- h- i- j-

James KYLE, b-29 Oct 1867, c-John COX, admr., d-$2000, e-John TAYLOR, Davis BATES, f-15 Feb 1868, g- h- i- j- (See release recorded in Deed Book ZZ, p. 682)

Mathew TAYLOR, b-29 Oct 1867, c-George BATES, admr., d-$40,000, e-Davis BATES, George BLYMYER, f- g- h- i- j-

Henry COMFORT, b-8 Nov 1867, c-Elizabeth COMFORT, admx., d-$600, e-Jno. A. McKEE, Martin ORT, f-7 Dec 1867, g- h- i- j-

Stephen A. HINDS, b-13 Nov 1867, c-J. W. HINDS, admr., d-$3000, e-T. G. BELL, R. M. KINSLOE, f-30 Nov, 1867, g- h- i- j-

John STROUP, b-23 Dec 1867, c-Martin L. STROUP, Henry BRIDGE, extrs., d-no bond, e- f-8 Jan 1868, g- h- i- j-

Sarah TAYLOR, b-27 Dec 1867, c-J. W. HORTON, exor., d-no bond, e- f- g- h- i- j-

Arthur WOODS, b-31 Dec 1867, c-John HOYT, admr., d-$150, e-[?looks like Mrs?, could be William] MANN, J. B. SELHEIMER, f- g-24 Aug 1868, h-$589.11, i-$834.00, j-$244.89, estate

Samuel SAGER, b-22 Jan 1868, c-Thompson G. BELL, admr., d-$500, e-George MOYER, Wm. CREIGHTON, f-7 Feb 1868, g- h- i- j-

Frederick EVERHART, b-23 Jan 1868, c-Mathew McCLINTICK, admr d-$2000, e-Henry J. GOSS, Joseph YETTER, f-20 Feb 1868, g-24 Aug 1868, h-$258.21, i-$240.77, j-$17.44, administrator

Daniel YODER, b-29 Jan 1868, c-Michael YODER, Solomon YODER, admrs., d-$8000, e-Jared KAUFFMAN, Joshua HARSHBERGER, f-18 Feb 1868, g- h- i- j-

Daniel KNEPP, b-10 Feb 1868, c-Nicholas HARTZLER, admr., d-$1000, e-Simon KENNAGY, J. W. HORTON, f-28 Feb 1868, g-For settlement, see release recorded in Deed Book QQ, p. 253, h- i- j-

Mary DOAK, b-10 Feb 1868, c-Mary VANZANDT, admrx., d-$1600, e-W. P. VANZANDT, A. J. ATKINSON, f-19 Mar 1868, g- h- i- j-

Page 228, Frame 246

Catharine MORRISON, b-3 Mar 1868, c-A. F. GIBBONEY, exor., d-no bond, e- f- g- h- i- j-

Moses MOIST, b-7 Mar 1868, c-M. F. H. KINSEL, W. R. BRATTON, admrs., d-$2500, e-Jacob STINE, Albert HORNING, f-25 Mar 1868, g- h- i- j-

Thomas FRITZ, b-28 Mar 188 [1868?], c-Wm. MACKLIN, Hugh McKEE, exors., d-no bond, e- f-8 Apr 1868, g- h- i- j-

William BISHOP, b-4 Apr 1868, c-Wm. JOHNSON, admr., d-$100, e-David CHRISWELL, John McGRAW, f- g- h- i- j-

Henry H. SPRIGGLE, b-13 Apr 1868, c-Joseph SPRIGGLE, d-$200, e-Saml. YOCUM, S. H. McCOY, f- g- h- i- j-

Joseph ZOOK, b-17 Apr 1868, c-Jonas ZOOK, exor., d-no bond, e- f-1 May 1868, g- h- i- j-

Dr. Henry KAUFFMAN, **b**-11 May 1868, **c**-Abrm. KAUFFMAN, admr., **d**-$500, **e**-Richeson BRATTON, Kurtz KAUFFMAN, **f**-11 Jun 1868, **g**- **h**- **i**- **j**-

Michael RUBLE, **b**-23 May 1868, **c**-Joseph RUBLE, Saml. L. RUBLE, admrs., **d**-$25,000, **e**-Jacob RINSEL, Geo. BLYMYER, **f**-1 Jun 1868, **g**- **h**- **i**- **j**-

John KANAGY, **b**-20 May 1868, **c**-Simeon YODER, exor., **d**-no bond, **e**- **f**-4 Jun 1868, **g**- **h**- **i**- **j**-

Fanny McGIRK, **b**-2 Jun 1868, **c**-James McGIRK, admr., **d**-$1200, **e**-Henry AURAND, J. C. BLYMYER, **f**-11 Jun 1868, **g**- **h**- **i**- **j**-

William BARR, **b**-18 Jun 1868, **c**-J. D. BARR, J. O. CAMPBELL, exors., **d**-no bond, **e**- **f**-25 Jul 1868, **g**- **h**- **i**- **j**-

John FLEMING, **b**-19 Jun 1868, **c**-Jos. M. FLEMING, exor., **d**-no bond, **e**- **f**-24 Dec 1868, **g**- **h**- **i**- **j**-

John T. STONEROAD, **b**-2 Jul 1868, **c**-Martha STONEROAD, extx., **d**-no bond, **e**- **f**-31 Jul 1868, **g**- **h**- **i**- **j**-

Page 229, Frame 247

Caleb STRALEY, **b**-24 Jul 1868, **c**-Peter BAREFOOT, exor., **d**-no bond, **e**- **f**-11 Aug 1868, **g**- **h**- **i**- **j**-

John YOUNTZ, **b**-11 Aug 1868, **c**-William YOUNTZ, admr., **d**-$200, **e**-William CREIGHTON, Forest SWYERS, **f**-19 Aug 1868, **g**- **h**- **i**- **j**-

Saml. NIGHTSINGER, **b**-25 Aug 1868, **c**-Chas. STRATFORD, admr., **d**-$100, **e**-Jno. A. McKEE, H. J. WALTERS, **f**- **g**- **h**- **i**- **j**-

Jane ANDERSON, **b**-29 Aug 1868, **c**-Saml. H. McCOY, admr., **d**-$600, **e**-Jno. C. SIGLER, Thompson G. BELL, **f**-17 Oct 1868, **g**- **h**- **i**- **j**-

Alexander ORR, **b**-29 Aug 1868, **c**-Wm. A. ORR, Exor., **d**-no bond, **e**- **f**-5 Sep 1868, **g**- **h**- **i**- **j**-

Hugh McKEE, **b**-5 Sep 1868, **c**-Andrew J. McKEE, exor., **d**-no bond, **e**- **f**-27 Nov 1868, **g**- **h**- **i**- **j**-

Martha ANDERSON. **b**-5 Sep 1868, **c**-Saml. H. McCOY, admr., **d**-$600, **e**-Thos. McCORD, Jno. WOLFKILL, **f**-4 Nov 1868, **g**- **h**- **i**- **j**-

Anthony PETER, **b**-2 Oct 1868, **c**-Jno. H. PETER, admr., **d**-Wm. STEININGER, Daniel SNOOK, **e**-10 Oct 1868, **f**- **g**- **h**- **i**- **j**-

Elizabeth TREASTER, **b**-15 Oct 1868, **c**-John EBY, admr., **d**-$500, **e**-Anthony FELIX, Jos. A. MAJOR, Chas. W. STAHL, **f**- **g**- **h**- **i**- **j**-

David CULP, **b**-4 Nov 1868, **c**-Samuel WATTS, admr., **d**-$200, **e**-Abrm. GRASSMIRE, R. M. TAYLOR, **f**-21 Nov 1868, **g**- **h**- **i**- **j**-

Hugh ALEXANDER, b-4 Nov 1868, c-John ALEXANDER, exor., d-no bond, e- f- g- h- i- j-

Geo. W. THOMAS, b-24 Nov 1868, c-Chas. E. THOMAS, Adelia E. THOMAS, admrs., d-$20,000, e-Wm. RUSSELL, Jas. BURNS, f-8 Dec 1868, g- h- i- j-

Joseph BROUGHT, b-3 Dec 1868, c-Anna C. BROUGHT, extx., d-no bond, e- f-29 Dec 1868, g- h- i- j-

Page 230, Frame 248

Jacob KENNAGY, b-6 Jan 1869, c-David HOOLEY, d-$1000, e-Shem ZOOK, George ELDER, f- g- h- i- j-

John DUNMIRE, b-7 Jan 1869, c-Henry S. PRICE, d-$500, e-George HANAWALT, John [GORTER/GORUR?], f-30 Jan 1869, g- h- i- j-

Charles DANIELS, b-13 Jan 1869, c-Elias PENEPACKER, d-$500, e-Saml. H. McCOY, John KAYES, f- g- h- i- j-

Joel DEVAULT, b-28 Jan 1869, c-Abagail DEVAULT, d-$3000, e-S. J. BRISBIN, J. C. GUSS, f- g- h- i- j-

William BARGER, b-6 Feb 1869, c-Samuel H. McCOY, extr., d-no bond, e- f-20 Feb 1869, g- h- i- j-

Lydia CRISSMAN, b-3 Apr 1869, c-Winchester J. McCARTHY, d-no bond, e- f- g- h- i- j-

Margaret [SUIGART] [possibly SWIGART], b-27 Feb 1869, c-Abraham R. SUIGART, d-$500, e-A. R. SUIGART, M. F. H. KNISEL, f-27 Mar 1869, g- h- i- j-

Frederick FRANCIS, b-6 Mar 1869, c-Jacob FRANCIS, extr., d-no bond, e- f- g- h- i- j-

Augustine WAKEFIELD, b-12 Mar 1869, c-Amor W. WAKEFIELD, William H. SWANZEY, d-$4000, e-William WILLIS, William C. VINES, f- g- h- i- j-

David ROSS, b-22 Mar 1869, c-William W. ROSS, d-$800, e-Gen. Jno. ROSS, C. A. ATKINSON, f- g- h- i- j-

Peter HOUSER, b-1 Mar 1869, c-C. W. STAHL, d-$400, e-J. A. McKEE, G. N. HART, f-23 Mar 1869, g- h- i- j-

Mary STRUNK, b-6 Mar 1869, c-Samuel STRUNK, d-$800, e-Saml. STRUNK, J. M. STRUNK, f-27 Mar 1869, g- h- i- j-

Timothy G. STERRETT, b-27 Mar 1869, c-Robert STERRETT, Samuel STERRETT, d-$800, e-Harry BOOK, William S. CALWELL, f- g- h- i- j-

Jane SMITH, **b**-6 Apr 1869, **c**-J. S. [CLISE], **d**-$8000, **e**-[Charles] NAGANY, O. P. SMITH, **f**- **g**- **h**- **i**- **j**-

George W. GRAHAM, **b**-9 Apr 1869, **c**-Walter GRAHAM, extr., **d**-no bail, **e**- **f**-9 May 1870, **g**- **h**- **i**- **j**-

Page 231, Frame 249

Daniel BROUGHT, **b**-24 Apr 1869, **c**-Sylvester BROUGHT, extr., **d**-no bail, **e**- **f**- **g**- **h**- **i**- **j**-

William James BURNS, **b**-24 Apr 1869, **c**-Jos. S. WAREAM, **d**-$8000, **e**-Mitchel JONES, James BURNS, **f**-6 Aug 1869, **g**- **h**- **i**- **j**-

Margaret BEATY, **b**-4 May 1869, **c**-Peter BEATY, **d**-$200, **e**-Peter BEATY, [Albert HONIG], **f**- **g**- **h**- **i**- **j**-

Henry ARNOLD, **b**-4 May 1869, **c**-Catharine ARNOLD, **d**-$2000, **e**-Peter BEATY, G. W. [NESSER], **f**- **g**- **h**- **i**- **j**-

Sophia BURKHOLDER, **b**-5 May 1869, **c**-Matilda FIRTH, **d**- **e**- **f**- **g**- **h**- **i**- **j**-

Christopher HANAWALT, **b**-8 May 1869, **c**-Saml. HANAWALT, R. S. GAMBLE, **d**-$2000, **e**-Elijah MORRISON, David HEISTER, **f**- **g**- **h**- **i**- **j**-

Jacob YEAGER, **b**-17 May 1869, **c**-Jeremiah M. YEAGER, **d**-$500, **e**-Elias HOFFNAGLE, Jesse MENDENHALL, **f**- **g**- **h**- **i**- **j**-

William SOLTERMAN, **b**-19 Jun 1869, **c**-Catherine SOLTERMAN, extx., **d**- **e**- **f**- **g**- **h**- **i**- **j**-

Jemima HARSHBARGER, **b**-22 Jun 1869, **c**-David H. HARSHBARGER, admin., **d**-1000, **e**- **f**- **g**- **h**- **i**- **j**-

Caleb STRALEY, Jr., **b**-22 Jun 1869, **c**-Julia C. STRALEY, James J. COTTLE, **d**- **e**- **f**- **g**- **h**- **i**- **j**-

John ORT, **b**-12 Jul 1869, **c**-John HAMILTON, Martin ORT, extrs., **d**-no bail, **e**- **f**-6 Aug 1869, **g**- **h**- **i**- **j**-

Charles K. [DAIRE], **b**-13 Jul 1869, **c**-Andrew REED. extr.. **d**-no bail, **e**- **f**- **g**- **h**- **i**- **j**-

Valentine SPIGGLEMEYER, **b**-29 Jul 1869, **c**-Reuben HOOK, admr., **d**-$500, **e**-Henry ZERBE, Martin L. STROUP, **f**-21 Aug 1869, **g**- **h**- **i**- **j**-

David RAMLER, **b**-28 Aug 1869, **c**-Margaret RAMLER, extx., Wm. H. SMITH, extr., **d**-no bail, **e**- **f**-11 Sep 1869, **g**- **h**- **i**- **j**-

Mary Ann THOMAS, **b**-6 Sep 1869, **c**-Charles NAGANY, extr., **d**-no bail, **e**- **f**- **g**- **h**- **i**- **j**-

Sarah McCOY, **b**-9 Sep 1869, **c**-James McCORD, admr., **d**-$6000, **e**-J. A. McKEE, J. W. McCORD, **f**-18 Sep 1869, **g**- **h**- **i**- **j**-

John B. MILLER, b-15 Sep 1869, c-Anthony FELIX, d-$4000, e-[illegible, maybe Arnis JSAOB???], Geo. BLYMYER, f-7 Oct 1869, g- h- i- j-

* * * * *

NOTE: Looking ahead, it appears that the columns previously occupied by g- h- i- j- information are being phased out. In a few pages, they will eventually start adding detailed information about date and time of death. Therefore, we will be discontinuing the use of those last four letters in order to streamline the transcription process. If they ever reappear in the records, we will resume. The last column (f-) is now date of filing inventory. The clerks' handwriting has also deteriorated. Will do my best, but no guarantees. If it looks possible, please go look at it for yourself. That's why the Frame number has been included.

* * * * *

Page 232, Frame 250

John [McDOWELL or McDANELL?], b-24 Sep 1869, c-John D. NAGANY, [Jos.] WAGNER, d-$2000, e-D. W. WOODS, A. P. BLYMYER, f-28 Oct 1869

Mary S. SAMPLE, b- [26] Sep 1868, c-George W. ELDER, Esq., admr., d-$4000, e-]Wm.] WILLIS, f-27 Sep 1869

Benjamin WION, b-28 Sep 1869, c-John [R. GARVER], admr., d-$500, e-Jno. R. GARVER, R. M. TAYLOR, f-27 Nov 1869

Susan STEELY, b-26 Oct 1869, c-Moses FLOYD, admr., d-$4000, e-Montgomery MORRISON, Wm. RUSSELL, f-5 Nov 1869

William ALLISON, b-1 Nov 1869, c-Joseph ALLISON, extr., d- e- f-

Elizabeth TAYLOR, b-3 Nov 1869, c-J. P. TAYLOR, Saml. McWILLIAMS, extrs., d- e- f-30 Nov 1869

William J. POSTLETHWAIT, b-4 Nov 1869, c-John VANZANDT, admr., d-$1600, e-Samuel D. POSTLETHWAIT, Jno. VANZANT[sic], f-4 Jan 1870

John GLICK, b-13 Nov 1869, c-John PEACHEY, extr., d- e- f-14 Dec 1869

Elizabeth STRODE, b-9 Nov 1869, c-Isaac STRODE, extr., d- e- f-28 Jan 1870

Joseph STEUART, b-25 Nov 1869, c-Thompson G. BELL, admr., d-$1000, e-T. G. BELL, Wm. CREIGHTON, f-25 Feb 1870

Mary DEAN, b-2 Dec 1869, c-Joseph D. DEAN, admr., d-$200, e-Joseph D. DEAN, George DOBSON, f-9 Aug 1871

Jacob RHEAM, b-9 Dec 1869, c-Isaac RHEAM, admr., d-$500, e-Elias RHEAM, James BURNS, f-9 Dec 1869

Nancy TAYLOR, b-15 Dec 1869, c-John D. BARR, extr., d-no bail, e- f-

John SEAMAN, b-16 Dec 1869, c-Jacob BOLINGER, extr., d-no bail, e- f-

Holmes MACLAY, b-1 Dec 1869, c-David MACLAY, Saml. MACLAY, d-$1000, e-Jos. H. MACLAY, f-28 Dec 1869

Mrs. Sarah BROUGHT, b-1 Jan 1870, c-George FETZER, admr., d-$2000, e-Jno. ALEXANDER, Seth BENNER, f-20 Jan 1870

William H. McNITT, b-4 Jan 1870, c-Ira THOMPSON, Peter BAREFOOT, extrs., d- e- f-19 Jan 1870

John YEALTER, b-10 Jan 1870, c-John & Samuel YEALTER, admr, d-$1500, e-Thomas YOUNGMAN, John P. TAYLOR, f-15 Jan 1870

Edmond BENNETT, b-10 Jan 1870, c-Joel ZOOK, extr., d- e- f-10 Feb 1870

John MOTEER, b-3 Feb 198-. c-Jessee W. HORTON, extr., d- e- f-2 Mar 1870

John BOWERSOX, b-17 Feb 1870, c-Michael & Saml. BOWERSOX, extrs., d- e- f-18 Mar 1870

John PEACHEY, b-23 Feb 1870, c-Christian B. PEACHEY, d-$13,000, e-Jonathan PEACHEY, Adam HAMAKER, Henry [ZORLE, TORLE?], f-23 Mar 1870

Page 133, Frame 251

Christian B. YODER, b-2 Mar 1870, c-Jonathan N. YODER, admr., d-$600, e-Adam YODER, Jesse W. HORTON, f-26 Mar 1870,

Jacob STUTER, b-8 Mar 1870, c-Theressa STUTER, admr., d-$500, e-Nathaniel STUTER, Adam S. STALEY, f-15 Apr 1870

John ROBB, b-29 Mar 1870, c-Benjamin NORTON, admr., d-$600, e-George MACKLIN, Seth BENNER, f-18 Apr 1870

John GONDER, b-12 Apr 1870, c-John S. GONDER, extr., d- e- f-3 May 1870

J. A. McKEE, b-16 Apr 1870, c-A. W. McKEE, George McKEE, extrs., d- e- f-7 May1870

Hugh McKEE, b-22 Apr 1870, c-George McKEE, admr. de bonis non, d-$1000, e-A. W. McKEE, Saml. RILAND, f-

Peter G. SNOOK, b-30 Apr 1870, c-Daniel H. SNOOK, admr., d-$500, e-Isaiah KNEPP, Daniel SNOOK, f-26 May1870

Christian AMHEISER, b-7 May 1870, c-Joseph S. WAREAM, admr., d-$500, e-Adam HAMAKER, J. C. BLYMYER, f-

Peter WERTZ, b-18 May 1870, c-Samuel H. McCOY, d-$500, e-H. G. MARTIN, f-

Margaret HARDY, b-1 May 1870, c-Chas. HENDERSON, extr.,, d- e- f-7 May 1870

John RONK, b-20 May 1870, c-C. RONK, Chas. HIMELSBAUGH, d-$1000, e-Abraham KAUFFMAN, Jonas HERSHBARGER, f-9 Jun 1870

David ZOOK, b-28 May 1870, c-Joel ZOOK, Simeon K. ZOOK, extrs., d- e- f-29 Jun 1870

John WILSON, Sr., b-31 May 1870, c-Mary S. WILSON, John W. WILSON, Andrew CAMPBELL, extrs., d- e- f-25 Jun 1870

Mary COMFORT, b-1 Jun 1870, c-Saml. COMFORT, admr., d-$3000, e-Wm. K. GRAHAM, Adam HAMAKER, f-29 Jun 1870

James BICE, b-1 Jun 1870, c-William BICE, d-$500, e-D. M. CONTNER, f-22 Jun 1870

Benjamin BYLER, b-6 Jun 1870, c-Jonathan PEACHEY, d-$5000, e-John PEACHEY, C. B. PEACHEY, f-16 Jun 1870

Solomon KINTZER, b-16 Jun 1870, c-Andrew REED, extr., d- e- f-28 Jun 1870

Margaret [MORGAN?], b-29 Jun 1870, c-William HUEY, extr., d- e- f-23 Jun 1870,

Dr. Thos. [VANVALZAH], b-8 Jul 1870, c-Thos. H. VANVALZAH, admr., d-$15,000, e-Ezra D. PARKER, David VANVALZAH, f-

Miles C. WILSON, b-22 Jul 1870, c-J. T. WILSON, H. S. WILSON, admrs., d-$4000, e-J. W. WILSON, f-[2] Aug 1870

Page 234, Frame 252

Catharine MIERLEY, b-23 Jul 1870, c-John CHILCOTE, extr., d- e- f-26 Aug 1870

Joseph [BROUER?], b-26 Jul 1870, c-[Elizabeth] BROUER, admx., d-$3000, e-Samuel BROUER, Francis H. MILLER, f-26 Aug 1870

John CRISSMAN, b-9 Aug 1870, c-Peter BAREFOOT, John M. CRISSMAN, extrs., d- e- f-9 Sep 1870

Jane [McDONELL], b-10 Aug 1870, c-T. M. UTTLEY, admr., d-$500, e-Adam HAMAKER, H. J. WALTERS, f-

Peter LAMM, b-23 Aug 1870, c-Harriett C. LAMM, extx., d- e- f-

[Gracie] **HOUSHOLDER**, **b**-3 Sep 1870, **c**-Russel P. JOHNSTON, James F. MATEER, admrs., **d**-$200, **e**-Geo. B. [REIKORD], **f**-23 Sep 1870

Jonathan McWILLIAMS, **b**-15 Sep 1870, **c**-Saml. McWILLIAMS, extr., **d**- **e**- **f**-15 Oct 1870

Joseph YODER, **b**-17 Sep 1870, **c**-Joshua YODER, Joshua HARSHBERGER, admrs., **d**-$1000, **e**-D. M. [DUET], **f**-15 Oct 1870

Grier SAYERS, **b**-3 Oct 1870, **c**-William SAYERS, admr., **d**-$1000, **e**-William A. PECHT, B. Carrel WHARTON, **f**-28 Oct 1870

John B. SMELKER, **b**-15 Oct 1870, **c**-Sarah SMELKER, T. B. SMELKER, extrs., **d**- **e**- **f**-

Samuel BOTTEICHER, **b**-17 Oct 1870, **c**-William B. BRATTON, admr., **d**-$600, **e**-A. B. ROSS, Elisha GRAHAM, **f**-5 Nov 1870

Joseph KEARNS, **b**-22 Oct 1870, **c**-John W. KEARNS, admr., **d**-$2500, **e**-Joseph SIGLER, John KEARNS, **f**-21 Nov 1870

David CANDER, **b**-2 Nov 1870, **c**-C. G. CANDER, extx., **d**- **e**- **f**-12 Nov 1870

Sophia ROUSCHE, **b**-3 Nov 1870, **c**-Christian B. PEACHEY, admr., **d**-$500, **e**-J. MILLIKEN, Danl. EISENBISE, **f**-25 Nov 1870

Robert ELLIS, **b**-17 Nov 1870, **c**-James ELLIS, admr., **d**-$400, **e**-William S. ELLIS, John HAYES, Jr., **f**-30 Nov 1870

William J. W. BRISBIN, **b**-28 Nov 1870, **c**-William MANN, extr., **d**- **e**- **f**-12 Feb 1871

William SAYER, **b**-7 Feb 1871, **c**-Henry BOOK, extr., **d**- **e**- **f**-22 Feb 1870

Page 235, Frame 253

Hon. Ephraim BANKS, **b**-9 Feb 1871, **c**-Jane Ann BANKS, Thadeus BANKS, **d**-no bail, **e**- **f**-8 Mar 1871

Samuel H. TAYLOR, **b**-1- Feb 1871, **c**-Andrew REED, admr., **d**-$3500, **e**-Alexander REED, James [MANOR], **f**-7 Mar 1871

Sarah A. [GINCHER], **b**-18 Feb 1871, **c**-Amos W. MITCHELL, **d**-$200, **e**-John A. McKEE, Augustus FROXEL, **f**-18 Mar 1871

Sarah H. NOURSE, **b**-23 Feb 1871, **c**-John T. NOURSE, admr., **d**-$300, **e**-Jas. S. GALBRAITH, Abraham [GORSER], **f**-9 Mar 1871

Joel DEVAULT, **b**-27 Feb 1871, **c**-David HOUGH, Eliza HOUGH, admin. De Bonis Non), **d**-$3000, **e**-Peter SPANGLER, Henry FRYSINGER, **f**-

Daniel SNOOK, **b**-4 Mar 1871, **c**-Rebecca SNOOK, extx., **d**- **e**- **f**-

William G. HENDERSON, **b**-9 Mar 1871, **c**-George C. HENDERSON, admr., **d**-$2200, **e**-Benjamin RHODES, Jno. GLASGOW, **f**-7 Apr 1871

William J. McCOY, b-18 Mar 1871, c-T. F. McCOY, Esq., admr., d-$500, e-J. G. McCOY, N. H. BRATTON, f-17 Apr 1871

Andrew BREHMAN, b-18 Mar 1871, c-Jane BREHMAN, admx., d-$500, e-Jacob BREHMAN, Joseph STRUNK, f-25 Mar 1871

Jacob ZOOK, b-18 Mar 1871, c-Sarah ZOOK, Simeon H. YODER, admrs., d-$2000, e-A. P. BLYMYER, Jos.. S. WAREAM, f-28 Mar 1871

Elizabeth B. ALEXANDER, b-4 Apr 1871, c-John ALEXANDER, extr., d-no bail, e- f-

Houston ALEXANDER, b-8 Apr 1871, c-James ALEXANDER, admr., d-$500, e-[J. T.] McCLURE, Geo. BATES, f-

Jacob STEIN, b-8 Apr 1871, c-Henry STEIN, extr., d- e- f-29 Apr 1871

Ann M. SEMPLE, b-17 Apr 1871, c-A. W. CAMPBELL, extr., d- e- f-26 Apr 18871

Samuel C. BROWN, b-29 Apr 1871, c-Anna BROWN, extx., d- e- f-

Martin KINZER, b-12 May 1871, c-Alexander REED, admr., d-$1000, e-John HENRY, John REED, f-13 Jun 1871

Page 236, Frame 254

William NALE, b-13 May 1871, c-Henry L. CLOSE, admr., d-$1500, e-D. F. MILLIKEN, Crawford KYLE, f-12 Jun 1871

Isaac SNOOK, b-16 May 1871, c-Peter BAREFOOT, admr., d-$1000, e-Joseph WAGNER, Jos. P. BLYMYER, f-1 Jul 1871

Margaret WILEY, b- 16 May 1871, c- George W. WILEY, admr., d- $500, e- Joshua MORRISON, Chas. W. STAHL, f-27 May 1871

William HAMILTON, b-19 Jun 1871, c-John K. RHODES, admr., d-$500, e-John K. RHODES, T. M. UTTLEY, f-22 Jul 1871

Jacob J. KLINE, b-10 Jul 1871, c-Mrs. Matilda KLINE, admx., d-$500, e-Chas. RITZ, f-

Gideon YODER, b-15 Jul 1871, c-Joel ZOOK (potter), extr., d- e- f-27 Jul 1871

Noah HARTZLER, b-27 Jul 1871, c-Jonas HARSHBARGER, Christian H. YODER, admrs., d-$2000, e-William HARSHBARGER, Christian MOIST, f-26 Aug 1871

William THOMPSON, b-10 Aug 1871, c-James THOMPSON, W. J. THOMPSON, extrs., d- e- f-

William K. STROUP, b-28 Aug 1871, c-Thomas STROUP, admr., d-$400, e-J. H. JACOBS, D. MUTTHERSBAUGH, f-

Robert FORSYTHE, **b**-7 Oct 1871, **c**-John C. SIGLER, admr., **d**-$25,000, **e**-Ames [Amos] HOOT, Joseph SIGLER, **f**-

R. H. McCLINTIC, **b**-5 Sep 1871, **c**-Isabella McCLINTIC, extx., **d**- **e**- **f**-

S. [Ults???] WILSON, **b**-19 Oct 1871, **c**-John W. WILSON, admr., **d**-$4000, **e**-J. Taylor WILSON, John R. [GERSER?], **f**-16 Nov 1871

Jacob KNEPP, **b**-28 Nov 1871, **c**-Jacob KNEPP, John LUKENS, admrs., **d**-$900, **e**- **f**-22 Dec 1871

Jacob GLICK, **b**-1 Dec 1871, **c**-Samuel A. GLICK, **d**-$1000, **e**-J. M. BULICK, Jonas ZOOK, **f**-29 Dec 1871

Michael BUOY, **b**-26 Dec 1871, **c**-W. H. BRATTON, extr., **d**- **e**- **f**-16 Jan 1872

John ROOP, **b**-30 Dec 1871, **c**-John SWARTZELL, J. T. ROOP, admrs., **d**-$2000, **e**-Wm. M. GILLMORE, Wm. SWINEHART, **f**-6 Jan 1872

Page 237, Frame 255
Elizabeth R. MITCHELL, **b**-29 Dec 1871, **c**-Andrew REED, extr., **d**-no bail, **e**- **f**-22 Jan 1872

John [GARL], **b**-3 Jan 1872, **c**-John HOFFMAN, admr., **d**-$500, **e**-J. L. HIMES, S. BENNER, **f**-5 Jan 1872

Mary ELLIS, **b**-10 Jan 1872, **c**-William S. ELLIS, admr., **d**-$500, **e**-David F. MILLIKEN, Thomas DUNN, **f**-16 Jan 1872

John HOYT, **b**-15 Jan1872, **c**-William CREIGHTON, admr., **d**-$5000, **e**-Jeremiah YEAGER, William MANN, **f**-6 Feb 1872

Mary FORSYTHE, **b**-22 Jan 1872, **c**-Mathew FORSYTHE, admr., **d**-$10,000, **e**-John C. SIGLER, Geo. BLYMYER, **f**-24 Jan 1872

Ellen McVEY, **b**-27 Jan 1872, **c**-John R. McVEY, admr., **d**-$1000, **e**-A. J. ATKINSON, John McVEY, **f**-20 Feb 1872

Jacob ZOOK, **b**-7 Feb 1872, **c**-David J. ZOOK, admr., **d**-$6000, **e**-Jacob ZOOK, Samuel KAUFFMAN, **f**-24 Jul 1872

Mary RHEAM, **b**-2 Mar 1872, **c**-Elias RHEAM, admr., **d**-$500, **e**-Henry STELLER, **f**-

Christian KAUFFMAN, **b**-19 Mar 1872, **c**-Emanuel KAUFFMAN, extr., **d**- **e**- **f**-

R. F. ELLIS, **b**-21 Mar 1872, **c**-Nancy Jane ELLIS, extx., **d**- **e**- **f**-26 Mar 1872

James TURNER, **b**-4 Apr 1872, **c**-Joseph McCULLOCH, **d**-$3000, **e**-Geo. W. ELDER, Geo. W. WILEY, **f**-

Francis KING, **b**-8 Apr 1872, **c**-Jacob MILLER, **d**-$3000, **e**-John HERSHBERGER, Jacob MILLER, **f**-22 May 1872

John A. STERRETT, **b**-10 Apr 1812, **c**-John C. SIGLER, admr., **d**-$20,000, **e**-W. LIND, Wm. RUSSELL, **f**-24 Apr 1872

John STRONG, **b**-20 Apr 1872, **c**-Saml. H. McCOY, Saml. S. STRONG, **d**-$2000, **e**-Wm. GRAHAM, J. S. BROUGHT, **f**-30 Apr 1872

Samuel KLINE, **b**-14 May 1872, **c**-Peter BAREFOOT, admr., **d**-$500, **e**-James N. KLINE, James C. [McNITT?] **f**-21 Jun 1872,

Samuel STAYROOK, **b**-24 May 1872, **c**-Charles BRATTON, Jr., **d**-$2000, **e**-W. H. BRATTON, Jonathan KAUFMAN, **f**-19 Jun 1872

Page 238, Frame 256

John MOIST, **b**-5 Jun 1872, **c**-Jonathan KAUFMAN, Chas. BRATTON, Jr., **d**-$1000, **e**-W. H. BRATTON, Henry HARTZLER, **f**-19 Jun 1872

Rosanna HAZLETT, **b**-7 Jun 1872, **c**-Hannah HAZLETT, extx., **d**- **e**- **f**-27 Jun 1872

Robert WAGNER, **b**-8 Jun 1872, **c**-George WAGNER, **d**-$1000, **e**-Benjamin GILL, William SHILLING, **f**-18 Jun 1872

Samuel KNEPP, **b**-19 Jun 1872, **c**-William A. ORR, **d**-$500, **e**-Reuben KNEPP, **f**-18 Jul 1872

Elias AURAND, **b**-6 Jul 1872, **c**-Roswell E. AURAND, **d**-$1000, **e**-James WREN, Henry ZERBE, **f**-17 Aug 1872

Rev. John THRUSH, **b**-18 Jul 1872, **c**-Rachael THRUSH, extx., **d**-no bail, **e**- **f**-

John DIPPLE, **b**-13 Aug 1872, **c**-Anna Margaret DIPPLE, admx., **d**-$1000, **e**-George PETERS, Henry PETERS, **f**-

Richard GALLAHER, **b**-23 Aug 1872, **c**-D. W. WOODS, extr., **d**-no bail, **e**- **f**-24 Aug 1872

John M. McCOY, **b**-2 Oct 1872, **c**-John R. McCOY, admr., **d**-$500, **e**-T. F. McCOY, **f**-

Jacob CORRELL, **b**-3 Oct 1872, **c**-Elijah MORRISON, extr., **d**- **e**- **f**-22 Oct 1872

John VANZANDT, Sr., **b**-12 Oct 1872, **c**-George W. COULTER, admr., **d**-$500, **e**-Felix NORTON, Jr., William [MATHEWS???], **f**-9 Nov 1872

Susannah STUCKEY, **b**-15 Oct 1872, **c**-Peter BAREFOOT, admr., **d**-$500, **e**-J. C. MAYES, Samuel R. SPANGLER, **f**-

Samuel SHEARER, **b**-19 Oct 1872, **c**-Nancy SHEARER, **d**-$500, **e**-Wm. R. McKEE, John A. SHIMP, **f**-

Daniel EBRIGHT, **b**-30 Oct 1872, **c**-Jacob [KINZEL], **d**-$500, **e**-Samuel FINKEL, Robert MARTIN, **f**-30 Nov 1872

Solomon BYLER, **b**-9 Nov 1872, **c**-Joel ZOOK, extr., **d**- **e**- **f**-25 Nov 1872
Nathaniel WILSON, **b**-30 Nov 1872, **c**-N. C. WILSON, admr., **d**-$4000, **e**-Wm. S. WILSON, Geo. W. ELDER, **f**-29 Dec 1872

Page 239, Frame 257
Catharine STEELY, **b**-16 Jan 1873, **c**-David G. LANTZ, extr., **d**- **e**- **f**-24 Jan 1873
Mary Ann KYLE, **b**-16 Jan 1873, **c**-John B. KYLE, extr., **d**- **e**- **f**-
Jonas MOIST, **b**-22 Jan 1873, **c**-Joseph RONK, extr. **d**- **e**- **f**-10 Feb 1873
John LEPLEY, **b**-25 Jan 1873, **c**-Margaret C. LEPLEY, James BAILEY, admrs., **d**-$2000, **e**-Nathan FRANK, Henry ZERBE, **f**-20 Feb 1873
Samuel S. WOODS, **b**-13 Feb 1873, **c**-David W. WOODS, William H. WOODS, extrs., **d**- **e**- **f**-7 Mar 1873
Jacob STUMPFF, **b**-13 Feb 1873, **c**-William A. ORR, admr., **d**-$1000, **e**-Joseph SNOOK, Jonathan PETER, **f**-12 Mar 1763
Eliel McVEY, **b**-14 Feb 1873, **c**-John R. McVEY, **d**- **e**- **f**-
Henry FIKE, **b**-22 Feb 1873, **c**-Wm. H. FIKE, Geo. HANAWALT, **d**-$1000, **e**-William B. BRATTON, J. C. MILLER, **f**-
Thomas McCORMICK, **b**-27 Feb 1873, **c**-John SETTLE, admr., **d**-$1500, **e**-Saml. H. McCOY, [G. T.?] McCORMICK, **f**-5 Mar 1873
John FOLK, **b**-28 Feb 1873, **c**-Amos FOLK, admr., **d**-$600, **e**-Peter HOFFMAN, Thomas ARNOLD, **f**-21 Mar 1873
John MARKLEY, **b**-17 Mar 1873, **c**-Samuel ROLAND, admr., **d**-$500, **e**-David MUTHERSBAUGH, [N.] W. HOFFMAN, **f**-18 Mar 1873
James BAILEY, **b**-20 Mar 1873, **c**-Joseph CAMPBELLl, extr., **d**- **e**- **f**-14 Apr 1873.
John TEATS, **b**-21 Mar 1873, **c**-Aaron M. SHOOP, **d**-$500, **e**-James M. GILL, Simon YEAGER, **f**-15 Apr 1873
William [HOUENSTINE], **b**-3 Apr 1873, **c**-Albert [STINSBRYER], admr., **d**-$500, **e**-Samuel RICHARD, John F. GIBBONEY, **f**-2 May 1873
Lewis LEOPOLD, **b**-10 Apr 1873, **c**-Geo. A. LEOPOLD, Joseph M. OWENS, **d**-$3000, **e**-Samuel H. McCOY, Lewis OWENS, **f**-12 Apr 1873
Christeena HARTZLER, **b**-14 Apr 1873, **c**-Nicholas HARTZLER, **d**-$8000, **e**-Joshua HARSHBARGER, J. M. DACHENBACH, **f**-

Page 240, Frame 258

Hetty SHEAFFER, b-2 May 1873, **c**-R. G. SHAW, extr., **d**- **e**- **f**-14 May 1873

Rebecca BAREFOOT, **b**-12 May 1873, **c**-Peter BAREFOOT, admr., **d**-$200, **e**-Henry L. CLOSE, James C. McNITT, **f**-30 May 1873

Robert DORMAN, **b**-27 May 1873, **c**-Thompson DORMAN, **d**- **e**- **f**-23 Jun 1873

Augustus STINE, **b**-5 Jun 1873, **c**-Jos. RHODES, James E. STINE, **d**-$2000, **e**-John F. STINE, David RHODES, **f**-24 Jun 1873

Francis M. YINGLING, **b**-9 Jun 1873, **c**-Lydia Elizabeth YINGLING, admr., **d**-$500, **e**-P. M. ORT, Jos. S. WAREAM, **f**-21 Jul 1873

John W. KEARNS, b-8 Mar 1873, **c**-Joseph W. KEARNS, extr., **d**- **e**- **f**-24 Mar 1873

Cina E. McKEE, b-14 Jul 1873, **c**-John McKEE, admr., **d**-$500, **e**-John A. SHIMP, Wm. R. McKEE, **f**-14 Aug 1873

Henry GARVER, b-23 Jul 1873, **c**-Elisha BRATTON, admr., **d**-$5000, **e**-W. H. BRATTON, T. F. McCOY, **f**-28 Aug 1873

William SNOOK, **b**-29 Jul 1873, **c**-Joseph SNOOK, **d**-$3000, **e**-William A. ORR, Jos. S. WAREAM, **f**-27 Aug 1873

E. M. ROBINSON, **b**-29 Jul 1873, **c**-Maj. John BRADY, **d**- **e**- **f**-1 Sep 1873

John YOUTZEY, **b**-4 Aug 1873, **c**-George HOFFMAN, admr., **d**-$500, **e**-Jacob MILLER, McClelland YOUTZEY, **f**-4 Sep 1873

Jacob GAFF, **b**-9 Aug 1873, **c**-David HEISTER, admr., **d**-$500, **e**-W. H. BRATTON, Aaron MOIST, **f**-25 Aug 1873

Benjamin NORTON, Sr., **b**-11 Aug 1873, **c**-Elizabeth E. NORTON, exec., **d**- **e**- **f**-

Henry CLUM, **b**-12 Aug 1873, **c**-Geo. W. ELDER, **d**-$800, **e**-James NICHOLS, Peter CLUM **f**-

Robert INGRAM, **b**-11 Aug 1873, **c**-Larisea T. INGRAM, extx. **d**- **e**- **f**-

C. C. HOOVER, b-15 Aug 1873, **c**-John M. MOHLER, Robert COOPER, extrs., **d**- **e**- **f**-25 Aug 1873

Page 241, Frame 259

James HUGHES, Sr., b-12 Sep 1873, **c**-James HUGHES, Jr., **d**-$500, **e**-A. J. ATKINSON, R. M. KINSLOE, **f**-Time of filing inventory, 25 Sep 1873

John BRINDLE, b-13 Oct 1873, **c**-Josiah BRINDLE, admr., **d**-$300, **e**-A. C. MAYES, Henry [TARBE], **f**-8 Nov 1873

David HOOLEY, **b**-10 Nov 1873, **c**-Christopher HOOLEY, admr., **d**-$30,000, **e**-John D. NAGANEY, Samuel MACLAY, Christian MYERS, **f**-4 Dec 1873

James FORGY, **b**-6 Oct 1873, **c**-Adam LEFFORD, Robt. FORGY, Jr., **d**- **e**- **f**-27 Oct 1873

Ephraim ROSS, b-20 Nov 1873, **c**-John M. MOHLER, **d**-$300, **e**-Henry N. FRANK, Sylvester B. WEBER, **f**-

John KIBE, **b**-6 Dec 1873, **c**-Ira THOMPSON, extr., **d**- **e**- **f**-

Samuel WITHROW, **b**-22 Dec 1873, **c**-Wm. MACKLIN, David WITHROW, W. J. McCARTHY, extrs., **d**- **e**- **f**-17 Jan 1873

Wilbur F. CUBBISON, **b**-28 Jan 1874, **c**-Wm. R. GRAHAM, admr., **d**-$1200, **e**-Saml. H. McCOY, John CLARKE, **f**-16 Feb 1874

George W. FILSON, **b**-13 Feb 1874, **c**-Joseph FILSON, **d**-$300, **e**-Mitchell JONES, David M. [STINE], **f**-14 Feb 1874

Isaac PRICE, **b**-18 Mar 1874, **c**-John B. PRICE, Henry BOOK, extrs., **d**- **e**- **f**-25 Apr 1874

Simon GRO, **b**-27 Mar 1874, **c**-Austin GRO, William YODER, extrs., **d**- **e**- **f**-20 Apr1874

Rebecca B. MATHEWS, b-23 Mar 1874, **c**-John B. SELHEIMER, admr., **d**-$500, **e**-John SELHEIMER, [Jos.] B. McFADDEN, **f**-

Margaret TODD, b-30 Mar 1874, **c**-George SHEAHAN, admr., **d**-$50, **e**-David EISENBISE, John McKEE, **f**-

Joseph ZEIGLER, **b**-21 Apr 1874, **c**-Henry L. CLOSE, **d**-$1000, **e**-Thos. MAYES, C. [WAGINEY], **f**-7 May 1874

Susannah SNORK, **b**-8 May 1874, **c**-Joseph SNORK, **d**-$500, **e**-Mathew McCLINTIC, **f**-Filed 20 Jun 1874

Sarah C. McCORMICK, **b**-9 May 1874, **c**-John SETTLE, admr., **d**-$2000, **e**-Geo. W. ELDER, Jas. T. McCORMICK, **f**-2 Jun 1874

John [AIGHTHERT], **b**-26 May [1874], **c**-Joseph S. [IRCRZORN], **d**-$2000, **e**-William R. GRAHAM, Mitchell JONES, **f**-Filed 20 Jun 1874

* * * * * * Housekeeping note: Column **f**-'s title has now been changed to "Inventory Filed." * * * * * *

Page 242, Frame 260

Charles BELLAMY, **b**-5 Jun 1874, **c**-J. R. WIRT, **d**-$200 **e**-Jos. McFADDEN, W. H. BRATTON, **f**-25 Aug 1874

Robert McFARLAND, b-13 Jun 1874, **c**-David STINE, Jr., extr., **d**- **e**- **f**-8 Jul 1874

Robert HORNING, b-27 Jun 1874, c-Adam LOFFORD, J. R. WIRT, d-e- f-25 Aug 1874

James W. STERRETT, b-7 Jul 1874, c-Margaret W. STERRETT, admx., d-$1500, e-A. P. MANN, William CREIGHTON, f-28 Jul 1874

Nancy HOLDEN, b-7 Jul 1874, c-John HOLT, admr., d-$600, e-W. R. GRAHAM, Mitchell JONES, f-

Joseph BRANNAN, b-20 Jul 1874, c-Thomas H. BRANNAN, admr., d-$200, e-Geo. S. HOFFMAN, John KNISELY, f-17 Aug 1874

Fannie BRENNEMAN, b-6 Aug 1874, c-Abraham BRENNEMAN, Oliver SHIMP, d-$5000, e-Nathan FRANK, Jos. S. WAREAM [looks like WOREAM], f-22 Aug 1874

John REAM, b-15 Aug 1874, c-Isaac REAM, admr., d-$1200, e-William T. [SHORUP], Michael MOYER, f-16 Aug 1874

George KNEPP, b-25 Aug 1874 c-Isaiah KNEPP, Simon KNEPP, admrs., d- e- f-16 Sep 1874

John B. PRICE, b-26 Aug 1874, c-Barbara PRICE, extx., d- e- f-22 Sep 1874

John [MORT], b-4 Sep 1874, c-Henry McAULEY, admr., d-$100, e-Henry McAULEY, D. M. KLINE, f-

Samuel MYERS [looks like an N in both places, but must be an M], b-5 Sep 1814, c-Peter S. MYERS, admr., d-$20,000, e-Andrew SPONAGLE, George SHAHEN, f-7 Nov 1874

Levi ERDLY, b-18 Sep 1874, c-Henry P. ERDLY, extr., d- e- f-

Richeson BRATTON, b-19 Sep 1874, c-Wm. R. BRATTON, Joseph R. BRATTON, d-$2000, e-W. C. BRATTON, Gideon HARSHBERGER, f-20 Oct 1874

F. H. [[BIRUN???]], b-21 Sep 1874, c-Marietta [[BIRUN???]], d-$2000, e-G. R. [[SNYEIGER??]], f-26 Sep 1874

George [SNORZETL] [NOTE: Could it be SWORZETL?], b-21 Sep 1874, c-Henry L. CLOSE, admr., d-$2400, e-[W. T. CLOSE], Peter BAREFOOT, f-15 Oct 1874

Page 243, Frame 261

Charles W. STAHL, b-21 Sep 1874, c-Jos. S. WAREAM, admr., d-$500, e-John A. McKEE, P. M. ORT, f-8 Oct 1874

Frank HAGGERTY, b-28 Sep 1874, c-Jos. S. WAREAM, extr., d- e- f-17 Oct 1874

William CAVANAUGH, b-13 Oct 1874, c-Catherine CAVANAUGH, admx., d-$300, e-Geo. LEGVOLD, Joseph M. OWENS, f-

Casper DULL, b-3 Oct 1874, c-J. J. DULL, D. M. DULL, A. J. DULL, C. P. DULL, extrs., d- e- f-5 Nov 1874

Harrison MANBECK, b-3 Nov 1874, c-John HENRY, extr., d- e- f-14 Nov 1874

Sarah IRWIN, b-26 Oct 1874, c-Abram [STOUFFER?], admr., d-$300, e-Mitchell JONES, f-30 Oct 1874

George SELLERS, b-29 Oct 1874, c-Geo. W. SOUL, admr A.C.T.A., d-$600, e-Joseph McCULLOCH, M. JONES, f-10 Nov 1874

John [HAINES?], Sr., b-27 Dec 1874, c-Mitchell JONES, admr., d-$2000, e-[E. C.] KEARNS, John McDONELL, f-

Lawrence LYNCH, b-22 Dec 1874, c-Samuel AURAND, admr., d-$300, e-Martin ORT, Henry ALBRIGHT f-

Elizabeth [HARRINGER], b-26 Dec 1874, c-Peter BAREFOOT, admr., d-$200, e-Christian NYERS, f-14 Jan 1875

Anna POSTLETHWAIT, b-21 Dec 1874, c-Thos. H. CREAMER, extr., d- e- f-

Edward WEATON, b-7 Jan 1875, c-Jacob S. KING, admr., d-$8000, e-Albert HAZLETT, G. W. CONTNER, f-23 Jan 1875

David KNEPP, b-13 Jan 1875, c-Mrs. Elizabeth KNEPP, admx., d-$300, e-James G. McCOY, Joseph R. BRATTON, f-

James WHARTON, b-19 Jan 1875, c-Daniel S. WHARTON, Benjamin C. WHARTON, extrs., d- e- f-

Sarah BLOOM, b-2 Feb 1875, c-John BAUM, admr., d-$6000, e-William WILLIS, f-2 Feb 1875

Mary Ann ATKIN, b-10 Feb 1875, c-John S. REED, admr., d-Chas. STRATFORD, Jr., John A. McKEE, e- f-

Page 244, Frame 262

Chester CAUGHLING, b-15 Feb [1875], c-Mary J. CAUGHLING, extx., d-no bail, e- f-

Dr. Geo. W. HOOVER, b-22 Feb 1875, c-Mrs. Catharine HOOVER, admx., d-$6000, e-Jas. PARKER, f-

Mary S. KEIFHABER, b-3 Mar 1875, c-F. J. KEIFHABER, John GLASGOW, extrs., d- e-F. G. FRANCISCUS, f-17 Jul 1875

Samuel MURFIN, b-4 Mar 1875, c-Catharine MURFIN, James L. POSTLEWAIT[sic], extrs., d-no bail, e- f-

Henry BOWERSOX, Sr., b-9 Mar 1875, c-William A. ORR, admr., d-$8000, e-James WRAY, John WRAY, f-12 Apr 1875

Ann Barbara [STEFFY], b-13 Mar 1875, c-John William BROCK, extr., d-no bail, e- f-

Samuel D. MOLSON, b-18 Mar 1875, c-Joseph McCULLOCH, admr., d-$1500, e-R. W. PATTON, G. W. [SOULT?], f-12 Apr 1875

Mrs. Rachel WILLS, b-31 Mar 1875, c-James F. WILLS, extr., d-no bail, e- f-

Hiram McCLENAHEN, b-24 Mar 1875, c-Peter BAREFOOT, admr., d-$3000, e-Jas. C. McNITT, Reed SAMPLE, f-

Mary M. BECKLEY, b-7 Apr 1875, c- d- e- f-

James CUPPLES, b-23 Apr 1875, c-Thompson G. BELL, admr., d-$1600, e-Samuel H. McCOY, J. C. SIGLER, f-19 May 1875

Mrs. Elizabeth YODER, b-24 Apr 1875, c-Samuel K. YODER , admr., d-$3000, e-John BAUM, f-18 May 1875

William MITCHELL, b-28 May 1875, c-A. W. MITCHELL, A. P. MITCHELL, extrs., d-$3000, e-A. P. BLYMYER, f-24 Jun 1875

Margaret HOGLE, b-26 May 1875, c-Gilbert HOGLE, extr., d-no bail, e- f-

Isaac WARD, b-3 May 1875, c-Samuel MUSSER, admr., d-$600, e-Wm. MANN, f-8 May 1875

Sarah YODER, b-27 May 1875, c-Yost Z. YODER, extr., d-no bail, e-William R. GRAHAM, f-

Peter SHARP, b-29 May 1875, c-Noah SHARP, d-no bail, e- f-18 Jun 1875

Joel ZOOK, b-25 May 1875, c-C. G. YODER, John D. ZOOK, admrs., d-$2000, e-Simeon K. ZOOK, Jos. H. MACLAY, f-15 Jun 1875

Andrew HAZLETT, b-1 Jun 1875, c-Nicholas HARTZLER, Thomas J. HAZLETT, admrs., d-$5000, e-David [but could be Daniel!] YODER, A. P. BLYMYER, f-12 Jun 1875

William MILLER, b-2 Jun 1875, c-Joseph MILLER, admr., d-$4000, e-Robert W. MILLER, Wm. H. BROUGHT, f-23 Jun 1875

Mrs. Ann SWARTZELL, b-4 Jun 1875, c-Joseph SWARTZELL, admr., d-$20,000, e-John SWARTZELL, Andrew SWARTZELL, f-19 Jun 1875

Robert STERRETT, b-__ Jun 1875, c-H. C. VANZANT, Samuel STERRETT, admrs., d-$600, e-J. W. WILSON, Henry ZERBY, f-10 Jun 1875

John ALEXANDER, b-11 Jun 1875, c-John H. ALEXANDER, admr., d-$1000, e-Reed SAMPLE, Jas C. McNITT, f-29 Jun 1875

Miss Elizabeth KERNY/KENNY?, **b**-16 Jun 1875, **c**-John W. WILSON, admr., **d**-$12.00 or $1200?, **e**-Samuel STERRETT, D. M. CONTNER, **f**-29 Jun 1875

Mathew FORSYTH, **b**-22 Jun 1875, **c**-Horace J. [CULBERTSON], admr., **d**-$1600, **e**-J. C. SIGLER, William RUSSELL, **f**-29 Jun 1875, died 13 Jun 1875, 6:30 p.m. at his residence in Derry Twp.

* * * * *NOTE: At this point, it appears that the time and place of death is being added at the end. Times will be entered on 24-hour basis from now on. The notation "XX:XX M" is somewhat ambiguous. * * * * *

Alexander DORMAN, **b**-28 Jun 1875, **c**-W. C. McCLENAHEN, extr., **d**-no bail, **e**- **f**- Died 8 Jun 1877 [sic, but probably 1875?] at 15:30 at residence in Decatur Twp.

Joseph POSTLETHWAIT, **b**-3 Jul 1875, **c**-Mrs. Louisa POSTLETHWAIT, extx., **d**-no bail, **e**- **f**-Died 26 Jun 1875 at 5:40 at residence in Newton Hamilton

Page 245, Frame 263

Jacob GLASS, **b**-8 Jul 1875, **c**-Levi C. GLASS, admr., **d**-$800, **e**-Jonathan L. BYLER, Jonathan S. ZOOK, **f**-31 Jul 1875, died 28 Jun 1875 at 4:45 at residence in Union Twp

Mrs. Mary J. McNITT, **b**-13 Jul 1875, **c**-Jacob R. ELIOTT, admr., **d**-$6000, **e**-A. HARSHBERGER, A. N. GRAFF, **f**-Died 13:00 at residence in Armagh Twp.

David RHODES, **b**-5 Aug 1875, **c**-Joseph RHODES, admr., **d**-$800, **e**-Peter RHODES, [Levi] RHODES **f**-Died 7 May 1875 at "12. m." at his residence in Oliver Twp.

Susannah FRANCIS, **b**-20 Aug 1875, **c**-Henry YETTER, admr., **d**-$60, **e**-A. HULL, A. YETTER, **f**-Died 26 Jun 1874, Wyanna, Macon, Missouri

Gideon YODER, **b**-23 Aug 1875, **c**-J. S. KING, admr. DBN, **d**-$14,000, **e**-David J. ZOOK, D. H. YODER **f**-

William BALDWIN, **b**-24 Aug 1875, **c**-John C. SHEAHEN, admr., **d**-$500 **e**-Jos. STRODE, James McFARLANE, **f**-Died 23 May 1875, 4:00, residence in Granville Twp.

William B. HOFFMAN, **b**-27 Aug 1875, **c**-Geo S. HOFFMAN, admr., **d**-$6000, **e**-John A. SHIMP, Wm. WILLIS, **f**-Died 14 May 1875, 22:00, residence in Lewistown

Joseph BURKHOLDER, b-28 Aug 1875, **c**-Margaret BURKHOLDER, G. T. SIGLER, admrs., **d**-$4000, **e**-D. M. KLINE, Jac. C. BLYMYER, **f**-Died 11 Aug 1875 at 1:00 at res. in Decatur Twp.

Mary BURLEW, b-3 Sep 1875, **c**-Alexander BURLEW, admr., **d**-$200, **e**-Joshua MORRISON, Henry A. WALTERS, **f**-Died 31 Aug 1875, 9:00 at [looks like "his"?] res. in Lewistown Borough

Christian BROWN, b-4 Sep 1875, **c**-Adam A. BROWN, admr., **d**-$2000, **e**-Wm. W. GILMORE, John M. McAULEY, **f**-Died 29 Sep 1875[sic, suspect clerk's error; probably 29 Aug?] at 9:00 at res. in Armagh Twp. Letters vacated on account the subsequent finding of a last Will & Testament of said Decedent upon Petition of A. A. BROWN to Judges of Orphans' Court 11 Jan 1876 and Letters Testamentary granted to said A. A. BROWN.

Gideon PEACHEY, b-14 Sep 1875, **c**-Jacob N. YODER, extr., **d**-no bail, **e**- **f**-Died 8 Sep 1875 at 4:30 at res. in Menno Twp.

Ellen C. NORTON, b-28 Sep 1875, **c**-J. K. RHODES, extr., **d**-no bail, **e**- **f**-Died 15 Sep 1875 at 11:00 at res. in Newton Hamilton

Samuel ZOOK, b-6 Oct 1875, **c**-Levi GLASS, admr., **d**-$1000, **e**-John HARTZLER, David ZOOK, **f**-Died 4 Oct 1875 at 10:00 at res. in Union Twp.

J. CRISWELL & Ann CRISWELL, b-7 Oct 1875, **c**-J. Vance CRISWELL, extr., **d**-no bail, **e**- **f**-J. CRISWELL died 28 Jun 1874 and Anna CRISWELL died 29 Sep 1875 at res. in McVeytown

Phillip MILLER, b-20 Oct 1875, **c**-Mrs. Elizabeth MILLER, extx., **d**-[no bail], **e**- **f**-Died 19 Sep 1875 at 10:00 in Harrisburg

John HEADINGS, b-22 Oct 1875, **c**-Joseph M. FLEMING, admr., **d**-$1000, **e**-J. S. RAKERD, A. W. CAMPBELL, **f**-Died 9 Oct 1875 at res. in Menno Twp.

Jacob V. SIGLER, b-28 Oct 1875, **c**-J. H. SIGLER, E. P. SIGLER, admrs., **d**-$4000, **e**-Geo. BLYMYER, Jacob C. BLYMYER, **f**-Died 18 Sep 1875 at 12:30 at res. in Derry Twp.

Page 246, Frame 264

John KANAGY, b-12 Nov 1875, **c**-John YODER, admr. D.B.N., **d**-$4000, Jonas YODER, C. B. PEACHEY, **e**- **f**-

E. L. BENEDICT, b-15 Nov 1875, **c**-Margaret U. BENEDICT, Horace J. CULBERTSON, extrs., **d**-no bail, **e**- **f**-Died 7 Nov 1875 at 17:45 at res. in Lewistown. Letters Testamentary on Estate of E. L. BENEDICT as to Mrs. M. U. BENEDICT revoked and vacated at Court 10 Jan 1877. See Orphans' Court Docket No. 13, page 194.

Jacob HEADINGS, b-15 Nov 1875, **c-**Isaac HEADINGS, admr., **d-**$2000, **e-** Dr. Samuel MACKY, John D. NAGNEY, **f-**Died 11 Nov 1875 at 7:00 at res. in Menno Twp.

William DILLON, b-18 Nov 1875, **c-**Milton L. BROSIUS, extr., **d-**no bail, **e- f-**18 Nov 1875, died 29 Sep 1875 at 2:00 at res. in Derry Twp.

J. Ritz BURNS, b-27 Nov 1875, **c-**Peter SPANGLER, admr., **d-**$10,000, **e-**C. RITZ, M. MORRISON, **f-**Died 15 Nov 1875 about 7:00; found dead in Alleghany Mountains 15 miles from Phillipsburg, Centre County, Pa., with gun shot would [sic, probably meant to be wound] in mouth.

Margaret EXTINE, b-10 Dec 1875, **c-**Joseph McCULLOCH, admr., **d-**$500, **e-**R. W. PATTON, J. S. RAKERD, **f-**Died 6 Dec 1875 at 14:00 at res. in Lewistown.

Jane C. HOYT, b-16 Dec 1875, **c-**William CREIGHTON, extr., **d-**no bail, **e- f-**Died 13 Dec 1875 at 10:15 at res. in Brown Twp.

Thomas ROOP, b-22 Dec 1985. **c-**David HARSHBARGER, John H. MITCHELL, admrs., **d-**$6000, **e-**James G. McCOY, W. H. BRATTON, **f-**Died 25 Nov 1875 at 5:00 at res. in Bratton Twp.

Elizabeth LOTZ, b-24 Dec 1875, **c-**John BAUM, extr., **d-**no bail, **e- f-**

Lewis OWENS, b-24 Dec 1875, **c-**Catharine OWENS, extx., **d-**no bail, **e- f-**Died 10 Dec 1875 at 1:00 at res. in Granville Twp.

Wm. DECKER, b-27 Dec 1875, **c-**R. M. JOHNSON, admr., **d-**$1000, **e- f-**

Jacob SALTZMAN, b-1 Jan 1876, **c-**H. C. VANZANDT, admr., **d-**$1000, **e-**Saml. STERRETT, J. K. MUTHERSBAUGH, **f-**Died at 14:00 at res. in Decatur Twp.

Samuel B. HAINES, b-28 Jan 1876, **c-**James S. RAKERD, admr., **d-**$600, **e-**Jos. M. FLEMING, **f-**Died 12 Dec 1875 at 20:00 at res. in Derry Twp.

Christian BROWN, b-11 Jan 1876, **c-**Adam A. BROWN, extr., **d-**no bail, **e- f-**

Isabella P. MacDONALD, b-13 Jan 1876, **c-**A. A. MacDONALD, admr. C. T. A., **d-**$500, **e-**Jos. H. MACLAY, **f-**Died 27 Jan 1875 at 22:00 at res. in Glendower, Virginia.

Page 247, Frame 265

John GOSS, b-28 Jan 1876, **c**-Henry GOSS, Joseph GOSS, admrs., **d**-$1000, **e**-Peter W. HOFFMAN, Abraham GOSS, **f**-Died 4 Dec 1876 [probably 75] at 7:00 at res. in Decatur Twp.

Christian J. PEACHEY, b-11 Feb 1876, **c**-Jonas ZOOK, admr., **d**-$5000, **e**-John PEACHEY, W. A. GILMORE, **f**-Died 6 Feb 1876 at 18:00 at res. in Menno Twp.

Henry BRINDLE, b-24 Feb 1876, **c**-Adam STALEY, admr., **d**-$300, **e**-Amos S. EALY, John M. EALY, **f**-Died 15 Feb 1876 at 9:00 at res. in Union Twp.

Simon WEBBER, b-29 Feb 1876, **c**-Vance C. AURAND, admr., **d**-$1500, **e**-Phillip PEFFER, John AURAND, **f**-Died 16 Feb 1876 at 7:00 at res. in Oliver Twp.

Homer BENEDICT, b-7 Mar 1876, **c**-Mrs. M. U. BENEDICT, admx., **d**-$500, **e**-J. S. RAKERD, F. G. FRANCISCUS, **f**-Died 26 Oct 1871 at 4:00 at res. in Lewistown

Mary OLIVER, b-9 Mar 1876, **c**-John Shannon OLIVER, extr., **d**-no bail, **e**- **f**-Died 24 Feb at 9:30 at res. in Oliver Twp.

John SUNDERLAND, b-9 Mar 1876, **c**-John GLASGOW, Samuel A. SUNDERLAND, **d**-$1000, **e**-J. A. DYSART, J. K. RHODES, **f**-Died 2 Mar 1876 at 21:20 at res. in Wayne Twp.

James PARKER, b-9 Mar 1876, **c**-Mrs. Hannah C. PARKER, extx., **d**-no bail, **e**- **f**-Died 1 Mar 1876 at 4:35 at res. in Lewistown

Joseph MILLIKEN, b-11 Mar 1876, **c**-D. W. WOODS, R. M. PATTON, extrs., **d**-no bail, **e**- **f**-

James SHEERER, b-3 Apr 1876, **c**-Cyrus SHEERER, Joshua HARSHBERGER, extrs., **d**-no bail, **e**- **f**-Died 9 Mar 1876 at 10:00 at res. in Bratton Twp.

Sarah OATENKIRK, b-5 Apr 1876, **c**-William M. HEADINGS, **d**-no bail, **e**- **f**-Died 21 Mar 1876 at 11:00 at res. in Menno Twp.

John STUMPFF, b-6 Apr 1876, **c**-Wm. A. ORR, admr., **d**-$50, **e**-J. K. RHODES, **f**-Died 5 Feb 1876 at 24:00 at res. in Centre[sic] County

Thomas POSTLETHWAIT, b-11 Apr 1876, **c**-Theo. H. [CREMER], admr. C. T. A., **d**-Jac. S. SHADE, J. SMUCKER, **e**- **f**-Died in 1862

Robert W. SHAW, b-15 Apr 1876, **c**-Emma M. SHAW, admx., **d**-$1000, **e**-Henry ZERBE, **f**-Died 4 Apr 1876 at 16:00 at res. in Derry Twp.

Elizabeth HOOLEY, b-15 Apr 1876, **c**-Martha HOOLEY, admx., **d**-no bail, **e**-D. R. GRAHAM **f**-

Isaac YODER, b-17 Apr 1876, c-Christ. L. YODER, Solomon L. YODER, admrs., d-no bail, e- f-5 Apr 1876 at 10:00 at res. in Union Twp.

Mrs. Sarah SIGLER, b-17 Apr 1876, c-H. P. SIGLER, admr., d-$4000, e-Andrew SWARTZELL, f-Died 10 Apr 1876 at 14:00 at res. in Brown Twp.

Elizabeth MILLIKEN, b-1 May 1876, c-D. W. WOODS, d-no bail, e-A. P. BLYMYER f-

George STRUNK, b-9 May 1876, c-Henry STRUNK, John SHADLE, d-no bail, e- f-Died 13 Apr 1876 at 4:00 at res. in Brown Twp.

Zachariah ROTHROCK, b-20 May 1876, c-John E. McCORD, admr., d-$300, e-John ROTHROCK, Joseph CLINGER, f-Died 5 Mar 1876 at 8:00 at res. in Oliver Twp.

Margaret STONEROAD, b-5 Jun 1876, c-Ella M. PATTERSON, admx., d-no bail, e- f-Died 29 May 1876 at 19:30 at res. in Lewistown

F. A. [NEWPERT], b-9 Jun 1876, c-John BAUM, extr., d-no bail, e- f-Died 1 Jun 1876 at 2:00 at res. in Lewistown

Richard ALLISON, b-22 Jun 1876, c-R. K. ALLISON, David ALLISON, extrs., d-no bail, e- f-Died 1 Jun 1876 and 16:00 at res. in Menno Twp.

Page 248, Frame 266

Catharine KURTZ, b-26 Jun 1876, c-Eli KURTZ, extr., d-no bail, e- f-Died 21 Jun 1876 at 11:00 at res. in Menno Twp.

William MONTGOMERY, b-7 Jul 1876, c-Sophia MONTGOMERY, admx., d-$600, e-John BAUM, R. H. MONTGOMERY, f-Died 11 Jun 1876 at 10:00 at res. in Lewistown

William DECKER, Sr., b-13 Jul 1876, c-R. M. JOHNSON, admr. D.B.N., d-$300, e-J. K. RHODES, J. S. RAKERD, f-

B. J. SILLS, b-13 Jul 1876, c-Sarah A. SILLS, admx., d-$600, e-John SWARTZELL, T. F. McCOY, f-Died 17 Jun 1876 at 11:00 at res. in Lewistown

Phillip WATTS, b-20 Jul 1876, c-Jesse W. HORTON, admr., d-$300, e-Jno. B. SELHEIMER, Jos. L. ROPER f-Died 26 May 1876 at res. in Union Twp.

G. V. MITCHELL, b-28 Jul 1876, c-Lizzie R. MITCHELL, admx., d-$1200, e-Robt. TAYLOR, John HENRY, f-Died 21 Jul 1876 at 14:00 at res. in Brown Twp.

William HARPER, b-19 Aug 1876, c-John McDOWELL, extr., d-no bail, e- f-Died 15 Aug 1876 at 23:00 at Wm. SWINEHART's Hotel in Reedsville, PA

John S. YOUNG, **b**-22 Aug 1876, **c**-Christian B. PEACHEY, admr., **d**-$300, **e**-A. W. CAMPBELL, Jonas YODER, **f**-[Died] 5 Aug 1876 at 4:00 at res. in Union Twp.

Daniel EISENBISE, **b**-29 Aug 1876, **c**-Jacob GOOD, extr., **d**-no bail, **e**- **f**-Died 24 Aug 1876 at 18:00 at res. in Lewistown

Annie LANTZ, **b**-30 Aug 1876, **c**-David G. LANTZ, extr., **d**-no bail, **e**- **f**-Died 30 Jul 1876 at 7:30 at res. in Menno Twp.

William W. GILMORE, **b**-26 Sep 1876, **c**-R. M. GILMORE, Saml. [WILLS], extrs., **d**-no bail, **e**- **f**-Died 31 Aug 1876 at 5:00 at res. in Brown Twp.

Simon YEAGER, **b**-2 Oct 1876, **c**-J. M. YEAGER, extr., **d**-no bail, **e**- **f**-Died 29 Sep 1876 at 19:00 at res. in Derry Twp.

George DOBSON, **b**-3 Oct 1876, **c**-Mrs. Hannah DOBSON, admx., **d**-$150, **e**-Joseph KNEPP, Henry S. DOBSON, **f**-Died 30 Aug 1876 at 15:00 at res. in Armagh Twp.

William MANN, **b**-4 Oct 1876, **c**-Mrs. Mary J. MANN, admx., **d**-$500, **e**-Thos. P. COCHRAN, Geo. W. ELDER, **f**-Died 17 May 1876 at about 11:00 on the Ohio River Steamboat Disaster

Thomas N. BULICK, **b**-6 Oct 1876, **c**-Jno. M. BULICK, admr., **d**-$500, **e**-Jas. M. BULICK, Jos. [probably Jas.] S. RAKERD, **f**-Died 18 Feb 1874[sic] at 2:00 at res. in Union Twp.

John [HERSHBERGER], **b**-14 Oct 1876, **c**-[Jno.] MILLER, extr., **d**-no bail, **e**- **f**-Died 27 Sep 1876 at 15:00 at res. in Bratton Twp.

Salome BYLER, **b**-25 Oct 1876, **c**-Joel ZOOK, extr., **d**-no bail, **e**- **f**-Died 5 Oct 1876 at 19:00 at res. in Union Twp.

A. W. McCORMICK, **b**-25 Oct 1876, **c**-Geo. T. McCORMICK, admr., **d**-$400, **e**-John C. ROSS, W. C. BRATTON, **f**-Died 16 Sep 1876 at 1:00 at res. in Altoona P.R.R. Track.

Page 249, Frame 267

Peter F. LOOP, **b**-30 Oct 1876, **c**-Elizabeth A. LOOP, Geo. BATES, admrs., **d**-$500, **e**-T. H. VAN VALZAH, S. J. BRISBON, **f**-Died

Cyrus HOPPLE, **b**-13 Nov 1876, **c**-Sarah HOPPLE, admx., **d**-$600, **e**-J. S. WAREAM, J. S. [GARRETT], **f**-Died 13 Sep 1874 at 13:30 at res. in Greenville Twp.

Shem H. YODER, **b**-21 Nov 1876, **c**-Jacob D. ZOOK, Erie[sic] YODER, admrs., **d**-$1600, **e**-Saml. B. WILLS, Samuel YODER, **f**-Died 10 Nov 1876 at 13:00 at res. in Menno Twp.

James McCORD, b-28 Nov 1876, **c**-John A. McKEE, admr., **d**-$50, **e**-Jos. S. WAREAM, P. M. ORT, **f**-

Hugh KENNEDY, b-5 Dec 1876, **c**-John W. WILSON, admr., **d**-$2500, **e**-Christian H. YODER, Joseph W. FLEMING, **f**-Died 23 Nov 1876 at 21:00 at res. in Menno Twp.

Susannah DUNMIRE, b-2 Dec 1876, **c**-Joseph DUNMIRE, extr., **d**-no bail, **e**- **f**-Died 25 Aug 1876 at "12 M" at res. in Oliver Twp.

Anna C. SMITH, b-5 Dec 1876, **c**-Jacob KRISE, admr., **d**-$50, **e**-Irvin WILKEY, Edward REED, **f**-

Catharine MOIST, b-7 Dec 1876, **c**-Wm. R. BRATTON, admr., **d**-$1000, **e**-Wm. C. BRATTON, W. H. BRATTON, **f**-Died 30 Nov 1876 at "12 M." at res. in Oliver Twp.

Mary KNEPP, b-15 Dec 1765, **c**-Wm. A. ORR, R. E. AURAND, extrs., **d**-no bail, **e**- **f**-

Henry ZERBE, b-22 Dec 1876, **c**-Hannah M. ZERBE, Charles A. ZERBE, admrs., **d**-$16,000, **e**-Amos HOYT, John W. SHAW, **f**-Died 16 Dec 1876 at 9:00 at res. in Lewistown

John ROSS, b-28 Dec 1876, **c**-John ATKINSON, admr., **d**-$2000, **e**-Wm. [MACKLIN], David STINE, Jr., **f**-Died 13 Dec 1876 at 14:00 at res. in McVeytown.

Eliza ROSENBOROUGH, b-5 Jan 1877, **c**-Wm. H. SWANZEY, admr., **d**-$100, **e**-Saml. M. WILLIAMS, J. English WEST, **f**-Died 29 Nov 1876 at ___ at res. in McVeytown

Saml. B. KING, b-16 Jan 1877, **c**-Joel ZOOK, extr., **d**- **e**- **f**-Died 7 Dec 1876 at 6:00 at res. in Union Twp.

Wm. B. STRUNK, b-6 Jan 1877, **c**-Saml. H. McCOY, admr., **d**-$600, **e**-Owen OWENS, Jos. M. OWENS, **f**-Died 17 Nov 1877 and 1:00 at res. in Granville Twp.

Benjamin HOW, b-6 Feb 1877, **c**-Daniel S. ZOOK, extr., **d**-no bail, **e**- **f**-Died 3 Feb 1877 at 5:00 at res. in Derry Twp.

Achsah WERTZ, b-10 Feb 1877, **c**-Samuel H. McCOY, admr., **d**-$1400, **e**-J. J. BROUGHT, Wm. MINEHART, **f**-Died 4 Feb 1877 at 23:00 at res. in Granville Twp.

W. R. McDOWELL, b-26 Feb 1877, **c**-J. M. SHAVER, admr., **d**-$2000, **e**-E. MORRISON, Jonathan McDOWELL, **f**-Died 10 Feb 1877 at 23:00 at res. in Wayne Twp.

Page 250, Frame 268

Joseph R. HANAWALT, b-3 Mar 1877, **c-**M. F. H. KINSEL, extr., **d-**no bail, **e- f-**Died 14 Feb 1877 at 14:00 at res. in Oliver Twp.

John DREES, b-20 Mar 1877, **c-**Joseph D. ULSH, Jacob W. DREES, extrs., **d-**no bail, **e- f-**Died 13 Mar 1877 at res. in Decatur Twp.

John SHADE, b-22 Mar 1877, **c-**B. F. SHADE, John GLASGOW, admrs., **d-**$3000, **e-**J. T. CALDWELL, J. K. RHODES, **f-**Died 8 Mar 1877 at 15:00 at res. in Wayne Twp.

Charles M. BELL, b-28 Mar 1877, **c-**Peter BAREFOOT, extr., **d-**no bail, **e- f-**Died 22 Feb 1877 at 7:00 at res. in Armagh Twp.

George BROUGHT, b-31 Mar 1877, **c-**John HAMILTON, admr., **d-**$50, **e-**John A. McKEE, A. T. HAMILTON, **f-**

Elizabeth LANE, b-5 Apr 1877, **c-**William H. SUNDERLAND, extr., **d-**no bail, **e- f-**Died 1 Apr 1877 at 6:00 at res. in Wayne

William F. STROUP, b-11 Apr 1877, **c-**Jesse W. HORTON, admr., **d-**$50, **e-**J. W. FLEMING, E. C. BIGLOW, **f-**Died 25 Feb 1877 at 5:30 at res. in Belleville, Pa.

Mrs. Sarah R. ROSS, b-19 Apr 1877, **c-**A. B. ROSS, Geo. H. MACKLIN, admrs., **d-**$600, **e-**Robert FORGY, Jr., J. B. SELHEIMER, **f-**Died 1 Jan 1876 at res. in McVeytown [NOTE: Next entry was 1876 corrected to 1877]

Alexander HAMILTON, b-24 Apr 1877, **c-**Geo. W. BOWERSOX, admr., **d-**$1300, **e- f-**Died 27 Mar 1877 at 17:00 at res. in Wayne

James BELL, b-25 Apr 1877, **c-**Peter BAREFOOT, admr., **d-**$50, **e-**J. R. ELLIOTT, J. C. McNITT, **f-**Died 1 Jul 187[5] at res. C. M. BELL in Armagh Twp.

Mrs. Elizabeth STRALEY, b-14 May 1877, **c-**Peter BAREFOOT, admr., **d-**$2000, **e-**J. R. ELLIOTT, Reed SAMPLE, **f-**Died 8 May 1877 at res. in Armagh Twp.

Ann M. McCORMICK, b-18 May 1877, **c-**Geo. T. McCORMICK, admr., **d-**$300, **e-**John BAUM, W. S. SETTLE, **f-**Died 5 Dec 1876 at 18:30 in
—

George MITCHELL, b-21 May 1877, **c-**John ATKINSON, admr., **d-**$4000, **e-**C. P. DULL, E. CONRAD, **f-**Died 6 May 1877 at 2:00 at rs. in Bratton Twp.

Adam H. SUNDERLAND, b-19 May 1877, **c-**Hannah M. SUNDERLAND, extx, **d-**no bail, **e- f-**Died 26 Apr 1877 at 23:15 at res. in Oliver Twp.

Eliza B. FLEMING, **b**-23 May 1877, **c**-Saml. B. WILLS, extr., **d**-no bail, **e**- **f**-Died 5 May 1877 at 22:00 at res. in Union Twp.

Page 251, Frame 269
John CUTMAN, **b**-10 Jul 1877, **c**-Mortimer WHITWORTH, admr., **d**-$300, **e**-W. H. SWANZEY, W. S. SETTLE, **f**-ied 7 Apr 1877 at 19:00 at res. in Oliver Twp.
Gabriel ALLEN, **b**-3 Aug 1877, **c**-Martha A. ALLEN, admx., **d**-$400, **e**-Levi ALLEN, John McKEE, **f**-Died 20 Jul 1877 at 13:00 at res. in Oliver Twp.
George WOODS, **b**-10 Aug 1877, **c**-John BAUM, extr., **d**-no bail, **e**- **f**-Died 6 Aug 1877 at 5:00 at res. in Derry Twp.
Michael BOWERSOX, **b**-16 Aug 1877, **c**-Henry BOWERSOX, John M. BOWERSOX, admrs., **d**-$2000, **e**-William STUMPFF, Reuben SHAWVER, **f**-Died 26 Jul 1877 at 2:30 at res. in Decatur Twp.
Mrs. Ann BROWN, **b**-4 Sep 1877, **c**-Dr. Saml. MACLAY, extr., **d**-no bail, **e**- **f**-Died 24 Aug 1877 at 23:00 at res. in Armagh Twp.
Jacob STINE, **b**-26 Sep 1877, **c**-Cyrus STINE, Jno. F. STINE, admrs., **d**-$2000, **e**-Benjamin GILL, James E. STINE, **f**-Died 23 Aug 1877 at 9:00 at res. in Oliver Twp.
Jno. BURKHOLDER, **b**-26 Sep 1877, **c**-Jacob McCAULY, extr., **d**-no bail, **e**- **f**-Died 22 Sep 1877 at 19:00 at res. in Decatur Twp.
Mrs. Sarah SIGLER, **b**-12 Oct 1877, **c**-Geo. T. SIGLER, extr., **d**-no bail, **e**- **f**-Died 31 Aug 1877 at 15:00 at res. in Decatur Twp.
G. W. WOODS, **b**-15 Oct 1877, **c**-Mary Ellen WOODS, extx., **d**-no bail, **e**- **f**-Died 25 Sep 1877 at 17:20 in Borough of Lewistown
Augusta M. WEAVER, **b**-17 Oct 1877, **c**-S. Percy McREA, admr., **d**-$2000, **e**-C. C. MILLER, Theo. MAHER, **f**-Died 22 Aug 1877 at 11:30 at res. in McVeytown
Peter RHODES, **b**-15 Oct 1877, **c**-J. K. RHODES, admr., **d**-$600, **e**-Wm. A. ORR, David HEISTER, **f**-Died 29 Sep 1877 at 8:00 at res. in Bratton Twp.
Wm. J. THOMPSON, **b**-20 Oct 1877, **c**-Ner THOMPSON, admr., **d**-$1500, **e**-M. R. THOMPSON, Peter BAREFOOT, **f**-Died 16 Sep 1877 at 22:00 at res. in Sunberry, Snyder Co.
Joseph PRICE, **b**-20 Oct 1877, **c**-Sarah J. PRICE, admx., **d**-$200, **e**-William PRICE, W. S. CUSTER, **f**-Died 26 Mar 1877 at 19:30 at res. in Lewistown

William A. TAYLOR, b-22 Oct 1877, **c-**Samuel H. McCOY, admr., **d-**$500, **e-**J. K. RHODES, George SETTLE, **f-**Died 12 Oct 1877 at 20:00 at res. in Bratton Twp.

Thomas Augustus WORRALL, b-8 Nov 1877, **c-**Jno. BAUM, T. F. McCOY, extrs., **d-**no bail, **e- f-**Died 30 Oct 1877 at 23:00 [could be 11:00] at res. in Lewistown Borough

William CLAY, b-20 Nov 1877, **c-**Ann CLAY, admx., **d-**$300, **e- f-**Died 29 Mar 1873 at 9:00 at res. in Granville Twp.

Page 252, Frame 270

James M. TAYLOR, b-10 Dec 1877, **c-**Jacob CASNER, admr., **d-**$150, **e-**Jeremiah KNEPP, J. K. RHODES, **f-**Died 4 Nov 1877 at 21:00 in Wayne Twp.

Mary [YEANEK or ZEANEK?], b-11 Dec 1877, **c-**D. M. KLINE, extr., **d-**no bail, **e- f-**Died 1 Nov 1877 at 10:00 at res. in Derry Twp.

Francis GOCHNAUR, b-14 Dec 1877, **c-**Henry PRINTZ, admr., **d-**$300, **e-**Chas. PRICE, H. E. PRINTZ, **f-**Died 29 Mar 1877 at 6:30 at res. in Juniata Co., Pa.

John McNITT, b-7 Jan 1878, **c-**A. D. McNITT, J. S. McNITT, extrs., **d-**no bail, **e- f-**Died 28 Dec 1877 at 18:30 at res. in Armagh Twp.

William MORRISON, b-7 Jan 1878, **c-**T. M. UTTLEY, admr., **d-**$200, **e-**T. F. McCOY, **f-**Died 22 Sep 1877 at ___ at res. in Lewistown

R. MARTIN, b-22 Jan 1878, **c-**H. J. WALTERS, extr., **d-**no bail **e- f-**Died 22 Jan 1878 at 8:45 at res. in Lewistown.

Archibald VANDYKE, b-23 Jan 1878, **c-**Jno. GLASGOW, Archibald VANDYKE, extrs., **d-**no bail, **e- f-**Died 23 Jan 1878 at 16:00 at res. in Oliver Twp.

Daniel BEARLEY, b-29 Jan 1878, **c-**R. H. McCLINTOC, admr., **d-**$100, **e-**J. S. RAKERD, Jos. W. FLEMING, **f-**Died 23 Jun 1877 at about 9:00 at res. in Lewistown

George ELLIS, b-25 Feb 1878, **c-**John M. SHADLE, admr., **d-**$1000, **e-**LaFayett WEBB, Henry FRANK, **f-**Died 2 Apr 1878 at about 18:00 in Kansas.

Eliza McCURDY, b-6 Mar 1878, **c-**T. F. McCOY, extr., **d-**no bail, **e- f-**Died 7 Dec 1877 at res. in Clearfield Co.

David F. MILLIKEN, b-6 Mar 1878, **c-**John HENRY, admr., **d-**$3000, **e-**E. C. KYLE, H. J. TAYLOR, **f-**Died 18 Jan 1878 at 4:00 at res. in Brown Twp.

Mary BORLAND, b-7 Mar 1878, c-Nicholas HARTZLER, extr., d-no bail, e- f-Died 26 Feb 1878 at 19:00 at res. in Allenville

Eliza McCORD, b-25 Mar 1878, c-Saml. H. McCOY, extr., d-no bail, e-f-Died 13 Mar 1878 at 17:00 at res. in McVeytown

Elizabeth SIGLER, b-29 Mar 1878, c-Johnston SIGLER, admr., d-$1000, e-John A. McKEE, C. S. [HUBLERT?], f-Died 9 Nov 1877 in Wisconsin

John KAUFFMAN, b-9 Apr 1878, c-Christian KAUFFMAN, Sarah KAUFFMAN, extrs., d-no bail, e- f-Died 30 Mar 1878 at 6:00 at res. in Union Twp.

Wm. R. MORRISON, b-11 Apr 1878, c-Mary K. MORRISON, admx., d-$800, e-R. M. KINSLOE, f-Died 12 Mar 1878 at 6:00 at res. in Wayne Twp.

W. B. PRICE, b-22 Apr 1878, c-Joseph McCULLOCH, d-$2000, e-R. W. PATTON, f-Died 27 Oct 1876 at res. in Granville Twp.

Catharine GLICK, b-23 May 1878, c-John PEACHEY, extr., d- e- f-Died 19 May 1878 at 1:00 at res. in Menno Twp.

Henry HARTZLER, b-18 Jun 1878, c-David HARSHBARGER, extr., d-e- f-Died 11 Jun 1878 at 2:00 at res. in Bratton Twp.

Priscilla BRIGGS, b-16 Jul 1878, c-[James SWISHER], admr., d-$100 [this area is a little muddled; don't live or die by it], e-Wm. C. VINES, Robt. B. FORSYTH, f-

John ALEXANDER, b-19 Jul 1878, c-R. M. TAYLOR, admr., d-$6000 e-H. F. TAYLOR, Saml. McWILLIAMS, J. P. TAYLOR, f-Died 11 Jul 1878 at 7:00 at res. in Brown Twp.

R. N. [possibly U.?] JACOB, b-25 Jul 1878, c-D. W. WOODS, d-$5000, e-Amos HOOT, T. F. McCOY, f-Died 21 Jul 1878 at 10:00 at res. in Lewistown

Page 253, Frame 271

Jonathan BYLER, b-13 Aug 1878, c-Eli BYLER, admr., d-$6500, e-H. P. TAYLOR, f-Died 6 Aug 1878 at 21:00 at res. in Menno Twp.

Wm. CHESTNUT, b-14 Aug 1878, c-John BAUM, admr., d-$200, e-Joseph McFADDEN, f-Died 6 Nov 1876; found on the mountain with gun shot wound [Dead]

Felix NORTON, b-22 Aug 1878, c-L. V. POSTLETHWAIT, admr., d-$500, e-S. D. POSTLETHWAIT, f-Died 16 Aug 1878 at 12 M [?], at res. in Newton Hamilton

Mary SEIBERT, **b**-4 Sep 1878, **c**-R. H. WHARTON, admr., **d**-$500 **e**-F. D. BEYER, Wm. HARTZLER, **f**-Died 8 Nov 1876 at 19:00 at res. in McVeytown

Adam SEIBERT, **b**-4 Sep 1878, **c**-R. H. WHARTON, admr., **d**-$500, **e**-F. D. BYER, Wm. HARTZLER, **f**-Died 11 Aug 1878 at 8:00 while on a visit in Kansas

Isaac BRUSH, **b**-26 Aug 1878, **c**-Jno. W. WILSON, extr., **d**-no bail, **e**- **f**-Died 30 Jun 1878 at 19:00 at res. in Menno Twp.

Thomas JOHNSTON, **b**-12 Sep 1878, **c**-S. B. STINE, H. J. JOHNSTON, extrs., **d**- **e**- **f**-Died 31 Aug 1878 at 5:25 at res. in Wayne Twp.

Silas ALEXANDER, **b**-26 Sep 1878, Thomas R. ALEXANDER, extr., **c**- **d**- **e**- **f**-Died 19 Sep 1878 at 10:30 at res. in Union Twp.

Benjamin NORTON, **b**-20 Sep 1878, **c**-[Jacob] [ink blot in middle of his name] NORTON, **d**-$1000, **e**-Jno. K. RHODES, **f**-Died 18 Aug 1878 at 15:00 at the Newton Hamilton Camp Grounds

Elisha BRATTON, **b**-1 Oct 1878, **c**-Jos. R. BRATTON, W. C. BRATTON, extrs., **d**-no bail, **e**- **f**-Died 18 Sep 1878 at 5:00 at res. in McVeytown Borough

Samuel COMFORT, **b**-7 Oct 1878, **c**-A. W. PORTER, admr., **d**-$600, **e**-W. C. PORTER, Nathan KENNEDY, **f**-Died 10 Aug 1878 at 15:00 at res. in Lewistown Borough

William HEDDINGS, **b**-23 Oct 1878, **c**-Jonathan PEACHEY, extr., **d**- **e**-**f**-Died 16 Oct 1878 at 17:00 at res. in Union Twp.

Susan CHESTER, **b**-24 Oct 1878, **c**-J. R. ELLIOTT, extr., **d**-no bail, **e**- **f**-Died 14 Oct 1878 at 23:30 at res. in Armagh Twp.

John CULP, **b**-30 Oct 1878, **c**-Mary KULP[sic], admx., **d**-$500, **e**- R. H. McCLINTIC, **f**-Died 19 Oct 1878 at 13:30 at res. in Lewistown Borough

Elizabeth Ann LOOP, **b**-9 Nov 1878, **c**-Silas WRIGHT, extr., **d**- **e**- **f**-Died 6 Nov 1878 at 21:28 at res. in Lewistown Borough

Elizabeth HESS. **b**-20 Nov 1878, **c**-Samuel HESS, admr., **d**-$500 **e**-Joseph McFADDEN, Geo. S. HOFFMAN, **f**-Died 30 Oct 1878 at 8:30 at res. in Lewistown Borough

John ROBB, **b**-23 Nov 1878, **c**-Jno. [ROBERTSON], admr. D.B.N., **d**-$1800, **e**- **f**-

William McCLELLAN, **b**-27 Nov 1878, **c**-J. W. WILSON, extr., **d**- **e**- **f**-Died 24 Nov 1878 at 2:00 at res. in Menno Twp.

Robert McNITT, **b**-29 Nov 1878, **c**-Peter BAREFOOT, extr., **d**- **e**- **f**-Died 18 Nov 1878 at 16:00 at res. in Armagh Twp.

Samuel HEMPHILL, b-30 Nov 1878, c-Mary Ann HEMPHILL, extx., d- e- f-Died 15 Jul 1878 at 12 M. at res. in Lewistown Borough

Jane McCLELLAN, b-4 Dec 1878, c-R. P. MACKY, Jr., Jos. H. [MACKY], extrs., d- e- f-Died 18 May 1878 at 4:00 at res. in Menno Twp.

Harriet J. MARK, b-16 Dec 1878, c-W. W. MARK, admr., d-$8000, e-Jno. W. SHAW, Chas. A. ZERBE, f-Died 8 Dec 1878 at 19:00 on steps of Presbyterian Church on Brown Street, Lewistown Borough

Joseph ALEXANDER, b-17 Dec 1878, c-N. B. ALEXANDER, admr., d-$2000, e-N. A. ELDER, J. NORTH, f-Died 26 Oct 1878 at 3:00 at res. of his son N. B. in Juniata Co.

Daniel KING, b-20 Dec 1878, c-Jacob S. KING, Jonas Y. KING, extrs., d- e- f-Died 15 Dec 1878 at 15:00 at res. in Menno Twp.

Sevor [probably something like Sevier?] YODER, b-20 Dec 1878, c-Solomon ZOOK, admr., d-$500, e-Jac. S. KING, L. Z. YODER, f-Died 16 Dec 1878 at 7:00 at res. in Union Twp.

Page 254, Frame 272

Nancy McDONALD, b-25 Dec 1878, c-Samuel B. STINE, admr., d-$200, e-Geo. W. COULTER, David R. STINE, f-Died...

N. B. ALEXANDER, b-27 Dec 1878, c-W. R. and R. _____, extrs., d-no bail, e- f-Died on 19 Dec 1878 at 1:00 at res. in Union Twp.

George SHEHAN, b-9 Jan 1879, c-Robert F. CUPPLES, admr., d-$300, e-James L. GOODWIN, Martin ORT, f-Died 25 Dec 1878 at 12 M. at res. in Granville Twp.

Adam PETER, b-10 Jan 1879, c-Wm. F. [SPETH], d-$100, e-W. S. SETTLE, Wm. BRATTON, A. BRATTON, f-Died 17 May 1877 at unknown hour at res. in Lewistown Borough

Jeremiah GROVE, b-11 Jan 1879, c-Mary M. GROVE, A. B. McNITT, admrs., d-$400, e-O. P. SMITH, W. S. SETTLE, f-Died 22 Dec 1878 at 6:20 at res. in Armagh Twp.

Catharine BECK, b-11 Jan 1879, c-John D. MILLER, extr., d-no bail, e- f-Died 21 Feb 1879 [sic] at 21:00 at res. in Wayne Twp.

Andrew MABEN, b-30 Jan 1879, c-L. M. [FUNT], admr. CTA, d-$100, e-W. C. McCLENAHEN, Peter BAREFOOT, f-Died 28 Dec 1878 at 12:00 M at res. in Armagh Twp.

Jonathan DETWEILER, b-31 Jan 1879, c-Solomon Z. DETWILER, extr., d- e- f-Died 25 Jan 1879 at 20:00 at res. in Menno Twp.

William GIBBS, b-4 Feb 1879, c-Catharine GIBBS, admx., d-$100, e-Jno.
S. GARRETT, S. A. MARKS, f-Died 27 Jan 1879 at 18:30 at [Selin's]
Grove by railroad–accident

Joseph HAFFLY, b-13 Feb 1879, c-Jos. CAMPBELL, Miles HAFFLY,
extrs., d- e- f-Died 7 Feb 1879 at 19:00 at res. in Union Twp.

Peter A. BLACK, b-19 Feb 1879, c-Andrew F. BLACK, admr., d-$400,
e-Reed SAMPLE, J. C. McNITT, f-Died 19 Jan 1879 at 17:00 at res.
in Armagh Twp.

John FILSON, b-21 Feb 1879, c-John SWARTZELL, extr., d- e- f-Died
18 Feb 1789 at 21:00 at res. in Armagh Twp.

Francis MORGAN, b-24 Feb 1879, c-Nicholas HARTZLER, John
MORGAN, admrs., d-$4000, e-George WEILER, Jno. F.
KAUFFMAN, f-Died 13 Feb 1879 at 8:00 at res. in Menno Twp.

Henry J. HINEMAN, b-4 Mar 1879, c-Mary M. HINEMAN, admx., d-
$100, e-William W. FEAR, f-Died 8 Feb 1879 at 11:30 at junction of
PRR & Lewistown [?Division?], killed coupling cars

James I. COTTLE, b-7 Mar 1879, c-Roseana COTTLE, Jesse J.
COTTLE, extrs., d- e- f-Died 12 Jun 1878 at 22:00 at res. in Armagh
Twp.

John SETTLE, b-7 Mar 1879, c-W. S. SETTLE, admr., d-$500, e-Jno. S.
GARRETT, T. F. McCOY, Jno. A. McKEE, f-Died 28 Feb 1879 at ___
at res. in Oliver Twp.

William HARDY, b-8 Mar 1879, c-Wm. M. HARDY, admr., d-$5000, e-
John JENKINS, f-Died 18 Jan 1879 at 23:00 at res. in McVeytown

Isabella [BLANCHER], b-11 Mar 1879, c-S. A. McCLINTIC, extr., d- e-
f-Died 2 Mar 1879 at 12:00 M at res. in Armagh Twp.

Jacob HOOVER, b-17 Mar 1879, c-Samuel E. HOOVER, extr., d- e- f-
Died 12 Mar 1879 at 11:30 at res. in Derry Twp.

Jacob SHARER, b-19 Mar 1879, c-J. W. SHARER, J. M. SHARER,
extrs., d- e- f-Died 12 Mar 1879 at 22:00 at res. in Wayne Twp.

Michael SHILLING, b-1 Apr 1879, c-A. M. INGRAM, d-$150, e-J. H.
MILLER, Jas. WRAY, f-Died 4 Mar 1879 at 23:00 at res. in Decatur
Twp.

Page 255, Frame 273

R. C. CRAIG, b-3 Apr 1879, c-Francis C. CRAIG, admr., d-$500, e-J. C.
CRAIG, M. D. CRAIG, f-Died 26 Mar 1879 at 8:45 at res. in Newton
Hamilton, Pa.

Eliza BUTLER, b-5 Apr 1879, **c**-Geo. W. ELDER, extr., **d**-no bond, **e**- **f**-Died 1 Apr 1879 at 17:00 at res. in Lewistown

Mary S. WILSON, b-14 Apr 1879, **c**-John W. WILSON, admr., **d**-$3000, **e**-John HENRY, J. W. FLEMING, **f**-Died 22 Sep 1878 at ___ at res. in Menno Twp.

Christian C. ZOOK, b-21 Apr 1879, **c**-Jos. B. ZOOK, Jno. B. ZOOK, admrs., **d**-$7000, **e**-M. S. ZOOK, Jacob H. ZOOK, **f**-Died 26 Mar 1879 at 7:00 at res. in Brown Twp.

Jacob FOCHT, b-26 Apr 1879, **c**-Barbara FOCHT, exts., **d**-no bond, **e**- **f**-Died 27 Apr 1879 at 11:00 at res. in Menno Twp.

Solomon KING, b-1 May 1879, **c**-Barbara A. KING, extx., **d**-no bond, **e**- **f**-Died 16 Apr 1879 at 15:00 at res. in Menno Twp.

Magdalena HOOK, b-9 May 1879, **c**-Reuben HOOK, admr., **d**-$300, **e**-Cha. A. ZERBE, Nathan FRANK, **f**-Died 14 Apr 1879 at 2:00 at res. in Decatur Twp.

Reed SAMPLE, b-12 May 1879, **c**-Andrew REED, extr., **d**-no bond, **e**- **f**-Died 6 May 1879 at 19:00 at res. in Armagh Twp.

Mary A. SHEAFFER, b-16 May 1879, **c**-William T. SHEAFFER, extr., **d**-no bond, **e**- **f**-Died on 12 May 1879 at 18:00 at res. in Newton Hamilton, Pa.

James THOMPSON, b-21 Jun 1879, **c**-Albert THOMPSON, admr., **d**-$100, **e**-Saml. STERRETT, U. R. THOMPSON, **f**-Died 4 Feb 1879 at 10:00 ___ at res. in Armagh Twp.

Ann H. MANN, b-25 Jun 1879, **c**-A. S. KERLIN, admr., **d**-$100, **e**-C. M. MANN, Jno. B. SEILHEIMER, **f**-Died 17 Jun 1879 at 1:00 at res. in Brown Twp.

Jacob ORT, b-28 Jun 1879, **c**-J. A. McKEE, extr., **d**-no bond, **e**- **f**-Died 1 Jun 1879 at 16:00 at res. in Granville Twp.

John HAMILTON, b-5 Jul 1879, **c**-Jno. ROBERTSON, admr., **d**-$1000, **e**-A. J. ATKINSON, J. K. RHODES, **f**-Died 31 Jul 1879 at 3:00 at res. in Newton Hamilton

Isaac GEARHART, b-14 Jul 1879, **c**-Emanuel GEARHART, extr., **d**-no bond, **e**- **f**-Died 11 Jul 1879 at 10:00 at es. in Derry Twp.

Mary HOOLEY, b-5 Aug 1879, **c**-Christopher HOOLEY, extr., **d**-no bond, **e**- **f**-Died 3 Aug 1879 at 3:30 at res. in Armagh Twp.

Geo. STRODE, b-6 Aug 1879, **c**-A. C. STRODE, **d**-$500, **e**-Isaiah COPLIN, W. S. SETTLE, **f**-Died 11 May 1879 at 12:00 M at res. in Granville Twp.

David MOIST, b-15 Aug 1879, **c**-Mary E. MILLER, admx., **d**-$2500, **e**-David H. MILLER, Wm. H. MOORE, **f**-Died 15 Jul 1879 at 22:30 at res. in Wayne Twp.

Sarah YODER, b-20 Aug 1879, **c**-Saml. K. YODER, admr., **d**-$4000, **e**-Christian L. YODER, John BAUM, **f**-Died 14 Aug 1879 at 3:00 at res. in Union Twp.

John ZOOK, b-4 Sep 1879, **c**-Jacob S. KING, extr., **d**-no bond, **e**- **f**-Died 24 Aug 1879 at 23:00 at res. in Union Twp.

William F. SHAW, b-11 Oct 1879, **c**-Mary M. SHAW, Oliver F. SHAW, extrs, **d**-no bond, **e**- **f**-Died 27 Seo 1768 at 5L99 at res, in Lewistown

Chas. M. MANN, b-25 Oct 1879, **c**-James H. MANN, admr., **d**-$10,000, **e**-Geo. W. ELDER, Rufus C. ELDER, **f**-Died 20 Oct 1879 at 2:00 at es. in Brown Twp.

Page 256, Frame 274

David HARTZLER, b-27 Oct 1879, **c**-Jonas ZOOK, extr., **d**-no bond, **e**- **f**-Died 20 Oct 1879 at 10:00 at res. in Menno Twp.

Sarah M. TITTLE, b-1 Nov 1879, **c**-A. A. BROWN, extr., **d**-no bond, **e**- **f**-Died 27 Dec 1878 at ___ at res. in Armagh Twp.

Margaret G. HAMILTON, b-7 Nov 1879, **c**-Alfred F. HAMILTON, extr., **d**-no bond, **e**- **f**-Died 2 Nov 1879 at 10:00 at res. in Lewistown

Isaac PLANK, b-8 Nov 1879, **c**-Saml. Y. PLANK, admr., **d**-$12,000, **e**-Jonathan PLANK, Christian K. YODER, **f**-4 Nov 1879 at 4:30 at res. in Union Twp.

James BURNS, b-11 Nov 1879, **c**-Jno. C. SIGLER, Andrew REED, extrs., **d**- **e**- **f**-Died 26 Oct 1879 at 20:00 at res. in Lewistown

Michael MILLER, b-13 Nov 1879, **c**-J. W. HOUGH, admr., **d**-$1000, **e**-James FIROVED, Henry [DUESE], **f**-Died 26 Oct 1879 at 20:00 at res. in Derry Twp.

Walter GRAHAM, b-15 Nov 1879, **c**-Wm. R. GRAHAM, **d**-$300, **e**-J. S. RAKERD, T. F. McCOY, **f**-Died 20 Oct 1879 at 22:00 at res. in Armagh Twp.

Mary E. BLYMYER, b-15 Nov 1879, **c**-Andrew REED, extr., **d**-no bond, **e**- **f**-Died 2 Nov 1879 at 18:00 at res. in Lewistown

Susan ROTHROCK, b-21 Nov 1879, **c**-S. J. BRISBEN, admr., **d**-$300, **e**-Geo. W. ELDER, Joseph McCOLLOCH, **f**-Died 19 Oct 1879 at +++ at res. in Lewistown

Jane SUNDERLAND, b-22 Nov 1879, **c**-John L. SUNDERLAND, admr., **d**-$300, **e**-J. K. RHODES, A. ROTHROCK, **f**-Died 17 Oct 1879 at 8:00 at res. in Wayne Twp.

William C. PORTER, b-5 Dec 1879, **c**-A. W. PORTER, admr., **d**-$900, **e**-Silas GLASCOW[sic], Saml. H. McCOY, **f**-Died on 27 Nov 1879 at 22:00 at res. in Lewistown

Frederick PECHT, b-30 Dec 1879, **c**-Isaiah PECTH [sic], extr., **d**-no bond, **e**- **f**-Died 26 Nov 1879 at 18:00 in res. in Armagh Twp.

Elizabeth FOSSELMAN, b-19 Jan 1880, **c**-Geo. W. ELDER, extr., **d**-no bond, **e**- **f**-Died 15 Jan 1880 at 20:00 at res. in Lewistown

Sarah E. MAYES, b-10 Jan 1880, **c**-J. M. WOODS, admr., **d**-$100, **e**-D. W. WOODS, Saml. S. WOODS, **f**-Died on 11 Aug 1879 at ___ at res. in Lewistown

James F. MATERS, b-12 Jan 1880, **c**-Joseph M. FLEMING, extr., **d**-no bond, **e**- **f**-Died 19 Dec 1879 at 21:00 at res. in Menno Twp.

James F. McNEAR, b-23 Jan 1880, **c**-J. B. EWING, admr., **d**-$500, **e**-J. K. RHODES, A. J. ATKINSON, **f**-Died 19 Dec 1879 ___ at res. in Wayne Twp.

N. W. STERETT, b-7 Feb 1880, **c**-A. S. STERETT, John R. STERETT, extrs., **d**-no bond, **e**- **f**-Died 18 Dec 1879 at 5:00 at res. in Armagh Twp

Elizabeth C. LINDSEY, b-24 Feb 1880, **c**-W. M. DOUGHMAN extr., **d**-no bond, **e**- **f**-Died 12 Feb 1880 at 13:00 at res. in Newton Hamilton

J. Laird BRICKER, b-28 Feb 1880, **c**-Joseph McCULLOCH, admr., **d**- **e**- **f**-Died 9 Feb 1879 at 12:00 PM [24:00?] at res. in Lewistown

John RUBLE, b-13 Mar 1880, **c**-Aaron RUBLE, extr., **d**-no bond, **e**- **f**-Died 4 Mar 1878 at 12:00 M at res. in Granville Twp.

John SPIGLERMOYER, b-18 Mar 1880, **c**-A. M. INGRAM, admr., **d**-$100, **e**-B. SPIGLERMOYER, Howard AURAND, **f**-Died 11 Feb 1880 at 12:00 M at res. in Decatur Twp.

Page 257, Frame 275

Benedictk STUCKEY, b-23 Mar 1880, **c**-Peter BAREFOOT, extr., **d**-no bond, **e**- **f**-Died 6 Mar 1880 at 19:00 at res. in Brown Twp.

William MOLSON, b-23 Mar 1880, **c**-T. M. UTTLEY, admr., **d**-$150, **e**-T. F. McCOY, **f**-Died 5 Jan 1879 at 1:00 at res. in Lewistown Bor.

Saml. F. MORRISON, b-6 Apr 1880, **c**-M. J. MORRISON, admr., **d**-$50, **e**-James FIROVED, Wm. O. THRUSH, **f**-Died 8 Jun 1879 at 12:00 M at res. in Lewistown Borough

Lucinda PAYNE, b-13 Apr 1880, **c-**Peter BAREFOOT, admr., **d-**$100, **e-** W. S. DELLETT, S. R. SPANGLER, **f-**Died on 19 Jan 1880 at 7:00 [___] at res. in Armagh Twp.

Sarah CAVANAUGH, b-9 Apr 1880, **c-**John CAVANAGH, admr., **d-**$75, **e-**Saml. H. McCOY, Alvin SHIMP, **f-**Died 9 Apr 1880 at 12:00 at res. in Granville Twp.

David A. McALISTER, b-13 May 1880, **c-**Wm. J. YEAGER, admr., **d-** $2000, **e-**James H. MANN, **f-**Died 10 May 1880 at 14:00 at res. in Brown Twp.

Charles ROMICK, b-21 May 1880, **c-**Charles F. ROMICK, admr., **d-** $600, **e-**Joseph W. McAULEY, **f-**Died 27 Mar 1880 at 14:00 at res. in Derry Twp.

Joseph Z. KING, b-22 May 1880, **c-**Joel ZOOK, admr., **d-**$8000, **e-** Christian L. YODER, **f-**Died 30 Apr 1880 at 15:00 at Belleville, suddenly.

Mrs. Sydney M. VANZANDT, b-26 May 1880, **c-**H. M. VAN ZANDT, admr., **d-**$2000, **e-**A. H. SHEAFFER, F. E. STICKNEY, **f-**Died 5 May 1880 at 12:00 P.M. at son's res. in Granville Twp.

John BEAVER, b-28 May 1880, **c-**Robert BEAVER, Jacob BEAVER, admrs., **d-**$1000, **e-**Henry STEIN, Geo. REIGLE, **f-**Died 22 Apr 1880 at 22:00 at res. in Decatur Twp.

Joseph HOSTETLER, b-31 May 1880, **c-**Christian Y. YODER, extr., **d-** no bond, **e- f-**Died 2 May 1880 at 10:00 at res. in Menno Twp.

Jno. DENGLER, b-1 Jun 1880, **c-**Mary DENGLER, admx., **d-**$600, **e-**Jno. RIDEN, Peter BAREFOOT, **f-**Died 20 May 1880 at 15:00 at Roring [sic] Springs, Blair Co., Pa.

Arabella VANZANT, b-8 Jul 1880, **c-**T. C. VANZANDT, extr., **d-**no bond, **e- f-**Died 17 Feb 1880 ___ in Newton Hamilton.

Jacob HOSTETLER, b-~~12 Jul 1880~~ written above is 22 Mar 1881, **c-** ~~Christian L. YODER, extr.~~, written above is Lea HOSTETLER, extx., **d-**no bond, **e- f-**Died 13 Jun 1880 at 12:00 at res. in Union Twp.

Charles PRICE, b-14 Jul 1880, **c-**Louisa PRICE, admx., **d-**$2600, **e-**John DAVIS, D. MUTTHERSBOUGH, **f-**Died 2 Jul 1880 at 19:00 near Selensgrove, Snyder County, Pa.

Christian FRAINE, b-17 Jul 1880, **c-**Geo. K. FRAINE, **d-**$500, **e-**Henry STETLER, H. J. SEINBARGER, **f-**Died 24 Jun 1880 at 18:00 at res. in Decatur Twp.

Mrs. Cathrine E. FRAKER, b-20 Jul 1880, **c-**A. H. SHAFFER, extr., **d-** no bond, **e- f-**Died 1 Jun 1880 at 23:00 at res. in Lewistown

Sarah C. STRUNK, b-31 Jul 1880, c-A. R. STRUNK, admr., d-$500, e-Wm. H. STRUNK, Geo. A. LEOPOLD, f-Died 11 Jun 1880 at 12:00 P.M. at res. in Brown Twp.

Sarah STINE, b-2 Aug 1880, c-John ATKINSON, extr., d-no bond, e- f-Died 20 Jul 1880 at 12:00 A.M. at res. in Bratton Twp.

John McKEE, b-11 Aug 1880, c-Eliza Ann McKEE, extx., d-no bond, e-f-Died 12 May 1880 at 8:00 at res. in Granville Twp.

Freman N. SHIPTON, b-6 Sep 1880, c-Peter BAREFOOT, d-$600, e-Jacob R. ELIOTT, J. C. McNITT, f-Died 13 Aug 1880 at ___ at res. in Armagh Twp.

Page 258, Frame 276

Elizabeth ALLISON, b-14 Sep 1880, c-Saml. B. WILLS, admr., d-$200, e-Saml. MITCHELL, R. M. GILLMORE, f-Died 5 Aug 1880 at 5:00 at res. in Menno Twp.

Joseph HOOT, b-20 Sep 1880, c-Sallie HOOT, admx., d-$200, e-Amos HOOT, Isaiah COPLIN, f-Died 26 Aut 1880 at 19:00 at res. in Lewistown

Elizabeth HEINLEY, b-24 Sep 1880, c-Samuel MITCHELL, extr., d-no bond, e- f-Died 9 Sep 1880 at 5:00 at res. in Derry Twp.

John D. TAYLOR, b-4 Oct 1880, c-Henry P. TAYLOR, admr., d-$50,000, e-Alex. REED, R. M. TAYLOR, f-Died 29 Sep 1880 at 12:00 M. at res. in Brown Twp.

Ann WALTERS, b-4 Oct 1880, c-H. McC. WALTERS, extr., d- e- f-Died 30 Sep 1880 at 10:00 at res. in McVaytown

H. M. DUNMIRE, b-13 Oct 1880, c-John C. SIGLER, admr., d-$1000, e-C. H. HENDERSON, f-Died 22 Sep 1880 at 12:00 M at res. in Derry Twp.

David T. KLINE, b-6 Nov 1880, c-David M. KLINE, admr., d-$600, e-David A. STROUP, H. C. VANZANT, f-Died 20 Oct 1880 at 4:00 at res. in Decatur Twp.

Mary MILLER, b-25 Oct 1880, c-Christian Y. YODER, extr., d-no bond, e- f-Died 19 Sep 1880 at 15:00 at res. in Union Twp.

Elizabeth GARVER, b-26 Nov 1880, c-Jonathan K. HARTZLER, extr., d- e- f-Died 22 Nov 1880 at 00:00 at res. in Oliver Twp.

William ROSS, b-13 Dec 1880, c-C. P. DULL, admr., d-$2000, e-Andrew REED, D. M. DULL, f-Died 28 Nov 1880 at 3:00 at res. in McVeytown, Pa.

Shem ZOOK, b-23 Dec 1880, c-Jonathan K. HARTZLER, extr., d-no bond, e- f-Died 17 Dec 1880 at 3:00 at res. in Bratton Twp.

(End of W. V. B. COPLIN's Term 5 Jan 1881)

Julian SHERRER [female], b-13 Jan 1881, c-Jacob MILLER, Joseph WINTER, extrs., d-no bond, e- f-Died 9 Jan 1881 at 14:00 at res. in Bratton Twp.

Mary LARIMER, b-24 Jan 1881, c-J. R. WIRT, extr., d-no bond, e- f-Died 14 Jan 1881 at 9:00 at res. in McVeytown

Elizabeth DENNIS, b-5 Feb 1881, c-Jonas HARSBARGER[sic], extr., d-no bond, e- f-Died 6 Jan 1881 at 00:00 at res. in Bratton Twp.

Saml. GEARHEART, b-9 Feb 1881, c-J. R. WIRT, d-$500, e-J. K. RHODES, W. H. BRATTON, f-Died 27 Jan 1881 at 11:30 at res. in Oliver Twp.

Elizabeth VINCENT, b-14 Feb 1881, c-T. M. UTTLEY, admr C.T.A., d-$200, e-T. F. McCOY, D. E. ROBISON, f-Died 14 Jul 1878 [sic] at 10:00 at res. in Lewistown

John RUPERT, b-18 Feb 1881, c-Adam RUPERT, J. H. ALLEN, admrs., d-$3000, e-S. J. SWIGART, Jacob MILLER, f-Died 5 Feb 1881 at 5:00 at res in Oliver Twp. (Died Suddenly)

Thomas G. KEARNS, b-24 Feb 1881, c-Mary E. KEARNS, H. C. VANZANT, C. T. A., d-$3000, e-E. C. KEARNS, Saml. STERRETT, f-Died 14 Jan 1881 at 2:00 at res. in Decatur Twp.

Page 259, Frame 277

Charles BRATTON, b-25 Feb 1881, c-Charles BRATTON, Jr., d-$1500, e-W. H. BRATTON, J. A. WOODRUFF, f-Died 13 Nov 1880 at 21:30 at res. of daughter in Lewistown

Joseph MOIST, b-18 Mar 1881, c-Joseph WINTER, d-$600, e-Jacob MILLER, Geo. HOFFMAN, f-12 Mar 1881 at 13:00 at res. of Mrs. FRENCH in Bratton Twp. "Died Suddenly"

Asenath JEFFRIES, b-19 Mar 1881, c-David HANAWALT, C. T. A., d-$200, e-Jno. SAILOR, Jno. MORRISON, f-Died 11 Mar 1881 at [13:30] at res. in Wayne Twp.

William WILSON, b-23 Mar 1881, c-Jefferson Taylor WILSON, extr., d-no bond, e- f-Died 14 Mar 1881 at 3:00 at res. in Wayne Twp.

Matilda BELL, b-24 Mar 1881, c-John K. BELL, extr., d-no bond, e- f-Died 3 Mar 1881 at 22:00 at res. in Decatur Twp.

William PAYNE, **b**-27 Mar 1881, **c**-Geo. W. PAYNE, **d**-$100, **e**-S. G. SHANNON, W. V. B. COPLIN, **f**-Died 27 Mar 1881 at 2:00 at res. of nephew in Renova, Clinton Co.

Mary SHATSAR, **b**-1 Apr 1881, **c**-David SHATSAR, **d**-$100, **e**-John BAUM, W. S. SETTLE, **f**-Died 20 Jul 1876 at 19:00 at res. of Geo. MARTIN. "Died Suddenly"

Sarah KAUFFMAN, **b**-15 Apr 1881, **c**-Christian KAUFFMAN, extr., **d**-no bond, **e**- **f**-Died 27 Feb 1881 at 10:00 at res. in Union Twp.

Mary TAYLOR, **b**-19 Apr 1881, **c**-Peter BAREFOOT, **d**-$600, **e**-Saml. SPANGLER, Jno. McDOWELL, **f**-Died 11 Apr 1881 at 20:00 at res. of Jno. CHAMBERLAIN in Armagh Twp.

James N. POSTLETHWAITE, **b**-26 Apr 1881, **c**-James S. RAKERD, **d**-$300, **e**-J. A. DYSART, J. K. RHODES, **f**-Died 8 Jan 1881 at 22:00 at res. in Newton Hamilton

Robert P. McCLAY, **b**-9 May 1881, **c**-Jno. O. CAMPBELL, Jos. K. McCLAY, **d**-$4000, **e**-Joseph CAMPBELL, J. Taylor WILSON, **f**-Died 20 Apr 1881 at 15:00 at res. in Union Twp.

John KEMMERLING, **b**-19 May 1881, **c**-Erastus KEMMERLING, William ORR, **d**-no bond, **e**- **f**-Died 14 May 1881 at 1:00 at res. in Decatur Twp.

Elizabeth BAIRD, **b**-19 May 1881, **c**-William BAIRD, admr., **d**-$1000, **e**-James H. MANN, J. M. YEAGER, **f**-Died 5 Apr 1881 at 12:00 at res. of H. RUBLE in Granville Twp.

John ALLEN, **b**-25 May 1881, **c**-Joseph McCULLOCH, extr., **d**-no bond, **e**- **f**-Died 14 May 1881 at 12:00 at res. in Lewistown Borough

Mary MABERR, **b**-16 Jul 1881, **c**-Peter BAREFOOT, extr., **d**-no bond, **e**- **f**-Died 3 Jul 1881 at 21:00 at res. in Milroy, Armagh Twp.

Frederick BICKLE, **b**-18 Jul 1881, **c**-Jno. A. WAREAM, **d**-$500, **e**-A. HULL, D. M. KLINE, **f**-Died 15 Jun 1881 at 20:00. Drown in Kishacoquillas Creek near Lewistown in Mifflin Co.

John HAMILTON, **b**-28 Jul 1881, **c**-D. E. ROBESON, admr., **d**-$100, **e**-D. W. WOODS, T. M. UTTLEY, **f**-Died 20 Sep 1879 at ___ at res. in Lewistown

Mary MARKS, **b**-30 Aug 1881, **c**-Mary E. CONTNER, admx., **d**-$1200, **e**-William WILLIS, Jos. A. FICKTHORN, **f**-Died 30 Aug 1881 at 4:30 at res. in Lewistown

Page 260, Frame 278

Theodore HAEBER, b-8 Sep 1881, **c**-Willhelmina HAEBER, **d**-no bond, **e**- **f**-Died 27 Aug 1881 at 00:25 at res. in Lewistown

Mary REED, b-29 Sep 1881, **c**-T. G. BELL, Jas H. ALEXANDER, extrs., **d**-no bond, **e**- **f**-Died 27 Sep 1881 at 2:00 at res. in Derry Twp.

Hamilton KAUFFMAN, b-3 Oct 1881, **c**-George A. LEOPOLD, **d**-$1200, **e**-Albert B. STRUNK, S. S. STRONG, **f**-Died 21 Sep 1881 at 20:00 at res. in Oliver Twp.

Williamson CUMMINGS, b-20 Oct 1881, **c**-Samuel CUMMINGS, **d**-$1000, **e**-Saml. KAUFFMAN, Sarah A. CUMMINGS, **f**-Died 24 Sep 1881 at 21:30 at res. in Union Twp.

Samuel YOCUM, b-4 Nov 1881, **c**-Joseph McCULLOCH, admr., **d**-$1000, **e**-T. F. McCOY, W. S. SETTLE, **f**-Died 14 Oct 1881 at ___ P.M. at res. in Lewistown

Rosanna DAVIS, b-14 Nov 1881, **c**-C. P. DULL, extr., **d**-no bond, **e**- **f**-Died 20 Oct 1881 at 6:00 at res. in McVeytown

John ALEXANDER, b-13 Dec 1881, **c**-W. C. ALEXANDER, [E.b.n.vc?], **d**-$700, **e**-J. C. KEARNS, James M. GOODHART, **f**-Additional bond filed on account of assets afterward discovered. See Bond Book No. 9, p. [404, maybe 444?]

John R. McCARTHEY, b-13 Dec 1881, **c**-J. W. McCARTHEY, H. C. McCARTHEY, **d**-$2000, **e**-R. M. KINSLOE, J. K. RHODES, **f**-Died 14 Nov 1881 at 9:00 at res. in Wayne Twp.

Martha STONEROAD, b-15 Dec 1881, **c**-Joseph McCULLOCH, extr., **d**-no bond, **e**- **f**-Died 12 Dec 1881 at 4:00 at res. in Lewistown

Jane B. ALEXANDER, b-29 Dec 1881, **c**-Wm. C. ALEXANDER, extr., **d**-no bond, **e**- **f**-Died 28 Oct 1881 at 1:00 at res. of J. C. KEARNS in Mifflin Co.

Daniel BAKER, b-30 Dec 1881, **c**-Joseph BAKER, extr., **d**-no bond, **e**- **f**-Died 24 Dec 1881 at 22:00 at res. in Derry Twp.

Fanny YODER, b-4 Jan 1882, **c**-Daniel F. YODER, admr., **d**-$4500, **e**-A. [Z.] PEACHEY, David PEACHEY, **f**-Died 26 Dec 1881 at 00:00 at res. of Daniel F. YODER, Menno Twp.

Jonathan A. PEACHEY, b-4 Jan 1882, **c**-Abraham [Z.] PEACHEY, **d**-$8000, **e**-Daniel F. YODER, David PEACHEY, **f**-Died 30 Dec 1881 at 9:00 at res. in Menno Twp.

Catharine McLAUGHLIN, b-18 Jan 1882, **c**-J. R. WIRT, extr., **d**-no bond, **e**- **f**-Died 16 Dec 1881 at 23:00 at res. in McVeytown, Mifflin

Amos MARTZ, b-1 Feb 1882, c-David WASSON, admr., d-$300, e-Alfred HULL, J. K. RHODES, f-Died 24 Jan 1882 at 2:00 at res. in Derry Twp.

Geo. W. THOMAS, b-3 Feb 1882, c-Armilda A. THOMAS, admx. d. b. n. c. t. a., d-$10,000, e-Lydia S. THOMAS, Harriet S. THOMAS, f-

Mary J. CUBBESON, b-16 Feb 1882, c-Geo. T. GARDNER, extr., d-no bond, e- f-Died 13 Feb 1882 at 17:00 at res. in Lewistown

Geo. W. SPIGLEMOYER, b-11 Mar 1882, c-J. W. McMANAMY, d-$300, e-Catharine E. KRICK, Wm. SEPLEY, f-Died 6 Apr 1877 at 17:00 at res. in Decatur Twp.

Page 261, Frame 279

Frank E. STICKNEY. b-13 Mar 1882, c-Mary T. STICKNEY, admx., d-$150, e-Andrew REED, Joseph STICKNEY, f-Died 21 Feb 1882 at 14:00 at res. in Lewistown Borough

Sarah TAYLOR, b-25 Mar 1882, c-Samuel C. HEISTER, d-$500, e-Henry H. KAUFFMAN, J. K. RHODES, f-Died 12 Mar 1882 at 8:00 at res. Saml. C. HEISTER in Wayne Twp.

Samuel WILSON, b-30 Mar 1882, c-Lewis HESSER, admr., d-$2000, e-David McKINSTRY, Christian [RUNK], f-Died ___ Jun 1880 at 16:00 at res. in Bratton Twp.

John WELSH, b-3 Apr 1882, c-Michael J. WELSH, d-no bond, e- f-Died 29 Mar 1882 at 1:00 at res. in Derry Twp.

George FOSTER, b-3 Apr 1882, c-John GLASGOW, d-$600, e-David STINE, Jr., John F. STINE, f-Died 3 Apr 1882 at 3:00 at his res. in Wayne Twp.

Philip SNOOK, b-20 Apr 1882, c-Amos SNOOK, d-$1500, e-Jacob [I.] GOSS, Isaac S. GOSS, f-Died 15 Apr 1882 at 14:00 at res. in Armagh Twp.

Isaac KNEPP, b-21 Apr 1882, c-Peter BAREFOOT, d-$2000, e-Jas. C. McNITT, Saml. R. SPANGLER, f-Died 31 Mar 1882 at 23:00 at res. in Armagh Twp.

Mary A. HEMPHILL, b-10 May 1882, c-W. W. [TURET?], extr., d-no bond, e- f-Died 5 May 1882 at 3:00 at res. in Lewistown

Louisa CAROTHER, b-13 May 1882, c-A. J. ATKINSON, admr., d-$6000, e-William WILLIS, Allen SCHOCH, f-Died 7 May 1882 at 5:00 at res. of A. J. ATKINSON in Lewistown

Catherine STRATFORD, b-22 May 1882, **c-**Charles STRATFORD, Sr., **d-**$2000, **e-**J. English VREST, D. R. STRATFORD, **f-**Died 17 May 1882 at 10:00 at res. in Derry Twp. (Vacate by order of the Court)

Samuel PRICE, b-1 Jun 1882, **c-**William CREIGHTON, **d-**$3000, **e-**A. J. ATKINSON, R. M. PRICE, **f-**Died 3 May 1882 at 13:00 at res. of Nancy PRICE in Derry Twp.

Jacob BRENEMAN, b-2 Jun 1882, **c-**Susan BRENEMAN, Jno. A. McKEE, **d-**no bond, **e- f-**Died 16 May 1882 at 6:00 at res. in Lewistown Borough

Jacob R. ELIOTT, b-7 Jun 1882, **c-**Peter BAREFOOT, admr., **d-**$1500, **e-**James C. McNITT, Saml. R. SPANGLER, **f-**Died 18 May 1882 at 20:00 at res. in Armagh Twp.

William SOLES, b-7 Jun 1882, **c-**William S. SETTLE, admr., **d-**$1000, **e-**John S. GARRETT, David GROVE, **f-**Died 2 Jun 1882 at 14:30 at res. in Lewistown Borough

Robert CUMMINS, b-17 Jun 1882, **c-**Catharine A. CUMMINS, **d-**no bond, **e- f-**Died 27 May 1882 at 23:00 at res. in Armagh Twp.

Catherine STRATFORD, b-19 Jun 1882, **c-**Charles STRATFORD, extr., **d-**no bond, (nuncupative will), **e- f-**Died 17 May 1882 at 10:00 at res. in Derry Twp.

Rachel McCORD, b-24 Jun 1882, **c-**Saml. H. McCOY, **d-**$1000, **e-**T. G. BELL, J. K. RHODES, **f-**Died 17 Jun 1882 at 1:00 at res. in Granville Twp.

Page 262, Frame 280
Ann SIGLER, b-5 Jul 1882, **c-**Belinda AIKEN, **d-**no bond, **e- f-**Died 3 Jul 1882 at 3:00 at res. of Mrs. B. AIKEN in Lewistown

Mary ZOOK, b-21 Jul 1882, **c-**Jonas ZOOK, **d-**$5000, **e-**Christian ZOOK, D. W. WOODS, **f-**Died 6 Jul 1882 at 13:00 at res. in Menno Twp.

John G. McCORD, b-6 Aug 1882, **c-**Saml. H. McCOY, **d-**$300, **e-**J. K. RHODES, Geo. W. SOULT, **f-**Died 16 May 1882 at 3:00 at res. in Oliver Twp.

Eva JONES, b-7 Aug 1882, **c-**John L. ESTWORTHY[sic; appears to be ESWORTHY?], **d-**no bond, **e- f-**Died 26 Jul 1882 at 15:00 at res. of John ESTWORTHY in Granville Twp.

Wm. W. HAMAKER, b-15 Aug 1882, **c-**Mary B. HAMAKER, **d-**no bond, **e- f-**Died 3 Aug 1882 at 7:00 at res. in Lewistown. Vacated by order of Court dated 11 Jan 1883. See Orphans' Court Docket No. 14.335.

James B. DORMAN, b-1 Sep 1882, **c-**Wm. A. ORR, extr., **d-**no bond, **e- f-**Died 21 Aug 1882 at 8:00 at res. in Decatur Twp.

Eliphas C. BIGELOW, b-9 Sep 1882, **c-**Jesse W. HORTON, **d-**$10,000, **e-**Richard BRINDLE, Lewis E. SCHUCHT, **f-**Died 25 Aug 1882 at 3:30 at res. in Belleville

William H. FIKE, b-14 Sep 1882, **c-**M. M. McLAUGHLIN, **d-**$200, **e-**Henry BOSSINGER, James [maybe FIROVED?], **f-**Died 21 Aug 1882 at 14:00 at res. in Bratton Twp.

Joseph S. WAREAM, b-25 Sep 1882, **c-**Mabel J. WAREAM, **d-**$250, **e-**La Fayette WEBB, W. V. B. COPLIN, **f-**Died 20 Feb 1880 at 18:00 at res. in Lewistown

John LAWVER, b-28 Sep 1882, **c-**Jacob LAWVER, William A. ORR, **d-**$500, **e-**Frederick LASH, Wm. LEPLEY, **f-**Died 5 Aug 1882 at 13:30 at res. in Decatur Twp.

Nancy LOCKWOOD, b-8 Oct 1882, **c-**Jos. M. FLEMING, **d-**no bond, **e- f-**Died 17 Sep 1882 at 3:00 at res. in Menno Twp.

Philip HASSENPLUG, b-3 Nov 1882, **c-**Peter BAREFOOT, extr., **d-**no bond, **e- f-**Died 28 Oct 1882 at 16:00 at res. of A. J. AITKENS in Siglerville

Daniel TICE, b-3 Nov 1882, **c-**Gideon M. TICE, **d-** $100, **e-**John DAVIS, J. H. C. THOMAS, **f-**Died 2 Aug 1882 at 6:00 at res. in Lewistown. Died Suddenly.

Geo. A. SOULT, b-3 Nov 1882, **c-**Eliza A. SOULT, **d-**$1000, **e-**Saml. H. McCOY, Jos. McFADDEN, Laurence SHEPPARD, **f-**Died 4 Oct 1882 at 1:00 at res. in Granville Twp.

Elijah MORRISON, b-10 Nov 1882, **c-**Saml. W. NORTON, Albert HAZELETT, B. E. MORRISON, **d-**no bond, **e- f-**Died 30 Oct 1882 at 22:00 at res. in Wayne Twp.

Catharine RHEAM, b-17 Nov 1882, **c-**D. W. WOODS, extr., **d-**no bond, **e- f-**Died 30 Sep 1882 at 6:00 at the res. of Michael MOYER in Derry Twp.

William M. WIMER, b-18 Nov 1882, **c-**John M. WIMER, **d-**$300, **e-**J. K. RHODES, **f-**Died 14 Nov 1882 at 9:00 at res. in Lewistown from gun shot wound

John G. LIGHTNER, b-25 Nov 1882, **c-**Nicholas HARTZLER, **d-**$1000, **e-**Jos. W. FLEMING, J. K. HARTZLER, **f-**Died 19 Nov 1882 at 6:30 at res. in Allenville, Mifflin County

John [BEAR], b-9 Dec 1882, c-Samuel H. McCOY, d-$2000, e-Walter L. OWENS, Laurence SHEPHERD, f-Died 31 Aug 1882 at 12:30 at res. in Granville Twp.

Page 263, Frame 281

Polly SAWVER, b-14 Dec 1882, c-William A. ORR, George KRICK, d-$2000, e-John L. BROWER, Andrew SNOOK, f-Died 20 Sep 1882 at 1:00 at res. of Geo. KRICK, Decatur Twp.

Jacob KRICK, Sr., b-14 Dec 1882, c-George KRICK, William A. ORR, d-$2000, e-John L. BROWER, Andrew SNOOK, f-Died 6 Nov 1882 at 6:00 at res. in Decatur Twp.

Rosanna ERWIN, b-20 Dec 1882, c-Jacob R. WIRT, extr., d-no bond, e-f-Died 13 Dec 1882 at 5:00 at res. in McVeytown. Letters testamentary to Jacob R. WIRT vacated at his petition. See Orphans' Court Docket No. 14, p. 35, for order of Court.

Abram BRENEMAN, b-22 Dec 1882, c-Sarah A. BRENEMAN, Reuben [T. ILY??? guessing TULLY], d-$1500, e-Saml. MUSSER, Geo. S. RUBLE, f-Died 1 Dec 1882 at 2:00 at res. in Oliver Twp.

Franklin CAUM, b-27 Dec 1882, c-Edmund S. DOTY, Jr., d-$200, e-Joseph McFADDEN, J. K. RHODES, f-Died 29 Nov 1882 at 14:20 at his res. in Granville Twp.

Martin GILL, b-30 Dec 1882, c-John WILSON, d-$2000, e-James H. MANN, Jno. B. SELHEIMER, f-Died 13 Nov 1882 at 4:30 at res. in Derry Twp.

Margaret BUCHAN[sic], b-4 Jan 1883, c-Joseph McCULLOCH, admr. C. T. A., d-$1000, e-T. F. McCOY, J. K. RHODES, f-Died on or about 28 Dec 1882 having been found dead in her bed on that day at res. in Granville Twp.

James BUCHAN[sic], b-4 Jan 1883, c-Samuel J. BRISBIN, admr. C. T. A., d-$1000, e-J. K. RHODES, Jno. A. McKEE, f-Died on or about 18 Dec 1882 having been found dead in his bed on that day at res. in Granville Twp.

Charles A. REDELIN, b-4 Jan 1883, c-M. L. BROSIUS, d-$600, e-Jno. B. SELHEIMER, Jno. A. McKEE, f-Died 27 Nov 1882 at 15:00 near res. in Derry Twp., the result of an accident.

Jonas LAYMAN, b-11 Jan 1883, c-David A. HOSTETLER, d-$200, e-Saml. B. HOSTETLER, James S. RAKERD, f-Died 19 Dec 1882 15 10:30 at res. in Menno Twp.

J. A. TOWNSEND, b-13 Jan 1883, c-T. W. TOWNSEND, d-no bond, e- f-Died 9 Jan 1883 at 22:00 at res. in Lewistown

Geo. S. HUNT, b-16 Jan 1883, c-Saml. J. BRISBIN, d-$1500, e-T. F. McCOY, J. K. RHODES, f-Died 13 Jan 1883 at 15:00 at res. of John HUNT in Derry Twp.

Rosanna ERWIN, b-18 Jan 1883, c-William H. ERWIN, admr. C. T. A., d-$12,000, e-James E. STINE, W. E. RHODES, f-

John C. SIGLER, b-19 Jan 1883, c-Amanda M. SIGLER, and Joseph M. WOODS, d-$40,000, e-D. W. WOODS, Caroline A. SIGLER, f-Died 14 Jan 1883 at 11:00 at res. in Lewistown

Wm. W. HAMAKER, b-22 Jan 1883, c-Saml. J. BRISBIN, admr. C. T. A., d-$3000, e-Geo. S. HOFFMAN, Jos. E. WILLIAMS, f-

David CUMMINGS, b-27 Jan 1883, c-A. Taylor KYLE, d-$1000, e-John D. BARR, R. [M.] TAYLOR, f-Died ___ about the year 1877 in Lake City, Minnesota

Hugh AIKENS, b-3 Oct 1883, c-Jno. A. AIKENS, Wm. H. AIKENS, admrs., d-$600, e-Jno. S. HOUTZ, James C. McNITT, f-Died 24 Jan 1883 at 10:00 at res. in Armagh Twp.

Elizabeth H. TAYLOR, b-9 Feb 1883, c-John P. TAYLOR, J. Beatty HENRY, extrs., d-no bond, e- f-Died 17 Jan 1883 at 15:00 at the St. Cloud Hotel in Philadelphia

John H. BROUGHT, b-10 Feb 1883, c-William H. BROUGHT, d-$2500, e-Sylvester BROUGHT, J. K. MUTHERSBAUGH, f-Died 30 Jan 1883 at 10:30 at res. in Granville Twp.

David S. McNITT, b-19 Feb 1883, c-John McNITT, extr., d-no bond, e- f-Died 30 Jan 1883 at 17:00 at res. in Brown Twp.

Page 264, Frame 282

Daniel NAFZINGER, b-20 Feb 1883, c-Jonas YODER, d-$3000, e-J. KAUFFMAN, J. SHADLE, f-Died 13 Feb 1883 at 9:00 at res. in Oliver Twp.

Elizabeth S. CAMPBELL, b-1 Mar 1883, c-Andrew W. CAMPBELL, d-$6000, e-Joseph CAMPBELL, James H. MANN, f-Died 7 Feb 1883 at 19:00 at res. in Union Twp.

Marjory OLIVER, b-1 Mar 1883, c-Joseph CAMPBELL, d-no bond, e- f-Died 18 Feb 1883 at 23:00 at res. in McVeytown

John C. WHISLER, b-3 Mar 1883, c-Michael M. McLAUGHLIN, d-$100, e-A. W. CORRELL, Wm. ROUNDTREE, f-Died 20 Mar 1880 at 19:00 at res. in McVeytown

Henry R. PRICE, **b**-5 Mar 1883, **c**-William R. PRICE, **d**-$2000, **e**-David M. KLINE, Daniel J. PRICE, **f**-Died 1 Mar 1883 at 15:00 at res. in Granville Twp.

Sarah J. BOTTORFF, **b**-7 Mar 1883, **c**-John WILSON, **d**-$1500, **e**-James H. MANN, J. M. YEARGER, **f**-Died 27 Nov 1879 at ___ at res. in Derry Twp.

Gideon M. TICE, **b**-8 Mar 1883, **c**-Hannah M. TICE, admx., **d**-$4000, **e**-John DAVIS, Henry N. FRANK, James M. THOMAS, **f**-Died 27 Feb 1883 at 4:00 at res. in Lewistown

Margaret F. PARKER, **b**-15 Mar 1883, **c**-Thomas D. PARKER, **d**-$1600, **e**-F. G. FRANCISCUS, Catharine J. HOOVER, **f**-Died 1 Sep 1882 at 20:45 at res. in Derry Twp.

Robert STERRETT, **b**-19 Mar 1883, **c**-William S. STERRETT, **d**-no bond, **e**- **f**-Died 8 Mar 1883 at 7:00 at res. in Armagh Twp.

David HOUGH, **b**-20 Mar 1883, **c**-Joseph McCULLOCH, **d**-$1000, **e**-J. K. RHODES, W. S. SETTLE, **f**-Died 7 Mar 1883 at 20:00 at res. in Granville Twp.

Lizzie KAUFFMAN, **b**-23 Mar 1883, **c**-John E. KAUFFMAN, admr. C.T.A., **d**-$2500, **e**-Jared KAUFFMAN, Johnathan KAUFFMAN, **f**-Died 28 Feb 1883 at 1:00 at res. in Bratton Twp.

John CONTNER, **b**-27 Mar 1883, **c**-Ellen CONTNER, **d**-$300, **e**-M. R. THOMPSON, A. A. BROWN, **f**-Died 6 Aug 1882 at 4:00 at res. in Armagh Twp.

Mary STULL, **b**-9 Apr 1883, **c**-Jeremiah L. SLAGLE, **d**-no bond, **e**- **f**-Died 17 Mar 1883 at 12:00 at res. in Menno Twp.

John POSTLETHWAIT. **b**-10 Apr 1883, **c**-North A. POSTLETHWAIT, James A. DYSART, **d**-no bond, **e**- **f**-Died 7 Apr 1883 at 3:00 at res. in Wayne Twp.

John R. WOOD, **b**-12 Apr 1883, **c**-W. Henry PLATT, **d**-$200, **e**-William S. SETTLE, Chas. S. MARKS, **f**-Died 5 Apr 1883 about 1:00 (A.M. or P.M.?). Killed in Ore Bank in Decatur Twp.

Elizabeth HAFFLY, **b**-19 Apr 1883, **c**-Joseph CAMPBELL, extr., **d**-no bond, **e**- **f**-Died 15 Apr 1883 at 18:00 at res. in Union Twp.

Samuel J. SHIRE, **b**-21 Apr 1883, **c**-William B. LUKENS, **d**-$200, **e**-Joseph TAYLOR, J. K. RHODES, **f**-Died 27 Jul 1882 at 7:00 at res. in Wayne Twp.

Philip MERTZ, **b**-30 Apr 1883, **c**-Philip D. MERTZ, **d**-$4000, **e**-Henry STERN, David A. STROUP, **f**-Died 25 Apr 1883 at 5:30 at res. in Derry Twp.

John T. WILSON, **b**-9 May 1883, **c**-Jefferson T. WILSON, **d**-$4000, **e**-Saml. B. WILES, Andrew CAMPBELL, **f**-Died 1 May 1883 at 22:00 at res. in Menno Twp.

<u>Page 265, Frame 283</u>

George BUCKLEY, **b**-10 May 1883, **c**-Samuel W. PETERSON, **d**-$2500, **e**-R. M. KINSLOE, Elisha FIELDS, **f**-Died 18 Apr 1883 at 18:30 at res. in Wayne Twp.

Geo. M. D. CASNER, **b**-17 May 1883, **c**-Isabella P. CASNER, **d**-$100, **e**-Zachariah ROTHROCK, J. S. RAKERD, **f**-Died 8 May 1883 at 13:00 at Lewistown Junction by accident at Coal Hoister

George PETERS, **b**-19 May 1883, **c**-Samuel J. BRISBIN, **d**-$100, **e**-Jno. A. McKEE, Saml. H. BERRYHILL, **f**-Died 17 Mar 1883 at 21:00 at res. in Lewistown

James CLIMANS, **b**-29 May 1883, **c**-Emanuel B. [HORENCAME], **d**-$300, **e**-John BOOHER, J. K. RHODES, **f**-Died 23 Jun 1882[sic] at 9:00 at res. in Wayne Twp.

Eliza CLIMANS, **b**-1 Jun 1883, **c**-Alfred SIMON, **d**-$600, **e**-Alpheus [RINCIN], T. F. McCOY, **f**-Died 10 May 1883 at 2:00 at res. in Wayne Twp.

James M. MARTIN, **b**-9 Jun 1883, **c**-S. Martin BELL, **d**-no bond, **e**- **f**-Died 1 Jun 1883 at 16:30 at res. in Derry Twp.

Sarah OSBURNE, **b**-25 Jun 1883, **c**-Joseph McCULLOCH, **d**-$1000, **e**-A. H. SHEAFFER, Geo. K. McCLINTIC, **f**-Died 24 Feb 1882 at 20:00 at the James ECLEBARGER [res.] in Lewistown

John GAFF, **b**-3 Jul 1883, **c**-L. V. POSTLETHWAITE, **d**-$100, **e**-T. M. UTTLEY, Jno. K. RHODES, **f**-Died 14 Dec 1878[sic] at 18:00 at res. in Wayne Twp.

James J. LASHELL, **b**-11 Jul 1883, **c**-Margaret LASHELL, **d**-$600, **e**-Jos. H. MORRISON, David W. WOODS, **f**-Died 3 Jul 1883 at 3:30 at res. in Union Twp.

James A. DORMAN, **b**-23 Jul 1883, **c**-Geo. W. KEARNS, **d**-no bond, **e**-**f**-Died 17 Jul 1883 at 2:00 at res. of Geo. W. KEARNS in Decatur Twp.

Joseph BYLER, **b**-31 Jul 1883, **c**-Jonathan L. BYLER, [Sem.] L. BYLER, **d**-no bond, **e**- **f**-Died 18 Jul 1883 at 14:00 at res. in Union Twp.

John McCONNEL, **b**-6 Aug 1883, **c**-Thomas J. WILSON, **d**-no bond, **e**-**f**-Died 24 Jun 1883 at 14:00 at res. in Menno Twp.

Dr. Charles FREDERICI, b-7 Aug 1883, **c**-Samuel J. BRISBIN, **d**-$500, **e**-T. F. McCOY, John A. McKEE, **f**-Died 2 Aug 1883 at 17:00 at the Alms House, Mifflin Co.

John KYLE, b-3 Sep 1883, **c**-James KYLE, **d**-$2000, **e**-D. W. WOODS, Henry TAYLOR, **f**-Died 24 Jul 1883 at 20:00 at res. in Brown Twp.

Matilda BOOK, b-14 Sep 1883, **c**-Henry BOOK, **d**-no bond, **e**- **f**-Died 3 Sep 1883 at 1:00 at res. in Derry Twp.

John PRESTON, b-29 Oct 1883, **c**-E. C. KEARNS, ~~Daniel K. GISE~~, (Daniel K. GISE being a non resident and having failed to file a bond and having filed a renunciation, letters were granted to E. C. KEARNS, the other extr.), **d**-no bond, **e**- **f**-Died 1 Oct 1883 at 9:00 at res. in Decatur Twp.

Felix McCLINTIC, b-20 Oct 1883, **c**-Peter BAREFOOT, **d**- **e**- **f**-Died 6 Oct 1883 at 11:00 at res. in Armagh Twp.

David M. KLINE, b-29 Oct 1883, **c**-T. M. UTTLEY, Joseph McCULLOCH, **d**-no bond, **e**- **f**-Died 21 Oct 1883 at 7:00 in res. in Lewistown

Page 266, Frame 284

Hannah YODER, b-12 Nov 1883, **c**-Saml. CUMMING, **d**-no bond, **e**- **f**-Died 6 Nov 1883 at 4:00 at res. in Brown Twp.

Robert M. ALEXANDER, b-15 Nov 1883, **c**-Geo. V. ALEXANDER, **d**-$800, **e**-Robert M. TAYLOR, A. G. GIBBONEY, **f**-Died 7 Apr 1881 at 16:00 in Culpeper Co., Va., having gone there for benefit of his health

Ira R. ALEXANDER, b-15 Nov 1883, **c**-Geo. V. ALEXANDER, **d**-$800, **e**-R. M. TAYLOR, A. G. GIBBONEY, **f**-Died 15 Sep 1883 at 20:00 in Stutsman Co., Docotah Teritory

Saml. MUTHERSBAUGH, b-19 Nov 1883, **c**-Wm. S. MUTHERSBAUGH, **d**-$1500, **e**-Johnson MUTHERSBAUGH, Julian MUTHERSBAUGH, **f**-Died 14 Nov 1883 at 20:00 at res. in Decatur Twp.

Geo. T. SIGLER, b-24 Nov 1883, **c**-Phebe E. SIGLER, T. W. TOWNSEND, **d**-$10,000, **e**-Jos. SIGLER, E. C. KEARNS, **f**-Died 14 Nov 1883 at 7:00 at res. in Decatur Twp.

Charles McCORMICK, b-28 Nov 1883, **c**-L. V. POSTLETHWAIT, **d**-$1000, **e**-Saml. D. POSTLETHWAIT, J. K. RHODES, **f**-Died 17 Nov 1883 at res. in Wayne Twp.

George **FETZER**, **b**-20 Dec 1883, **c**-A. W. PORTER, admr. C.T.A., **d**-$10,000, **e**-T. F. McCOY, W. W. MARKS, **f**-Died 14 Dec 1883 at 9:00 at res. in Lewistown

Mary R. **ROTHROCK**, **b**-11 Jan 1884, **c**-Joseph McCULLOCH, **d**-$400, **e**-J. S. RAKERD, W. S. SETTLE, **f**-Died 14 Nov 1883 at 20:00 or 21:00 at Insane Asylum in Dauphin Co.

Samuel **HAFFLY**, **b**-14 Jan 1884, **c**-Andrew W. CAMPBELL, **d**-$1200, **e**-Jefferson T. WILSON, J. Milton CAMPBELL, **f**-Died 17 April 1883 at Fargo, Dacota Territory

Abraham **PEACHEY**, **b**-21 Jan 1884, **c**-David PEACHEY, John PEACHEY, **d**-no bond, **e**- **f**-Died 15 Jan 1884 at 17:00 at res. in Menno Twp.

Sarah **KEPPERLING**, **b**-26 Jan 1884, **c**-Solomon S. WAGNER, admr. C.T.A. **d**-$1000, **e**-John M. CRISSMAN, Ira THOMPSON, **f**-Died 8 Jan 1884 at 5:00 at res. in Armagh Twp.

Isabella **ROOP**, **b**-1 Feb 1884, **c**-Elias PENEPACKER, **d**-no bond, **e**- **f**-Died 18 Jan 1884 at 23:00 at res. in Bratton Twp.

Sophia **PRESTON**, **b**-16 Feb 1884, **c**-Elias C. KEARNS, **d**-no bond, **e**- **f**-Died 13 Feb 1884 at 21:00 at res. in Decatur Twp.

John H. **KURTZ**, **b**-19 Feb 1884, **c**-Jacob C. YODER, **d**-$2000, **e**-Jonathan S. ZOOK, Jonathan N. YODER, **f**-Died 12 Feb 1884 at 15:00 at res. in Union Twp.

Chestina **BRINDLE**, **b**-27 Feb 1884, **c**-Christian B. PEACHEY, **d**-no bond, **e**- **f**-Died 23 Feb 1884 at 9:00 at res. in Union Twp.

Yost **YODER**, **b**-27 Feb 1884, **c**-Jonathan L. BAYLER, **d**-no bond, **e**- **f**-Died 26 Jan 1884 at 23:00 at res. in Union Twp.

Mary **STERRETT**, **b**-28 Feb 1884, **c**-William A. STERRETT, **d**-no bond, **e**- **f**-Died 22 Feb 1884 at 10:00 at res. in Armagh Twp.

Martha **KING**, **b**-10 Mar 1884, **c**-Christian G. YODER, **d**-no bond, **e**- **f**-Died 3 Mar 1884 at 23:00 at res. in Menno Twp.

Henry **GIBBONEY**, **b**-22 Mar 1884, **c**-H. C. VANZANT, **d**-$200 **e**-Joseph SIGLER, Saml. STERRETT, **f**-Died 2 Mar 1884 at 16:00 at res. in Decatur Twp.

Barbara **ZOOK**, **b**-24 Mar 1884, **c**-John YODER, **d**-no bond, **e**- **f**-Died 14 Mar 1884 at 10:30 at res. in Union Twp.

David J. **HOOLEY**, **b**-28 Mar 1884, **c**-Jacob C. YODER, **d**-no bond, **e**- **f**-Died 14 Mar 1884 at 18:00 at res. in Union Twp.

Shem **YODER**, **b**-31 Mar 1884, **c**-Yost YODER, **d**-no bond, **e**- **f**-Died 22 Mar 1884 at 20:00 at res. in Union Twp.

Page 267, Frame 285

Joseph KYLE, Sr., **b**-19 Apr 1884, **c**-W. B. KYLE and A. T. KYLE, **d**-no bond, **e**- **f**-Died 28 Nov 1879 at 4:00 at res. in Brown Twp.

David WEILER, **b**-19 May 1884, **c**-John B. FLOYD, **d**-$15,000, **e**-Moses FLOYD, A. J. ATKINSON, **f**-Died 6 May 1884 at 5:00 at res. of Jno. B. FLOYD in Union Twp.

Samuel YODER, **b**-28 May 1884, **c**-Levi B. YODER, Jacob H. ZOOK, **d**-no bond, **e**- **f**-Died 19 May 1884 at 12:00 at res. in Union Twp.

Martha SEACHRIST, **b**-6 Jun 1884, **c**-Christian SEACHRIST, **d**-$200, **e**-Jesse MENDENHALL, W. S. SETTLE, **f**-Died 13 Apr 1884 at 18:00 at res. of C. SEACHRIST, DerryTwp.

Mary RUBLE, **b**-7 Jun 1884, **c**-Geo. H. SWIGART, **d**-$1500, **e**-Henry SWIGART, Saml. S. RUBLE, **f**-Died 30 Apr 1884 at 12:00 at res. in Oliver Twp.

Sarah R. SIMS, **b**-21 Jun 1884, **c**-Mary M. [LOND], **d**-no bond, **e**- **f**-Died 6 Jun 1884 at 4:30 at Harrisburg, Dauphin Co., Pa.

Arthur B. LONG, **b**-27 Jun 1884, **c**-Geo. H. LONG, David W. WOODS, **d**-(Geo. H. LONG being a non-resident of Penna. gave Bond in $200), **e**-Ann E. LONG, C. S. HURLBUT, John S. LONG, **f**-Died 23 Jun 1884 at about 21:00 at res. in Lewistown

Alice R. WILKINSON, **b**-28 Jun 1884, **c**-W. H. BROSIUS, Jos. L. PENNOCK, **d**-no bond, **e**- **f**-Died 22 Jun 1884 about 5:00 at res. of M. L. BROSIUS in said county

Laura J. CLEMENS, **b**-19 Jul 1884, **c**-John CLEMENS, extr., **d**-no bond, **e**- **f**-Died 9 Jul 1884 at about 18:30 at res. in Reedsville

Dr. John H. BELL, **b**-21 Jul 1884, **c**-Eliza A. BELL, **d**-$600, **e**-T. G. BELL, Geo. G. FRYSINGER, **f**-Died 24 Mar 1884 at about 21:00 at res. in Lewistown

John MARSDEN, **b**-25 Jul 1884, **c**-Robert D. CAMPBELL, **d**-no bond, **e**- **f**-Died 14 Jul 1884 at 19:30 at res. of R. D. CAMPBELL, Union Twp.

Joseph CLINGER, **b**-29 Jul 1884, **c**-Jno. C. CLINGER, Jas. H. CLINGER, **d**-no bond, **e**- **f**-Died 19 Jul 1884 at 23:50 at res. of Jno. C. CLINGER in Derry Twp.

Samuel RODGERS, **b**-2 Aug 1884, **c**-Isaac H. RODGERS, **d**-no bond, **e**- **f**-Died 25 Jul 1884 at 20:00 at res. in Derry Twp.

Harriet J. MARKS, **b**-13 Aug 1884, **c**-David W. WOODS, **d**-no bond, **e**- **f**-Died 10 Aug 1884 at 14:00 at res. in Lewistown Borough

Caroline HENZE, b-2 Sep 1884, **c**-Clarisa L. HENZE, admx. C.T.A., **d**-$500, **e**-[J. C.] BURKHOLDER, John BARR, **f**-Died 16 Aug 1884 at 6:00 at res. in Decatur Twp.

Jacob HAM, b-6 Sep 1884, **c**-T. A. W. WEBB, **d**-no bond, **e**- **f**-Died 11 Aug 1884 at 23:15 at res. of T. A. W. WEBB, Mifflin Co.

Lizzie B. WHEITSEL, b-11 Oct 1884, **c**-James E. WHEITSEL, **d**-no bond, **e**- **f**-Died 24 Jan 1884 at 20:00 at res. in Menno Twp.

Abraham KITTING, b-31 Oct 1884, **c**-Sarah C. KITTING, **d**-no bond, **e**- **f**-Died 23 Oct 1884 at 7:00 at res. in Lewistown Borough

Francis MILLIKEN, b-11 Nov 1884, **c**-John MILLIKEN, **d**-no bond, **e**- **f**-Died 23 Oct 1884 at 20:00 at res. in Derry Twp.

Page 268, Frame 286

William FOY, b-17 Nov 1884, **c**-Sarah Ellen FOY, **d**-no bond, **e**- **f**-Died 10 Nov 1884 at 17:00 at res. in Derry Twp.

Sarah C. KITTING, b-22 Nov 1884, **c**-D. R. STRATFORD, **d**-no bond, **e**- **f**-Died 21 Nov 1884 at 2:00 at res. in Derry Twp.

Abraham KITTING, b-26 Nov 1884, **c**-Saml. J. BRISBIN, admr C.T.A., **d**-$5000, **e**-David GROVE, James FIROVED, **f**-Died 23 Oct 1884 at 7:00 at residence in Lewistown.

Adam HAMAKER, b-28 Nov 1884, **c**-David G. HAMAKER, **d**-no bond, **e**- **f**-Died 22 Nov 1884 at 4:00 at res. in Lewistown

Josiah W. KENNEDY, b-4 Dec 1884, **c**-Samuel J. BRISBIN, **d**-$100, **e**-John KENNEDY, James FIROVED, **f**-Died 29 Nov 1884 at 2:00 at res. in Lewistown

John DAVIDSON, b-8 Dec 1884, **c**-Peter BAREFOOT, **d**-$1000, **e**-W. S. DELLETT, W. S. SETTLE, **f**-Died 27 Nov 1884 at 10:00 at res. in Armagh Twp.

Henry T. MITCHELL, b-9 Dec 1884, **c**-A. Taylor KYLE, **d**-$1500, **e**-Robert M. TAYLOR, Andrew W. CAMPBELL, **f**-Died 1 Dec 1884 between 6:00 and 8:00 at the hotel of Jas. [MINZAY? MINRAY?], Mifflintown, Pa.

Matilda E. HINDS, b-8 Jan 1885, **c**-Thompson G. BELL, **d**-$6000, **e**-S. M. BELL, Francis J. McCOY, **f**-Died 28 Oct 1884 at 2:00 at res. of T G. BELL, Derry Twp.

Nancy HEADDINGS, b-15 Jan 1885, **c**-John W. WILSON, **d**-no bond, **e**- **f**-Died 12 Jan 1885 at 14:00 at res. in Menno Twp.

Stephen H. MILLER, b-6 Feb 1885, **c**-Samuel L. BROWER, **d**-no bond, **e**- **f**-Died 14 Jan 1885 at 17:30 at res. in Decatur Twp.

Elizabeth BOTTEICHER, b-14 Feb 1885, **c**-Geo. W. BOTTEICHER, **d**-$100, **e**-Isaac LONG, M. M. McLAUGHLIN, **f**-Died 14 Oct 1880 at res. of Geo. W. BOTTEICHER in Bratton Twp.

Charles RITZ, b-23 Feb 1885, **c**-Andrew REED, **d**-no bond, **e**- **f**-Died at 10:30 at res. in Lewistown Borough

Lavina McKINNEY, b-28 Feb 1885, **c**-Charles A. McKINNEY, **d**-bond, **e**-Jos. S. McKENNY[sic], Geo. V. McKENNY[sic], **f**-Died 23 Feb 1885 at 8:00 at res. in Lewistown Borough

Geo. WEILER, b-2 Mar 1885, **c**-Francis R. WEILER, **d**-no bond, **e**- **f**-Died 18 Feb 1885 at 10:00 at res. in Menno Twp.

John THOMPSON, b-25 Mar 1885, **c**-Jas. P. THOMPSON, **d**-no bond, **e**- **f**-Died 22 Mar r1885 at 21:00 at re. in Newton Hamilton

Washington C. NELSON, b-27 Mar 1885, **c**-Jonathan PEACHEY, **d**-$1500, **e**-John W. WILSON, John M. FLEMING, **f**-Died 15 Mar 1885 at 9:00 at res. in Belleville, Mifflin Co.

Ann GALLAHER, b-28 Mar 1885, **c**-James K. MUTTHERSBAUGH, **d**-$200, **e**-Martin ORT, Daniel HARTLEY, **f**-Died 15 Jan 1885 at 21:00 at res. in Granville Twp., Pa.

Alexander KINLEY, b-4 Apr 1885, **c**-Charles NAGINEY, **d**-no bond, **e**- **f**-Died 18 Jan 1885 at 8:00 at res. in Derry Twp.

Page 269, Frame 287

Rosannah ALEXANDER, b-8 Apr 1885, **c**-James B. SMITH, **d**-no bond, **e**- **f**-Died 29 Mar 1885 at 9:00 at res. of W. J. EHRENFELD, Armagh Twp.

Margaret BURKHOLDER, b-16 Apr 1885, **c**-J. Clark BURKHOLDER, E. Adalaid BURKHOLDER, **d**-$10,000, **e**-John M. BEATTY, Chas. B. SIGLER, **f**-Died 20 Mar 1885 at 8:00 at res. in Lewistown

Jonathan Y. BYLER, b-17 Apr 1885, **c**-Saml. K. YODER, **d**-$500, **e**-Christian L. YODER, Solomon ZOOK, **f**-Died 9 April 1885 at 2:00 at res. in Union Twp.

Jane DULL, b-2 May 1885, **c**-J. R. WIRT, **d**-no bond, **e**- **f**-Died 16 Apr 1885 at 12:00 at res. in McVeytown.

John POLLOCK, b-16 May 1885, **c**-Jno. T. POLLOCK, Wm. J. POLLOCK, **d**-no bond, **e**- **f**-Died 14 Apr 1885 at 7:00 at res. in Wayne Twp.

Amos HOOT, b-10 Jun 1885, **c**-David W. WOODS, admr. C.T.A., **d**-$20,000, **e**-Joseph McFADDEN, Chas. H. HENDERSON, **f**-Died 1 Jun 1885 at 19:30 at res. in Lewistown Borough

Hugh McCLELLAND, b-13 Jun 1885, **c-**H. Mc. WALTERS, admr. B. N., **d-**$100, **e-**J. R. WIRT, L. WEBB, **f-**

[Gartrub] SHARP, b-20 Jun 1885, **c-**Noah SHARP, **d-**no bond, **e- f-**Died 28 Mar 1885 at 9:00 at res. in Brown Twp.

Mary DAVIS, b-7 Jul 1885, **c-**Rachel A. DAVIS, **d-**no bond, **e- f-**Died 20 Jun 1885 at 21:00 at res. in Lewistown

James NICHOLS, b-9 Jul 1885, **c-**James N. HOFFMAN, **d-**no bond, **e- f-**Died 1 Jul 1885 at 2:00 at res. in Lewistown

Mary J. BEAR, b-5 Aug 1885, **c-**W. L. OWENS, **d-**no bond, **e- f-**Died 26 Jul 1885 at 11:00 at res. in Granville Twp.

William SHILLING, b-7 Sep 1885, **c-**Martin A. PRICE, **d-**$100, **e-**Wm. S. STAYNER, Jeremiah PRICE, **f-**Died 23 May 1880 at res. in Granville Twp., about 3:00 [a.m.?]

Michael D. BROWN, b-18 Sep 1885, **c-**Joseph McCULLOCH, **d-**$1000, **e-**T. F. McCOY, R. W. PATTON, **f-**Died 6 Sep 1885 at res. in Derry Twp. at 11:30.

John B. MILLER, b-30 Sep 1885, **c-**James M. HEISTER, **d-**$200 **e-** Saml. W. NORTON, John T. [LANE], **f-**Died 29 Aug 1885 at res. in Newton Hamilton at 19:00

Ann E. GISEWHITE, b-14 Nov 1885, **c-**John LOCKE, **d-**no bond, **e- f-**Died 11 Oct 1885 at res. in Reedsville at 3:00.

John SNOOK, b-25 Nov 1885, **c-**John D. SNOOK, **d-**$400, **e-**Henry SNOOK, Howard AURAND, **f-**Died 13 Nov 1885 at res. in Armagh Twp at 7:00.

Henry BURLEW, b-27 Nov 1885, **c-**Geo. B. BURLEW (Chas. A. BURLEW the other extr. renounced) **d-**no bond, **e- f-**Died 21 Nov 1885 at res. in Wayne Twp. at 12:00 p.m.

John B. WAKEFIELD, b-3 Dec 1885, **c-**Letitia A. WAKEFIELD, **d-**$3000, **e-**Adam P. RUPERT, J. K. RHODES, **f-**Died 7 Nov 1885 at res. in Bratton Twp. at 19:00

Nancy J. GOODWIN, b-12 Dec 1885, **c-**John W. WILSON, **d-**no bond, **e- f-**Died 14 Nov 1885 at res. in Union Twp. at 8:00

Page 270, Frame 288

James KIBE, b-8 Jan 1886, **c-**Peter BAREFOOT, **d-**$1000, **e-**Ner THOMPSON, John D. NAGINEY, **f-**Died 30 Dec 1885 about 21:00 at res. in Armagh Twp.

Eliza KLINE, b-18 Jan 1886, **c**-Martha J. SCOTT, **d**-$300, **e**-Clarissa A. KLINE, Geo. W. ELDER, **f**-Died 10 Jan 1886 about 22:00 at res. of Mrs. SCOTT in Decatur Twp.

Christian PEACHEY, b-20 Jan 1886, **c**-John PEACHEY, **d**-no bond, **e**-**f**-Died 11 Jan 1886 about 11:45 at res. in Menno Twp.

Joseph W. McAULEY, b-19 Feb 1886, **c**-Joseph M. WOODS, **d**-$1000, **e**-D. W. WOODS, Thos. H. VAN VALZAH, **f**-Died 24 Jan 1886 about 20:00 at res. in Derry Twp.

Lydia GAFF, b-1 Mar 1886, **c**-Henry CORNELIUS, **d**-no bond, **e**- **f**-Died 18 Dec 1885 about 6:00 at res. of Henry CORNELIUS

Lewis REEL, b-1 Mar 1886, **c**-Christian Z. YODER, **d**-$100, **e**-Christian PEACHEY, Jonas Z. PEACHEY, **f**-Died May ___ 1883 at 16:00 at res. in Union Twp.

Francis McCLURE, b-8 Mar 1886, **c**-John T. McCLURE, **d**-$30,000, **e**-J. Beatty HENRY, Davis HENRY, **f**-Died 21 Feb 1886 at 10:00 at res. in Lewistown

Jacob C. HERTZLER, b-23 Mar 1886, **c**-Jonathan K. HERTZLER, **d**-no bond, **e**- **f**-Died 18 Mar 1886 at 5:00 at res. in Menno Twp.

George ORR, b-30 Mar 1886, **c**-Margaret ORR, **d**-$600, **e**-James FIROVED, John KINLEY, **f**-Died 17 Mar 1886 about 4:00 at res. in Derry Twp.

Sarah [CONENAUGH], b-3 Apr 1886, **c**-John C. SWIGART, **d**-$500, **e**-S. J. SWIGART, Jos. STRODE, **f**-Died 9 Apr 1880 at 24:00 (12:00 P.M.) at res. in Granville Twp.

Henry KLIPPERT, b-6 Apr 1886, **c**-Henry R. KLIPPERT, **d**-no bond, **e**-**f**-Died 27 Mar 1886 about 1:00 at res. in Bratton Twp.

Anna LANTZ, b-9 Apr 1886, **c**-Wm. H. GLASS, **d**-no bond, **e**- **f**-Died 30 Mar 1886 at 20:00 at res. in Allenville, Pa.

T. W. TOWNSEND, b-12 Apr 1886, **c**-H. J. CULBERTSON, **d**-no bond, **e**- **f**-Died 7 Apr 1886 at 1:00 at res. in Lewistown

Christian MOIST, b-27 Apr 1886, **c**-Jonas HARSHBARGER, **d**-no bond, **e**- **f**-Died 24 Apr 1886 at 15:00 at res. in Bratton Twp.

John M. CUMMINS, b-1 May 1886, **c**-N. C. WILSON, **d**-$1000, **e**-C. P. DULL, A. HULL, **f**-Died 10 Aug 1879 at about 0:00 at Atlantic City, N.J.

Philip FICKES, b-5 May 1886, **c**-William H. FICKES, **d**-$1200, **e**-T. A. CRISSMAN, A. S. HARSHBERGER, **f**-Died 7 Apr 1886 at about 7:00 at res. in Siglerville, Pa.

Thomas MILLER, b-8 May 1886, **c-**Henry STETLER, **d-**$1000, **e-**Henry STEIN, Aaron SINGLEY, **f-**Died 7 Apr 1886 ___ ___ ___ at res. in Decatur Twp.

Philip S. KEARNS, b-11 May 1886, **c-**J. C. KEARNS, Willis F. KEARNS, **d-**no bond, **e- f-**Died 5 May 1886 at 17:25 at res. in Decatur Twp.

Mary BRINDLE, b-12 May 1886, **c-**Albert G. GIBBONEY, **d-**no bond, **e- f-**Died 4 May 1886 at 19:00 at res. in Belleville, Pa.

Jane P. ELLIOTT, b-24 May 1886, **c-**D. W. WOODS, **d-**no bond, **e- f-**Died 19 Apr 1886 at 7:00 at res. in Lewistown.

Page 271, Frame 289

Nancy PRICE, b-25 May 1886, **c-**Henry BOOK, admr. C.T.A., **d-**$1000, **e-**Reuben M. PRICE, A. J. ATKINSON, **f-**Died 18 May 1886 at 22:00 at res. in Derry Twp.

Elijah YOUTZEY, b-1 Jun 1886, **c-**William YOUTZEY, **d-**$1000, **e-**Jonas HARSHBARGER, H. G. BRATTON, **f-**Died 17 May 1886 at 21:00 at res. in Bratton Twp.

William T. CUMMINGS, b-8 Jun 1886, **c-**John McNITT, **d-**$1000, **e-**Jno. D. BARR, R. M. TAYLOR, **f-**Died 1 Sep 1879, shot near Nevada, California.

Samuel S. SEACHRIST, b-15 Jun 1886, **c-**John C. SEACHRIST, Jno. GLASGOW, **d-**$2000, **e-**Wm. P. WITHEROW, J. W. HINDS, **f-**Died 19 Mar 1886 at 19:00 at res. in Wayne Twp.

Benjamin A. BRADLEY, b-25 Jun 1886, **c-**J. R. WIRT, **d-**no bail, **e- f-**Died 21 May 1886 at 23:00 at res. in McVeytown, Pa.

John SMITH, b-28 Jun 1886, **c-**Samuel J. SMITH, **d-**$100, **e-**H. C. KINSLOE, C. H. HENDERSON, **f-**Died 6 Apr 1885 at 18:00 at res. in Wayne Twp.

John A. MATHEWS, b-14 Jul 1886, **c-**Elizabeth A. MATHEWS, W. S. SETTLE, **d-**no bail, **e- f-**Died 9 Jul 1886 at 7:30 at res. in Granville Twp.

George SMITH, b-28 Jul 1886, **c-**Miles HAFFLEY, **d-**$1000, **e-**Felix SMOKER, Jno. R. GARVER, **f-**Died 5 Jul 1886 at 5:00 at res. in Union Twp.

William RUSSELL, b-4 Aug 1886, **c-**J. L. RUSSELL, D. W. WOODS, **d- e- f-**Died 28 Jul 1886 at 16:00 at res. in Lewistown.

John M. BEATTY, b-16 Aug 1886, **c**-Joseph M. WOODS, admr. C.T.A., **d**-$18,000, **e**-D. W. WOODS, Joseph McFADDEN, **f**-Died 5 Jul 1886 at 3:00 at res. in Lewistown

Adam RANKIN, b-16 Aug 1886, **c**-Ellen RANKIN, W. W. ROYER, **d**-no bond, **e**- **f**-Died 7 Aug 1886 at 16:00 at res. in Lewistown

W. R. ALEXANDER, b-17 Aug 1886, **c**-G. V. ALEXANDER, **d**-$100, **e**-Joseph McCULLOCH, H. G. BRATTON, **f**-Died 2 Apr 1886 at 4:00 at res. in Esler, Dakota [Territory]

Mary ALEXANDER, b-24 Aug 1886, **c**-S. J. ALEXANDER, **d**-$400, **e**-R. M. TAYLOR, H. F. TAYLOR, **f**-Died 8 Jun 1886 at 1:00 at res. in Armagh Twp.

Chas. MATHEWS, b-31 Aug 1886, **c**-S. J. BRISBIN, **d**-$100, **e**-H. J. WALTERS, La Fayette WEBB, **f**-Died 15 Jan 1886 sometime in the night at Pine Grove Forge, Cumberland County

M. P. WAKEFIELD, b-16 Sep 1886, **c**-Emma G. WAKEFIELD, **d**-$5000, **e**-David GROVE, James FIROVED, **f**-1 Sep 1886 at 18:00 at res. in Lewistown

Elenora C. SPETH, b-17 Sep [1886], **c**-Darwin C. SMITH, **d**-no bond, **e**- **f**-Died 9 Sep 1886 at 7:00 at res. in Granville Twp.

Wm. J. KYLE, b-20 Sep 1886, **c**-Laura M. KYLE, **d**-$1300, **e**-Jas. M. GOODHART, F. A. MEANS, **f**-Died 28 Aug 1886 at 13:00 at res. in Baltimore, MD.

Wm. S. CALDWELL, b-27 Sep 1886, **c**-Wm. Scott CALDWELL, Geo. W. CALDWELL, **d**-no bond, **e**- **f**-Died 28 Aug 1886 at 22:00 at res. in Granville Twp.

John D. NAGINEY, b-2 Oct 1886, **c**-M. M. NAGINEY, R. A. NAGINEY, Capt. R. J. McNITT, **d**-no bail, **e**- **f**-Died 14 Sep 1886 at 5:10 at res. in Milroy.

Page 272, Frame 290

James RENNINGER, b-5 Oct 1886, **c**-Lewis RENNINGER, **d**-$400, **e**-Jared KAUFFMAN, Geo. HUFFMAN, **f**-Died 15 Sep 1886 at 13:00 at res. in Bratton Twp.

James M. BULICK, b-15 Oct 1886, **c**-John W. WILSON, **d**-no bond, **e**- **f**-Died 8 Oct 1886 at 00:30 at res. in Union Twp.

Catharine ALEXANDER, b-26 Oct 1886, **c**-James B. SMITH, **d**-no bond, **e**- **f**-Died 11 Oct 1886 at 15:00 at res. in Armagh Twp.

John TREASTER, **b**-11 Nov 1886, **c**-Peter BAREFOOT, **d**-$3000, **e**-W. C. McCLENAHEN, Wm. A. MICHAEL, **f**-Died 30 Apr 1886 at 15:00 at res. in Armagh Twp.

Hannah S. McFARLANE, **b**-20 Nov 1886, **c**-Rose A. E. McFARLANE, **d**-$3000, **e**-Jas. McFARLANE, Geo. W. ELDER, **f**-Died 7 Oct 1886 at 11:00 at res. of her son James McFARLANE

John BOAS, **b**-7 Dec 1886, **c**-George W. BOLLINGER, **d**-$300, **e**-Geo. [A. LAPOLD], Allen SCHOCH, **f**-Died 10 Sep 1886 at 8:30 at res. in Oliver Twp.

Joseph SWARTZELL, **b**-11 Dec 1886, **c**-Francina SWARTZELL, **d**- **e**- **f**-Died 5 Dec 1886 at 22:00 at res. in Armagh Twp.

Hannah HANAWALT, **b**-24 Dec 1886, **c**-Joseph HANAWALT, **d**-$600, **e**-Samuel R. HANAWALT, David HANAWALT, **f**-Died 3 Dec 1886 at 22:30 at res. in Wayne Twp.

Emily ELLIOTT, **b**-6 Jan 1887, **c**-Joseph McCULLOCH, **d**-$3600, **e**-Geo. W. ELDER, M. A. PRICE, **f**-Died 1 Mar 1874 at 14:00 at res. in Lewistown Borough

Nath. KENNEDY, **b**-7 Jan 1887, **c**-John KENNEDY, James FIROVED, **d**-no bond, **e**- **f**-Died 5 Jan 1887 at 20:30 at res. in Kewistown

Ezra M. HOOPES, **b**-11 Jan 1887, **c**-Peter BAREFOOT, **d**-$1000, **e**-Ner THOMPSON, Ira THOMPSON, **f**-Died 24 Dec 1886 at 13:32 at res. in Armagh Twp.

R. A. MEANS, **b**-21 Jan 1887, **c**-F. A. MEANS, R. H. MEANS, **d**- **e**- **f**-Died 5 Jan 1887 at 18:00 at res. in Derry Twp.

Frank C. WOLF, **b**-25 Jan 1887, **c**-Samuel PARKER, **d**-$500, **e**-A. F. KLINE, Geo. MYERS, **f**-Died 23 Jan 1887 at 3:00 at res. of A. F. KLINE in Lewistown

John S. REED, **b**-27 Jan 1887, **c**-Elizabeth REED, **d**-$100, **e**-John A. McKEE, Wm. H. REED, **f**-Died 22 Jan 1887 at 22:00 at res. in Lewistown

I. Isabella CALDWELL, **b**-28 Jan 1887, **c**-Alva M. CALDWELL, **d**- **e**- **f**-Died 6 Dec 1886 at 13:00 at res. in Oliver Twp.

Mrs. E. J. KNOTWELL, **b**-2 Feb 1887, **c**-H. R. KNOTWELL, **d**-$100, **e**-Jno. A. McKEE, S. L. COOPER, **f**-Died 27 Jul 1886 at 6:15 at res. in Lewistown

James ALEXANDER, **b**-4 Feb 1887, **c**-Robert A. ALEXANDER, L. L. HAUGHAWOUT, **d**-$25,000, **e**-C. A. ALEXANDER, Z. M. ALEXANDER, E. R. ALEXANDER, **f**-Died 28 Sep 1886 at 5:00 at res. in Union Twp.

William HAWLK, b-14 Feb 1887, **c**-W. S. DELLETT, **d**-$500, **e**-John H. COULTER, Elias HUFFNAGLE, **f**-Died 7 Jan 1887 at 23:00 at res. in Milroy

Catherine KING, b-24 Feb 1887, **c**-Yost HARTZLER, **d**-$400, **e**-Benj. HARTZLER, Jos. McCULLOCH, R. M. GILMORE, **f**-Died 21 Feb 1887 at 17:00 at res. in Menno Twp.

Page 273, Frame 291

Saml. LIGHTER, b-29 Mar 1887, **c**-Joseph McCULLOCH, **d**-$[300] **e**-Geo. W. ELDER, S. J. BRISBIN, **f**-Died 13 Apr 1882, Granville Twp.

Robert DIXON, b-29 Mar 1887, **c**-John YODER, **d**- **e**- **f**-[NOTE: The record seems to be omitting "Died" from this point on; may add in for clarity] 16 Mar 1887 at 10:00 at res. in Union Twp.

John McLAUGHLIN, b-6 Apr 1887, **c**-James ROSENBERRY, **d**- **e**- **f**-Died 4 Apr 1887 at about 6:00 at res. in Wayne Twp.

Wm. PARKER, b-8 Apr 1887, **c**-James WRAY, **d**-$500, **e**-Frederick LASH, John WRAY, **f**-Died 28 Mar 1887 at about 9:10 at res. in Decatur Twp.

Margaret TREASTER, b-20 Apr 1887, **c**-Adam A. BROWN, **d**-$1000, **e**-Lott ARMSTRONG, Thomas DEPO, **f**-Died 6 Apr 1887 at about 21:00 at res. of D. O. TREASTER, Armagh Twp.

Geo. C. WAKEFIELD, b-4 May 1887, **c**-G. H. MACKLIN, Andrew McKEE, Jr., **d**-$3000, **e**-David STINE, Jr., Wm. WILLIS, **f**-Died 22 Apr [1887] at 17:30 at res. in Oliver Twp.

William SLEUSTER, b-23 May 1887, **c**-T. F. McCOY, **d**-$100, **e**-Jos. McFADDEN, D. M. RITTENHOUSE, **f**-Died 21 May [1887] at [7:00] at res. in Lewistown

James CRUTCHLEY, b-17 Jun 1887, **c**-Sarah A. CRUTCHLEY, extx., **d**- **e**- **f**-Died 2 March [1887] at 2:00 at res. in Lewistown

John HAYES, Jr., b-20 Jun 1887, **c**-Rebecca J. HAYES, admx., **d**-$2000, **e**-W. J. HAYES, Jno. REED, **f**-Died 24 Mar [1887] at 22:00 at res. in Brown Twp.

Henry W. HOFFMAN, b-30 Jun 1887, **c**-Elizabeth L. HOFFMAN, **d**-$4000, **e**-Jno. KLEIN, W. C. HOFFMAN, **f**-[Died in] Camden, New Jersey

Wilhelmina HAEBER, b-8 Jul 1887, **c**-Magdalena BUSHE, extx., **d**- **e**- **f**-Died 2 Jul 1887 at 7:55 at res. in Lewistown

John W. ROBISON, b-18 Jul 1887, **c**-W. M. DOUGHMAN, George W. ROBISON, **d**- **e**- **f**-

Jonathan P. YODER, b-20 Jul 1887, c-Jonas HARSHBARGER, d-$200, e-Jacob MILLER, Lewis HESSER, f-Died 24 Jun 1887 at noon at res. in Bratton Twp.

Sidney I. LYON, b-27 Jul 1887, c-A. W. CAMPBELL, d-$4000, e-Jos. CAMPBELL, John A. CAMPBELL, f-Died 8 Jul 1887 at about 8:30 at res. of Mrs. OLIVER, McVeytown

Jane McKEE, b-4 Aug 1887, c-J. Strode McKEE, d- e- f-Died 19 Jul 1887 at about 20:00 at res. of J. Strode McKEE, Lewistown

Joseph SNYDER, b-13 Aug 1887, c-Mrs. Anna SNYDER, Wm. [G.] ROPER, d-$5000, e-F. A. MEANS, C. H. HENDERSON, f-Died 31 Jul 1887 at 13:40 at res. in Granville Twp.

John HARRIS, b-18 Aug 1887, c-A. W. PORTER, d-$50, e-T. B. REED, H. J. WALTERS, f-Died June 1883 at res. in Lewistown

Frances G. AURAND, b-20 Aug 1887, c-Harrison AURAND, extr., d- e- f-9 Aug 1887 at about 6:00 at res. in Granville Twp.

John CAMP, Sr., b-23 Aug 1887, c-Peter BAREFOOT, admr. C.T.A., d-$600, e-J. C. McCLINTIC, Ira THOMPSON, f-

Elizabeth C. McCLINTIC, b-24 Aug 1887, c-Hugh McCLINTIC, extr., d- e- f-Died 12 Aug 1887 about 18:00 at res. of father in Armagh Twp.

Joseph YEATTER, b-24 Aug 1887, c-Henry STETLER, d-$800, e-M. G. DRUCKEMILLER, Reuben O. STETLER, f-Died 9 Feb 1884 at res. in Decatur Twp.

Mrs. Anna Eliza LONG, b-29 Aug 1887, c-D. W. WOODS, extr., d- e- f-Died 24 Aug 1887 at about 20:30 at res. of Dr. C. H. HURLBUT in Lewiston

Julia Ann RHODES, b-6 Sep 1887, c-John M. QUARRY, extr., d- e- f-Died 30 Aug 1887 about 18:00 at res. of Jno. M. QUARRY in Oliver Twp.

Page 274, Frame 292

Aaron MOIST, b-8 Sep 1887, c-Abraham MOIST, Moses MOIST, d-$1000, e-Lewis HESSER, f-Died 19 Aug 1887 at about 10:00 at res. in Bratton Twp.

Felix SMOKER, b-12 Sep 1887, c-J. E. SMUCKER[sic], extr., d- e- f-Died 1 Aug 1887 at about 12:30 at res. in Lewistown

Mrs. Sarah M. CRISSWELL, b-19 Sep 1887, c-Henry STETLER, d-$600, e-James FIROVED, J. A. STINEBARGER, f-Died 5 Apr 1885 at about 5:00 at res. in Decatur Twp.

Elizabeth CORNELIUS, b-28 Sep 1887, **c**-John MYERS, **d- e- f**-Died 6 Aug 1887 at about 7:00 at res. in Oliver Twp.

Henry PRINTZ, b-15 Oct 1887, **c**-Samuel KILLIAN, admr., **d**-$200, **e**-Wm. W. TROUT, John G. WHITE, **f**-Died 8 Oct 1887 at about 22:00 at res. in Lewistown

J. English WEST, b-20 Oct 1887, **c**-Annie S. WEST, **d- e- f**-Died 23 Mar at about 9:00 at res. in McVeytown

Sarah J. HOLLAND, b-22 Oct 1887, **c**-Samuel H. McCOY, **d**-$1600, **e**-W. G. C. MINEHART, Joseph McFADDEN, **f**-Died 22 Oct 1887 at 4:30 at res. of Mrs. HERRINGTON of Granville Twp.

Sarah YODER, b-7 Nov 1887, **c**-Shem K. YODER, extr., **d- e- f**-Died 11 Sep 1887 at 13:00 at res. in Brown Twp.

Adam HARTZLER, b-10 Nov 1887, **c**-Jacob K. DETWEILER, extr., **d- e- f**-Died 3 Nov 1887 at 22:00 at res. in Menno Twp.

Simon STROUP, b-4 Nov 1887, **c**-George T. GARDNER, **d**-$100, **e**-H. C. VANZANDT, Lebiah STUMPFF, **f**-Died 6 Jul 1887 at 11:00 at res. in Decatur Twp.

Mrs. Nancy J. ELLIS, b-11 Nov 1887, **c**-Mary M. KEPLER, **d**-$12,000, **e**-James H. MAN[sic], Jno. B. SELHEIMER, **f**-Died 30 Oct 1887 at 12:30 at res. in Lewistown

Reuben KAUFFMAN, b-14 Nov 1887, **c**-Levi KAUFFMAN, extr., **d- e- f**-Died 22 Oct 1887 at 00:30 at res. in Bratton Twp.

Sarah NAGINEY, b-10 Dec 1887, **c**-Peter BAREFOOT, extr., **d- e- f**-Died 30 Nov 1887 at 13:00 at res. in Armagh Twp.

John FULTZ, b-13 Dec 1887, **c**-Miles HAFFLY, **d- e- f**-Died 5 Dec 1887 at 21:45 at res. in Union Twp.

Augustus J. KUHN, b-24 Dec 1887, **c**-Susanna M. K. STANLY[sic], Winfield Scott STANLEY, **d- e- f**-Died 3 Dec 1887 at 6:15 at La Fayette Hotel, Philadelphia

Jacob H. ZOOK, b-4 Jan 1888, **c**-Christian C. ZOOK, admr., **d**-$600, **e**-Joseph H. ZOOK, Seth K. YODER, **f**-Died 26 Dec 1887 at 19:00 at re. in Brown Twp.

W. J. LUCAS, b-11 Jan 1888 **c**-Wm. A. ORT, **d**-$400, **e**-John K. RHODES, John L. BROWER, **f**-Died 3 Jan 1888 at 18:00 at res. in Derry Twp.

William U. BUNNELL, b-13 Jan 1888, **c**-N. C. WILSON, admr., **d**-$2000, **e**-W. C. BUNNELL, J. B. SELHEIMER, **f**-Died 19 Nov 1887 at 23:00 at res. of A. C. MAYES in Lewistown

Enoch ZOOK, b-19 Jan 1888, c-David H. ZOOK, Enoch A. ZOOK, d- e- f-Died 11 Jan 1888 at 23:00 at res. in Union Twp.

John S. (or C.) SECREST, b-31 Jan 1888, c-Wm. P. WITHROW, d- e- f-Died 25 Jan 1888 at 6:00 at res. in Wayne Twp.

Isaac SNOOK, b-3 Feb 1888, c-Samuel SHIREY, admr., d-$800, e-John SHIREY, John L. BROWER, f-Died 19 Jan 1888 at 11:00 at res. in Brown Twp.

Isaac WALLS, b-9 Feb 1888, c-C. Penrose DULL, d- e- f-Died 3 Jan 1888 about 21:30 at res. in [Mattawana], Bratton Twp.

Page 275, Frame 293

Nancy M. THOMPSON, b-17 Feb 1888, c-Mary T. STICKNEY, extx., d- e- f-Died 9 Feb 1888 at about 17:00 at res. in Lewistown

William C. VINES, b-22 Feb 1888, c-Joseph M. WOODS, d- e- f-Died 17 Feb 1888 at 2:00 at res in Lewistown

Solomon KAUFFMAN, b-23 Feb 1888, c-Mary E. KAUFFMAN, d-$3000, e-Levi FELKER, John C. SHAHEN, f-Died 10 Feb 1888 at 1:30 at res. in Oliver Twp.

Sarah J. LANE, b-2 Mar 1888, c-John T. LANE, d-$3000, e-J. K. RHODES, W. C. BRATTON, f-Died 24 Aug 1886 at 18:00 at res. in Newton Hamilton

David STINE, Sr., b-5 Mar 1888, c-John GLASGOW, extr., d- e- f-Died 25 Feb 1888 at 10:00 at res. in Wayne Twp.

Rebecca J. McKALIPS, b-10 Mar 1888, c-Mahlon McKALIPS, d-$800, e-Henry P. ALEXANDER, J. C. BELL [NOTE: It looks like an "E" on the end of the name, but I think it is just a flourish], f-Died 11 Jan 1888 at 11:30 at res. in Derry Twp. [Another process on p. 281.]

John HAYES, Sr., b-19 Mar 1888, c-James W. HAYES, d- e- f-Died 14 Mar 1888 at 14:00 at res. in Union Twp.

Margaret C. GRIMMINGER, b-22 Mar 1888, c-John S. GRIMMINGER, d-$100, e-Joseph McCULLOCH, James S. RAKERD, f-Died 2 Oct 1884 at 9:00 at Mrs. MORAN's in Altoona, Blair, Pennsylvania

Levi ZOOK, b-27 Mar 1888, c-Jacob K. DETWEILER, d-$1000, e-David H. ZOOK, Ismael [T.] YODER, f-Died 2 Oct 1884 at 22:00 at res. in Oliver Twp.

John SNYDER, b-31 Mar 1888, c-R. H. MEANS, A. S. McKEE, d-$2000, e-F. A. MEANS, J. Strode McKEE, f-23 Mar 1888 at 16:00 by accident on mountain near his home in Granville Twp.

Eve Anna MYERS, **b**-31 Mar 1888, **c**-S. E. GRIMM, **d**- **e**- **f**-Died 19 Mar 1888 at 5:00 at res. in Granville Twp.

Peter BEATTY, **b**-10 Apr 1888, **c**-J. R. WIRT, **d**- **e**- **f**-Died 3 Apr 1888 about 7:00 at res. in McVeytown

Charles LEHR, **b**-12 Apr 1888, **c**-Isaac SHIREY, **d**-$100, **e**-H. M. ULSH, Samuel LAWVER, **f**-Died 12 Dec 1887, found burned to death in his res. at Decatur Twp.

Jacob H. SPIGLEMYER, **b**-14 Apr 1888, **c**-C. Stewart GARRETT, **d**-$400, **e**-Jos. McCULLOCH, La Fayette WEBB, **f**-Died 6 Apr 1888 at about 6:00 at res. in Decatur Twp.

Sallie Ann TAYLER, **b**-4 May 1888, **c**-Fanny Brown STRUNK, **d**- **e**- **f**-Died 16 Apr 1888 at 13:00 at res. in Armagh Twp.

Christian SEACHRIST, **b**-5 May 1888, **c**-George SEACHRIST, **d**- **e**- **f**-Died 25 Apr 1888 at 7:00 in res. in Derry Twp.

Philip SHADE, **b**-11 May 1888, **c**-J. K. HARTZLER, **d**-$1000, **e**-A. ROTHROCK, J. R. WIRT, **f**-Died 24 Apr 1888 at 6:00 at res. in Wayne Twp.

John BARDINE, **b**-22 May 1888, **c**-Mrs. Ellen BARDINE, Samuel BARDINE, **d**- **e**- **f**-Died 5 May 1888 at 12:30 at res. in Wayne Twp.

Solomon K. BYLER, **b**-22 May 1888, **c**-Moses P. YODER, **d**- **e**- **f**-Died 3 May 1888 at 14:00 at res. in Union Twp.

J. Howard ALEXANDER, **b**-29 May 1888, **c**-Rhoda A. ALEXANDER, **d**-$400, **e**-Jos. McCULLOCH, William WILLIS, **f**-Died 22 Oct 1887 at 10:00 at res. in Union Twp.

Lydia ZOOK, **b**-1 Jun 1888, **c**-Menno S. ZOOK (of Brown Twp., **d**-$2000, **e**-John B. ZOOK, Eli B. ZOOK, **f**-Died 23 May 1888 at 10:00 at res. in Brown Twp.

Moses MILLER, **b**-9 Jun 1888, **c**-D. W. WOOD, **d**- **e**- **f**-Died 2 Jun 1888 at 10:30 at res. of Albert STEINBARGER in Granville Twp.

Moses PEACHEY, **b**-23 Jul 1888, **c**-Barbara PEACHEY, **d**- **e**- **f**-Died 18 Jun 1888 at 14:00 in res. in Menno Twp.

Alex. H. SHEAFFER, **b**-28 Jul 1888, **c**-Ellen E. SHEAFFER, **d**- **e**- **f**-Died 20 Jul 1888 at 16:20 at res. of J. W. WILLIAMS, Lewistown

Marie DIGGS, **b**-3 Aug 1888, **c**-James H. MANN, **d**- **e**- **f**-Died 19 Jul 1888 at 1:15 at res. in Lewistown

John KAYS, **b**-15 Aug 1888, **c**-J. M. WOODS, **d**-$1000, **e**-D. W. WOODS, T. F. McCOY, **f**-Died 3 Aug 1888 at res. in Granville Twp.

Catharine J. YODER, **b**-24 Aug 1888, **c**-Benjamin HARTZLER, **d**- **e**- **f**-Died 15 Aug 1888 at 9:00 at res. in Menno Twp.

Page 276, Frame 294

[NOTE: Time of death seems to be omitted at this point. They will resume shortly.]

George MOLSON, **b**-3 Sep 1888, **c**-Mary MOLSON, extx., **d**- **e**- **f**-Died 10 Aug 1888 at res. in Lewistown

Robert KENNEDY, **b**-4 Sep 1888, **c**-Joseph M. WOODS, **d**-$5600, **e**-D. W. WOODS, C. Stewart GARRETT, **f**-Died 16 Aug 1888 at res. in Kildrum, Antrim, Ireland

Thomas MOORE, **b**-10 Sep 1888, **c**-John R. MOORE, **d**-$2000, **e**-Sarah J. MOORE, Marten ORT, **f**-Died 4 Aug 1888 in Granville Twp.

John GEPHART, **b**-11 Sep 1888, **c**-Hannah C. GEPHART, **d**-$100, **e**-W. H. FELIX, C. S. GARRETT, **f**-16 Aug 1888 by accident at Rail Road Bridge in Mifflin County

Elias C. KEARNS, **b**-11 Sep 1888, **c**-Nancy J. KEARNS, **d**-$3000, **e**-Abram STOUFFER, H. A. FELIX, **f**-13 Aug 1888 at res. in Derry Twp

John CARSON, **b**-22 Sep 1888, **c**-W. D. TAYLOR, **d**-$1500, **e**-R. M. TAYLOR, J. P. TAYLOR, **f**-14 Sep 1888 at res. in Brown Twp.

John CUPPLES, **b**-25 Sep 1888, **c**-Wm. KREPPS, J. R. WIRT, **d**- **e**- **f**-Died 16 Sep 1888 at res. of Wm. KREPPS in Bratton Twp.

John D. BYLER, **b**-8 Oct 1888, **c**-Jacob S. KING, Rufus A. BYLER, **d**-$1500, **e**-Levi L. BYLER, John S. BYLER, **f**-Died 31 Aug 1888 in res. in Menno Twp.

John H. DEWEES, **b**-15 Oct 1888, **c**-Emily J. DEWEES, **d**-$500, **e**-D. W. WOODS, Mary E. RUSSELL, **f**-Died 9 Dec 1883 in Thomasville, North Carolina

Eliza A. KIBE, **b**-22 Oct 1888, **c**-Sarah M. KIBE, **d**-$400, **e**-James B. McNITT, W. S. DELLETT, **f**-7 Oct 1888 at res. of J. & J. McNITT, Armagh Twp.

Jacob LEPLEY, **b**-20 Oct 1888, **c**- **d**-$600 **e**-Ephraim LEPLEY, Moses YETTER, **f**-Died 17 Oct 1888 at res. in Decatur Twp.

John A. RUSH, **b**-20 Nov 1888, **c**-John C. SHAHEN, **d**-$800, **e**-W. H. BINGERMAN, Geo. W. AULTS, **f**-Died 13 Nov 1888 at res. in Oliver Twp.

Harry SOLES, **b**-24 Nov 1888, **c**-Olive SOLES, **d**- **e**- **f**-Died 16 Nov 1888 in res. in Lewistown Borough

Abraham BROWN, **b**-7 Dec 1888, **c**-The Fidelity Insurance Trust and Safe Deposit Co., of Philadelphia, **d**-$17,000, **e**-The Fidelity Insurance Trust and Safe Deposit Co., **f**-Died 15 Nov 1888 in Mattawana, Pa.

Joseph F. DULL, **b**-13 Dec 1888, **c**-D. M. DULL, **d**-$5000, **e**-J. K. RHODES, Jno. A. WAREAM, **f**-Died 18 Oct 1888 at res. in McVeytown

George W. BYERS, **b**-20 Dec 1888, **c**-John M. BYERS, **d**-$500, **e**-David McKERR, S. J. BRISBIN, **f**-Died 15 Dec 1888 at res. in McVeytown

Mary BRATTON, **b**-21 Dec 1888, **c**-Nannie J. DULL, Margaret H. STINE, **d**- **e**- **f**-Died 2 Dec 1888 at res. of Mrs. STINE, McVeytown

Susanna HENRY, **b**-8 Jan 1889, **c**-Adam A. BROWN, **d**-$250, **e**-John A. SHUMAKER, Ira THOMPSON, **f**-25 Jan 1888 at 10:00 at res. in Armagh Twp.

Davis McKean CONTNER, **b**-10 Jan 1889, **c**-J. T. WILSON, **d**- **e**- **f**-Died 3 Jan 1889 about 22:00 at res. in Menno Twp.

Robert Finley ELLIS, **b**-11 Jan 1889, **c**-Wm. IRWIN, admr. C.T.A., **d**-$200, **e**-Geo. W. ELDER, Rufus C. ELDER, **f**-Died about Mar 1872 at res. in Lewistown.

Joseph HARTZLER, **b**-15 Jan 1889, **c**-J. Taylor WILSON, **d**-$3000, **e**-Robert F. WILSON, J. W. WILSON, **f**-Died 28 Dec 1888 at about 3:00 at res. in Menno Twp.

Robert U. MARKS, **b**-23 Jan 1889, **c**-Mrs. Ellen D. MARKS, **d**-$2000, **e**-J. R. McCOY, J. M. SELHEIMER, **f**-8 Jan 1889 at about 00:30 at res. of J. J. McCLURE in Philadelphia, Pa.

Wm. M. AITKINS, **b**-1 Mar 1889, **c**-Mrs. M. J. AITKENS, **d**-$800, **e**-Henry W. BARR, Joseph M. WOODS, **f**-Died [10] Feb 1889 at 9:30 in res. in Siglerville, Armagh Twp.

Jacob FINKEL, **b**-5 Mar 1889, **c**-Jno. W. WILSON, **d**-$1000, **e**-R. F. WILSON, J. J. WILSON, **f**-Died 30 Dec 1888 at 1:00 at res. in Belleville, Union Twp.

Robt. B. FORSYTH, **b**-12 Mar 1889, **c**-Mrs. Kate B. FORSYTH, **d**- **e**- **f**-Died 21 Feb 1889 at 20:00 at res. in Derry Twp.

Robert TAYLOR, **b**-25 Mar 1889, **c**-R. M. TAYLOR, J. P. TAYLOR, **d**- **e**- **f**-Died 14 Mar 1889 at 4:30 in res. in Brown Twp.

Page 277, Frame 295
Geo. W. THOMAS, **b**-3 Apr 1889, **c**-Joseph McCULLOCK, admr. D.B.N. C.T.A., **d**-$10,000, **e**-T. F. McCOY, W. S. SETTLE, **f**-

Jesse MENDENHALL, **b**-8 Apr 1889, **c**-E. E. MENDENHALL, W. H. MENDENHALL, **d**- **e**- **f**-Died 3 Apr 1889 about 20:00 at res. in Derry Twp.

John C. McCREARY, b-11 Apr 1889, c-Mary B. McCREARY, d- e- f-Died 14 Jun 1888 at 13:00 at Harrisburg Insane Asylum

Geo. H. WILLIAMS, b-19 Apr 1889, c-James E. WOOMER, d-$100, e-Wm. ROUNTREE, John MARTIN, f-Died 8 Mar 1889 at 21:00 in railroad accident at or near Middleburg, Snyder County

A. Taylor KYLE, b-10 Apr 1889, c-Lizzie R. M. KYLE, W. B. KYLE, d-$4000, e-John D. BARR, J. Beatty HENRY, f-Died 5 Apr 1889 at 23:00 at res. in Brown Twp.

Lucinda SIGLER, b-29 Apr 1889, c-Chas. B. SIGLER, d-$5000, e-W. A. ORR, J. Clark BURKHOLDER, f-Died 17 Apr 1889 at 9:45 at res. in Decatur Twp.

Lydia S. THOMAS, b-15 May 1889, c-Harriet L. THOMAS, admr. C.T.A., d-$5000, e-Jos. McCULLOCH, D. W. WOODS, f-Died 13 Oct 1888 at 9:00 at res. in Lewistown

Armilda A. THOMAS, b-15 May 1889, c-Harriet L. THOMAS, extx., d- e- f-Died 24 Mar 1889 at 16:00 at res. in Lewistown

Jane Ann BANKS, b-15 May 1889, c-Andrew REID, extr., d- e- f-Died 10 May 1889 at 19:00 at res. in Lewistown

John THRELKELD, b-21 May 1889, c-Joseph McCULLOCH, d-$50, e-J. M. WOODS, S. J. BRISBIN, f-Died 26 Jul 1884 at 4:30 at res. in Lewistown

Joel PEACHEY, b-11 Jun 1889, c-A. Z. PEACHEY, d-$2000, e-Solomon PEACHEY, John GARVER, f-Died 25 May 1889 at 20:00 at res. in Menno Twp.

Wm. R. PRICE, b-15 Jul 1889, c-B. C. CUBBISON d-$2500, e-Wm. BROWN, Danl. J. PRICE, f-Died 26 Jun 1889 at 22:00 at res. in Derry Twp.

James KALPETZER, b-17 Jul 1889, c-Joseph KLINE, d-$5600, e-Jos. S. GOSS, Frank P. DECKER, T. A. WAGNER, f-Died 24 Jun 1889 about 15:00 at res. in Decatur Twp.

Henry PETER, b-22 Jul 1889, c-Wm. S. SETTLE, d- e- f-Died 19 Jul 1889 at 11:00 at res. in Lewistown Borough

George FORSYTHE, b-3 Aug 1889, c-J. M. WOODS, d-$32,000, e-D. W. WOODS, T. F. McCOY, f-Died 25 Jun 1889 at 17:00 at res. in Lewistown Borough

Wm. McNITT, b-7 Aug 1889, c-Robert B. McNITT, Wm. B. McNITT, d- e- f-Died 7 Jul 1889 at 23:00 at res. in Armagh Twp.

Wm. L. CLOSE, b-7 Aug 1889, c-Peter BAREFOOT, d- e- f-Died 31 Aug 1888 at 12:00 P.M. at res. in Armagh Twp.

Mary A. NICHOLS, b-6 Aug 1889, **c**-Joseph McCULLOCH, **d- e- f**-Died 3 Aug 1889 at 14:40 at res. in Lewistown Borough

Barbara PLANK, b-22 Aug 1889, **c**-Joshua ZOOK, **d**-$15,000, **e**-Jonathan PLANK, D. R. ZOOK, **f**-Died 26 Jul 1889 at 22:00 at res. in Union Twp.

James WILSON, b-27 Aug 1889, **c**-Wm. H. WILSON, Wm. B. LUKENS, **d**-$12,000, **e**-D. C. RHODES, W. S. STAYNER, **f**-Died 15 Jul 1889 at 21:00 at res. in Wayne Twp.

Saml. Y. PLANK, b-3 Sep 1889, **c**-Jacob K. DETWEILER, **d**-$3000, **e**-David H. ZOOK, David YODER, **f**-Died 13 Aug 1889 at 11:00 at res. in Union Twp.

Jacob HOUSER, b-9 Sep 1889, **c**-J. VANZANT, C. VANZANT, **d**-$900, **e**-W. F. KEARNS, Lebiah STUMPFF, **f**-Died 16 Mar 1889 at 20:00 at res. of B. F. HOUSER of Derry Twp.

John M. MITCHELL, b-16 Sep 1889, **c**-Samuel MITCHELL, **d- e- f**-Died 2 Aug 1889 at 23:00 at res. in Derry Twp.

Page 278, Frame 296

Ephraim BANKS, b-18 Sep 1889, **c**-Andrew REED, admr. d.b.n. c.t.a. **d**-$1500, **e**-H. P. TAYLOR, S. B. WEBER, **f**-

W. W. HORRELL, b-23 Sep 1889, **c**-Geo. F. HORRELL, **d**-$150, **e**-A. HULL, La Fayette WEBB, **f**-Died 18 Jul 1889 about 3:00 at res. in Menno Twp.

Henry McAULEY, b-27 Sep 1889, **c**-David H. McAULEY, **d- e- f**-Died 15 Sep 1889 at 20:30 at res. in Armagh Twp.

Elias HUFFNAGLE, b-28 Sep 1889, **c**-Jos. HUFFNAGLE, **d- e- f**-Died 11 Sep 1889 at 13:00 at res. in Derry Twp.

Henry STETLER, b-1 Oct 1889, **c**-Reuben O. STETLER, **d**-$1600, **e**-Simon KNEPP, Simon KREPS, **f**-26 Sep 1889 at 20:00 at res. in Decatur Twp.

Christian G. YODER, b-2 Oct 1889, **c**-Israel T. YODER, **d- e- f**-Died 2 Sep 1889 at 23:30 at res. in Union Twp.

Benj. K. GARDNER, b-8 Oct 1889, **c**-W. W. TROUT **d- e- f**-Died 27 Sep 1889 at 23:00 at res. in Lewistown

Thompson G. BELL, b-12 Oct 1889, **c**-S. M. BELL, **d- e- f**-Died 28 Sep 1889 at 14:00 at res. in Derry Twp.

Elizabeth E. BURKHOLDER, b-17 Oct 1889, **c**-Isaac DREESE **d- e- f**-Died 8 Oct 1889 at 16:00 at res. in Newton Hamilton

Laressa T. INGRAM, b-19 Oct 1889, c-George F. GARDNER, d- e- f-
Died 16 Oct 1889 at 11:30 at res. in Decatur Twp.

Ephraim HAZLETT, b-25 Oct 1889, c-Louisa HAZLETT, d-$10,000, e-
Jacob S. KING, S. M. PEACHEY, f-27 Sep 1889 at 14:00 by Railroad
Accident at Ardheims Siding at Huntingdon Co., Pa.

Nancy RONK, b-4 Nov 1889, c-J. R. WIRT, d-$500, e-C. P. DULL, J. B.
SELHEIMER, f-Died 5 Aug 1889 at ___ at res. in Bratton Twp.

Peter PRINTZ, b-11 Nov 1889, c-Wm. PRINTZ, d-$4000, e-James
PRINTZ, Joseph McCULLOCH, Wm. S. SETTLE, f-Died 20 Aug
1881 at 18:00 at res. of his daughter in Lewistown

J. O. CAMPBELL, b-14 Nov 1889, c-A W. CAMPBELL, d- e- f-Died 29
Oct 1889 at 9:30 at res. in Union Twp.

Jacob KNEPP, b-12 Dec 1889, c-Jacob LAWVER, d-$100, e-Edward
YETTER, Rufus KNEPP, f-Died 16 Nov 1889 at 17:00 at res. in
Decatur Twp.

John W. SHAW, b-27 Dec 1889, c-John W. SHAW, d- e- f-Died 8 Dec
1889 at 14:00 at res. in Lewistown

Margaret J. ALLISON, b-3 Jan 1890, c-James ALLISON, d-$4000, e-
David ALLISON, Saml. W. ALLISON, f-Died 16 Feb 1889 at 17:00
at res. in Menno Twp.

Page 279, Frame 297

George G. COUCH, b-9 Jan 1890, c-Maria McVey COUCH, d- e- f-Died
11 Dec 1889 at 3:00 in res. in McVeytown

Mahala TICE, b-10 Jan 1890, c-Samuel KILLIAN, d-$300, e-W. W.
TROUT, Thomas STRANG, f-Died 30 Dec 1889 at 6:55 at res. in
Lewistown

Philip L. LEE, b-13 Jan 1890, c-H. J. CULBERSON, d-$4000, e-S. B.
WEBER, J. M. GOODHART, f-25 Dec 1889 at St. Louis, Missouri

William W. MURPHY, b-24 Jan 1890, c-M. M. McLAUGHLIN, d-$500,
e-S. R. H. MONTGOMERY, George MYERS, f-Died 20 Jan 1890 at
17:00 at res. in Lewistown

Frederick J. KIEFHABER, b-11 Feb 1890, c-Ferd KIEFHABER, d-
$5000, e-J. K. RHODES, J. Roller McCOY, f-Died 26 Feb 1888 at
9:00 at res. in Wayne Twp.

James L. PHILIPS, b-22 Feb 1890, c-John FROCK, d-$100, e-George
SEARER[sic], Aaron SINGLEY, f-Died 12 Feb 1890 at 16:45 at res.
in Decatur Twp.

Maria L. HAMILTON, b-24 Feb 1890, **c**-H. C. KINSLOE, **d**-$2200, **e**-C. H. HENDERSON, T. J. MAHON, **f**-Died 7 Jan 1890 at 5:52 at res. in Newton Hamilton

Margaret J. ALLISON, b-25 Feb 1890, **c**-David ALLISON, debonis non, **d**-$5000, **e**-J. G. ALLISON, H. L. LOCKWOOD, **f**-Died 16 Feb 1889 at 17:00 at res. in Menno Twp.

James ALLISON, b-26 Feb 1890, **c**-James G. ALLISON, **d**-$2000, **e**-David ALLISON, S. W. ALLISON, **f**-Died 7 Feb 1890 at 10:00 at res. in Menno Twp.

Julia A. MABEN, b-28 Feb 1890, **c**-John A. McKEE, **d**- **e**- **f**-Died 24 Feb 1890 at 14:00 at res. of George BROWN in Lewiston

Joseph RENNINGER, b-4 Mar 1890, **c**-Gideon HARSHBERGER, **d**-$1200, **e**-Joshua HARSHBERGER, H. W. FORGY, **f**-Died 19 Feb 1890 at 7:00 at res. in Bratton Twp.

Elizabeth COMFORT, b-11 Mar 1890, **c**-D. W. WOODS, **d**- **e**- **f**-Died 25 Feb 1890 at 1:30 at res. of Robt. McKEE in Lewistown

Isaac LEWIS, b-15 Mar 1890, **c**-John PUGH, **d**-$50, **e**-W. S. SETTLE, C. Stewart GARRETT, **f**-Died at res. in Granville Twp.

James S. GALBRAITH, b-24 Mar 1890, **c**-Samuel J. BRISBIN, **d**-$1400, **e**-C. S. GARRETT, La Fayette WEBB, **f**-Died 21 Mar 1890 at 23:00 at res. of Jno. M. NOLTE in Lewistown

Brown McNITT, b-25 Mar 1890, **c**-John McNITT, **d**- **e**- **f**-Died 23 Jan 1890 at 7:30 at res. in Armagh Twp.

William B. LUKENS, b-25 Mar 1890, **c**-Catharine LUKENS, **d**-$700, **e**-Jos. A. FICHTHORN, Robt. FORGY, Jr., **f**-Died 30 Oct 1890 at 22:00 at res. in Wayne Twp.

David PEACHEY, b-31 Mar 1890, **c**-Abraham Z. PEACHEY, **d**- **e**- **f**-Died 21 Mar 1890 at 17:00 at res. in Menno Twp.

Harriet C. HOUCK, b-14 Apr 1890, **c**-J. E. SMUCKER, **d**-$5000, **e**-Elias PENNYPACKER, John A. McKEE, **f**-Died 14 Jan 1888 at 2:00 at res. in Wayne Twp.

John MILLER, b-16 Apr 1890, **c**-J. D. MILLER, W. C. MILLER, **d**- **e**- **f**-Died 5 Apr 1890 at 17:00 at res. in Wayne Twp.

A[l]bert S. STROUP, b-18 Apr 1890, **c**-Emma L. STROUP, **d**-$350, **e**-John A. McKEE, S. S. RUBLE, **f**-Died 10 Apr 1890 at 17:30 at res. in Lewistown

Barbara PETER, b-13 May 1890, **c**-James H. PETER, **d**- **e**- **f**-Died 25 Apr 1890 at 2:00 at res. in Decatur Twp.

John M. SHADLE, b-15 May 1890, c-Mrs. E. A. SHADLE, d-$1200, e-G. A. SIGLER, S. M. SHADLE, f-Died 16 Jun 1889 at 21:00 at res. in Lewistown

Annie E. BURNS, b-19 May 1890, c-Joseph McCULLOCH, d-$500, e-T. F. McCOY, W. S. SETTLE, f-Died 11 May 1890 at 8:40 at res. in Lewistown

Samuel HARVEY, b-2 Jun 1890, c-S. [W.] NORTON, J. L. POSTLEWAIT[sic], d- e- f-Died 24 May 1890 at +++ at res. in Wayne Twp.

George S. RUBLE, b-18 Jun 1890, c-Serena RUBLE, d-$1800, e-J. A. MYERS, S. L. RUBLE, f-Died 14 May 1890 at 9:00 at the Station house in Mattawana

Samuel H. McCOY, b-2 Jul 1890, c-Rachel Jane McCOY, S. E. McCOY, d- e- f-Died 8 Jun 1890 at 2:00 at res. in Granville Twp.

James FRY, b-2 Jul 1890, c-Lydia FRY, d-$100, e-W. S. SETTLE, Jacob YOUTZY, f-Died 29 Jun 1890 at 17:00 at res. in Derry Twp.

Page 280, Frame 298

Saml. TREASTER, b-12 Jul 1890, c-Peter BAREFOOT, d- e- f-Died 7 Jul 1890 at 15:00 at res. in Armagh Twp.

Mary STUCKEY, b-16 Jul 1890, c-Christian KAUFFMAN, d- e- f-Died 11 Jul 1890 at 20:00 or 21:00 at res. in Brown Twp.

John B. HUMMEL, b-16 Jul 1890, c-Sarah C. HUMMEL, d- e- f-Died7 Dec 1888 at 23:00 at res. in Decatur Twp.

Jacob DEAN, b-19 Jul 1890, c-M. L. WEST, d-$200, e-R. J. McNITT, W. S. DELLETT, f-Died 20 Jun 1890 at 5:00 at res. in Armagh Twp.

John WILL, b-19 Jul 1890, c-Leah WILL, d- e- f-Died 12 Jul 1890 at 10:00 at res. in Decatur Twp.

Lydia PEACHEY, b-22 Jul 1890, c-A. Z. PEACHEY, d- e- f-Died 18 Jul 1890 at 17:00 at res. in Menno Twp.

Moses KREPS, b-26 Jul 1890, c-A. J. KREPS, d- e- f-Died 14 Jul 1890 at 23:00 or 00:00 at res. in Granville Twp.

Geneora S. CAMPBELL, b-25 Aug 1890, c-Jacob R. STINE, admr., d-$600, e-J. T. CALDWELL, John F. STINE, f-Died 2 May 1890 at 13:00 at the res. of Jacob R. STINE

Benjamin P. HOGLE, b-29 Aug 1890, c-Rachel HOGLE, extx., d- e- f-Died 17 Aug 1890 at 9:30 at res. in Lewistown

Elizabeth RUSSELL, **b**-30 Aug 1890, **c**-Wm. RUSSELL, S. A. ROTHROCK, **d**-no bond, **e**- **f**-Died 15 Aug 1890 at 9:30 at res. in Bratton Twp.

Margaret FICHTHORN, **b**-30 Aug 1890, **c**-Jos. A. FICHTHORN, C.T.A., **d**-$500, **e**-William WILLIS, W. W. FICHTHORN, **f**-Died 26 Aug 1890 at 8:00-10:00 at res. in Lewistown

W. H. CORNELIUS, **b**-8 Sep 1890, **c**-N. C. WILSON, C.T.A., **d**-$1000, **e**-Jno. B. SELHEIMER, F. F. McCOY, **f**-Died 1890 at res. in Oliver Twp.

A. J. PENEPACKER, alias John A. PARKER, **b**-10 Sep 1890, **c**-Elias PENEPACKER, **d**-$270, **e**-B. C. CUBBISON, M. K. THOMPSON, **f**-Died 8 Sep 1890 at 7:00 at res. of Elias PENEPACKER in Derry Twp.

Robert A. WILLS, **b**-19 Sep 1890, **c**-Joseph K. HOOLEY, **d**-$450, **e**-M. R. THOMPSON, J. A. WAREAM, **f**-Died 11 Sep 1890 at 2:00 at res. in Union Twp.

Samuel McK. FLEMMING, **b**-22 Sep 1890, **c**-John M. FLEMMING, **d**-$2000, **e**-J. H. MORRISON, S. W. FLEMMING, **f**-Died 26 Aug 1890 at 18:00 at res. in Menno Twp.

Ann W. TRIMBLE, **b**-24 Sep 1890, **c**-Joseph F. ROTHROCK, **d**- **e**- **f**-Died 5 Sep 1890 at 7:00 at res. of Dr. A. ROTHROCK in McVeytown

Franklin SIPE, **b**-27 Sep 1890, **c**-Ephraim LEPLEY, **d**-$300, **e**-Reuben HOOK, George SEARER, **f**-Died 15 Sep 1890 at 3:00 or 4:00 at res. in Decatur Twp.

Sarah HAFFLY, **b**-22 Oct 1890, **c**-Joseph CAMPBELL, **d**-no bond, **e**- **f**-Died 17 Oct 1890 at 00;00 at res. in Union Twp.

Mary M. KYLER, **b**-22 Oct 1890, **c**-Ann E. KNEPP, **d**-no bond, **e**- **f**-Died 17 Oct 1890 at 11:45 at res. of Wm. KNEPP in Lewistown

William T. SMITH, **b**-27 Oct 1890, **c**-A. W. CAMPBELL, **d**-$800, **e**-J. W. WILSON, J. T. WILSON, **f**-Died 27 Aug 1890 at 1:00 or 2:00 at res. in Union Twp.

George W. STARR, **b**-7 Nov 1890, **c**-Jas. B. STARR, **d**-$50, **e**-Jas. W. STARR, H. J. WALTERS, **f**-Died 20 Jul 1882 at 19:00 at res. of Jas. W. STARR in Derry Twp.

Magdalena BUSCHE, **b**-13 Nov 1890, **c**-N. C. WILSON, **d**-$50, **e**-C. P. DULL, H. J. WALTERS, **f**-Died 5 Jan 1890 at res. of Mrs. VOGLE in Philadelphia

William HARSHBARGER, **b**-29 Nov 1890, **c**-Gideon HARSHBARGER, Joshua HARSHBARGER, **d**-$1500, **e**-David HARSHBARGER,

Emanuel BYLER, **f**-Died 9 Nov 1890 at 5:00 or 6:00 at res. in Bratton Twp.

Mahlon McKALIPS, b-11 Dec 1890, **c**-J. C. BELL, C.T.A., **d**-$1400, **e**-V. D. STONEROAD, Jas H. ALEXANDER, **f**-Died 27 Nov 1890 at 7:00 at res. in North Derry Twp.

Frederick BAKER, b-18 Dec 1890, **c**-James BAKER, **d**-$600, **e**-Alfred BAKER, **f**-Died 2 Dec 1890 at 11:00 at res. in Derry Twp.

Ellen M. REYNOLDS, b-25 Dec 1890, **c**-George W. ELDER, extr., **d**- **e**-**f**-Died 17 Dec 1890 at 11:30 at res. in Carlisle, Pennsylvania

James SHAHEN, b-27 Dec 1890, **c**- **d**- **e**- **f**-Died 17 Dec 1890 at 10:30 at res. in Granville Twp.

Page 281, Frame 299

Rebecca J. McKALIPS, b-6 Jan 1891, **c**-J. C. BELL, d.b.n., **d**-$2000, **e**-V. D. STONEROAD, C. S. GARRETT, **f**-Died 11 Jan 1888 at 11:30 at res. in Derry Twp. [Seems to be a second record for her; previous one on p. 275]

Saml. B. WILLS, b-9 Jan 1891, **c**-J. M. WOODS, **d**-$100, **e**-D, W, WOODS, Jos. M. OWENS, **f**-Died at res. in Union Twp.

William FIELDS, b-9 Jan 1891, **c**-C. C. FIELDS, G. A. FIELDS, extrs. **d**-**e**- **f**-Died 6 Jan 1891 at 13:50 at res. in Union Twp.

John WAGNER, b-19 Jan 1891, **c**-S. C. MONAHON, **d**-$70, **e**-George MYERS, James SMITH, **f**-Died 12 Jan 1891 at 3:00 at res. of George WAGNER in Derry Twp.

Joseph TAYLOR, b-23 Jan 1891, **c**-Castor TAYLOR, **d**- **e**- **f**-Died 12 Jan 1891 at 12:00 M at res. in Wayne Twp.

John W. ALLISON, b-26 Jan 1891, **c**-Saml. W. ALLISON, **d**- **e**- **f**-Died 21 Dec 1891 at 7:00 at res. in Menno Twp.

Thomas RODGERS, b-2 Feb 1891, **c**-Saml. EWING, Jas. A. DYSART, **d**- **e**- **f**-Died 25 Jan 1891 at 8:00 at res. in Newton Hamilton

Jane VANZANT, b-10 Feb 1891, **c**-Wm. H. EWING, **d**-$100, **e**-J. K. RHODES, Jos. MAHON, **f**-Died 6 Feb 1891 at 5:00 at res. in Newton Hamilton

Robert BRANAN, b-12 Feb 1891, **c**-James H. BRANAN, **d**-$1000, **e**-Clarissa KLINE, H. A. WALTERS, **f**-Died 16 Jan 1891 at 9:00 at res. in Granville Twp.

Joel MOIST, b-13 Feb 1891, **c**-J. R. WIRT, **d**-$100, **e**-George HUFFMAN, A. S. MOIST, **f**-Died 15 Jan 1891 at 5:00 at res. in Bratton Twp.

Edward COLEMAN, b-23 Feb 1891, **c**-Austin COLEMAN, **d**-$350, **e**-Amos FOLK, Abraham RABUCK, **f**-Died 12 Feb 1891 at 3:00 at res. in Decatur Twp.

Eliza STEEL, b-10 Feb 1891, William T. SHIMP, **d**- **e**- **f**-Died at res. in Granville Twp.

George W. SEACHRIST, b-2 Mar 1891, **c**-Maggie SEACHRIST, **d**-$100, **e**-W. W. TROUT, A. T. HAMILTON, **f**-Died 21 Dec 1891 at res. in Derry Twp.

Harry ULSH, b-18 Mar 1891, **c**-John ULSH, **d**-$400, **e**-Wm. KEARNS. L. E. SCHUCHT, **f**-Died 9 Mar 1891 at 4:00 or 5:00 at Railroad Bridge, Snyder County

Jacob PETER, b-25 Mar 1891, **c**-Joseph SNOOK, **d**-$700, **e**-Israel MOYER, Michal LYTER, **f**-Died 20 Feb 1891 at 14:15 at res. in Decatur Twp.

Rebecca H. MOYER, b-25 Mar 1891, **c**-Israel MOYER, **d**-$200, **e**-Joseph SNOOK, Michael LYTER, **f**-Died 29 Dec 1890 at 16:00 at res. in Decatur Twp.

John A. WOLFKILL, b-27 Mar 1891, **c**-George A. WOLFKILL, **d**-$200, **e**-Geo. S. HOFFMAN, John A. WAREAM, **f**-Died 19 Mar 1891 at 8:40 at res. in Bratton Twp.

Mary KERR, b-18 Apr 1891, **c**-James KERR, **d**-$200, **e**-Peter BAREFOOT, La Fayette WEBB, **f**-Died 13 Mar 1891 at 21:00 at res. in Armagh Twp.

John SPEESE, b-18 Apr 1891, **c**-John LOCKE, **d**-$5000, **e**-W. H. FELIX, R. H. MONTGOMERY, **f**-Died 8 Apr 1891 at 21:00 at res. in Lewistown

William HENRY, b-20 May 1891, **c**-Margaret A. HENRY, John REED, **d**- **e**- **f**-Died 29 Apr 1891 at 3:00 at res. in Brown Twp.

William CREIGHTON, b-21 May 1891, **c**-I. T. CREIGHTON, **d**- **e**- **f**-Died 8 May 1891 at 6:00 at res. of Saml. MUSSER in Derry Twp.

Sarah FLEMING, b-27 May 1891, **c**-S. J. BOYER, **d**- **e**- **f**-Died 19 May 1891 at 3:30 at res. in Armagh Twp.

Jacob ELLINGER, b-1 Jun 1891, **c**-John ELLINGER, **d**- **e**- **f**-Died 27 May 1891 at 4:00 at res. of Robt. MILLER in Brown Twp.

Wm. M. HEADINGS, b-5 May 1891, **c**-J. M. HEADINGS, **d**-$300, **e**-Jos. WALLACE, Jas. G. HEADINGS, **f**-Died 27 Mar 1891 at 10:00 at res. in Menno Twp.

Charles NAGINEY, **b**-2 Jun 1891, **c**-J. C. NAGINEY, **d**-$3500, **e**-R. J. McNITT, W. D. TAYLOR, **f**-Died 17 May 1891 at 7:00 at res. in Armagh Twp.

Charles C. MILLER, **b**-2 Jun 1891, **c**-Caroline MILLER, **d**-$1000, **e**-A, LOTZGAZELLE, R. H. MYERS, **f**-Died 8 May 1891 at 10:30 at res. in Granville Twp.

Levi SWIGART, **b**-20 Jun 1891, **c**-Joseph H. SWIGART, **d**-$800, **e**-Amos NAFZINGER, S. Harvey SWIGART, **f**-Died 1 Jun 1891 at 6:20 at res. in Oliver Twp.

Reuben SHAWVER, **b**-24 Jun 1891, **c**-John SHAWVER, **d**-$600, **e**-M. STINE, Aaron SINGLEY, **f**-Died 15 Jun 1891 at 4:00 at res. in Decatur Twp.

James CULBERSON, **b**-24 Jun 1891, **c**-James O. CULBERSON, **d**- **e**- **f**-Died 4 Jun 1891 at 14:00 at res. in Menno Twp.

Page 282, Frame 300

Mary B. McDOWELL, **b**-26 Jun 1891, **c**-John McDOWELL, Maggie J. PARKER, **d**-$12,000, **e**-Horace J. CULBERTSON, George L. RUSSELL, **f**-Died 8 Apr 1891 at 11:20 at res. of A. H. PARKER in Brown Twp.

James B. HENRY, **b**-30 Jun 1891, **c**-J. E. HENRY, W. H. TAYLOR, **d**-$8000, **e**-Davis HENRY, Jno. J. THOMPSON, **f**-Died 21 Jun 1891 at 17:00 at res. in Brown Twp.

Mary E. RUSSELL, **b**-1 Jul 1891, **c**-J. M. WOODS, **d**- **e**- **f**-Died 16 Jun 1891 at 16:40 at res. in Lewistown

Henry DOBSON, **b**-3 Jul 1891, **c**-Joseph KNEPP, **d**-$150, **e**-Amos DEAN, C. S. GARRETT, **f**-Died 23 Jun 1891 at 19:00 or 20:00 at res. in Armagh Twp.

George TWEED, **b**-29 Jul 1891, **c**-Lewis H. RHODES, **d**-$2000, **e**-Jacob R. STINE, John L. BERRYMAN, **f**-Died 6 Jul 1891 at 00:15 at res. in Wayne Twp.

Rebecca RODGERS, **b**-7 Aug 1891, **c**-Mary RODGERS (now DIESLANG), **d**- **e**- **f**-Died 2 Aug 1891 at 19:30 at res. in Union Twp.

Mary M. RIDEN, **b**-10 Aug 1891, **c**-S. J. BRISBIN, extr., **d**- **e**- **f**-Died 27 Jul 1891 at 23:00 at res. of Mrs. L. LOWMIDLER in Lewistown

Peter CLUM, **b**-25 Aug 1891, **c**-T. F. McCOY, **d**-$4000, **e**-Jos. McFADDEN, Jos. McCULLOCH, **f**-Died 22 Aug 1891 at 15:00 at res. in Lewistown

George Albert SIGLER, b-31 Aug 1891, **c**-Horace J. CULBERTSON, **d**-
e- **f**-Died 29 Aug 1891 at 21:00 at res. in Lewistown

Rebecca SNOOK, b-9 Sep 1891, **c**-Adam A. BROWN, **d**- **e**- **f**-Died 5 Sep
1891 at ___ at res. in Siglerville, Armagh Twp.

James PATTON, b-17 Sep 1891, **c**-Robert A. PATTON, extr., **d**-$500, **e**-
A. E. PATTON, W. M. GIBBONEY, **f**-Died 10 Jul 1891 at 4:00 at res.
in Menno Twp.

Elizabeth MOIST, b-3 Oct 1891, **c**-Jonas HARSHBARGER, **d**-$2500, **e**-
Wm. FRENCH, R. C. ELDER, **f**-Died 19 Apr 1886 at ___ at res. in
Bratton Twp.

A. W. SIGLER, b-10 Oct 1891, **c**-George R. SIGLER, Wm. G. SIGLER,
d- **e**- **f**-Died 24 Sep 1891 at 8:20 at res. in Decatur Twp.

Robert GILLILAND, b-12 Oct 1891, **c**-James E. GILLILAND **d**- **e**- **f**-No
data entered

Elizabeth H. BEATTY, b-Mary E. BEATTY, M. Agnes BEATTY, **c**- **d**-
e- **f**-Died 17 Sep 1891 at 9:50 at res. in Newton Hamilton

Barbara MILLER, b-3 Nov 1891, **c**-Joseph MILLER, **d**-$400, **e**-A. D.
MILLER, Saml. RITTENHOUSE, **f**-[There appears to be an
inexplicable double entry for her death—]Died 12 Oct 1891 at 10:00
at res. in Armagh Twp. and Died 6 Oct 1891 at 10:00 at res. in Derry
Twp.

Sarah YOST, b-4 Nov 1891, **c**-W. H. GLASS, **d**-$150, **e**-John A. WEBB,
J. P. GETTER, **f**-Died 21 Aug 1890 at at res. in Menno Twp.

Jacob KRICK, b-10 Nov 1891, **c**-S. L. BROWER **d**-$1000, **e**-Levi
KLINE, Henry A. ERB, **f**-Died 24 Oct 1891 at ___ at res. of Jackson
RAGER in Decatur Twp.

Mary Ann VANZANDT, b-12 Nov 1891, **c**-T. M. UTTLEY, extr., **d**- **e**-
f-Died 13 Jun 1891at ___ at res. of E. J. EWING in Jersey City, N. J.

Samuel COGLEY. b-19 Nov 1891, **c**-George W. COGLEY, **d**-$7800, **e**-J.
H. MORRISON, H. M. GIBBONEY, **f**-Died 3 Nov 1891,at 5:00 at res.
of Reuben AXE, in Union Twp.

William KARSTETTER, b-24 Nov 1891, **c**-Levi F. KARSTETTER, **d**-
$400, **e**-H. SINGLEY, H. A. MOODIE, **f**-Died 25 Oct 1891 at 17:00
at res. in Decatur Twp.

John H. CRIST, b-30 Nov 1891, **c**-Wm. S. SETTLE, **d**-$1600, **e**-Joseph
McCULLOCH, Saml. J. BRISBIN, **f**-Died 22 Nov 1891 at 18:00 at res.
in Lewistown

John R. HOOPES, b-2 Dec 1891, **c**-Asenath HOOPES, **d**- **e**- **f**-Died 25
Nov 1891 at 11:30 at res. in Derry Twp.

Abraham SPICHER, b-4 Dec 1891, c-Joel SPICHER, d-$400, e-John C. ZOOK, John S. YODER, f-Died 26 Nov 1891 at 20:30 at res. in Brown Twp.

James C. CRAIG, b-5 Dec 1891, c-S. W. NORTON, d-$500, e-James S. NORTON, Rufus C. ELDER, f-Died 19 Nov 1891 at 16:00 at res. in Newton Hamilton

George W. COULTER, b-15 Dec 1891, c-J. C. COULTER, d-$3200, e-George W. STINE, Saml. B. STINE, f-Died 20 Oct 1891 at 14:00 at res. in Wayne Twp.

Lucy HOWENSTINE, b-19 Dec 1891, c-Jacob STEINBARGER, d-$4000, e-Henry STEIN, P. D. MERTZ, f-Died ___ Mar 1891 at ___ at res. in Derry Twp.

Mary Ann MOORE, b-22 Dec 1891, c-Saml. J. HAVICE, Lewis REED, d- e- f-Died 12 Dec 1891 at 1:30 at res. in Armagh

Page 283, Frame 301 [Duplicated on Frame 302]

Malinda BERGER, b-24 Dec 1891, c-Joseph McCULLOCH, d-$100, e-T. F. McCOY, W. S. SETTLE, f-Died 23 Aug 1885 at 2:00 at res. in Derry Twp.

Anna Eliza WISE, b-7 Jan 1892, c-Charles B. WISE, admr., d-$1000, e-Lawrence R. STROUP, James M. BENNETT, f-Died 31 Dec 1891 at 6:00 at res. in Union Twp.

Judith ORT, b-18 Jan 1892, c-John BAUM, extr., d- e- f-Died 14 Jan 1892 between 3:00 and 7:00 at res. in Granville Twp.

Nancy WILSON, b-21 Jan 1892, c-R. F. WILSON, admr., d-$100 e-Joseph McCULLOCH, J. M. WOODS, f-Died 3 Nov 1877 at ___ at res. in Menno Twp.

R. H. LEE, b-26 Jan 1892, c-Mary [W.?] LEE, extx., d- e- f-Died 28 Dec 1891 at 23:00 at res. in Derry Twp.

James HILL, b-5 Feb 1892, c-W. P. STEVENSON, admr., d-$1000, e-Saml. McWILLIAMS, James MACKLIN, f-Died 27 Jan 1892 at 22:00 at res. in Oliver Twp.

Jane WILLIAMS, b-15 Feb 1892, c-Saml. J. BRISBIN, admr., d-$1000, e-C. S. GARRETT, David GROVE, f-Died 12 Mar 1892 at 23:30 at res. in Derry Twp.

Simeon H. YODER, b-23 Feb 1892, c-Noah SHARPE, d-$600, e-Davis HENRY, Eli PEACHEY, f-Died 31 Jan 1892 at 6:00 at res. in Brown Twp.

Henry H. WHITE, **b**-16 Mar 1892, **c**-Clarissa W. FULTZ, extx., **d**- **e**- **f**-Died 22 Feb 1892 at 5:00 at res. in Menno Twp.

Fannie B. STRUNK, **b**-17 Mar 1892, **c**-H. C. STRUNK, admr., **d**-$700, **e**-Geo. S. HOFFMAN, Robt. W. STRUNK, **f**-Died 3 Mar 1892 at 19:00 at res. in Armagh Twp.

John SAYLOR, **b**-19 Mar 1892, **c**-Wm. E. SAYLOR, John D. SAYLOR, **d**-$3000, **e**-L. V. POSTLETHWAITE, H. C. KINSLOE, **f**-Died 7 Mar 1892 at 15:00 at res. in Wayne Twp.

David M. ZOOK, **b**-31 Mar 1892, **c**-Jonathan B. ZOOK, A. D. ZOOK, **d**- **e**- **f**-Died 25 Mar 1892 at 7:30 at res. in Menno Twp.

John COX, **b**-2 Apr 1892, **c**-Mary M. MITCHELL, **d**-$1500, **e**-John CAMP, Edw. KRICHBAUM, **f**-Died 22 Feb 1892 at 15:30 at res. of Danl. CLECK in Armagh Twp.

Jacob MOHLER, **b**-4 Apr 1892, **c**-John M. MOHLER, **d**- **e**- **f**-Died 4 Mar 1890 at between 8:00 and 11:00 at res. in Derry Twp.

A. W. GRAFF, **b**-15 Apr 1892, **c**-Caroline GRAFF, Roland THOMPSON, A. L. HAMILTON, **d**- **e**- **f**-Died 5 Apr 1892 at 6:00 at res. in Armagh Twp.

C. C. ZOOK, **b**-16 Apr 1892, **c**- Joseph F. ZOOK, admr., **d**-$1100, **e**-John H. ZOOK, Joel SPICHER, **f**-Died 7 Apr 1892 at 20:00 at res. in Brown Twp.

Landrum BUCHANAN, **b**-23 Apr 1892, **c**-Samuel T. MOORE, c.t.a., **d**-$100, **e**-Andrew SWARTZELL, John CAMP, **f**-Died 29 Mar 1892 at 7:00 at son's res. in Armagh Twp.

Samuel P. TREASTER, **b**-23 Apr 1892, **c**-Louisa J. TREASTER, J. H. HAVICE, **d**-$600, **e**-J. C. NAGINEY, James R. TREASTER, **f**-Died 20 Apr 1892 at 3:00 at res. in Armagh Twp.

John HAVICE, **b**-26 Apr 1892, **c**-Saml. J. HAVICE, W. H. HAVICE, **d**-$400, **e**-Philip J. HAVICE, Lewis REED, **f**-Died 4 Apr 1892 at 7:00 at res. in Armagh

Henry KLIPPART, **b**-2 May 1892, **c**-J. R. WIRT, admr., **d**-$500, **e**-C. P. DULL, Anthony McAULEY, **f**-Died 17 Apr 1892 at 18:00 at res. in Bratton Twp.

William McKENDREE, **b**-2 May 1892, **c**-Catharine McKENDREE, **d**-$250, **e**-H. C. KINSLOE, H. B. WHARTON, **f**-Died 21 Apr 1892 at 18:00 at res. in Wayne Twp.

Christian MYERS, **b**-4 May 1892, **c**-Peter BAREFOOT, **d**-$6000, **e**-Kate M. MYERS, Adam HENRY, **f**-Died 21 Apr 1892 at 5:45at res. in Armagh Twp.

George H. SHILLING, b-11 Jun 1892, **c**-R. E. AURAND, **d**-$200, **e**-W. J. AURAND, H. H. SPIGLEMYER, **f**-Died __ May at __ at res. in Decatur Twp.

George BUFFINGTON, b-11 Jun 1892, **c**-W. L. OWENS, **d**-$1000, **e**-J. M. OWENS, F. J. McCOY, **f**-Died ___ at ___ at res. in Derry Twp.

Joseph McCULLOCH, b-15 Jun 1892, **c**-W. S. SETTLE, extr. **d**- **e**- **f**-Died 25 May 1892 at ___ at res. in Lewistown

Mary Matilda SAYLOR, b-21 Jun 1892, **c**-R. M. MAGEE, extr., **d**- **e**- **f**-Died 31 May 1892 at 4:00 at res. in New York City

William CRISSMAN, b-29 Jun 1892. **c**-Israel CRISSMAN, A. J. MILLER, **d**- **e**- **f**-Died 25 Jun 1892 at ___ at res. in Derry Twp.

Page 284, Frame 303

Thomas M. WEILER, b-[5] July 1892, **c**-Jos. M. GALBRAITH, **d**-$600, **e**-John REED, Jos. KELLEY, **f**-Died 25 Jun 1892 at 17:00 at Herndon, Northumberland County

Abram STOUFFER, b-19 Jul 1892, **c**-Celinda J. STOUFFER, **d**-$10,000, **e**-George RUDISILL, H. A. FELIX, **f**-Died 10 Jul 1892 at 5:00 at res. in Lewistown

Joseph McFADDEN, b-27 Jul 1892, **c**-Chas. J. McFADDEN, **d**-$15,000, **e**-Frances McFADDEN, John B. SELHEIMER, **f**-Died 23 Jul 1892 at 1:00 at res. in Lewistown

Jesse LEPLEY, b-29 Jul 1892, **c**-T. A. WAGNER, **d**-$150, **e**-John LEPLEY, George BENFER, **f**-Died 27 Jun 1892 at 11:00 at res. in Decatur Twp.

Erastus KEMBERLING, b-30 Jul 1892, **c**-E. W. KEMBERLING **d**-$300, **e**-James WRAY, A. SINGLEY, **f**-Died 21 May 1892 at 18:00 at res. in Decatur Twp.

John A. YODER, b-1 Aug 1892, **c**-John YODER, **d**-$3000, **e**-Christian Z. YODER, John B. SELHEIMER, **f**-Died 18 Jun 1892 at 13:00 at res. in Union Twp.

John LONGWELL, b-3 Aug 1892, **c**-Peter BAREFOOT, **d**- **e**- **f**-Died 30 Jul 1892 at 22:00 or 23:00 at res. in Armagh Twp.

John G. KAUFFMAN, b-17 Aug 1892, **c**-John C. KAUFFMAN, Joas KAUFFMAN, **d**- **e**- **f**-Died 13 Aug 1892 at 18:30 at res. in Union Twp.

Elizabeth HART, b-20 Aug 1892, **c**-Joseph HART, **d**- **e**- **f**-Died 29 Feb 1892 at 20:00 at res. in McVeytown

Philip MURPHY, b-20 Aug 1892, **c**-T. Speer DICKSON, **d**-$100, **e**-Saml. McWILLIAMS, J. M. WOODS, **f**-Died 18 Apr 1892 at 3:00 at res. in Oliver Twp.

Sarah A. SHUMAKER, b-23 Sep 1892, **c**-John A. SHUMAKER **d**- **e**- **f**-Died 9 Sep 1892 at 3:00 at res. in Brown Twp.

David H. KING, b-7 Oct 1892, **c**-Jacob S. KING, **d**-$300, **e**-C. H. KING, Jonathan PLANK, **f**-Died 28 Sep 1892 at 9:00 at res. in Menno Twp.

Christen R. CAMPBELL, b-10 Oct 1892, **c**-William B. MACLAY, **d**- **e**- **f**-Died 20 Sep 1892 at 16:20 at res. in Union Twp.

David YETTER. b-21 Oct 1892, **c**-Irvin YETTER, M. S. SNOOK, **d**-$800, **e**-Daniel SNOOK, Thomas ARNOLD, **f**-Died 23 Sep 1892 at 6:00 at res. in Decatur Twp.

Jacob HOOVER, b-2 Nov 1892, **c**-William J. SHAW, **d**-$16,000, **e**-J. K. RHODES, William WILLIS, **f**-Died ___ at ___ at res. in ___

Samuel E. HOOVER, b-2 Nov 1892, **c**-G. H. BELL, **d**-$300, **e**-S. M. BELL, L. H. RUBLE, **f**-Died 24 Oct 1892 at 22:30 at res. in Derry Twp.

Eleanor THATCHER, b-3 Nov 1892, **c**-Saml. T. MOORE, **d**-$300, **e**-Andrew SWARTZELL, John C. McCLINTIC, **f**-Died 6 Oct 1892 at ___ at res. in Armagh Twp.

Charles S. MARKS, b-10 Nov 1892, **c**-M. M. McLAUGHLIN, **d**-$300, **e**-John S. GROFF, A. B. GROFF, **f**-Died 22 Oct 1892 at ___ at res. of J. L. MARKS

Martha WISE, b-16 Nov 1892, **c**-John W. WILSON, **d**-$200, **e**-R. F. WILSON, Wm. H. TAYLOR, **f**-Died 4 Nov 1892 at 9:00 or 10:00 at res. in Union Twp.

Samuel WORLEY, b-1 Dec 1892, **c**-Hannah WORLEY, **d**-$250, **e**-Peter BAREFOOT, J. C. McNITT, **f**-Died 13 Oct 1892 at 17:00 near res. in Armagh Twp.

John A. RAGER, b-3 Dec 1892, **c**-Adam A. BROWN, **d**-$500, **e**-Leo F. TREASTER, Chas. B. McCLENAHEN, **f**-Died 26 Nov 1892 at a.m. at res. in Armagh

Levi PECHT, b-3 Dec 1892, **c**-J. Robert STERRETT, **d**-$5000, **e**-W. S. STERRETT, A. B. McNITT, **f**-Died 4 Nov 1892 at 2:00 at res. in Armagh Twp.

Saml. D. POSTLETHWAITE, b-7 Dec 1892, **c**-L. V. POSTLETHWAITE, S. H. POSTLETHWAITE, **d**- **e**- **f**-Died 28 Nov 1892 at 10:00 at res. in Newton Hamilton

John STEEL, **b**-9 Dec 1892, **c**-Jane G. STEEL, Samuel STEEL, **d**-$500, **e**-Lebiah STUMPFF, Simon KNEPP, **f**-Died 16 Nov 1892 at 18:00 at res. in Decatur Twp.

Martin L. LEITZELL, **b**-10 Dec 1892, **c**-Stuart M. LEITZELL, **d**-$600, **e**-Henry A. WALTERS, Henry BOSSINGER, **f**-Died 6 Dec 1892 at 8:00 at res. in Granville Twp.

Daniel WEDER, **b**-24 Dec 1892, **c**-Isaac F. WEDER, A. A. BROWN, **d**-$1600, **e**-Jos. KELLEY, W. S. DELLETT, **f**-Died 13 Dec 1892 at 16:30 at res. in Brown Twp.

Henry LEHR, **b**-27 Dec 1892, **c**-Mina A. LEHR, **d**- **e**- **f**-Died 13 Dec 1892 at 1:20 at res. in Armagh Twp.

Page 285, Frame 304
Samuel M. PEACHEY, **b**-3 Jan 1893, **c**-Jacob B. HARTZLER, **d**- **e**- **f**-Died 21 Dec 1892 at 22:00 at res. in Menno Twp.

Annie E. KINSLOE, **b**-12 Jan 1893, **c**-Harry B. WHARTON, **d**- **e**- **f**-Died 1 Jan 1893 at 18:23 at res. in Newton Hamilton

Sophia K. YEAGER, **b**-13 Jan 1893, **c**-Thomas J. NOVINGER, **d**- **e**- **f**-Died 4 Jan 1893 at 8:00 at res. in Decatur Twp.

William S. BELL, **b**-30 Jan 1893, **c**-James Clark BELL, **d**- **e**- **f**-Died 16 Jan 1893 at 11:00 at res. of J. C. BELL in Derry Twp.

Alexander CRESWELL, **b**-1 Feb 1893, **c**-Saml. STERRETT, **d**-$100, **e**-H. C. VANZANT, Isaac HENRY, **f**-Died 7 Sep 1887 at 1:00 at res. in Decatur Twp.

Mary Ann SIGLER, **b**-4 Feb 1893, **c**-Ira H. SIGLER, **d**-$800, **e**-J. Clark WILSON, Johnson MUTTHERSBAUGH, **f**-Died 30 Apr 1892 at 6:00 at res. in Armagh Twp.

Susanna COGLEY, **b**-10 Feb 1893, **c**-George W. COGLEY, **d**-$1300, **e**-W. M. GIBBONEY, M. O. WATTS, **f**-Died 22 Jan 1893 at 5:30 at res. in Union Twp.

Rebecca BARTLE, **b**-24 Feb 1903. **c**-Wm. P. BREHMAN, **d**-$100, **e**-Wm. S. SETTLE, John A. McKEE, **f**-Died 9 Jun 1892 at ___ at res. of Mary BREHMAN in Oliver Twp.

Francis A. McCOY, **b**-22 Feb 1893, **c**-Mary J. McCOY, **d**- **e**- **f**-Died 17 Feb 1893 at 6:10 at res. in Granville Twp.

Sarah McCLELLAN, **b**-27 Feb 1893, **c**-Cornelius McCLELLAN, **d**-$400, **e**-Irvin C. DIMM, William W. TROUT, **f**-Died 26 Jan 1893 at 23:30 at res. in McVeytown

Thomas McCORD, b-28 Feb 1893, **c**-Jacob ESTERLINE, N. A. McCORD, **d**-$250, **e**-J. Roller McCOY, J. Harvey CLINGER, **f**-Died 19 Feb 1893 at 4:25 at res. in Bratton Twp.

Catharine MITCHELL, b-1 Mar 1893, **c**-Wm. S. SETTLE, **d**- **e**- **f**-Died ___ at ___ at res. in Granville Twp.

Mary EHRENFELD, b-3 Mar 1893, **c**-Morris M. NAGINEY, **d**- **e**- **f**-Died 19 Oct 1892 at 10:00 at res. in Armagh Twp.

Martha J. SCOTT, b-13 Mar 1893, **c**-Bruce W. VANZANT, **d**- **e**- **f**-Died 8 Mar 1893 at ___ at res. in Lewistown

Frany KING, b-14 Mar 1893, **c**-Jacob C. YODER, **d**-$2000, **e**-Joseph B. HOSTETLER, Moses P. YODER, **f**-Died 1 Mar 1893 at 8:00 at res. in Union Twp.

Andrew SWARTZELL, b-22 Mar 1893, **c**-Anna M. SWARTZELL, **d**-$800, **e**-Leo F. TREASTER, G. W. LINTHURST, **f**-Died 16 Feb 1893 at 1:10 at res. in Armagh Twp.

Levi M. PEACHEY, b-22 Mar 1893, **c**-Solomon PEACHEY, **d**- **e**- **f**-Died 15 Mar 1893 at 7:00 at res. in Menno Twp.

Margaret HAZLETT, b-25 Mar 1893, **c**-William HUEY, **d**-$800, **e**-James C. HAZLETT, Henry A. FELIX, **f**-Died 20 Mar 1893 at 14:00 at res. in Menno Twp.

Joseph YETTER, b-8 Apr 1893, **c**-T. A. WAGNER, W. J. TREASTER, **d**- **e**- **f**-Died 1 Apr 1893 at 5:00 at res. in Decatur Twp.

Joseph NEWMAN, b-15 Apr 1893 **c**-Keturah A. NEWMAN, **d**-$300, **e**-C. H. HENDERSON, Wm. S. SETTLE, **f**-Died 9 Apr 1893 at 12 M at res. in Derry Twp.

Noah E. PENEPACKER, b-18 Apr 1893, **c**-Edith PENEPACKER, **d**-$100, **e**-C. M. SHULL, La Fayette WEBB, **f**-Died 7 Apr 1893 at 15:30 at res. in Lewistown

Frances ZOOK, b-22 Apr 1893, **c**-Joseph Z. KANAGY, **d**- **e**- **f**-Died 16 Apr 1893 dead in bed at res. in Menno Twp.

Solomon KAUFFMAN, b-26 Apr 1893, **c**-Jared KAUFFMAN, **d**- **e**- **f**-Died 11 Apr 1893 at 10:00 or 11:00 at res. of Jared KAUFFMAN in Bratton Twp.

Sarah MILLER, b-29 Apr 1893, **c**-Saml. L. BROWER, **d**- **e**- **f**-Died 3 Apr 1893 at 14:00 at res. in Decatur Twp.

George W. LEWIS, b-2 May 1893, **c**-Oscar R. LEWIS, **d**-$5000, **e**-Samuel MUSSER, Samuel MITCHELL, **f**-Died 11 Apr 1893 at 17:00 at res. in Derry Twp.

John C. HOOLEY, b-2 May 1893, c-Stephen M. HOOLEY, d-$13,500, e-Peter Y. KING, Joseph A. HOOLEY, W. H. TAYLOR, f-Died 26 Apr 1893 at 21:00 at res. in Brown Twp.

Moses YETTER, b-2 May 1893, c-Jacob LAWVER, d-$600, e-Andrew SNOOK, Reuben KNEPP, f-Died 8 Apr 1893 at 14:00 at res. in Decatur Twp.

Charles STRATFORD, Sr., b-5 May 1893, c-Laura ANDERSON, W. J. PIERCE, d- e- f-Died 1 May 1893 at 00:22 at res. of Laura ANDERSON

Joseph SIGLER, b-12 May 1893, c-Saml. S. SIGLER, d-$200, e-S. K. RUSSELL, W. H. GOSS, f-Died 28 Apr 1893 at 13:12 at res. in Decatur Twp.

John B. HARTSWICK, b-31 May 1893, c-Francina HARTSWICK, d-$200, e-Jas. S. RAKERD, La Fayette WEBB, f-Died 1 May 1893 at 10:20 at res. in Armagh Twp.

Page 286, Frame 305

Sarah H. POLLOCK, b-13 Jun 1893, c-John T. POLLOCK, d-$1200, e-John GLASGOW, J. R. WIRT, f-Died 7 May 1893 at 8:00 at res. in Wayne Twp.

Elizabeth M. RODGERS, b-1 Jul 1893, c-Harry H. DEAMER, d-$100, e-Wm. H. KITTING, C. H. HENDERSON, f-Died 22 Apr 1885 at ___ at res. in Lewistown

Elias W. DIXON, b-8 Jul 1893, c-J. R. WIRT, d- e- f-Died 3 Jul 1893 at 9:30 at res. in Oliver Twp.

Matilda M. BELL, b-1 Aug 1893, c-S. A. McCLINTIC, d- e- f-Died 8 Jun 1893 at 12:00 M at res. of S. A. McCLINTIC in Armagh Twp.

Jacob FOGLEMAN, b-2 Aug 1893, c-G. H. BELL, d-$600, e-L. H. RUBLE, S. M. BELL, f-Died 29 Jul 1893 at 14:00 at res. in Granville Twp.

Sarah B. YOUTZY, b-14 Aug 1893, c-John A. YOUTZY, d- e- f-Died f-Died 7 Jul 1893 at 22:00 at res. of Alfred CAROTHERS in Huntingdon County

William H. RAMSEY, b-24 Aug 1893, c-R. A. NAGINEY, d-$2000, e-R. J. McNITT, M. M. NAGINEY, f-Died 22 Jul 1893 at 15:30 at res. in Armagh Twp.

Robert MILLIKEN, b-29 Aug 1893, c-C. G. MILLIKEN, d.b.n.c.t.a, d-$200, e-Jas. M. TAYLOR, Joseph HARKNESS, f-Died 20 Nov 1855 at 10:00 at res. in Brown Twp.

Daniel DECKER, **b**-5 Sep 1893, **c**-William P. BREHMAN, **d**-$800, **e**-Levi FELKER, Wm. S. SETTLE, **f**-Died 23 Aug 1893 at 12 M at res. in Oliver Twp.

Hannah SWISHER, **b**-11 Sep 1893, **c**-John K. RHODES, **d**-$100, **e**-R. W. INGRAM, B. F. WHITE, **f**-Died 28 Jun 1893 at ___ at res. in Newton Hamilton

John ARBOGAST, **b**-11 Sep 1893, **c**-Mrs. Lizzie MILLER, **d**-$400, **e**-W. R. McKEE, J. Roller McCOY, **f**-Died 5 Sep 1893 at 15:00 near res. in Granville Twp.

Mattie HOOLEY, **b**-16 Sep 1893, **c**-John HOOLEY, **d**- **e**- **f**-Died 13 Sep 1893 at 5:00 at res. of J. B. HOOLEY in Brown Twp.

Jonathan SHOWALTER, **b**-16 Sep 1893, **c**-R. E. AURAND, **d**- **e**- **f**-Died 12 Sep 1893 at 7:00 at res. in Decatur Twp.

John BROUGHT, **b**-23 Sep 1893, **c**-Austin Z. BROUGHT, **d**- **e**- **f**-Died 24 Aug 1893 at 6:25 at res. in Granville Twp.

Rachel KREPPS, **b**-28 Sep 1893, **c**-Lawrence KREPPS, **d**-$600, **e**-William BINGERMAN, Lewis H. RUBLE, **f**-Died 24 Aug 1893 at 22:00 at res. of B. F. WHITE in Lewistown

George GOSS, **b**-3 Oct 1893, **c**-John P. TAYLOR, **d**-$200, **e**-Thos. J. FROW, W. H. McCLELLAN, S. S. WOODS, **f**-Died 21 Sep 1893 at 3:00 at res. in Kleck, Brown Twp.

Annie PRICE, **b**-4 Oct 1893, **c**-Lewis H. RUBLE, **d**-$600, **e**-G. H. BELL, B. F. WHITE, **f**-Died 8 Sep 1893 at 22:00 at res. in Granville Twp.

Anna HOGLE, **b**-5 Oct 1893, **c**-Gilbert HOGLE, **d**- **e**- **f**-Died 3 Dec 1892 at 6:30 at res. in Lewistown

Rosanna NORTON, **b**-7 Oct 1893, **c**-Samuel W. NORTON, **d**-$2000, **e**-J. W. NORTON, D. C. NIPPLE, **f**-Died 26 Jan 1890 at ___ at res. of Geo. HAFFLY in Huntingdon County

David LEAHY, **b**-10 Oct 1893, **c**-Martha J. LEAHY, **d**-$200 **e**-A. HULL, E. E. BURLEW, **f**-Died 29 Sep 1893 at P.M. at res. in Lewistown

Aaron DIFFENDERFER, **b**-26 Oct 1893, **c**-Charles L. DIFFENDERFER, **d**-$500, **e**-Peter D. YODER, James C. HAZLETT, **f**-Died 15 Oct at 7:30 at res. in Menno Twp.

Levi H. MUMDORF, **b**-27 Oct 1893, **c**-J. R. WIRT, **d**-$200, **e**-E. CONRAD, Geo. L. RUSSELL **f**-Died 24 Oct 1892 at 13:45 in Huntingdon County

Lewis THOMAS, **b**-31 Oct 1893, **c**-Saml. D. BAPTIST, **d**-$100, **e**-Lycurgus LAW, Rachel STEVENS, **f**-Died 24 Oct 1893 at 15:00 at res. in Lewistown

Sarah F. SHAW, b-2 Nov 1893, c-John K. RHODES, d- e- f-Died 30 Oct 1893 at 9:15 at res. in Brown Twp.

<u>Page 287, Frame 306</u>

Samuel SHADE, b-8 Nov 1893, c-J. B. M. SHADE, Philip SHADE, d-$100, e-John T. CALDWELL, B. F. SHADE, f-Died 27 Oct 1893 at 00:30 at res. in Wayne Twp.

Henry L. CLOSE, b-11 Nov 1893, c-James H. CLOSE, d-$400, e-James B. SMITH, Christ. HOSTETTLER, f-Died 9 Sep 1893 at 17:30 at res. in Armagh Twp.

F. M. COULTER, b-13 Nov 1893, c-J. R. WIRT, A. R. HESSER, d- e- f-Died 27 Oct 1893 at 16:30 at res. in McVeytown

Francis JEFFERSON, b-17 Nov 1893, c-Rachel A. STEVENS, d- e- f-Died 11 Nov 1893 at 6:00 at res. of Rachel A. STEVENS in Lewistown

Peter F. GOSS, b-21 Nov 1893, c-Jacob LAWVER, d-$1400, e-William GOSS, W. C. ERB, f-Died 15 Nov 1893 at 3:30 at res. in Decatur Twp.

Rebecca ZEIGLER, b-22 Nov 1893, c-Uriah S. ZEIGLER, Charles D. ZEIGLER, d-$2000, e-J. P. TAYLOR, W. D. TAYLOR, f-Died 22 Nov 1893 at 7:40 at res. in Brown Twp.

Jane GALLAHER, b-24 Nov 1893, c-Harry MUTHERSBAUGH, d- e- f-Died 13 Nov 1893 at 10:00 at res. of J. K. MUTHERSBAUGH in Granville Twp.

William H. BAIR, b-25 Nov 1893, c-Annie E. BAIR, d- e- f-Died 20 Feb 1893 at 10:50 at res. in Derry Twp.

Abraham HARSHBERGER, b-30 Nov 1893, c-A. S. HARSHBERGER, d- e- f-Died 5 Nov 1893 at 2:00 at res. in Armagh Twp.

N. C. WILSON, b-9 Dec 1893, c-William A. WILSON, d- e- f-Died 17 Apr 189[1] at 18:00 at res. of Wm. A. WILSON in McVeytown

Sarah SILLS, b-19 Dec 1893, c-William T. SHILLING, d-$400, e-Alvin SHIMP, Benj. F. WHITE, f-Died 15 Dec 1893 at 23:25 at res. of Mary M. SHILLING in Lewistown

James H. ALEXANDER, b-22 Dec 1893, c-Susanna ALEXANDER, M. R. ALEXANDER, d- e- f-Died 19 Oct 1893 at 16:00at res. in Derry Twp.

Jacob ZERBY, b-27 Dec 1893. c-James G. ZERBY, d-$4000, e-Thos. H. BAILEY, T. A. W. WEBB. f-Died 21 Nov 1893 at 13:00 at res. in Menno Twp.

John B. SELHEIMER, b-27 Dec 1893, c-Joseph M. SELHEIMER, d-$10,000, e-Eliza S. SELHEIMER, Eleanor B. SELHEIMER, W. G.

SELHEIMER, H. C. SELHEIMER, Mary L. SELHEIMER, Lizzie BECKWITH, **f**-Died 16 Dec 1893 at 17:00 at res. in Lewistown

Mathias GOSS, **b**-28 Dec 1893, **c**-T. A. WAGNER, **d**-$600, **e**-Levi KLINE, Edward B. KLINE, **f**-Died 10 Dec 1893 at __ at res. in Decatur Twp.

Christian ZOOK, **b**-2 Jan 1894, **c**-Joseph C. ZOOK, **d**- **e**- **f**-Died 16 Dec 1893 at 11:30 at res. in Menno Twp.

William A. ORR, **b**-3 Jan 1894, **c**-Allan A. ORR, **d**-$1600, **e**-John K. RHODES, R. W. INGRAM, **f**-Died 23 Dec 1893 at 16:00 at Nelsonville, Ohio

Susan H. MOHLER, **b**-9 Jan 1894, **c**-Edward M. HOWE, **d**-$100, **e**-J. U. HOWE, Wm. HOWE, **f**-Died 23 Nov 1893 at 16:00 at Waynesburg, Franklin County

John M. SMOKER, **b**-15 Jan 1894, **c**-Levi DETWEILER, **d**-$1400, **e**-Jacob B. ZOOK, John YODER, **f**-Died 10 Jan 1894 at 8:00 at res. in Union Twp.

John SHULTZ, **b**-23 Jan 1894, **c**-Aaron M. SHOOP, **d**- **e**- **f**-Died 20 Dec 1893 at 6:30 at res. in Derry Twp.

Mary Jane SIGLER, **b**-26 Jan 1894, **c**-George T. GARDNER, **d**- **e**- **f**-Died 3 Jan 1893[sic] at 14:00 at res. in Decatur Twp.

Lon B. ROPER, **b**-1 Feb 1894, **c**-J. J. HUNT, **d**-$1500, **e**-T. B. REED, S. HULL, C. H. HENDERSON, **f**-Died 16 Dec 1893 at 6:30 at res. in Lewistown

Thomas MAYES, **b**-3 Feb 1894, **c**-A. C. MAYES, **d**- **e**- **f**-Died 14 Jan 1894 at 5:30 at res. in Lewistown

Page 288, Frame 307

William McCORMICK, **b**-16 Feb 1894, **c**-Christian B. PEACHEY, **d**- **e**- **f**-Died 8 Feb 1894 at 7:00 at res. in Union Twp.

Jacob A. HARTZLER, **b**-21 Feb 1894, **c**-Joseph B. HOSTETLER, **d**-$1200, **e**-John YODER, Levi Z. HARTZLER, **f**-Died 16 Jan 1894 at 6:30 at res. in Union Twp.

Marshal DEPKA, **b**-21 Feb 1894, **c**-M. O. DWYER, **d**- **e**- **f**-Died 1 Feb 1894 at 12:00 P.M. at res. in Derry Twp.

Charles B. SIGLER, **b**-21 Feb 1894, **c**-Geo. R. SIGLER, Jas. H. MUTHERSBAUGH, M. M. McLAUGHLIN, **d**- **e**- **f**-Died 17 Feb 1894 at 16:30 at res. in Decatur Twp.

Samuel H. TAYLOR, b-23 Feb 1894, **c**-Samuel EWING, **d**- **e**-Wm. H. EWING, D. C. NIPPLE, **f**-Died 11 Feb 1894 at 9:00 at res. in Newton Hamilton

Joseph L. ROPER, b-28 Feb 1894, **c**-Richard BRINDLE, **d**- **e**-Jonathan S. ZOOK, Henry S. WILSON, **f**-Died 3 Jan 1894 at 10:00 at res. in Union Twp.

Alfred HULL, b-1 Mar 1894, **c**-J. M. WOODS, extr., **d**- **e**- **f**-Died 25 Feb 1894 at 19:00 at res. in Lewistown

Sarah KAUFFMAN, b-9 Mar 1894, **c**-George KAUFFMAN, **d**-$100, **e**-Wm. B. BRATTON, Jacob CASNER, **f**-Died 10 Apr 1890 at 22:00 at res. in Bratton Twp.

John McNABB, b-14 Mar 1894, **c**-William J. McNABB, **d**-$30,000, **e**-James R. FLEMING, John W. WILSON, **f**-Died 2 Mar 1894 at 19:55 at res. in Union Twp.

John B. NICKEE, b-2 Apr 1894, **c**-E. Bruce ALEXANDER, **d**-$300, **e**-T. J. FROW, John B. FLOYD, **f**-Died 2 Mar 1894 at 19:00 at res. of Jos. BYLER in Union Twp.

John H. MILLER, b-6 Apr 1894, **c**-Mary M. MILLER, **d**- **e**- **f**-Died 19 Mar 1894 at 17:10 at res. in Lewistown

William WILLIS, b-12 Apr 1894, **c**-J. Irvin QUIGLEY, **d**-$70,000, **e**-Susan WILLIS, Catharine COLEMAN, Anthony McCAULEY, **f**-Died 5 Apr 1894 at 1:55 at res. in Lewistown

Vesta A. McNITT, b-14 Apr 1894, **c**-John A. McNITT, **d**- **e**- **f**-Died 31 Jan 1894 at 2:30 at res. in Armagh Twp.

Benjamin SPIGELMOYER, b-21 Apr 1894, **c**-Henry H. SPIGELMOYER, **d**-$200, **e**-Walter BAKER, R. D. SALTZMAN, **f**-Died 13 Apr 1894 at 6:00 at res. in Decatur Twp.

Frederick HAWKE, b-23 Apr 1904. **c**-Mary C. HAWKE, J. C. SWIGART, **d**-$2500, **e**-S. J. SWIGART, John C. SHAHEN, **f**-Died 8 Apr 1894 at 1:30 at res. in Lewistown

Mary Jane McNITT, b-25 Apr 1894, **c**-Nancy Margaret McNITT, **d**- **e**- **f**-Died 15 Mar 1894 at 11:00 at res. in Armagh Twp.

Sarah J. HOLLAND, b-27 Apr 1894, **c**-Joseph M. WOODS, c.t.a., **d**-$1200, **e**-La Fayette WEBB, D. W. WOODS, **f**-Died22 Oct 1887 at 4:30 at res. of Mrs. Herrington in Granville Twp.

Elizabeth MITCHELL, b-4 May 1894, **c**-Thompson MITCHELL, **d**-$1200, **e**-D. E. ROBESON, J. K. RHODES, **f**-Died 1 May 1894 at 22:30 at the Mansion House in McVeytown

David C. APPLEBY, **b**-25 May 1894, **c**-Margaret A APPLEBY, **d**- **e**- **f**-Died 6 May 1894 at 19:00 at res. in Derry Twp.

Charlotte FORSYTH, **b**-26 May 1894, **c**-Mary L. REED, **d**-$50,000, **e**-Alexander REED, John McDOWELL, Andrew REED, **f**-Died 17 May 1894 at 2:30 at res. in Lewistown

Elizabeth YODER, **b**-31 May 1894, **c**-Jacob B. ZOOK, **d**-$2800, **e**-Adam YODER, John K. YODER, **f**-Died 10 May 1894 at 13:00 at res. in Union Twp.

Louis CASSEY, **b**-13 Jun 1894, **c**-J. R. WIRT, Andrew CASSEY, **d**-$4000, **e**-C. P. DULL, John F. STINE, **f**-Died 25 May 1894 between 14:00 and 16:00 at res. in Oliver Twp. (sudden)

Benjamin F. MILLER, **b**-18 Jun 1894, **c**-Jane Elizabeth MILLER, **d**- **e**-**f**-Died 28 May 1894 at 5:00 at res. in Lewistown

Silas GLASGOW, **b**-6 Jun 1894, **c**-Rufus C. ELDER, **d**- **e**- **f**-Died 1 Jun 1894 at 2:00 at res. in Granville Twp.

Page 289, Frame 308

Martin D. ROWE, **b**-11 Jul 1894, **c**-A. A. BROWN, admr., **d**-$300, **e**-W. S. DELLETT, Wm. H. LINTHURST, **f**-Died 2 Jun 1893 at __ at res. in Brown Twp.

Catharine WERTS, **b**-16 Jul 1894, **c**-Geo. F. STACKPOLE, **d**-$1000, **e**-Andrew C. STRODE, T. B. REED, **f**-Died 26 Jun 1894 at 5:00 at res. of Eliza STACKPOLE in Lewistown

John SAGER, **b**-26 Jul 1894, **c**-Samuel STERRETT, **d**-$250, **e**-L. H. RUBLE, G. H. BELL, **f**-Died 23 Jul 1894 at 11:00 at res. of Saml. SMITH in Derry Twp.

Sarah C. HUMMEL, **b**-1 Aug 1894, **c**-T. J. NOVINGER, **d**-$900, **e**-W. H. TAYLOR, John C. SHAHEN, **f**-Died 27 Jul 1894 at 18:00 at res. in Decatur Twp.

Joseph SNOOK, **b**-3 Aug 1894, **c**-Samuel STERRETT, **d**-$300, **e**-John C. STRAHEN, S. S. SIGLER, H. C. VANZANT [might belong to the next entry], **f**-Died 27 Jul 1894 at __ at res. in Decatur Twp.

John L. BROWER, **b**-4 Aug 1894, **c**-G. H. BELL, **d**-$500, **e**-L. H. RUBLE, S. M. BELL, **f**-Died 8 Jul 1894 at 23:10 at res. of Francina HARTSWICK in Armagh Twp.

Hugh McClellan WALTERS, **b**-7 Aug 1894, **c**-Jennie W. BACON, **d**- **e**-**f**-Died 19 Jun 1894 at 17:30 at res. of Jennie W. BACON in Hannibal, Missouri

Ammon M. SMITH, b-7 Aug 1894, **c**-Mollie R. SMITH, **d**-$1200, **e**-Robt. H. MYERS, Wm. IRWIN, **f**-Died 29 Jul 1894 at 12:35 at res. in Decatur Twp.

John I. SMITH, b-7 Aug 1894, **c**-Roswell E. AURAND, **d**-$400, **e**-Thos. J. NOVINGER, Henry H. SPIGELMYER, **f**-Died 5 Jul 1894 at 16:30 at res. in Decatur Twp.

Ephraim MORRISON, b-8 Aug 1894, **c**-Joseph H. MORRISON, **d- e- f**-Died 17 Jul 1894 at 17:30 at res. in Brown Twp.

William LEWIS, b-17 Aug 1894, **c**-William H. ERWIN, **d**-$600, **e**-Wm. P. STEVENSON, Jno. GLASGOW, **f**-Died 15 Jul 1894 at 9:00 at res. in Bratton Twp.

Mary E. MARKS, b-28 Aug 1894, **c**-Rufus C. ELDER, **d**-$10,000, **e**-Geo. W. ELDER, Herman S. ELDER, **f**-Died 23 Aug 1894 at 23:30 at res. in Lewistown.

Susannah WEILER, b-18 Sep 1894, **c**-Jephtha H. PEACHEY, **d- e- f**-Died 11 Sep 1894 at 13:00 at res. in Menno Twp.

Abraham ROTHROCK, b-18 Sep 1894, **c**-Jos. T. ROTHROCK, J. R. WIRT, **d- e- f**-Died 9 Sep 1894 at 00:45 at res. in McVeytown

Phebe B. ROTHROCK, b-18 Sep 1894, **c**-Jos. T. ROTHROCK, **d- e- f**-Died 14 Sep 1894 at 6:00 at res. in McVeytown

Margaret J. FLECK, b-22 Sep 1894, **c**-John D. BARR, **d- e- f**-Died 13 Sep 1894 at 12:00 M at res. in Brown Twp.

Peter ANTHONY. b-24 Sep 1894, **c**-John W. WILSON, **d- e- f**-Died 4 Sep 1894 at 12:00 M at res. of C. K. SMOKER in Union Twp.

Lewis TREASTER, b-26 Sep 1894, **c**-James M. TREASTER, **d**-$300, **E**-T. A. WAGNER, John LEPLEY, **f**-Died 9 Sep 1894 at 19:00 at the Nat. Encampment Pittsburg Pa.

Mary A. SPIGELMYER, b-27 Sep 1894, **c**-William F. SPIGELMYER, **d**-$500, **e**-William D. GIFT, Robert F. KREBS, **f**-Died 4 Sep 1894 at 3:40 at res. of Admr. [administrator] in Snyder Co.

Frederick LASH, b-8 Oct 1894, **c**-W. L. LASH, **d**-$1000, **e**-J. R. McCOY, B. F. WHITE, **f**-Died 5 Oct 1894 at 8:00 at res. in Decatur Twp.

John DAVIS, b-8 Oct 1894, **c**-W. W. TROUT, **d- e- f**-Died 10 Sep 1894 at 10:20 at res. in Lewistown

Joseph CAMPBELL, b-10 Oct 1894, **c**-J. Milton CAMPBELL, **d- e- f**-Died 6 Oct 1894 at 22:42 at res. in Union Twp.

Pauline HULL, b-15 Oct 1894, **c**-Joseph M. WOODS, **d**-$700, **e**-D. W. WOODS, Andrew C. STRODE, **f**-Died 11 Sep 1894 at 9:30 at res. in Lewistown

Reuben L. PETER. b-5 Nov 1894, c-Della R. PETER, d-$600, e-Isaac C. SNOOK, James H. PETER, f-Died 12 Oct 1894 at 8:15at res. in Decatur Twp.

Jacob C. BLYMYER, b-19 Nov 1894, c-Tillie BLYMYER, d- e- f-Died 12 Nov 1894 at 5:25 at res. in Lewistown

Joseph WINTER, b-20 Nov 1894, c-J. R. WIRT, d-$1000, E-E. CONRAD, Geo. L. RUSSELL, f-Died 29 Oct 1894 at 22:30 at res. in Bratton Twp.

Page 290, Frame 309

James S. BRISBIN, b-11 Dec 1894, c-John P. TAYLOR, d-no bond, e- f-Died 14 Nov 1894 at 00:30 at res. in Brown Twp.

Frederick LASH, b-12 Dec 1894, c-W. L. LASH, admr. c.t.a., d-$1000, e-J. Roller McCOY, B. F. WHITE, f-Died 5 Oct 1894 at 8:00 at res. in Decatur Twp.

Charles E. THOMAS, b-28 Dec 1894, c-Elizabeth J. THOMAS, d-no bond, e- f-Died 1 Nov 1892 at 3:00 at res. in Phila.

Matthew McCLINTIC, b-29 Dec 1894, c-Thomas J. HAZLETT, d-no bond, e- f-Died 23 Dec 1894 at 1:00 at res. in Decatur Twp.

Joseph RHODES, b-3 Jan 1895, c-W. E. RHODES, d-$1000, e-W. P. STEVENSON, J. R. WIRT, f-Died 27 Apr 1892 at 17:30 at res. of W. E. RHODES in Oliver Twp.

George W. CRISSMAN, b-10 Jan 1895, c-S. H. CRISSMAN, d-$100, e-Isaac BOBB, R. H. SANKEY, f-Died 7 Oct 1894 at 3:30 at res. in Armagh Twp.

Wilson W. NALE, b-14 Jan 1895, c-H. W. AIKENS, d-$500, e-John M. CRISSMAN, Isaiah PECHT, f-Died 24 Jan 1890 at 23:00 at res. in Armagh Twp.

Albert HORNING, b-17 Jan 1895, c-C. P. DULL, d-$4000, e-Joe SELHEIMER, S. B. WEBER, f-Died 23 Dec 1894 at 10:00 at res. in Oliver Twp.

William H. DAVIES, b-22 Jan 1895, c-W. C. DAVIES, d- e- f-Died 8 Jun 1892 at 4:00 or 5:00 at res. in Lewistown

Daniel FIELDS, b-4 Feb 1895, c-La Fayette WEBB, d-$200, e-T. J. FROW, T. B. REED, f-Died 23 Jan 1895 at 1:00 at res. in Lewistown

J. T. MAHON, b-11 Feb 1895, c-Eliza E. MAHON, d- e- f-Died 1 Feb 1895 at 20:00 at res. in Lewistown

Thomas DEPO, b-23 Feb 1895, **c**-Harvey A. BRITTAIN, **d**-$100, **e**-C. E. RAMSEY, John CULBERSON, **f**-Died 18 Dec 1895 at 5:00 at res. in Armagh Twp.

William M. REIGLE, b-1 Mar 1895, **c**-Sarah L. REIGLE **d**- **e**- **f**-Died 11 Feb 1895 at 2:10 at res. in Derry Twp.

John S. HOUTZ, b-21 Mar 1895, **c**-Mollie E. HOUTZ, **d**- **e**- **f**-Died 18 Mar 1895 at 12:40 at res. in Lewistown

Mary CULBERTSON, b-6 Apr 1895, **c**-W. Robert PECHT, **d**-$1400, **e**-Isaiah PECHT, John CULBERTSON, Wm. H. CULBERTSON, **f**-Died 8 Sep 1894 at 8:00 at res. in Armagh Twp.

A. F. KLINE, b-13 Apr 1895, **c**-Perie KLINE, **d**- **e**- **f**-Died 2 Apr 1895 at 12:00 M at res. in Lewistown

Amanda BRININGER, b-20 Apr 1895, **c**-J. K. RHODES, **d**-$100, **e**-A. A. ORR, G. G. FRYSINGER **f**-Died __ at __ at res. in Lewistown

William M. FLEMING, b-23 Apr 1895, **c**-William W. FLEMING, **d**- **e**-**f**-Died 17 Apr 1893 at 15:00 at res. in Brown Twp.

Benjamin F. FOLK, b-4 May 1895 **c**-Annie M. FOLK, **d**-$500, **e**-Geo. W. KEARNS, Isaac HENRY, T. J. NOVINGER **f**-Died 27 Apr 1895 at 19:30 at res. in Decatur Twp.

Page 291, Frame 310

David F. MOORE, b-17 May 1895, **c**-Evanna MOORE, **d**-$100, **e**-John M. CRISSMAN, Solomon H. WAGNER, **f**-Died 1 Jan 1895 at 2:00 at res. in Armagh Twp.

Eliphas WIAN, b-18 May 1895, **c**-William J. PIERCE, **d**-$300, **e**-Ephraim WIAN, W. W. TROUT, **f**-Died ___ at __ at res. in Lewistown

Crawford KYLE, b-21 May 1895, **c**-Mary E. KYLE, **d**-$1000, **e**-James R. BEATTY, W. B. KYLE, **f**-Died 7 May 1895 at 5:00 at res. in Brown Twp.

Jacob S. KING, b-27 May 1895, **c**-Levi DETWEILER, Jacob H. PEACHEY, **d**-$1000, **e**- **f**-Died 19 May 1895 at 7:15 at res. in Menno Twp.

F. G. FRANCISCUS, b-12 Jun 1895, **c**-James P. FRANCISCUS, Katharine FRANCISCUS, ad. c.t.a., **d**-$40,000, **e**-Catharine J. HOOVER, T. F. McCOY, J. E. WILLIAMS, J. W. HUGHES, A. B. SPANOGLE, J. A. MUTHERSBOUGH, James C. HAZLETT, **f**-Died 7 Jun 1895 at 4:00 at res. in Lewistown

Thomas LONGWELL, b-23 Jul 1895, **c**-John R. LONGWELL, **d**- **e**- **f**-Died 7 Apr 1883 at 21:00 at res. in Armagh Twp.

Lebbeus BIGELOW, b-12 Aug 1895, **c-**Priscilla A. BIGELOW, **d-**$300, **e-**E. B. BIGELOW, W. J. HAYES, **f-**Died 30 Jul 1895 at 00:55 at res. in Greenwood Furnace, Huntingdon Co., Pa.

Caroline A. SIGLER, b-22 Aug 1895, **c-**D. W. WOODS, J. M. WOODS, **d- e- f-**Died 11 Aug 1895 at 15:00 at res. in Lewistown

Martin ORT, b-24 Aug 1895, **c-**Nancy E. ORT, Lawrence G. ORT, **d-**$1000, **e-**John H. SNYDER, Harrison AURAND, **f-**Died16 Aug 1895, at 2:40 at res. in Granville Twp.

Jonas YODER, b-30 Sep 1895, **c-**David Z. YODER, John BYLER, **d- e- f-**Died 16 Sep 1895 at 4:00 at res. in Menno Twp.

Sarah E. TOWNSEND, b-8 Nov 1895, **c-**H. J. CULBERTSON, **d- e- f-**Died 22 Oct 1895 at 23:00 at res. in Lewistown

Margaret B. FORGY, b-13 Nov 1895, **c-**W. P. STEVENSON, Jas MACKLIN, **d- e- f-**Died 7 Nov 1895 at 9:00 at res. in McVeytown

Matilda KLINE, b-15 Nov 1895, **c-**C. M. SHULL, **d- e- f-**Died 10 Nov 1895 at 2:00 at res. in Lewistown

Jacob PETER, b-16 Nov 1895, **c-**Emanuel PETER. admr. d.b.n., **d-**$300, **e-**John LEPLEY, Jacob KREPP, **f-**Died 20 Feb 1891 at 14:15 at res. in Decatur Twp.

Samuel HOFFMAN, b-25 Nov 1895, **c-**George HOFFMAN, **d-**$600, **e-**Elmer HOFFMAN, J. A. WAREAM, **f-**Died 18 Sep 1895 at 21:00 at res. in Bratton Twp.

Christian B. PEACHEY, b-30 Nov 1895, **c-**Rufus S. PEACHEY, admr. c.t.a, **d-**$1200, **e-**William HAYES, Geo. E. BRINDLE, **f-**Died 18 Nov 1895 at 1:00 at res. in Union Twp.

David E. ROBESON, b-27 Oct 1895, **c-**Rufus C. ELDER, **d- e- f-**Died 20 Oct 1895 at 6:00 at res. in Lewistown

Page 292, Frame 311

Robert M. KINSLOE, b-3 Dec 1895, **c-**H. Clay KINSLOE, **d-**$100, **e-**H. B. WHARTON, C. H. HENDERSON, **f-**Died 1 Apr 1890 at 1:30 at res. in Newton Hamilton.

Elizabeth HUFFNAGLE, b-7 Dec 1895, **c-**Joseph HUFFNAGLE, **d-**$600, **e-**J. C. HAZLETT, George MOYER, **f-**Died 14 Aug 1895 at 12:00 M at res. of Jacob SMITH in Derry Twp.

Salome B. YODER, b-20 Dec 1895, **c-**Tobias M. YODER, Jacob H. PEACHEY, extrs., **d- e- f-**Died 9 Dec 1895 at 15:30 at res. in Menno Twp.

Rebecca E. SMITH, b-10 Jan 1896, **c-**Carlton A. SMITH, **d- e- f-**Died 23 Dec 1895 at 13:30 at res. in Lewistown

Rebecca STERRETT, b-15 Jan 1896, **c-**Woods STERRETT, **d- e- f-**Died 11 Jan 1895 at 20:00 at res. in Armagh Twp.

Peter BAREFOOT, b-16 Jan 1896, **c-**Robert J. McNITT, **d- e- f-**Died 10 Jan 1896 at 23:05 at res. in Armagh Twp.

Porter LAUGHLIN, b-23 Jan 1896, **c-**W. P. STEVENSON, **d-**$2700 **e-**Saml. McWILLIAMS, J. T. McWILLIAMS, **f-**Died 25 Dec 1894 at 10:00 at res. in Wayne Twp.

William HOWE, b-28 Jan 1896, **c-**Jacob U. HOWE, Ed. M. HOWE, **d-**$6000, **e-**Saml. RICHARD, Wm. F. BURLEW, **f-**Died 14 Jan 1896 at at res. in Derry Twp.

Magdalena BEILER, b-1 Feb 1896, **c-**Enos H. PEACHEY, c.t.a., **d-**$600, **e-**Michael YODER, Wm. J. HAYES, **f-**Died 7 Jan 1896 at 11:30at res. of Jonathan D. KAUFFMAN in Union Twp.

Mary A. ALLISON, b-11 Feb 1896, **c-**S. W. ALLISON, **d-**$6000, **e-**J. C. HAZLETT, H. L. LOCKWOOD, **f-**Died 4 Mar 1895 at 23:00 at res. of David ALLISON in Menno Twp.

Harriet MARKLEY, b-11 Feb 1896, **c-**G. H. BELL, admr. c.t.a., **d-**$800, **e-**L. H. RUBLE, [S.] M. BELL, **f-**Died 29 May 1895 at __ at res. in Derry Twp.

Mrs. Maggie LASHELL, b-12 Feb 1896, **c-**Warner UTTS, **d-**$7000, **e-**Joseph MORRISON, Hampson UTTS, **f-**Died 21 Jan 1896 at 22:30 at res. in Union Twp.

Mary KEILER, b-12 Feb 1896, **c-**Joseph M. WOODS, **d-**$100, **e-**D. W. WOODS, Wm. S. SETTLE, **f-**Died 30 May 1882 at __ at res. in Lewistown

Mary L. REED, b-18 Feb 1896, **c-**Thomas B. REED, **d-**$2500, **e-**G. B. WEBER, A. C. STRODE, **f-**Died 27 Jan 18896 at 8:00 at res. in Granville Twp.

John C. BRENEMAN, b-7 Mar 1896, **c-**Horace J. CULBERTSON, **d- e- f-**Died 24 Dec 1896 (5 written above) at 6:00 at res. in Oliver Twp.

James E. FREED, b-9 Mar 1896, **c-**William W. THOMAS, **d-**$200, **e-**J. A. WAREAM, James M. THOMAS, **f-**Died 31 Mar 1889 at __ at res. in Derry Twp.

Mary SMUCKER, b-11 Mar 1896, **c-**John YODER, **d-**$6000, **e-**D. H. SMUCKER, J. Z. YODER, **f-**Died 4 Mar 1896 at 9:00 at res. in Union Twp.

Isaac SNOOK, **b**-17 Mar 1896, **c**-Saml. L. BROWER, d.b.n., **d**-$100, **e**-Andrew REED, Jacob N. YODER, **f**-Died 6 May 1872 at __ at res. in Armagh Twp.

Samuel KAUFFMAN, **b**-20 Mar 1896, **c**-John F. KAUFFMAN, **d**-$400, **e**-Jacob N. YODER, Joseph Z. YODER, **f**-Died 14 Mar 1896 at 3:56 at res. in Union Twp.

Daniel YODER, **b**-31 Mar 1896, **c**-Peter D. YODER, **d**- **e**- **f**-Died 22 Mar 1896 at 18:00 at res. in Menno Twp.

Mary A. ARNOLD, **b**-11 Apr 1896, **c**-Wm. J. TREASTER, **d**- **e**- **f**-Died 31 Mar 1896 at 7:10 at res. in Decatur Twp.

Andrew P. MARTIN, **b**-28 Apr 1896, **c**-Lavinia B. MARTIN, **d**-$4000, **e**-Margaret U. MARTIN, W. W. TROUT, **f**-Died 8 Feb 1894 at 22:00 at res. in Lewistown

Margaret A. APPLEBY, **b**-28 Apr 1896, **c**-James S. RAKERD, **d**- **e**- **f**-Died 15 Mar 1896 at 19:45 at res. in Derry Twp.

Thomas F. McKEE, **b**-4 May 1896, **c**-Mary M. SHAW, **d**- **e**- **f**-Died 21 Apr 1896 at 5:00 at res. of Mary M. SHAW in Lewistown

Mary A. BAILEY, **b**-2 May 1896, **c**-C. H. BAILEY, T. W. BAILEY, **d**-$100, **e**-H. C. BAILEY, J. M. HUNTER, **f**-Died 14 Apr 1896 at 18:00 at res. in ___

Page 293, Frame 312

Huston McCORMICK, **b**-9 Apr 1896, **c**-H. J. CULBERTSON, **d**- **e**- **f**-Died __ Apr 1896 at __ at res. in Derry Twp.

James G. McCOY, **b**-27 May 1896, **c**-T. F. McCOY, **d**-$100, **e**-Wm. S. SETTLE, La Fayette WEBB, **f**-Died 16 Apr 1896 at 19:00 at res. in McVeytown

Frances HOFFMAN, **b**-10 Jun 1896, **c**-Geo. S. HOFFMAN, **d**-$1000, **e**-Wm. H. HOFFMAN, Fred. BOSSINGER, **f**-Died 18 Jan 1896 at 23:00 at res. in Lewistown

Emanuel KAUFFMAN, **b**-25 Jun 1896, **c**-C. K. HOSTETLER, D. D. KAUFFMAN, **d**-$200, **e**-A. L. FOCHT, C. H. KING, J. Y. ZOOK, **f**-Died 17 Jun 1896 at 00:00 at res. The Hahneman Hospital in Philadelphia

Hannah WORLEY, **b**-2 Jul 1896, **c**-G. W. LINTHURST, **d**-$250, **e**-John A. CAMP, J. C. McNITT, **f**-Died 6 Apr 1896 at 6:00 at res. in Milroy

S. W. SHADLE, **b**-8 Jul 1896, **c**-Mrs. E. A. SHADLE, **d**- **e**- **f**-Died 26 Jun 1896 at 15:30 at res. in Lewistown

Daniel C. YODER, b-28 Jul 1896, c-Israel T. YODER, d- e- f-Died 23 Jul 1896 at 18:00 at res. in Menno Twp.

Emily A. MARTIN, b-29 Jul 1896, c-Frances M. MARTIN, d- e- f-Died 16 Jul 1896 at 11:00 at res. in Derry Twp.

Rebecca J. STRODE, b-5 Aug 1896, c-A. C. STRODE, d-$10,000, e-John WILSON, Thos. B. REED, f-Died 16 Jul 1896 at 22:00 at res. of Isaac STRODE in Culver, Kansas

Mary WHEATON, b-7 Aug 1896, c-T. A. W. WEBB, admr. c.t.a., d-2600, e-Thos. H. BAILEY, J. B. HARTZLER, f-Died ___ at between 16:00 and 19:00 at res. in Menno Twp. [note: no ditto marks under previous line's date, so not sure]

John CULBERTSON, b-11 Aug 1896, c-James A. DYSART, d-$400, e-J. M. SHAVER, G. B. EWING, f-Died 18 Jul 1896 at 15:00 at hospital in Hagertown, Md.

Frank FOX, b-18 Aug 1896, c-A. W. SMITH, d-$300, e-W. W. TROUT, R. H. MYERS, f-Died 10 Aug 1896 at 23:15 at res. of Dale HECK in Lewistown

Robert FORGY, b-21 Aug 1896, c-Henry W. FORGY, d- e- f-Died 4 Aug 1896 at 18:00 at res. in Wayne Twp.

M. Agnes BEATTY, b-22 Aug 1896, c-Mary E. BEATTY, d-$1000, e-G. L. RUSSELL, And. REED, f-Died 12 Jul 1893 at 14:00 at res. in Armagh Twp.

Margaret SHANK, b-1 Sep 1896, c-J. C. McNITT, d- e- f-Died 7 Mar 1896 at __ at res. in Armagh Twp.

Lydia GREEN, b-7 Sep 1896, c-Wm. A. WILSON, d- e- f-Died 2 Sep 1896 at 23:00 at res. in Oliver Twp.

Franey RHIEL, b-5 Oct 1896 c-A. D. ZOOK, d- e- f-Died 30 Sep 1896 at 16:00 at res. in Menno Twp.

David A. HOSTETLER, b-7 Oct 1896, c-Solomon PEACHEY, d-$2000, e-David H. YODER, Geo. L. RUSSELL, f-Died 2 Oct 1896 at 1:30 at res. in Menno Twp.

Mary Ann SPEESE, b-17 Oct 1896, c-D. W. WOODS, d- e- f-Died 24 Sep 1896 at 7:00 at res. in Lewistown

Christian MYERS, b-24 Oct 1896, c-Adam HENRY, admr. d.b.n., d-$100, e-J. R. STERRETT, La Fayette WEBB, f-Died 21 Apr 1892 at 5:45 at res. in Armagh Twp.

Elizabeth GLASS, b-24 Oct 1896, c-Jesse W. HORTON, d- e- f-Died 14 Oct 1896 at 23:00 at res. in Union Twp.

Page 294, Frame 313

Margaret A. CLAY, **b**-4 Nov 1896, **c**-J. R. WIRT, **d**- **e**- **f**-Died 20 Mar 1896at at res. in McVeytown

Isaac PLANK, **b**-9 Nov 1896, **c**-Jonathan PLANK, d.b.n., **d**-$150, **e**-Henry S. WILSON, Mattie A. PLANK, **f**-Died 4 Nov 1879 at __ at res. in Union Twp.

George SWARTZELL, **b**-11 Nov 1896, **c**-Samuel L. SWARTZELL, d.b.n., **d**-$150, **e**-J. R. STERRETT, W. B. McNITT, **f**-Died 21 Aug 1874 at 6:00 at res. in Armagh Twp.

James KYLE, **b**-11 Nov 1896, **c**-Joseph W. KYLE, **d**-$100, **e**-Wm. H. TAYLOR, A. Reed HAYES, **f**-Died __ Nov 1888 at 5:00 at res. in Brown Twp.

Samuel McCLAY, M.D., **b**-13 Nov 1896, **c**-Jos. H. MACLAY, **d**-$1600, **e**-Wm. B. MACLAY, La Fayette WEBB, **f**-Died 17 Dec 1891 at __ at res. in Armagh Twp.

Rev. Robert M. WALLACE, **b**-26 Nov 1896, **c**-Mary R. WALLACE, **d**-$12,000, **e**-J. P. FRANCISCUS, Annie R. WALLACE, **f**-Died 15 Jun 1896 at 11:00 at res. in Lewistown

Thomas STROUP, **b**-27 Nov 1896, **c**-Millie H. STROUP, **d**-$100, **e**-Isabella M. MUTHERSBOUGH, **f**-Died 3 Aug 1890 at 1:00 at res. in Lewistown

Henry RENNINGER, **b**-3 Dec 1896, **c**-William RENNINGER, **d**-$100, **e**-J. K. MILLER, J. E. RONK, **f**-Died 17 May 1892 at 23:00 at res. in Bratton Twp.

E. E. LOCKE, **b**-3 Dec 1896, **c**-Maria B. MITCHELL, **d**-$150, **e**-Frank E. MANN, Wm. H. MANN, **f**-Died 22 Feb 1883 at __ at res. in Lewistown

Oliver P. SMITH, **b**-18 Nov 1896, **c**-James B. SMITH, Jno. P. TAYLOR, **d**- **e**- **f**-Died 21 Aug 1896 at 13:00 at res. in Armagh Twp.

Felix McCLINTIC, **b**-8 Dec 1896, **c**-S. A. McCLINTIC, **d**-$300, **e**-J. C. EHRENFELD, C. T. ROSSMAN, **f**-Died 6 Oct 1883 at 3:30 at res. in Armagh Twp.

David J. SMITH, **b**-14 Dec 1896, **c**-William WERTS, **d**- **e**- **f**-Died 8 Dec 1896 at 9:00 at res. of William WERTS in Wayne Twp.

John McCORMICK, **b**-15 Dec 1896, **c**-John C. SWIGART, **d**-$100, **e**-R. H. MEANS, Jno. C. SHAHEN, **f**-Died 5 Nov 1896 at 12:40 at res. of Wm. GEEDY in McVeytown

Margaret C. LEPLEY, **b**-17 Dec 1896, **c**-Saml. B. STINE, **d**- **e**- **f**-Died 5 Nov 1896 at 12 M at res. in Wayne Twp.

Joseph H. MORRISON, b-21 Dec 1896, **c**-Wm. M. GIBBONEY, Vannie GRAFT, **d**- **e**- **f**-Died 12 Dec 1896 at 20:00 at res. in Union Twp.

George W. RARICK, b-28 Dec 1896, **c**-Mary M. RARICK **d**- **e**- **f**-Died 16 Dec 1896 at 8:30 at res. in Lewistown

R. Bruce FOUST, b-31 Dec 1896, **c**-William A. STINE, **d**-$300, **e**-Samuel R. STINE, Geo. T. COOPER, **f**-Died 7 Dec 1896 at 4:00 at res. in Wayne Twp.

Almira W. PENEPACKER, b-4 Jan 1897, **c**-George B. PENEPACKER, **d**-$400, **e**-Geo. H. PEARSON, J. K MUTHERSBOUGH, **f**-Died 19 Dec 1896 at 22:00 at res. of G. B. PENEPACKER in Granville Twp.

Abner THOMPSON, b-16 Jan 1897, **c**-Edward J. THOMPSON, **d**-$750, **e**-Joseph KELLEY, Andrew REED, **f**-Died 6 Mar 1866 at __ at res. in Lewistown

Joseph HARKNESS, b-28 Jan 1897, **c**-John REED, **d**-$2000, **e**-John WILSON, J. R. STERRETT, **f**-Died 12 Jan 1897 at __ at res. in Brown Twp.

Kate A. SAYLOR, b-1 Feb 1897, **c**-Catharine E. SAYLOR,. **d**-$250, **e**-La Fayette WEBB, David GROVE, **f**-Died 20 Jan 1897 at 7:40 at Methodist Hospital in Philadelphia

George W. EARNEST, b-2 Feb 1897, **c**-Jas. L. POSTLETHWAITE, **d**-$1000, **e**-H. C. KINSLOE, J. C. McDOWELL, **f**-Died 20 Jan 1897 at 15:00 at Ryde Station in Wayne Twp.

James BAILEY, b-13 Feb 1897, **c**-Thos. H. BAILEY, **d**-$150, **e**-James C. HAZLETT, Thos. J. HAZLETT, **f**-Died 21 Mar 1873 at 16:00 at res. in Brown Twp.

Elizabeth A. MONTGOMERY, b-17 Feb 1897, **c**-Robert H. MONTGOMERY, **d**-$200, **e**-Benjamin F. WHITE, C. B. BRENEMAN, **f**-Died 22 Sep 1896 at 9:00 at res. in Hospital in Philadelphia

James FIROVED, b-18 Feb 1897, **c**-Sarah B. FIROVED, **d**-$100, **e**-John KENNEDY, William R. CLARKE, **f**-Died 31 Oct 1893 at 14:30 at res. in Lewistown

James D. RAMSEY, b-23 Feb 1897, **c**-Adam A. RAMSEY, G. Howard RAMSEY, **d**-$100, **e**-J. R. STERRETT, C. E. RAMSEY, **f**-Died 24 Feb 1896 at 7:00 at res. in Armagh Twp.

William R. McKEE, b-27 Feb 1897, **c**-John A. McKEE, **d**-$200, **e**-A. C. STRODE, Joe W. SELHEIMER, **f**-Died 20 Feb 1897 at 15:45 at res. of Jno. A. McKEE in Lewistown

James M. BROWN, b-1 Mar 1897, **c**-A. S. HARSHBERGER, **d**-$55, **e**-W. W. FICHTHORN, R. H. McCLINTIC, **f**-Died 26 Apr 1896 at __ A.M., at res. in Beloit, Kansas

Page 295, Frame 314
Phillip HARDMAN. b-3 Mar 1897, **c**-E. P. MANN, **d**-$3500, **e**-Jeremiah M. YEAGER, Robert H. McCLINTIC, **f**-Died 25 Feb 1897 at 11:10 at res. in Derry Twp.
James B. KELLEY, b-5 Mar 1897, **c**-John K. RHODES, **d**-$4000, **e**-John G. WHITE, Robert H. MYERS, **f**-Died 26 Feb 1897at 18:20 at res. in Lewiston
Abner ROBINS, b-5 Mar 1897, **c**-John A. McKEE, **d**- **e**- **f**-Died 2 Aug 1884 at __ at res. in Lewiston
Margaret J. NORTON, b-10 Mar 1897, **c**-John W. NORTON, **d**-$600, **e**-John K. RHODES, S. W. NORTON, **f**-Died 17 Aug 1896 at 17:00 at res. in Newton Hamilton
Freeman N. SHIPTON, b-11 Mar 1897, **c**-Lewis W. HOOVER, **d**-$100, **e**-A. E. HOOVER, John RIDEN, **f**-Died 13 Aug 1880 at __ at res. in Milroy, Pa.
Abraham B. GARVER, b-17 Mar 1897, **c**-A. Rush GIBBONEY, **d**-$2000, **e**-Harrison H. GIBBONEY, H. Foster TAYLOR, **f**-Died 9 Mar 1897 at __ at res. in Brown Twp.
John TAYLOR, b-2 Apr 1897, **c**-John H. TAYLOR, **d**-$150, **e**-Saml. A. McCLINTIC, Gruber H. BELL, **f**-Died __ Jun [no dittos] at at res. in Osborne Co., Kansas
Anna MYERS, b-9 Apr 1897, **c**-Charles BOOK, **d**- **e**- **f**-Died 5 Apr 1897 at 5:00 at res. in Bratton Twp.
Elizabeth KANAGY, b-16 Apr 1897, **c**-Israel T. YODER, **d**- **e**- **f**-Died 2 Apr 1897 at 22:00 at res. in Union Twp.
Mathew R. PATTON, b-23 Apr 1897, **c**-J. H. PEACHEY, **d**- **e**- **f**-Died 11 Apr 1897 at 11:00 at res. in Menno Twp.
Sarah KING, b-24 Apr 1897, **c**-Jacob C. YODER, **d**-$5000, **e**-Jonathan S. ZOOK, Joseph B. HOSTETLER, **f**-Died 11 Apr 1897 at 15:30 at res. in Union Twp.
Elizabeth R. ANDREWS, b-30 Apr 1897, **c**-I. T. ANDREWS, **d**-$900, **e**-N. Sargent ROSS, H. C. BRENEMAN, **f**-Died 25 Dec 1897 [maybe 1896?] at 19:00 at res. in Lewistown
Daniel F. YODER, b-6 May 1897, **c**-John K. YODER, David C. PEACHEY, **d**- **e**- **f**-Died 28 Apr 1897 at 6:00 at res. in Menno Twp.

Johanna KINSEL, b-8 May 1897, c-W. C. DAVIES, d-$350, e-Peter DREYER, Frank W. SILLS, f-Died 25 Nov 1894 at 22:20 at res. in Lewistown

Benjamin A. SIGLER, b-10 May 1897, c-D. Clark NIPPLE, M.D., d- e- f-Died 7 May 1897 at 6:57 at res. in Newton Hamilton

Elizabeth HERTZLER, b-14 May 1897, c-David HARSHBARGER, d- e- f-Died 9 May 1897 at 11:40 at res. in Bratton Twp.

John PEACHEY, b-20 May 1897, c-Jonas Z. PEACHEY, d- e- f-Died 15 May 1897 at 13:30 at res. in Menno Twp.

Mary M. NORRIS, b-24 May 1897, c-A. Wilson NORRIS, d- e- f-Died 17 May 1897 at 18:50 at res. of W. T. ODELL in Lewistown

William RUSLER, b-25 May 1897, c-William B. MACLAY, d- e- f-Died 13 May 1897 at 14:00 at res. in Union Twp.

Jacob KNEPP, b-25 May 1897, c-James G. KNEPP, d-$200, e-James MACKLIN, J. R. WIRT, f-Died 20 May 1897 at 22:45 at res. in McVeytown

Elizabeth STRUNK, b-1 Jun 1897, c-W. P. STEVENSON, d-$1000, e-Saml. McWILLIAMS, J. T. McWILLIAMS, f-Died 10 Apr 1897 at 2:00 at res. in Bratton Twp.

Joseph E. WILLIAMS, b-4 Jun 1897, c-Saml. J. BRISBIN, d-$2000, e-C. H. HENDERSON, G. L. RUSSELL, f-Died 26 Apr 1897 at 17:00 at res. in Lewistown

William H. SWIGART, b-14 Jun 1897, c-John C. SWIGART, d-$100, e-Andrew C. STRODE, La Fayette WEBB, f-Died 27 May 1897 at 6:50 at res. of B. J. YETTER in Granville Twp.

Miles HAFFLY, b-24 Jun 1897, c-William J. HAFFLY, d-$200, e-J. K. DETWEILER, A. D. BYLER, f-Died 13 Jun 1897 at 15:30 at res. in Union Twp.

Margaret A. MURRAY, b-26 Jun 1897, c-George W. MURRAY, d-$1000, e-S. B. WEBER, George S. HOFFMAN, f-Died22 May 1897 at 22:00 at res. in Lewistown

Alfred KLINE, b-28 Jun 1897, c-Charles H. KLINE, d-$300, e-Mary S. KLINE, John KLINE, f-Died 14 Jun 1897 at 2:15 at res. in Derry Twp.

David SHATZER, b-28 Jun 1897, c-Saml. J. BRISBIN, d-$900, e-George L. RUSSELL, Richard SHATZER, f-Died 29 Jun 1893 at 19:00 at res. in Lewistown

Henry S. PRICE, b-30 Jun 1897, c-George W. RUBLE, d-$800, e-John C. SHAHEN, Wm. H. BINGERMAN, f-Died 6 Jun 1897 at 17:00 at res. in Oliver Twp.

Page 296, Frame 315

Joseph H. ALTER, **b**-8 Jul 1897, **c**-Martha ALTER, **d**- **e**- **f**-Died 28 Jun 1897 at 16:00 at res. in Lewistown

John A. BROUGHT, **b**-8 Jul 1897 **c**-Anna G. BROUGHT **d**- **e**- **f**-Died 4 Oct 1896 at 1:00 at res. in Lewistown

Jacob HARTZLER, **b**-13 Jul 1897 **c**-Joseph A. KANAGY, **d**- **e**- **f**-Died 3 Jul 1897 at 10:00 at res. in Menno Twp.

Leonard S. WOLFKILL, **b**-14 Jul 1897, **c**-Eva S. WOLFKILL, **d**- **e**- **f**-Died 11 Apr 1897 at 11:30 at res. in Lewistown

M. Irvin MOWERY, **b**-17 Jul 1897, **c**-G. H. PEARSON, **d**-$600, **e**-F. J. McCOY, G. A. LEOPOLD, **f**-Died 11 Jul 18897 at 6:20 at res. in Granville Twp.

Esther MORRISON, **b**-20 Jul 1897, **c**-Martha E. MORRISON, **d**-$100, **e**-Allen A. ORR, J. K. RHODES, **f**-Died 17 Jan 1880 at 2:00 at res. in Newton Hamilton

Robert C. GRAHAM, **b**-20 Jul 1897, **c**-Emma J. GRAHAM, **d**-$100, **e**-V. J. McKIM, Joseph KELLEY, **f**-Died 16 Jul 1895 at 21:00 at res. in Derry Twp.

Harry HOFFMAN, **b**-10 Aug 1897, **c**-La Fayette WEBB, **d**-$2500, **e**-Wm. H. TAYLOR, A. W. NALE, **f**-Died 24 Jul 1897at 20?30 at the German Hospital in Philadelphia

K. Agnes NEWMAN, **b**-27 Aug 1897, **c**-Samuel MYERS, **d**-$100, **e**-Henry SMITH, David SMITH, **f**-Died 7 Mar 1897 at 23:40 at res. in Yeagertown

Elizabeth McCOY, **b**-28 Aug 1897, **c**-James N. HOFFMAN, **d**- **e**- **f**-Died 8 Aug 1897 at 18:00 at res. of Wm. N. HOFFMAN in Lewistown

John BARGER, **b**-6 Sep 1897, **c**-Margaret M. BARGER, **d**-$500, **e**-Robert A. DELLETT, W. S. DELLETT, **f**-Died 21 Aug 1897 at 11:50 at res. in Armagh Twp.

W. W. FOCHT, **b**-6 Sep 1897, **c**-T. A. W. WEBB, **d**-$3500, **e**-J. B. HARTZLER, T. H. BAILEY, Jacob K. METZ, **f**-Died 15 Aug 1897 at 9:30 at res. in Menno Twp.

David NORTON, **b**-10 Sep 1897, **c**-L. . POSTLTHWAITE c.t.a., **d**-$1000, **e**-S. W. NORTON, J. W. NORTON, **f**-Died 11 Sep 1892 at __ at res. in Wayne Twp.

Hugh McCLELLAND, **b**-13 Sep 1897, **c**-Jennie W. BACON, **d**-$300, **e**-J. R. WIRT, G. H. MACKLIN, **f**-Died ___ at __ at res. in Union Twp.

James R. BEATTY, **b**-23 Sep 1897, **c**-John K. BEATTY, **d**-$1000, **e**-James B. SMITH, John D. STERRETT, **f**-Died 13 Sep 1897 at 15:30 at res. in Armagh Twp.

Joseph M. FLEMING, **b**-4 Nov 1897, **c**-Joseph T. FLEMING, **d**-$3200, **e**-R. T. FLEMING, Samuel N. FLEMING, **f**-Died12 Oct 1897 at 17:00 at res. in Menno Twp.

Maria E. PATTON, **b**-6 Nov 1897, **c**-H. Maria PATTON, **d**-$100, **e**-T. F. McCOY, Robert W. PATTON, Jr., **f**-Died 22 Jan 1896 at 5:45 at res. in Washington, D.C.

Annie E. LANTZ, **b**-9 Nov 1897, **c**-John W. WILSON, **d**-$100, **e**-W. J. McNABB, John T. WILSON, **f**-Died 28 Sep 1896 at __ at res. in Union Twp.

Sarah J. LEVY, **b**-11 Nov 1897, **c**-Susan CALLAHAN, **d**-$100, **e**-Samuel H. CALLAHAN, Benjamin F. WHITE, **f**-Died 2 Jun 1897 at 23:30 at res. in Lewistown

Mary E. STREILEY, **b**-15 Nov 1897, **c**-Frank J. STREILEY, **d**-$1500, **e**-Joseph KELLEY, Elizabeth CUNNINGHAM, William HOLLIS, **f**-Died 6 Nov 1897 at 2:30 at res. in Brown Twp.

Barbara HOOLEY, **b**-24 Nov 1897, **c**-A. Z. PEACHEY, **d**- **e**- **f**-Died 17 Nov 1897 at 4:00 at res. of Jonathan HOOLEY in Brown Twp.

Mary C. HURLBUT, **b**-26 Nov 1897, **c**-J. M. WOODS, **d**- **e**- **f**-Died 19 Nov 1897 at 11:00 at res. in Lewistown

David HANAWALT, **b**-7 Dec 1897, **c**-Walker PETERSON, **d**- **e**- **f**-Died 26 Nov 1897 at 16:00 at res. in Wayne Twp.

Rebecca E. ANDREWS, **b**-17 Dec 1897, **c**-James K. ANDREWS, **d**- **e**- **f**-Died 10 Dec 1897 at 16:40 at res. in Wayne Twp.

Page 297, Frame 316

Harriet WIGHTMAN, **b**-11 Jan 1898, **c**-Wm. S. SETTLE **d**- **e**- **f**-Died 9 Jan 1898 at __ at res. in Lewistown

Simon KREPS, **b**-31 Jan 1898, **c**-David L. KREPS, John A. KREPS, **d**-$800, **e**-H. H. RHEAM, George W. KEARNS, **f**-Died 19 Jan 1896 at 9:00 at res. in Decatur Twp.

Margaret J. HAFFLY, **b**-5 Feb 1898, **c**-A. D. BYLER, **d**-$100, **e**-Joseph Z. YODER, J. Y. ZOOK, **f**-Died 31 Jan 1898 at 16:30 at res. in Union Twp.

Noah R. ROMIG, **b**-10 Feb 1898, **c**-Simon ROMIG, Simon H. OLDT, **d**-$1200, **e**-John SHIREY, Reuben J. SMITH, **f**-Died 1 Feb 1898 at 4:00 at res. in Armagh Twp.

Margaret E. WILSON, b-11 Feb 1898, **c-**J. R. WIRT, c.t.a., **d-**$400, **e-** George L. RUSSELL, B. F. SHEIBLEY, **f-**Died 14 Jan 1898 at 14:00 at res. in Oliver Twp.

Elizabeth McCURDY, b-22 Feb 1898, **c-**C. M. SHULL, **d- e- f-**Died 18 Feb 1898 at 9:40 at res. in Lewistown

Michael YODER, b-5 Mar 1898, **c-**Joseph I. YODER, **d- e- f-**Died 24 Feb 1898 at 18:30 at res. in Brown Twp.

Ephraim WIAN, b-8 Mar 1898, **c-**William H. WIAN, **d-**$100, **e-**J. I. QUIGLEY, John G. WHITE, **f-**Died 2 Mar 1898 at 5:30 at res. in Lewistown

John WATTS, b-8 Mar 1898, **c-**William H. ERWIN, **d-**$800, **e-**Jos. R. BRATTON, W. P. STEVENSON, **f-**Died 1 Mar 1898 at 18:00 at res. in McVeytown

John T. LANE, b-9 Mar 1898, **c-**George M. LANE, **d- e- f-**Died 4 Mar 1898 at 8:45 at res. in Newton Hamilton

Elizabeth J. JACOB, b-17 Mar 1898, **c-**A. Wilson JACOB, **d-**$15,000, **e-** Mary W. JACOB, Robert U. JACOB, **f-**Died 12 Mar 1898 at 18:40 at res. in Lewistown

Lewis HOUSER, b-18 Mar 1898, **c-**James C. HOUSER, **d-**$2000, **e-**Geo. W. LINTHURST, S. W. BROWN, A. E. GETZ, **f-**Died 13 Mar 1898 at 3:10 at res. in Armagh Twp.

Catharine CONRAD, b-24 Mar 1898, **c-**A. C. STRODE, **d-**$100, **e-**T. B. REED, J. M. WOODS, **f-**Died __ Mar 1898 at __ at res. in Granville Twp.

Sallie E. HARTZLER, b-26 Mar 1898, **c-**David K. HARTZLER, Lydia R. HARTZLER, **d-**$400, **e-**David H. YODER, Solomon PEACHEY, **f-** Died 21 Jan 1898 at 21:10 at res. in Menno Twp.

James C. ROBESON, b-5 Apr 1898, **c-**Elizabeth C. ROBESON, **d- e- f-** Died 31 Mar 1898 at 3:15 at res. of W. F. ROBESON in Pittsburg, Pa.

Christian P. YODER, b-9 Apr 1898, **c-**Jacob D. YODER, **d-**$1000, **e-** Solomon PEACHEY, Joshua HARSHBARGER, **f-**Died 20 Dec 1895 at P.M. at res. in Menno Twp.

Sarah E. GREER, b-13 Apr 1898, **c-**William GREER, **d-**$600, **e-**Joseph KELLEY, Wm. H. KOHLER, **f-**Died 12 Jul 1890 at 12 M at res. in Armagh Twp.

John T. F. FIELDS, b-20 Apr 1898, **c-**George A. FIELDS, **d- e- f-**Died 16 Apr 1898 at 19:00 at res. in Newton Hamilton

Henry BOSSINGER, b-2 May 1898, **c**-William F. BOSSINGER, **d**-$300, **e**-Fred BOSSINGER, George S. HOFFMAN, **f**-Died 23 Apr 1898 at 23:15 by accident in Granville Twp.

Ernest H. BURGHART, b-18 May 1898, **c**-Wm. H. KITTING, **d**- **e**- **f**-Died 14 Apr 1898 at 14:00 at res. of Jere. KNEPP in Lewistown

James E. GILLILAND, b-6 Jun 1898, **c**-Dr. W. T. BROWNING. **d**- **e**- **f**-Died 22 May 1898 at 19:00 at res. in Newton Hamilton

Adam YODER, b-13 Jun 1898, **c**-Jacob B. ZOOK, **d**-$700, **e**-C. Z. YODER, D. L. BYLER, **f**-Died 26 Apr 1898 at 10:00 at res. in Union Twp.

John D. BARR, b-W. B. KYLE, W. B. MACLAY, **c**- **d**- **e**- **f**-Died 28 May 1898 at 00:15 at res. in Brown Twp.

Joseph STRODE, b-28 Jun 1898, **c**-Amor A. STRODE, **d**- **e**- **f**-Died 18 May 1898 at 2:00 at res. in Oliver Twp.

Emma BOLLINGER, b-1 Jul 1898, **c**-John W. SWIGART, **d**-$200, **e**-S. Harvey SWIGART, George A. LEOPOLD, **f**-Died 24 Jun 1898 at 6:00 at res. in Oliver Twp.

Page 298, Frame 317

Maria KNEPP, b-11 Jul 1898, **c**-William J. TREASTER, **d**- **e**- **f**-Died 31 Oct 1897 at 11:00 at res. in Decatur Twp.

A. F. GIBBONEY, b-14 Jul 1898, **c**-A. F. GIBBONEY, Wm. K. GIBBONEY, **d**- **e**- **f**-Died 8 Jul 1898 at 7:00 at res. in Union Twp.

Margaret J. HORNING, b-22 Jul 1898, **c**-C. P. DULL, **d**- **e**- **f**-Died 29 Mar 1898 at 2:00 at res. in Oliver Twp.

Peninah NEWMAN, b-5 Aug 1898, **c**-J. H. PEACHEY, **d**-$100, **e**-La Fayette WEBB, J. C. HAZLETT, **f**-Died 1 Jul 1894 at __ at res. in Menno Twp.

Daniel GROSS, b-1 Sep 1898, **c**-William B. GROSS, **d**- **e**- **f**-Died 28 Aug 1898 at 15:10 at res. in Lewistown

Hannah M. QUIGLEY, b-1 Sep 1898, **c**-J. Irvin QUIGLEY, **d**-$16,000, **e**-W. W. FICHTHORN, Susan WILLIS, **f**-Died 5 Aug 1898 at 5:00 at res. in Lewistown

Robert A. McKEE, b-26 Aug 1898, **c**-Annie E. McKEE, **d**- **e**- **f**-Died 15 Jul 1898 at 4:00 at res. in Lewistown

William A. SANKEY, b-16 Sep 1898, **c**-Margaret E. SANKEY, **d**-$1500, **e**-J. Roller McCOY, David GROVE, **f**-Died 13 Aug 1898 at 20:00 at res. in Lewistown

Joel ZOOK, b-4 Oct 1898, **c**-Joseph B. HOSTETLER, **d**-$600, **e**-Christian L. YODER, Solomon ZOOK, **f**-Died 13 Sep 1898 at 2:00 at res. in Union Twp.

Lewis E. SCHUCHT, b-17 Oct 1898, **c**-John D. SCHUCHT, Saml. E. SCHUCHT, **d**-$3000, **e**-Jeremiah KNEPP, S. L. BROWER, **f**-Died 13 Oct 1898 at 5:30 at res. in Lewistown

Henry M. GRASSMYER, b-19 Oct 1898, **c**-Jas. S. GRASSMYER, G. A. GRASSMYER, **d**-$800, **e**-William YODER, William YOUTZY, **f**-Died 16 Oct 1898 at 5:45 at res. in Bratton Twp.

John ROTHROCK, b-28 Oct 1898, **c**-S. H. ROTHROCK, **d**-$1000, **e**-Oliver J. ROTHROCK, John T. ROTHROCK, **f**-Died 25 Jun 1898 at 19:00 at res. in Derry Twp.

Samuel LAWVER, b-11 Nov 1898, **c**-Geo. W. KEARNS, H. P. ERTLEY, **d**- **e**- **f**-Died 2 Nov 1898 at 6:00 at John WRAY's res. in Decatur Twp.

Robert M. TAYLOR, b-11 Nov 1898, **c**-H. Foster TAYLOR, **d**-$8000, **e**-William D. TAYLOR, **f**-Died 6 Oct 1898 at 6:00 at res. in Brown Twp.

James E. WOOMER, b-25 Nov 1898, **c**-Ellen R. WOOMER, **d**-$200, **e**-John R. WOOMER, Robert W. PATTON, **f**-Died 22 Sep 1898 at __ at Burnham Work in Derry Twp.

Stephen HARSHBARGER, b-6 Dec 1898, **c**-William HARHBARGER, **d**-$300, **e**-G. W. KREPPS, Fred. BOSSINGER, **f**-Died 8 Feb 1897 at 9:00 at res. in Bratton Twp.

Mary A. CONTNER, b-21 Dec 1898, **c**-N. Kennie WHARTON, **d**-$20,000, **e**-Harry B. WHARTON, Geo. H. PECHT, Mary E. CONTNER, **f**-Died 29 Nov 1898 at 7:30 at res. in Menno Twp.

Edward M. ZERBE, b-22 Dec 1898, **c**-Frank. J. ZERBE, **d**-$4000, **e**-Jeremiah KNEPP, Chas. H. HENDERSON, **f**-Died 11 Dec 1898 at 9:00 at res. of Mr. DAVIS near Barre in Huntingdon Co.

Andrew L. CASSEY, b-27 Dec 1898, **c**-Mary L. CASSEY, D. R. STINE, **d**-$6000, **e**-Jonas HARSHBARGER, John F. STINE, William C. FRENCH, Jacob R. STINE, **f**-Died 15 Dec 1898 at 21:00 at his Lumberman's Shanty in Oliver Twp.

Amanda CASNER, b-29 Dec 1898, **c**-Jacob CASNER, **d**-$100, **e**-William A. BRATTON, John H. WHITEHEAD, **f**-Died 3 Mar 1897 at 3:00 at res. in Wayne Twp.

Page 299, Frame 318

George KRICK, **b**-3 Jan 1899, **c**-Hiram KRICK, **d**-$3000, **e**-Lawrence KRICK, Lucinda C. KRICK, **f**-Died 12 Dec 1898 at 3:00 at res. in Decatur Twp.

Abraham M. GRASSMYER, **b**-13 Jan 1899, **c**-John C. SWIGART, **d**- **e**- **f**-Died 31 Dec 1898 at 7:45 at res. in Bratton Twp.

John S. ROOK, **b**-4 Feb 1899, **c**-W. J. ROOK, H. W. AIKENS, **d**-$300, **e**-J. Roller McCOY, C. M. SHULL, **f**-Died __ Jan 1895 at 20:00 at res. in Lewistown

John HENRY, **b**-9 Feb 1899, **c**-Davis HENRY, **d**-$200, **e**-A. W. NALE, Jos. A. HOOLEY, **f**-Died __ Nov 1867 at 5:00 at res. in Brown Twp.

Rev. Andrew H. PARKER, **b**-20 Feb 1899, **c**-Maggie J. PARKER, **d**-$30,000, **e**-John McDOWELL, George L. RUSSELL, **f**-Died 1 Feb 1899 at 17:15 at res. in Brown Twp.

William A. MOORE, **b**-21 Feb 1899, **c**-John GLASGOW, John S. LEFFERD, **d**- **e**- **f**-Died 15 Feb 1899 at 15:00 at res. in McVeytown

Henry BOOK, **b**-22 Feb 1899, **c**-D. W. WOODS, J. M. WOODS, **d**- **e**- **f**-Died ___ at __ at res. in Granville Twp.

Mary CLARK, **b**-24 Feb 1899, **c**-W. H. ERWIN, **d**-$100, **e**-William A. WILSON, E. CONRAD, **f**-Died 14 Apr 1894 at 5:00 at res. in McVeytown

Katie M. BOYER, **b**-27 Feb 1899, **c**-Fred J. BOYER, **d**- **e**- **f**-Died 12 Jan 1899 at 23:45 at res. in Union Twp.

William H. EWING, **b**-6 Mar 1899, **c**-Susan EWING, C. B. EWING, **d**- **e**- **f**-Died 26 Feb 1899 at 21:30 at res. in Newton Hamilton

Caroline LAWVER, **b**-7 Mar 1899, **c**-George W. KEARNS, **d**-$2000, **e**-Reuben GOSS, John A. KREPS, Robert H. KRICK, **f**-Died 1 Mar 1899 at 2:00 at res. in Decatur Twp.

Catharine YODER, **b**-9 Mar 1899, **c**-John YODER, **d**-$5000, **e**-Christian Z. YODER, A. Reed HAYES, **f**-Died 7 Feb 1899 at 5:30 at res. in Union Twp.

Henry A. MOODIE, **b**-13 Mar 1899, **c**-J. W. HORNBERGER, **d**-$300, **e**-Chas. W. McELHOE, William STUMPFF, **f**-Died 10 Feb 1899 at 3:30 at res. in Decatur Twp.

Frances J. SIGLER, **b**-16 Mar 1899, **c**-Saml. S. SIGLER, Laura E. THOMPSON, **d**- **e**- **f**-Died 7 Mar 1899 at 4:25 at res. in Decatur Twp.

Christian B. ZOOK, **b**-21 Mar 1899, **c**-C. G. MILLIKEN, **d**-$1000, **e**-W. D. TAYLOR, John B. ZOOK, **f**-Died 13 Mar 1899 at 21:10 at res. in Brown Twp.

Cyrus K. MARK, **b**-22 Mar 1899, **c**-Ellen A. PARKER, **d**- **e**- **f**-Died 7 Mar 1899 at 17:00 at res. in Lewistown

Samuel MITCHELL, **b**-23 Mar 1899, **c**-Elder C. MITCHELL, J. Brown MITCHELL, **d**- **e**- **f**-Died 14 Jan 1899 at 11:00 at res. in Derry Twp.

Mary NAFTSINGER, **b**-27 Mar 1899, **c**-Mary HARSHBARGER, **d**-$250, **e**-Jacob MILLER, J. C. SWIGART, **f**-Died 8 Feb 1899 at 20:00 at res. in Bratton Twp.

John P. METZ, **b**-3 Apr 1899, **c**-S. B. METZ, **d**-$1200, **e**-Jacob K. METZ, Harry K. METZ, **f**-Died 21 Jan 1899 at 22:00 at res. in Menno Twp.

John G. GILLILAND, **b**-10 Apr 1899, **c**-Henrietta E. GILLILAND, E. P. SHADE, **d**-$200, **e**-William SHADE, J. A. WAREAM, **f**-Died 27 Mar 1899 at 15:40 at res. in Wayne Twp.

Eliza M. CHESTNUT, **b**-10 Apr 1899, **c**-John A. McKEE, **d**-$100, **e**-Wm. S. SETTLE, David GROVE, **f**-Died 11 Feb 1897 at 5:00 at The State Hospital in Harriburg

Charles HIMMELSBAUGH, **b**-24 Apr 1899, **c**-Thaddeus D. HIMMELSBAUGH, **d**-$200, **e**-W. F. ROCHE, Henry MILLER, **f**-Died 10 May 1897 at 3:30 at res. in Bratton Twp.

Page 300, Frame 319

Thomas COCHRAN, **b**-6 May 1899, **c**-D. C. NIPPLE, **d**-$600, **e**-John M. SMELKER, J. K. RHODES, **f**-Died 20 Apr 1899 at 13:30 at res. in Wayne Twp.

Mary MORRISON, **b**-12 May 1899, **c**-S. W. NORTON, **d**- **e**- **f**-Died 14 Apr 1899 at 15:25 at res. in Huntingdon

Augustus J. KUHN, **b**-17 May 1899, **c**-A. Reed HAYES, **d**-$20,000, **e**-R. J. HAYES, John REED, H. F. TAYLOR, **f**-Died 3 Dec 1887 at 6:15 at in The La Fayette Hotel, Philadelphia

Susan PRICE, **b**-20 May 1899, **c**-John C. SHAHEN, **d**- **e**- **f**-Died 7 May 1899 at 7:30 at res. in Oliver Twp.

Sarah ZOOK, **b**-20 May 1899, **c**-Solomon PEACHEY, **d**-$800, **e**-Rufus C. ELDER, La Fayette WEBB, **f**-Died 11 May 1899 at 16:00 at res. in Menno Twp.

James W. RAMSEY, **b**-27 May 1899, **c**-Adam A. RAMSEY, **d**-$100, **e**-J. Charles EHRENFELD, **f**-Died 1 May 1899 at 18:45 at res. in Armagh Twp.

Ambrose COULTER, **b**-6 Jun 1899, **c**-Jennie McCLELLAN, **d**-$500, **e**-Benjamin MATHERS, Frank B. McCLELLAN, **f**-Died 23 Jul 1881 at 10:00 at res. in McVeytown

Alexander REED, **b**-28 Jun 1899, **c**-Mary L. REED, **d**- **e**- **f**-Died 5 Jun 1899 at 15:15 at res. in Brown Twp.

Margaret SMOKER, **b**-11 Jul 1899, **c**-Ada J. SHEESLEY, **d**- **e**- **f**-Died 26 May 1899 at 20:00 at res. in Lewistown

Samuel McWILLIAMS, **b**-31 Jul 1899, **c**-J. T. McWILLIAMS, **d**- **e**- **f**-Died 13 Apr 1899 at 20:00 at res. in McVeytown

Jared KAUFFMAN, **b**-5 Aug 1899, **c**-Harry G. KAUFFMAN, **d**-$100, **e**-John E. KAUFFMAN, J. A. FRENCH, **f**-Died 10 May 1899 at 5:30 at res. in Bratton Twp.

Thomas F. McCOY, **b**-19 Aug 1899, **c**-Joseph M. WOODS, **d**- **e**- **f**-Died 21 Jul 1899 at 9:00 at res. in Lewistown

Margaret E. WILSON, **b**-19 Aug 1899, **c**-William A. WILSON, **d**-$100, **e**-Harry G. KAUFFMAN, A. Reed HAYES, **f**-Died 14 Jan 1898 at 14:00 at res. in Oliver Twp.

Katie M. BOYER, **b**-29 Aug 1899, **c**-Richard YOUNG, **d**-$100, **e**-John T. WILSON, J. Robert STERRETT, **f**-Died 12 Jan 1899 at 23:45 at res. in Union Twp.

George ARNOLD, **b**-12 Sep 1899, **c**-D. J. ARNOLD, **d**-$100, **e**-Allen A. ORR, A. Reed HAYES, **f**-Died 9 Sep 1899 at 17:30 at res. of D. J. ARNOLD in Granville Twp.

John KOUGH, **b**-12 Sep 1899, **c**-Miles R. KOUGH, **d**-$100, **e**-William T. ROCHE, Gottlieb SIDES, **f**-Died 27 Aug 1899 at 15:00 at res. in McVeytown

John WALLS, **b**-8 Sep 1899. **c**-William H. ERWIN, **d**-$100, **e**-W. P. STEVENSON, Wm. R. BRATTON, **f**-Died 28 Feb 1898 at 19:00 at res. of Isaac H. WALLS in Altoona, Blair Co.

Martha A. GETTYS, **b**-6 Oct 1899, **c**-John W. WILSON, **d**- **e**- **f**-Died 2 Oct 1899 at 19:00 at res. in Union Twp.

Lewis REED, **b**-13 Oct 1899, **c**-Mary E. REED, **d**-$400, **e**-William B. McNITT, Joseph G. McNITT, **f**-Died 7 Sep 1899 at 3:00 at res. in Armagh

Mary ZOOK, **b**-14 Oct 1899, **c**-C. G. MILLIKEN, **d**-$1600, **e**-Noah SHARP, Henry A. WALTERS, **f**-Died 28 Apr 1898 at 15:00 at res. in Union Twp.

Samuel MILLER, **b**-25 Oct 1899, **c**-Joseph A. MILLER, **d**-$2000, **e**-La Fayette WEBB, **f**-Died 20 Jan 1898 at 11:45 at res. of F. H. WENTZ in Lewistown

William PATTON, **b**-31 Oct 1899, **c**-Wm. L. PATTON, **d**- **e**- **f**-Died 11 Oct 1899 at 00:30 at res. in Menno Twp.

Kurtz KAUFFMAN, **b**-11 Nov 1899, **c**-J. B. HARSHBARGER, **d**-$250, **e**-D. P. YODER, D. R. STINE, **f**-Died 4 Nov 1899 at 11:00 at res. in Bratton Twp.

Frederick J. BOYER, **b**-16 Nov 1899, **c**-Richard YOUNG, **d**- **e**- **f**-Died 23 Aug 1899 at 14:30 at res. in Union Twp.

Mary Martha HETRICK, **b**-21 Nov 1899, **c**-G. H. BELL, **d**-$100, **e**-L. H. RUBLE, S. M. BELL, **f**-Died 3 Aug 1899 at __ P.M. at res. in Lewistown

Page 301, Frame 320

John RIDEN, **b**-23 Nov 1899, **c**-G. B. Mc. RIDEN, J. R. LONGWELL, **d**- **e**- **f**-Died 17 Nov 1899 at 18:30 at res. in Armagh Twp.

Margaret McLAUGHLIN, **b**-27 Nov 1899, **c**-M. M. McLAUGHLIN, **d**-$1200, **e**-C. H. HENDERSON, H. A. WALTERS, **f**-Died 11 Nov 1899 at 10:30 at res. in Lewistown

John ATKINSON, **b**-Wm. M. ATKINSON, **c**- **d**- **e**- **f**-Died 20 Sep 1899 at 00:30 at res. in Bratton Twp.

Edward W. FOSNOT, **b**-28 Nov 1899, **c**-H. J. FOSNOT, **d**-$1000, **e**-C. H. HENDERSON, George L. RUSSELL, **f**-Died 22 Nov 1899 at 7:15 at res. in Lewistown

Margaret Jane CAMPBELL, **b**-6 Dec 1899, **c**-J. Milton CAMPBELL, **d**-$5000, **e**-A. W. CAMPBELL, John A. CAMPBELL, **f**-Died 14 Nov 1899 at 16:10 at res. in Union Twp.

Christian K. PEACHEY, **b**-7 Dec 1899, **c**-Nancy PEACHEY, A. Z. PEACHEY, **d**- **e**- **f**-Died 26 Nov 1899 at 12:25 at res. in Union Twp.

Rudolph KLINE, **b**-19 Dec 1899 **c**-Abram B. KLINE, **d**-$1000, **e**-B. Ella KLINE, R. W. KLINE, **f**-Died 11 Dec 1899 at 7:30 at res. in Granville Twp.

NOTES ON INDEXING PRACTICES

- Numbers in bold type indicate the deceased individual who is the subject of the record; an identical non-bold entry indicates another person with the same name on that page
- The compiler attempted to group similar names together or at least cross reference them to each other (she is also fallible); if they were similar but in close proximity in the index, they were not grouped
- Readers are advised to review the whole alphabetical section for the name of interest and look at the original entries of anything that looks close to that name; the frame numbers have been added in the text to make that easier

INDEX OF NAMES

NOTE: Combining all; look for specific given names of interest

FORGY (continued)
  Robert. 69, 97, 138, 141,
                    144, 281
  Robert, Jr.. . . . . 203, 214, 256
  Robert, Sr.. . . . . **144**
  William. 79, 97
FORSCANON (see FONCANON)
FORSTER
  John. 125
FORSYTH, FORSYTHE
  Charlotte. 171, **274**
  George.. . . . . **253**
  Kate B.. 252
  Marg. 171
  Mary. **171, 199**
  Mathew, Matthew. . . . 73, **133**,
                    171, 199, **207**
  Robert (R.). . 9, 11, 13, 15, 22,
    24, 25, 29, 33, 64, **73, 199**
  Robert B... . . . . 217, **252**
FOSNOT
  Edward W.. . . . . **294**
  H. J.. 294
FOSSELMAN
  Elizabeth. **223**
FOSTER
  George.. . . . . **229**
  John. **125**
  Joseph. **43**
  Margaret. **131**
FOULTON
  Samuel.. 51
FOUST
  R. Bruce. **283**
FOWLER
  William E.. 131
FOX
  Frank. **281**

FOY
  Sarah Ellen. 239
  William. **239**
FRAINE
  Christian. **224**
  George K.. 224
FRAKER
  Cathrine E., Mrs... 224
FRAMPTON
  Samuel.. . . . . **6**
  William. 22
FRANCIS
  Frederick. **192**
  Jacob. 192
  Susannah. **207**
FRANCISCUS
  Francis G. (F. G.). . . 144, 159,
                205, 210, 234, **277**
  James P. (J. P.). 277, 282
  John. 100
  Katharine.. 277
  Louis P.. . . . . **144**
FRANK
  Henry.. 216
  Henry N.. . . . . 203, 234
  Nathan. 181, 201, 204, 221
  Nathaniel. 161
  Samuel.. . . . . 150, 154
FRANKS
  R. R.. 136
  Samuel.. 152
  Theo.. 164
FRAZER
  William. 29
FREDERICI
  Charles, Dr.. . . . . **236**
FREDERICK
  John. 4

MONAHAN, MONAHON
James. **155**
Mary. **69**
Michael M. (M. M.). . 23, 25,
27, 28, 32, 33, 35, 38,
49-51, 60, 69, 100, 119
S. C.. 259
MONKS
William. 9
MONTGOMERY
Elizabeth A.. . . . . **283**
John. 3, 92, 94
Moses (M.). 135, 142, 148, 158
Richard. 38, 79, 86, **144**
Robert. **85**
Robert H. (R. H.).. . 142, 211,
255, 260, 283
Samuel. **3, 27**
Sophia. 211
William. **19, 50**, 117, 149, **211**
MONTOOTH
Mary. 21, 40
William. **21, 40**
MOODIE
Henry A. (H. A.). . . . 262, **291**
MOODY
Mathias. 123, **127**
MOOLZER
John. 61
MOOR
William A.. 138
MOORE
Andrew. **5**
Ann. **69**
Archibald.. . . . . 28, **59**
David F.. . . . . **277**
Elizabeth. 52
Evanna.. 277
Francis.. . . . . 25, 72, 86

George. **52, 72, 86**
George H.. 173
Henry.. . . . . **3**
Howard. 52
Isabella.. . . . . 5, **80**
James. **5**, 25
Jane. 72
Jesse.. . . . . **43**
John. 2, 5, 69, **80**
John H... . . . . **187**
John R... 251
Joshua, Revd... 156
Mary Ann. **263**
Moses.. . . . . 32, 43
Rebecca. **105**
Robert. **25**
Samuel M., Revd.. 182
Samuel T... . . . . 264, 266
Sarah J.. 251
Thomas. **251**
Thomas W.. 80
William. **32**
William A. (W. A.). . 105, 154,
167, 186, **291**
William H. 222
William W.. 43
MOOREHOUSE
Peter.. . . . . **24**
MOOTZER
John. 61, 106
MORAN
_____, Mrs.. 249
Hugh. 118, **153**
MORGAN
Francis.. . . . . 175, **220**
John. 220
Joseph. **11**, 11
Margaret. **196**
Robert. **108**

WILLS (continued)
Rachel, Mrs.. . . . . **206**
Robert A.. . . . . **258**
Robert E.. 167
Samuel.. . . . 151, 167, **178**, 212
Samuel B.. . . . . 135, 212, 215,
225, **259**
Thomas. **167**
William. **151, 183**
William R.. . . . . 156, 180
WILSON
A. C.. 166
A. L.. . . . . 121, 122
Abraham. **81**
Abraham S. (A. S.). . . . 76, 78,
93, 94, 102-106, 110-112,
114, 121, 174
David.. . . . . 10, **61**
George.. 2, 5, 43, 61, 109, 122,
145, 147, 168, **175**
Henry.. . . . . 94, **120, 148**
Henry S. (H. S.).. . . . 184, 196,
273, 281
Hugh. 81
J. Campbell.. . . . . **169**
J. Clark. 267
J. H.. 183
J. J.. 252
J. T.. . . 175, 188, 196, 252, 258

> *Editor's note: Because there are two*
> *candidates for the initials J. T. in the*
> *area, only the ones with a Taylor and/or*
> *Jefferson association will be combined.*
> *I still suspect that J. T. here is Jefferson*
> *rather than John T. Of course, I may be*
> *wrong!*

James.. . 37, 41, 114, **115**, 179,
183, **254**
Jefferson Taylor. . . . 199, 226,

227, 235, 237, 252
John.. . . . 8, **33**, 44, 48, 56, 61,
76, **107**, 118, 232,
234, 280, 283
John B.. 182
John F.. 168
John T.. . . . . . . **235**, 287, 293
John W. (J. W.) .175, 177, 178,
196, 199, 206, 207, 213,
218, 221, 239-241, 244,
252, 258, 266, 273, 275,
287, 293
John, Sr.. . . . . 177, **196**
Joseph C.. 168
Josiah. 43, 75
Margaret E.. . . . . **288, 293**
Margaret F.. . . . . **178**
Mary. . . . **39, 50, 75**, 120, **178**
Mary S.. . . . . 196, **221**
Miles C.. . . . . **196**
N. C.. . . . . 177, 201, 242, 248,
258, **271**
Nancy. **263**
Nathaniel.. . . . 81, 86, 98, 105,
111, 135, **201**
Richard. 36, **37**
Robert. 12, 46, 58
Robert F. (R. F.). 252, 263, 266
S. [Ults?].. . . . . **199**
Samuel.. . . . . **229**
Sarah. **174**
Sarah W.. . . . . **178**
Thomas. 19, **43**, 43, 50, **55**, 140
Thomas J.. . . . . 115, 162, 164,
168, 235
William. 2, 3, 14, 22, 127,
138, 156, 159, 160,
169, **226**
William A.. 271, 281, 291, 293

YODER (continued)
Veronica. **174**
William. 203, 290
Yost. **237**, 237
Yost Z.. 206
YOKAM, YOKEM (see also
YOCAM)
Isaiah. 14, 15
John. 12, 14, 64
YOST
Isaac.. . . . . 20, 21, **78**
Jacob. 3, 4, 18, **20**
Mary. **78**
Sarah. **262**
YOTTER
Abraham. 27
Christian. 46
Christly. 13
Jacob. 13, 27
YOUNG
Anthoney. . . 23-25, 30, 31, 68,
85, 107
Conrad. 7
David. **140**
Elizabeth. 85, **108**
John. **41**
John S.. . . . . **212**
Levi, Jr.. 69
Mary. 41
Richard. 293, 294
YOUNGMAN
Thomas. 195
YOUNTZ
John. **191**
William. 191
YOUTZEY *[see also next two]*
Elijah. 155, **243**
John. **202**
McClelland. 202
William. 243

YOUTZY
Jacob. 257
John A.. 269
Michael. 142
Sarah B.. . . . . **269**
William. 290
YUTSEY, YUTZEY
Elijah. 138
Michael. 95, **138**, 138
ZEANEK
Mary. **216**
ZEIGLER
Charles D.. 271
Daniel (D.).. . . . 139, 142, 148,
154, 156
Joseph. 172, **203**
Rebecca. **271**
Uriah S.. 271
ZELNER
Samuel L.. 182
ZERBE (see also ZERBY)
Charles A.. . . . . 213, 219, 221
Edward M.. . . . . **290**
Frank J.. 290
Hannah M.. 213
Henry. 138, 178, 183, 189,
193, 200, 201, 210, **213**
ZERBY (see also ZERBE)
Henry. 206
Jacob. **271**
James G.. 271
ZIMERMAN
Nathan. 186
ZOOK
A. D.. . . . . 264, 281
Abraham. . . 60, 110, 137, **154**
Barbara. **237**
Benjamin. 183
C. C.. . . . . **264**
Catharine. **178**

www.ingramcontent.com/pod-product-compliance
Lightning Source LLC
Chambersburg PA
CBHW060130280326
41932CB00012B/1476